A Fireside Book Published by Simon & Schuster

The American Book of the Dead™

The Definitive

Grateful Dead®

Encyclopedia

Oliver Trager

FIRESIDE
Rockefeller Center
1230 Avenue of the Americas
New York, NY 10020

FIRESIDE and colophon are registered trademarks
of Simon & Schuster Inc.

Designed by Richard Oriolo

Manufactured in the United States of America

10   9   8   7   6   5   4   3

Library of Congress Cataloging-in-Publication Data

Trager, Oliver.
The American book of the Dead : the definitive encyclopedia of the Grateful
Dead / Oliver Trager.
p.   cm.
1. Grateful Dead (Musical group)—Miscellanea.   I. Title.
ML421.G72T67 1997
782.42166'092'2—dc21   97-29769
[B]   CIP
                                                                                                        MN

ISBN 0-684-81402-1

Acknowledgments

My name may be up there in lights, but books, among other endeavors in life, are, thankfully, group gropes. Naturally, I would like to humbly thank all those I can remember who so selflessly contributed to making *The American Book of the Dead* all that it is.

Front and center, I would like to bow down in supplication to my agent Doveen Schecter for selling the project, former Simon & Schuster editor David Dunton for buying it, and my editor Mary Ann Naples for nurturing it. Kudos should also be directed S&S's way for the thoughtful work and assistance of Carlene Bauer, Laurie Chittenden, Matthew Shine, and Shawn Dahl, who made me literate.

Acknowledgments should further be spread to my colleagues and former colleagues at Facts On File: Jamie Warren for thinking up the project in the first place, Marc Greene for talking about and jamming with me, Jo Stein, Jeff Golick, Jeff Jackson, Gary Krebs, Walter Kronenberg, and William Meyers.

In that this tome is a synthesis of all that has been written and archived about the Grateful Dead, special thanks needs to be paid to those writers who went where no one had gone before and brought back the ore I have attempted to smelt: Blair Jackson, David Gans, the folks at *DeadBase*, *Relix*, *Dupree's Diamond News*, *Unbroken Chain*, and *Guitar Player*.

I think that the graphic material presented here really makes this book special. Thank you Bob Minkin, Ed Perlstein, Michael Schulman, and Mitch Blank at Archive Photos, the New York Public Library for the Performing Arts at Lincoln Center, Chris Walklet, Joe Slomka, and Richard Berner.

Richard Berner (as solid a cat as you'd ever want to meet) should also be given a special tip of the hat for providing not only me but also the universe at large with some of the best concert tapes (Grateful Dead and otherwise) on this sweet swingin' sphere. Thank you also to Lance Neal and New York's Pacifica Radio affiliate, WBAI-FM, for their great Dead show *Morning Dew,* from which I was able to gather hundreds of hours of audio material. Deeper into the tapers' section, let me finally thank anyone and everyone I was privileged to trade tapes with over the years.

As you might expect, several individuals in the Dead's organization were particularly helpful. A heartfelt thank-you to Elena Chieffo, Peter McQuaid, Alan Trist, and Dennis McNally (for being the patron saint of all mensches).

Lastly and firstly, my wife, Elaine, and son, Cole, are the best. Elaine, thank you for giving me the psychic and physical space to make this book a reality.

For the Grateful (Elaine and Cole)
and the Dead (Chuck and Steve)

How to Use This Book

Most of the entries are fairly self-explanatory even for those not familiar with the Grateful Dead's recorded legacy. One symbol used throughout that may be the cause of some confusion looks like this: >. It is used to indicate seamless segues from song to song. For example, if you come across something that looks like "Scarlet Begonias">"Fire on the Mountain," it means that the music flows from "Scarlet Begonias" into "Fire on the Mountain" without a pause.

The following is provided for further ease of use.

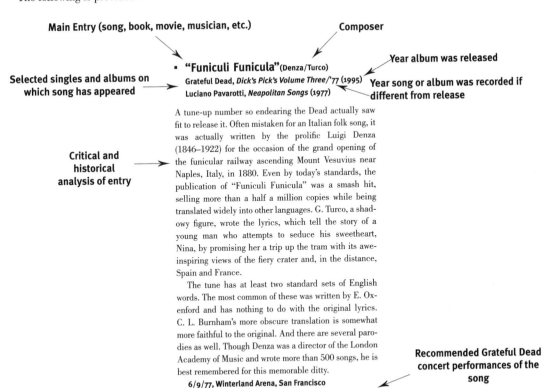

Main Entry (song, book, movie, musician, etc.)

Composer

Year album was released

Selected singles and albums on which song has appeared

- **"Funiculi Funicula"** (Denza/Turco)
Grateful Dead, *Dick's Pick's Volume Three*/'77 (1995)
Luciano Pavarotti, *Neapolitan Songs* (1977)

Year song or album was recorded if different from release

Critical and historical analysis of entry

A tune-up number so endearing the Dead actually saw fit to release it. Often mistaken for an Italian folk song, it was actually written by the prolific Luigi Denza (1846–1922) for the occasion of the grand opening of the funicular railway ascending Mount Vesuvius near Naples, Italy, in 1880. Even by today's standards, the publication of "Funiculi Funicula" was a smash hit, selling more than a half a million copies while being translated widely into other languages. G. Turco, a shadowy figure, wrote the lyrics, which tell the story of a young man who attempts to seduce his sweetheart, Nina, by promising her a trip up the tram with its awe-inspiring views of the fiery crater and, in the distance, Spain and France.

The tune has at least two standard sets of English words. The most common of these was written by E. Oxenford and has nothing to do with the original lyrics. C. L. Burnham's more obscure translation is somewhat more faithful to the original. And there are several parodies as well. Though Denza was a director of the London Academy of Music and wrote more than 500 songs, he is best remembered for this memorable ditty.

6/9/77, Winterland Arena, San Francisco
4/8/82, Onondaga County War Memorial, Syracuse, New York

Recommended Grateful Dead concert performances of the song

Cross-references are in SMALL CAPITAL letters. Songs written by the Grateful Dead, Grateful Dead albums, and members of the Grateful Dead, including Robert Hunter, are not cross referenced.

The First Days

Jerry Garcia was smiling. And when Jerry Garcia smiled, the entire cosmos seemed to smile with him. The Dead were barreling towards the climax of another show that began in the far-gone-isphere, hitched a ride on the tailfin of a Venusian trolley car, took a right on Chuck Berry Boulevard, crashed through the Great Wall of China, ran a stop sign in a Black Hole, picked up Bob Dylan's grandmother in Merle Haggard's backyard, took five at a juice bar on the asteroid belt before nestling on one of Saturn's rings where Salvador Dalí dueled Stravinsky in a best of infinity ping-pong match.

Sound familiar? I was twelve years old on that sultry Sunday in June 1969. With school recently out my friends and I earnestly whiled away the afternoon in Central Park playing baseball (softball according to our parents) on the Great Lawn and checking out the scene at Bethesda Fountain where there was always more than enough gawk material to last a couple of New York minutes. As we approached the ornamental fountain known as the Angel of the Waters in the psychic epicenter of the park, the bright strains of country rock drifted from the nearby bandshell.

"It's the Dead, man," said a bearded hippie with hair down to his ass.

"The what?" we must have said with clueless expressions to which the hippie (slinging his arm over his girlfriend's shoulders) just shrugged. We followed him and most of the crowd over to the bandshell. A band was beginning to warm up with a series of songs that seemed pretty foreign to ears still having a hard time digesting the Beatles' *Magical Mystery Tour*. With my wanna-be "mod" haircut, flared chinos, and musical sensibility that felt more at home with the Monkees than the Stones, my decidedly un-hippie aesthetic was faux Carnaby Street all the way down to my penny loafers.

The look of the band didn't help much either. A long-haired space child wearing a dashiki closed his eyes and scratched indecipherable rhythm licks, the bass player grinned the grin of a demon hipster as he thumped away, an organ player who looked like our math teacher peered suspiciously from behind his rack, the drummers chased each other into a thunderous abyss, and the lead guitarist (a wily son-of-a-gun with pigtails and a bushy beard) seared his beatific flights of guitar fancy that soared and crashed into our unprepared little skulls. By the time a bad-ass biker type in a cowboy hat ambled up to the mike and began wailing with the meanest gutbucket blues and mouth organ this end of Chicago's South Side, we were seriously spooked.

Later, as the group was immersing itself in a deep sonic ozone that more approximated a jet taking off than anything my buddies and I would then classify as music (much less "rock" music), we removed ourselves to the periphery of the scene and just stood there marveling at a swarm of writhing, dungareed bodies. The police presence was virtually nonexistent and clouds of marijuana smoke soon hovered over the landscape. Someone offered us a hit but we just giggled. Much to our utter shock, horror, delight, and gratitude, one young woman briefly shed her attire and pranced through the crowd with a rose in her mouth à la *Carmen*. Meanwhile, a young dude sat cross-legged next to us in a meditative reverie as he contemplated a burning candle oozing hot red wax over his clenched fist. At some point, an anti-War protester tried to take the stage, but even he seemed to know his mission was misbegotten and quickly begged off. Yes, it was quite the spectacle—maybe even a little more than my friends and I had bargained for . . . but only a little.

I was still shell-shocked when I dragged myself home for dinner that night. "How was your softball game?" my mom asked as she poured some pasta into a pot of boiling water.

"Huh? Oh . . . it was *amazing*," was about all I could manage.

"Oh, that's nice, dear."

If she had only known. If I had only known. No, I didn't get on the bus that afternoon or, then again, maybe I did. Who can really say? Looking back, it was certainly a bookend to the following quarter century and change of my life in general and Grateful Dead experience in even more general.

It wasn't until some years later—the summer of 1974 to be precise—that, while working as a counselor at a summer camp in Vermont, I had my Grateful gestalt in the form of *Workingman's Dead*. "Uncle John's Band," in particular, seemed to hit some resonant, still undefined and forever lost chord, within my soul. A few of my friends and I even mustered a passable version of the song at the annual camp talent show, drawing the desired reprimand for including the dreaded expletive "goddamn" in our purposely unedited rendition.

Upon returning home at summer's end, I was pleased to discover that my younger sister (back then, anyway, she was way hipper than I) had *Workingman's* and a few other Dead LPs by her hi-fi: *American Beauty*, *Live Dead*, and *Vintage Dead*. I soon added *Europe '72* and the eponymous "Skull and Roses" to that collection as well as my first GD bootleg (tape trading was ridiculously unheard of then) which I scarfed up at Free Being, a little hole-in-the-wall record shop on Second Avenue just south of St. Mark's Place in the East Village. A friend's brother had a nice little collection of boots that helped while away the afternoons we were supposed to be spending gearing up for our SATs.

Simultaneously, I was getting my first real exposure to Dylan, jazz, and a taste of that experience venturing into grottoes like the Village Vanguard and Slugs to check out Mingus, Pharoah Sanders, Elvin Jones, Ornette Coleman, and Sun Ra while tripping the night fantastic on the sidewalks of New York.

Devouring those albums and opening my ears at the Vanguard, I started making the connections that I suppose formed the basis of this book. By comparing renditions of songs and tracking down original versions I commenced a self-imposed tutorial on Grateful Dead music and all its various configurations that may continue until the day I join Jerry.

As I entered my freshman year at college, I hankered for another taste of the Dead. Unfortunately, this was smack-dab in the middle of the band's mid-1970s "retirement" and there was some very real question (more like cold panic) if they would ever tour again. I caught Kingfish at a crazy rock-a-thon in Trenton, stood outside the Bottom Line with my ear pressed against the glass in a half-futile attempt to hear the Legion of Mary, attended my first Garcia Band show at the Beacon Theater, but had yet to see/hear the Dead again.

So when, in spring of 1976, the rumors of a new Dead tour turned out to be true, I found myself cramped in the back of an old pickup truckin' ticketless to that evening's show at the Boston Music Hall. Ducats were easy to come by (this was still well before the era of "miracle tickets"). When the lights dimmed and the crowd let out at that special howl I would come to love almost as much as the concert, I was standing off comfortably to the right of the stage about twenty rows back. The band started with "Might as Well," a new song that seemed to dovetail perfectly with my little adventure. The rest of the first set was equally apropos as the Dead mixed the familiar ("Mama Tried," "Tennessee Jed," "Candyman," and "Brown-Eyed Women") with material that was still, to me, vaguely familiar ("Cassidy" and "Scarlet Begonias") and totally unfamiliar ("Looks Like Rain" and "Lazy Lightning").

I remember thinking how happy and loose the band appeared and how much like their images they seemed to be: professorial Phil dancing his fingers over the strings of the bottom registers, slick Weir shakin' things up with his charismatic stage flash, the drummers just like they were back in Central Park that day—pursuing each other in cosmic battle, Keith Godchaux hunched over his grand piano spicing the flow with jazzy runs up the keyboard, Donna sashaying to the mic for her background vocals, and Jerry—the frumpy hero—so free and easy with his smile and guitar magic. It seemed like I'd been there before.

While exploring the Music Hall's catacombs in search of a *pissoir* and loose joints during the break (I found both), I experienced one of those flashes that can happen anywhere but seemed particularly potent in the Grateful Dead universe: I realized I had visited this venue many years before as part of a magical day with my father that included a game at Fenway Park and a film (*Those Magnificent Men in Their Flying Machines*) at a Gilded Age theater 'twixt Boston Common and the Combat Zone a decade earlier. Synchronicity spoken here.

Scrambling back to my seat to share this news with my friends, the band launched into the delirious "St. Stephen." I knew I had found a home. In some ways, perhaps, I've never left.

The following two decades have been partly spent in pursuit of that slippery Grateful Dead muse as a roadmap to my soul finding these feet at some of the strangest of places trying to look at it right: hitching a ride at the Holland Tunnel entrance to the last Roosevelt Stadium show where Phil ruled, cramming into a Volvo for the spring '77 tour including an Ithaca show that was a throwback to some Dionysian rite, hopping freight trains to Boulder, Colorado, for the fifteenth-anniversary concerts, swearing off sacramental assistance after being too far gone to really enjoy a front-row seat at one of the acoustic revivals at San Francisco's Warfield Theater in 1980, neatly tying in a visit to a Sante Fe girlfriend in '83 with some real Grateful Dead magic that included an apocalyptic thunderstorm and a rainbow in the course of a single afternoon, catching "St. Stephen" at the Garden a month later, burning outside the Spectrum in '85 when my friend with a ticket pulled a no-show (his car died on the Jersey Turnpike), doing July Fourth with Dylan and the Dead in '87, finding "Dark Star" and much more at the '89 Meadowlands epiphany, interviewing the band in '93 for an article that went terribly bum, and, finally, joining Jerry's Central Park wake.

In all there were seven U.S. presidents, about a hundred shows, two thousand and one adventures, a thousand more tapes, and a million smiles in Deadland. But, in the end, my Grateful Dead journey is the same as yours. We came to the music in different ways, perhaps, drew different inspirations from it, sent different balls of light at each other and stageward, but we forged it all into the marrow of our souls.

Even more than two years after Jerry Garcia's death it's still a bit hard not to peek back over our shoulders down the road from where the long, strange trip has come and wonder if the band was ever here at all. Mostly, though, I like to look up the pike . . . furthur.

A Grateful Dead studio album disguised as Bob Weir's solo debut, *Ace* is filled with spunky dynamism ("Greatest Story Ever Told"), an ethereal exploration ("Playing in the Band"), good-time rock ("One More Saturday Night"), polka rock ("Mexicali Blues"), and a tender naturalistic ballad ("Looks Like Rain"). Many Deadheads consider this version of "Playing in the Band" an example of the Dead at their musically intuitive peak.

▪ Aces Back to Back: A Guide to the Grateful Dead (book)/Scott W. Allen 124 pp. Pierce Axiom, 1992.

This history of the band appears to have been assembled primarily using others' work as source material. Allen, an earnest believer, apparently never interviewed any band members but he includes hundred of long, unattributed quotes. Though it is amateurishly written and published, Deadheads will find plenty of information and GD deification in this disorganized vanity affair.

▪ The Acid Test: A Sound City Production (record from the 1966 Acid Tests) Sound City Productions, 1966.

KEN KESEY released this slice of Acid Test life and though it gives an aural Polaroid of the doings, it does make one wonder what all the fuss was about. Guess you just had to be there.

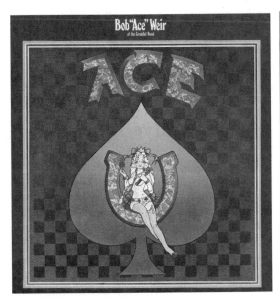

(© Grateful Dead Merchandising, Inc.)

▪ Ace/Bob Weir

Warner Bros. BS 2627, 1972; LP reissue GD BS/2627; CD reissue GDCD 4004. Produced by everyone involved.

"Greatest Story Ever Told," "Black Throated Wind," "Walk in the Sunshine," "Playing in the Band," "Looks Like Rain," "Mexicali Blues," "One More Saturday Night," "Cassidy"

Ed Bogus–string arrangements on "Looks Like Rain." Dave Torbert–bass on "Greatest Story Ever Told."

• Acid Tests

Perhaps more than any other advent in the primordial fomentation of the Grateful Dead, the 1965 and 1966 Acid Tests were to forever inform the band's aesthetic. When LSD was still legal, KEN KESEY and the Merry Pranksters hosted free-form, audience participatory, multimedia West Coast events featuring films, projections, tape loops, ambient microphones, and "Electric Kool-Aid."

During his graduate-school stint at Stanford University, Kesey (along with Robert Hunter) was introduced to psychedelics as a paid volunteer in government-run experiments at Palo Alto's VA hospital. It wasn't long before unauthorized amounts of LSD were finding their way to Kesey's bungalow on Perry Lane, the college town's bohemian enclave that included, according to *The Electric Kool-Aid Acid Test,* Tom Wolfe's neo-journalistic account of the era, "a wild-haired kid named Jerry Garcia" who was living just four blocks away at a communal household known as the Chateau. Kesey, a budding novelist, soon began throwing parties with his LSD-spiked venison chili serving as the catalyst.

The fallout from the bacchanals was so interesting that Kesey and company decided to re-create them as public spectacles. With a one-dollar admission for everyone, "performers" and "audience" alike, the Acid Tests became the template for the three decades of Grateful Dead experience which followed.

"The Acid Test was the prototype for our whole basic trip," Garcia related to *Rolling Stone* in 1970. "But nothing has ever come up to the level of the way the Acid Test was. It's just never been equaled really, or the basic hit of it never developed out . . . It was something more incredible than just rock & roll and a light show; it was just a million times more incredible. It was incredible because of the formlessness, because of the thing of people wandering around wondering what was going on . . . and stuff happening spontaneously and people being prepared to accept any kind of thing that was happening, and to add to it . . . Everybody was creating. Everybody was doing everything. That's about the simplest explanation."

In 1981, Garcia elaborated on the music the Dead shared at the event. "The nice thing about the Acid Test was that we could play or *not.* And a lot of times we'd play for maybe a *minute* and then we'd lose it and have to leave—'This is too weird for me!' On the other hand, sometimes we'd play, and there was no pressure on us

because people didn't come to see the Grateful Dead, they came for the Acid Test; it was the whole event that counted. Therefore we weren't in the spotlight, so when we did play, we played with a certain kind of freedom you rarely get as a musician. Not only did we not have to fulfill expectations about us, we didn't have to fulfill expectations about *music,* either. So in terms of being able to experiment freely with music, it was amazing."

Garcia elaborated to David Jay Brown and Rebecca Novick in a 1995 interview first published in *Relix,* "The thing that was fun about those days was that nothing was expected of us. We didn't have to play. [*Laughter*] We weren't *required* to perform. People came to the Acid Tests for the Acid Test, not for us.

"So there were times when we would play two or three tunes or even a couple of notes and just stop. We'd say, 'To hell with it, we don't feel like playing!' It was great to have that kind of freedom because before that we were playing five sets a night, fifty minutes on, ten minutes off, every hour. We were doing that six nights a week and then usually we'd have another afternoon gig and another night-time gig on Sunday. So we're playing a lot!

"So all of a sudden, you're at the Acid Test and hey, you didn't even have to play. Also we weren't required to play anything even acceptable. We could play *whatever* we wanted. So it was a chance to be completely free-form on every level. As far as a way to break out from an intensely formal kind of experience, it was just what we needed, because we were looking to break out."

Typically, NEAL CASSADY, the hipster saint who bridged the gap between the Beat Generation and the hippies by inspiring Jack Kerouac's *On the Road* and driving Furthur, Ken Kesey's bus of Merry Pranksters, across the country, was the madcap MC with a non-stop space rap that would have impressed Lord Buckley *and* Ice-T.

Attired in red, white, and blue jumpsuits, Kesey and the Merry Pranksters added to the mayhem while jamming on the Thunder Machine, a sound sculpture created by Ron Boise.

• *Acoustic Disc 100% Handmade Music Volume 1*/Various artists
Acoustic Disc ACDS-8, 1993. Produced by DAVID GRISMAN.

This fine sampler from David Grisman's first seven Acoustic Disc releases includes music from a tantalizing array of artists. Along with a couple of cuts from their

Jerry Garcia/David Grisman outing, the album offers Deadheads a bonus cut of "Louis Collins," a traditional folk song arranged by Garcia and featuring guitar virtuoso Tony Rice trading hot licks with Garcia and Grisman.

"*Addams Family* Theme" (Vic Mazzy)

The Dead have always tweaked their audience with a strange mix of filler material usually thrown in when "technical difficulties" arose. This popular riff that Jerry Garcia and Brent Mydland played around with in the late 1980s was composed by Hollywood songwriter Vic Mazzy (who also gave us the *Green Acres* theme) for *The Addams Family,* the hit television show (1964–66) based on the ghoulish characters created in *The New Yorker* magazine cartoons of Charles Addams. Addams was, in real life, as eccentric as his cartoons. Late in life, he was married in a pet cemetery.

The Adventures of Panama Red /New
RIDERS OF THE PURPLE SAGE
Columbia PC 32450, 1973. Produced by Norbert Putnam.

The Dead began easing away from the New Riders in the mid-1970s but Robert Hunter's "Kick in the Head" and harmony vocals by Donna Godchaux on "Important Exportin' Man" and "L.A. Lady" are the two Grateful Dead contributions to this, the last great NRPS disc.

Aesthetics of the Grateful Dead: A Critical Analysis (book) /David Womack
192 pp. Flying Public Press, 1991.

Writer and musician David Womack's book is perhaps the most idiosyncratic tome ever published on the Grateful Dead. Eschewing the standard overview, Womack tackles the published criticism of the group's recorded output, paying special attention to the infamous scathing review by rock critic Dave Marsh, who had written of the Dead's "patchouli-oil philosophy." Womack does a good job in his exploration of Robert Hunter's lyrics, giving an in-depth analysis and uncovering such things as the relationship between "Dark Star" lyrics and the poetry of T. S. Eliot.

As a fan's notes, Womack's small-press, album-by-album exposition of the band's commercial releases is right-on in its discussion of the scope of Grateful Dead music.

"Aiko-Aiko"
See "Iko-Iko"

"Ain't It Crazy" (SAM "LIGHTNIN'" HOPKINS)
Lightnin' Hopkins, *Hootin' the Blues* (1962), *Lightnin!* (1990), *The Complete Prestige/Bluesville Recordings/'63* (1991)
Singles: "Lovin'" Sam ("Spo-Dee-O-Dee") Theard (1934), Oscar's Chicago Swingers (1936), State Street Swingers (1936).

One of the earliest tunes in the Dead's repertoire, this riotously raunchy Pigpen vehicle steeped in sexual innuendo was originally performed in their embryonic acoustic unit, MOTHER MCCREE'S UPTOWN JUG CHAMPIONS. Deadheads have sometimes misidentified the title of this tune as "The Rub" in their tape collections.

Lightnin' Hopkins is credited with the song's authorship, but the song actually goes back at least as far as the vaudeville era.
7/2/71, Fillmore West, San Francisco

Airto
See **Airto Moreira**

"Alabama Getaway" (Garcia/Hunter)
Grateful Dead, *Go to Heaven* (1980), *Dick's Picks Volume Five/'79* (1996), *Dick's Picks Volume Six/'83* (1996), *The Arista Years* (1996)

Often incorrectly taken as a comment on the recent departure of Alabama-bound bandmates Keith and Donna Godchaux from the Dead in 1979, this tune, referenced with imagery from the Twenty-third Psalm, is difficult to interpret accurately. It's as if Garcia edited a longer Hunter yarn into a breezy shorthand, loosely describing a relationship with a difficult acquaintance.

Regardless, the song was a concert perennial in the early 1980s before slowly dropping out of sight in 1989, only to be revived with a bang in 1995.

The Dead performed "Alabama Getaway" on *Saturday Night Live* in April 1980, and the song began to get significant airplay on album-oriented rock stations across the country and was even played on a number of AM stations. Garcia was delighted with the airplay "Alabama Getaway" received and laughingly declared, "That's incredible—we were sure our very first record was going to be a hit."

Even with the airplay, record sales for the single were flat and the Dead had another near-miss. *Go to Heaven,* however, did make the Top 30 and gained the band legions of new fans.

Some of Hunter's references are worthy of note here.

The line "Majordomo Billy Bojangles sit down and have a drink with me" would seem a nod to black tap dancer William Robinson who used the stage name "Mr. Bojangles" and who was immortalized in Jerry Jeff Walker's song of the same title.

"Majordomo" is later repeated in the song's lyrics "Twenty-third Psalm majordomo, reserve me a table for three, down in the valley of the shadows, just you Alabama and me." A majordomo is the head steward of a large house and the Twenty-third Psalm reads: "Even though I walk through the valley of the shadow of death, I fear no evil; for Thou art with me."

8/16/80, Mississippi River Festival, Edwardsville, Illinois

10/9/82, Frost Amphitheater, Palo Alto, California

4/19/87, Irvine Meadows Amphitheater, Irvine, California

▪ "Alice D. Millionaire" (Grateful Dead)

This tune, which appears on a 1966 rehearsal tape and two very early Grateful Dead set lists, is a blustery Pigpen love plea as well as a veiled tongue-in-cheek ode to their patron saint in sound and psychedelics, Augustus Owsley Stanley III, a.k.a. Bear. The song's title was reportedly inspired by a *Los Angeles Times* story about Owsley headlined "The LSD Millionaire" shortly before the October 6, 1966 illegalization of the psychedelic in California.

10/31/66, California Hall, San Francisco

▪ "All Along the Watchtower" (BOB DYLAN)

Bob Dylan, *John Wesley Harding* (1968), *Bob Dylan at Budokan* (1978), *Biograph* (1985), *MTV Unplugged* (1995)

Bob Dylan and THE BAND, *Before the Flood* (1974)

Bob Dylan and Grateful Dead, *Dylan & the Dead*/'87 (1989)

Grateful Dead, *Dozin' at the Knick*/'90 (1996)

Jimi Hendrix, *Electric Ladyland* (1968), *Smash Hits* (1969), *Isle of Wight* (1971), *Kiss the Sky* (1984), *Live & Unreleased: The Radio Show* (1989)

Brewer and Shipley, *Weeds* (1969)

Affinity, *Affinity* (1970)

Dave Mason, *Dave Mason* (1974), *Certified Live* (1976)

Spirit, *Future Games (A Magical Khauana Dream)* (1977)

Johnny Fuzzy Kruz and the Mind Explosions, *Electric Jam for Feet and Brain* (1990)

Most of the world is familiar with this haunting Bob Dylan masterpiece from Jimi Hendrix's deservedly heralded but overplayed *Electric Ladyland* version. "All Along the Watchtower" was, in fact, Hendrix's only Top 40 single, hitting No. 20.

Hendrix's rendition impressed the song's composer as well. As Dylan wrote in the liner notes of his 1985 *Biograph* album: "I liked Jimi Hendrix's record of this and ever since he died I've been doing it that way. Funny though, his way of doing it and my way of doing it weren't that dissimilar; I mean the meaning of the song doesn't change like when some artists do other artists' songs. Strange, though, how when I sing it I always feel like it's a tribute to him in some kind of way . . . I was thinking about him the other night—I really miss him a lot, him and Lennon. 'All Along the Watchtower' probably came to me during a thunder and lightning storm. I'm sure it did."

Dylan has essentially kept the song as a constant in his set-list rotation since he resumed touring in 1974 and there are six very different but equally effective versions of "All Along the Watchtower" in his commercially available catalogue.

The song, with its apocalyptic aura and musical flexibility, had seemed a Grateful Dead natural a long time before they started performing it in preparation for their short 1987 summer tour with Dylan. It was one of the few songs the Dead worked up for the Dylan tour to find life in their concerts long after that still controversial union.

Bob Weir's desperate delivery of the song is reminiscent of his own "Estimated Prophet" but it is Garcia's soaring solos in which the Dead made their cover of "All Along the Watchtower" all their own.

6/20/87, Greek Theater, Berkeley, California

7/12/87, Giants Stadium, East Rutherford, New Jersey (with Bob Dylan)

7/2/88, Oxford Plains Speedway, Oxford, Maine

5/21/92, Cal Expo Amphitheater, Sacramento, California

▪ *Alleys of the Heart* (book)/ROBERT M. PETERSEN, introduction by Robert Hunter.
140 pp. Hulogos'i, 1988.

The highway dust, stale coffee, reveries, and ecstasies of Bobby Petersen's picaresque life are evident in every phrase from this book of collected poems—his only—which should sit alongside Kerouac and Ginsberg on the shelf of every true or budding hipster. Best known as the wordsmith behind such Dead classics as "Unbroken Chain" and "New Potato Caboose," Petersen's book shows he should be remembered for more.

ALLEYS of the HEART

The Collected Poems of
Robert M. Petersen

(Courtesy of Hulogos'i Communications)

- **"Alligator"** (Hunter/Grateful Dead)
  Grateful Dead, *Anthem of the Sun* (1968), *Dick's Picks Volume Four/'70* (1996)

This Pigpen vehicle included lyrics written by the singer, Robert Hunter, and the band as a whole. A blustery affair, "Alligator" worked as a swaggering showcase for the vocalist and as a loose musical groove from which the band launched into extended and high-powered jams.

While Hunter's lyrics evoke a distinct *Zap Comix* sensibility with their exaggerated description of the titled reptile, they also operate as anarchist allegory with references to burning down the Fillmore Auditorium and Avalon Ballroom in an apparent swipe at those who were profiting off the San Francisco scene, musically, socially, and spiritually.

According to Hunter in *A Box of Rain*, his book of collected lyrics, "This was the first set of my lyrics recorded by the Dead. I got paid two hundred fifty dollars from the record advance for *Anthem of the Sun* with which I bought a used car and headed north to Seattle, where I tried to make a living restringing beads from

Goodwill for a friend's boutique. I made about five dollars at this occupation. The car broke down, which was okay, since I couldn't afford gas for it, so I hitchhiked back to S.F. and decided to hang in there with the Dead."

The only Grateful Dead original performed by Pigpen in the late 1960s, "Alligator" was changed considerably from Hunter's demo. As Hunter told Blair Jackson in 1986, "My melody was a lot different. I was just writing a blues. Pigpen wrote some of those lines in there, too, like that line 'contracted union . . .' You can tell which ones are Pigpen."

When Mickey Hart first joined the group for a September 1967 gig at San Francisco's Straight Theater, the Dead plunged into a nonstop two-hour rendition of "Alligator," initiating and cementing the percussionist's future participation with them.

1/22/68, Eagles Ballroom, Seattle
12/12/69, Thelma Theater, Los Angeles
1/16/70, Springer's Inn, Portland, Oregon
4/29/71, Fillmore East, New York

- **"All I Have to Do Is Dream"** (Felice and Boudleaux Bryant)
  Everly Brothers, single (1958), *The Very Best of the Everly Brothers* (1965), *The Everly Brothers Show* (1970)
  Richard Chamberlain, *Richard Chamberlain* (1963)
  Bobbie Gentry, *Bobbie Gentry & Glen Campbell* (1968)
  Terry Reid, *Rogue Waves* (1979)

As the Dead's only legitimate teenage heartthrob, it was natural that Bob Weir brought a few Everly Brothers tunes to the band early in their career. The sincere-but-syrupy "All I Have to Do Is Dream" was one of these. There is only one known Grateful Dead performance, from when they reorganized themselves as Weir's sometimes cowboy cover band, Bobby Ace and the Cards from the Bottom of the Deck.

6/11/69, California Hall, San Francisco

- # The Allman Brothers Band
  Duane Allman–born November 20, 1946, Nashville, Tennessee; died October 29, 1971, Macon, Georgia. Gregg Allman–born December 8, 1947, Nashville, Tennessee. Richard "Dickey" Betts–born December 12, 1943, West Palm Beach, Florida. Berry Oakley–born April 4, 1948, Chicago, Illinois;

died November 11, 1972, Macon, Georgia. Jai Johnny Johanson (a.k.a. Jaimoe)–born John Lee Johnson July 8, 1944, Ocean Springs, Mississippi. Butch Trucks–born Claude Hudson Trucks Jr. May 11, 1947, Jacksonville, Florida.

Dixie's answer to the Grateful Dead, the Allman Brothers set the standard for Southern rock that has never been equaled much less really challenged by the genre they invented, defined, and redefined. Little Feat, Lynyrd Skynyrd, the Marshall Tucker Band, and a host of boogie bands hailing from below the Mason Dixon have come and gone since the Allmans first hit in the late 1960s but only the Brothers remain in the ring— survivors in every sense of the word. But though they remain a vigorous, exciting band, nothing they do can compare with the band's halcyon days that ended when guitarist Duane Allman met his maker in a 1971 motorcycle accident.

In the few short years before that dreadful day, the Allman Brothers Band established an awesome reputation for their concerts, rivaling the Dead's for both length and ecstatic peaks. The twin lead guitars of Duane and Dickey Betts was a perfect one-of-a-kind blend that spearheaded some of rock's most gloriously soaring jams.

The band's story begins, of course, with Duane and Gregg, products of the early baby boom that followed World War II. Because their father died when they were very young, their mother was forced to work to support the family, which she moved to Daytona Beach, Florida, in 1959. A year later, the younger Gregg received a guitar for Christmas and Duane a motorcycle. After wrecking the bike, Duane traded in the broken parts for another guitar and the two were off to the woodshed.

Within a year they had started their own band and were making their first public appearances at local teen dances displaying their quickly developing chops on the standard repertoire of the era. But the brothers loved the blues and taught themselves many of their early songs by listening to the popular late night R&B radio shows that featured the likes of Muddy Waters, J. B. Hutto, Little Walter, and Robert Johnson.

After participating in an integrated group called the House Rockers, the Allman Joys (a pun on the candy bar) was formed in 1965 and began working the go-go circuit that included stops in such Southern cities as Jacksonville, Atlanta, and Mobile and led to their first single on the Dial label, Willie Dixon's "Spoonful."

The next few years were spent in Los Angeles where, working in a glitzy studio band called the Hourglass, the brothers became increasingly disenchanted with the mainstream music industry and returned to Florida. Joining a group called the 31st of February headed by drummer Butch Trucks, they began to cross paths with a band led by guitarist Dickey Betts that included bassist Berry Oakley. Along with Jai Johnny Johanson, another drummer on the scene, the musicians began to informally jam and slowly come together as the first incarnation of the Allman Brothers Band.

As these studio get-togethers began pleasing and surprising the participants, they engaged Phil Walden, a Macon, Georgia, manager to handle them. After *The Allman Brothers Band*, the debut 1969 LP that won stellar reviews, Walden booked the band on the first of a number of tours of major cities throughout the United States. Gaining word-of-mouth attention as one of the best blues-rock bands on the scene, the group's second LP, *Idlewild South*, became a hit and got them plenty of gigs as they moved across the territories in a Winnebago trailer-bus.

Their appearances at the Fillmore East became the stuff of legend. At one December 1970 show, they were in such rare form that the crowd kept calling them back for encore after encore until finally they gave up the stage to the headline group, Canned Heat, at half past three in the morning.

Their third album, *The Allman Brothers Band at Fillmore East*, a two-record set cut during a March 1971 run at Bill Graham's fabled abode, still stands as one of rock's great live releases. Featuring amazing interplay within highly dynamic arrangements, the marathon jams never stumble. "Hot 'Lanta," "In Memory of Elizabeth Reed," and "Whipping Post" were a few of the blazing tracks that helped spread the gospel of the Allman Brothers Band.

It was around this time that the Allman Brothers began sharing the bill and sometimes jamming with the Grateful Dead. The Bros. had opened the famous mid-February 1970 concerts that produced the Dead's *Bear's Choice* and the much loved 2/13 version of "Dark Star." Two nights earlier, Duane and Gregg had joined the Dead onstage with Fleetwood Mac's Peter Green for an exploratory "Spanish Jam" and swamp "Love Light."

When the Dead were playing their last Fillmore East

shows in late April 1971 Duane once again appeared and actually led the boys through searing versions of "Sugar Magnolia," "It Hurts Me Too," and "Beat It on Down the Line." The Dead really stepped back and let Duane rip on that night.

Sadly, it was Duane's adieu to the Dead and this world as he was dead by year's end. His Allman brethren were in not much better shape when Oakley was killed in a similar motorcycle accident nearly a year to the day later, not three blocks from where Duane lost his life. Enough to make you believe in voodoo.

Eat a Peach, a record released not long after Duane's death and featuring some wonderful outtakes from the Fillmore East gigs plus the heavenly "Blue Sky," didn't do much to help swallow these bitterest of pills.

The band reunited behind Gregg and Dickey but their fortunes declined in a painfully slow tailspin, although not before one last moment of musical glory with the Grateful Dead at some gigs in the summer of 1973, most notably the Watkins Glen powwow in upstate New York and the fantabulous Washington, D.C., jam at RFK Stadium that displayed some of both groups' most sublime music.

The balance of the 1970s and virtually the entire 1980s was a veritable lost weekend for the Allman Brothers. Drugs, alcohol, and various and ill-advised personnel changes contributed to tarnishing the band's rep despite the occasional decent album. And Gregg's short-lived, high-profile marriage to Cher didn't exactly help matters much either.

But the 1989 release of *Dreams*, a thoughtfully compiled box set containing highlights of the Allman Brothers' entire career, engendered a heartfelt renaissance drawing many enthusiastic teenagers who were not even a twinkle in their parents' eyes when Duane was tearing up his axe. The group responded with tour after white-hot tour and a mix of studio and live recordings harkening back to their best of their roots. With Warren Haynes on second lead guitar giving Betts a run for his money every night, the Allman Brothers threaten to replace the Dead as improvisational rock's elder statesmen in the wake of Jerry Garcia's passing.

• *Allman Brothers Band—Fillmore East Feb. '70*/THE ALLMAN BROTHERS BAND
Grateful Dead Merchandising GDCD 4063. Recorded Fillmore East, New York City, February 1970. Produced and recorded by Owsley Stanley.

"In Memory of Elizabeth Reed," "Hoochie Coochie Man," "Statesboro Blues," "Trouble No More," "Outskirts of Town," "Whipping Post," "Mountain Jam"

The February 13 and 14, 1970, shows at the Fillmore East are not merely the stuff of legend because of the amazing performances by the Grateful Dead. No, there was another band, hailing from below the Mason-Dixon line and making its New York City debut, that almost stole the show on those nights (and early mornings). Fortunately, the Dead's soundman and benefactor, Owsley Stanley, was in the habit of recording the opening bands, thus resulting in this surprise release from the archives featuring a maturing but still red-hot Allman Brothers Band blazing through a handful of their incandescent blues.

• *Almost Acoustic*/Jerry Garcia Acoustic Band
Concensus Reality/Grateful Dead Records GDCD4005, 1989. Produced by Sandy Rothman. Recorded live, fall of 1987.
"Swing Low, Sweet Chariot," "Deep Elem Blues," "Blue Yodel #9 (Standin' on the Corner)," "Spike Driver Blues," "I've Been all Around This World," "I'm Here to Get My Baby Out of Jail," "I'm Troubled," "Oh, the Wind and Rain," "The Girl at the Crossroads Bar," "Oh, Babe, It Ain't No Lie," "Casey Jones," "Diamond Joe," "Gone Home," "Ripple"
Jerry Garcia–guitar/vocals. DAVID NELSON–guitar/vocals. Sandy Rothman–mandolin/dobro/vocals. JOHN KAHN–bass. Kenny Kosek–fiddle. David Kemper–snare drum.

In 1987, Garcia returned to the arena of acoustic performance when he put together a crack string band built around his old bluegrass friends David Nelson and Sandy Rothman for a series of gigs on both coasts. The fruits of these well-conceived and well-received concerts and those that followed over the next year, *Almost Acoustic* went after and captured that elusive "high lonesome" sound so prevalent in the country blues and bluegrass of Garcia's many musical heroes, most notably that cherished American musical icon Bill Monroe.

In the liner notes to the album, Rothman recalled the genesis of the collaboration. "In 1964, twenty-three years before these shows were recorded, Jerry, David, and I were playing together in the early Bay Area folk music scene. After all the intervening years, we spontaneously got together again to sing and play. This time, Jerry played rhythm and lead guitar (instead of banjo),

David played rhythm and lead (instead of mandolin), and I played mandolin and dobro (instead of guitar) and some banjo (but not on these selections). We don't know why it happened this way. . . . We think of this as a mostly acoustic, not-quite-bluegrass, progress report for our friends, our fans, and people who love this music."

This earthy, soulful and superbly recorded album finds the ensemble mining many strata of traditional American music. Highlights of the disc include Jimmie Rodgers's "Blue Yodel #9," Mississippi John Hurt's "Spike Driver Blues," and the eerie chestnut, "Oh, the Wind and Rain."

- **"Althea"** (Garcia/Hunter)
  Grateful Dead, *Go to Heaven* (1980), *Without a Net* (1990), *Dick's Picks Volume Six*/'83 (1996)

Garcia and Hunter have penned many tunes about women and the madness they are sometimes said to drive men to ("Valerie," "Rosemary," "Sugaree"). Such a song is "Althea"—a playful but realistic scenario of two flawed and suspicious people looking for love. What makes "Althea" stylistically more interesting than these other songs is that it is relayed as a conversation being recalled by the narrator. He tells Althea what's bothering him and she always has the perfect comeback.

Commitment, free-spiritedness, and staunch bachelorhood are some of the themes dealt with here, complemented with a warm score that gave the Dead room for volcanic instrumental expression.

In this conversational song Hunter has infused a hefty dose of the Bard. The line "You may be a clown on the burying ground or just another pretty face / You may meet the fate of Ophelia to sleep and perchance to dream" directly links with a scene from *Hamlet*, one of Shakespeare's darkest plays. After Ophelia has committed suicide in the tragedy, two clowns dig her grave. They unearth a skull, which Hamlet later holds during his "Alas, poor Yorick" soliloquy. Earlier, before the suicide, Hamlet himself questioned, "To be or not to be," and mused about the hereafter: "To die, to sleep—to sleep—perchance to dream" concluding that "dread of something after death" made people unwilling to flee the burdens of life.

"You may be Saturday's child all grown old" refers to the famous proverbial nursery rhyme regarding the attributes an individual acquires according to the day of the week on which they were born. Hunter may have also

been influenced by "To Althea from Prison," by Richard Lovelace, a seventeenth-century poem which deals with unrequited love.

  11/5/79, The Spectrum, Philadelphia
  8/31/85, Manor Downs, Austin, Texas
  7/19/90, Deer Creek Music Center, Noblesville, Indiana
  6/12/91, Coliseum, Charlotte, North Carolina

- **Amagamalin Street**/Robert Hunter
  Relix RRLP-RRCD 2003, 1984.
  "Roseanne," "Amagamalin Street," "Gypsy Parlor Light," "Rambling Ghost," "Ithaca," "Don't Be Deceived," "Taking Maggie Home," "Out of the City," "Better Bad Luck," "Streetwise," "Face Me," "Where Did You Go?," "13 Roses"
  Robert Hunter–acoustic guitar, vocals. Vaclav Berosini–bass. Roy Blumenfeld–drums. JOHN CIPOLLINA–electric guitar. Jorma Kaukonen–electric guitar. MERL SAUNDERS–keyboard. Rodney Albin–violin.

In this self-described "audio novel" mixing minimalist, sub-folk arrangements with detailed writing focusing on character, Robert Hunter unveiled an ambitious, extended work that exists *way* outside the realm of the commercial mainstream. Rendered as a narrative not unlike the rock operas of the early 1970s, *Amagamalin Street* succeeded where that much-disparaged concept failed.

Painting a dramatic portrait of the hard-core Ameri-

can underbelly, Hunter evokes Dylan, Johnny Cash, Kris Kristofferson, Jerry Jeff Walker, and Leonard Cohen. Split into two distinct sections, the story, *Amagamalin Street*, is partly narrated by Chet, a devil-may-care skirt-chaser. In true picaresque fashion we hear about the dissolution of his relationship with Roseanne (a girlfriend who he led to prostitution), a burgeoning romance with Maggie (a dropout who has seen better days), and his friendship with Murphy (a Vietnam vet who is the sole voice of approximate sanity).

Many elements of Hunter's aesthetic, social, and karmic concerns that imbue his work with the Grateful Dead are in evidence here as well. Aimless wandering, desperate characters whose lives are determined by chance events and the possibility of redemption are always at the fore.

(Courtesy of Warner Bros. Records)

- ### *American Beauty*
  Warner Bros. WS 1893, 1970. Produced by the Grateful Dead.
  "Box of Rain," "Friend of the Devil," "Sugar Magnolia," "Operator," "Candyman," "Ripple," "Brokedown Palace," "Till the Morning Comes," "Attics of My Life," "Truckin'"
  Dave Torbert–bass on "Box of Rain." DAVID NELSON– electric guitar on "Box of Rain." DAVID GRISMAN– mandolin on "Friend of the Devil" and "Ripple." Howard Wales–organ on "Candyman" and "Truckin'," piano on "Brokedown Palace." Ned

Lagin–piano on "Candyman." NEW RIDERS OF THE PURPLE SAGE collaborated musically throughout the album.

Picking up where *Workingman's Dead* left off, the band continued to explore traditional, acoustic-based American music with their own original songs. The Dead's sixth album found them moving further into vocal harmony which, up until this point, had not been one of their stronger talents.

From the opening strains of "Box of Rain," the album exudes a warmth that carries throughout. A testament to *American Beauty*'s importance is that all of the songs except "Operator" and "Till The Morning Comes" remained as evergreen compositions in the Grateful Dead's performance repertoire.

A final note, the album's cover art (designed by the famed Mouse/Kelly team) renders the album's title to be read also as "American Reality."

- ### "And We Bid You Goodnight"
  (Traditional)
  Grateful Dead, *Live/Dead* (1969), *Dick's Picks Volume Four/'70* (1996), *Dozin' at the Knick/'90* (1996)
  Tom Constanten, *Nightfall of Diamonds* (1992)
  The Pindar Family, *The Real Bahamas* (1965), *The Music Never Stopped/'65* (1995)
  Incredible String Band, *The Hangman's Beautiful Daughter* (1968)
  Aaron Neville, *Warm Your Heart* (1991)

The Dead sometimes used this soft, gospel-infused tune, sung a cappella, to close their shows in the late 1960s and early 1970s, a tradition they revived in 1989. These earlier renditions often found the band incorporating many more verses into the song than their *Live / Dead* offering, giving these versions a rousing, down-home flavor reminiscent of a turn-of-the-century tent show or Baptist revival meeting.

The Dead also grafted the "And We Bid You Goodnight" theme as an instrumental coda to their performances of "Goin' Down the Road Feelin' Bad."

The Dead probably learned "And We Bid You Goodnight" from the Pindar Family's performance of the song on the 1965 Nonesuch album *The Real Bahamas*, an LP popular amongst folkies. One of the singers, Jenny Pindar, was the sister of the Bahamas' most renowned musical figure, guitarist Joseph Spence, which some suggest explains the Caribbean lilt found in the Dead's treatment of the song.

The song is overflowing with biblical references. One verse in particular is worthy of examination:

But His rod and His staff they comfort me.
Tell *A* for the ark, that wonderful boat
Tell *B* for the Beast at the ending of the wood
You know it ate all the children who would not be good.

Fittingly, each of these lines references a biblical death or disaster. The rod and staff is drawn from an almost identical line in the Twenty-third Psalm. Of course, the "*A* for the ark" is Noah's ark, which saved its passengers from the great flood. The "*B* for the beast" tells a story from the second book of Kings. At one point in the story, the prophet Elijah is mocked by some young boys who he cursed in the name of the Lord. Suddenly, two female bears charged out of the woods and slaughtered the children.

Finally, the lines "Walkin' in Jerusalem just like John / I go walkin' in the valley of the shadow of death" recounts the story of John the Baptist who preached that the Messiah was coming soon. Unfazed by the consequences of this, he told King Herod that Herod's marriage to the wife of his deceased brother violated God's law. Angering the wife, she demanded that John's head be brought to her on a silver platter and was not disappointed.

2/13/70, Fillmore East, New York (Dick's Picks Volume Four [1996])
4/29/71, Fillmore East, New York
10/16/89, Brendan Byrne Arena, East Rutherford, New Jersey

▪ *Angel Clare* /Art Garfunkel
Columbia KC 31472, 1973. Produced by Art Garfunkel and Roy Halee.

In September 1973 Garcia made an unusual appearance as a supporting musician on "Down in the Willow Garden," a track on Garfunkel's debut solo album. Despite the likes of some heavyweight recording artists on the scene, Garcia seemed irritated when recalling his contribution to the album in a 1981 interview with Blair Jackson and David Gans. "One time I did a session for Art Garfunkel and it turned out every little note, every lick, every moment of what I was doing—which was an overdub in a *sea* of overdubs—[was planned out]. It wasn't like he wanted me to play a part, but he definitely wanted to discuss *everything* in advance. Everything I did, I did four or five times."

▪ "A Night at the Family Dog"
(television program)

On February 4, 1970, the San Francisco affiliate of PBS videotaped the Dead, Jefferson Airplane, and Santana for a one-hour, edited mini-concert. Broadcast the following December, the reel features micro-sets by each band and concludes with a "super-jam" with members of all three groups.

The Dead performed a number of selections for the taping but their excellent renditions of "Hard to Handle" and "China Cat Sunflower">"I Know You Rider" are the best extant example of cinematic Dead from this ripe period of their career. Despite the needless slow-mo edits and superfluous female dancers, the tape is a classic.

Incidentally, the "Hard to Handle" footage from this special found its way into the Dead's own *Backstage Pass* video twenty years later.

▪ *Anthem of the Sun*
Warner Bros. WS 1749, 1968. Produced by the Grateful Dead and Dave Hassinger.
"That's It for the Other One: I. Cryptical Envelopment, II. Quadlibet for Tenderfeet, III. The Faster We Go, the Rounder We Get, IV. We Leave the Castle," "New Potato Caboose," "Born Cross-Eyed," "Alligator," "Caution (Do Not Stop on the Tracks)"

The Dead's second album, an ambitious compositional experiment mixing live and studio recording, is still regarded as quintessential San Francisco psychedelia. As Garcia commented on the concept behind *Anthem of the Sun*, "We weren't making a record in the normal; we were making a collage. We were trying to do something completely, which didn't even have to do with a concept. It had to do with an approach that's more like electronic music or concrete music, where you are actually assembling bits and pieces toward an enhanced nonrealistic representation."

Though the LP is not for the uninitiated, the Dead kick out long, lyrical jams on "The Other One," "New Potato Caboose," and "Caution." Phil Lesh can be heard taking a short Miles Davis–influenced trumpet solo on "Born Cross-Eyed."

THE GRATEFUL DEAD
❖
ANTHEM OF THE SUN

(Courtesy of Warner Bros. Records)

Still, *Anthem* is the Dead's most unconventional album and remains more decidedly experimental than most of the popular music released in 1968. Many groups fed off the creative spirit engendered in the 1967 "Summer of Love," but all of them kept one foot firmly planted in the mainstream. That there isn't anything on the album that sounds, even remotely, like a single is a testament to the Dead's uncompromising attitude toward their art.

Taking a 180-degree turn from their first album, which was grounded in tradition, *Anthem* shows the band at its most extreme. *Anthem*'s first side is a rock masterpiece with the main theme of "The Other One" leading into some beautiful musique concrète that results in "Caboose." The end of "Caboose" is a driving solo by Garcia that builds to a frenzy thanks to Lesh's bass and the drummer's billowing effects.

Writing in the September 1968 *Rolling Stone*, Jim Miller pointed out that "The mixture of electronic and serious music achieved by Edgard Varèse on 'Deserts' stands as one of the most impressive achievements in this area; on their own terms the Dead have achieved a comparable blend of electronic and electric music. For this reason alone *Anthem of the Sun* is an extraordinary event."

Discussing the relative care with which the band approached the recording of *Anthem* in comparison to their first album, Garcia pointed out, "The second record

went the whole other way. We were going to work on it, make sure it sounded good, really get into recording, and go on some trips with it. We recorded for a couple of weeks in L.A., experimentally, and accomplished absolutely nothing.

"Then we went to New York . . . and got our producer [Dave Hassinger] so excited that he quit. We were being so weird, and he was only human, after all, and he didn't really have to go through all that . . ."

The band's relationship with Hassinger, as well as their unusual approach to studio creation, was not helped when Phil Lesh invited his friend Tom "T.C." Constanten to contribute to the album. As T.C. recounted, "The final part of 'That's It for the Other One' was an overlay of several live performances, whence it gets that depth; it's a remarkable effect. They wanted to take that up and swirl it into an explosion, and out of the ashes of that would stealthily enter the warm, misty waves of 'New Potato Caboose.'

"At one point I dived into the piano, having pulled the string on a gyroscope and put it against the sounding board. The sound is not unlike that of a chainsaw being taken into it. I wasn't able to see it because of the sightlines in the studio, but I'm told that Hassinger cleared his seat by fully a foot and a half when he heard it. They managed to calm him down, however, and actually the piano wasn't damaged at all."

After a final blowout with the Dead over Weir's "Born Cross-Eyed" (the guitarist wanted the producer to help him create the sound of "thick air"), Hassinger quit. That left Garcia and Lesh to fend for themselves as producers.

The two worked for about six months at San Francisco's Columbus Recorders, smoking large quantities of marijuana and putting together a substantial number of two-track tapes of concerts from a tour of the Northwest in early 1968. Although they lost many generations of sound from overdubbing they created what Lesh once aptly described as a "pillow of sound."

A final note concerns the source concert that comprised the bulk of the album. As Lesh recalled to David Gans in *Playing in the Band*, "The gig that became the core tape of *Anthem of the Sun* was the one Garcia talked about in the movie [*The Grateful Dead Movie*], where he 'threw me down the stairs' because I stopped playing for a while. I got lost and stopped. I couldn't figure out what was going on.

"He said, 'Motherfucker, you *play!*—mumble mumble.' He just kinda pushed me out of the way.

"That was the first act of violence that any one of us had ever directed toward another one. It blew my mind, for about six or eight hours . . . 'You ever touch me again . . . ' You know how it is.

"And of course, the first thing he said to me the next day was. 'Hey, I'm sorry,' and I said, 'Hey, forget it.' That's all you can really say.

"That was one night we weren't high on acid. We were just playin'. If you're not on drugs and you play shit like that, I dunno—maybe it makes you wired-er, more edgy. We were trying too hard. . . .

"The tape was so hot that we didn't connect it with that incident for a while. I think Jerry was the first one who recognized it. He told me about it, and I said, 'Are you shittin' me?'

"Even after all that misunderstanding, we used *those* tapes of that night: St. Valentine's Day 1968, at the Carousel Ballroom. We used that for the core of 'The Other One' and 'Alligator.' "

As has often been the case, not everyone in the band was pleased with the music being made at the time or its enshrinement on vinyl. According to Bill Kreutzmann's 1989 interview with Blair Jackson, "It was kind of strange. There was a lot of layering and manipulation in the studio, obviously, but if the end result is cool then that's fine with me. To be real honest, I wasn't all that involved with *Anthem of the Sun*. I didn't feel like I participated that much in that music; it didn't 'get me,' if you know what I mean. It wasn't my cup of tea particularly. If I listened to the record right now I might eat my words, but my memory is I wasn't that thrilled with it. I thought then—and actually I still think this way sometimes—that some of the double drum stuff makes the music seem less concise. Sometimes less is more."

The album's title was drawn from a piece of ancient Egyptian music Lesh uncovered in a report by archaeologist Paul Schliemann. The report described the discovery of a tomb containing the remains of a huge orchestra that included sixty-five instruments, eighty singers, and a single skull.

Bill Walker, an artist friend of Constanten, painted the fire-wheel mandala on the album cover, which included psychedelically camouflaged renderings of the band members. According to Walker, those representations were the musicians' "subtle energy patterns" he had observed emanating from them while they performed. The artwork was inspired by a 1967 New Year's Eve LSD and yagé trip Walker and Constanten experienced in an area of the Nevada desert known as the Valley of the Sun.

As for Constanten, he made up most of the oddly named segments on the album denoting where the music clearly changed so the band could receive royalties for more than just one song.

Phil Lesh remixed *Anthem* in 1972 and it was rereleased. The remix was released again in 1976 with a white cover instead of a purple one. When the CD was released, the original mix was restored.

■ **"Antwerp's Placebo"** (Hart/Kreutzmann)
Grateful Dead, *Go to Heaven* (1980)

This slice of "Drumz"/"Space" appeared with a curious title on the Dead's first album with Brent Mydland.

■ ***Aoxomoxoa***
Warner Bros. WS 1790, 1969. Produced and arranged by the Grateful Dead.
"St. Stephen," "Dupree's Diamond Blues," "Rosemary," "Doin' That Rag," "Mountains of the Moon," "China Cat Sunflower," "What's Become of the Baby," "Cosmic Charlie"
Marmaduke (John Dawson), DAVID NELSON, Peter Grant, Wendy, Debbie, Mouse

One of the first attempts at sixteen-track recording, this eerie studio concoction layers acoustic, keyboard, and voicing textures with offbeat rhythmic arrangements. While "St. Stephen" and "China Cat Sunflower" became instant audience favorites, a couple of cuts, particularly "What's Become of the Baby," are still downright inaccessible.

Discussing the album's construction with Jann Wenner and Charles Reich in 1971, Garcia said, "The next record was really a continuation of the *Anthem of the Sun* trip—called *Aoxomoxoa*—a continuation in the style of having a complex record. When we started, *Aoxomoxoa* was an eight-track record and then all of a sudden there was a sixteen-track recorder in the studio, so we abandoned our entire eight-track version and went to sixteen-track to start all over again. Now, at the time we were sipping STP during our session, which made it a little weird—in fact, very weird. We spent too

(*Courtesy of Warner Bros. Records*)

much money and too much time on that record; we were trying to accomplish too much, and I was being really stupid about a lot of it, because it was material, some new tunes that I had written, that I hadn't really bothered to teach anyone in the band, and I was trying to record them from the ground up, and everybody was coming in and doing overdubs. It was weird, we went about it in a very fragmentary way. We didn't go about it as a group at all.

"Now, I like that record, personally, just for its weirdness, really. There are certain feelings and a certain kind of looseness that I kinda dig; but it's been our most unsuccessful record. It was when Hunter and I were both being more or less obscure, and there are lots of levels on the verbal plane in terms of the lyrics being very far-out. Too far-out, really, for most people.

"That was one of my pet records 'cause it was the first stuff that I thought *was* starting to sound like how I wanted to hear songs sound.

"It was great fun. *All* the music is on the tapes, the tapes were well recorded, and the music is well-played, and everything on it is really *right*. It's just that it was our first adventure with sixteen-track, and we tended to use up *every* track, and then when we were mixing, we were all of us trying to mix. Well, *we* couldn't; somebody might be able to. Anyway, it came out mixed by committee. A lot of the music was just lost in the mix; a lot of what was really there on the tape. But I really had fun remixing it. The remixes are admittedly somewhat sim-

pler, and I left out a lot of what seemed unnecessary to the content of the stuff. I just got farther into trying to make it sound like what I hoped it would sound like in the first place.

"That record is one of my pets. I really like it. I was always sorry that it came out so fucked up and then didn't sell and all. It was one our most expensive ones—it might've been *the* most expensive one."

Over the years Garcia cooled his own enthusiasm regarding the record, confiding to David Gans in 1981, "A lot of the *Aoxomoxoa* songs are overwritten and cumbersome to perform. They're packed with lyrics or musical changes that aren't worth it for what finally happens with the song. But at that time, I wasn't writing songs for the band to play—I was writing songs to be writing songs.

"Those were the first songs Hunter and I did together, and we didn't have the craft of songwriting down. We did things that, in retrospect, turned out to be unwise from the point of view that it's important for the musicians to enjoy playing the tune; the performances never sound anything but strained.

"Most of the *Aoxomoxoa* songs worked their way out of our repertoire; nobody in the band really expresses any interest in playing them . . . Even 'China Cat Sunflower' is marginal."

Aoxomoxoa marked the beginning of a serious Garcia-Hunter songwriting partnership, with Hunter providing the lyrics and Garcia and Lesh composing the music. As Hunter recalled the process some years later: "When we lived together in Larkspur, the way we'd write a song was I'd sit upstairs banging away at my three chords for days and days working something out. By the time I had it worked out, through the thin walls he'd heard everything I was doing. I'd come down and hand him this sheet of paper, and he'd say 'Oh, that's interesting.' And he'd play the whole arrangement of it right away, because he'd heard what I was doing and heard where it was going."

The Dead wanted to call the album *Earthquake Country*, but Rick Griffin, the late artist who rendered the album cover design, insisted on calling it *Aoxomoxoa*. Griffin had become obsessed with palindromes at that particular stage of his drawing and the Dead went along with his persuasions. A final note of trivia concerns the album's back cover. Courtney Love, our mid-1990s grunge diva, is reportedly pictured as a child in the spectral "family" portrait. Love's father, Hank Harrison, was among those in the Dead's camp at the time, so the allegation is not without plausibility.

▪ *Apocalypse Now* (soundtrack)
Elektra DP 90001, 1979.

"Francis wanted me to paint a picture of the jungle. He kept telling me, 'Make the jungle come alive!' Well, when I started out, I didn't have all the colors to make the picture Francis wanted, so I went out and *made* them. This was to be music of the spheres."

This, according to Mickey Hart, was the inspiration of the construction of "The Beast," a huge drum setup that gave Hart and Bill Kreutzmann another musical dimension in the late 1970s.

Francis Ford Coppola's monumental film was released at the same time as this motion picture soundtrack, which included atmospheric jungle music with an ensemble led by Hart.

Inviting some of his closest musical colleagues to "go up the river" with him, Hart remembered the process of creation: "We laid out the instruments so we could walk through the room without stumbling and make the music flow, like the river. Sometimes we got lost in it, just like Kurtz [the crazed protagonist of the film, played by Marlon Brando]. Just about everyone involved with *Apocalypse Now* got 'Kurtzed' at one time or another."

The sessions for the soundtrack lasted for about ten days and the recordings (made on both audio and videotape) were used by Coppola in the second half of the film and over the closing credits in the 35-millimeter version. Ultimately Coppola got exactly what he paid for: music that captured the primitivism of the jungle and Man himself.

Some of the Rhythm Devils' contribution to the film was included on the soundtrack album but a better representation of their efforts can be heard on *The Apocalypse Now Sessions*.

See also **The Rhythm Devils Play River Music: The Apocalypse Now Sessions**

▪ "Are You Lonely for Me Baby" (Bert Berns)
Freddie Scott, single (1967)
Otis Redding and Carla Thomas, *King and Queen* (1967)
Goliath, *Goliath* (1969)

Although Bob Weir sang "Are You Lonely for Me Baby" only once, just before the band stormed the Continent in 1972, the song was written by Bert Berns, an important figure in New York music during the 1960s.

Born Bert Russell in 1929, Berns composed various R&B and soul standards including "Twist and Shout" (with Phil Medley) and "Piece of My Heart." Later he made a brief foray into the British scene and produced Van Morrison's early records.

Though he was trained at the Julliard School of Music, Berns was a true product of Tin Pan Alley, where he worked as song-plugger, music copyist, composer, talent scout, A&R man, and producer. Berns operated at the crossroads of the new teenage pop and the emerging soul style which allowed "Twist and Shout," with its Latin-influenced rhythm typical of many Berns compositions, to be a crossover hit for the Beatles and the Isley Brothers. He scored a similar success with soul songs he wrote for Solomon Burke ("Cry to Me" and "Everybody Needs Somebody to Love"), which were covered by the Rolling Stones, among others.

Before his surprising death of a heart attack on New Year's Eve 1967, Berns had owned his own label, recorded Lulu, virtually discovered Them, taken over LEIBER AND STOLLER'S duties as Atlantic's resident songwriter/producer, been the guiding force behind such classic Drifters tracks as "Under the Boardwalk," scored big pop hits in England with the McCoys' "Hang on Sloopy," and recorded Neil Diamond's first tracks. Janis Joplin scored a big hit with Berns's "Piece of My Heart" a year after his death.

3/25/72, Academy of Music, New York

▪ *The Arista Years*
Arista 07822-18934-2, 1996.
"Estimated Prophet," "Passenger," "Samson & Delilah," "Terrapin Station: Lady with a Fan, Terrapin Station, Terrapin, Terrapin Transit, At a Siding, Terrapin Flyer, Refrain," "Good Lovin'," "Shakedown Street," "Fire on the Mountain," "I Need a Miracle," "Alabama Getaway," "Far from Me," "Saint of Circumstance," "Dire Wolf," "Cassidy," "Feel Like a Stranger," "Franklin's Tower," "Touch of Grey," "Hell in a Bucket," "West L.A. Fadeaway," "Throwing Stones," "Black Muddy River," "Foolish Heart," "Built to Last," "Just a Little Light," "Picasso Moon," "Standing on the Moon"

Compilation albums never quite seem up to snuff and *The Arista Years* once again fits that bill. With nary a

(Courtesy of Arista Records)

bonus track to be found on this two-disc set, the collection groups songs chronologically by album with severe top-heaviness on the *In the Dark* and *Built to Last* material, boasting five selections each from those albums, while only including one cut (the great "Eyes of the World" with Branford Marsalis) from the stellar *Without a Net*. Similar brevity is given the *Reckoning* and *Dead Set* material, while nearly the entire *Terrapin Station* album is included. Who makes these decisions, anyway?

Liner notes by Blair Jackson and Richard Gehr help to soften the blow of laying out *mucho dinero* for yet another weasely record company product.

- **"Around and Around"**
  See **"Round and Round"**

- **Around the World (for a Song)** / Various Artists
  Rykodisc RCD 00217, 1991. Produced by Mickey Hart.
  "Udu Chant" (Mickey Hart); "Sweet Sixteen (DIGA RHYTHM BAND); "Blow Wind Blow" (DZINTARS: THE LATVIAN WOMEN'S CHOIR); "Akiwowo," "Kori" (BABATUNDE OLATUNJI); "The Groom" (MUSIC OF UPPER AND LOWER EGYPT); "Dry Sand of the Desert" (Mickey Hart, AIRTO, FLORA PURIM); "Tov L'Hodot" (GOLDEN GATE GYPSY ORCHESTRA); "Mwashah" (HAMZA EL DIN); "Bamboo Jew's Harp" (VOICES OF THE RAINFOREST); "Compound" (Rhythm Devils); "Alop and Jor" (HARIPRASAD — ZAKIR

HUSSAIN); "Raga: Bageshree" (Ustad Sultan Khan); "Yamantaka" (THE GYUTO MONKS); "Grand Entry Song" (Songs of the Great Lakes Indians); "Sky Water" (Mickey Hart)

A musical "ticket to ride," this unique sampler highlights the major sources of Mickey Hart's Rykodisc project, The World.

- **The Asphalt Jungle Boys**
  See **Mother McCree's Uptown Jug Champions**

- **Astronauts and Heretics** / Thomas Dolby
  Giant 24478, 1992.
  Garcia takes a bow on "Beauty of a Dream," a track from this overlooked Thomas Dolby album.

- **"At a Siding"** (Grateful Dead)
  Grateful Dead, *Terrapin Station* (1977)

An elastic jam which punctuated the Dead's "Terrapin Station" suite on vinyl made only one concert appearance.
  3/18/77, Winterland Arena, San Francisco

- **At the Edge** / Mickey Hart
  Rykodisc RCD 10124, 1990. Produced by Mickey Hart.
  "#4 for Gaia," "Sky Water," "Slow Sailing," "Lonesome Hero," "Fast Sailing," "Cougar Ran," "The Eliminators," "Brainstorm," "Pigs in Space"
  Mickey Hart–whistles, rainstick, rattles, forest zone (processed crickets), Matrix-12, Roland D-50 and Emulator II, processed bell, remo toms, raindrops, sit gongs (hollow log), Englehart Comet Bells (metal percussion), kalimba (thumb piano), cowbells, dundun (talking drum), panpipes, trap set, agogo (double bell), wood blocks, whistles, Matrix-12, Devil Chasers (bamboo concussion sticks), bass drum, tar, cowbells, spatial processing. Jerry Garcia–forest zone, electric guitar, guitar synthesizer. ZAKIR HUSSAIN–processed tabla, duggi tarang (tuned metal drums), tar (frame drum), processed tabla, shakers, dholak (double-headed cylinder drum), tabla. Joze Lorenzo–berimbau (musical bow). Sikiru Adepoju–dundun. BABATUNDE OLATUNJI–djembe (wooden hourglass drum), balafon (pentatonic marimba), cowbells, shekere (beaded gourd rattle), Englehart hex bells, slit gong. Creek Hart–Linn 9000 drum

samples. Taro S. Hart–Kawasaki electronic drums. AIRTO MOREIRA–extended voice and beast.

Though this companion to Hart's first book, *Drumming at the Edge of Magic*, has an all-star lineup, many compositions serve better as ambient music. However, the main Garcia track, "The Eliminators," is striking and recalls the best of the Dead's "Space" presentations.

As Hart told Blair Jackson in 1990, "I composed it at different times during the period I was researching the book. I was heavily into reading the literature on the subject of day and night, and it was even in my dreams. The instruments that naturally come to life in those dreams should come to life in your dream songs, become part of your code. So these are just little rumblings that I brought back from that side; little dream songs."

For instance, when Hart was studying trance-inducing instruments, the compositions he was working on began taking on some of the elements of that particular research. Obviously Hart didn't set out to cut a mainstream product but rather a nonliteral soundtrack to his book. Without trying to specifically re-create what he chronicled in the tome, he captured the spirit and aural imagery of the rarefied terrain that he covered on paper. In fact, some of the musicians and much of their music never made the final cut, because Hart simplified his vision of the album during production.

A lot of what ended up being pressed was processed from acoustic sounds Hart captured and manipulated on a computer. For example, Mickey counted 161 individual raindrop sounds on the album alone. He became so involved with including recorded examples of nature on the disc that he began trading sounds with filmmaker George Lucas, who drew on his own special-effects library for the endeavor.

As Hart told Jackson, "It was primal because I was studying prehistory, a time before man organized sounds. The whistles and sounds of nature—that's where we got our language and our music. We started mingling with these sounds until it became music."

In regards to the difficulties and joys of collaborating with such a diverse ethnic and musical crew, Hart told Jackson, "Zakir and I laid a couple of basics together, but most of it was overdubbed. When Olatunji would come in we'd talk about it for hours and try different things. Sometimes he or Zakir would come in, I'd talk about what I was after, and *wham*—'That's it!' But it's hard to describe what you hear in a dream, and sometimes it's hard to remember your dreams clearly. So you have to search and try to hold on to that original vision as well as you can."

▪ "Attics of My Life" (Garcia/Hunter)
Grateful Dead, *American Beauty* (1970)

A somber, melancholic ballad, "Attics of My Life" is an early Robert Hunter call to inspiration in a manner he dramatically explored with the "Terrapin Station" suite a decade later. "Attics" was performed about fifteen times in 1970 and once in 1972 before being shelved for about seventeen years and returning to the Dead's playlist in 1989. Imbued with hopeful introspection, the song is filled with many of Hunter's signature ellipses. An ear bends to hear a tune, eyes close to see, and petals unfold in a dreamland conjured either by the singer or the one to whom he is singing.

6/24/70, Capitol Theater, Port Chester, New York

9/8/91, Madison Square Garden, New York

9/24/94, Berkeley Community Theater, Berkeley, California

- **"Baba O'Riley"** (Pete Townshend)
  The Who, *Who's Next* (1971), *The Kids Are Alright* (1979)
  Pete Townshend and Friends, *I Am* (1970)

Thirty seconds of spiraling solo synthesizer opens the Who's finest studio LP and its most famous track. Eventually the piano, voice, drums, bass, and guitar join in, but it's the tension between Roger Daltrey's leonine roar and Pete Townshend's tuneful pleading on the guitar that gives "Baba O'Riley" its drama. "Baba O'Riley" was named after Meher Baba, Pete Townshend's spiritual guru, and Terry Riley, the electronic composer who was Townshend's musical mentor. Riley's *A Rainbow in Curved Air* inspired Townshend's use of looping synthesizer riffs in "Baba O'Riley."

According to Townshend, "This was a number I wrote while I was doing these experiments with tapes on the synthesizer. Among my plans was to take a person out of the audience and feed information—height, weight, autobiographical details—about the person into the synthesizer. The synthesizer would then select notes from the pattern of that person. It would be like translating a person into music. On this particular track I programmed details about the life of Meher Baba and then provided the backing for the number."

"Teenage Wasteland," the starting point for Townshend's imaginary generation in their search to find nirvana, became a timeless Who entity in Daltrey's hands, and the outright disgust with the post-Woodstock decline in culture was rarely matched in rock.

Vince Welnick may have had some of this in mind when he began singing "Baba O'Riley" with the Dead in the spring of 1992. Situated on the front end of a medley that paired it with the Beatles' "Tomorrow Never Knows," "Baba O'Riley" was employed almost exclusively as an encore vehicle for the band. As Vince told *The Grateful Dead Almanac*, the band's house organ, in 1995, "With 'Baba O'Riley,' I just started playing the intro and Billy [Kreutzmann] just jumped right in. Pretty soon the whole band was all over it like a cat on a mouse. The way it got put together with 'Tomorrow Never Knows' was just a coincidence: Bobby Weir happened to bring that song into rehearsal on the same day."
  5/25/92, Shoreline Amphitheater, Mountain View, California
  6/14/92, Giants Stadium, East Rutherford, New Jersey (with Steve Miller)

- **"Baby What You Want Me to Do"**
  (Jimmy Reed)
  Jimmy Reed, *The Best of Jimmy Reed* (1960)
  ETTA JAMES, *Etta James Rocks the House* (1964)
  Bill Cosby, *Bill Cosby Sings* (1966)
  Elvis Presley, *Elvis—A Legendary Performer, Vol. 2* (1968)
  The Everly Brothers, *A Date with The Everly Brothers* (1961), *The Everly Brothers Show* (1970)
  Hot Tuna, *Yellow Fever* (1975)
  John Cale, *Helen of Troy* (1975)
  Maureen Tucker, *Mojadkatebarry* (1987)

Jimmy Reed's "Baby What You Want Me to Do" hit the Top 10 of the R&B charts in 1960 and was covered by a wide range of artists.

With Brent Mydland handling the vocals, the Dead only performed "Baby What You Want Me to Do" a few times in the early and mid-1980s. But their first rendition of the song, backing up Etta James at the 1982 New Year's Eve show, was the most memorable.

> **12/31/82, Oakland Auditorium Arena, Oakland, California**

- ### *Backstage Pass* (video)

  Directed by Justin Kreutzmann. Produced by Gillian Grisman. Music producer: John Cutler. Sound Designer: Bob Bralove. Animation: Xaos. Grateful Dead Merchandising, 1992.

  "Hard to Handle," "Fearless Groove," "The Other One," "Easy to Love You," "She Belongs to Me," "Infrared Roses Revisited"

This kaleidoscopic six-song, thirty-five-minute video journey through the Dead's history opens with Ron "Pigpen" McKernan belting out an incendiary "Hard to Handle." The presentation includes rare, never-before-seen or heard footage and music of the Dead from their jugband days through the Acid Tests, the Fillmore era, and the legendary performances in Egypt to a 1992 "unplugged" cover of Bob Dylan's "She Belongs to Me" featuring Garcia, Weir, and Lesh trading vocal leads. An added attraction of the video is some of the best animation this side of *Who Killed Roger Rabbit?*

- ### "Bad Moon Rising" (JOHN FOGERTY)

  Creedence Clearwater Revival, *Green River* (1969), *Chronicle* (1976), *The Concert* (1980)
  Emmylou Harris, *Evangeline* (1981)
  Stretch Marks, *What D'Ya See?* (1987)

John Fogerty joined the Dead onstage during their set at the free concert honoring Bill Graham several days after the impresario's tragic death in a California helicopter crash. "Bad Moon Rising," a portentous song in the Creedence Clearwater Revival catalogue, was one of several one-off performances the Dead performed with Fogerty that bittersweet afternoon.

> **11/3/91, Polo Field. Golden Gate Park, San Francisco**

- ### Joan Baez

  Born January 9, 1941, Staten Island, New York

Because she was a central figure in the folk revival of the early 1960s, Joan Baez's once-in-a-lifetime soprano and consistent commitment to pacifist-humanist politics in

Joan Baez *(Archive Photos/Peter D. Whitney)*

her music and her life sustained a career that has spanned four decades. It has also made her a natural influence on and collaborator with the Grateful Dead.

Baez's upbringing certainly predisposed her to a life of progressive politics and music. Her father was a Mexican-born physicist who was a UNESCO consultant and a Quaker. She grew up in California and in Boston, where she first made contact with the New England folk-music community of the late 1950s. Not yet twenty years old, she was quickly recognized as one of the most gifted interpreters of the traditional Child ballads, named after Francis J. Child, the most important folk scholar of the nineteenth century. Child's collection and codification of English and Scottish material became *the* basic source for singers of traditional songs.

Baez accompanied herself on guitar and was the hit of the 1959 Newport Folk Festival and in 1960 she cut the first of seventeen remarkable albums for Vanguard. Including songs from Leadbelly ("House of the Rising Sun") and the Carter Family ("Wildwood Flower"), Baez's first record also contained a harrowing version of the tragic Scottish ballad "Mary Hamilton."

As with most of the younger folk musicians of the era, Baez was an outspoken supporter of causes from the early antinuclear movement to civil and human rights. The anthem of the burgeoning "movement," "We Shall Overcome," was a feature of her early concerts. But it wasn't until she met Bob Dylan that she began performing contemporary songs and, soon, writing her own. She repaid Dylan by introducing him to her folk audiences in 1963 and prolifically, if unoriginally, interpreting his songs. This eventually led her to record *Any Day Now,* a double-album of Dylan material, in 1968. She also covered Phil Ochs's "There But for Fortune," with which she had a 1965 hit single in Britain.

But when Dylan drifted away from protest songs, Baez and many of her peers veered away from him. Putting her political actions where her voice was, she helped found the Institute for Non-Violence in California and withheld her taxes in protest of U.S. defense spending for a few years. Her break from Dylan was also a response to his turn to electric music and her discomfort with rock music was always evident. A graphic depiction of their separation can be uncomfortably glimpsed in *Don't Look Back,* D. A. Pennebaker's film vérité about Dylan's 1965 tour of England.

Eventually she broadened her horizons with a series of six albums recorded in Nashville between 1968 and 1973. With these efforts, Baez discovered an appropriate amplified mode to display her repertoire, which now included contemporary country and singer/songwriter material. *One Day at a Time,* released in 1970, was the most critically acclaimed of the Nashville albums and mixed old songs such as "Joe Hill" (about the turn-of-the-century labor organizer) with the Rolling Stones' "No Expectations" and social commentary on Steven Young's "Seven Bridges Road." In 1971 she had her only Top 10 hit in the U.S. with a pedestrian working of the Band's "The Night They Drove Old Dixie Down," which appeared on her album *Blessed Are.* A testament to her growing confidence as a writer was the publication of *Daybreak,* a collection of her notebook jottings and drawings.

In 1968 Baez married David Harris, an anti–Vietnam War activist who was later arrested and jailed for resisting the draft. Though they had a son, Gabriel, in 1969, the couple separated in 1971. Gabe would become a second-generation Deadhead.

Perhaps the best commingling of her art and politics can be found on the B side of her 1973 album *Where Are You Now, My Son?* which was devoted to an extended composition incorporating tapes she made during a United States air raid on Hanoi which occurred while she was visiting Vietnam with a peace delegation.

The fruits of Baez's maturing songwriting skills blossomed through a series of recordings in the mid-1970s and came to full flower with *Diamonds and Rust* in 1975. The record was a minor hit and much of its material, including the title track, was an account of her relationship with Dylan ten years before. Baez sang the song when she reunited with Dylan on his Rolling Thunder Revue tours of 1975 and 1976. Baez again joined Dylan for his 1984 tour of Europe but her experiences with the enigmatic troubador remained decidedly mixed.

Though Baez's records lost some of their consequence over the course of the next decade, she continued to attract large international audiences for her concerts, which were often linked to political causes, such as Nicaragua's Sandinista revolution, about which she made a film, *There But for Fortune,* in 1982.

For a period in the 1980s she was a woman without a record label and, when asked if this was a result of a political blacklisting in the Reagan era, Baez quipped, "I don't think they would care whether I was a communist or a fascist if I would commit myself to making platinum singles."

Her commitment to human justice was again dramatically evidenced in the 1990s when she ventured to Bosnia to bring attention to the genocidal conflict in that tortured region of the world. In August 1966, Baez had joined the Dead and other musicians onstage for a rousing "Midnight Hour" in a concert that benefited a children's day camp. But it wasn't until December 1981 that she united with the band for a trio of concerts. The first of these was a Baez-organized bill advertised as "Dance for Disarmament." Baez joined the Dead for a rare acoustic set that included an unusual mix of cover tunes and Joanie originals: "ME AND BOBBY MCGEE," "Children of the '80s," "Lucifer's Eyes," "Warriors of the Sun," "BYE BYE LOVE," "BARBARA ALLEN," "You Find Me," "Where Have All the Heroes Gone," "Oh Boy," "Lady Di," and "The Boxer." Just two weeks later, Baez joined the Dead for the final two shows of their Oakland Auditorium New Year's run that included similarly obscure acoustic sets.

Almost exactly six years later, Weir, Jerry Garcia, and Garcia Band bassist John Kahn performed acoustically for an AIDS Emergency Fund benefit concert organized by Baez. After a rousing set that included old and new selections, Baez joined them on "Dark Hollow," "The Turtle Dove," and "Knockin' on Heaven's Door."

▪ "Ballad of Casey Jones" (Traditional)

Singles: Mississippi John Hurt (1928), De Ford Bailey (1928), Charles "Cow Cow" Davenport (1930), Henry Truvillion (1933), Cornelius Steen (1933), John and Rochelle French (1935), Will Weldon (1936), Jesse James (1936), Ed Cobb (1937), John Floyd (1939), Arthur ("Brother-in-Law") Armstrong (1940), Asa Ware (1942)
Jerry Garcia Acoustic Band, *Almost Acoustic* (1989)
Jerry Garcia/DAVID GRISMAN, *Shady Grove* (1996)
Johnny Cash, *Blood, Sweat and Tears* (1963)
Furry Lewis, *Shake 'Em on Down* (1961), *In His Prime/'27* (1988)

Not to be confused with "Casey Jones," the Garcia/Hunter rocker on *Workingman's Dead*, "The Ballad of Casey Jones" was recorded under many other titles and variously known as "Casey Jones," "Casey Jones Blues," "Kassie Jones," and "Southern Casey Jones." The Dead performed this song a couple of times in 1970 when they were opening their lengthy three-set concerts with an acoustic presentation. It was more commonly covered by Garcia during his acoustic shows during the 1980s and early 1990s.

5/15/70, Fillmore East, New York

▪ "Ballad of Frankie Lee and Judas Priest" (BOB DYLAN)

Bob Dylan, *John Wesley Harding* (1968)

A delightful tale of temptation and its consequence. Dylan's delivery and harmonica work carried this brittle warning when it was first released on his influential *John Wesley Harding* album. So it was with some surprise that Dylan revived it for his concerts with the Grateful Dead in 1987. A poorer song choice probably couldn't have been made for the large stadium venues at which these shows took place in that "Frankie Lee and Judas Priest" has the elongated feel of a shaggy dog story, a comic tall tale in the frontier-ballad style with echoes of Mark Twain and Robert Service. Dylan pulls off a dozen jokes in the song and because of this, it really deserves to be *listened* to and was an inappropriate selection for crowds of 70,000.

7/6/87, JFK Stadium, Philadelphia (with Bob Dylan)

▪ "Ballad of a Thin Man" (BOB DYLAN)

Bob Dylan, *Highway 61 Revisited* (1965), *At Budokan* (1978), *Real Live* (1985)
Bob Dylan and THE BAND, *Before the Flood* (1974)

One of Bob Dylan's most frightening songs, "Ballad of a Thin Man," is a haunting blues about a mysterious Mr. Jones who just does not seem to understand the world around him. Mr. Jones, one of Dylan's greatest archetypes, is a Philistine who does not see, a person who does not reach for the right questions. He piously pays his social dues through self-serving tax deductions, pays to watch freak shows but doesn't like the entertainment, is superficially educated and well bred but not very smart about the things that count.

Dylan freaks have, naturally, spent years debating if Mr. Jones is based on a real individual and who that person may be, with everybody from Pete Seeger to Joan Baez to a *Time* magazine reporter named Jeffrey Jones and anything in between thrown up for speculation. More probably, Mr. Jones is a composite.

Dylan has performed the song throughout his career, reinventing it with each phase and shade of his ever-shifting persona, and the song was one of the highlights during his 1987 concerts with the Grateful Dead. Within a year of those shows, Weir effectively trotted out "Ballad of a Thin Man" for an all-too-brief two-show run.

But it was Garcia who articulated the song's essence in his 1981 interview with David Gans and Blair Jackson: "It tells that person who's lame that they're lame, why they're lame, which is a very satisfying thing to do. Certainly something everybody knows about."

> **7/12/87, Giants Stadium, East Rutherford, New Jersey (with Bob Dylan).**
>
> **4/1/88, Brendan Byrne Arena, East Rutherford, New Jersey**

• "Banana Boat (Day-O)"

(Belafonte/Burgess/Attaway)

HARRY BELAFONTE, *Calypso* (1957), *Pure Gold* (1975), *Day-O & Other Hits* (1990)

Stan Freberg, single (1957)

Raffi, *Baby Beluga* (1977)

Yellowman, *Live at Reggae Sunsplash* (1983)

The Main Attraction, *By Request* (1989)

Kidsongs, *Cars Boats, Trains & Other Things That Go* (1992)

Red Grammer, *Red Grammer's Favorite Sing Along Songs* (1993)

Frankie Paul, *Killer Reggae* (1994)

B. B. Shawn, *Finding My Way* (1996)

Harry Belafonte spearheaded the mid-1950s calypso craze in America with his third album, *Calypso*, in 1956. Although he started out as a more conventional pop artist, the LP, along with his clear diction, pure voice, and strikingly handsome features, made him a national sensation.

According to the original album's liner notes, " 'Day-O' is based on the traditional work songs of the gangs who load the banana boats in the harbor at Trinidad. The men come to work with the evening star and continue to work through the night. They long for daybreak when they will be able to return to their homes. All their wishful thinking is expressed in the lead singer's plaintive cry: 'Day-O, Day-O . . .' The lonely men and the cry in the night spell overtones of symbolism which are universal."

The Dead only performed the peppy "Day-O" at two 1987 concerts with the Neville Brothers leading the charge on vocals.

> **12/31/87, Coliseum Arena, Oakland, California**

• The Band

Jaime Robbie Robertson–born July 5, 1943, Toronto, Ontario. Richard Manuel–born April 3, 1943, Stratford, Ontario, died March 4, 1986, Florida. Garth Hudson–born August 2, 1937, London, Ontario. Rick Danko–born December 9, 1943, Simcoe, Ontario. Levon Helm–born May 26, 1940, Marvell, Arkansas.

Placing themselves staunchly on the side of tradition rather than novelty, the Band made two important contributions to the music of the 1960s and 1970s. In helping Bob Dylan go "electric" in the mid-1960s they turned rock music on its ear. Additionally, their own critically acclaimed albums, particularly *Music from Big Pink* (1968) and *The Band* (1969), were seen as part of the "maturing" of rock 'n' roll. While their peers often dabbled in the superficial, the Band was determined to place their music in an earlier context. Like John Ford's westerns that portray an idyll of a bygone America, the Band looked at the northern half of the continent with a fresh eye and their songs honorably celebrated the country's downtrodden. The sepia-toned aura of their albums prompted critic Greil Marcus to write, "Their music gave us a sense that the country was richer than we guess."

It was this period of the Band's work that directly influenced the Grateful Dead's 1970 albums *Workingman's Dead* and *American Beauty* (among other artists).

But, like the Dead, the Band did not develop their unique aesthetic overnight. Pieced together in Canada by Ronnie Hawkins, the reliable, hard-traveling Arkansas-bred rockabilly artist, they hit the road for a tour that lasted a decade. Hawkins recruited the future members of the Band one by one as his backing group, the Hawks. They had a Canadian hit with Bo Diddley's "WHO DO YOU LOVE?," a 1963 recording on which Robertson's stinging lead-guitar lines were already evident. As the Hawks developed musically, they were inspired to leave Hawkins and bill themselves as Levon and the Hawks after the drummer Levon Helm, the only Yank in the crew.

Honed by years of touring, their distinctive vocal and instrumental interplay began to develop a cult following on the East Coast by the mid-1960s. But it was in 1965 when they worked on John Hammond's *So Many Roads* on Vanguard and were invited by Bob Dylan to back him up on his groundbreaking electric tour that their reputation as cultural mavericks was sealed. Robertson was one of the studio musicians involved with Dylan's mercurial *Blonde on Blonde* album in 1966 and the Band (sans Levon Helm, who was temporarily replaced on drums by Mickey Jones) can be heard on the pirated recordings of Dylan's truly extraordinary 1966 concerts, as well as on a live "Just Like Tom Thumb's Blues" released as a late-sixties B-side.

When Dylan cracked up his motorcycle and body in 1966, the Band followed him to Woodstock, New York, where their relaxed woodshedding with the singer/songwriter resulted in *The Basement Tapes*, the widely bootlegged recordings that were officially released in 1975. *The Basement Tapes* also found Danko, Manuel, and Robertson writing their own material and collaborating with Dylan ("Tears of Rage" and "This Wheel's on Fire," both of which appeared on their debut album).

With its natural sound (there was no overdubbing) and plaintive vocals, *Music from Big Pink* was their critically acclaimed 1968 premiere that often featured Helm, Danko, and Manuel switching vocals within the same song. The compositions, including "I Shall Be Released," "We Can Talk," "Chest Fever," and the ever-popular "The Weight" (later covered by the Grateful Dead and a host of others), cemented the Band's reputation as stellar songwriters in their own right.

Showing no sophomore slump with a similarly eclectic offering in their 1969 follow-up album, *The Band*, they scored their biggest pop hit, "Up on Cripple Creek." Like its predecessor, the LP explored simple truths through a range of characters and stories. The following string of albums—*Stage Fright* (1970), *Cahoots* (1971), *Rock of Ages* (1972), and *Moondog Matinee* (1973)—added to their fascination with tribulation through original work and pointed cover material.

With the road, of course, never far away the Band sharpened their presentation, culminating in *Rock of Ages*, a live album recorded at New York City's Academy of Music on New Year's Eve 1973. The halcyon days of the Band were capped by their appearance with the Grateful Dead and the ALLMAN BROTHERS at the Watkins Glen concert, which attracted some 600,000 revelers in August 1973. Their reunion with Bob Dylan on his much-overlooked 1974 *Planet Waves* album and widely heralded tour of the same year (documented on 1974's *Before the Flood*) resulted in perhaps their best work from this period.

Tensions within the group, though, compounded by the grind of touring and a pair of increasingly conservative albums, led to their decision to disband. But it was a parting that was not without classy fanfare. With director Martin Scorsese they filmed and recorded their final concert at San Francisco's Winterland on Thanksgiving 1976. Regarded as the greatest rock 'n' roll concert film, *The Last Waltz* featured guest appearances from Dylan, Neil Young, Dr. John, Eric Clapton, the Staples Singers, Muddy Waters, Neil Diamond, Van Morrison, and their old stomping partner, Ronnie Hawkins.

While all the members pursued solo careers, Robertson's was easily the most significant. He turned to films, writing the music for many of Scorsese's later work and writing, producing, and starring in *Carny* (1980). Robertson returned to recording with *Robbie Robertson* (1988), a successful but conservative comeback, and *Storyville* (1991), a concept album that drew on the Band's earlier aesthetic sensibility. "Broken Arrow," a song from Robertson's self-titled disc, became a radio hit for Rod Stewart from his 1991 album *Vagabond Heart*, and was a late Grateful Dead concert inclusion performed by Phil Lesh.

The group re-formed without Robertson in the early 1980s and toured through the mid-1990s despite the loss of Richard Manuel, who hanged himself in a Florida hotel room in 1986. They shared several bills with the Grateful Dead in 1983 and 1984, stealing the 10/22/83 show at the Carrier Dome in Syracuse, New York.

Inducted into the Rock and Roll Hall of Fame in 1994, the Band performed a tense reunion set with Robertson (and without Helm) at the ceremonial shindig.

- ## "Banks of the Ohio" (Traditional)
  Paul Clayton, *Bloody Ballads* (1961)
  JOAN BAEZ, *Joan Baez, Volume 2* (1961), *The Joan Baez Country Music Album* (1979)
  Blue Sky Boys, *The In Concert '64* (1991)
  Porter Wagoner, *The Carroll County Accident* (1969)
  Grandpa Jones, *Fifty Years of Bluegrass Hits, Vol. 2* (1985)
  The Carter Family, *Wildwood Flower* (1988)
  Ann Richmond Boston, *The Big House of Time* (1990)
  Bill Monroe and Doc Watson, *Live Duet Recordings 1963–1980* (1993)

A diabolical song, "Banks of the Ohio" is a murder ballad that steers clear of the usual pregnant-sweetheart theme. While the version the Dead performed with Joan Baez in 1981 does not stray from her rendition of the song in which a young man kills his girl because she rejects his marriage proposal, some versions indicate family opposition to the union as a reason for the girl's refusal. Though similar in theme to various British broadside ballads, versions of this song have been reported only in America.

Many traditional songs in the Baez songbook originally appeared in what were commonly known as "broadside ballads." Practically from the inception of printing, ballad and song material were published on one side of single sheets of paper of various sizes, often wider than they were long, and sold for a few pennies by street singers and hawkers at country fairs and on the streets of cities throughout Europe and, later, in the New World as well. Though the artistry of these compositions is generally regarded as being of a lower order than those of the older traditional ballads (because they were knocked off by hack scriveners in the employ of the printers), the ballad sheets helped bring these songs into the oral tradition. When that occurred, many of them were smoothed out and transformed from journalistic pap into minor oral masterpieces.

12/31/81, Oakland Auditorium Arena, Oakland, California (with Joan Baez)

• "Barbara Allen" (Traditional)

Singles: Nick Marlor (1936), Queen Hule Hines (1939)
The Everly Brothers, *Songs Our Daddy Taught Us* (1958), *The Reunion Concert* (1991)
JOAN BAEZ, *Joan Baez Vol. 2* (1961)
The Hillmen, *The Hillmen* (1963)
Art Garfunkel, ANGEL CLARE (1973)
Dame Clara Butt, *The Heart of the Empire* (1993)
Dolly Parton, *Heartsongs* (1994)
Edward Flower and Joel Brown, *Chords & Thyme: English Folksongs for Guitar* (1994)

Another tune the Dead performed with Joan Baez but very rarely otherwise, "Barbara Allen" is one of the best known and most widely sung of all British traditional ballads. In both the Old World and in America, most variants of the song strongly resemble one another. This probably relates to its frequent publication in songsters, chapbooks, penny garlands, and on broadsides since the seventeenth century.

12/12/81, Fiesta Hall, County Fairgrounds, San Mateo, California (with Joan Baez)

• "Barbed Wire Whipping Party" (Grateful Dead)

Recorded in October 1968, this *Aoxomoxoa* outtake never made it to the concert stage. The reason for that may have had something to do with the method the Dead chose to record the gnarly instrumental in the studio. Using newly acquired sixteen-track recording gear that could create a cascade effect whereby sound recorded on one track was played back a split second later and rerecorded on the next track and then again until all sixteen tracks had been utilized. According to Garcia, "We all had microphones and headphones and hoses coming from a tank of nitrous oxide. When you'd play something, it came back sixteen times. You can imagine how confusing that was on nitrous oxide—immediately it turned into total gibberish."

• John Perry Barlow

Born October 3, 1947, Jackson Hole, Wyoming

Perhaps the last place you would have expected to find a key member of America's slowest rising show business act is in a Wyoming barn at dawn assisting a heifer in the last stages of a tough birth. Or surfing the Internet, digging deep into the digital ocean of electronic communications. Or conferring with fellow Republicans on the steps of Cheyenne's Capitol building. But any of the above locales are familiar territory to John Barlow, the lyricist responsible for a score of the Dead's fiery passion plays.

A prep-school chum of Bob Weir's, Barlow, like Robert Hunter, was a poet and novelist who happened to be a longtime friend of the musicians before being drafted into the songwriting ranks. Though somewhat less prolific than Hunter, Barlow's collaborations with Weir have endured as concert centerpieces. Barlow also began writing with Brent Mydland in a short-lived collaboration that ended when the keyboardist died of a drug overdose in 1990.

Barlow's childhood was straight out of a storybook. The product of generations of farmers and ranchers and the son of a state senator, Barlow was raised on Bar

Cross cattle ranch in Pinedale, Wyoming, often riding on horseback through the snow in order to attend a one-room schoolhouse or putting in twelve-hour days on a tractor by the time he was eleven. But when his rebellious streak got the better of him (and began threatening his father's political career), he was summarily shipped off to Fountain Valley High, a Colorado Springs, Colorado, prep school where he met and immediately bonded with another miscreant by the name of Bob Weir. Even though Weir was expelled after a year and the two didn't see each other for the next five, they stayed in touch through the mid-1960s. Just as music was Weir's entree to a more constructive form of anarchy, literature and theology were Barlow's. He had pulled himself up by his academic bootstraps and entered Wesleyan College in Middletown, Connecticut, where he studied with the likes of Jerzy Kosinski and John Cage while associating himself with the radical political and psychedelic vangard as student council president. He graduated with honors in 1969 with a degree in comparative religion.

Barlow reunited with Weir in 1967 at a New York City Dead concert but it wasn't until some years hence that he was pushed in the direction of songwriting. His first flush of songs for and with Weir in the early years stood the test of time and included "Mexicali Blues," "Cassidy," "Looks Like Rain," and "Black-Throated Wind." These songs, which appeared on Weir's solo debut album *Ace*, enlivened the Dead's concerts and spurred the two to continue collaborating. They wrote songs of freedom ("Estimated Prophet"), celebration ("The Music Never Stopped"), eschatology ("Throwing Stones"), and community ("Let It Grow"), but the overriding fruit of their labors was compositions that underscored Weir's declaration of "misfit power," something the Dead and their followers seemed to take to heart. "Lost Sailor," "Saint of Circumstance," "Feel Like a Stranger," and "Picasso Moon" were perhaps the best examples of this sensibility in a well-crafted song cycle that sharpened through the years.

In 1971, Barlow began operating the Bar Cross Land and Livestock Company, a large cow-calf operation in Cora, Wyoming, where he grew up. He continued to do so until he sold it in 1988. In 1990, he and Mitchell Kapor founded the Electronic Frontier Foundation, an organization promoting freedom of expression in digital media, of which he currently serves as vice chairman. A writer and lecturer on subjects relating to the virtualization of society, Barlow is a contributing editor of numerous publications, including *Communications of the ACM*, *Microtimes*, and *Mondo 2000*. He is also a contributing writer for *Wired*. Barlow is a recognized expert on computer security, virtual reality, digitized intellectual property, and the social and legal conditions arising in the global network of connected digital devices. He is probably the only former

John Barlow with Bob Weir, Debbie and Carlos Santana, and Bill Graham, backstage at the Cow Palace, San Francisco, 12/31/76.
(© Ed Perlstein)

Republican county chairman in America willing to call himself a hippie mystic without lowering his voice, and though he was declared by *Utne Reader* to be among "100 Visionaries Who Could Change Your Life," he is generally content to work on changing his own. Finally, according to his Internet Web site (http://eff.org/~barlow/barlow.html), "He recognizes that there is a difference between information and experience and he vastly prefers the latter."

He is the father of three daughters and lives in Wyoming, New York, on the road, and in cyberspace.

▪ *Baron Von Tollbooth and the Chrome Nun*/Paul Kantner, Grace Slick, David Freiberg
Grunt BFL 1-0148, 1973.
"Ballad of the Chrome Nun," "Fat," "Flowers of the Night," "Walkin," "Your Mind Has Left Your Body," "Across the Board," "Harp Tree Lament," "White Boy (Transcaucasian Airmachine Blues)," "Fishman," "Sketches of China"

Garcia is everywhere on this Airplane (and pre–Jefferson Starship) spin-off project, contributing guitar, pedal steel, and banjo parts to all but a couple of the tunes on the album. Mickey Hart also joins the potpourri—along with David Crosby, Jorma Kaukonen, Jack Casady, and the Pointer Sisters—on what amounts to an interesting but uneven brew.

Additionally Robert Hunter contributed the lyrics and David Freiberg the melody to "Harp Tree Lament," a song on this album. According to Hunter, the song's title was drawn from "a piobaireachd for Highland pipe." Go figure.

"YOUR MIND HAS LEFT YOUR BODY" eventually found its way as a very intermittent but luscious instrumental jam at about fourteen Dead shows between 1973 and 1993.

▪ *Baru Bay* (cassette tape)/Bob Weir
Hyperion, 1995. Produced by Bob Weir and Wendy Weir.
"Baru Bay," "Baru Dance"
Bob Weir–guitar, narration. Mandawuy Yunupingu–vocals, tribal chanting. John Lawrence–synthesizer, guitar. Bill Hendrickson–drums, synthesizer, blima (clapsticks). Stephen Kent, Mark Growdon–yidaki (didgeridoo).

The raw, unchanged beauty of Baru Bay, Australia, is captured in the Weirs' story, which is narrated by Bob on the first side of this cassette accompanying the release of their spirited and colorful children's book of the same name. Recorded with some noted local musicians, side two features an atmospheric and geographically and spiritually specific composition by John Lawrence and Bill Hendrickson illustrating the essence of the Weirs' mysterious children's tale.

▪ *Baru Bay: Australia* (book)/ Bob Weir and Wendy Weir
40 pp. Hyperion, 1995. 40 color illustrations.

The success of *PANTHER DREAM: A STORY OF THE AFRICAN RAINFOREST* allowed Bob Weir and his sister Wendy to turn their talents to the environment of the world's coral reefs. With both books, the authors reach a wide general audience, from educators to children. Their fresh approach to learning combines narration, music, sound effects, and Ms. Weir's colorful illustrated text.

In *Baru Bay*, readers are introduced to the aboriginal people who live in Baru Bay, Australia, descendants of people who have lived in the area since the "dreamtime," the time of creation. It is this nether realm that Tamara, a young Australian girl, sets out to explore. During her adventures, Tamara not only learns about the ancestral traditions of the Land Down Under, but also discovers its natural underwater beauty when she snorkels through the coral reef.

The Weirs explained their approach to the project this way:

"In October 1992, we went to Australia to research Baru Bay . . . loaded with cameras and DAT recording equipment, we stepped off the plane to begin an experience that influences our lives to this day. We dove the Great Barrier Reef and were amazed at the beauty and diversity of marine life. We hiked through rainforests to record the sounds as they change at dawn and dusk. We stayed with Mandawuy Ynupingu, leader of the aboriginal rock band Yothu Yindi, in the Gumatj community outside of Nhulunbuy where we enjoyed warm friendship and generosity.

"In writing for children, we look through our eyes as children. We show the beauty of life so that when they grow older they will want to save this beauty for both themselves and their children. In reading and listening to *Baru Bay*, we want children to be filled with the wonder of life in and around a coral reef, the excitement of adventure, and the joy of new experiences. We want them to learn the value of unity, of staying together. We want to reinforce their innate understanding that there is no difference between people who are black and those who are white. The story, pictures, and sounds are all based upon reality and are woven together to encourage the child's imagination."

▪ The Beach Boys

Brian Wilson–born June 20, 1942, Hawthorne, California. Dennis Wilson–born December 4, 1944, Hawthorne, California; died December 26, 1983, Marina del Rey, California. Carl Wilson–born December 21, 1946, Los Angeles, California. Mike Love–born March 15, 1941, Los Angeles, California. Al Jardine–born September 3, 1942, Lima, Ohio. Bruce Johnston–born June 24, 1945, Chicago, Illinois.

The Grateful Dead's involvement with the Beach Boys was one of their more bizarre, if short-lived, collaborative efforts. The sheer strangeness of the April 27, 1971, one-night stand smack in the middle of the Dead's final string of concerts at the Fillmore East was compounded by the wholesome reputation of the Southern California pop group. An overlooked footnote to the event was that the Dead and the Beach Boys had shared a North Carolina bill three days before the Fillmore concert so the meeting was probably set into motion then.

At that 1971 Fillmore show, the Beach Boys made a surprise appearance late in the second set and joined the Dead for an equally unlikely group of tunes. They began with run-throughs of two Leiber and Stoller classics "SEARCHIN'" and "RIOT IN CELL BLOCK #9," Brian Wilson's 1965 hit "HELP ME RHONDA," and a tongue-in-cheek version of Merle Haggard's "OKIE FROM MUSKO-GEE," and CHUCK BERRY's "JOHNNY B. GOODE." In between, the Beach Boys performed rich renditions of "Good Vibrations" and "I Get Around" without the Dead.

As evidenced from the tapes of the show, the union was a spirited and oddly complementary one. But the Grateful Dead and the Beach Boys had more in common than might first meet the eye. Just as the Dead continually extended themselves and pushed the envelope of their genre, Brian Wilson led the Beach Boys to transform the boundaries of pop music.

The most commercially successful American group of

the 1960s, the Beach Boys have recorded and toured well into the 1990s. Ironically, compilations of early material—the first "oldies" album to top the American charts—sold better than their new releases.

Reared in a middle-class suburb of Los Angeles, the Wilson brothers, their cousin Mike Love and friend Al Jardine formed various singing ensembles in the early 1960s, settling on the Beach Boys. The group had a series of hit surfing songs and anthemic teenage California fantasies. While these early recordings celebrated the sun and surf leisure of California's youth, their work by the end of the decade saw a new perspective in which adolescent anguish and loss of innocence played a strong part. The wistful replaced the brash as Brian Wilson took control of their recording career. But in the mid-1960s drug abuse and a nervous breakdown prompted Wilson to take refuge from the Beach Boys and rest of the world. Their 1966 gem, *Pet Sounds,* with its convention-stretching studio techniques and trenchant pop songwriting was released at the beginning of this withdrawal as Brian Wilson seemed to be at the peak of his powers, ever-refining his gift for complex harmonies. This transformation prompted critic Michael Wood to point out that "the sad beauty" of the Beach Boys stems from the fact that "there is a strange melancholy—even in their early energetic songs—a note of mourning as they sing of the happy days a-surfin'."

Brian Wilson's touch continued to bring success with such intricate productions as "Good Vibrations" in 1966 and "Heroes and Villains" a year later. But as his work and behavior became increasingly erratic (and he had, in true Proustian mode, confined himself to his bed), the Beach Boys began to decline as a shaping force in popular music by the early 1970s.

Without Brian, the group churned out two records a year and toured endlessly, but these gigs began to take on the trappings of a "nostalgia" show—a role the band seemed quite comfortable with.

But they also continued to make news. In 1982, they were the center of public brouhaha when James Watt, President Ronald Reagan's interior secretary, unsuccessfully attempted to prevent them from performing a July Fourth concert on the Mall in Washington, D.C. In December 1983, Dennis Wilson drowned in a California boating accident.

Despite lingering psychological problems, Brian Wilson slowly emerged from his isolation and, in 1995, released *I Just Wasn't Made for These Times,* an album of Beach Boys recordings and solo songs. The album also served as the soundtrack to an identically titled documentary film about Wilson released at the same time.

- ### *Bear's Choice*
  See *History of the Grateful Dead Vol. 1 (Bear's Choice)*

- ### "Beat It on Down the Line" (JESSE FULLER)
  Jesse Fuller, *The Lone Cat* (1958)
  Grateful Dead, *Grateful Dead* (1967), *Steal Your Face* (1976), *Dick's Picks, Volume Seven/'74* (1997)
  Stackabones, *Stackabones* (1992)

The Dead have always had a lot of fun performing "Beat It on Down the Line," particularly with the song's signature multibeat introduction. At one 1985 concert, this introduction, usually eight beats, was extended to an unbelievable forty-five!

Lyrically the song is typical of much of Jesse Fuller's work with an emphasis on escape from the travails of life and the shackles of labor to a community of acceptance and freedom. His original recording of "Beat It on Down the Line" appeared on his 1961 album *The Lone Cat*. As a Bay Area blues fixture, the Dead had a long-standing familiarity with Fuller's records and live performances.

One of the Dead's most-performed songs, the band trotted it out more than 300 times as a super-charged, rockabilly first-set hand grenade.

6/13/69, Convention Center, Fresno, California
5/18/72, Kongressaal, Munich
3/21/73, Memorial Auditorium, Utica, New York
12/27/83, San Francisco Civic Auditorium, San Francisco
3/24/91, Knickerbocker Arena, Albany, New York

- ### "Beer Barrel Polka" (Lew Brown/Jaromir Vejvoda)
  Andrews Sisters, *In Blossom* (1978), *50th Annversary Celebration, Vol. 1* (1987)
  Roy Clark/Buck Trent, *Banjo Bandits* (1978)
  James Moody, *Sweet and Lovely* (1989)
  Liberace, *The Golden Age of Television, Vol. 1* (1991)

Some of the Dead's music, particularly their cowboy numbers such as "Mexicali Blues and "Big River," has a distinct polka hop to it. So it is no wonder that they included the most popular polka as frequent filler while the techies attended to equipment difficulties.

Based on the Czech song "Skoda Lasky," "Beer Barrel Polka" was introduced to the United States by Will Glahe and his Musette Orchestra. The Andrews Sisters helped make "Beer Barrel Polka" into one of the top sheet-music and jukebox favorites of its era.

2/9/73, Roscoe Maples Pavilion, Palo Alto, California

- ### *Before Time Began* / NEW RIDERS OF THE PURPLE SAGE / DAVID NELSON
  Relix Records RRLP 2024, 1986.

In late 1969, Jerry showed up at Pacific High Recording, one of the Bay Area's first-class recording studios, to lay down tracks for the embryonic New Riders of the Purple Sage including John Dawson's "Henry," "Last Lonely Eagle," and "Cecilia," and the Garcia/Hunter/Dawson composition "All I Ever Wanted."

- ### Harry Belafonte
  Born Harold George Belafonte, March 1, 1927, New York City

It may seem ironic that the man best remembered as "The King of Calypso" was born in New York City's Harlem district. But having spent part of his childhood in Jamaica, Harry Belafonte was steeped in the culture he celebrated on a string of popular records released in the 1950s. However, Belafonte's greater significance is arguably as a patron and supporter of black musicians, a role culminating in his efforts to organize the USA for Africa famine-relief benefit recording in 1985.

After a three-year stint in the navy and an apprenticeship at New York's American Negro Theater Workshop, Belafonte rose to prominence with the gathering momentum of the folk-music revival. He made the rounds of the Greenwich Village clubs and cafes, including the legendary Village Vanguard, performing a selection of West Indian songs. This led to a starring role in *Carmen Jones*, the cinematic adaptation of the Oscar Hammerstein musical, and a recording contract with RCA Victor.

Recorded in 1956, the *Calypso* album was one of the first cross-over smash hits in postwar America. The album contains "BANANA BOAT (DAY-O)," a version of the traditional work song, which was a Top 5 hit in the

United States and Europe. The Tarriers, a white folk group, had an even more successful cover version of the song soon after, and Stan Freberg had a hit with a satirical version in 1957. More than three decades later, "Banana Boat" was memorably featured in one of the set pieces of the 1988 film *Beetlejuice.*

"Banana Boat," of course, was briefly covered by the Dead but there were two other Belafonte songs that caught the Dead's fancy: "Man Smart, Women Smarter" and "Matilda."

Belafonte continued to churn out the hits including "Island in the Sun" and "Mary's Boy," which, in 1957 and 1958, was the first single to sell a million copies in Britain. He continued to appear in films and, during the 1960s, made the occasional concert appearance, the most highly regarded of which was preserved on the live double album *Belafonte at Carnegie Hall.*

The singer has sometimes been accused of diluting traditional West Indian music, but he argues that he has allowed the music to reach wider audiences. Belafonte retained a commitment to the advancement of black culture by uniting some of his peers who enjoyed success through the folk revival. He has also demonstrated keen business savvy with his control over his own artistic career. Undoubtedly, his highest-profile gesture was the leading role he played in the USA for Africa recording, "We Are the World." This, in turn, led to the recording of

Paradise in Gazankulu with black South African musicians in 1985.

Belafonte's progressive artistic expression continued in 1995 with his appearance in *White Man's Burden,* a futuristic allegorical film with John Travolta, and *Kansas City,* Robert Altman's celebration of 1930s jazz, in 1996.

▪ "Believe It or Not" (Garcia/Hunter)

The Dead briefly interjected this simple, blunt, declarative love song into their set lists in 1988 but dropped it in 1990 after it failed to make the cut for their *Built To Last* disc. "Believe It or Not" was only performed seven times. Composed in the mold of two Garcia Band tunes—"Gomorrah" and Louis Armstrong's "Lucky Old Sun" (from which it borrows an instrumental figure)—the live versions had a big, built-up climax reminiscent of the great Stax/Volt tunes from R&B utopia.

According to Hunter, his contribution was a country & western lyric reminiscent of the type of song "I remember hearing coming from tavern jukeboxes in 1948, when my father would stop in to have a few while I waited out in the car."

Garcia was surprised by the reaction the song received. As he told Blair Jackson for *Golden Road* in

Harry Belafonte.
(ARCHIVE PHOTOS)

1988, "Like when we were rehearsing 'Believe It or Not' it was [shrugs] 'Eh. Big deal.' But when we performed it the first time, it had an amazing reception. It was an amazingly emotional moment. I had no idea that song would have that kind of effect; on me even."

10/21/88, Reunion Arena, Dallas

3/22/90, Copps Coliseum, Hamilton, Ontario

• Luciano Berio

Born 1925

It makes perfect sense that Phil Lesh and Tom Constanten were both students of Luciano Berio, an underappreciated influence on Grateful Dead music.

Of all the prominent figures of his generation, Berio is regarded as the most prodigal and encyclopedic, drawing on a range of sources that reach from the poetry of Dante to the politics of Martin Luther King, Jr., and the operas of Monteverdi to the riffs of modern jazz. Like Béla Bartók, his output includes beautiful settings of traditional folk songs. But he has also embraced all of the major musical developments of the modern era, including electronic music, musical theater, and lyrics using quotations and collage. Described as a musical "omnivore," Berio writes music that possesses a dynamic lyricism that links him to the great Italian tradition of Verdi and Puccini.

The 1950s were Berio's formative years and he spent as much time in the studio as in the concert hall. Two of his early works, *Omaggio a Joyce* and *Visage*, stand as some of the era's seminal electronic music. Many of these works incorporated the recorded voice of his then-wife Cathy Berberian, a mezzo-soprano whose vocal gifts were matched by a vivid stage presence, which was exploited to the fullest in the pieces Berio wrote for her. In *Recital*, for instance, the performer is asked to enact the nervous breakdown of a neurotic concert singer.

Berio's vocal music, however, was not just concerned with theatrical role-playing or with re-creating the beauties of Italian bel canto for contemporary audiences, but with the very nature of language and speech itself. In *Circles* (another piece written for Berberian), the singer's movement in a circle around the stage is mirrored by a musical circle in which three poems by e. e. cummings are progressively deconstructed into their constituent phonetic parts and then reconstructed. *Circles* itself had a certain amount of cult popularity in the late 1960s as "drug music." Berio may have been courting the youth

Luciano Berio. *(The New York Library for the Performing Arts)*

market when he told Rosanna Dalmonte and Balint Varga that "Music allows young people to move into an alternative space, not necessarily a reassuring and optimistic one, because it is partially determined by the real world. . . . However, anyone entering that space can in some measure adapt it to his own needs, and even creatively live there."

A similar experiment underpinned *O King* (1967) for mezzo and five instruments, in which the words "O Martin Luther King" are gradually constructed out of their vowel sounds. *King* was later incorporated into *Sinfonia* (1969), one of three major vocal and orchestral works from the 1960s—with *Epiphanie* (1962) and *Laborintus* (1965)—that perfectly demonstrate the omnivorousness of Berio's music. *Epiphanie* sets words by Marcel Proust and Bertolt Brecht (among others) in a variety of vocal styles ranging from the extravagantly ornamented to the monotonously spoken, interlaid with orchestral movements, while *Laborintus 2* uses speaker, singers, orchestra, and jazz musicians to explore a welter of texts organized around the poetry of Dante. Beriophiles often cite the third movement of *Sinfonia* as an extraordinary example of his powers. Here he builds a musical labyrinth around the third movement of Mahler's *Symphony No. 2* and passages from Samuel Beckett's *The Unnamable.*

Berio's appropriation of other people's words and music hasn't aspired to the complexity found in *Sinfonia.* In the earlier work *Folksongs* (1964), he incorporated transcriptions of folk songs from around the world (including one by Berio himself) for soprano and ensemble. *Folksongs* is one of his most accessible and popular works. Two decades later it was followed by transcriptions of works by de Falla, Mahler, and Brahms. Folk music continued to be an important source of material in pieces such as *Voci* (1984), a haunting recomposition of Sicilian folk melodies for viola and orchestra.

Berio's taste for recomposition and collage runs throughout his work, as does his love of the theatrical. The best of Berio's work achieves a remarkable synthesis of extended theatrical techniques and large-scale means, albeit one that owes little to traditional operatic models. These works show Berio transforming the experimental fervor of his earlier work into a musical language of greater restraint and consistency.

Lesh and Constanten were students of Berio's at Mills College in 1962, and the connections between what Berio and the Dead brought to their audiences is not hard to fathom. Like their elder, the rock group mixed all the elements of the musical universe around them while incorporating contemporary theatrical philosophies into their notion of what a rock band was, mixing high literary ambition with political and community significance.

Upon crossing paths with Lesh in Europe in the late 1980s, Berio is said to have asked his former student if he was still "Grateful Deading."

· *Berkeley in the Sixties* (film)
1990

This self-described documentary includes archival footage of the Dead performing "Dancing in the Streets" and "Viola Lee Blues."

· Chuck Berry
Born Charles Edward Berry, October 18, 1926, San Jose, California

The very definition of *rock & roll,* Chuck Berry's style of songwriting, guitar playing, and stage persona was one of the major influences on *all* who followed. His career has been erratic, tarnished by brushes with the law, poor professional decisions, and a brusque personality. He remains an elusive subject, though, with many details of his life obscure, even after he published an autobiography. This enigmatic artist floats in the realm of the great American blues mystique.

Growing up in St. Louis, where his parents sang in a Baptist church choir, Berry strayed from the flock and wound up spending time in a reform school following a robbery conviction. He then trained as a beautician in night school but soon found his true calling: music. In the early 1950s he led a popular St. Louis blues trio and began integrating a range of influences into his own developing style. Of the guitarists he credited with influencing his guitar improvisations, T-Bone Walker (as well as technical innovator Les Paul and jazz virtuoso Charlie Christian) reigned supreme in Berry's rhythmic formation. Additionally, the vocal approach formalized by Nat "King" Cole, and Louis Jordan's witty jump blues were models for Berry's modernized lyric approach.

In 1955 Berry commenced his recording career when Muddy Waters steered the rocker and his demo tape ("Ida Red") to Leonard Chess's Chicago label. After Chess made him rerecord the song, a tribute to an automobile, as "Maybellene," the visionary DJ Alan Freed (credited as cowriter) helped popularize the record, which became one of rock & roll's first bona fide hits.

Berry was able to replicate the successful formula through the late 1950s with glorious hymns to the new music capturing the teenage exuberance of the era: "Roll Over Beethoven," "Rock & Roll Music," "School Day," "Carol," "Sweet Little Sixteen," and, of course, "JOHNNY B. GOODE," his signature anthem.

While many of his releases were not hits, their impact on popular music and cultural was enormous. By the end of the 1960s, the Berry *oeuvre* was avidly studied and practiced by everyone from the Rolling Stones to the most casual garage band. Though all attempted to recapture Berry's primal edge, the tribal guitar firepower emanating from his Guild was nontransferable.

These were the songs and the sounds which the Grateful Dead picked up on as choices for some of their cover material and compositional methodology. Along with "Johnny B. Goode," Weir incorporated "PROMISED LAND" (Berry's colorful road song) and "ROUND AND ROUND" (a.k.a. "Around and Around," a show-stopping raveup if there ever was one) into his repertoire, while Garcia trotted out the hardscrabble "Let It Rock" both with the Dead and his own groups. Both employed the

Berry model in creating some of their own work as well, most notably "One More Saturday Night" and "Alabama Getaway."

Berry's chart success mirrored his popularity as a live act. His patented "duckwalk," a crouching cross-stage hop that he unveiled in the ecstatic froth of a spasmatic solo, was a visible crowd-pleasing device landing him cameos in several rock films, including *Rock, Rock, Rock* (1956), *Mr. Rock and Roll* (1957) and *Go, Johnny, Go* (1959). Perhaps the best example of Berry's live show from this period was captured in *Jazz on a Summer's Day*, Bert Stern's highly-regarded documentary of the 1958 Newport Jazz Festival.

Berry's 1962 conviction and eventual two-year imprisonment in Indiana for an immorality charge concerning a teenage girl employed at his nightclub only heightened his reputation as an outlaw hero to the burgeoning generation of rock enthusiasts, primarily white middle-class American teenage boys. Upon his release from jail in 1964, he was more popular than ever thanks to the growing number of white rock bands playing his songs. Picking up where he left off before his incarceration, Berry continued to appeal to the adolescent muse with several classics: "Nadine," "No Particular Place to Go," and "It Wasn't Me."

By the mid-1960s, the Beatles had popularized Berry's "Roll Over Beethoven" and "Rock & Roll Music," the Stones had released "Come On" on their first single, and BOB DYLAN's first Top 40 single, "Subterranean Homesick Blues," drew partly on "Too Much Monkey Business," a famous Berry "botheration" song.

Berry formed alliances with the rock community (and courted its fans) during the 1960s and early 1970s resulting in "Concerto in B Goode," an eighteen-minute, heavy-rock instrumental, a live album with the STEVE MILLER Band, a recording date with the British rock elite (*London Sessions*), and the risqué "My Ding-a-Ling" (backed by the Average White Band), which garnered him a surprise transatlantic hit in 1972.

Despite being relegated to the rock 'n' roll revival circuit, Berry retained a fairly high-profile position during the 1970s, capped by his appearance in the 1977 film *American Hot Wax*, based on the career of Alan Freed.

Throughout his career Berry was the consummate road warrior and developed a compelling "lone wolf" mystique, blowing into a town the day of a gig, handpicking local musicians as his backup band and demanding cash payment from the concert promoter *before*

he performed. These acerbic qualities were captured in *Hail! Hail! Rock 'n' Roll*, the volatile 1987 autobiographical concert film in which Keith Richards acted as musical director.

That Chuck Berry was among the last opening acts for the Grateful Dead show seemed to bring the musical and cultural lineage full circle. Garcia expressed the sentiments of many of his contemporaries when he noted that "Maybe Chuck Berry was the first rock musician because he was one of the first blues cats to listen to records, so he wasn't locked into the blues idiom."

- ### "Bertha" (Garcia/Hunter)
  #### Grateful Dead, *Grateful Dead* (Skull and Roses) (1971), *Hundred Year Hall*/'72 (1995)
  #### Los Lobos, *Deadicated* (1991), *Just Another Band from L.A.* (1993), *Furthur* (1996)

Leave it to the Grateful Dead to compose a song that was inspired by a temperamental electric fan. According to Garcia during his 1971 interview with Charles Reich and Jann Wenner, "Bertha is a big electric fan that we used to have in the office upstairs. Colossal electric fan, and you'd plug it into the wall, and it would hop along on the ground. It was this huge motor and way overpowered and the fan was a little off kilter and it would bounce around and bang up and down. And it would blow this tremendous gale wind. It was the only air conditioning that we had at the time, and if you left it for a minute, it would crash into the wall and chew a big piece out of it. It was like having a big airplane propeller, you know, live, you know, running around."

Actually the song is a bit deeper than that, offering words of warning that reverberate through the Dead canon with funk and spunk. The Garcia-sung rocker was often used to commence concerts and for a time in the late 1970s was effectively paired with the Dead's later reworking of the venerable bar-band cover song "Good Lovin'." Around this same time, the song's dramatic qualities were significantly enhanced when the band reconfigured its structure so that the soloing was placed between the second and third verses rather than adjacent to the final chorus.

8/6/71, Hollywood Palladium, Hollywood, California
1/15/78, Selland Arena, Fresno, California
6/10/90, Cal Expo, Sacramento, California
6/25/92, Soldier Field, Chicago

- ## "Betty and Dupree" (Traditional)

    Singles: Walter Taylor (1930), Kingfish Bill Tomlin (1930), Blind Willie Walker (1930), Georgia White (1935), Walter Roberts (1936), Buena Flint (1939), Jack Kelley (1939), Meade Lux Lewis (1939), Sonny Terry and Brownie McGhee (1952)

    Sonny Terry and Brownie McGhee, *The Folkways Years* (1960)

    Chuck Willis, *Atlantic Rhythm & Blues, Vol. 2/'58* (1991), *Stroll On* (1994)

    Pink Anderson, *Ballad & Folksinger* (1961)

    Paul Clayton, *Bloody Ballads* (1961)

    Peter, Paul and Mary, *See What Tomorrow Brings* (1965)

    Muddy Waters, *Muddy, Brass & The Blues* (1967)

    Alexis Korner, *I Wonder Who* (1967)

    Big Joe Duskin, *Cincinnati Stomp* (1979)

    Bob Gibson and Hamilton Camp, *Revisited* (1988)

Variously recorded as "Betty and Dupree," "Diamond Buyer Blues," "Diamond Ring," "Diamond Ring Blues," "Dupree," "Dupree Blues," and "New Dupree Blues," this resonant chestnut is integral to the American folk songbook. Based on a true story, "Betty and Dupree" was the cornerstone composition for the Garcia/Hunter original "Dupree's Diamond Blues," but is only known to be performed by the Dead at one of their very early concerts.

12/1/66, The Matrix, San Francisco

- ## *Between Rock & Hard Places: A Musical Audiobiodyssey* (book)/Tom Constanten

    252 pp. Hulogos'i, 1992. Contains a few musical scores and astrological diagrams, annotated bibliography (books pertaining to keyboards), and an extensive discography, list of compositions, and performances.

Keyboardist Tom Constanten was only with the Dead for about three years but he left his mark at the great shows in the late 1960s. He has also fiercely pursued an independent career with its predictable pillar-to-post hardships, all of which are addressed with plucky wordplay in his highly self-styled "audiobiodyssey."

A self-acknowledged eccentric, T.C. tells his life story with a breezy honesty that belies his intact, if weathered, soul.

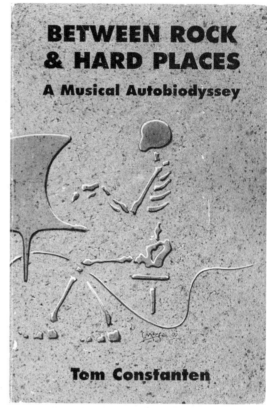

(Courtesy of Hulogos'i Communications)

- ## *Be What You Want To*/ Link Wray

    Polydor PD 5047, 1973. Produced by Thomas Jefferson Kaye.

When Link Wray cut the breathtaking instrumental "Rumble" in 1954, he introduced to the world the fuzz-tone guitar sound and the idea of distortion as part of the guitarist's aural arsenal.

Born Lincoln Wray in Fort Bragg, North Carolina, on May 2, 1930 (some sources put his birth as late as 1935), the part–Native American played in various country and then rock & roll groups with his brothers Doug and Vernon. A musical simulation of a bar brawl, "Rumble" didn't hit the charts until 1958, several years after it was first recorded.

Wray was *way* ahead of his time as he uninhibitedly attacked the guitar in a manner that owed much to soul-blues in his creation of one great instrumental after another built primarily on chordal themes. As the godfather of the power chord, Wray's music contained the groundbreaking roots of heavy metal, easily ten years before it came into being. Wray was a key influence on Pete Townshend and Jeff Beck, among others, and recorded sporadically throughout his career, becoming wilder in his approach and proving that one is never too old to rock & roll.

Wray continued to make his presence known well into the 1990s, contributing to the soundtrack for Terry Gilliam's apocalyptic cinematic manifesto *12 Monkeys.*

Along the way, Wray released *Be What You Want To,* on which Garcia played pedal steel guitar solos ("Tucson, Arizona" and "Riverbend") as well as wild electric guitar ("Walk Easy, Walk Slow"). David Bromberg and members of Commander Cody's Lost Planet Airmen also help out on this piece of Garcia obscura.

▪ "Big Boss Man" (Al Smith/Jimmy Reed)

Jimmy Reed, *Greatest Hits of Jimmy Reed Vol. 1* **(1960),** *Jimmy Reed at Carnegie Hall* **(1961),** *The New Jimmy Reed Album* **(1967),** *Big Boss Blues* **(1989),** *The Music Never Stopped: The Roots of the Grateful Dead* **(1995)**
Grateful Dead, *Grateful Dead* **(Skull and Roses) (1971)**
KINGFISH, *LIVE '85* **(1986)**
Mance Lipscomb, *Mance Lipscomb Vol. 3* **(1964)**
The Astronauts, *Everything is A-OK* **(1964)**
Pretty Things, single (1964), *Live at the Heartbreak Hotel* **(1984)**
Standells, single (1965)
Bill Cosby, *Bill Cosby Sings* **(1966)**
Elvis Presley, *Clambake* **(1967)**
Jerry Lee Lewis, *Memphis Beat* **(1967)**
B. B. King, *Six Silver Strings* **(1985)**

Pigpen sang this modern working-stiff blues with the Dead during his era as the band's frontman. Garcia picked it up for the occasional surprise reading throughout the 1980s and early 1990s.

Jimmy Reed cowrote "Big Boss Man" with Al Smith, his manager/producer, and had a big hit with the tune in 1961.

Born Mathias James Reed on September 6, 1925, in Dunleith, Mississippi, Reed was among the most influential bluesmen of the 1950s and 1960s. Selling more records during this period than any other blues artist except B. B. King, Reed was noted for his rhythmically relaxed style that was uncommonly accessible. Rooted in the Delta tradition, his sweet sound touched both blacks and whites, an impact that can be heard on the Rolling Stones and BOB DYLAN. He stroked his audiences with his laid-back blues—shying away from the gritty, urgent approach with which Muddy Waters and Howlin' Wolf hammered their listeners. Because he hit a responsive chord so instantly, it's no surprise that he regularly crossed over onto the pop charts. His nonthreatening vocals, tender harmonica playing, and walking bass passages were infectious.

Eddie Taylor, Reed's boyhood friend and constant companion with whom he first traveled to Chicago in 1943, rightly received much of the credit for Reed's success. It was Taylor who created the rhythms that powered Reed's blues. Reed's wife, Mary Lee "Mama" Reed, should also not be overlooked, as she was the author of many of his lyrics. But it was Reed who projected the warmth and easy feel of his compositions and made his repertoire so distinctive and popular.

After serving in the Navy at the tail end of World War II, Reed and Taylor teamed up playing small clubs in the Chicago area. With Reed on guitar, harp, and vocals and Taylor on guitar, the two made their first recording for the Chance label in 1953. An audition with Chess records failed, but Vee-Jay Records recognized them as a viable antidote for Chess's harder-edged catalog and signed them.

From 1955 through 1961, Reed churned out a dazzling string of hits, including "You Don't Have to Go," "Ain't That Lovin' You Baby," "You Got Me Dizzy," "Honest I Do," "Baby What Do You Want Me to Do," "Bright Lights Big City," and "Big Boss Man."

Reed's success eventually landed him gigs at Carnegie Hall, the Apollo Theater and, thanks to the Rolling Stones' covers of some of his songs, England, where he had become a marquee attraction. While some have suggested that his arrangements lack spark, there is no denying their compositional excellence.

Reed continued to tour and record until the end of his life but his bouts with alcoholism had a deleterious effect on both. He died on August 29, 1976, in Oakland, California. Fifteen years after his death he was inducted into the Rock and Roll Hall of Fame.

7/2/71, Fillmore West, San Francisco
12/31/89, Oakland Coliseum Arena, Oakland, California (with Bonnie Raitt)
6/16/90, Shoreline Amphitheater, Mountain View, California

- ### "Big Boy Pete" (Don Harris/Dewey Terry)
  Don and Dewey, single (1960), *Jungle Hop* (1991), *The Specialty Story* (1994)
  The Olympics, single (1960, 1965), *Cruisin'* (1965), *The Official Record Album of the Olympics* (1984), *All-Time Greatest Hits* (1991)
  Tidal Waves, single (1965)
  The Marathons, *Meet the Marathons* (1965)
  The Righteous Brothers, *Just Once in My Life* (1965)
  Paul Revere & the Raiders, *Here They Come* (1967)

Leave it to Pigpen to have intermittently worked this rollicking rarity into the Dead's early repertoire as a group sing-along. Weir resurrected it a dozen years after Mr. Pen's passing for a one-night only, concert-igniting performance in 1985.

Like twin Little Richards wailing in tandem, Don Harris and Dewey Terry cut a bushel of blistering, but DOA, rockers for Specialty Records between 1957 and 1959 only to see other acts revive their songs to much greater acclaim. Don and Dewey were both born in 1938 and raised in Pasadena, California, and joined a group called the Squires with whom they briefly recorded before branching off on their own. Harris eventually exchanged his guitar for a violin in the 1960s and, billed as "Sugarcane" Harris, sawed his rocked-out fiddle for the likes of John Mayall and Frank Zappa.

The Olympics, a black doo-wop quartet based in Los Angeles, had a hit with "Big Boy Pete," Don and Dewey's 1960 novelty song. But, when they rerecorded and released the song five years later as "Big Boy Pete '65," it flopped.

Formed in 1957 by lead singer Walter Ward, most of the group were products of the same Los Angeles, California, high school. After signing with Demon, they were assigned two songwriters, Fred Smith and Cliff Goldsmith, with whom they became expert practitioners of a song form virtually unique to the United States: the novelty song. Their first and biggest hit, "Western Movies," (complete with gunshots and ricochet effects) in 1958, was followed by a string of equally unlikely hits. These included "(I Wanna) Dance with the Teacher," "Shimmy Like Kate," "The Bounce," and "Good Lovin'," popularized by the Young Rascals and extensively covered by the Grateful Dead. "Hully Gully," another minor hit by the Olympics, was performed by the Dead at their unusual concert at Amsterdam's Melk Weg on 10/16/81.

In keeping with their reputation as masters of the gimmick, Rhino released a compilation of their hits, *The Official Record Album of the Olympics,* when the 1984 Olympic Games were taking place in L.A.

> 9/6/69, The Family Dog, San Francisco
> 9/20/70, Fillmore East, New York
> 11/21/85, Henry J. Kaiser Convention Center, Oakland, California

- ### "Big Breasa" (Traditional)

A single-show special, "Big Breasa" appeared at one of Weir's Bobby Ace and the Cards from the Bottom of the Deck acoustic concerts.

> 4/19/70, Family Dog at the Great Highway, San Francisco

- ### "Big Railroad Blues" (Noah Lewis)
  CANNON'S JUG STOMPERS, *The Complete Works 1927–1930* (1992), *The Music Never Stopped: Roots of the Grateful Dead* (1995)
  Grateful Dead, *Grateful Dead* (Skull and Roses) (1971), *Dick's Picks Volume One /'75* (1993), *Hundred Year Hall/'72* (1995)

Like MERLE HAGGARD's "MAMA TRIED," "Big Railroad Blues" is another classic yarn of a lost soul who failed to heed his mother's warnings. This spirited song of loss and desperation actually takes place on a freight train where its antihero narrator keeps his "cold iron bed" while bemoaning his sorry state and awaiting his fate. "Big Railroad Blues" provided a chance for Garcia to let loose with his axe *and* his voice. A Grateful Dead perennial, "Big Railroad Blues" was performed nearly 170 times over a quarter century.

> 9/20/70, Fillmore East, New York
> 4/5/71, Manhattan Center, New York (Skull and Roses)
> 11/19/72, Hofheinz Pavilion, Houston
> 9/21/73, The Spectrum, Philadelphia
> 10/10/80, Warfield Theater, San Francisco
> 4/1/84, Marin County Veterans Auditorium, San Rafael, California

- ### "Big River" (Johnny Cash)
  Johnny Cash, *I Walk the Line* (1964), *Strawberry Cake* (1976)
  Grateful Dead, *Steal Your Face* (1976), *One From the Vault /'75* (1991), *Dick's Picks Volume One/'73* (1993), *Dick's Picks Volume Five/'79* (1996), *Dick's*

Picks Volume Six/'83 (1996), *Dick's Picks Volume Seven/'74* (1997)
Stoneground, *Family Album* (1972)
Beat Farmers, *The Pursuit of Happiness* (1987)

Johnny Cash waxed this picaresque poem when he was recording for Sun Records and co-conspiring with labelmates Jerry Lee Lewis, Carl Perkins, and Elvis Presley in the mid- and late 1950s. A chronicle of a smitten wastrel's unsuccessful search for his elusive lover as they venture down the Mississippi River, "Big River" recalls the spirit of Mark Twain's riverboat Americana.

Johnny Cash. *(The New York Public Library for the Performing Arts)*

Johnny Cash, "The Man in Black," was born on February 26, 1932, in Kingsland, Arkansas, and was as troubled as he was talented, an erratic comet blasting across the horizon of mid-twentieth-century American music. His genius, which was apparent in both his songwriting and performances, allowed his popularity to reach far beyond the boundaries of country & western and into the realms of folk and popular music as well.

With a style and sensibility that shared much with Woody Guthrie, Cash, a man of complex personality, cast himself as a teacher of the rural poor. The poverty and daily fight for survival in his youth no doubt contributed to the many zeniths and nadirs he would experience later in life. Bent by decades of sharecropping, tragedy, and near tragedy, the Cash family was a proud one. After he nearly died of starvation in infancy, Cash's childhood consisted of a dirt farmer's shack, five brothers and sisters, cotton patches to be labored in, and a fundamentalist Bible indoctrination by a determined mother and work-weary father. Part of his upbringing took place in a federal government resettlement colony in Dyess, Tennessee, the 1937 flooding of which he recalled in "Five Feet High and Rising." His songs and attitude would later contain the fragments and undertones of these hardest of hard times.

Despite the sudden death of two brothers, the family stayed together, tirelessly working their plot. But Johnny finally began to break away from his kin by enlisting in the Air Force when he was 22. It was while stationed in Germany that he first took up the guitar and made his first stabs at songwriting.

He relocated in Memphis, Tennessee, upon his discharge and joined forces with guitarist Luther Perkins and bassist Marshall Grant. Billing themselves as Johnny Cash and the Tennessee Two they auditioned for and won a Sun Records contract, quickly scoring a big country hit with "Cry, Cry, Cry" and a pop chartbuster "I Walk the Line." Ultimately becoming his signature tune, "I Walk the Line," with its pared down simplicity, was his most representative Sun recording.

But after a trio of pop hits with Sun in 1958 ("Ballad of a Teenage Queen," "Guess Things Happen That Way," and Charlie Rich's somber "The Ways of a Woman in Love"), Cash became dissatisfied with the label's patriarch and rock & roll evangelist, Sam Phillips, and joined Columbia.

Cash's magic touch continued, especially after he was teamed with Don Law, a producer who had handled everybody from Robert Johnson to Lester Flatt and Earl Scruggs. More traditionally inclined than most producers, Law nurtured Cash's down-home tastes as the singer returned to the spare sound of his premiere work.

But the acid test for Cash wasn't the continued popularity and high sales of his singles but the thoughtful, organic albums from which they were drawn. Taken as a whole, they represent some of the first concept albums in the folk idiom. *Ride This Train*, an American travelogue released in 1960, was the first of these and was followed three years later by *Blood, Sweat and Tears*, which praised the American working man. A collection of Indian protest songs, *Bitter Tears*, was released in 1964 and revealed a further shade of this recording artist's progressive sensibilities.

Always on tour throughout the decade, Cash's reputation as a top-flight act grew tremendously, and he was featured on both country & western and major-network variety shows. He also became a favorite with folk-music audiences, headlining many large festivals and performing in clubs across the country.

Piecing together a folk troupe to complement and augment his own concerts, Cash met June Carter of the Carter Family, one of country music's most enduring institutions.

International fame came to Cash with the release of his live album *At Folsom Prison* in 1968, his guest appearance on BOB DYLAN's *Nashville Skyline* (for which he wrote the liner notes) and his cover of Shel Silverstein's comedic "A Boy Named Sue," which became a megahit.

His libertarian beliefs and drug use (which abated in the late 1960s) had never put him as a member in good standing among the Nashville elite. Nevertheless, he was lauded by his peers in the industry and was offered a primetime television show in 1969. Undoubtedly the show's high water mark was Bob Dylan's 1969 appearance on which the two reprised their *Nashville Skyline* duet, "Girl from the North Country."

Cash turned toward religion in the early 1970s, releasing *The Man in Black* (featuring a duet with evangelist Billy Graham) in 1971 and *Gospel Road* in 1973. But his spiritual declarations once again kept him at a distance from country music's mainstream which was embracing the "outlaw" movement in the 1970s.

After a series of personal and professional setbacks, Cash returned with *Highwayman*, a highly successful 1986 concept album recorded with Kris Kristofferson, Willie Nelson, and Waylon Jennings. Concurrently, he was turning both to the contemporary writers of the day (such as Bruce Springsteen and Nick Lowe) and to the music of the 1950s to rekindle the flames of his first inspirations.

By the mid-1990s, with the release of *American Recordings* and his appearance at the 1992 Bob Dylan celebration at Madison Square Garden, Cash had secured himself a place in the pantheon of twentieth-century American music.

Weir handled the "Big River" vocals in the song's Grateful Dead incarnation remaining true to the Cash original. At their best, the Dead turned "Big River" into a soaring country polka recalling the best of Bob Wills and the Texas Playboys.

6/10/73, RFK Stadium, Washington, D.C.
7/13/76, Orpheum Theater, San Francisco
9/20/88, Madison Square Garden, New York

■ "Bird Song" (Garcia/Hunter)
Jerry Garcia, *Garcia* (1972)
Grateful Dead, *Reckoning* (1981), *Without a Net* (1990)

A tender ode evoking the beauty of nature and love, "Bird Song" grew over the years into a flowering tour-de-force jam session. "Bird Song" found its place near the end of the first set in 1981 and developed into a mini–"Dark Star" allowing the band to explore fascinating textural terrain.

After introducing "Bird Song" in 1971 and performing it several dozen times over the next two years, the Dead dropped "Bird Song" until 1980 when it was revisited as a surprise choice during the Dead's acoustic performances in the autumn of that year. Immediately and permanently working it back into their concerts, "Bird Song" took on the role of a first-set voyage. The song also occasionally appeared during Garcia's acoustic gigs in the 1980s.

Hunter wrote the song in specific response to Janis Joplin's death and in *A Box of Rain*, his collection of lyrics, the verse is inscribed "For Janis."

8/27/72, Old Renaissance Fair Grounds, Veneta, Oregon
11/22/72, Municipal Auditorium, Austin, Texas
10/29/80, Radio City Music Hall, New York
3/7/81, Cole Field House, Landover, Maryland
8/20/83, Frost Amphitheater, Palo Alto, California
7/15/84, Greek Theatre, Berkeley, California
10/3/87, Shoreline Amphitheater, Mountain View, California
6/8/90, Cal Expo Amphitheater, Sacramento, California
4/1/91, Coliseum, Greensboro, North Carolina

■ "Blackbird" (Lennon/McCartney)
The Beatles, *The Beatles* (The White Album) (1968)

Paul McCartney, *Wings over America* (1975)
Billy Preston, *Music Is My Life* (1973)
Crosby, Stills and Nash, *Allies* (1983)
Rande Harris, *A Little o' This 'n' That* (1995)

Paul McCartney was supposedly inspired to compose "Blackbird" after reading a newspaper report concerning race riots in the U.S. He wrote, sang, and recorded "Blackbird" for the Beatles' White Album, originally recording the song solo in one of the Abbey Road studios on June 11, 1968. John Lennon was simultaneously experimenting with sound effects for "Revolution 9" next door, which led Paul to double-track his voice in parts of the official release of "Blackbird." The Beatles also utilized *Volume Seven: Birds of a Feather*, a sound-effects record, to get the sound of singing blackbirds added to the track.

The Beatles never performed "Blackbird" but Paul dusted off the number for his 1975–76 tour with Wings after including it on their album *Wings over America*.

The Grateful Dead tried "Blackbird" as an encore at a couple of concerts in the summer of 1988. But the high harmonies were a little much for the group's vocal abilities and these versions ended up being little more than ragged crowd-pleasers.

Weir did far more justice to the tune in his performances of "Blackbird" with Rob Wasserman in the years that followed.

6/23/88, Alpine Valley Music Theater, East Troy, Wisconsin

8/8/95, Central Park, New York (Bob Weir, Rob Wasserman et al.)

▪ Black Mountain Boys

See *Almost Acoustic* and **Mother McCree's Uptown Jug Champions**

▪ "Black Muddy River" (Garcia/Hunter)

Grateful Dead, *In the Dark* (1987), *The Arista Years* (1996)

A gospel-inspired ballad that closed their much-lauded *In the Dark* release, "Black Muddy River" served the Dead best as a low-key but heartfelt encore when they performed it regularly in the late 1980s. The song was briefly revived in 1995 and was the last song Jerry Gar-

cia sang as a lead vocalist when it was included as the first of a two-song encore at the Dead's final July 9, 1995, Soldier Field concert in Chicago.

With its allusions to the Old Testament (the line "I can't tell my pillow from a stone" seems lifted from Genesis 28), some of the notions found in the last work of Irish poet W. B. Yeats ("When I can't hear the song for the singer" recalls Yeats's inability to perceive the "dancer from the dance"), and an implicit confrontation with death, "Black Muddy River" finds Hunter dealing with the sobering introspection that accompanies the acknowledgment of mortality.

As Hunter told David Gans in 1988, "Black Muddy River" was "Just an examination of what it's like to be forty-five years old. It's just a good look into the deep dark well, and the heart resonances in that area. And a statement of individual freedom, that no matter what happens, I have this black muddy river to walk by.

"I hesitate to define it for you—I could talk about what I mean by 'black muddy river,' and I don't mean a literal river running around. It's a deeply meaningful symbol to me, and I think just a little thought into, like, archetypal subconscious resonances gives you all you need to know about what we're talking about here. And past that you're setting it in concrete, and just as soon as that's done, that's not what it meant it all."

12/27/86, Henry J. Kaiser Convention Center, Oakland, California

▪ "Black Peter" (Garcia/Hunter)

Grateful Dead, *Workingman's Dead* (1970), *Bear's Choice* (1973), *What a Long Strange Trip It's Been* (1977), *Dozin' at the Knick*/'90 (1996)
The Palookas, *Classical Music* (1989)

A man singing from his deathbed is not a common subject for most rock groups. Yet this pensive folk blues graced Dead shows from its 1970 acoustic premiere. Since the mid-1970s "Black Peter" has served as a common late-second-set, downshift device.

According to Hunter's notes in *A Box of Rain*, his book of collected lyrics: "I wrote this as a brisk piece like Kershaw's 'Louisiana Man.' Garcia took it seriously, though, dressing it in subtle changes and a mournful tempo. The bridge verse—'See here how everything lead up to this day . . .' —was written after the restructuring of the piece and reflects the additional depth of possibility provided for the song by his treatment."

That particular verse stands as one of Hunter's most encompassing, moving from the macro to the micro with a quick brushstroke in its description of the dying man's last reflections.

But Black Peter is also a common character in folklore, the traditional counterpart to St. Nicholas who, in tales from the Netherlands, carries "bundles of switches to beat naughty children." Additionally, in *The Once and Future King*, T. H. White's retelling of King Arthur's childhood, a character named Black Peter figures in the famous "Sword and the Stone" story.

In memory of Garcia, Patti Smith performed "Black Peter" with her band in the autumn of 1995.

7/14/70, Euphoria Ballroom, San Rafael, California

6/23/74, Jai-lai Fronton, Miami

10/27/79, Cape Cod Coliseum, South Yarmouth, Massachusetts

5/21/82, Greek Theatre, Berkeley, California

4/8/89, Riverfront Arena, Cincinnati, Ohio

▪ "Black Queen" (Stephen Stills)
Stephen Stills, *Stephen Stills* (1970)

Stephen Stills's "Black Queen" appeared on his self-titled debut album, which started his solo career with much promise. The album featured a cast of rock luminaires including Jimi Hendrix, Eric Clapton, David Crosby, Graham Nash, John Sebastian, and Rita Coolidge. The opening cut, "Love the One You're With," was a smash hit. Stills's warm, weathered voice is used to great effect on most of these tracks, but his overbearing organ work muffles some of Hendrix's lead guitar.

The Dead only performed "Black Queen" twice, both times with Stills sharing the stage. In 1969, Stills joined them at the Thelma Theater for a presentation of the newly composed song and then again nearly fourteen years later for a very different rendition on the first night of a memorable two-gig New Jersey run in 1983.

12/10/69, Thelma Theater, Los Angeles

4/16/83, Brendan Byrne Arena, East Rutherford, New Jersey

▪ "Black-Throated Wind" (Weir/Barlow)
Bob Weir, *Ace* (1972)
Grateful Dead, *Steal Your Face* (1976), *Dick's Picks Volume Seven/'74* (1997)

A hitchhiker simultaneously running away from and confronting his past propels this Weir/Barlow adventure with autobiographical overtones. The song tells the story of a man on the road and down on his luck, describing the loneliness of the American night and recalling the decisions that resulted in his current, feral predicament.

The Dead introduced "Black-Throated Wind" in 1972 as a first-set gem and performed it scores of times through 1974. Like many Dead songs, the band and singer save their best for the climax: Garcia wails on his guitar while Weir seems a man possessed in deciding to go back home and "Turn around, that's what I'm a gonna do!" Great stuff. But, despite their obvious affinity for "Black-Throated Wind," the Dead shelved it in 1974 and kept it there for the next sixteen years.

"Black-Throated Wind" was written around the same time as "Greatest Story Ever Told." As Weir told David Gans in 1981, the weather and spirits were contributing factors in the song's composition. "It was a process—it took me a while. I was snowed in in this little cabin in Wyoming with Barlow, a guitar, a typewriter, and a bottle of whiskey. The catalyst, a bottle of Wild Turkey 101. We just sort of pounded away at it. That one's a fairly strange song—I intend to redo the lyrics on it, and it may resurface."

Weir did rework and reintroduce the song in 1990. By the end of the year he had returned to the original lyrics and the song remained in semiregular rotation through 1995 often as a partly acoustic reading in its last couple of years as a Dead vehicle. The later versions of the song, however, never quite captured the on-the-lam fever of the 1972-74 versions.

8/21/72, Berkeley Community Theater, Berkeley, California

9/21/74, Palais des Sports, Paris

3/25/94, Nassau Veterans Memorial Coliseum, Uniondale, New York

▪ *Blows Against the Empire*/Paul Kantner
RCA LSP 444, 1970. RCA CD 3868-2-R.

In the true fashion of the San Francisco rock community, Garcia, Hart, and Kreutzmann assist their old friends on this Jefferson Airplane spinoff project. The Airplane's unity was a bit diffuse when the record was made and the final, good but sloppy, result demonstrated that. Several of their albums were recorded under true anarchistic conditions with Airplane members going into the studio with whoever was around—group members and friends—some of whom later became members. Between 1970 and 1974, their albums were credited to a wide variety of people and aggregations, with tracks from numerous different sessions.

On *Blows Against the Empire*, Garcia plays some well-oiled, if muted, lead guitar on "Starship," banjo on "Let's Get Together," and pedal steel on "Have You Seen the Stars Tonite." Additionally, Garcia and Hart teamed with Paul Kantner and Paul Sawyer on "XM," a strange piece of electronic noise that they presumably "perform" on because they are credited with "writing" it.

- **"Blow Away"** (Mydland/Barlow)
  Grateful Dead, *Built to Last* (1989), *Dozin' at the Knick*/'90 (1996)

One of Brent Mydland's best musical contributions to the Dead's repertoire, "Blow Away" lent itself well to the band's improvisational approach and, late in Mydland's life, found its place as a burning first-set closer. A driving uptempo but typically bitter Mydland effort describing a romantic falling-out, "Blow Away" could have evolved into a good segue number had Mydland not unexpectedly passed away in 1990. Many Deadheads suggested the song's dynamic chord changes should have been revived as an instrumental in homage to the late keyboardist.

  3/16/90, Capital Centre, Landover, Maryland

- ***Bluegrass Reunion***/Various Artists
  Acoustic Disc ACC-4, 1992.
  "Back Up and Push (theme)," "She's No Angel," "I'm Just Here to Get My Baby Out Of Jail," "The Fields Have Turned Brown," "To Love and Live Together," "I'm Blue, I'm Lonesome," "Pigeon Roost," "Down Where the River Bends," "Love Please Come Home," "Letter From My Darlin'," "Is This My Destiny?," "Ashes of Love," "Is It Too Late Now?," "Little Maggie," "Will You Miss Me When I'm Gone?," "Back Up and Push (theme)"
  Red Allen–guitar, vocals. DAVID GRISMAN–mandolin, vocals. Herb Pederson–banjo, vocals. Jim Buchannan–fiddles, vocals. Jim Kerwin–bass. Jerry Garcia–lead vocals on "Ashes of Love," guitar on "Is This My Destiny?"

(Courtesy of Acoustic Disc)

Garcia's two-song contribution to this fine bluegrass album featuring some of the genre's heavyweights shows that he had barely missed a beat on his return to the acoustic finger-picking arena.

- ***Blue Incantation***/Sanjay Mishra
  Rain Dog Records RDR 098, 1995. Produced by Sanjay Mishra.

Sanjay Mishra, an Indian guitarist who is as firmly rooted in raga as he is in psychedelic rave, put out this sonically pure, spiritually atmospheric album, which included Garcia contributions on three cuts: "Monsoon," "Clouds," and "Nocturne/Evening Chant." Mishra grew up playing in an Indian rock band that covered the Dead in spades and he rises to the occasion in this outing with his mentor.

- ***Blues for Allah***
  Grateful Dead/United Artists/YA494G, 1975. Produced by the Grateful Dead.
  "Help on the Way"›"Slipknot!"›"Franklin's Tower," "King Solomon's Marbles," "Stronger Than Dirt or Milkin' the Turkey," "The Music Never Stopped," "Crazy Fingers," "Sage and Spirit," "Blues for Allah," "Sand Castles & Glass Camels," "Unusual Occurrences in the Desert"
  Steven Shuster–reeds and flute.

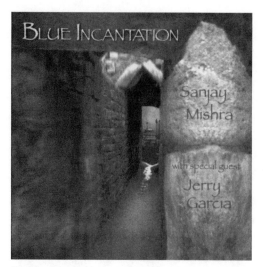

(Courtesy of Akar Music)

The Dead return to form on this powerful disc made during the band's hiatus from the rigors of touring in 1975. *Blues for Allah* crackles with energy. "Help on the Way," "Franklin's Tower," and "The Music Never Stopped" be-

(© Grateful Dead Merchandising, Inc.)

came high points of many a Dead show but the lengthy (and murky) title track, which takes up most of the album's second side, was performed only a few times around the time of the album's release.

Chiseled from jams in Weir's home studio, *Blues for Allah* sparkles with contradictions and anomalies. Although the album remains a showcase for the Dead's technical chops (often absent from the band's official releases), half of the album never found its way into regular concert inclusion. Yet *Allah* still sounds warm and intimate with its homespun hippie intelligence that was often lost amid the sacral circuses Dead shows came to epitomize by bridging the musical gap between hot jamming and outside musical adventure.

In a 1991 conversation with Blair Jackson, Garcia confirmed the notion that the album was constructed from the ground up rather than by individual band members bringing in a batch of songs and fine tuning them. "In fact we kind of made a ground rule for that record: Let's make a record where we get together every day and we don't bring anything in. The whole idea was to get back to that band thing, where the band makes the main contribution to the evolution of the material. So we'd go into the studio, we'd jam for a while, and then if something nice turned up we'd say, 'Well, let's preserve this little hunk and work with it, see if we can't do something with it.' And that's how we did most of the album. . . . A lot of it went through metamorphoses that normally would take quite a long time. We sort of forced them through."

Hunter was equally involved with the in-studio creative process. "This was not a terribly good way for a lyricist to work, because they'd say, 'Okay, we're ready for the words for this right now.' So I'd try something: 'How about this? No? How about this?' 'Yeah, that'll do.' Bam! And on it would go. So I got involved in that immediacy process, too. I must say I prefer to sit back and toy with things a little bit more. So a method that might work nicely with a musical instrument might not work as well with language."

A final note: *Blues For Allah* may be the only album in Western music history that includes a lyric sheet in Arabic, Sanskrit, and English.

- **"Blues for Allah"** (Garcia/Hunter)
  Grateful Dead, *Blues for Allah* (1975), *One from the Vault/*'75 (1991)
  HENRY KAISER, *ETERNITY BLUE* (1995)
  Joe Gallant, *THE BLUES FOR ALLAH PROJECT* (1996)

Considering the immense popularity of the album on which this ambitious but convoluted composition appears, it is somewhat surprising that the Grateful Dead only performed "Blues for Allah" three times. But the song's obtuseness and built-in space relegated it to the band's repertory trash heap. Conversely, the few outings the Dead gave "Blues for Allah" were uniformly gratifying and very different from one another, especially considering they were performed within several months of one another in 1975. The Dead also performed two unusual instrumental jams built on the composition's modal structure in 1981 and again in 1984.

The suite wasn't any easier to compose. Commenting on its collaborative in-studio composition, Hunter and Garcia remembered the difficulty with Blair Jackson in 1991. Hunter gave a glimpse of the high pressure he received from the band: "But 'Blues for Allah,' specifically, I remember them saying to me, 'Dammit, we need the line right now!'

"I find that song holds up well in the current situation, though it also has a basic naivete—sort of 'Why can't we just be friends?' But some of the lines in there work still: 'The ships of state sail on mirage and drown in sand.'"

Garcia concurred. "Oh, that song was a bitch to do! When we got toward the end of the album we had some time restrictions and we started working pretty fast. But until then we'd been pretty leisurely about it.

"That song was another totally experimental thing I tried to do. In terms of the melody and the phrasing and all, it was not of this world. It's not in any key and it's not in any time. And the line lengths are all different."

Recalling the lyrical inspiration, Garcia told Jackson, "We were talking about King Faisal [of Saudi Arabia] in the studio, 'cause an article came up about him in *Newsweek* or something. And I remember being blown away when it said that Faisal owned a third of the world's wealth or something like that. One guy?"

In his 1982 interview with David Gans, Mickey Hart described some of the unusual occurrences that transpired in the recording studio. "We miked a box of crickets, and throughout the second side of *Blues for Allah* there are crickets on the basic track. We slowed them down, sped 'em up, played them backwards at half speed. . . . They sounded like whales and they sounded like chirping birds.

"We made this thing called 'The Desert.' Garcia was engineering, and I was in the studio. I played all my little percussion things—bells, metal, glass. We made about a twenty-minute track . . . and he gated it with a vocal gate, a VCA [voltage-controlled amplifier]. He was saying 'Al-lah'—the desert says 'Allah.' You don't hear a voice—you hear the desert saying the word in place of his voice.

"After we were finished, we let the crickets go on Weir's mountain. We liberated them after the session. We'd kept them alive, fifty of them, and we miked the box. And for years after, Weir had exotic crickets outside his house."

3/23/75, Kezar Stadium, San Francisco (with keyboardists MERL SAUNDERS **and Ned Lagin)**

- ### *The Blues for Allah Project*/Joe Gallant **and Illuminati**
  Knitting Factory Works, 188, 1996. Produced by Joe Gallant. Recorded live at the Knitting Factory, New York City, January 13–14, 1996.
  "Invocation," "Help on the Way"› "Slipknot!"› "Franklin's Tower," "King Solomon's Marbles," "The Music Never Stopped," "Crazy Fingers," "Sage and Spirit," "Prelude," "Blues for Allah," "Sand Castles & Glass Camels," "Unusual Occurrences in the Desert"

This sweeping jazz orchestration of the Dead's 1975 *Blues for Allah* recorded at a live New York City gig is a freewheeling twenty-one-piece band salute to a great Dead album. While Gallant alternately anchors and animates the quixotic blend of jazz, folk, rock, funk, reggae, and cabaret on bass guitar, it's his flair as an arranger that keeps the music fresh and surprising.

(Courtesy of Knitting Factory Records)

Those who have had the privilege of checking out Joe Gallant (a New York bassist, composer, and arranger) and his band Illuminati have seen a future for Grateful Dead music . . . and he is it! Gallant's celebratory explorations of the Dead's jazz and worldly diversity were heralded in his 1994 album *Code of the West* and his 1996 presentation of the *Blues for Allah* suite. His bicoastal repertory event suggested one way for the Dead's music to continue and thrive.

Gallant founded Illuminati as a trio in 1982, slowly building it to at least a sixteen-piece big band by the mid-1990s. As a composer, arranger, and bassist, Gallant caught the attention of Phil Lesh, who featured him on his "Eyes of Chaos/Veil of Order" radio show with Gary Lambert. Illuminati's version of "Unbroken Chain" on their *Code of the West* album was considered a catalyst for the Dead's decision to finally perform the song in 1995. Lambert subsequently asked Gallant if he would be interested in arranging *Blues for Allah* for a twenty-piece jazz orchestra to commemorate the twentieth anniversary of its release.

(Courtesy of Summertone Records)

▪ *Blues from the Rainforest . . . A Musical Suite . . .* / MERL SAUNDERS
Summertone Records S2CD-01/S2CS-16, 1990; reissue
Grateful Dead Merchandising GDCD 3901.
"Blues from the Rainforest," "Sunrise over Haleakala,"
"Blue Hill Ocean Dance," "Afro Pearl Blue," "Dance of the Fireflies," "Sri Lanka"

Merl Saunders's dedication to progressive music and political ideals was already well established when he committed himself to this environmentally conscious release coinciding with the Dead's own activism in rainforest preservation. The album mixes atmospheric instrumentals with sound effects Saunders collected in Hawaii.

Hailed as the "Dark Star" of the 1990s, this first Garcia/Saunders collaboration in way too many years featured the ultimate evolution of the space jam into a more integrated musical idiom. Garcia and Saunders picked up where they left off back in the 1970s, playing off each other's improvisations, while expressing the mood and feeling of the dying Amazon rainforest on this new age/environmental release.

As Saunders told Jim Rosenthal of *Relix* in 1990: "This is more than just a song with some political and social relevance. I wanted to musically re-create the

falling of the trees and the crying of the forest. It's as if the forest is talking and telling the people who are exploiting it to get lost."

But this is not just music for the granola-crunching, crystal-wearing crowd either—no redundant meanderings of ambient sounds that typify new age music here—as Saunders strikes a balance between environmental

Jerry Garcia and Merl Saunders during the recording of *Blues from the Rainforest*. (Photo: Linda Jacobson courtesy of Summertone Records)

music and the experimental electronic blending of synthesizers, percussion, and Garcia's guitar mastery.

- ### *Bobby and the Midnites*/Bobby and the Midnites
  Arista AL9568, 1981. Produced by Gary Lyons.
  "Haze," "Too Many Losers," "Far Away," "Book of Rules," "Me, Without You," "Josephine," "(I Want to) Fly Away," "Carry Me," "Festival"
  Bob Weir–guitar, vocals. Billy Cobham–drums, vocals. Bobby Cochran–guitar, vocals. Alphonso Johnson–bass, vocals. Mathew Kelly–harmonica, vocals. Brent Mydland–keyboards, vocals. John Barlow–lyrical supervision.

The genesis of Bob Weir's second stab at forming another band after bowing out of Kingfish came at, of

(*Courtesy of Arista Records*)

all places, a conference of the National Association of Music Merchants in Philadelphia, Pennsylvania, around 1978. Jeff Hasselberger, then a marketing director for Ibanez instruments and with whom Weir had been designing guitars, invited the guitarist and a number of other musicians (including Alphonso Johnson on bass, Billy Cobham on drums, and Bobby Cochran on guitar) to perform as part of the trade show. Weir and company had such an enjoyable time performing that they decided to regroup as Bobby and the Midnites, take to the road, and cut a disc. By then

the unit included the Dead's Brent Mydland on keyboards.

Ostensibly a Weir spinoff diversion in the early 1980s, the Midnites went through several personnel changes but toured extensively, performing upwards of one hundred shows between June 1980 and September 1984, when the band hung it up for good.

The name of the band had an unusual source. According to Weir's 1981 conversation with David Gans, "It came to me in a flash, along with the album cover. The infamous cat and the fiddle, the reincarnation of Midnite the Cat. Midnite the Cat was a fixture on a TV show called *Andy's Gang*. I remember it from the very dawn of my memory; when I was a real little kid, that show was on TV. Just about all I really remember about the show was the cat. He had a little cigar-box podium and he played the fiddle. I guess he was some sort of puppet—had me fooled at the time. . . .

"That picture [on the album cover] more or less came to me. I drew a rough sketch and gave it to Vic Moscoso, and he made it just perfect."

This album, one of two the Midnites produced, was not unlike their live shows, easily shifting from rock & roll to fusion-jazz to funk to New Orleans R&B to gospel. Several of the songs ("Josephine," "Festival," and "Book of Rules") survived this disc and their outings with the Midnites to be included in Weir's various subsequent solo tours.

Weir plays straight-ahead guitar-rock songs on the album, singing forlorn love songs that are earnest enough even if, as a whole, they come off as a collection of half-baked wannabe hits from someone who had spent much of his career finding success by doing just the opposite. (The album did medium-poor business, only staying on the charts for a couple of months.)

- ### *Book of the Dead* (book)/Photographs by Herb Greene; Foreword by Robert Hunter.
  158 pp. Delacorte Press/Delta Books, 1990.

Having shot some of the most memorable photographs of the Dead through the years, Herb Greene published this oversized but unpretentious collection. Greene was a young commercial photographer living in the Haight-Ashbury when the post-Beat, post-Beatle, LSD-inspired subculture took root and flowered in ballrooms filled with flashing lights, colorful graphics, and adventurous, eclectic music. Working as a staff photographer for a local department store by day and a chronicler of the street scene by night, Greene developed a strong professional reputation. He shot the cover of the JEFFERSON AIRPLANE's *Surrealistic Pillow* and provided Alton Kelly with shots of the Dead used in the cover collage of the band's 1966 eponymous debut album.

Greene earned a Grammy nomination in 1974 for his art direction of the Pointer Sisters' second LP, *That's a Plenty*, and an exhibition of his '60s images toured the country for a couple years in the early 1990s. While some photographers specialize in performance reportage, Greene's oeuvre is the portrait.

The Dead always seemed to loosen up for Greene's formal and informal sessions. The book represents a series of encounters with friends and fellow travelers in the late 1960s, 1979 and 1987. An added bonus to the portfolio is a foreword by Robert Hunter.

▪ "Born Cross-Eyed" (Weir)
Grateful Dead, single, *Anthem of the Sun* (1968), *What a Long Strange Trip It's Been* (1977)

Wild, weird, and distinctly Bob Weir, "Born Cross-Eyed" was an early autobiographical evaluation by the young guitarist and the perfect tune to conclude the first side of the Dead's monumental *Anthem of the Sun* LP. Weir was, in fact, born cross-eyed and dyslexic and the song has a kind of dizzying angularity that is a good aural approximation of the latter infirmity. It is, however, Phil Lesh's short Miles Davis–influenced trumpet solo that steals the show on this high-energy but dated release.

Of the song's skittish feeling, Mickey Hart pointed out that the band "started 'Born Cross-Eyed' on the second beat and left the *one* completely blank. That made everything in the song seem off-kilter. It's a rhythmic and aural illusion; it tricks the ear."

The engineering of the song was not without its adventures either. Recalling the band's difficult relationship with Warner Bros.'s producer Dave Hassinger, Weir said: "I had a song called 'Born Cross-Eyed.' We'd more or less done the basic track and some overlays, and I was describing how I wanted the song. There was a little bit of tension in the studio, but I was oblivious to it; I was into brown rice at the time and wasn't taking any drugs—zero—but I was pretty spaced, anyway.

"I was describing how I envisioned the song, and [Dan] Healy and Hassinger were hassling over something. The song got quiet at one point, and so I announced, 'Right here I want the sound of thick air.' I couldn't describe it back then, because I didn't know what I was talking about. I do know now: a little bit of white noise and a little bit of compression. I was thinking about something kind of like the buzzing that you hear in your ears on a hot, sticky summer day.

"So I said, 'Dave, right here I want the sound of thick air.'

"Dave Hassinger threw up his hands and said, 'Thick air. He wants the sound of THICK AIR. *Thick air!* He wants the sound of thick air'—over and over again, as he's walking out of the studio.

"That was the end of Dave Hassinger and the Grateful Dead. It wasn't exactly my fault, but I think I was the straw that broke the camel's back."

2/14/68, Carousel Ballroom, San Francisco

▪ "Born on the Bayou" (JOHN FOGERTY)
Creedence Clearwater Revival, *Bayou Country* (1969), *Live in Europe* (1974), *The Concert* (1980)
Little Richard, *King of Rock n' Roll* (1971)
The Broken Homes, *Born on the Fourth of July* soundtrack (1991)

John Fogerty was not born on the bayou, yet much of the Berkeley, California–bred musician's best work evokes the distinct essence of Mississippi Delta swamp rock. "Born on the Bayou" first appeared on Creedence's second album, *Bayou Country*, which found the band's unique crunch already well developed. The song has remained a classic-rock staple and still receives ample radio airplay.

When Fogerty joined the Dead onstage during the memorial concert for Bill Graham, "Born on the Bayou" led off their little four-song mini-set.

11/3/91, Polo Field, Golden Gate Park, San Francisco

▪ "The Boxer" (Paul Simon)
Simon and Garfunkel, *Bridge over Troubled Water* (1970), *Greatest Hits* (1972), *The Concert in Central Park* (1982)
Paul Simon, *Paul Simon in Concert: Live Rhymin'* (1974), *Paul Simon's Concert in Central Park* (1991), *Born at the Right Time* (1993)
BOB DYLAN, *Self Portrait* (1970)
Chet Atkins, *Pickin' My Way* (1971)
Emmylou Harris, *Roses in the Snow* (1980)
JOAN BAEZ, *European Tour* (1981)
The King's Singers, *Good Vibrations* (1993)

How could they miss? Between Paul Simon's (born October 13, 1942, Newark, New Jersey) brilliant song craftsmanship, Art Garfunkel's sweet, airy choirboy upper tenor, and their combined delicate harmonic vocal interplay, Simon and Garfunkel earned the distinction of being the most successful folk-pop duo of the 1960s and early 1970s.

What most people don't know is that the duo had been seriously working together as early as 1955, registering their originals at the Library of Congress. Under the pseudonyms Tom and Jerry, they got a record deal in 1957 while still in high school and had their first single ("Hey Schoolgirl") hit No. 49 nationally, landing them a spot on television's *American Bandstand.*

Although they went to separate colleges, they continued collaborating and reunited as Simon and Garfunkel in 1964. The twosome's first album,*Wednesday Morning 3 AM*, was a straightforward folk effort mixing covers with originals, that failed to sell. But within that failure smoldered the coals of success. Without informing the partners, Tom Wilson, the album's producer, took a track from the album, overdubbed a complete rock orchestration, and remixed it as a single. The song, "The Sounds of Silence," soared to the No. 1 position for two weeks and boosted *Wednesday Morning 3 AM* to No. 30. When the dust cleared, Simon's writing was being mentioned in the same breath as Dylan and Lennon/McCartney, but much of his best writing was yet to come.

Huge commercial and artistic fanfare accompanied their next four releases: *Parsley, Sage, Rosemary and Thyme; Bookends;* the soundtrack album from the movie *The Graduate;* and *Bridge over Troubled Water.* Simon and Garfunkel broke up during the recording of *Bridge over Troubled Water* because Simon was becoming increasingly frustrated by his partner's absence while pursuing a career in acting.

With Joan Baez taking the lead, the Dead performed Paul Simon's wistful debt to *Requiem for a Heavyweight* at one 1981 concert.

12/12/81, Fiesta Hall County Fairgrounds, San Mateo, California (with Joan Baez)

- **"Box of Rain"** (Lesh/Hunter)
  Grateful Dead, *American Beauty* (1970)
  Robert Hunter, *Jack o' Roses* (1979), *Box of Rain* (1991)
  Nicky Holland, *Nicky Holland* (1992)
  Toni Brown, *Blue Morning* (1996)

Regarded as one of the Dead's poetic masterpieces, "Box of Rain" was the perfect choice to lead off the Dead's *American Beauty* album and was Phil Lesh's most beloved concert staple.

In a 1978 conversation with David Gans, Robert Hunter described this rare collaboration with Lesh. " 'Box of Rain' was an exceptionally quick song. I took the cassette home, and I started writing before I was through listening to it. The second listen, I neatened the lyrics up, and that was that."

In *A BOX OF RAIN*, his own collection of lyrics, Hunter wrote that "Phil Lesh wanted a song to sing to his dying father and had composed a piece complete with every vocal nuance but the words. If ever a lyric 'wrote itself,' this did—as fast as the pen would pull."

Upbeat yet cautious, clear yet mysterious, "Box of Rain" is about as close to Zen folk as a tune by Robert Hunter can get. While much Grateful Dead music lends itself to and encourages improvisation among its members and subjective interpretation among its listeners, this song is about texture. Always on the verge of revelation, "Box of Rain" is open to wide interpretation—ever-shifting and expansive in its ultimate paradoxical meanings.

The Dead performed the song frequently in 1973 and 1974 and it was virtually Lesh's only vocal lead in those days. However, when the bassist suffered a severe, acute vocal-chord injury from singing backup at too high a range, "Box of Rain" was shelved for about a decade. By 1983 Lesh was healed, and he resumed singing "Box of Rain" three years later. Not only did it remain in constant rotation after that, but it appeared in a variety of capacities: show opener, first-set jewel, second-set segue fodder, and encore.

"Such a long, long time to be gone and a short time to be there," reads the song's last line. How poignantly appropriate then that "Box of Rain" was the final song performed by the Grateful Dead.

12/11/72, Winterland Arena, San Francisco
3/21/73, Memorial Auditorium, Ithaca, New York
1/25/93, Coliseum Arena, Oakland, California

- **A Box of Rain**/Robert Hunter
  Rykodisc RCD 10214, 1991. Produced by Robert Hunter.
  "Box of Rain," "Scarlet Begonias," "Franklin's Tower,"
  "Jack Straw," "Brown-Eyed Women," "Reuben &
  Cerise," "Space," "Deal," "Promontory Rider,"
  "Ripple," "Boys in the Barroom," "Stella Blue"

This predominantly live album amounts to an excellent "greatest hits" retrospective of the Dead's primary lyricist, Robert Hunter. Hunter's treatments of the tunes are, as always, vastly different from those the Grateful Dead performed but his interpretations shed new literary light on their many shades and nuances. Though he's never been known for his abilities as a cutting-edge musician, *A Box of Rain* nevertheless demonstrates Hunter's often-overlooked acoustic finger-picking talents.

- ### *A Box of Rain* (book)/Robert Hunter
  Viking Penguin, 1990.

Released simultaneously with his *A Box of Rain* CD, this book is a comprehensive collection containing Robert Hunter's work with and without the Grateful Dead. It also includes lyrics to some unreleased Dead tunes and "unedited" versions of the songs before Garcia and company reshaped and altered them to better suit their performance needs. The book is a demonstration of Hunter's personal as well as artistic transformation.

- ### *Boz Scaggs*/Boz Scaggs
  Atlantic 19166, 1969.

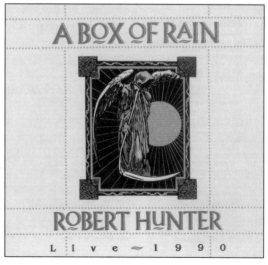

(Courtesy of Rykodisc)

"I'm Easy," "I'll Be Long Gone," "Another Day (Another Letter)," "Now You're Gone," "Finding Her," "Look What I Got," "Waiting on a Train," "Loan Me a Dime," "Sweet Release"

Featuring crack accompaniment by the Muscle Shoals house band, Boz Scaggs's Jann Wenner–produced solo

Phil Lesh, Grand Prix Racecourse, Watkins Glen, New York, 7/28/73. (*Photo: Richard Berner*)

debut is a near masterwork, mingling the pathos and heartache of oldtime honky-tonk with the celebration and redemption of southern soul. On this diverse outing, Duane Allman turns in some of his hottest licks on "Loan Me a Dime," an extended blues dirge, and Scaggs is marvelous on his revamping of Jimmie Rodgers's classic hobo song, "Waiting on a Train."

Donna Godchaux (then Donna Jean Thatcher) was a member of that standard Muscle Shoals Studio unit, lending backup vocals to this as well as many other fine records produced from the Alabama musical nexus.

· Bob Bralove

MIDI master Bob Bralove was a relative newcomer to the Grateful Dead, only working with them full time since the summer of 1987, when he was hired to help explore the potential of the newest generation of sophisticated electronic musical technology. His passion and training in all things musical and electronic made it possible to hear Garcia launch into a rainbow solo with what sounded more like an Andean flute than an electric guitar. Bralove employed an array of sounds that seldom resemble the instruments they are being played on, which include oboes, accordions, fiddle, and saxophones.

· Candace Brightman

Long after the liquid, prismatic images of the Joshua Light Show's halcyon days at the Fillmores had faded from the backdrop at Grateful Dead concerts, the right illumination to suit the ever-changing musical mood was magically provided by Candace Brightman, who had been "doing lights" for the band since 1972. Long gone, too, are the days when she would run an entire show from a regular audience seat with a shoebox-sized controller. By the 1990s she relied on sophisticated computer programs, state-of-the-art electronics, and some of the best lighting technicians in the business to help her pull it all together. Though Brightman had to stay on top of each spontaneous nuance in the music during a concert to add just the right coloration, she said, "When the band is playing really well, any lighting seems to work."

· "Bring Me My Shotgun" (Traditional)

The Grateful Dead are only known to have played this archaic folk song, probably of Appalachian Mountain origin, as an acoustic-set inclusion at one concert.

7/12/70, Fillmore East, New York

· "Brokedown Palace" (Garcia/Hunter)

Grateful Dead, *American Beauty* **(1970),** *Dead Set*
    (1981), *Dick's Picks Volume Five/'79* **(1996),** *Dozin'*
    at the Knick/'90 **(1996)**
HENRY KAISER, *ETERNITY BLUE* **(1995)**

A natural encore selection, the Dead regularly performed this melancholic gospel lullaby since introducing it in 1970. "Brokedown Palace" was often performed at the end of a tour or a multi-night run at a single venue lending a personal touch to the concert site. A sense of faded glory permeates the tune, a quiet acknowledgment that perhaps the best times have already passed.

8/6/71, Hollywood Palladium, Hollywood, California
4/30/84, Nassau Veterans Memorial Coliseum,
    Uniondale, New York

· "Broken Arrow" (J. Robbie Robertson)

Robbie Robertson, *Robbie Robertson* **(1987)**
Rod Stewart, *Vagabond Heart* **(1991)**

Phil Lesh brought Robbie Robertson's "Broken Arrow" to the Dead in 1993 and frequently performed it thereafter. Rod Stewart had a hit with the tune just around the same time the Dead began performing "Broken Arrow," and it represents one of the few Top 40 hits the Dead played when the song was near its peak of commercial popularity.

With its elemental, ritualistic imagery, "Broken Arrow" draws on Robertson's Native American heritage, fitting the Dead's aesthetic, musical, and social concerns to a T.

3/30/95, The Omni, Atlanta

· *David Bromberg*/David Bromberg

Columbia C31753, 1973. Produced by David Bromberg.

David Bromberg was already a well-known folkie before this album proved he was a top-notch songwriter and winning vocalist as well. As he mixes folk, blues, rock, and jug-band music it was natural that he should enlist Garcia, Lesh, Kreutzmann, and Keith Godchaux to contribute to his solo debut. There is no credit listing on the album, but "Diamond Lil" and "Demon in Disguise" have Grateful Dead written all over them.

- ### "Brown-Eyed Women" (Garcia/Hunter)
  Grateful Dead, *Europe '72* **(1972),** *What a Long Strange Trip It's Been* **(1977),** *Dick's Picks Volume Five/'79* **(1996),** *Dick's Pick's Volume Seven/'74* **(1997)**
  Robert Hunter, *Box of Rain* **(1991)**

Recalling the days of yore and the best of the Band's evocation of rowdy nineteenth-century frontierism, this warm, nostalgic song tinged with tragedy was a Grateful Dead concert regular since 1971. It is also one of the few examples of the historian in Robert Hunter as he draws on his roots and upbringing in the Pacific Northwest's fanciful "Bigfoot County," referencing Prohibition, the Great Depression, and the lifestyles of the destitute and hopeless.

The song's title has long been the source of confusion over the years. On the cover of *Europe '72* it was originally listed as "Brown-Eyed Woman" yet nowhere in the song is that lyric sung. According to Hunter, this was a classic case of a typographical error resulting in the song being copyrighted incorrectly.

- **8/21/72, Berkeley Community Theater, Berkeley, California**
- **5/8/77, Barton Hall, Ithaca, New York**
- **1/15/78, Selland Arena, Fresno, California**
- **6/30/85, Merriweather Post Pavilion, Columbia, Maryland**

- ### *Brujo*/NEW RIDERS OF THE PURPLE SAGE
  Columbia PC 33145, 1975.

By the mid-1970s, the Dead's involvement with the New Riders was pretty minimal and the only Grateful Dead connection on this album is the song "Crooked Jungle" with its Robert Hunter lyrics copenned with David Nelson.

- ### *Built to Last*
  Arista AL19-8634, 1989.
  "Foolish Heart," "Just a Little Light," "Victim or the Crime," "Standing on the Moon," "Blow Away," "Picasso Moon," "Built to Last," "I Will Take You Home," "We Can Run"

On Halloween 1989, the Dead released *Built to Last*, an album on which each member of the group approached recording from a completely different angle. Each player worked in his own studio from one basic

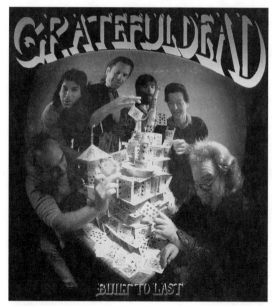

(Courtesy of Arista Records)

rhythm track, a process that Garcia called mechanistic on the surface, but one that he felt produced some interesting results, including songs with such timely concerns as drug addiction and world ecology.

Hailed as a superbly recorded (but generally weaker) followup to their *In the Dark* success, *Built to Last* finds keyboardist Brent Mydland taking center stage for the first time in his underappreciated tenure with the Grateful Dead, with four contributions. Mydland's "Blow Away" and Bob Weir's "Picasso Moon" (both composed with John Perry Barlow) and the Garcia/Hunter tunes "Foolish Heart" and "Standing on the Moon" are easily the album's standouts.

Calling the album "solid if unspectacular" in *The Nation*, Gene Santoro wrote: "It's not a great album . . . [but] when they're playing as well as they're playing now, their balletic, democratic communication validates the old slogan: 'There is nothing like a Grateful Dead concert.'"

- ### "Built to Last" (Garcia/Hunter)
  Grateful Dead, *Built to Last* **(1989),** *The Arista Years* **(1996)**

"Built to Last," the title track to the Dead's 1989 studio album, is a slow-tempo retrospection on Grateful Dead durability. The song humbly acknowledges the importance of staying power and shuns the Warholian "fifteen minutes of fame" ethic so prevalent and implicit in the disposable machinations of popular culture. But the song is about more than the band and their surprising (even to them) longevity. Anything—a friendship, a marriage, a family—better have a strong foundation if it is to survive the inevitable challenges of life.

The Dead performed the song many times after introducing it in 1988, dropping it from their concerts after the death of Brent Mydland, perhaps as a testament to the frailty of all unions.

7/17/89, Alpine Valley Music Theater, East Troy, Wisconsin

- ### *Built to Last: Grateful Dead 25th Anniversary Album* (book)/Jamie Jensen
  96 pages, 120 photographs. Plume/New American Library, 1990.

A band-endorsed, magazine-style softcover book, *Built to Last* serves more as an exaggerated concert program than a serious investigation of the Grateful Dead muse.

- ### "Bye Bye Love" (Felice and Boudleaux Bryant)
  The Everly Brothers, single (1956), *They're Off and Running* (1958), *The Very Best of the Everly Brothers* (1965)
  Simon and Garfunkel, *Bridge over Troubled Water* (1970)

Before the Everly Brothers hit the big time, they had moved from their native Kentucky to Nashville, playing the local clubs and waiting for their first break. It was the mid-1950s and the country was the in throes of rockabilly fever wrought by Elvis and Jerry Lee Lewis. The brothers got their first record deal in 1957 and while searching for new material by making the rounds of local music publishers, they met the songwriting team of Felice and Boudleaux Bryant at Acuff-Rose. The Bryants played them "Bye Bye Love," a new composition, and the Everlys decided to record it. Thus commenced a long association with the Bryants that lasted for many years and produced a series of hits. Sparked by the high-pitched, close harmonizing of traditional country music and bluegrass, "Bye Bye Love" was the Everlys' first smash, rising to the top of the charts in 1957.

The Dead included "Bye Bye Love" in two of their 1981 acoustic sets with Joan Baez.

12/12/81, Fiesta Hall, County Fairgrounds, San Mateo, California

C

- ## "Calibration"
  ### (television program)

In 1969 the Dead were videotaped with the Quicksilver Messenger Service for a local San Francisco television mini-concert on which the Dead performed "Easy Wind" and "Candyman" among others.

- ## "California Earthquake" (Rodney Crowell)
  ### Rodney Crowell, *Ain't Living Long Like This* (1978)
  ### The Seldom Scene, *The New Seldom Scene Album* (1976)

The Dead broke out this tune for two October 1989 concerts on the East Coast in recognition of the Bay Area quake that occurred during their fall tour that year. The first of these performances was at the Philadelphia Spectrum just three days after the quake. The Dead worked up their version during the soundcheck of that night's concert, with Garcia singing lead on the slow, folksy ballad.

Though the song has an old-timey, days of yore sensibility, it is a recent addition to the American songbook, having been penned in the late 1970s by Rodney Crowell.

A consummate singer/songwriter, Crowell was born on August 7, 1950, and "grew up in Houston off of Wayside Drive" (as he sings in the lyrics of Waylon Jennings's "I Ain't Living Long Like This"), latching onto everything from Hank Williams to Chuck Berry and Elvis.

Crowell performed in his father's local country bar band when he was growing up, moving to Nashville in the mid-1970s in search of a recording career but finding only work as a lounge singer. He stuck it out and before long he caught a career-making break playing guitar in Emmylou Harris's Hot Band, earning a reputation for his evaluation of material and for his arranging smarts. Songwriting and producing credits followed with projects that included Guy Clark, Sissy Spacek, and Crowell's now ex-wife Rosanne Cash (their breakup was the stuff of tabloid wet dreams).

Described as "country shuffle," Crowell's records are a grab bag of musical influences and collaborations that, at one point, even included Booker T. Jones of Booker T. and the MG's. With his slightly left-of-center attitude, Crowell's subjects are typical country ones that have made his songs appealing to other recording artists as cover material.

10/20/89, The Spectrum, Philadelphia

- ## "Candyman" (Garcia/Hunter)
  ### Grateful Dead, *American Beauty* (1970), *Dead Set* (1981)

Garcia and Hunter displayed a penchant for reinterpreting chestnuts from the folk and blues traditions virtually from the outset of their collaboration. Their version of "Candyman" draws on both the sexual and violent nature of the title character celebrated in the music of the early Southern blues. Considerably more salacious than Hunter's more convoluted tale, these original, rural Southern versions featured lines like

"He's got a stick of candy nine inches long" that would still raise the hackles of Tipper Gore. Likewise, Hunter's opening line, "Come all you pretty women . . ." is drawn from the narrative form of numerous older songs that invite the listener to hear the tale. Like its predecessors, the Dead's Candyman is liable to return to town, woo the women, win the craps games, and settle old scores before returning to the dark vacuum from whence he came.

The Dead had included "Candyman" in both their electric and acoustic sets since 1970, its shadowy character kept fresh by steady readings.

Of Deadheads' reaction to the song, Hunter pointed out to Blair Jackson in 1988 that "There's the line in 'Candyman' that always gets the big cheers: 'If I had a shotgun, I'd blow you straight to hell.' The first time I ran into that phenomenon was when I went to the movie *Rollerball* and saw the people were cheering the violence that was happening. I couldn't believe it. I hope that people realize that the character in 'Candyman' is a character, and not me."

Mr. Benson, the character who is threatened with death by shotgun blast, has his antecedents in the folk-blues canon and may be based on T. A. Binford, the county sheriff of Harris County, Texas, from 1918 to 1937, who was involved in the infamous Houston Mutiny of 1917. Leadbelly mentions Binford in his classic "Midnight Special" but, over time, other songsters changed the name to Benson and he became a codification similar to Mr. Charlie in the blues idiom and referenced in the Grateful Dead song of the same title.

11/22/72, Municipal Auditorium, Austin, Texas

10/27/79, Cape Cod Coliseum, South Yarmouth, Massachusetts

3/31/85, Cumberland County Civic Center, Portland, Maine

• Gus Cannon/Cannon's Jug Stompers

Born September 12, 1883, in Red Banks, Mississippi, Gus Cannon was a veteran of the black medicine shows in the early years of the twentieth century. But it was as the founding father and leader of Cannon's Jug Stompers by which he left his indelible mark on the decades following.

Cannon absorbed the raw, earthy blues of the Mississippi Delta as a youth and settled in Memphis in 1916 when the musical identity of that burgh was beginning to take shape. In addition to the early blues influence, Can-

non was also steeped in the pop, folk, and old minstrel songs absorbed during his years on the road which was

CANNON'S JUG STOMPERS

(© R. Crumb/Shanachie Entertainment)

reflected in his diverse and inventive banjo style. Along with a more traditional approach to the instrument, he was known to set the banjo on his lap and slide a knife up and down its neck, similar to the method employed by bottleneck blues guitarists.

Cannon sang, played banjo, and told jokes with the traveling shows. During the years of World War I he met Noah Lewis, a virtuoso harmonica player hailing from Henning, Tennessee whose harp work injected the good-timey music with a lethal case of the blues. Cannon formed his Jug Stompers in 1928 with Lewis and three lesser known members: guitarists Ashley Thompson, Hosea Woods, and Elijah Avery. Memphis was the center of the jug craze that swept the region in the late 1920s. Cannon capitalized on the fad by rigging a jug around his neck enabling him to simultaneously pluck the banjo and blow into the jug.

Despite the continuing popularity of jug band music in the South through the mid-1930s, the Depression had stymied any chances at recording. Cannon continued to intermittently perform with members of the Jug Stompers but, as the jobs petered out, he was relegated to busking in Memphis's W. C. Handy Park.

Twenty years later he recorded for the Folkways label, which led to gigs at folk and blues festivals and clubs during the 1960s. His longevity also resulted in appearances in two documentary films, *The Blues* and *The Devil's Music: A History of the Blues*. "Walk Right In," a tune of his written some years before, was recorded by the Rooftop Singers, topping the pop charts in 1963.

It was Cannon's earlier music, though, that ignited

the jug band revival of the early 1960s—repopularized most successfully by Jim Kweskin's Jug Band. Kweskin's music reached California and was a partial inspiration for one of the earliest incarnations of the Grateful Dead, Mother McCree's Uptown Jug Champions, which featured some Cannon material also covered by Kweskin. Eventually several tunes from the Cannon canon became integral parts of the Dead's repertoire, including "Viola Lee Blues" and "Big Railroad Blues."

Cannon lived to see the fruits of his musical labor pass on to a new generation by the time he died at ninety-six on October 15, 1979, in Memphis.

■ "Can't Come Down" (WARLOCKS)
The Warlocks, EMERGENCY CREW demo (1965)

Before the Warlocks became the Grateful Dead and Robert Hunter began contributing the lyrics that helped shape their vision, the band composed a handful of hippie-dippy songs which quickly wound up in the trash bin. "Can't Come Down" is one such example of these songs which were dated even as they were written. The Warlocks recorded "Can't Come Down" for their first demo tape in November 1965 and they are only known to have performed it once.

1/7/66, The Matrix, San Francisco

■ *Captain Trips: A Biography of Jerry Garcia* (book)/Sandy Troy
288 pp. Thunder's Mouth Press, 1994.

As the first official Garcia-centric biography, Sandy Troy's investigation of the Dead's leading man goes where no one had gone before. But the book suffers from its press-clip construction and does not include a single interview collected for the purposes of giving any new insights into what made its subject tick. Still, the book gives a more than adequate overview of Garcia's life and music.

■ "Cardboard Cowboy"

A song of unknown authorship and origin with driving Jefferson Airplane–like music and lyrics, "Cardboard Cowboy" is only known to have been sung by Weir at one particularly hot, early Grateful Dead show.

7/17/66, Fillmore Auditorium, San Francisco

■ *Carry On*/Country Joe McDonald
Ragbaby/Shanachie 8019, 1996.

An old Garcia/McDonald track, "Lady with the Lamp," from the sessions that produced *Superstitious Blues* appears on this McDonald release.

■ "Casey Jones" (Garcia/Hunter)
Grateful Dead, *Workingman's Dead* (1970), *Steal Your Face* (1976), *Dick's Picks Volume Four*/'70 (1996)
Warren Zevon with David Lindley, *Deadicated* (1991)
Wailing Souls, *Fire on the Mountain: Reggae Celebrates the Grateful Dead* (1996)

Although the song is obviously their own, Garcia and Hunter took a page from the folk tradition in their recasting of an old American story—a real train wreck that occurred on the Illinois Central Railroad's Chicago–New Orleans lines April 30, 1900. Just as in the Dead's version, the engineer John Luther Jones (nicknamed K.C. or Casey because he hailed from Cayce, Kentucky), left the station with an overdue train at quarter to nine. Determined to make up ninety-five minutes of lost time, Jones highballed the locomotive down the dangerous "Cannon Ball Run" towards Canton, Mississippi. As the train hurtled down a one-hundred-mile straightway, Jones apparently did not see (or ignored) a switchman flashing a lantern warning of a disabled train ahead. Realizing a wreck was inevitable, Jones ordered the fireman to jump but stayed with the train himself, pulling the whistle and jerking the air brake hose as the train plowed into the stationary freight train's caboose. According to legend, his body was found with hands still clutching the whistle and the brake.

The tragedy soon became the stuff-of-legend songwriting fodder, with the story mythologized to the point that writers, both white and black, from South Carolina to Oregon, claimed the wreck occurred in their backyard.

Contrary to their audience's perception of this driving rocker as an affirmation of hedonism, the Dead composed their "Casey Jones" as a tract warning of cocaine's pitfalls. Commenting on this in his 1971 conversation with Charles Reich, Garcia said, "It's got a split-second little delay, which sounds very mechanical, like a typewriter almost, on the vocal, which is like a little bit jangly, and whole thing is, well . . . I always thought it's a pretty good musical picture of what cocaine is like. A little bit evil. And hard-edged. And also that sing-songy thing, because that's what it *is*, a sing-songy thing, a little melody that gets in your head."

Despite this claim, the song's signature phrase ("Driving that train, high on cocaine") seems not to have filtered down to the population at large. "Casey Jones" has been intermittently banned from radio airplay and was rarely included in the Dead's later concert repertoire.

Robert Hunter threw in his two cents during his 1988 discussion with Blair Jackson: "I said the bad word—cocaine—and put it in a somewhat romanticized context and people look at that as being an advertisement for cocaine, rather than what a close inspection of the words will tell you."

Regardless of its composer's sentiments, "Casey Jones" has always been a crowd pleaser.

Discussing the song's genesis, Garcia commented in 1971, "He [Robert Hunter] wrote the words . . . and the words were just so exquisite, they were just so perfect that I just sat down with the words, picked up the guitar and played the song. It just came out."

As Hunter told Jeff Tamarkin of *Relix* in 1986, "I was working on songs for the *Workingman's Dead* album and I had written down in my notebook: 'Drivin' that train, high on cocaine, Casey Jones you'd better watch your speed.' I thought that was very, very funny. I didn't think of it as a song or anything else, and just went on writing other songs. Some time later I came back to it, and thought there might be a song there.

"We were working it, playing it for Stills and Crosby, just jamming on it, and then we decided to record it. Then there came up the question of the word *cocaine*. This was a time when this was still a very risky word, as was *goddamn* in 'Uncle John's Band.' I said, 'Give me some time to think about it,' and I tried to write other concepts. I wrote 'Drivin' that train, whippin' that chain.' No. 'Luggin' propane.' No. I just tried any way to get away from it and there just was no way. That was the line for the song, and it had to go on in."

There has also been some speculation that the song is an allegorical interpretation of Neal Cassady and the Merry Pranksters.

10/4/70, Winterland Arena, San Francisco

6/22/73, P.N.E. Coliseum, Vancouver, British Columbia, Canada

11/5/79, The Spectrum, Philadelphia

▪ Neal Cassady
Born February 8, 1926, Denver, Colorado; died February 3, 1968, San Miguel de Allende, Mexico

As the wild-eyed, mercury-tongued, picaresque spirit driver of Jack Kerouac's first transcontinental adventure and Furthur, Ken Kesey's bus filled to the gills with his band of Merry Pranksters, Neal Cassady single-handedly steered the Beat Generation into the Summer of Love and way, way beyond.

Cowboy, pool-hall hustler, con man, jive-talker, workingman, cosmic visionary, family man, heartbreaker, and heartmaker, Cassady was an incongruous mix who inspired the core of the Beats and those who followed in their frazzled wake. Allen Ginsberg dedicated his first epic poem, *Howl*, to him and he appears in John Clellon Holmes's early Beat novel *Go*. But it was as Dean Moriarty in Jack Kerouac's *On the Road* that the Cassady legend begin to infiltrate the staid American landscape of the late 1950s.

But much to the chagrin of some of his most ardent adherents, Cassady wrestled with conflicting urges of experiencing the shared dreams of a higher, freer life and the mundane reality of employment. Fast-talking and hard-living, he also loved his second wife Carolyn and their two children yet yearned to take off with his buddies on another wild, transcontinental road adventure.

The early years of Cassady's life were as desperate as any in the Great Depression. Born in the backseat of a jalopy, he moved from skid row flop house to skid row flop house on Denver's Larimer Street with his alcoholic father. A ripe candidate for the reform schools and juvenile prisons in which he spent his adolescence, Cassady still found time to hot-wire cars and whisk his girlfriends into the Rockies for steamy joy rides. Cassady left a minuscule written legacy, but *The First Third*, a posthumously released City Lights publication, includes a marvelously evocative memoir of his formative experiences and efforts to escape the hobo jungles of his hometown. Part of his self-education was a highbrow reading list including the likes of Proust and Schopenhauer.

But his fortunes took a surprise turn when he ventured to New York with LuAnne Henderson, his fifteen-year-old bride, to visit Hal Chase, a Denver friend who was a student at Columbia University and friends with Kerouac and Ginsberg. The young East Coast writers were instantly taken with Cassady, whose energetic sincerity, Adonis-like good looks and penchant for the extreme made him *the* prototype/archetype beat hero. Along with William Burroughs, this core quartet, with their marijuana and amphetamine-fueled all-night rap sessions, planted the seeds for what became the Beat Generation. Their existential and artistically driven lives were from then on marked by honesty, loyalty, and an acknowledgment of the sacred aspects of everyday life.

Cassady was not an artist per se. One might say that he wrote with his feet, living his art, which was his life. No doubt his ability to intuitively free associate with his own highly codified form of free spoken word was among his contributions to the culture he helped spawn.

After splitting with LuAnne, Cassady settled down and married Carolyn Cassady in 1948, living in Los Gatos, California, a Bay Area suburb near San Jose. There he worked as a brakeman for the Southern Pacific railroad. But according to Carolyn Cassady's memoirs and Kerouac's letters, they were also years of confusion, frustration, and heartache for the threesome. Despite Cassady's wanderlust and disregard for the conventions of the accepted norm, Carolyn stood by him and their two children.

Kerouac's rise to literary fame and shame with the 1957 publication of *On the Road* also brought Cassady into the not necessarily desired realm of the culturally notorious. A year later, he was set up by undercover narcotics agents, convicted of marijuana possession and sent to San Quentin for a two-year sentence. Upon his release, he was barred from resuming his job with the railroad and was forced to live out his parole as a tire recapper in Los Gatos. A return to his old ways eventually resulted in a 1960 divorce from Carolyn.

Always the scenemaker, Cassady began infiltrating the burgeoning Bay Area vanguard in the early 1960s, hooking up with Ken Kesey and his Band of Merry Pranksters at their LSD-fueled Acid Tests in California. Revered by the emerging next generation of the Beats, Neal took the wheel of Furthur, the Pranksters' visionary road bus that roamed America from 1964 to 1966 in a conscious effort to expose the U.S. of A. to higher consciousness through higher living.

Along with inspiring the Grateful Dead, Cassady performed with them as well. At least one of these impromptu gigs was recorded and the surviving tape of a July 1967 show (which many early Deadheads received as an acetate insert in Hank Harrison's *The Dead Book*) reveals Cassady at his most fabulously weird doing a numeric stream-of-consciousness James-Joyce-by-way-of-Svengali tongue-twister with the Dead riffing on "Turn On Your Love Light" behind him.

Remembering Cassady's influence on their scene, Garcia once said, "It wasn't as if he said, 'Jerry, my boy, the whole ball of wax happens here and now.' It was watching him move, having my mind blown by how deep he was, how much he could take into account in any given moment and be really in time with it. Neal represented a model to me of how far you could take it in the individual way, in the sense that you weren't going to have a work, you were going to *be* the work. Work in real time, which is a lot like a musician's work. I was oscillating at the time. I had originally been an art student and was wavering between one man/one work or being involved in something that was dynamic and ongoing and didn't necessarily stay any one way. And also something in which you weren't the only contributing factor. I decided to go with what was dynamic and with what more than one mind was involved."

Kesey also released a couple of Cassady audio tapes that were recorded in the heyday of the Acid Tests and reveal a similar high level of musical, if scattered, free association. But like some of John Coltrane's late music, the more the listener sticks with this stuff the more its linguistic architecture makes sense.

Cassady tumbled through the exciting, turbulent times, flipping his omnipresent ballpeen hammer as he discoursed and rapped with exhilarating abandon whether at the Acid Tests or on Haight Street. Cassady's excesses began to take their toll on his powerful constitution as his erratic demeanor increasingly estranged even those with whom he was closest.

Soon after driving the Dead's equipment truck on their first cross-country tour in late 1967 and early 1968, he ventured to San Miguel de Allende in central Mexico with some friends. A few days short of his forty-second birthday, after a hard night of partying, Cassady left the house of a lover to pick up what he called his "magic bag"—a package containing letters from Kerouac and Ginsberg as well as a Bible—that he had left at the train station. Meeting up with a Mexican wedding party, he downed a few Seconals, drank some tequila, and set off in a hard rain to walk to Celaya, a small town fifteen miles down the tracks. Discovered comatose the next morning by a group of Indians, he passed away later that day.

Cassady's spirit never left the Grateful Dead. In two different songs, "The Other One" and "Cassidy," the Dead pay homage to a man as mercurial as any cultural cipher.

It was Kerouac, though, who was eulogizing Cassady even while he was still alive. As he wrote in the last paragraph of *On the Road:* "So in America when the sun goes down and I sit on the old broken-down river pier watching the long, long skies over New Jersey and sense all that raw land that rolls in one unbelievable huge bulge over to the West Coast, and all that road going, all the people dreaming in the immensity of it, and in Iowa I know by now the children must be crying in the land where they let the children cry, and tonight the stars'll be out, and don't you know that God is Pooh Bear? The evening star must be dropping and shedding her sparkler dims on the prairie, which is just before the coming of complete night that blesses the earth, darkens all rivers, cups the peaks and folds the final shore in, and nobody knows what's going to happen to anybody besides the forlorn rags of growing old, I think of Dean Moriarty, I even think of Old Dean Moriarty the father we never found, I think of Dean Moriarty."

- ## "Cassidy" (Weir/Barlow)
  Bob Weir, *Ace* (1972)
  Grateful Dead, *Reckoning* (1981), *Without a Net* (1990), *The Arista Years* (1996)
  Suzanne Vega, *Deadicated* (1991)
  Lasana Bandale, *Fire on the Mountain: Reggae Celebrates the Grateful Dead* (1996)

A song of passionate wanderlust and quiet ceremony, "Cassidy" pays homage to both Beat Generation progenitor NEAL CASSADY and the birth of Cassidy Law, the daughter of Eileen Law, an old Grateful Dead friend and coworker.

Law, who later comanaged the band's in-house ticket service, recalled, "I lived in a tent behind Weir's house when I was pregnant and I'd hear him playing these beautiful riffs in the house while I practiced my breathing exercises.

"I had decided on the name before she was even born because I thought it sounded good for either a boy or a girl. I don't think she's ever really liked the name, though."

Weir's recollections regarding the song's composition are equally organic. "While she was having the child, I was sitting out in the living room scratching on the ol' guitar, and this song just kinda made its presence known. I named it 'Cassidy' because it was born the same day as Cassidy Law. I had the song for about a year and a half before I started on my solo album. Barlow finished it about a week before we recorded it. I folded up the paper and put it in my pocket.

"I recorded a basic track with my guitar and Billy's drums and then I overdubbed a couple of rhythm guitars and a lead track. It added up to this sort of lush, slightly out-of-tune, angular sound I wanted. When I broke out the words and applied them to the melody—for the first time, really—they fit perfectly. By the second verse, Donna was singing harmony. The whole thing was relatively effortless."

Commenting on the song's lyrics, Barlow confirmed that "I was thinking about Neal Cassady's departure and Cassidy Law's arrival as being part and parcel of one another—not like reincarnation, but more the way the cycle works. So what that song is is a wave goodbye to Neal and a hallo to Cassidy."

"Cassidy" is a dramatic, naturalistic composition with many challenging chord changes that allow the Dead dynamic musical exploration, and it was often performed late in the first sets of their concerts when the band was sufficiently warmed up and focused. But it is also a deeply literate song with Barlow referencing Psalm 81 with his lines "Blow the horn and tap the tambourine." Additionally, the term "catch colt," which is used in the song, is defined, according to the *Dictionary of American Regional English*, as "the offspring of a mare bred accidentally and, by extension, a child born out of wedlock" a thematic undercurrent to the composition. Perhaps coincidentally, the citation is attributed to one "Cassidy."

As Weir told Blair Jackson in 1989: "I generally try to place a song like 'Cassidy' later in the set so we're pretty much warmed up and loosened up and have some sense as players what our parameters are for the evening, so we can just let fly. I think 'Bird Song' is the same way for Garcia."

Despite having performed the song over three hundred times since introducing it in 1974 and mining its inherent open-ended improvisational qualities, the Dead only began utilizing "Cassidy" as a segue device allowing them to jam into other songs in the early 1990s. "Cassidy" was also a favorite inclusion in the Dead's 1980 acoustic sets.

5/7/77, Boston Garden, Boston
10/28/77, Soldiers and Sailors Memorial Hall, Kansas City, Kansas
10/23/80, Radio City Music Hall, New York
5/3/87, Frost Amphitheater, Palo Alto, California
6/20/88, Alpine Valley Music Theater, East Troy, Wisconsin
5/27/93, Cal Expo Amphitheater, Sacramento, California

■ **"Cathy's Clown"** (Don Everly/Phil Everly)
The Everly Brothers, *A Date with the Everly Brothers* (1961), *The Golden Hits of the Everly Brothers* (1962), *The Very Best of the Everly Brothers* (1965)
Reba McEntire, *Reba Live* (1989)
You Am I, *Hi Fi Way* (1996)

"Cathy's Clown" is significant in the Everly Brothers history as it was the first hit they scored after landing a lucrative deal with the newly formed Warner Bros. Records in 1960. The deal marked their move to Los Angeles but was also a sour end to their artistic relationship with Felice and Boudleaux Bryant, who copenned their earliest work.

The Dead are only known to have covered "Cathy's Clown" twice. Both renderings were in a semi-acoustic form as part of Weir's mostly Grateful Dead band Bobby Ace and the Cards from the Bottom of the Deck.

4/17/70, Family Dog, San Francisco

■ ***Cats Under the Stars*/**Jerry Garcia Band
Arista AB 4160, 1978 (reissued as AC/ARCD-85835)
Produced by Jerry Garcia.
"Rubin and Cherise," "Love in the Afternoon," "Palm Sunday," "Cats Under the Stars," "Rhapsody in Red," "Rain," "Down Home," "Gomorrah"
Jerry Garcia–guitar, vocals. Keith Godchaux–vocals, keyboard. Donna Godchaux–vocals. JOHN KAHN–basses, keyboards, guitars, orchestration. Ron Tutt–drums, percussion. MERL SAUNDERS–organ. Maria Muldaur–backup vocal on "Gomorrah" and "Love in the Afternoon." Steve Shuster–flutes,

(Courtesy of Arista Records)

clarinet, saxophone. Brian and Candy Godchaux–violins.

Garcia, with good reason, often referred to *Cats Under the Stars* as his most satisfying solo album. As well structured as it is recorded, the outing is an excellent amalgam of Garcia and Hunter's musical and folklorist passions: mythology ("Rubin and Cherise"), Ellingtonia ("Down Home"), biblical allusion ("Gomorrah"), gospel ("Palm Sunday"), rock ("Rhapsody in Red"), and the good old love song ("Love in the Afternoon").

In addition to Donna Godchaux giving perhaps her best recorded performance on the Beatlesque "Rain," several of these tunes remained Jerry Garcia Band staples since their introductions at his concerts in the late 1970s. But the album failed to break into the Top 100 and remains a vastly underrated Jerry Garcia album.

Garcia told Blair Jackson in 1991 that, as far as he was concerned, *Cats Under the Stars* was "my most successful record—even though it's my least successful record! . . . I always loved it and it never went anywhere. . . . I'll never understand it!"

A final note on the album concerns a detail involved in its recording schedule. The Garcia Band was set to take a month-long break from recording the album so drummer Ron Tutt could return to his steady gig: providing the backbeat for the Elvis Presley tour. But Elvis "left the building" and, within a week, recording was able to resume.

- ### The Cauldron Journey of Healing/Nicki Scully
  Cauldron Records/CAU 3, 1990.

A super-esoteric item, Garcia and Roland Barker contributed a musical score to this meditation tape from the wife of the Dead's former manager Rock Scully.

- ### "Caution (Do Not Stop on Tracks)"
  (Grateful Dead/Ron McKernan)
  Grateful Dead, *Anthem of the Sun* (1968), *Dick's Picks Volume Four*/'70 (1996)

Voodoo rock at its very harrowing best, this bluesy raga with its "Peter Gunn"–style theme featured Pigpen's narration of a visit to a gypsy woman who holds the key to his romantic tribulation.

The Dead performed "Caution" numerous times from 1967 through 1972 and occasionally broke it out as an instrumental jam session even after Pigpen's passing.

Bob Weir once described the song's evolution: "How the 'Caution' jam developed is we were driving around listening to the radio, like we used to do a lot, and the song 'Mystic Eyes' by Them was on, and we were all saying, 'Check this out! We can do this!' So we got to the club where we were playing and we warmed up on it. We lifted the riff from 'Mystic Eyes' and extrapolated it into 'Caution,' and I think Pigpen just made up the words."

> **2/14/68, Carousel Ballroom, San Francisco**
> **3/16/68, Carousel Ballroom, San Francisco**
> **12/12/69, Thelma Theater, Los Angeles**
> **2/14/70, Fillmore East, New York (*Dick's Picks Volume Four*).**
> **4/14/72, Tivoli Concert Hall, Copenhagen**
> **10/19/74, Winterland Arena, San Francisco**

- ### "C.C. Rider" (Traditional)
  Singles: Gertrude "Ma" Rainey (1924), Blind Lemon Jefferson (1927), Alfred Lewis (1930), Kansas City Kitty (1934), LEADBELLY (1935), Wea Bea Booze (1942), Carl Perkins (1969), Therapy? (1994)
  Grateful Dead, *Dick's Picks Volume Five*/'79 (1996), *Dick's Picks Volume Six*/'83 (1996)
  Big Bill Broonzy, *The Young Big Bill Broonzy*/'34 (1968)
  Jimmy Witherspoon, *The Spoon Concerts* (1959), *Live at the Mint* (1996)
  LIGHTNIN' HOPKINS, *Country Blues* (1960), *The Complete Aladdin Recordings* (1991)
  Ella Fitzgerald, *These Are the Blues* (1963)

Ian and Sylvia, *Ian & Sylvia* (1963)
Mississippi John Hurt, *Memorial Anthology* (1964)
B. B. King, *Confessin' the Blues* (1966)
Cher, *All I Really Want to Do* (1965)
The Everly Brothers, *Beat and Soul* (1965)
Alexis Korner, *I Wonder Who* (1967)
Richie Havens, *Electric Havens* (1966)
The Animals, *Animalization* (1966), *Star Portrait* (1971)
CHUCK BERRY with the Steve Miller Band, *Live at the Fillmore Auditorium* (1968)
Street, *Street* (1968)
Dave Allen, single (1968), *Epitaph for a Legend* (1980)
Elvis Presley, *On Stage, February 1970* (1970)
Jerry Lee Lewis, *The "Killer" Rocks On* (1972)
Joe Williams, *Joe Williams Live* (1973)
Roy Buchanan, *In the Beginning* (1974)
Little Esther Phillips, *Confessin' the Blues* (1975)
Duke Ellington, *This One's for Blanton* (1975)
John Lee Hooker, *Sad and Lonesome* (1979)
La Vern Baker, *Live in Hollywood 1991* (1991)
Dakota Staton, *Dakota Staton* (1991)
Chuck Willis, *Stroll On*/'57 (1994)
Street Sounds, *Street Sounds* (1994)
Ray Charles, *Ray Charles Sings the Blues* (1995)
KINGFISH, *KINGFISH IN CONCERT*/'76 (1995)
Lonnie Johnson, *American Folk Blues Festival* (1995)
Milwaukee Slim, *Lemmon Avenue* (1995)
Junior Mance, *Softly as a Morning Sunrise* (1995)
Ramsey Lewis Trio, *Consider the Source* (1996)

Also recorded as "See See Rider," the title of this venerable blues is usually thought to refer not to someone's name but to a jilted lover's lament as heard in the song's commencing verse: "See, see Rider see what you have done." However some bluesologists insist that the "C.C." in question stands for "Carney Circuit Rider"— that is, a wastrel who works the carnival as it moves from town to town and misadventure to misadventure. Whatever its true lineage, "C.C. Rider" is among the oldest of country blues standards dating back to the days before recording equipment.

Gertrude "Ma" Rainey's 1925 Paramount 78 with her Georgia Jazz Band made the first popular release of the song. In fact, she and Lena Arant are credited with the composition on the record, and, over time, many have attributed Rainey with its authorship.

Though the validity of that may not hold much water,

Rainey's release was the probably the most influential. One of the most popular jazz and blues singers of the 1920s, her bands showcased the talents of at least a half-dozen members of the American musical pantheon, including Louis Armstrong, Kid Ory, Don Redman, Coleman Hawkins, Tampa Red, and Fletcher Henderson.

In the Grateful Dead universe, "C.C. Rider"—since its concert debut in 1979—worked well as an early-first-set Weir cover functioning in the same way as his interpretations of "Walkin' Blues," "Little Red Rooster," "Wang Dang Doodle," and a revolving handful of other blues classics.

6/30/85, Merriweather Post Pavilion, Columbia, Maryland

▪ *Chance in a Million*/ZERO

Whirled Records WRR 1960, 1994 (Rereleased by Horizon 69712-4050-2, 1995.)

"Chance in a Million," "Horses," "Catalina," "End of the World Blues," "Home on the Range," "Forever Is Nowhere," "Mercury Blues," "Roll Me After"

Martin Fierro–tenor saxophone. Steve Kimock–guitar. Greg Anton–drums. Judge Murphy–drums. Pete Sears–keyboards. Bobby Vega–bass. Liam Hanrahan–bass. JOHN KAHN–bass. Vince Welnick–keyboards, background vocals. Nicky Hopkins–keyboards. Robert Hunter–lyrics.

A loose configuration of core and peripheral Grateful Dead personnel, Zero is a Bay Area musical cooperative with a hard-jamming, bar-band sound. This debut CD, drawn from three live 1992 shows at San Francisco's Great American Music Hall, captures the band at a peak. Along with musical assistance from Vince Welnick and longtime Garcia Band bassist John Kahn, Robert Hunter contributed lyrics to the first five tunes included on this release.

▪ "Childhood's End" (Lesh)

Though the title of this '90s Phil Lesh composition references Arthur C. Clarke's famous science-fiction novel about a Martian invasion of Earth, "Childhood's End" is anything but spacey. It is, however, a sensitive statement about the passage of time and loss of innocence.

9/24/94, Berkeley Community Theater, Berkeley, California

▪ "Chimes of Freedom" (BOB DYLAN)

Bob Dylan, *Another Side of Bob Dylan* (1964)
The Byrds, *Mr. Tambourine Man* (1965)

One of the wonderful and underappreciated aspects of the Dylan/Dead concerts in the summer of 1987 was the number of rarely (if ever) performed Dylan songs that were resurrected for the purposes of the tour.

"Chimes of Freedom" was the jewel in the crown of these rarities. Its language, sweep, compassion, and universality make it one of Dylan's most profound song-poems—a triumph of word-color and metaphor encompassing humanity. Hearing "the chimes of freedom flashing" for the legion of the downtrodden, Dylan's noble affinity with the underdog is deftly crafted. Set during a dramatic lightning storm, the alliterative explosion of words is at once one of Dylan's most political songs, a heartrending love song that extends to all living creatures, and a paean to the inspirational qualities of nature.

Some literary scholars have specifically pointed to "Chimes of Freedom" in their arguments that place Dylan as a Romantic in the tradition of William Blake. They also argue that, similar to the poetic experiments of Rimbaud, Edgar Allan Poe, and Hart Crane, Dylan was dabbling in a technique known as "synesthesia"—extravagant and often violent imagery woven with an abundance of common vowels that can produce a surreal color effect.

5/87, Club Front, San Rafael, California (Dylan/Dead rehearsals)
7/10/87, JFK Stadium, Philadelphia

▪ "China Cat Sunflower" (Garcia/Hunter)

Grateful Dead, *Aoxomoxoa* (1969), *Europe '72* (1972), *Without a Net* (1990), *Hundred Year Hall/'72* (1995), *Dick's Picks Volume Four/'70* (1996)

Spiritually and musically linked at the hip with "I Know You Rider," the old folk- and country-blues jailhouse traditional, "China Cat Sunflower" represented one of the Dead's standout concert regulars for nearly three decades.

Despite its spidery melody, quirky beat, and nonsensically trippy lyrics, the song contains the salient elements of the Dead's classic work: intangible haiku powered by conversational guitar lines. Indeed, the song's thematic qualities lend themselves more to the realm of the Zen koan than they do anything remotely

Jerry Garcia, Golden Gate Park, San Francisco, 1968. (*Archive Photos*)

Western. Despite its lyrical fragmentation, "China Cat" is rife with equally fractured references. "Bodhi" may be a nod to Buddhism and the enlightenment the Buddha first experienced under a bodhi tree. "Leonardo words" may be a nod to the fact that Leonardo da Vinci could write in mirror script. "Krazy Kat" was the star of George Herriman's screwball comic-strip creation that appeared daily 1913–1944. The "Cheshire Cat" is drawn from Lewis Carroll's 1865 *Alice's Adventures in Wonderland*. Finally, "Queen Chinee" is a quote from an Edith Sitwell poem "Trio for Two Cats and a Trombone."

"China Cat Sunflower" was among the first lyrics Robert Hunter penned for the Grateful Dead. Temporarily relocated in New Mexico when Garcia contacted him with a formal invitation to contribute lyrics to the group, Hunter mailed them "China Cat" and "Alligator." A little known wrinkle to the song's evolution is that the lyrics that eventually became "The Eleven" were originally included as an addendum to "China Cat Sunflower."

As Hunter described the process of the song's creation to David Gans in 1978: "I think the germ of 'China Cat Sunflower' came in Mexico, on Lake Chapala. I don't think any of the words came, just the rhythms. I was writing things to these rhythms and, subsequently, I put some of the rhythms to these images.

"At one point I had a cat sitting on my belly and I was in a rather hypersensitive state. I followed the cat out to—I believe it was Neptune, but I'm not sure—and there were rainbows across Neptune and cats marching across this rainbow.

"All right, I wrote part of it in Mexico and part of it on Neptune!"

Separately, Hunter told Blair Jackson in 1991 that " 'China Cat' took a long time to write. I wrote it in different settings and added this and that to it. It was originally inspired by Dame Edith Sitwell, who had a way with words—I liked the idea of quick, clicky assonance and alliteration like 'See me dance the polka, said Mr. Wag like a bear, with my top hat and my whiskers, that tra-la-la trapped affair.' I just liked the way she put things together. I'd have to admit—that before you could trace it back—that there was some influence."

Jokingly referencing the song's poetic impenetrability in *A Box of Rain*, his book of collected lyrics, Hunter wrote, "Nobody ever asked me the meaning of this song. People seem to know exactly what I'm talking about. It's good that a few things in this world are clear to all of us."

Musically, the sublime joy of "China Cat Sunflower" was found in the driving interplay within the group as they instrumentally jammed from the song and into the "I Know You Rider" segue.

8/27/72, Old Renaissance Faire Grounds, Veneta, Oregon

5/19/74, Memorial Coliseum, Portland, Oregon

12/1/79, Stanley Theater, Pittsburgh

8/28/81, Long Beach Arena, Long Beach, California

8/24/85, Boreal Ridge, Soda Springs, California

7/29/88, Laguna Seca Recreation Area, Monterey, California

9/14/91, Madison Square Garden, New York

- **"China Doll"** (Garcia/Hunter)
Grateful Dead, *From the Mars Hotel* (1974), *Reckoning* (1981)
Suzanne Vega, *Deadicated* (1991)
DAVID MURRAY, *DARK STAR (THE MUSIC OF THE GRATEFUL DEAD)* (1996)

A dreamy, delicate tune with violent overtones of devastating and irreplaceable loss, "China Doll" is regarded among Deadheads as a minor Dead masterpiece. Often appearing as a second-set pace decelerator, the Dead also included this precious piece in their 1980 acoustic sets. Like much of Hunter's mid-1970s work, "China

Doll" dwells in the murky terrain of the hereafter and all that implies. It is a sad hymnal but imbued with an air of solace that points to the redemptive aspects of death. It's as if there is an unseen player in the song who is empathizing with the situation at hand and providing spiritual or physical comfort.

Of the cryptic lyrics, Hunter admitted the song was composed on the heels of a friend's suicide attempt and was originally titled "The Suicide Song." According to his 1988 interview with Blair Jackson, "I think it's a terrifying song. And then it's also got some affirmation of how it can be mended somehow. There's a bit of metaphysical content in there, which I kind of leave open, not that I subscribe or don't subscribe to it. At the time it resonated right. That song is eerie and very, very beautiful the way Jerry handles it."

A fascinating addendum to the song was a jazz arrangement worked up by tenor saxophonist David Murray in the year following Garcia's death when Murray's band performed their version of "China Doll" as a mournful jazz dirge owing something to the ballads of Charles Mingus and the shy romance of a Lester Young solo.

5/19/77, Fox Theater, Atlanta

10/6/80, Warfield Theater, San Francisco

6/24/84, Saratoga Performing Arts Center, Saratoga, New York

5/26/93, Cal Expo Amphitheater, Sacramento, California

▪ "Chinatown Shuffle" (Ron McKernan)

Pigpen was justifiably better known as a charismatic stage presence and earthy R&B interpreter than for his own compositions, which are few yet nevertheless uniformly stellar. "Chinatown Shuffle," a jump-blues with Hunteresque lyrics of karma and fate, ranks among his best and allowed him to let his theatrical mojo shine. A self-styled rock rumba about a Chinatown misadventure, the song can be heard as an amalgamation of Lightning Hopkins's "AIN'T IT CRAZY" and Pigpen's own "Operator."

12/31/71, Winterland Arena, San Francisco

▪ "Chinese Bones" (Robyn Hitchcock)
Robyn Hitchcock and the Egyptians, *Globe of Frogs* (1987)

Singer/songwriter Robyn Hitchcock developed a sizable cult following on the heels of the critical acclaim he received in the mid-1980s for his highly poetic, if somewhat obscure, songs.

Born in 1952 in London, England, Hitchcock first came to public attention in the late 1970s as the leader of the Soft Boys, a British band that cut three albums. A year after releasing an acoustic solo album (*I Often Dream of Trains*) in 1985, he founded Robyn Hitchcock and the Egyptians and, through 1993, released six albums.

Hitchcock has a considerable catalog, but neophytes are often steered to *Globe of Frogs*, the album on which "Chinese Bones" appears. Some idea of Hitchcock's highly imagistic folk-rock, an acquired taste, can be gleaned from the collection's Captain Beefheartish titles: "Tropical Fish Mandala," "Sleeping with Your Devil Mask," and "The Shapes Between Us Turn into Animals."

Hitchcock holds a worldview that combines radical ecology consciousness and benevolent cynicism. An official A&M Record bio gives an interesting glimpse into what he is all about: "My friends and family are all 'artists.' I have never met an ordinary person. But I am English and not so very exotic from a weeper full of fruit and fireworks. I'm six feet, two inches tall and made entirely of dead sea creatures. I have never wanted to be anything but a singer, although I'm basically a draughtsman. My songs are basically pictures. A song has no opinions. I want the pictures to be as intense as positive—ideally one glimpse would detonate the spectator permanently. But, inevitably, things are lost in translation. I have no ambition but am very persistent. The great thing about human beings is they can walk and eat at the same time."

As curiously cryptic as a Robert Hunter lyric, "Chinese Bones" was the most musically spacious and coolly exotic entry in the mini-set Suzanne Vega performed with the Grateful Dead during the 1988 Rainforest benefit, the only time the Dead played the song.

9/24/88, Madison Square Garden, New York

▪ John Cipollina
Born August 24, 1943, Berkeley, California; died May 29, 1989

As a founding member of Quicksilver Messenger Service, who, along with the Dead and the Jefferson Airplane, defined the San Francisco "acid rock" sound of the late 1960s, John Cipollina was at the vanguard of influential guitarists spawning on the left coast at the time. But his musical destiny may have been ordained from his birth—José Iturbi (1895–1980), the famous Spanish pianist who helped popularize classical music in America, was his godfather.

Born a twin in California, Cipollina lived in El Salvador and Guatemala until the age of six, when his family resettled in the Bay Area. Steeped in music and introduced to the piano by the age of two, John became attracted to the guitar in 1958 through the work of Elvis's guitarists Scotty Moore and James Burton, as well as the sonic exploits of Link Wray. Of Wray, Cipollina once said: "He could talk dirty with just a couple of licks on the guitar."

By the time Quicksilver Messenger Service came together, Cipollina was already a vet of the nascent Bay Area music scene, having played in bands that did everything from proto-garage rock, folk, and blues to bossa nova and flamenco. Cipollina often credited his long, flowing, melodic guitar lines to his integration of flamenco stylings into the electric-guitar sound.

When Beatlemania swept the world in 1964, Cipollina began meeting the men who would soon join him in his best known group. After some early shuffling, the primary Quicksilver unit was forged: Cipollina and Gary Duncan on guitar, David Freiberg on bass, Jim Murray on harmonica, and Greg Elmore on drums. Amazingly, not only did Cipollina and Freiberg share the same birthday, Duncan and Elmore shared theirs (September 4, 1969). Freiberg came up with the group's name, concluding that because four were Virgos and Murray was a Gemini they were all ruled by the planet Mercury. Because another name for Mercury is Quicksilver, the messenger of the gods, and Virgo is the servant, an alchemical combination would be appropriate. Hence, Quicksilver Messenger Service.

But while the Dead, the Airplane, Big Brother, and the Fish got their record deals and national tours, Quicksilver honed their sound in local clubs, becoming known for long, extended blues jams and developing a rabid following in the Bay Area.

From their birth in 1965 through many incarnations, reincarnations, and a couple of reunions, Quicksilver's performances and recordings were marked by Cipollina's expansive, funkified sting. Just a taste of *Happy Trails* and their renditions of "Who Do You Love" or

"Mona" should be revelation enough of the group's and the lead guitarist's enormous abilities.

Between Quicksilver rebirths, Cippolina formed the shortlived Copperhead, which recorded one eponymous album on Columbia in 1973. He was instrumental in the formation of the Dinosaurs, a Bay Area all-star band that included Robert Hunter, and Man, another came-and-went local band.

Cipollina lived for music and for years juggled gigs with a dozen bands through the late 1980s, including: Thunder and Lightning, Terry and the Pirates, Fish and Chips, Zero, Problem Child, Fish Stu, Rokey Sullivan, the Summer of Love All Stars, the Sounds of San Francisco, the Seven Deadly Sins, Silver Lightning, and Nickelsilver to name some.

In the late 1970s and early 1980s, Cipollina was a frequent guest guitarist at Dead shows, performing with the band no less than a dozen times between 1978 and 1983. And as a much-in-evidence San Francisco guitar god, he was playing Bay Area gigs with gusto that belied his true physical condition right up until his death, associated with emphysema, in 1989.

- **"Clementine"** (Woody Harris/Percy Montrose)
  Bobby Hackett, *The Da Da Strain* (1939)
  Duke Ellington, *The Complete Duke Ellington Songbook* (1957), *The Blanton-Webster Band* (1986)
  Bobby Darin, *The Bobby Darin Story* (1989), *Mack the Knife* (1991)
  Bing Crosby, *My Favorite Country Songs* (1996)

Everybody sang "Oh, My Darling Clementine" as a child. But only the Dead could instrumentally riff on this well-known folk song as a segue in a few of their more adventurous jams from 1968 and 1969. Basing it on Percy Montrose's 1884 song "Oh, My Darling Clementine," Woody Harris adapted the song for Bobby Darin, who had a popular recording of the updated version.

1/26/69, Avalon Ballroom, San Francisco

- **"Close Encounters"** (a.k.a. "Theme from *Close Encounters of the Third Kind*") (John Williams)
  Close Encounters of the Third Kind/soundtrack (1978)

At the height of its mass pop cultural omnipresence, the Dead surprised a Eugene audience with a one-of-a-kind jam off the *Close Encounters* theme before diving into a full-throttled version of "St. Stephen." The Dead did briefly return to this piece of pop culture by incorporating its main thematic riff into two 1989 space jams.

For anyone who never saw the film *Close Encounters of the Third Kind*—if that's possible—the music in question is the tonal means of communication between the humans and the extra-terrestrials. So it was with that special tongue-in-cheek knowledge this sole performance is cherished.

1/22/78, McArthur Court, University of Oregon, Eugene

- ## "Cocaine Habit Blues" (Traditional)
  Singles: Luke Jordan (1927), LEADBELLY (1933), Blind Jesse Harris (1937), Willie Storks (1942)
  Memphis Jug Band, *Double Album*/'30 (1990)
  David Van Ronk, *Inside David Van Ronk* (1962)
  The Byrds, *Untitled* (1970)
  Universe, *Universe* (1971)
  George Thorogood, *Move It on Over* (1973)

When Huddie "LEADBELLY" Ledbetter recorded the most popular early version of this song under its better known name, "Take a Whiff on Me," he captured the loose attitude toward cocaine shared by many black musicians in the 1920s and 1930s.

The Dead's short-lived inclusion of "Cocaine Habit Blues" in their 1970 acoustic sets probably worked as a nice historical nod to the subject matter also found in their anti-cocaine composition, "Casey Jones."

8/19/70, Fillmore West, San Francisco

- ## "Cold Rain and Snow" (Traditional)
  Grateful Dead, *Grateful Dead* (1967), *Steal Your Face* (1976), *Dick's Picks Volume Five*/'79 (1996)
  Shorty Bob Parker, single (1938)
  Obray Ramsey, *Obray Ramsey Sings Folksongs from Three Laurels* (1962), *The Music Never Stopped: Roots of the Grateful Dead* (1995)
  Pentangle, *A Maid That's Deep in Love* (1987)
  Muleskinner, *Muleskinner* (1973)
  Galaxy-Lin, *Galaxy-Lin* (1967)
  Arkansas Sheiks, *Whiskey Before Breakfast* (1976)
  Tom Constanten, *Fresh Tracks in Real Time* (1989), *Nightfall of Diamonds* (1991)
  The Bevis Frond, *A Psychedelic Psauna* (1991)
  HENRY KAISER, *ETERNITY BLUE* (1995)

An ancient white blues from the mountain-music tradition, probably the Blue Ridge Mountains of Virginia or North Carolina, "Cold Rain and Snow" is folk music in its purest form. It's a favorite among oldtimey groups, and determining a source for this rarely recorded plaint on the ravages of a particular woman is futile given its undetermined age and fuzzy regional origin.

Obray Ramsey, a banjoist and singer of oldtime mountain songs in western North Carolina during the 1950s and 1960s, recorded the most notable early version of "Cold Rain and Snow" in the late 1950s and it was probably the one to which Jerry Garcia was first exposed because the Dead's performance of "Cold Rain and Snow" bears a resemblance to this pressing. While Garcia was undoubtedly familiar with Ramsey's records, he might have been made aware of the song through Peter Rowan, who sang the song when he was the resident guitarist in Bill Monroe's band in the mid-1960s.

Just as the band enjoyed playing a tune like "One More Saturday Night" when they performed on the titled evening, the Dead tended to open shows on days of particularly inclement weather with "Cold Rain and Snow." One of the only songs the Dead performed throughout their career, "Cold Rain and Snow" was rearranged from a chugging rocker played at a breakneck speed into something almost resembling a torch song that was reminiscent of Ramsey's emotional, plaintive rendition.

4/29/71, Fillmore East, New York
10/12/84, Civic Center, Augusta, Maine

- ## Ornette Coleman
  Born March 19, 1930, Fort Worth, Texas

Of all the Olympian musicians with whom the Grateful Dead shared the stage, the most significant was a soft-spoken, unassuming gentleman improbably hailing from central Texas. Contrary to his sweet nature, Ornette Coleman has provoked more critical schizophrenia and outright hatred than almost any other jazz musician. Anecdotes about his formative years are the stuff of tragicomic legend: physically threatened onstage, having his horn confiscated and destroyed by an angry mob, or being left behind in Los Angeles by his bandleader after an ill-fated tour.

But mythology aside, one thing is certain—Ornette Coleman is one of the most important creators of twentieth-century music. His innovations and contributions helped shape all the jazz music that has come since he first hit the scene in the late 1950s. He baptized the "new wave" jazz revolution of the 1960s, maintaining

Ornette Coleman and Jerry Garcia, Oakland Coliseum, 2/23/93.
(Robert Minkin)

fresh technique and compositional innovation. But no matter how far out his music traveled or how contemporary it seemed, his playing never lost the wide open spaces of the Lone Star State, evoking images of cactus and tumbleweed, the scent of sage and jalapeño.

A loner from early childhood, Coleman was a Texan contemporary of King Curtis who played the alto saxophone in R&B bands before briefly moving to New Orleans. He relocated to Los Angeles in 1951 and spent the next seven years working as an elevator operator by day and developing his new music at night. With a small cabal of coconspirators (trumpeter Don Cherry, drummer Billy Higgins, and bassist Charlie Haden), Coleman began laying the musical groundwork that would alter the rest of his life.

Meeting with hostility from other musicians because their concept excluded the jazz conventions of chord changes and keys set forth in the wake of the be-bop revolution, Coleman's quirky quartet persevered nonethe-

less. This was most dramatically bared in dropping the piano and its obvious chord-changing capabilities from their ensemble.

The Coleman group did record an album for Contemporary that included a keyboard, but they were swiftly signed to Atlantic by Nesuhi Ertegun, who was developing the first avant-garde label with his brother Ahmet. Both brothers enthusiastically encouraged Coleman to pursue his muse.

Their first piano-less album was the prophetically titled *The Shape of Jazz to Come* (1959), on which they set the mold for all that would follow with compositions such as the masterful "Lonely Woman." Over the next three years, the group churned out an incredible seven albums, including *Change of the Century* in 1959, *This Is Our Music* in 1960, and *Ornette!* later that year, on which Haden was replaced by the prodigal Scott La Faro.

Combining avant-garde forms and sounds derived from traditional African-American music, Ornette's first albums divided the jazz community right down the middle into the Coleman followers and the non-believers who disregarded his approach as noisy gimmickry. Coleman playing a white plastic alto and Cherry a pocket trumpet (instruments that looked like toys) only gave the critics more to complain about.

The debate reached filibuster proportions in 1960 with the release of Coleman's most remarkable recording, *Free Jazz*. Featuring eight of the greatest jazz musicians of the mid-twentieth century (Coleman's quartet plus Eric Dolphy on bass clarinet, Freddie Hubbard on trumpet, LaFaro on bass, and drummer Higgins), the album showcased the talents of the ensemble spontaneously and collectively improvising for thirty-six minutes. In Grateful Dead terms, there could have been no "Dark Star" without *Free Jazz*.

Composer George Russell probably identified and best expressed Coleman's gift when he said, "Ornette seems to depend mostly on the overall tonality of the song as a point of departure for the melody . . . the melody and the chords of his compositions have an overall sound, which Ornette seems to use as a point of departure. This approach liberates the improviser to sing his own song, really, without having to meet the deadline of any particular chord."

For his part, Coleman once commented that "If I'm going to follow a preset chord sequence I may as well write out my solo."

After establishing a permanent residence in New

York City, Coleman eventually broke up the band and took a two-year sabbatical in the early 1960s, studying trumpet and violin, on which he performed and recorded with decidedly mixed results and reception. The first evidence of his use of these instruments could be heard on a pair of albums recorded live at the Golden Circle in Stockholm, Sweden, on a European tour with bassist David Izenson and drummer Charles Moffett.

Throughout the late 1960s and early 1970s, Coleman put together various units while developing his "harmolodic" theory of music, which focused on a series of attempts to broaden the standard American horizons of jazz. This development can be heard on *Crisis* (1969), an album with a politically radical agenda, on which he reunited with Cherry and Haden in a group that also included Ornette Denardo Coleman, the maestro's son, on drums, and tenor saxophonist Dewey Redman.

Coleman's evolving harmolodic concept can also be heard on *Science Fiction*, with Indian vocalist Asha Puthli, in 1971 and *Skies of America*, an orchestral piece performed by the London Symphony Orchestra in 1972. One of his most unusual collaborations of the 1970s took place in Morocco's Atlas Mountains where he performed and recorded with the legendary Master Musicians of Joujouka.

In the mid-1970s, Coleman formed Prime Time, an electric concept band featuring Denardo and steeped in harmolodic musical philosophy and technique. Their jazz-funk fusion mode resulted in one of Coleman's most popular albums, *Dancing in Your Head* (1977).

While Coleman continued to record and perform with Prime Time through the mid-1990s, he also involved himself with other projects of both a personal and commercial nature. For instance, he released *Song X*, a collaboration with the mainstream jazz guitarist Pat Metheny, in 1986. He also re-formed the classic quartet with Cherry, Haden, and Moffett for a series of concerts in 1986, sharing the bill with Prime Time at some engagements. Concurrently, he approved and was the subject of Shirley Clarke's fine 1986 documentary film, *Ornette: Made In America*, which focused on his return to Fort Worth to accept the keys to the city on the officially proclaimed Ornette Coleman Day.

It was in 1987 that he first crossed paths with the Grateful Dead. Denardo had attended a September 1987 Dead concert at Madison Square Garden and urged his father and pianist Cecil Taylor to join him on one of the following nights. Coleman was impressed and requested a private audience with the band. Ornette had been awed by the enthusiasm of the Deadheads. "They could have done anything up there and those people would have screamed. . . . I thought, 'Well, we could be friends here.' Because if these people here could be into this, they could dig what *we're* doing."

Within months, he invited Garcia to the Prime Time recording sessions that resulted in Coleman's 1988 *Virgin Beauty* album. In true harmolodic fashion, Garcia's contribution to three cuts ("3 Wishes," "Singing in the Shower," and "Desert Players") recede into the aural tapestry of Coleman's orchestral vision.

The musical union appeared to be short-lived, but on February 23, 1993, during the Dead's Mardi Gras show in Oakland, Coleman reemerged in Grateful Dead land. Prime Time opened the concert and was joined by Garcia for the final tune. Coleman returned the favor by appearing with the Dead midway through the second set when the guitarists were entering the thick of their "Space" jam. The music that followed amounts to one of the most unusual segments to both the Dead's and Coleman's recorded legacy. Perhaps because of its defined formlessness, the space section was most successful with Ornette layering his distinctive alto sounds over the shimmering cacophony. Moving into the Dead's highly modal "The Other One" was a wise choice, as its rhythm-based power allowed Coleman to continue his broad brush strokes. The music stalled somewhat with the segue into "Stella Blue," a languorous composition that gave the saxophonist little to do. But, in going into "TURN ON YOUR LOVE LIGHT," the Dead provided Coleman with the perfect show-ending raveup to let loose in the fashion of an oldtime, down-home Texas horn honker.

Assessing Coleman's performance with the Dead, Garcia told Jon Sievert of *Guitar Player* in 1993, "Influences for me are rarely that direct. It's just the exposure of having Ornette in my life. He's a wonderful model for a guy who's done what we did, in the sense of creating his own reality of what music is and how you survive within it. He's a high-integrity kind of person and just a wonderful man. It was great to have him play with us. It was such a hoot to hear him play totally Ornette and totally Grateful Dead at the same time without compromising either one of them. Pretty incredible. Good musicians don't do that thing of characterizing music. Like this is this kind of music and that is that kind of thing."

The musicians repeated the formula with similar results in December 1993 running through a nearly identical song list at the Sports Arena in Los Angeles.

What was particularly notable about both performances was the flexibility of all those involved. The Dead augment their style just enough to accommodate Coleman without alienating their audience while Ornette seems to enjoy playing both musical roles of rock & roller and aloof avant-gardist.

Despite his huge reputation, Coleman remains an under-appreciated and misunderstood American original well into the mid-1990s. He has alchemized from *enfant terrible* to guru without the commercial success desired by the big record companies though he has a loyal following.

- **"Comes a Time"** (Garcia/Hunter)
  Grateful Dead, *Hundred Year Hall*/'72 (1995)
  Jerry Garcia, *Reflections* (1976)

Literal and metaphorical vision is a common subtheme in Grateful Dead music and the blind are sometimes summoned to point the way to truth. In "Wharf Rat," a blind derelict is the carrier of revelation, and in "Comes a Time," a similarly impaired soul provides the solace to the footloose narrator.

A Garcia-sung ballad, "Comes a Time" was performed in both the first and second sets of Dead shows. Over time, however, it was used almost exclusively as an early second-set decelerator.

  4/11/72, City Hall, Newcastle upon Tyne, England
  6/12/76, Boston Music Hall, Boston
  7/13/85, County Fairgrounds, Ventura, California
  12/27/90, Coliseum Arena, Oakland, California

- ***Common Chord*** / DAVID GRISMAN **and Daniel Kobialka**
  Cymekob CYK803, 1993. Produced by David Grisman.

Jerry Garcia appears on "Ashokan Farewell," the first track of this unusual album featuring an ensemble of the finest classical, bluegrass, rock, and jazz players paying homage to the traditional music of America. A special highlight of the release is the appearance of Garcia's eldest daughter, Heather Garcia Katz, playing violin on the track with her dad.

- ***Compliments of Garcia*** / Jerry Garcia
  Round RX 102, 1974 (CD reissue GDCD 4009). Produced by JOHN KAHN.

(© Grateful Dead Merchandising, Inc.)

"Let It Rock," "When the Hunter Gets Captured by the Game," "That's What Love Will Make You Do," "Russian Lullaby," "Turn Out the Bright Lights," "He Ain't Give You None," "What Goes Around," "Let's Spend the Night Together"

Jerry Garcia–guitar, vocals. John Kahn–bass, arrangements. Arthur Adams–guitar. Michael O'Martin–piano, tack piano. Ron Tutt–drums. Bobbye Hall–congas, shakers, bells, wood block. Larry Carlton–guitar. MERL SAUNDERS–organ. Gene Connors–horn arrangements, trombone. Melvin Moore–trumpet. Jackie Kelso–baritone. Joel Tepp–clarinet. Richard Greene–violin. Amos Garrett–trombone. Clydie King, Merry Clayton, Patty–vocals. Geoff Muldaur–clarinet. Ben Benay–rhythm guitar. Sid Sharp–contractor. John Rotella–E-flat clarinet. Willie Green–B-flat clarinet. Julian Speer–bass clarinet. Ray Siegal–stand-up bass. Arnie Egilsson–bass. Terry Adams–cello. Nathan Rubin–violin. Sid Page–violin. Emily Van Valkenburgh–violin. Carl Pedersen–violin. Nancy Ellis–viola. Miriam Dye–viola. Judiyaba–cello.

Unlike Garcia's first solo album, *Compliments of Garcia* was not an extension of his Grateful Dead persona. Rather, this busman's holiday of a record was more an extension of the aesthetic he was forging with Merl

Saunders by bringing in horns and reeds to perform a series of wide-ranging covers including everything from the Rolling Stones' "Let's Spend the Night Together" to Irving Berlin's "Russian Lullaby."

Garcia returned to the studio to commence work on his second solo album in early 1974. Once again expanding his musical horizons, Garcia asked his friend and bassist John Kahn to produce the disc and help choose a collection of appropriate cover tunes. Kahn told Blair Jackson and Regan McMahon of *Golden Road* in 1987, "I would present him with a bunch of ideas, and he'd take the ones he liked and worked on those. It was mainly stuff that he wouldn't have ordinarily thought of, and I think that was part of the challenge for him—to try something that was really new to him."

Running through some thirty songs during the session, Kahn was impressed by Garcia's attitude: "I admired Jerry for being game for that stuff. A lot of performers wouldn't do something like that—stuff they're not familiar with—risking possible embarrassment of making mistakes."

No doubt Garcia was taking a chance with *Compliments*. Performing this type of music in a small club to an open-minded audience was one thing. Doing it on a record with large sums of money on the line was another matter entirely, and to assist in the execution of the project, Garcia brought in several studio musicians. While some critics suggested the album was indicative of a sophomore slump by not hitting the artistic paydirt of his debut solo album, *Compliments* was a moderate seller, reaching No. 49 in *Billboard*.

The final product was actually titled *Garcia*, just like his first solo effort. But it became known as *Compliments of Garcia* because of the promotional sticker that said "Compliments of" on the cover. When the Dead reissued the album in 1990, it was officially retitled *Compliments of Garcia*.

Much of this music stood the test of time with the various and sundry incarnations of the Garcia Band. "That's What Love Will Make You Do" became a juicy LEGION OF MARY nugget almost immediately, and Garcia worked some incredible magic into "Let's Spend the Night Together" with his last band playing guitar filigrees that rank as some of his finest solo work.

- ## "Confusion's Prince" (Garcia or Lesh)
  THE WARLOCKS, *EMERGENCY CREW* demo (1965)

Another dated-as-it-was-being-waxed WARLOCKS dud, "Confusion's Prince" describes a typical Haight-Ashbury trickster. Also known as "Mindbender," the song was a part of the Warlocks' thinly documented repertoire. In addition to their demo tape, there are only two known live versions.

1/7/66, The Matrix, San Francisco

- ## Tom Constanten
  Born March 19, 1944, Long Branch, New Jersey

During and since his short regular stint behind the keyboards for the Grateful Dead, Tom Constanten (better known as "T.C." to his friends and admirers) has been arguably the Dead's least understood member. Despite his contributions to *Anthem of the Sun* and *Live/Dead*, T.C. remains a bit of an anomaly in the Dead's legacy—an oval peg trying to fit into a round hole. But he lent a uniquely creative edge to the Dead's adventurous, ambitious material that helped guide the band away from its bluesy roots and toward another realm.

Born on the East Coast, Constanten spent most of his formative years in Las Vegas, where his stepfather was employed as a captain of waiters at the Sands Hotel in the early 1950s as the city was just beginning to spawn in all its inglorious neon glitz from the high chaparral desert. As T.C. was fond of punning (boy, is he ever!), "It's a nice place to live but I wouldn't want to visit there."

As a youngster, Constanten was a brilliant student and something of a musical prodigy—he began matriculating at the University of Nevada while still a high school student, composing orchestral pieces before he was twenty. Since he's someone who later helped steer the Dead toward their first dabblings in space music, it should come as little surprise that T.C. enrolled at the University of California at Berkeley in 1961 to major in astrophysics and not music. But after a semester of that and the continued company of a new friend, one Phil Lesh, he realized that his musical propensities were far more interesting, if not in accordance with his parents' desires.

Sharing a love for the emerging giants of the classical avant-garde (Karlheinz Stockhausen, Pierre Boulez, John Cage, and their future mentor, LUCIANO BERIO), Constanten and Lesh immersed themselves in studying this music to invoke the creative muses while composing their own pieces. Additionally, the Beat Generation continued to hold a strong grip over San Francisco and the two were habitués of City Lights Bookstore, where they devoured the latest Allen Ginsberg book, as they adhered to the bohemian lifestyle of the region and era.

Their initial experiences with Berio were as his students in 1962 and 1963 at Mills College in Oakland, which led Constanten to a two year apprenticeship with his guru in Darmstadt, West Germany and opportunities to pursue advanced studies with Stockhausen and Henri Pousseur in several European locales. Recalling the experience in 1993, T.C. told *Guitar Player*, "I was very much influenced by the people teaching there. But I was already wading out of the serial ocean. I had gotten to the point where I realized that, in terms of this listener's perception, the tone series is not where the piece is happening. It might be a convenient construct to enable you to throw some notes together but it's not what it is about the piece that communicates. Serialism was like a boat we had taken in crossing a lake. It was now hitting ground, and I was thinking, 'Hey time to get off.'"

Upon his return to the States in 1964, T.C. became interested in the possibilities of pop upon hearing the Beatles and Dylan. But just as Lesh was being drawn into the Warlocks, the first electrified version of the Grateful Dead, Constanten took a sharp turn by enlisting in the Air Force after receiving his draft notice. He later quipped to Blair Jackson in 1987 that "it seemed like a natural thing that I'd rather program a computer in Las Vegas than an M-16 in Vietnam."

During that Air Force stint, T.C. gained access to an IBM 1401 computer, which he used to compose several post-serialist works. He also wrote several orchestral works, which were performed by the Pops Orchestra in his hometown.

Living at home and working at the local base, Constanten managed quickly to make Squadron Member of the Month three times, receive a nomination from his base commander for Airman of the Year, and seriously experiment with psychedelics in the spectacular Vegas environs. Occasional trips to San Francisco kept his relationship with Lesh and the Dead fresh and by 1967 (still a good year away from his eventual Air Force release) he had collaborated with them on *Anthem of the Sun*, creating the prepared piano and tape music collage on "That's It for the Other One." On subsequent albums he added dimension to the band's equally experimental efforts, particularly on "St. Stephen" from *Live/Dead*, where his gently sustaining organ is a tightrope on which Jerry Garcia's quavering lead guitar work and vocals teeter.

On November 23, 1968, a day after his discharge

Tom Constanten, 1983.
(© Ed Perlstein)

from the Air Force, Constanten joined the Dead in Athens, Ohio, for his first concert and thus inaugurating what was arguably the Dead's most musically volatile phase. "Dark Star" was displayed at practically every concert and the sensible segue was perfected to an art. But a seven-piece band that included two drummers and two keyboardists created its own problems; the Dead were still grappling with the best way to present the keyboards in what was primarily a guitar band. T.C.'s solution was to wedge his organ runs between Garcia's melodic leads and Weir's skittish, off-beat rhythm work.

As captured on vinyl, Constanten's best work with the Dead can be found on *Aoxomoxoa*, recorded from the fall of 1968 through the spring of 1969. He expertly colored "Mountains of the Moon" with a haunting harpsichord line, added a period-piece calliope-like, hurdy-gurdy organ style to "Dupree's Diamond Blues," and injected "China Cat Sunflower" with some signature riffs.

Certainly, it was in the Dead's uncharted musical voyages where Constanten, with his background in the wild blue yonder, was at his best providing a distant quality to some of his playing, as airborne as one of Sun Ra's interstellar musical satellites weaving intricate patterns amid the freeform whirlpool of amorphous, sometimes dissonant sound. As he told Jackson: "I wanted to be able to say something and stay out of their way. You can have all kinds of musical activity side by side as long as it's in certain prescribed areas of the audible spectrum. Mahler was an expert at that—he'd have six, seven, eight things going on that you could hear clearly."

Though his role has been obscured over the years, Constanten is probably the individual responsible for shaping the band's sound for the balance of the 1960s, helping Lesh to push the band to the edges of experimental and improvisational chaos.

But as edge-pushing as the Dead's music was in 1969, the band began to implode, with T.C. drifting from the flock as he pursued musical projects in his spare time that were radically different from what the Dead were playing. It was also exacerbated by his increasing involvement in the Church of Scientology, which demanded abstinence from any drug use, making him a non-participant in the chemical sacraments of the time. Never able to totally overcome what even Lesh aptly described as "a certain stiffness" in his playing, T.C. left the band in 1970 by mutual decision during the infamous January 1970 New Orleans gigs when the Dead's drug bust "down on Bourbon Street" occurred.

For his part, T.C. pointed out in the 1993 *Guitar Player* profile, "The Grateful Dead, as freaky and far-out as they got, were Jerry Garcia's backup band to a large extent, and they still are. So there wasn't any room. The rainforest was already filled up. I was a seedling and I couldn't see any sunlight. On top of that, there was the amplification problem. There was always a problem in balancing the keyboard volume. You get Jerry Garcia with four [Fender] Twin Reverbs turned up to 10; his *mezzo-piano* was louder than my *forte*. My major frustration was not being able to find enough turf to even set up a tent in the sonic texture, and scarcely having time when there was a break to make something happen. I'd get to solo sometimes when Jerry would break a string, but even then he'd go back and string his guitar as fast as he could."

His decision to leave was partially influenced by an invitation to direct and write for *Tarot*, a famously delightful play blending myth and mysticism, rock and other music forms, which eventually enjoyed a successful 1971 off-Broadway reception in New York City around the same time he joined the Dead as a guest for their last Fillmore East run in April.

While his departure from the Dead may have deprived him of the type of notoriety he never seemed comfortable with anyway (if not the paychecks, which may have made it seem worthwhile), his lone wolf status did allow him to become an artist more on his own terms. For more than a quarter century after leaving the Dead, he supported himself by teaching piano in the Bay Area while keeping one foot in musical esoterica (composing and performing in a variety of obtuse and rarefied sets and settings) and the other foot firmly in the Grateful Dead omniverse playing keyboard with Henry Kaiser, Dead Ringers, Zero, and MERL SAUNDERS's Rainforest Band.

Between tours he devoted himself to a variety of home releases and small label recordings that merge his interpretations of the Dead and classical and traditional American music with his own complementary strain of original compositions. *Fresh Tracks in Real Time, Out-Sides,* and *Nightfall of Diamonds* include splendid examples of his continued dedication to composing and his self-styled "autobiodyssey," *Between Rock & Hard Places* (Hulogos'i, 1992) is a witty memoir chronicling his life within and without the Grateful Dead. As an "urban folk pianist," Constanten provided rambly, new-agey piano segues on *West Coast Weekend,* San

(Courtesy of Mauroy Records)

Francisco's answer to Garrison Keillor's *Prairie Home Companion* during the late 1980s and early 1990s.

Tom Constanten Live in Concert at the Piano

Mauroy Records CD2002, 1996. Recorded December 6, 1992 at the Old Fort Church in San Francisco.
"Duets from the Clavierubüing" (J. S. Bach), "Two Sonatas" (Cimarosa), "Sonata #30 in E, Opus 109" (Beethoven), "Four Klavierstücke" (Schumann, Brahms), "Two Preludes" (Claude Debussy), "Three Waltzes from the Waltz Project" (Harrison, Constanten, Glass).

More than programmatic allusion or pianistic innovation, Tom Constanten's entry into his musical vision quest signals a new direction in depiction of musical styles, whether of other continents or centuries.

Conversations with the Dead: The Grateful Dead Interview Book/David Gans

352 pages. Two eight-page glossy black and white photo inserts. Citadel Underground/Carol Publishing Group, 1991.

A Grateful Dead Midrash, David Gans's collection of interviews with the usual (and unusual) suspects comprises one of the most artistically insightful volumes ever put together about the band.

Cooking with the Dead (book)/Ellen Zipern

St. Martin's Press, 1995.

If being a Deadhead is a way of life, some would suggest that then, by logic, it must be a way of eating. The author of this one-of-a-kind cookbook is a Deadhead with a journalism degree who spent a year going to Dead shows around the country and getting to know the people who sell snacks of, by, and for Deadheads in the concert parking lots. Every recipe comes with a profile of the food seller, so the book is a sociological document as well as a cookbook.

"Cookbook" may not be quite the word. Since Deadheads gravitate to far-edge health-food theories, there's a lot of "fireless cuisine" here, such as the Wheel-of-creation-spiral-vegan-organic-no-electricity pizzas made from raw, sprouted wheat berries by someone known as Harvest Earth Heart. The recipes—mostly vegetarian snacks, often with mystical or health claims—will appeal strongly to some people and utterly repel others (the latter are also unlikely to sympathize with the complaints about how hard it is to get truly organic ginseng).

If you're looking this book over, bear in mind that Deadheads evidently use the word "fat" (or even "fatty") as a term of approval, not of nutritional content.

A final note: the book's cover features a smart takeoff of the Dead's premiere album.

"Corinna" (Weir/Hart/Hunter)

Weir introduced this funky percussive bewitchment in 1992. Like many of Weir's tunes it is sung from the perspective of the eternal outsider—a lovestruck hero whose goal of romantic union seems forever unrequited. Historically, it bears some thematic resemblance to "Corinna Corinna," the country-blues standard covered by many. The Dead's "Corinna" has a languid beat that suited it well for both singular first-set displays and as a second-set segue device.

1/25/93, Oakland Coliseum, Oakland, California

"Cosmic Charlie" (Hunter/Garcia/Lesh)

Grateful Dead, single, *Aoxomoxoa* (1969), *What a Long Strange Trip It's Been* (1977)

"Cosmic Charlie," a *Zap Comix*–like description of a typical Haight-Ashbury seeker, is a Deadhead favorite although it was not performed after 1976. Its strange melody and odd chord changes predisposed it to difficult concert execution. Outside of its semi-regular outings in the late 1960s and early 1970s, the Dead dusted it off and briefly reintroduced "Cosmic Charlie" in 1976 for a half-dozen outings.

Discussing the song's difficulty with David Gans and Blair Jackson in 1981, Garcia observed that "There's technically too much happening in a song like 'Cosmic Charlie' for us to be able to come up with a version of it that's comfortable to sing *and* play on stage. I never would have thought about that when I started writing songs; I didn't really realize you had to think about that stuff.

" 'Cosmic Charlie' is a recording song. Its weaknesses are part of what's musically clever about it but also part of what's cumbersome about performing it. The last time we worked it out was in 1976, and it was effective—sort of. We had a hell of a time getting through it, and the fact that it didn't stick as a piece of material tells me it's flawed. It's not quite *performable*."

Similarly, Garcia told Mary Eisenhart in 1987, "I've always liked 'Cosmic Charlie,' but it's just really a little too difficult. If I could figure out a way to either just sing or just play—but playing it and singing it is a bitch."

Regarding the lyrics, Hunter told Jeff Tamarkin of *Relix* in 1986, "That was done during a burst of songwriting when we were actually sitting down together saying, 'Okay, let's write some songs.' It's very psychedelic."

3/1/69, Fillmore West, San Francisco

5/2/70, Harpur College, Binghamton, New York

▪ Elizabeth "Libba" Cotten
Born January 1895, Chapel Hill, North Carolina; died June 29, 1987, Syracuse, New York

Although she probably never would have dreamed of calling herself an artist, Elizabeth Cotten was a creator of the highest order. Her soft, homespun music possessed an uncommon warmth and intimacy and drew on a range of regional American traditions: the country-blues, gospel, ragtime, and oldtime Appalachian mountain music.

Cotten played music her entire life, mostly for the entertainment of her family, and didn't begin recording or performing publicly until she was in her sixties. She did make up for lost time, however, by giving concerts into her nineties! Conversely, one of her most beloved songs, "Freight Train" was written when she was twelve years old and became a standard chestnut in the American folk-song canon. "Freight Train" was also one of the hits during the British "Skiffle" music craze, which engendered the Beatles.

Cotten was born and raised in North Carolina and taught herself how to play guitar. But, for undetermined reasons, she played it upside down and left-handed (something Jimi Hendrix was sometimes known to do), developing a unique two-finger picking style that influenced the folk revival of the 1950s.

Married at age fifteen, Cotten moved to Washington, D.C., after a divorce. While working at a local department store, she had a chance encounter that eventually led to her big break. One day during the Christmas season, she found a lost girl who had strayed from her mother while shopping. It turned out to be Peggy Seeger of the famous folk-singing family, which included her father, ethnomusicologist Charles Seeger, her mother, Ruth, and her brothers, Pete and Mike. One thing led to another and she was invited to work for the Seegers as a domestic.

Over time, Mike Seeger persuaded her to record for Folkways Records. *Folksongs and Instrumentals with Guitar* was the immaculate result and its acclaim enabled Cotten to perform at folk and blues festivals, including the prestigious Newport Folk Festival in 1964 and the Smithsonian Festival of Folklife from 1968 to 1971. In 1972 she was awarded National Folk Association's Burl Ives Award for her contribution to American folk music. She continued to record and perform through the 1970s and right up until a few months before her death in 1987, winning a Grammy in 1985 for her last album, *Elizabeth Cotten Live!*

The Grateful Dead performed one of Cotten's minor masterpieces, "Oh Babe, It Ain't No Lie." In addition, Garcia recorded "Freight Train" with DAVID GRISMAN on their 1993 album *Not for Kids Only*. Finally, Cotten's "Shake Sugaree" is often pointed to by Dead scholars as a partial inspiration for the Garcia/Hunter lament, "Sugaree." An oft-told tale of Garcia's generosity is that he suggested the Dead perform, record and release "Oh Babe, It Ain't No Lie" specifically to send a little royalty scratch Cotten's way, funds with which she immediately bought a new refrigerator.

▪ "Cowboy Song"

Virtually nothing is known about this probably mistitled song performed by Weir at one 1970 concert.

4/9/70, Fillmore West, San Francisco

"Crazy Fingers" (Garcia/Hunter)
Grateful Dead, *Blues For Allah* (1975), *One from the Vault*/'75 (1991)

A lilting Robert Hunter haiku with a spider-web reggae groove, "Crazy Fingers" was slow to catch on as a Grateful Dead concert regular. It wasn't until 1982 that the song was seriously incorporated by the band. "Crazy Fingers" is sometimes said to allegorically describe the fluidity of Garcia's intuitive digits as they glide across his guitar's fretboard. But the song's soft, meditative qualities paint a much broader portrait. Lush and vivid, the naturalistic landscapes it displays represent a near-perfect example of the marriage of words and music in a Grateful Dead song. This tranquillity is almost painterly, evoking Monet's series of water lily paintings or a Hokusai print.

In *A Box of Rain*, his book of collected lyrics, Hunter wrote: " 'Crazy Fingers' is a collection of haiku-style verses, mostly seventeen syllables, some more successful than others, with no connecting link other than similarity of mood."

Discussing with Blair Jackson in 1991 the evolution of the material on *Blues for Allah*, Garcia pointed out that "What became 'Crazy Fingers' originally had a hard rock & roll feel; it was completely different."

But, unlike most of the *Blues for Allah* material that was developed in the studio on the fly, "Crazy Fingers" was written beforehand as a page or two of haikus in Hunter's notebook that caught Garcia's eye and fancy.

6/3/76, Paramount Theater, Portland, Oregon
10/10/82, Frost Theater, Palo Alto, California
5/26/93, Cal Expo Amphitheater, Sacramento, California

"Cream Puff War" (Garcia)
Grateful Dead, *The Grateful Dead* (1967)

"Cream Puff War" rounded out the first side of the Dead's debut album and was presumably included in many of their early concerts, although only five taped versions have survived. A couple of those versions, however, demonstrate the Dead's ability, even very early in their career, to get the most out of a song. All the Dead's renditions of the song capture the exuberance (and goofiness) of the San Francisco sound.

Thematically, "Cream Puff War" describes a devious, mind-game playing acquaintance who gets his comeuppance. A put-down song in the tradition of Bob Dylan's mid-sixties best.

The song was revived by the Valentines, a Weir/Welnick pickup band that featured guitar virtuoso HENRY KAISER, at a 1995 Valentine's Day gig at San Francisco's revamped Fillmore. When Welnick suggested to Garcia that the Dead revive the morsel, Garcia agreed but said, "Only if *you* sing it!"

A final piece of trivia: "Cream Puff War" is, along with "Cryptical Envelopment," one of only two songs in the entire Grateful Dead catalogue credited solely to Jerry Garcia.

11/19/66, Fillmore Auditorium, San Francisco

Cross Between/Lamb
Warner Bros. WB 1920, 1971.

Although a note on the back cover of this album, which reads "Special thanks to Jerry Garcia," has been interpreted as an acknowledgment that Garcia contributed to this long lost (and some say thankfully forgotten) California disc, there is no evidence of any further collaboration.

Arthur "Big Boy" Crudup
Born August 24, 1905, Forest, Mississippi; died March 28, 1974, Nassawadox, Virginia; a.k.a. Elmore Jones, Elmer James, Percy Crudup

"THAT'S ALL RIGHT, MAMA" was the first song ever recorded by Elvis Presley at Sun Studios and, for that reason alone, its songwriter, Arthur "Big Boy" Crudup, was known as the "Father of Rock & Roll." The song, released on the Sun label in 1954, launched the King's career and explicitly linked the blues with primordial rock & roll.

But Crudup was more than a one-hit wonder. He wrote many classic blues songs like "Rock Me Mama," "Mean Ol' Frisco," and "My Baby Left Me," which were covered by the likes of B. B. King, Big Mama Thornton, and Bobby "Blue" Bland and remain part of the standard blues repertory. "That's All Right Mama" and "LOOK OVER YONDER'S WALL," a lesser-known Crudup performance, were briefly covered by the Grateful Dead.

Long before "That's All Right Mama" caught on with teenage whites, Crudup's energetic performances were popular among blacks, despite his technical lackings.

Still, the rhythmic power found in his ensembles prefigured the modernization of country blues and clearly influenced rockabilly.

Crudup began singing in gospel groups and church choirs in rural Mississippi and began playing the blues only after going to Chicago in 1939. Busking on street corners for spare change, Crudup was discovered and signed to the Bluebird label by Lester Melrose, a producer and talent scout regarded as the primary architect of the pre–World War II Chicago blues sound. But this relationship ended in 1947 when Crudup, a notoriously mediocre businessman, discovered Melrose was withholding royalties for his hit songs.

The experience soured Crudup on city life and he returned to Mississippi where he became a successful bootlegger while continuing to record with RCA through the early 1950s. Although he had toured frequently with Sonny Boy Williamson and Elmore James, Crudup quit the music business altogether by the mid-1950s.

He was rediscovered and coaxed out of retirement in the mid-1960s by Dick Waterman, a blues connoisseur, who had helped Crudup secure money owed him. Recommencing a recording career, Crudup was eventually the subject of a 1973 documentary based on his life, *Arthur Crudup: Born in the Blues*.

Whatever acclaim or fortune Crudup may have received late in his life was too little and too late, as he died near poverty.

• "Cryptical Envelopment (He Had to Die)" (Garcia)

Grateful Dead, *Anthem of the Sun* (1968), *Two from the Vault*/'68 (1992), *Dick's Picks Volume Four*/'70 (1996)

Garcia composed and performed this ambitious suite as an ode to NEAL CASSADY, a colleague and Beat Generation progenitor. Though they eventually dropped the prelude and coda to the work, it was an effective and still interesting achievement. Garcia briefly reintroduced "Cryptical" at a few 1985 concerts.

A sense of dark premonition and inevitable doom pervades the piece—it portrays Cassady's death taking on a meaning far greater than he or any of the participants in the Beat or hippie movements could have possibly realized.

The centerpiece of the composition is "The Other

One," a hard-driving modality with a hard-bop influence that the Dead performed almost more often than any other song in their repertoire.

Of the suite's opening lines, for which he is credited as author ["The other day they waited / The sky was dark and faded"], Garcia told Blair Jackson in 1991; "Seriously, I think that's an extension of my own personal symbology for 'The Man of Constant Sorrow'—the old folk song—which I always thought of as being a sort of a Christ parable. Something fuzzy like that. Fuzzy Christianity."

5/2/70, Harpur College, SUNY, Binghamton, New York
See also **"The Other One"**

• "Cumberland Blues" (Garcia/Hunter/Lesh)

Grateful Dead, *Workingman's Dead* (1970), *Europe '72* (1972), *What a Long Strange Trip It's Been* (1977)
Catch Valley Drifters, *Step Up to Big Pay* (1986)
Dead Ringers, *DEAD RINGERS* (1993)

The Dead's ode to blue-collarism, "Cumberland Blues" is an upbeat, uptempo nod to the rigors and sacrifices of basic, dignified survival. Inspired by the music of Appalachia, "Cumberland Blues" depicts the hard-driven characters whose toils in the dark dungeons of the region's mines have long been celebrated in white Southern musical traditions, most notably by Merle Travis.

Garcia's banjo-playing background is apparent in his guitar stylings through the many versions of this bluegrass rocker that captures that mercurial "high lonesome" sound so associated with that oeuvre.

Discussing the crossover between his banjo and guitar stylings, Garcia told Fred Stuckey of *Guitar Player* magazine in 1971, "My style has been characterized as picking every note, and that's a holdover from banjo—and also because I'm one of those guys who likes to hear every note. It's so easy to gloss over everything, but my reaction to that was that my phrasing got kind of stiff. When I listen to old tapes of myself, it's stiff . . . I used to be a pretty snappy banjo player. I think I worked harder at the banjo than I did at any other instrument. I got into the banjo just shortly after I got out of the Army, and I really, really worked at it. . . . There is no relationship between the two except for the fact that they are fretted instruments. My banjo chops are nothing like they once were. The banjo is the kind of thing where you've got to keep it up or else you lose your time. If I were to spend three or four weeks, I could get my banjo shit together; but there would have to be a reason for it. The reason I stopped playing banjo was because there wasn't anybody to play with and I've always been oriented along the lines of playing with somebody rather than playing by myself."

In *A Box of Rain*, Hunter wrote, "The best compliment I ever had on a lyric was from an old guy who'd worked at the Cumberland mine. He said: 'I wonder what the guy who wrote this song would've thought if he'd ever known something like the Grateful Dead was gonna do it.' "

5/15/70, Fillmore East, New York
4/14/72, Tivoli Concert Hall, Copenhagen, Denmark
6/30/74, Civic Center Area, Springfield, Massachusetts
7/15/84, Greek Theatre, Berkeley, California
5/1/88, Frost Theatre, Palo Alto, California
9/13/91, Madison Square Garden, New York
10/5/94, The Spectrum, Philadelphia

D

- ***Däfos***/Mickey Hart, Airto, FLORA PURIM

  Rykodisc 10108, 1989. Produced by Mickey Hart and
  AIRTO MOREIRA. Recorded live at San Francisco's
  Kabuki Theater in 1982 and 1983.

  "Dry Sands of the Desert," "Ice of the North," "Reunion
  I," "Reunion II," "Reunion III," "Saudacao Popular,"
  "Psychopomp," "Subterranean Caves of Kronos,"
  "The Gates of Dafos," "Passage."

  Mickey Hart–tar, saron, percussion, vocals, background
  vocals, berimbaus, beam, rain stick, tubular bells,
  the Beast. Shabda Kham–tar. Daniel Kennedy–tar.
  Mica Katz–tar. Khadija Mastah–tar. Ray Patch–tar.
  Habib Bishop–tar. Brian Crittenden–tar. Steve
  Douglas–woodwinds. Jody Diamond–saron. Flora
  Purim–percussion, vocals. Bobby Vega–electric
  bass. Airto Moreira–percussion, vocals. Marcos
  Antonio Dias–vocals. Batucaje–percussion, vocals,
  background vocals. Jose Lorenzo–percussion,
  vocals.

(Courtesy of Rykodisc)

With its thrilling, nearly overpowering sonics, this percussion-based voyage to a mythical country is an established audiophile classic, an extension of the approach used on the *Apocalypse Now* sessions. Mickey Hart and company engage in improvisations using different musicians interacting with varied groupings of percussion instruments. For instance, "Dry Sands of the Desert" features the sonorous saxophone of Steve Douglas in a sensual sea of eight tars, Egyptian drums resembling tambourines that make a warm and deeply resonant tone when tapped with fingertips or the heel of the hand.

When pressed by Blair Jackson in 1983 for the meaning of the word *däfos*, Hart told him, "It isn't really anything. It's a place that Airto and I conjured in our minds."

- ## Dance to the Beat of My Drum
  *See **Drums of Passion: The Beat***

• "Dancing in the Street" (Stevenson/Gaye/Hunter)

Martha and the Vandellas, single (1964), *Dance Party* (1965), *Greatest Hits* (1966), *Martha and the Vandellas Live!* (1967), *Flip Hits* (1983), *Greatest Command Performances* (1987)

Grateful Dead, *Vintage Dead* (1970), single, *Terrapin Station* (1977), *Dick's Picks Volume Three/'77* (1995), *Dick's Picks Volume Four/'70* (1996)

KINGFISH, *LIVE '85* (1986)

The Mamas and the Papas, *The Mamas and the Papas* (1967), *Farewell to the First Golden Era* (1967), *Creaque Alley* (1991)

Little Richard, *King of Rock 'n Roll* (1971)

Black Oak Arkansas, *Street Party* (1974)

Royals, *Spring '76* (1976)

John Hiatt, *Slug Line* (1979)

Fred Frith, *Gravity* (1980)

Van Halen, *Diver Down* (1982)

Mick Jagger and David Bowie, single (1985)

A No. 2 hit for Martha and the Vandellas in the summer of 1964, "Dancing in the Streets" is one of the most beloved Motown anthems from an era that passed all too quickly.

Born July 18, 1941, in Detroit, Michigan, Martha Reeves was the ultimate Motown product. She began working at the famed record company as a secretary but occasionally doubled as demo singer. When she was called upon to do some background vocals for Marvin Gaye, she parlayed her talents into a recording deal. As her star rose, the inevitable comparisons were made with the Supremes. But Reeves's incomparably earthier style was evidenced on "Heat Wave" and especially "Dancing in the Streets."

Of the famed "girl groups" from those golden days, Martha Reeves and the Vandellas were regarded as the most outspoken. When the 1967 African-American uprising turned violent in Detroit, the group was singing the song onstage in their hometown when word came from offstage of the riot's escalation. Naturally, they were forced to halt the show and tell everyone to go home and be with their families. The following weeks weren't much better for the Vandellas. It seemed that no matter where they went, civil unrest followed. When they finally began touring in Great Britain late in the summer, they were asked by an interviewer if "Dancing in the Street" was a call to revolution to which Reeves answered: "My Lord, it was a *party* song."

Indeed, the Motown brass knew they had captured lightning in a bottle with the Vandellas' perfect party music and it was a vein they mined successfully for several years to come. But as the 1960s closed shop, the group found the charts increasingly difficult to crack, and by the mid-1970s Martha's career had fizzled. Although she was largely confined to reprising her old hits, her magic transcends mere nostalgia when she hits the oldies circuit from time to time.

"Dancin'" was an intermittent but incredibly static inclusion at Dead shows, beginning in 1966, and showed hints of many musical styles in its volatile live presentations including traditions as varied as the Indian raga and late 1970s American disco.

The Dead's early versions of "Dancin'" stay pretty close to the original Vandellas arrangement. But within a couple of years they were stretching it out into mammoth snake-dance jams. After putting the song to rest for about five years, they resurrected it as a disco-style sendup and although this infuriated some Deadheads who thought the band was selling out to market pressures, this arrangement always kicked into high-octane performance overdrive. By the mid-1980s it had returned to its more traditional likeness and remained as an occasional cover through 1987.

7/3/66, Fillmore Auditorium, San Francisco

3/18/67, Winterland Arena, San Francisco

2/14/70, Fillmore East, New York (*Dick's Picks Volume Four*).

5/6/70, Kresge Plaza, MIT, Cambridge, Massachusetts

6/19/76, Capitol Theater, Passaic, New Jersey

4/22/77, The Spectrum, Philadelphia

5/11/86, Frost Amphitheater, Palo Alto, California

12/27/86, Henry J. Kaiser Convention Center, Oakland, California

• "Dark Hollow" (Traditional/Bill Browning)

Singles: Luke Jordan (1959), Jimmy Skinner (1959)

Grateful Dead, *History of the Grateful Dead Vol. 1 (Bear's Choice)* (1973), *Reckoning* (1981)

DAVID GRISMAN, *Early Dawg* (1966)

Muleskinner, *Muleskinner* (1973), *Live: Original Television Soundtrack* (1973), *A Potpourri of Bluegrass Jam* (1974)

The Seldom Scene, *Live at the Cellar Door* (1975)

David Bromberg, *Midnight on the Water* (1975)
Fred Travers, *Time After Time* (1992)

Country boy leaves girl behind to seek fame and fortune but finds only despair and loneliness is the theme of this Weir-sung plaint performed during the Dead's 1970 and 1980 acoustic sets. Also performed electric at two 1971 shows, "Dark Hollow" is one of the Dead's best tear-jerkers. A three-handkerchief song.

7/14/70, Euphoria Ballroom, San Rafael, California
11/8/70, Capitol Theater, Port Chester, New York
9/29/80, Warfield Theater, San Francisco

- **"Dark Star"** (Grateful Dead/Hunter)
  Grateful Dead, single (1968), *Live Dead* (1969), *What a Long Strange Trip It's Been* (1977), *Two from the Vault*/'68 (1992), *Dick's Picks Volume Two*/'71 (1995), *Dick's Picks Volume Four*/'70 (1996), *Dick's Picks Volume Seven*/'74 (1997)
  Tom Constanten, *Fresh Tracks in Real Time* (1989), *Nightfall of Diamonds* (1992)
  HENRY KAISER, *Those Who Know History Are Doomed to Repeat It* (1988), *Heart's Desire* (1990), ETERNITY BLUE (1995)
  Dead Ringers, DEAD RINGERS (1993)
  John Oswald and Grateful Dead, *Grayfolded* (1995)
  Solar Circus, *A Historical Retrospective* (1995)
  DAVID MURRAY, DARK STAR (THE MUSIC OF THE GRATEFUL DEAD) (1996)

"Dark Star" is the holy grail of Grateful Dead music. More than any single composition in their vast repertoire, "Dark Star" represents all that is "Grateful Dead" for nearly every Deadhead. And if it doesn't, it should.

Musically, the song is a modal endeavor, constructed along the lines of John Coltrane's more adventurous work, Miles Davis's "SO WHAT," or the open-ended ragas for which the music of India is most renowned. In performance, "Dark Star" evolved tremendously from the Dead's relatively short and accelerated renditions in 1967 to its elongated and sometimes formless presentations of the early 1970s.

"Dark Star" was among the earliest verse Robert Hunter composed for the Dead. Upon Hunter's reuniting with his friends in 1967 after a hiatus in New Mexico, Phil Lesh invited the poet to join the band for a gig in Rio Nido, a resort town on the Russian River north of San Francisco. As Hunter related to Jeff Tamarkin for *Relix* in 1986, "That was the first song I wrote with the Grateful Dead. We were down in Rio Nido, and I heard them playing it in the hall they were going to play. I just started scratching paper and got the 'Dark star crashes, pouring its light into ashes' part and I said, 'Why don't you try this with it? It worked well, and then they wanted more verses. I finished up the second set of verses back in San Francisco. I got up—I was staying at 710 Ashbury—one morning fairly early, about 10:30 or 11, and stumbled over to the Pandlehandle at Golden Gate Park. I was sitting there, getting stuck on a verse, when along came a hippie who handed me a joint. He asked me what I was doing, and I said I was writing a song called 'Dark Star.' He said, 'Oh.' That's pretty much the story."

Hunter's lyrics recall a twisted and psychedelic take on T. S. Eliot's "The Love Song of J. Alfred Prufrock." For example, Eliot's lines "Let us go then, you and I, while the evening is spread out against the sky like a patient etherised upon a table" become "Shall we go, you and I while we can? Through the transitive nightfall of diamonds" in the spectral landscape of "Dark Star." The early versions of "Dark Star" contained both sets of Hunter's lyrics bookending the marathon jam. But as the work developed, the inclusion of the lyrics became almost an afterthought. Sometimes one set of lyrics was sung, sometimes none at all.

There are almost two hundred surviving performances of the Dead lighting into "Dark Star" from the late 1960s and early 1970s. As a second-set centerpiece, the aural journey reflected the changes occurring within the band. Despite its inner convolutions, "Dark Star" followed a fairly straightforward pattern: a slow, melodic instrumental introduction arrives at the chorus that rapidly and atonally breaks down into electronic chaos from which a cosmically organic jam builds to high peaks of sublime agonizing ecstasy carrying the music through to the final chorus. There isn't an uninteresting rendition of "Dark Star," each one forming a distinct life of its own and taking both band and audience to where no one had gone before.

"Dark Star" already had achieved cult status among its adherents when the Dead all but ceased performing it between 1974 and 1989. After a few surprise displays in 1979 and 1984, it triumphantly returned in the 1989 fall tour for renewed interpretation (and adulation) until Garcia's passing.

2/22/69, Dream Bowl, Vallejo, California
2/27/69, Fillmore West, San Francisco (*Live/Dead*)
3/1/69, Fillmore West, San Francisco

3/29/69, Ice Palace, Las Vegas

6/14/69, Monterey Peninsula College, Monterey, California

5/23/69, Seminole Indian Village, West Hollywood, Florida

11/7/69, Fillmore Auditorium, San Francisco

2/13/70, Fillmore East, New York (*Dick's Picks Volume Four*)

6/24/70, Capitol Theater, Port Chester, New York

2/18/71, Capitol Theater, Port Chester, New York

7/31/71, Yale Bowl, New Haven, Connecticut

4/8/72, Wembley Empire Pool, London

5/18/72, Kongressaal, Munich

8/21/72, Berkeley Community Theater, Berkeley, California

8/27/72, Old Renaissance Faire Grounds, Veneta, Oregon

11/19/72, Hofheinz Pavilion, Houston

3/24/73, The Spectrum, Philadelphia

6/10/73, RFK Stadium, Washington, D.C.

8/1/73, Roosevelt Stadium, Jersey City, New Jersey

6/23/74, Jai-Alai Fronton, Miami

1/20/79, Shea's Buffalo Theater, Buffalo, New York

7/13/84, Greek Theatre, Berkeley, California

10/16/89, Brendan Byrne Arena, East Rutherford, New Jersey

10/26/89, Miami Arena, Miami

3/29/90, Nassau Veterans' Memorial Coliseum, Uniondale, New York (with Branford Marsalis)

10/31/91, Oakland Coliseum, Oakland, California

▪ *Dark Star: An Oral Biography of Jerry Garcia* (book)/Robert Greenfield
388 pp. Morrow Books, 1996.

As an antidote to Rock Scully's engrossing but gossipy and often inaccurate memoir, Robert Greenfield presents a view of Garcia's personal life from the vantage point of many Grateful Dead family members. The result is a juicy, sad, rapturous, and sometimes horrifying detail of Garcia's amazing and often painful life, with a funny mix of slime and objectivity. Owsley, Mountain Girl, Kesey, Barlow, Hart, Weir, Tiff Garcia, Manasha Matheson, Bill Graham, and a couple of Garcia's girlfriends are just some of the witnesses giving testimony in this sobering but compelling page-turner. The book is also a bit short on photos and lacks what all the other Garcia tomes do: a reasoned, educated analysis of Garcia's musical evolution and contribution.

(Courtesy of Astor Place Recordings)

▪ *Dark Star (The Music of the Grateful Dead)*/DAVID MURRAY
Astor Place Recordings TCD-4002, 1996. Produced by Herbie Miller.
"Shakedown Street," "Samson and Delilah," "Estimated Prophet," "Dark Star," "China Doll," "One More Saturday Night," "Shoulda Had Been Me"

David Murray finds common cause and ground with the Dead's music on this album inspired by his brief association in the mid-1990s with the Dead and the death of Jerry Garcia. Joined by an all-star cast of New York's youthful as well as veteran jazzsters (including alto saxophonist, flutist, and Sun Ra alum James Spaulding), Murray introduced the Grateful Dead's songs to an unusually receptive downtown jazz scene for the first time. He chose an atypical selection of material to pay homage—from the brassy struts of "Shakedown Street," luminous glow of "China Doll," and pure exuberance of "One More Saturday Night" to the interstellar realms of "Dark Star." To each, he brings a Mingus-like Midas touch to the Dead's music. An added bonus to the collection is "Shoulda Had Been Me," a piece from the Satchel Paige project Murray worked on with Bob Weir and on which Weir appears.

- ## "Darlin' Corey" (Traditional)
The Weavers, *The Weavers at Carnegie Hall* (1956)

"Darlin' Corey," a wild mountain banjo tune long a favorite of folksingers everywhere, is only known to have received the Grateful Dead treatment during a wild jam with Jorma Kaukonen in 1970.

Like "Little Maggie," its first cousin in song, and many another feral mountain-woman songs, gun-toting "Darlin' Corey" was popular among traditional singers in the Southern mountains. Bluegrass singers were particularly fond of the hard-living damsel, and the song is considered by some to be the bluegrass national anthem.

11/20/70, The Palestra, University of Rochester, Rochester, New York (with Jorma Kaukonen)

Reverend Gary Davis. (*The New York Public Library for the Performing Arts*)

- ## Reverend Gary Davis
Born April 30, 1896, Laurens, South Carolina; died May 5, 1972, Hammonton, New Jersey

One of the great characters and teachers of the blues, the Reverend Gary Davis was a gospel-blues singer whose gravelly, salt-of-the-earth vocals and complex fingerpicking technique on the six- and twelve-string guitar gave his music an overpowering vibrancy. His impact on both the blues and blues-flavored folk musicians is apparent in the guitar styles of John Cephas, Taj Mahal, and Jorma Kaukonen. Stefan Grossman, his most loyal

student as well as an influential tutor himself, produced many of Davis's later recordings and a fine Davis songbook. Davis also powered the folk and rock styles of BOB DYLAN, Dave Van Ronk, and Ry Cooder.

Along with Blind Blake and Blind Boy Fuller, Davis was a major force in the East Coast/Piedmont blues school. His virtuosity on the guitar was astounding. Davis had complete knowledge of the instrument displayed in his breathtaking ease of chording, blazing speed, and precision.

His music was singular in its synthesis of sacred and secular traditions. Davis made gospel and the blues Siamese twins using a performance and recording style that cherished emotional honesty and homespun folk qualities. A natural street preacher, his humorous, one-of-a-kind sermons made superb, ingenious use of his declamatory singing and virtually invented a genre: Holy Blues.

Through his long and prolific recording career, Davis left the blues some of its greatest standards, which have been reinterpreted by the score but never matched. "Samson and Delilah," "Candy Man," "Cocaine Man," and dozens of others seem as etched in stone as the tablets Moses brought down from the mountain.

But solid details of Davis's early life are sketchy at best and usually contradictory. For example, despite granting a number of interviews, he was coy when it came to confirming the cause of his blindness or even when it became complete. Accounts alternately trace the infirmity to birth, infancy, or adolescence. In addition, the age at which he taught himself the guitar, banjo, and harmonica are also debated, with some bluesologists claiming his proficiency was complete by the age of seven. Most agree that by 1910 he had joined a string band and began traveling the southeastern United States, finally settling in Durham, North Carolina, in the late 1920s, where he busked the blues on street corners. Within a couple of years Davis became interested in the gospel and was ordained as a Baptist minister in 1933. As he began to mix gospel music with the blues, he played at revival meetings and lumber camps, using both his thundering voice and guitar picking to testify.

During this period, probably in the 1920s, Davis met up with Blind Boy Fuller, another innovative guitar stylist who became his sometime pupil. In 1935 they ventured to New York City, where they recorded for the American Record Company. Though the label decided to promote Fuller, Davis eventually recorded for a variety of labels. Davis took to performing on the streets of Harlem, where he gained fame and notoriety as a unique, if generally misunderstood, blues-playing preacher.

As a teacher, Davis's reputation was massive, and many young, mostly white, folkies in search of the blues grail sought him out for pointers. While Jorma Kaukonen became perhaps his most famous pupil and Stefan Grossman his most ardent, Bob Weir made sure to seek out the charismatic bluesman when the Dead passed through New York in the early 1970s. Assessing Davis's influence, Weir told Jon Sievert of *Guitar Player* in 1981, "I never took any formal lessons from anybody except Reverend Gary Davis in 1971. I was a longtime fan of Davis's and always really liked his approach to guitar, because he played the whole instrument and only used two fingers to pick. Being blind, he didn't know what you can't do. Notes and lines just seemed to come at you from all different directions, and he seemed to have a way of tying them all together. He was just about to the end of his days when I met him and took a couple of lessons from him."

In 1993, Weir embellished on his experience with Davis in a follow-up discussion with *Guitar Player*'s Sievert. "Well, Reverend Gary Davis was my mentor. He was not just a great guitarist, he was also a great singer. I'd like to make that point. When I met him he was in his eighties, I guess. Blind as he'd ever been, but he still liked to have you park your girlfriend next to him. He liked that a lot. I'm quite sure he'll resurface as time goes on. He was so unique. People have this notion of what blues is supposed to sound like and it tends to gravitate towards Delta blues. You know, early blues is supposed to be Delta blues. And, of course, he played guitar like a stride piano mostly. Maybe his sound is a little too jolly for most people's confined or limited notion of what early blues is supposed to sound like.

"He also had a much more open notion of development. He wasn't as tightly structured by the blues as those other guys. If you accept style—and the blues is a style—as a set of limitations then those guys were confined in some ways."

In the same discussion with Sievert, Garcia appraised the Gary Davis legacy: "He always was kind of overlooked, but technically speaking he's definitely the best of them. And of course, what he plays isn't strictly blues either. It's not really the blues at all. It's really ragtime music. Gary Davis always reminded me of Ray Charles, you know what I mean. That similar voice, that kind of

gospel-style full chording. And his songs are structured similarly to those gospel long-form songs. . . .

"Gary Davis used to play things pretty much the same way he did on the record except there'd always be an unexpected point in there that wasn't on the record. There'd always be a new chorus or something that you hadn't heard. But I don't know whether that would be true for somebody like Robert Johnson, whose stuff sounds so incredibly worked out. It'd be interesting to know. There are a couple of outtakes—the second versions on that complete collection—that show he played them pretty much the same. At least from take to take. But that might only be true that month or that week or that year or whatever. It's hard to tell. . . .

"Gary Davis's stuff is a perfect example of that. There's a handful of early recordings of his where he does a couple of the classic tunes like 'Twelve Gates to the City,' and you can hear where they got to."

By the late 1950s, however, he had become, through his recordings and steady club appearances, a very much in-demand performer. With the folk revival in full swing, Davis became a fixture at the major folk festivals, including Newport and Mariposa in Toronto. His popularity led to an invitation to visit Great Britain with the Blues and Gospel Caravan in 1964 and a follow-up solo slate in 1965. An engaging entertainer, Reverend Davis was also the subject of at least three short films, including *Blind Gary Davis* in 1964.

It was in these twilight years that he cut his most memorable sides with the Prestige/Bluesville label, *When I Die I'll Live Again, Pure Religion!*, and *The Guitar and Banjo of Reverend Gary Davis*.

Davis continued to perform literally until the day he died. At the age of seventy-six, while en route to a 1972 concert in New Jersey, he suffered a fatal heart attack.

But his legacy only grew in the years since his passing. Jorma Kaukonen became a veritable Gary Davis jukebox through his career. But it was the Grateful Dead who were probably most responsible with generating the most royalties for the deceased master with their recordings and performances of two famous Reverend Gary Davis tunes, "Death Don't Have No Mercy" and "Samson and Delilah."

▪ "Days Between" (Garcia/Hunter)

"Days Between" was polished by Garcia and Hunter when the two holed up in Hawaii for an extended vacation in the winter of 1993. The baroque ballad is a melancholic and symbolic reflection on misspent energy and the middle-aged realization that the days between the ones that count are just as valuable.

An oddity in the lyrics concerns the use of the word *phantom* three times in one stanza. As Garcia explained to Anthony DeCurtis of *Rolling Stone* in 1993, "The *phantom* thing was funny, because first that line went, 'When ships with phantom sails set to sea on phantom tides.' I said, 'I want it to be something ships with phantom sails set to sea on phantom tides'—I want another two syllables.' So Hunter came up with a bunch of things, but then he said: 'What about *phantom?* Use *phantom* again.' Yeah, *right:* 'When *phantom* ships with phantom sails set to sea on phantom tides.' It worked perfectly. It has this ghostly, hollow quality—it's skeletal. So singing that song is like, *oooh,* it *works* for me. I get chills. It's that happy marriage of setting and sense."

> 3/17/93, Capital Centre, Landover, Maryland
> 3/28/94, Nassau Veterans Memorial Coliseum, Uniondale, New York

- ### "Day Tripper" (Lennon/McCartney)
  The Beatles, single (1965), *Yesterday . . . and Today* (1966), *The Beatles 1962–1966* (1973)
  Otis Redding, *Otis Redding's Dictionary of Soul* (1966), *Live in Europe* (1967)
  Jimi Hendrix and Curtis Knight, *Flashing* (1966)
  Jimi Hendrix, *Ballad of Jimi/'66* (1981), *My Best Friend/'66* (1981), *Radio One/'67* (1988)
  Fever Tree, *Fever Tree* (1968)
  James Taylor, *Flag* (1979)

Commonly, and perhaps mistakenly, thought to reference psychedelic drugs or, more possibly, a romantic tryst, "Day Tripper" is an ecstatic Beatles rocker, which hit Number One in early 1966. John Lennon wrote the song but did little to establish exactly what the song was about, once commenting that "Day Tripper" was a "drug type song in a way because she was a day tripper. I just liked the word tripper." At another juncture Lennon said, "Day trippers are people who go on a day trip, right? Usually on a ferryboat or something. But it was kind of, you know—you're just a weekend hippie."

"Day Tripper" was a well-received and downright fun inclusion in the Dead's set lists when they performed this Beatles classic a few times in the mid-1980s.

> 3/31/85, Cumberland County Civic Center, Portland, Maine

- ### *Dead Ahead* (video)/Produced by Grateful Dead, 1980 (re-released by Monterey Video, 1995).
  "Bird Song," "To Lay Me Down," "On the Road Again," "Ripple," "Don't Ease Me In"›"Lost Sailor"›"Saint of Circumstance"›"Franklin's Tower"›"Rhythm Devils"›"Fire on the Mountain," "Not Fade Away," "Good Lovin'"

Drawn from the Dead's monumental Radio City Music Hall concerts that capped their brief but bold return to acoustic performance, *Dead Ahead* is a Deadhead delight filled with esoteric song choices and inspired musicianship. While the performances are a bit on the sleepy side compared to the shows that spawned this release, the "Rhythm Devils" segment include some tasteful neo-psychedelic special effects, and the Franken and Davis comedy team was enlisted to goof around with the band. During one backstage bit, an overenthusiastic Franken "drops" Garcia's guitar.

- ### *DeadBase: The Complete Guide to Grateful Dead Song Lists*/John W. Scott, Mike Dolgushkin, and Stu Nixon

In an ongoing, already decade-long project chronicling the vast archive the Grateful Dead continue to leave in their aural wake, three collectors bridge the gap between the Aquarian and computer ages by compiling an exhaustive tome detailing the Dead's entire recording and performance catalog. *DeadBase*, published annually, includes such indispensable gnostic knowledge as set lists from practically every Dead, Garcia Band, and Weir solo show, how often a particular song has been played and who wrote it, year-by-year statistical breakdowns, reviews of concerts and tapes, and info on each venue the Dead have played. What the Elias Sports Bureau does for Major League Baseball these guys do for the Dead, deciphering every conceivable anality and banality while somehow making the stats human and fun. Where else could one go if they *just* had to know each time the band *didn't* play "One More Saturday Night" on a Saturday night or access forty anagrams for the words *grateful dead?* If you're collecting tapes but don't have *DeadBase,* you're not collecting tapes.

HANK HARRISON

- ### *The Dead Book* (book)/Hank Harrison
  Links Books, 1973; Celestial Arts, 1980; The Archives Press, 1972, 1985, 1990.

In its various incarnations, reprintings, and recastings, Hank Harrison's *Dead Book* series provided a new-journalism approach to the cultural milieu that informed the band's earliest days. Harrison was a manager for the WARLOCKS, but there isn't much historical *i* dotting or *t* crossing here. Rather, he presents a Tom Wolfe–inspired, novelistic, dadaist slice of Grateful Dead life, complete with sketches of all the core and periphery players in San Francisco's psychedelic passion play as well as great and rare photographs.

- ### *Dead Days* (book)/Herb Greene
  Grateful Dead Merchandising, 1994.

Photographer Herb Greene recycles his best work, those of others, and scrapbook ephemera in this high-end book of days.

- ## Deadheads

"You can't hop the freights anymore but you can chase the Grateful Dead around. You can have all your tires blow out in some weird town in the Midwest and you can get hell from strangers. You can have

something that lasts throughout your life as an adventure, the times you took chances. I think that's essential in anybody's life, and it's harder and harder to do in America. If we're providing some margin of that possibility, then that's great."—Jerry Garcia, 1993.

"They seem to be enjoying themselves. If I were fresh out of school, I can't imagine anything I'd rather do than just take up and travel around, following a band I really liked."—Bob Weir, 1992.

"Who are the Grateful Dead and why do they keep following me around?"—bumper sticker.

Deadheads. The very term conjures images of wild-eyed, acid-drenched, nubile, blond-haired, tie-dyed hippies migrating gypsy-like in weathered VW microbuses from show to show in their oft-derided quest for the peak Grateful Dead experience.

Deadheads. The subject of countless newspaper articles and television pieces, Web sites, police stings, two films, and at least one doctoral thesis.

Deadheads. Almost as long as there has been a Grateful Dead, there have been Deadheads, many of whom structured their lives around the late twentieth century's best known and longest running shindig. But since the success of the 1987 album *In the Dark*—which produced the group's only Top 10 single, "Touch of Grey"—the largest crop of budding Deadheads entered an unprepared fold and threatened to buckle the scene under its own weight. Venerable Dead venues like Berkeley's Greek Theatre and Morrison, Colorado's Red Rocks shrine said they could no longer handle the crowds the Dead attracted. More troubling were the local cops and politicians who didn't want the Dead in town, claiming they brought too much commotion, too many drugs, and, well, too many Deadheads. Even more disturbing were several controversial deaths that occurred at and around Dead shows in the late 1980s and early 1990s.

The Dead took steps to discourage the caravan atmosphere that had reached critical mass by urging the ticketless to stay at home, cracking down on the freewheeling vending markets that spontaneously regenerated in the parking lots outside shows, and planning their tour itineraries to hopscotch regions, making it difficult for their hardest-core fans to navigate their scruffy convoys in a spiraling vector toward Elysium.

At one point the band was forced to distribute a flyer that warned, "A Grateful Dead concert is for music, not for drug dealing. The problems we are experiencing mostly have to do with drug dealing outside our shows—it's the most visible, high-profile reason for anybody to have a problem with us. In other words, dealing makes us a target—so please don't buy or sell drugs at any of the shows. We're not the police, but if you care about this scene, you'll end this type of behavior so the authorities will have no reason to shut us down. We're in this together—so thanks."

Many Deadheads undertook the task of improving the mini-society by encouraging new Heads not to gate-crash, advising them on concert etiquette, and even talking them down from the occasional bum acid trip. One twelve-step clean and sober group, calling themselves the "Wharf Rats" (after the Dead song about a bloodied but unbowed wine derelict), met in the hallways between sets at every concert. Another sight not common at other rock events was groups, such as Greenpeace, distributing information about their various social and political causes.

To be fair, though the unreconstructed substrata of sixties-style society may comprise its most conspicuous (though relatively minuscule) ranks, the definition *Deadhead* can apply to anybody who enjoys Grateful Dead music and chooses to label themselves as such.

While an unbeliever might still claim that only 20,000 people in the entire world are Dead cultists, so blissed-out on the music that they materialized wherever the Dead performed on the face of the Earth, Deadheads compose a far-flung community that, in reality, inhabits the demographic grids generally encountered by all rock bands. Along with the twirling, swirling, and whirling hippie dervishes who filled the aisles and hallways at every show, a typical Grateful Dead concert also attracted large numbers of left-of-center, white middle-aged professionals, young working-class Americans, strait-laced students, preppies, yuppies, some elderly citizens, and, often, dozens of children.

Deadheads hold responsible positions in law, medicine, computer science, education, and other highly skilled fields. Stockbrokers, salesmen, entrepreneurs, actors, writers, artists, carpenters, craftspeople, and cab drivers, most Deadheads pursued their professional goals while looking forward to the odd Dead gig for rejuvenation and inspiration in a fan-friendly, low-testosterone rock & roll environment.

This is not to suggest that the legitimately obsessed don't inhabit this quirky universe. Perhaps its most unique denizens are the tapers—a subcult within a subcult. Since their earliest concerts, the Grateful Dead not only tacitly approved and encouraged but actually facilitated audience recordings. As a result, the Dead are indisputably the most recorded musicians in history. Tapes from nearly every performance since 1967 are the stuff of a huge above-ground trade and bartering network, with some collections numbering in the *thousands* of hours. One hip Alabama oral surgeon, for example, is known to accept tapes in lieu of monetary compensation for services rendered.

"When we're done with it, you can have it," was a frequent offer by Garcia (who followed and recorded his favorite bluegrass groups in the early 1960s) along with the plea that no money be exchanged for music not officially released—a request overwhelmingly honored by the tapeheads.

In 1984, when tension between concert attendees boogying and tapers hoping to preserve their delicate equipment and make optimal recordings reached a boiling point, the Dead responded by establishing a special tapers' section. After their segregation, the tapers created a kind of floating university of sound, producing hundreds of high-quality recordings at each concert. On any given night, a forest of microphones attached to eight-foot poles sprouted and pointed stageward from the tapers' section located in the back of the halls that the band played in. However, a few renegade tapers seeking ever higher-quality recordings could be found in the front rows, questioning authority.

Though the practice of pirate tape trading might contribute to the chronic insomnia suffered by some record-company executives, many bands began to look the other way when they saw a taper recording one of their shows, realizing, like the Dead did long ago, that the circulation of good-quality live tapes can only enhance reputation and spur legitimate record sales. Tapers have always maintained that the fruit of their sometimes exasperating efforts poses little threat to record profits, arguing that the desire for such recordings usually belongs only to the converted, who already possess a goodly number of the band's commercially available releases.

It's hard to determine how the demise of the Grateful Dead as a touring unit will affect the community of Deadheads in the future. Certainly, a number of Deadheads who followed the band on the road have glommed onto other bands such as Phish for spiritual and fiscal sustenance. Hard to determine, too, what impact the more assimilated will have on society through their own individual talents and concerns. Safe to say though, just like the bumper sticker says: "We Are Everywhere!"

- ## *Deadheads—An American Subculture* (video)/Flyin Eye Productions, 1991. Directed by Brian O'Donnell; produced by Flyin Eye Productions.

Brian O'Donnell's sixty-minute art documentary covers ten years of Deadhead culture. The video *vérité* takes an inside look at the artisans, magicians, musicians, and lunatics that make up the community of Grateful Dead devotees. Why Deadheads leave their schools, families, and jobs to be part of the ritualistic tribal celebrations of dance, drugs, and community as a twentieth-century phenomenon is explored in this time-capsuled document.

- ## *Deadicated*/Various Artists
  Arista ACD-8669, 1991. Produced by Ralph Sall.
  "Bertha" (performed by Los Lobos), "Jack Straw" (BRUCE HORNSBY and the Range), "U.S. Blues" (The Harshed Mellows), "Ship of Fools" (Elvis Costello), "China Doll" and "Cassidy" (Suzanne Vega), "Casey Jones" (Warren Zevon with David Lindley), "Uncle John's Band" (Indigo Girls), "Friend of the Devil" (Lyle Lovett), "To Lay Me Down" (Cowboy Junkies), "Wharf Rat" (Midnight Oil), "Estimated Prophet" (Burning Spear), "Deal" (Dr. John), "Ripple" (Jane's Addiction)

Until the release of *Deadicated*, proof of the Dead's impact on modern songsters was hard to come by. Their songs were rarely covered or recorded by other name artists and one was more likely to hear "Friend of the Devil" performed by the bar band at the local roadhouse on a Saturday night than on an album by a pop culture icon.

By contrast, *Deadicated* revealed new power in many of the Dead's best-known tunes when performed by the broad range of artists included on this labor-of-love production. The album is an appropriate marriage of songs and musicians, which takes some bold chances when it works against type. Jane's Addiction's harsh Gen-X send-up of "Ripple" is of particular note in this case and helped spread the Dead's gospel to ever-new frontiers of popular consciousness.

- ## *Dead Lyrics* (book)/Compiled by unknown author
  320 pp. Publisher unknown. Several original pen and ink drawings, photographs. Song and guest appearances index.

This super impossible-to-find paperback artifact was published in Germany and reeks of the type of devotion typical to the obsessed Deadhead. No more than typed-out lyrics on cheap, grainy paper, the book is nonetheless a valuable document in that it provides the words to many of the Dead's rarer and/or unreleased songs such as "Mason's Children" and "Mercy of a Fool."

- ## "Dead Man, Dead Man" (BOB DYLAN)
  Bob Dylan, *Shot of Love* (1981), single (live)/'81 (1989)

An underrated, fire-and-brimstone sneer from Bob Dylan's even more underappreciated *Shot of Love* album, "Dead Man, Dead Man" was more than just the tongue-in-cheek inclusion in the 1987 Dylan/Dead concert than the title might imply.

One of the last conscious born-again songs in Dylan's catalog, "Dead Man, Dead Man" is one of the most unrelenting. As Aidan Day observed in *Jokerman*, his 1988 study of Dylan's lyrics: "Measurement of the Last Things in Dylan's Christian lyrics is, in the last resort, ruled by a sense of the impending end of individual life. And the time that is so short is above all short for the master of bluff and proposition within the lyric-speaker's own identity. Time and again it is a conviction of his own depravity which traumatizes the speakers of these lyrics. 'Satan got you by the heel,' the speaker of 'Dead Man, Dead Man' warns that part of himself which is rooted in unredeemed nature, 'there's a bird's nest in your hair.'"

  7/26/87, Stadium, Anaheim, California (with Bob Dylan)

- ## *Dead Ringers*/Dead Ringers
  Relix Records RRCD2060, 1993.
  "Deep Elem Blues," "Mountains of the Moon," "Rosa Lee McFall," "Slidin' Delta," "Cumberland Blues," "Truckin'," "When I Paint My Masterpiece," "Deal," "Dark Star">"Gotta Serve Somebody," "Knockin' on Heaven's Door"
  Barry Flast–vocals, keyboards, acoustic guitar. DAVID NELSON–vocals, mandolin, electric guitar. Tom Constanten–keyboards. Fred Campbell–vocals, bass, acoustic guitar. Barry Sless–lead guitar, pedal steel. Bill Layman–bass on "Rosa Lee McFall."

(Courtesy of Arista Records)

Brian Godchaux–fiddle on "Deep Elem Blues."
Woody Vermeer–fiddle on "Knockin' on Heaven's
Door." Steve Berger–congas on "Knockin' on
Heaven's Door." Jeff Hobbs–sax on "Knockin' on
Heaven's Door."

Dead Ringers, a band spawned from the Grateful Dead family, is proof positive that the Dead's music will survive long past the band's physical demise.

The band's nucleus consists of Barry Flast (KINGFISH), Tom Constanten (Grateful Dead), and David Nelson (NEW RIDERS OF THE PURPLE SAGE, Almost Acoustic), and their choice of material draws on the Golden Age material from *Workingman's Dead, Aoxomoxoa,* and *American Beauty* because Constanten and Nelson were on those records.

As Constanten remarked, "We didn't learn it from sheet music and off a record. We were in there when it was being constructed and when it was built, and furthermore, we know who we are, we don't have anything to prove. We don't have to play like somebody."

Dead Ringers shows nimble versatility on this live record, with "Deal," "Dark Star," and particularly "Truckin'" seen as the supreme standouts.

▪ *Dead Set*

Arista A2L 8606 or AL9-8112, 1981. Produced by Dan
Healy, Betty Cantor-Jackson, Jerry Garcia.
"Samson and Delilah," "Friend of the Devil," "New

Minglewood Blues," "Deal," "Candyman," "Little
Red Rooster," "Loser," "Passenger," "Feel Like a
Stranger," "Franklin's Tower"›"Rhythm
Devils," "Space"›"Fire on the Mountain,"
"Greatest Story Ever Told," "Brokedown
Palace"

In the autumn of 1980, the Dead threw a party for themselves and their fans. The gala celebration spanned the continent with San Francisco's Warfield Theater and New York City's Radio City Music Hall opening their doors for weeks as exuberant, festive Deadheads reveled in the band's last monster three-set shows that opened with a cherished acoustic offering. Over the next year and half, the Dead released a couple of two-disc LPs as a souvenir of the event. Though this set is regarded as the less-compelling electric companion to the almost-acoustic *Reckoning,* the band burns on "Passenger," "Feel Like a Stranger," "Fire on the Mountain," and "Friend of the Devil" rearranged as a ballad. A good, if unmemorable, album.

▪ *Dead Tour* (book)/Alan Neal Izumi
172 pp. Relix, 1988.

It had to happen: a college town murder mystery centered around a Grateful Dead concert tour and its accordant culture. The band is never mentioned and the plot is fairly formulaic (Nero Wolfe this isn't), yet the novel is an interesting glimpse of the early 1980s Deadhead scene as captured in Alan Neal Izumi's genre-bender.

▪ *Dead Zone*
(CD collection)
Arista ACD6 8530, 1988.

Attempting to capitalize on the Dead's *In the Dark* cash-register bonanza, Arista released this glossy, high-end boxed collection that included the band's entire output for the label at that point: *Terrapin Station, Shakedown Street, Go to Heaven, Reckoning, Dead Set,* and *In the Dark.*

▪ **"Deal"** (Garcia/Hunter)
Jerry Garcia, *Garcia* (1972), *Jerry Garcia Band Live*
　　(1991)
Grateful Dead, *Dead Set* (1981)
Robert Hunter, *Box of Rain* (1991)
Dr. John, *Deadicated* (1991)
Dead Ringers, DEAD RINGERS (1993)

If one song can be pointed to as a model for and example of the Dead's evolution and maturation as reinventors of their own genre, it would have to be "Deal." For years after its concert debut in 1971, the band gave this cowboy rocker as straightforward a reading as anything in their songbook, varying little from the blueprint available on Garcia's debut solo album. But around 1980, the Dead grafted a jam built on the simple three-chord chorus that began taking the tune into the ionosphere.

Suddenly, what had been a rousing but formulaic first-set throwaway took on a new persona as a set-closing A-bomb leaving the audience hungering for more. Simultaneously, the Jerry Garcia Band developed their own blazing version during the 1980s.

In the same way John Coltrane's relentless musical and spiritual search can be traced through his many interpretations of "My Favorite Things," the Dead's ability to break new ground is revealed through the performance history of "Deal." Line up the hundreds of versions of the song and behold a slow, magical blossoming found within very few other artistic enterprises.

"Deal" has its roots in the archaic songs of the South. "Don't You Let That Deal Go Down" and "Last Bad Deal Gone Down" are a couple of oft-covered gambling songs popular with both card and craps players. Additionally,

Hunter pointed out in his 1986 interview with Robert O'Brian for *Relix,* "In songs like 'Deal,' there are almost definite instructions being given on how to approach things. This is the only gift that I can give in that way."

7/16/72, Dillon Stadium, Hartford, Connecticut
11/4/79, Civic Center, Providence, Rhode Island
12/28/82, Oakland Auditorium Area, Oakland,
　　California
8/20/83, Frost Amphitheater, Palo Alto, California
9/15/85, Devore Field, Chula Vista, California
2/9/86, Henry J. Kaiser Convention Center, Oakland,
　　California
6/21/89, Shoreline Amphitheater, Mountain View,
　　California
6/22/92, Star Lake Amphitheater, Burgettstown,
　　Pennsylvania

▪ **"Dear Mr. Fantasy"** (Capaldi/Wood/Winwood)
Traffic, *Mr. Fantasy* (1968), *Welcome to the Canteen*
　　(1971)
Michael Bloomfield and Al Kooper, *Live Adventures*
　　(1968)
Crosby, Stills, Nash & Young, *So Far: The Best of Crosby,*
　　Stills, Nash & Young (unreleased track) (1974)
Grateful Dead, *Without a Net* (1990)

A rock-radio lifer, Traffic's trippy treatise was an unusual collaboration by the group's three main members, Jim Capaldi, Chris Wood, and Steve Winwood, who handled the vocals on the 1967 track. Taking the cue from the San Francisco scene, members of Traffic decided to share a cottage in the English countryside and try their hand at communal living. After one particularly uplifting day, Capaldi wound down by doodling a drawing of a man manipulating the strings of a puppet holding a guitar. After finishing the drawing, he scribbled the words, "Dear Mr. Fantasy, play us a tune, something to make us all happy." Capaldi went to sleep. When he awoke the next day, he discovered that Winwood and Wood had written a song around the rendering he'd done. They added some words, worked out a larger arrangement and the rest is rock history.

Garcia sang the song with the Dead when they introduced it in 1984, but it became a late second-set anchor for Brent Mydland, usually paired with the Beatles' sublime "Hey Jude."

The Dead shared a few bills with Traffic in the late 1960s and in November 1970, members of Traffic jammed with the Dead at New York City's old Anderson Theater in the East Village at a concert benefiting the Hell's Angels. Twenty-four years later, in summer 1994, a reunited Traffic opened several stadium shows for the Dead, and Garcia joined his old friends for a "Dear Mr. Fantasy" jam.

6/9/90, Cal Expo Amphitheater, Sacramento, California

- **"Dear Prudence"** (Lennon/McCartney)
  The Beatles, *The Beatles* **(The White Album) (1968)**
  Jerry Garcia, *Jerry Garcia Band* **(1991)**
  Leslie West, *The Leslie West Band* **(1976)**
  Siouxsie and the Banshees, *Nocturne* **(1983),** *Hyaena* **(1984)**

Though the Dead only incorporated the melody from this beautiful Beatles tune into one 1982 instrumental jam, Garcia maintained it as a pensive but exhilarating staple of Jerry Garcia Band concerts for many years, performing "Dear Prudence" nearly two hundred times from 1979 through their last gigs in 1995.

As Garcia told Rip Rense of *Mix* magazine in 1987, "I'll tell you where *that* comes from. JOHN KAHN and I were driving somewhere when we heard this rhythm and blues version of 'Dear Prudence' on the radio. It had the most incredible groove to it. Years went by, and we were talking about tunes one day and remembered that. We didn't know anything about it—who recorded it or anything. We started looking around but we never found it. So we were trying to reconstruct what we felt it was sort of like. It's really our interpretation of an event that may or may not have happened. It's a great tune, and I had never thought about it as a tune until we heard this incredible R&B version with this amazing and relentless groove. So that's sort of a musical hallucination."

The song has a history steeped in the milieu and pop culture of the late 1960s. Prudence Farrow was the playful younger sister of the actress Mia Farrow. The Farrow sisters became friendly with the Beatles, who exposed Prudence to the philosophies of their spiritual teacher, Maharishi Mahesh Yogi. Prudence encouraged Mia to investigate the teachings of the guru, which eventually resulted in the two sisters journeying to India to study under the Maharishi. During their stay, Prudence became so serious that she turned into a near recluse, spending so much time meditating in her cottage that she rarely came out. The Beatles were studying with the Maharishi at the time and when they became aware of the situation, Lennon was asked to contact her and make sure she came out more often to socialize. (Later, all parties were to break with the guru with charges of sexual and/or spiritual misconduct.) The incident prompted Lennon to write "Dear Prudence." As he later said, "She'd been locked in for three weeks and was trying to reach God quicker than anyone else."

3/13/82, Centennial Coliseum, Reno, Nevada
11/26/88, Wiltern Theater, Los Angeles (Jerry Garcia Band)

- **"Death Don't Have No Mercy"** (REVEREND GARY DAVIS)
  The Reverend Gary Davis, *Pure Religion!* **(1960),** *4t Newport* **(1965)**
  Grateful Dead, *Live Dead* **(1969),** *Two from the Vault/'68* **(1992)**
  Hot Tuna, *Hot Tuna—Acoustic* **(1970),** *Splashdown* **(1975)**
  Jorma Kaukonen, *Too Hot to Handle* **(1986)**

This was the first treatment of several tunes associated with Reverend Gary Davis that the Dead attempted in concert. A dark, even frightening song describing the Grim Reaper's modus operandi, "Death Don't Have No Mercy" was sung by Garcia several dozen times through the late 1960s when it rounded out many of the Dead's multi-song jams from that era. The song had dropped out of sight for almost two decades when it surprisingly reappeared in the band's legendary fall 1989 concerts in which they dusted off and reintroduced several "long gone" numbers. While Garcia sang lead on the early versions, the singing duties were shared by Weir and Mydland in the song's last outings.

11/11/67, Shrine Exhibition Hall, Los Angeles
4/6/69, Avalon Ballroom, San Francisco
1/16/70, Springer's Inn, Portland, Oregon
10/9/89, Coliseum, Hampton, Virginia

- **"Death Letter Blues"** (Son House)
  Singles: Monette Moore (1924), Clara Smith, (1935)
  Son House, *Father of the Delta Blues* **(1965),** *Delta Blues and Spirituals* **(1995)**
  LEADBELLY, *King of the Twelve-String Guitar/'35* **(1991),** *Leadbelly's Last Session/'49* **(1953)**
  Geoff and Maria Muldaur, *Pottery Pie* **(1967)**
  Terry Robb, *Acoustic Blues Trio* **(1994)**
  Cassandra Wilson, *New Moon Daughter* **(1996)**

(© R. Crumb/Shanachie Entertainment)

Though there is no evidence that the Grateful Dead performed this stark Son House song, it was covered by Mickey and the Hartbeats, an abbreviated incarnation of the Grateful Dead that performed a few times in fall 1968 at San Francisco's famed bohemian hangout the Matrix.

The song, evidently a death-row plea, was one of Son House's better known, but whether the influential folk-blues musician actually wrote the song is still open to question. It has been suggested it was a Leadbelly song that he in turn learned from Blind Lemon Jefferson, the best of the early Texas bluesmen and Leadbelly's running mate in the 1920s. According to other testimonies, Son House's "Death Letter Blues" was directly responsible for the origin of Robert Johnson's famous "Walkin' Blues." House, whose influence in the Delta was considerable, recorded very little before World War II and it was not until 1964 that he recorded "Death Letter."

10/30/68, The Matrix, San Francisco

- **"Deep Elem Blues"** (Traditional)
  Singles: Ida May Mack (1928), Texas Bill Day (1929), the Lone Star Cowboys (1933), the Shelton Brothers (1935), Dallas Jamboree Jug Band (1935)

Grateful Dead, *Reckoning* (1981)
Jerry Garcia Acoustic Band, *Almost Acoustic* (1981)
Prairie Ramblers, *White Country Blues, 1926–1938: A Lighter Shade of White* (1993)
Jerry Lee Lewis, *Rare Tracks*/'56 (1989)
Kenny Baker and Josh Graves, *Bucktime!* (1973)
The Good Old Boys, *Pistol Packin' Mama* (1975)
Connie and Babe, *Down the Road to Home* (1995)

Until the 1930s, Dallas's Elm Street was the nexus of the city's notorious red-light district. Over time, the street name came to signify the area as a whole and the word Elm, in the great oral tradition, became corrupted first as Elem (or Ellem) and then as Deep Elem. Leadbelly and Blind Lemon Jefferson were among the rounders who performed and partied there, sharing the streets and saloons with an unlikely assortment of pimps, prostitutes, grifters, and flim-flamming politicians. Naturally, the neighborhood was romanticized in song and "Deep Elem Blues," describing the dangers lurking in the shadows, is one of the better known.

In the late 1980s, after years of neglect, Deep Elem actually became trendy, sporting many nightspots and spawning groups like Edie Brickell and New Bohemians.

The Dead primarily performed "Deep Elem Blues" during their 1970 and 1980 acoustic sets (it did make some electric appearances), and it covers the same thematic terrain as their own heady comment on urban blight, "Shakedown Street."

5/14/70, Meramec Community College, Kirkland, Missouri
10/13/80, Warfield Theater, San Francisco
8/27/83, Seattle Center Coliseum, Seattle, Washington

- ***Déjà Vu*/Crosby, Stills, Nash and Young**
  Atlantic SD 19118, 1970.

With all four members contributing great material, flawless harmonies, and thoughtful lyrics, *Déjà Vu*, CSNY's major triumph, displayed a broader musical scope than that found on *Crosby, Stills and Nash*. The disc represents state-of-the-art 1970s rock music and is the best example of CSNY's enormous stature and enduring legacy.

Garcia's pedal steel work on Graham Nash's "Teach Your Children" is probably his most well-known (if generally unheralded) licks. The song, a Top 20 hit, became a standard as the album topped the charts.

- **Demon in Disguise**/David Bromberg
  Columbia KC 31753, 1972.

Garcia and Lesh play on this early Bromberg album.

- **Desert Horizon**/Norton Buffalo
  Capitol 11847, 1978.

Remembered for his hot harmonica licks with Steve Miller and Commander Cody, Norton Buffalo put out a few decent melodic country-rock records in the late 1970s. Mickey Hart is credited as producer, engineer, and percussionist on the title track, which was recorded at his studio.

- **"Desolation Row"** (BOB DYLAN)
  Bob Dylan, *Highway 61 Revisited* (1965), *MTV Unplugged* (1995)

An apocalyptic portent as powerful as T. S. Eliot's "The Waste Land" and Allen Ginsberg's "Howl," "Desolation Row" is one of the most important songs in Bob Dylan's canon. Has any rock writer ever attempted so much in a single composition? Robin Hood, Einstein, Romeo, Cinderella, the Good Samaritan, Bette Davis, Ezra Pound, and T. S. Eliot himself, are just a few of those who make cameos in "Desolation Row" as Dylan reshapes the societal myths they represent into a bleak and brittle vision.

Perhaps because of its length and raw angularity, which may make it difficult to remember, Dylan has not performed the song much. But his second official release of "Desolation Row" on his *Unplugged* album in 1995 is markedly different than the original. In 1965 he performed the epic with a sneer, while his quiet, conspiratorial voice three decades later makes the corrosive song even more paranoid, if possible, than before.

Bob Weir tackled the lyrics with the Grateful Dead, and, while their versions are well-executed, the bitter, science-fiction nuances of "Desolation Row" have only been properly enunciated by its author. It was during the band's last performance of the song in July 1995 that an ugly gate-crashing incident occurred prompting calls within the Deadhead community to reevaluate themselves.

7/2/95, Deer Creek Music Center, Noblesville, Indiana

- **"Devil with a Blue Dress On"** (Frederick Long/William Stevenson)
  Singles: Shorty Long (1964)

Mitch Ryder and the Detroit Wheels, single (1966), *Sock It to Me!* (1967), *All Mitch Ryder's Hits* (1967), *Rev-Up: The Best of Mitch Ryder and the Detroit Wheels* (1990), *La Gash* (1992)
Bruce Springsteen, *No Nukes* (1980)

With its humorous spirit "Devil with a Blue Dress On" was an unusual tune for Brent Mydland to cover given his generally dour attitude toward the opposite sex when expressed in song.

Following the lead of Mitch Ryder and the Detroit Wheels—who first fused "Devil with a Blue Dress On" with "GOOD GOLLY MISS MOLLY," the 1958 Little Richard hit—and Bruce Springsteen's popular 1979 implementation of the medley, the Dead briefly displayed the tandem during three concerts in the autumn of 1987.

9/16/87, Madison Square Garden, New York

- **Devout Catalyst**/KEN NORDINE
  Grateful Dead Records GDCD 40152, 1991. Produced by DAN HEALY.
  "I Love a Groove," "Mr. Slick," "Inside of Us," "Aging Young Rebel," "Quatrains of Thought," "Spread Eagle & the Final Page," "Thousand Big Bangs," "Cracks in the Ceiling," "Ways of the Meek," "The Movie," "Zodiac Uprising," "Last Will"
  Ken Nordine–vocals. Tom Waits–vocals on "The Movie." Jerry Garcia–acoustic guitar. DAVID GRISMAN–mandolin. Howard Levy–keyboard and harmonica. Joe Craven–percussion. Jim Kerwin–acoustic bass.

The Dead renewed their ties with 1950s bohemia when they invited word jazz progenitor Ken Nordine to participate in their annual New Year's Eve celebration in 1990. Nordine, the airy Chicago-based vocal artist and basso profundo extraordinaire, is notable for his successful blend of poetry and bebop on a series of recordings in the late 1950s and 1960s. But when the idiom fell out of popularity, Nordine established himself as one of the most sought-after commercial voice-over practitioners in the biz while continuing to dispense his peculiar brand of whimsy on National Public Radio.

Nordine's New Year's gig with the Dead led to *Devout Catalyst*, an unusually well-received effort, especially given the implicit quirkiness of the personnel and material involved. With a musical groove that is pure "Grateful Dawg" (that unique aural amalgam occurring whenever Garcia and Grisman picked up their instruments in fretted collaboration), the music sensitively sculpts background environments for Nordine, who stays with them syllable for syllable. But it is Nordine's bizarre literary imagination and his planet-shaking chops that make this a hallmark spoken-word album that helped reignite the Beat Generation renaissance of the mid-1990s.

- **DGQ-20**/The DAVID GRISMAN Quintet
  Acoustic Disc ACD-20, 1996. Produced by David Grisman.

That Jerry Garcia appears on one track ("Dawgnation") is not the only reason to check out this amazing twenty-year retrospective of David Grisman's recording and performing units: The remaining thirty-seven selections are. Along with Garcia, all David Grisman Quartet members are represented and as many guest artists, including Vassar Clements, Al "Jazzbo" Collins, the Kronos Quartet, Jethro Burns, and the incomparable Stephane Grappelli. If there is one Grisman release to be stranded on a desert island with, this may be it.

- ## Dick's Picks Volume One
  Grateful Dead Records GDCD 40182, 1993. Produced and Recorded December 19, 1973, at Curtis Hixon Hall, Tampa, Florida, by John "Kidd" Candelario. Tape archivist: Dick Latvala.
  "Here Comes Sunshine," "Big River," "Mississippi Half-Step Uptown Toodleoo," "Weather Report Suite," "Big Railroad Blues," "Playing in the Band," "He's

(© Grateful Dead Merchandising, Inc.)

Gone">"Truckin'">"Nobody's Fault But Mine">"Jam">"The Other One">"Jam">"Stella Blue," "Around and Around"

The Dead inaugurated two archival series in the early 1990s. DAN HEALY's *From the Vault* project was the first in this successful and valuable reclamation project. But Dick Latvala, the band's official archivist and literal keeper of the vault, gave Healy a run for his money with his initial offering, *Dick's Picks Volume One*. And what a pick it was, the meat of a splendid December 1973 concert that captured the Grateful Dead at a peak of fluidity and real-time invention.

"Here Comes Sunshine," always a sublime demonstration when it was featured during this period, is taken up a few notches and worth the price of admission alone. "Playing in the Band" is also extended and exploratory. And while "Mississippi Uptown Half-Step Toodleoo" is still rather raw and embryonic, Weir's "Weather Report Suite" is given full, sensitive treatment. The long jam that includes "He's Gone," "Truckin'," "Nobody's Fault but Mine," "The Other One," and "Stella Blue" is a fine example of the band's ability to easily cut corners with a jazzy looseness that was only truly possible when Bill Kreutzmann was the sole drummer.

All of the participants and performances on *Dick's Picks* are sharp, each instrumentalist upping the ante for his band mates with each luscious lick.

The CD's packaging (and those in the series that followed it) is worthy of note in that it has a crude bootleg sensibility, designed around the concept of an old reel-to-reel tape box that still needs some dusting off. Thank God they did.

- ## Dick's Picks Volume Two
  Grateful Dead Records GDCD 4019, 1995. Recorded October 31, 1971, at Ohio Theater, Columbus, Ohio, by Rex Jackson. Tape archivist: Dick Latvala.
  "Dark Star">"Jam">"Sugar Magnolia," "St. Stephen," "Not Fade Away">"Going Down the Road Feeling Bad">"Not Fade Away"

A good, if somewhat disappointingly short, follow-up to his initial archival offering, *Dick's Picks Volume Two* is, nonetheless, a fine example of the Grateful Dead shortly after keyboardist Keith Godchaux joined the combo. "Dark Star" finds Phil Lesh taking the lead and turning the inspirational corners. "Sugar Magnolia" is just beginning to be stretched out in the "Sunshine Daydream" section. Likewise, "St. Stephen," in its last outing until 1976, is jammed in ways that seem to point to its later incarnations. Finally, the "Not Fade Away"> "Going Down the Road">"Not Fade Away" medley takes that then-common showstopper to new, dizzying heights—as if Garcia was cranking a Harley through a hall of mirrors.

The only complaint voiced among some tapeheads was the brevity of the release. Latvala's first pick contained two discs and a glance at the set list from which *Dick's Picks Volume Two* was drawn reveals any number of inclusions assuming the same high quality of master tape existed in the Dead's vault, that could have easily filled out another CD.

• *Dick's Picks Volume Three*

Grateful Dead Records GDCD 4022, 1995. Recorded May 22, 1977, at the Sportatorium, Pembroke Pines, Florida, by Betty Cantor-Jackson. Tape archivist: Dick Latvala.

"Funiculi Funicula," "The Music Never Stopped," "Sugaree," "Lazy Lightning">"Supplication," "Dancin' in the Streets," "Help on the Way"> "Slipknot!">"Franklin's Tower," "Samson and Delilah," "Sunrise," "Estimated Prophet">"Eyes of the World">"Wharf Rat">"Terrapin Station">"(Walk Me out in the) Morning Dew"

The Dead's 1977 spring tour holds many fond memories for Deadheads and tapeheads alike. The May 8 Ithaca,

New York, show in particular ranks high as one of the band's best but each show was inspired with a charged grace that was rarely matched. This Florida concert from later in the month finds the Dead razor sharp in a take-no-prisoners mode with *killer* versions of every selection. Keith Godchaux's contribution is particularly noteworthy as he fills in the spaces and accentuates the positive with the ESP of a great bebop pianist.

• *Dick's Picks Volume Four*

Grateful Dead Records GDCD 4023, 1996. Recorded February 13–14, 1970, at the Fillmore East, New York City, by Bear. Tape archivist: Dick Latvala.

"Introduction (by the Great Zacherle)," "Casey Jones," "Dancing in the Streets," "China Cat Sunflower">"I Know You Rider">"High Time," "Dire Wolf," "Dark Star" "That's It for the Other One">"Turn on Your Love Light," "Alligator">"Drums">"Me and My Uncle">"Not Fade Away">"Mason's Children">"Caution (Do Not Stop on Tracks)">"Feedback">"And We Bid You Goodnight"

In his first three releases, Dick Latvala had uncorked great but obscure shows in his fine archival series. For his fourth offering, Latvala took a 180-degree turn by sharing the Holy Grail of Grateful Dead performances—the meat of the February 13 and 14 Fillmore gigs. In various reader polls (including a number of recommendations in the book you now hold) these concerts have been frequently hailed as Grateful Dead Valhalla and

Grateful Dead at the Fillmore East, New York, 2/13/70. *(Amalie R. Rothschild/Corbis Bettmann)*

have been widely circulated for years. Yet this pristine release makes the music shine anew to even the most jaded tapehead vet. The Fillmore shows were unusually well-recorded for their time using the venue's excellent sound system, which was the only house PA that the band ever used. The mix is excellent, missing the monitor problems that plagued the band throughout the late 1970s. Recorded just weeks before the release of *Workingman's Dead*, there is perhaps no other moment when the Dead played songs so concisely *and* jammed with such sheer desire and curiosity. Perhaps the only thing missing here are any tracks from the acoustic sets from those nights, some of which ended up on *Bear's Choice*.

The three-disc set features seventeen tracks and includes the Dead's first-ever release of "Mason's Children," a treasured rarity, a heavyweight champion "Dark Star," and jamming that must serve as music to somebody's gods.

• *Dick's Picks Volume Five*

Grateful Dead Records GDCD 4024, 1996. Recorded December 26, 1979, at the Oakland Auditorium Arena. Tape archivist: Dick Latvala.

"Cold Rain and Snow," "C.C. Rider," "Dire Wolf," "Me and My Uncle">"Big River," "Brown-Eyed Women," "New Minglewood Blues," "Friend of the Devil," "Looks Like Rain," "Alabama Getaway">"Promised Land," "Uncle John's Band">"Estimated Prophet">"He's Gone">"The Other One">"Drums">"Not Fade Away">"Brokedown Palace">"Around and Around">"Johnny B. Goode," "Shakedown Street">"Uncle John's Band"

Since the inception of the Dead's archival release projects, Deadheads had been clamoring for a show from the Brent Mydland era. *Dick's Picks Volume Five* delivers just that: a complete concert (a first in the series) from early in the keyboardist's reign. This highly regarded but fairly uncommon reel is highlighted by a high-energy second set featuring one of the most unusual (and best) versions of "Uncle John's Band" and an over-the-top, post–"Estimated Prophet" jam that touches on everything from bluegrass to Coltrane to music befitting a soundtrack to a 1970s Blacksploitation film.

There are some rough spots here, but then, what would a Dead show be without those?

• *Dick's Picks Volume Six*

Grateful Dead Records GDCD 4026, 1996.

Recorded October 14, 1983, at the Hartford Convention Center. Tape archivist: Dick Latvala

"Alabama Getaway">"Greatest Story Ever Told," "They Love Each Other," "Mama Tried">"Big River," "Althea">"C.C. Rider," "Tennessee Jed," "Hell in a Bucket">"Keep Your Day Job," "Scarlet Begonias">"Fire on the Mountain" "Estimated Prophet">"Eyes of the World">"Spanish Jam">"The Other One">"Stella Blue">"Sugar Magnolia," "U.S. Blues"

Another cooking, three-disc show was archivist Dick Latvala's first plunge into the vast waters of the Dead's 1980s output and features blazing versions of just about everything. Standouts include "Greatest Story," "C.C. Rider," "Althea," "Scarlet">"Fire," a sinuous, exotic version of the rare "Spanish Jam," and a volcanic "Sugar Mag." Even "Day Job" is a welcome piece of madness on this inspired night.

• *Dick's Picks Volume Seven*

Grateful Dead Merchandising, GDCD 4027, 1997. Recorded September 1974, at Alexandra Palace, London. Tape Archivist: Dick Latvala.

"Scarlet Begonias," "Mexicali Blues," "Row Jimmy," "Black-Throated Wind," "Mississippi Half-Step Uptown Toodleoo," "Beat It on Down the Line," "Tennessee Jed," "Playing in the Band," "Weather Report Suite," "Stella Blue," "Brown-Eyed Women," "Big River," "Truckin' ">"Wood Green Jam">"Wharf Rat," "Me and My Uncle," "Not Fade Away">"Dark Star">"Spam Jam">"Morning Dew," "U.S. Blues"

About a month before entering their lengthy hiatus in 1974, the Dead visited Europe for a seven-concert tour of the Continent with stops in England, West Germany, and France, and played their hearts out. Culling the vaults for the best of the band's three-show run in London, archivist Dick Latvala creates a kind of dream concert with a percolating "Scarlet Begonias," a howling "Black-Throated Wind," a focused and spacey "Playing in the Band," an airtight "Weather Report Suite," and some stellar jams packed with favorites.

• **Bo Diddley**

Born Otha Ellas Bates McDaniel, December 30, 1928, McComb, Mississippi

Bo Diddley. *(Archive Photos/Frank Driggs Collection)*

An influential bluesman as well as a rock & roll progenitor, Bo Diddley may be the only guitarist to have a specific rhythm named after him, the famous "Bo Diddley Beat" (a.k.a. "Shave 'n a haircut, two bits"). He was also the only popular musician to have the gahunzas to name a song after *himself!* His signature guitar sound—thickly textured proto-funk—resists classification, and though he has sometimes been dismissed as a one-riff master, nothing could be further from the truth. Like Chuck Berry, Diddley falls somewhere between the blues and R&B-based rock, appealing to fans and practitioners of both genres.

Moving to Chicago as a young boy, Diddley aspired to a boxing career, and it was in the neighborhood gyms where he picked up his nickname. Well-versed in spiritual and sanctified church music, Diddley was also a student of classical music as well as a budding violinist. But when he heard John Lee Hooker's "Boogie Chillen" as a thirteen year old, he dropped it all for the guitar. He incorporated his church music roots into his sound, and the distinctive muscle apparent in many of his songs began to flex.

Diddley first recorded his blues-derived music with Chess Records in 1955, turning out the singles he became famous for: "Bo Diddley," "I'm a Man," "Mona," "Say Man," and "Hey, Bo Diddley." He also had some success with Willie Dixon's "You Can't Judge a Book by Its Cover." In 1958, Diddley moved to Washington, D.C., and it was there that he designed his trademark square guitar. Diddley toured with rock & roll package shows and made a series of novelty albums with catchy titles like *Bo Diddley Is a Gunslinger* (1960), *Bo Diddley Is a Lover* (1961), and *Bo Diddley Is a Twister* (1962). In 1963, when the guitar-heavy surfing craze hit rock, Diddley responded with albums like *Surfin' with Bo Diddley.*

Bo had an enormous effect on the British Invasion bands of the early 1960s but, as his popularity faded in the States, he took to the oldies circuit. He did briefly ride the wave of the black-power movement with *Black Gladiator,* an inspired, if commercially unsuccessful, album.

On March 25, 1972, at a legendary concert/party for the Hell's Angels at New York City's Academy of Music, Diddley opened for and then joined the Grateful Dead for one of their wilder first sets of the era, jamming freely through four of his better known songs: "Hey Bo Diddley," "I'm a Man," "Take It Off," and "Mona." Reporting on the event in the *Village Voice,* Patrick Carr wrote, "Saturday was their benefit for the Hell's Angels. Then they played as a backup band for Bo Diddley, ranged in a grinning line behind Big Bo's black-silk bulk, the best band he's ever likely to play with. It was party night, and their own set was loose."

Diddley has never stopped performing and, at one point, was hired as the opening act for some of the Clash's 1979 shows. His induction into the Rock and Roll Hall of Fame in 1987 led to a minor comeback that included a Nike sneakers commercial featuring the all-sports superstar Bo Jackson.

· Hamza El Din

The Grateful Dead invaded Cairo, Egypt, in September 1978, fulfilling a long-held dream to play in front of the Sphinx and the Great Pyramid. The three-night extravaganza, attended by a crowd of mostly befuddled Egyptians, was coproduced by the band and the Egyptian Ministry of Culture, with all proceeds going to the Department of Antiquities and Madame Jihan Sadat's (wife of then-Egyptian president Anwar Sadat) charity for handicapped children. The oud master Hamza El Din opened the event.

Acknowledged worldwide as the musical ambassador from Sudan, Hamza El Din is one of the great masters of the oud, a fretless lute popular throughout the Arab world. A celebrated composer, concert performer, and an emotional vocalist, Hamza is the person most responsible for keeping the musical traditions of Nubia alive.

Although Nubians, whose language is as richly poetic as Arabic and much like what was spoken in ancient Egypt at the time of the Pharaohs, have always used music to express themselves, the only indigenous instrument among the people of the upper Nile is a drum called the tar, prized for its three-dimensional resonance. (In Pharaonic temples there are hieroglyphic representations of people playing the tar.) Recognizing that a new medium was required to express the changing traditions of Nubia, Hamza went to what is now the Arab Institute of Music in Cairo to study the oud, which was not used in Nubia until he introduced it. A precursor to the lute through Moorish influence on Spain, the oud historically has been used in Middle Eastern music only as accompaniment to a singer, as a composition instrument, or in ensembles. Hamza developed its use as a solo instrument by elegantly combining Arabic music with his own.

Not much is known about Hamza's life and it is rumored that he spends much of his life on the outskirts of civilization, sometimes as a nomad. But it is also said he spends a considerable amount of time in Japan. Most of what is known about him is through his sketchy but long recording career beginning with the Vanguard and Nonesuch labels in the 1960s.

It was his relationship with the Grateful Dead that made him perhaps one of the most revered artists from the developing world. When the Dead visited Egypt for their trio of monumental (if poorly performed) concerts, it was Hamza El Din and his troupe of tar players and singers whom they invited to open the shows. As Hamza's group ended their sets, the Dead joined them for an extended foray into Hamza's "Ollin Arageed," a hypnotically enchanting vocal and percussion groove lasting for several minutes of the most exotic Grateful Dead music ever. Slowly, Hamza's group left the stage and the Dead slid into their music. These were undoubtedly the musical peaks of the Dead's Gizeh shows, touching musicians and audience alike. On the final night a total eclipse of the moon completed the mystical aura of the Dead's mission to the Middle East, which transpired at the height of the Camp David meetings between Israeli prime minister Menachem Begin and Egyptian president Sadat.

The Dead were so moved, in fact, that they invited Hamza to join them ten times in the succeeding twelve years, always returning to the mysterious "Ollin Arageed" for further coloring.

Mickey Hart helped popularize Hamza somewhat by remastering the oudist's 1978 album, *Eclipse*, and re-releasing it as part of "The World," the drummer's globally inclusive music project with Rykodisc.

Music of Nubia/Vanguard 79164 (1964)
Escalay: The Water Wheel/Nonesuch 72941 (1968)
Eclipse/Rykodisc 10103 (1978, 1988)

- **Diga/Diga Rhythm Band**
Round/United Artists RX 110 RX-LA600-G, 1976 (reissue Rykodisc RCD/RACS/RALP-0101, 1988). Produced by Mickey Hart.
"Sweet Sixteen," "Magnificent Sevens," "Happiness Is Drumming," "Razooli," "Tal Mala"
Mickey Hart–traps, gongs, timbales, timpani. ZAKIR HUSSAIN–tabla, folk drums, tar. Jim Loveless–marimbas. Jordan Amarantha–congos, bongos. Vince Delgado–dumbek, tabla, talking drum. Ray Spiegel–vibes. Tor Dietrichson–tabla. Aushim Chaudhuri–tabla. Arshad Syed–duggi tarang, nal. Joy Shulman–tabla. Peter Carmichael–tabla. Jerry Garcia–guitar on "Razooli" and "Happiness Is Drumming." Jim MacPhearson, Kathy MacDonald, and David Freiberg–vocals on "Razooli."

Mickey Hart's hiatus from the Grateful Dead between 1971 and 1974 was well spent if *Diga* is any indication of how he whiled away the years. Actually, *Diga* (an outgrowth of his work with the Diga Rhythm Band), represented a retrenchment in world music sounds and studies for the once and future Grateful Dead percussionist.

Though Hart was ostensibly the front man for the Diga Rhythm Band, the large ensemble was truly a joyous group effort as their sole album indicates. Most salient to Grateful Dead music, "Happiness Is Drumming," one of the disc's standout tunes, includes Garcia on lead guitar in a guest capacity and was later developed by the Dead into "Fire on the Mountain," a favored concert staple.

- ## *The Digital Domain: A Demonstration*
  ### Elektra/Asylum, 1983. Produced by Elliot Mazer and Loren Rush.

For those who must have everything, Mickey Hart assisted in the recording of "Helicopter," a track of an actual helicopter in flight for this novelty sampler.

- ## The Dinosaurs

While the 1970s were not very kind to most rock groups spawned in San Francisco during the 1960s, the Dinosaurs briefly figured out how to use that as a marketing and musical plus. Pieced together from bands of the past came a vibrant group of grizzled vets from the frontlines of the rock & roll wars. Featuring Robert Hunter on guitar and vocals, Quicksilver's JOHN CIPOLLINA playing lead guitar, Big Brother bassist Peter Albin, Airplane and NEW RIDERS OF THE PURPLE SAGE drummer Spencer Dryden, and guitarist Barry Melton from Country Joe and the Fish, the Dinosaurs never left the Bay Area, where they intermittently performed in the early and mid-1980s. Though they never recorded an album, their light-show-soaked concerts are cherished memories by all who saw them. The height of their commercial success was undoubtedly the 1982 New Year's concert they opened for the Grateful Dead.

- ## "Dire Wolf" (Garcia/Hunter)
  ### Grateful Dead, *Workingman's Dead* (1970), *Reckoning* (1981), *Dick's Picks Volume Four/'70* (1996), *Dick's Picks Volume Five/'79* (1996), *Grateful Dead: The Arista Years* (1996)

"Dire Wolf" is about as close as the Dead get to summoning their "bête noire," or "black beast," so common in world mythology. The unruly and devious subject behaves in a manner not dissimilar to the monstrous bird of Edgar Allan Poe's *The Raven* in its literary evocation of an onerous nemesis. Hunter addressed this in his 1986 interview with Robert O'Brian of *Relix*. "The dire wolf is the shadow of the man in the song who is dead at this point. It's a song by a ghost."

Thematically, the lyrics are reminiscent of the Dead's "Friend of the Devil" in which an unwinnable pact is made with the dreaded Lucifer. Similar high stakes are up for grabs in "Dire Wolf" with a card game recalling the symbolic chess match in Ingmar Bergman's 1957 film *The Seventh Seal* as the contest in which the outcome is never in question.

As Hunter told Jeff Tamarkin of *Relix* in 1986, "The imagery occurred to me in a dream. I woke up and grabbed a pencil before I was entirely awake and wrote the whole song down. I think I managed to capture the quality of the dream by writing it down before I was wide awake."

Set to a bright, folksy melody, the song takes place in the wintry dark and cold of Fennario, the same geographically vague locale where "PEGGY-O" (a.k.a. "Fennario"), the famous song of equally murky origin covered by the Dead, transpires.

A rollicking first-set regular since 1969, "Dire Wolf" was partially informed by the Zodiac Killer who stalked and terrorized the Bay Area during the song's composition and recording. Hence the chorus refrain, "Please don't murder me." Garcia also performed the song about thirty times in solo acoustic settings in the middle 1980s.

As Garcia told Paul Krassner in 1984, "That song got written when the Zodiac Killer was murdering in San Francisco. It was one of those things that was, like, every night I was coming home from the studio and I'd stop at an intersection and look around and if a car pulled up, ya know, it was like, 'This is it. I'm gonna die now.'

"It was like a game. Every night I was conscious of that thing. And that refrain got to be so real to me: 'Please don't murder me. *Please* don't murder me.'

"It was a coincidence in a way but it was also the truth of the moment."

Blues archaeologists will note that the plea also turns up in several old and new blues songs such as Li'l Son Jackson's "Charlie Cherry," which is loosely based on the 1964 murders of civil rights workers Andrew Goodman, Michael Schwerner, and James Chaney that inspired the film *Mississippi Burning*.

1/15/78, Selland Arena, Fresno, California

- ## Willie Dixon
  ### Born July 1, 1915, Vicksburg, Mississippi; died January 29, 1992, Burbank, California

"I Am the Blues!" shouts the title of Willie Dixon's autobiography and it is right. As a composer, producer, arranger, bass player, recording artist, session musician, talent scout, and Chess Records bandleader in the 1950s and early 1960s, Willie Dixon was *the* quintessential blues master. Dixon, along with Muddy Waters,

Willie Dixon. *(Archive Photos/Express Newspapers)*

cure the blues its rightful respect, protection, and recognition and to educate present and future generations about what he liked to call "the facts of life"—the blues. Blues Heaven also gives financial aid to destitute blues artists.

Much of Dixon's late work concerned itself with social consciousness, dedicated to world peace and improving the human condition. Appropriately, his last credit, "ETERNITY," a composition coauthored with Bob Weir, is Zen-like in its simple musing on the biggest of questions.

- **Dog Moon** (comic book)/Robert Hunter & Timothy Truman
  DC Comics-Vertigo, 1987.

One of the positive outgrowths of *Grateful Dead Comix* was the relationship Hunter struck with artist Timothy Truman. And while Truman may not be the graphic equivalent of Jerry Garcia as an outlet for Hunter's muse he should be credited with the creepy *Tales from the Crypt* sensibility of *Dog Moon*, an apocalyptic yarn in rhyme that concerns itself with lost souls and retribution. This is Hunter at his darkest.

- **"Doin' That Rag"** (Hunter/Garcia/Lesh)
  Grateful Dead, *Aoxomoxoa* (1969), *What a Long Strange Trip It's Been* (1977)

Though the obtuse lyrics to this tune are as impossible to comprehend as the song was evidently difficult to perform, the Dead did pull many explosive versions of "Doin' That Rag" out of their proverbial magic hats that were highlighted by a frenzied, cylindrical jam down the home stretch.

7/11/69, New York State Pavilion, Queens, New York

- **"Don't Ease Me In"** (Traditional)
  Grateful Dead, single (b/w "Stealin'") (1966); single, *Go to Heaven* (1980)
  Henry Thomas, *Texas Worried Blues*/'28 (1981), *The Music Never Stopped: Roots of the Grateful Dead* (1995)

This song is one of the Dead's earliest performed and most continuously played covers, reaching back to their jug band days in MOTHER MCCREE'S UPTOWN JUG CHAMPIONS, and the roots of "Don't Ease Me In" are firmly imbedded in the blues of rural Texas.

A Lone Star State songster, Henry "Ragtime Texas"

was the single most influential figure in the post–World War II Chicago-blues sound. "Hoochie Coochie Man," "I JUST WANT TO MAKE LOVE TO YOU," "Evil," "SPOONFUL," "I AIN'T SUPERSTITIOUS," "LITTLE RED ROOSTER," "Back Door Man," "Bring It on Home," and "MY BABE" are just a few of the many scores of compositions Dixon penned that have shaped the blues.

Of equal significance was the bond he helped forge between the blues and rock & roll. He recorded often with Chuck Berry in the late 1950s, and since the 1960s his classic songs have been covered by English and U.S. bands. Cream, Led Zeppelin, the Rolling Stones, and the Doors all tackled his material, passing on Dixon's mystique to new audiences. Willie Dixon's impact on the Grateful Dead was equally important. After Dylan and the Beatles, the eight Willie Dixon songs performed by the Dead are the most by any other single composer in their repertoire.

As much music as he gave people, Dixon gave back to the music and the people who made it, becoming the ambassador of the blues. In 1982, he created the Blues Heaven Foundation with royalty money from his song catalogue. The goal of the nonprofit organization (which continues to operate despite Dixon's passing) is to se-

Thomas recorded the first known version of the song in 1928 when he was fifty-four years old, just two years before his death. In fact, Thomas only began recording in 1927, cutting about two dozen sides by 1929, which have been compiled on many anthologies. His extant body of work reveals much about the songster tradition, which included black folk songs, jump blues, rags, dances, novelty tunes, and early blues.

Born sometime in 1874 near Big Sandy, Texas, Thomas's sharecropper parents were former slaves. After teaching himself the guitar and panpipes (a homemade reed instrument that creates a high-pitched, whistling sound), the teenage Thomas left home, worked on the Texas-Pacific Railroad and hoboed through the South, eking out an existence as an itinerant street musician. He is generally thought to have spent most of his life in East Texas but it is rumored he ventured to Chicago's Columbian Exposition in 1893 and the 1904 St. Louis World's Fair. All of his recordings, incidentally, were made in Chicago.

Because Thomas was old enough to recall the years in the late 1800s when the blues was in gestation, his recorded material is considered especially important to musicologists in helping to trace the blues back to its conception. "Don't Ease Me In" is a particularly good example of this. Unlike the Dead's version, Thomas references a high-profile Texas businessman by the name of Cunningham who was known to lease convicts to work his sugarcane fields along the Brazos River. Additionally, Thomas's biographer, Mack McCormick, suggests that "Don't Ease Me In" was commonly heard along the Brazos in various prison farms.

The song is a typical but upbeat bad-luck, got-done-wrong blues. However, the title phrase itself, "don't ease me in" is somewhat puzzling and would seem from the various versions to contain some kind of sexual innuendo.

Garcia never stopped singing this song with the Dead, who generally performed it as an uptempo first set closer or as an encore. In 1970, it received some acoustic attention when it was often used as the show opener. Always it served as a reminder of both the band's and the music's earliest moments.

7/14/70, Euphoria Ballroom, San Rafael, California

2/17/79, Coliseum Arena, Oakland, California (Weir on slide; Keith and Donna's last show)

5/3/87, Frost Amphitheater, Palo Alto, California

▪ "Don't Need Love" (Mydland)

If there was one tune that demonstrates Brent Mydland's soulfulness in performance this is it. It's a shame that the band never committed this song to disc while they had the chance. Typical of Mydland's compositions, "Don't Need Love" is alternately bitter and heartrending—the eternal outsider's statement on romance.

10/12/84, Civic Center, Augusta, Maine

▪ "Don't Think Twice, It's Alright" (BOB DYLAN)

Bob Dylan, *The Freewheelin' Bob Dylan* (1963), *At Budokon* (1979)

Bob Dylan and THE BAND, *Before the Flood* (1974)

JOAN BAEZ, *In Concert Part 2* (1963)

Peter, Paul and Mary, *In the Wind* (1963)

Johnny Cash, *Orange Blossom Special* (1965)

Wonder Who, single (1965)

Duane Eddy, *Duane Eddy Does Bob Dylan* (1966)

Sebastian Cabot, *Bob Dylan, poet* (1967)

Elvis Presley, *Elvis* (1973)

RAMBLIN' JACK ELLIOTT, *The Essential Ramblin' Jack Elliott* (1974), *Me & Bobby McGee* (1994)

Lenny Breau, *Lenny Breau Trio* (1985)

Bob Dylan wrote this kiss-off classic about Suze Rotolo, probably his first true love, with whom he was involved after his arrival in New York. Suze is the woman clutching the poet-waif's arm on the cover of *The Freewheelin' Bob Dylan*, his highly lauded, still-relevant breakthrough second album on which "Don't Think Twice, It's Alright" originally appeared. Rotolo's rancorous departure inspired her lover to pen this wry exercise in catharsis.

The song was an early commercial hit and widely recorded. But the majority of the covers miss Dylan's sardonic edge, stressing the song's saccharine aspect and ignoring its acidity. Even when Dylan transformed "Don't Think Twice" into a funky reggae affair with his big-band, Elvis Presley–style arrangements in 1978, the song's bitter wistfulness remained intact.

Dylan adapted the melody from Paul Clayton's interpretation of "Scarlet Ribbons for Her Hair." Clayton was a Greenwich Village folkie and a colleague of Dylan's who took his friend to legal task for the perceived infringement, eventually arriving at an out-of-court settlement.

By 1986, Dylan had joined forces with Tom Petty and

the Heartbreakers and embarked on a short summer tour opening for the Grateful Dead. During their Akron, Ohio, concert, the Dead coaxed Dylan onstage during their first set for a couple of ragged collaborations, including "Don't Think Twice."

7/2/86, Rubber Bowl, Akron, Ohio (with Bob Dylan)

• Dose Hermanos

One of the brighter aspects following in the wake of Garcia's passing was the swift grace with which the Grateful Dead musical family-at-large landed on its feet. Dose Hermanos, a keyboard duo consisting of BOB BRALOVE, the band's MIDI whiz, and Tom Constanten, their former keyboard practitioner from the late 1960s, made some appearances on both coasts in the winter of 1996. Their set consisted of consonant pieces, strafed with a California prettiness. Optimistic to a fault, Dose Hermanos mixed new wave music experimentalism with bits of pop textures and elements of the blues, as if uncovering some archaic musical form and quoting it.

Writing in the *Village Voice*, Richard Gehr described their January 1996 New York City Knitting Factory gig. "With their twinkling, punning helix lines and sheets of candy-colored calliope and harpsichord samples, [the duo] were by turns eloquent, tongue-tied, and portentous—just like da boyz themselves. Uh, were."

• *Double Dose*/The Heart of Gold Band

Whirled 01967, 1984 (CD reissue: Relix Records RRCD 2020, 1989). Produced by Greg Anton, Alan Trist, and JOHN CIPOLLINA.

"Stir It Up," "Watchin' the River Flow," "IT TAKES A LOT TO LAUGH, IT TAKES A TRAIN TO CRY," "Strange Man," "Lonesome Highway," "Ride Out," "Built for Comfort," "House of Wax," "Ready for Love," "Maybellene," "Solid Rock," "Golden Road," "KNOCKIN' ON HEAVEN'S DOOR," "Scarlet Begonias"

Keith Godchaux–piano, vocals. Donna Godchaux–vocals. Steve Kimock–guitar. Dexter LeBlanc–bass. Greta Rose–backup vocals. Don Gaynor–guitar. Bill Middlejon–guitar, vocals. Larry Klein–bass. Billy Travis–vocals. David McKay–bass. Mark Adler–piano.

After leaving the Dead in 1979, Keith and Donna Godchaux joined the Ghosts, a Northern California bar band. Though they gigged infrequently, the band devel-

oped a core following before changing their name to the Heart of Gold Band (after a line from "Scarlet Begonias") just before Keith was killed in a 1980 automobile accident.

The band went through a few personnel changes and recorded at various points with a surprisingly strong showing. *Double Dose* documents three versions of the group with a potpourri of very good studio tracks and ragged but fiery live cuts. The studio tracks showcase the songwriting abilities of guitarist Don Gaynor with smooth, relaxed uptempo rock. The original material ("Ride Out," "Built for Comfort," "House of Wax," and "Ready for Love") shows a band matured beyond their relatively short union.

There is also some predictable cover material on which Keith and Donna never sounded so good. The band takes the music to several Dead-like spaces, particularly in the jams that accompany "Scarlet Begonias" and Dylan's "Solid Rock."

Propelled by guitarist Steve Kimock, whose lava-hot stringwork almost steals the show, the album stands as a memorial to Keith and to what might have been.

• "Down in the Bottom" (WILLIE DIXON)

Singles: Augustus ("Track Horse") Haggerty (1934), Gabriel Browne (1943), Jubalairs (1943)

Howlin' Wolf, *The Genuine Article: The Best of Howlin' Wolf* (1960), *The Howlin' Wolf Album* (1969)

Walter Becker, *11 Tracks of Whack* (1994)

No one ever pillaged the blues' past like Willie Dixon. Here he dredges up "Meet Me in the Bottom," a 1930s favorite, and sets it to a galloping beat provided by Howlin' Wolf and company.

Bob Weir's enchantment with Dixon's blues is well acknowledged, and this composition is a further testament to Weir's debt to the great American artist. Echoing their treatment of "Minglewood Blues," the Dead sporadically performed "Down in the Bottom" in 1984 and 1985.

4/3/85, Providence Civic Center, Providence, Rhode Island

• *Down in the Groove*/BOB DYLAN

Columbia OC 40957, 1988. Produced by Bob Dylan (uncredited).

Dylanists jokingly disparage *Down in the Groove* as *Self-Portrait II*, after an earlier and similarly scorned hodge-podge. Bob Dylan hadn't written an album of entirely new material in three years and was able to muster only two originals and two collaborations for this, his thirty-second album.

By using a variety of bands from different sessions, *Down in the Groove* came off as a disappointing effort by someone who seemed to be getting bored with the whole idea of making records. This was the low ebb in Dylan's recording career with a result that was uninspired, haphazard, and shoddy.

But, it being a Bob Dylan album, the document is not without its interestingly weird strengths. Dylan's covers of the old folk chestnut "Shenandoah" (electrified here with a Bo Diddley beat) and the Stanley Brothers' haunting "Rank Strangers to Me" stand with his best interpretive work. And the inclusion of two Robert Hunter songs, "Silvio" and "The Ugliest Girl in the World," adds to the album's quirkiness.

Remembering how Dylan came to his songs, Hunter told David Gans in 1988: "You couldn't be easier to work with than Dylan. I brought the book—I think it had fifteen to seventeen songs—in to the Dead before we made *In the Dark*, of which "When Push Come to Shove" and "Black Muddy River" were selected. I took about three of them for the *Liberty* album, and Dylan took two of them for his album, set 'em and sent me a tape. That's what I call easy to work with! He just flipped through the songbook that was sitting there at Front Street, liked these tunes, put 'em in his pocket, went off, set 'em to music, recorded 'em, and . . . First time I met him he said [*imitating Dylan voice*] 'Eh, I just recorded two of your tunes!' And I said, 'Neat!'

"Bob Dylan doesn't have to ask a lyricist if he can do his tunes! Come *on*, man!

"I gotta just say this for the record: you got your Grammies, you got your Bammies, you got your Rock & Roll Hall of Fame—as far as I'm concerned, Bob Dylan has done two of my songs, and those other things sound far away, distant, and not very interesting."

For the recording session, Dylan included Garcia, Weir, and Mydland on backup vocals, but they are all but indistinguishable in the final wash.

• *Down on the Farm* / Little Feat
Warner Bros. WB 3345, 1979.

On the heels of Lowell George's production of the Dead's *Shakedown Street*, Keith Godchaux cowrote "Six Feet of Snow," on this last Little Feat album, released shortly after George's death.

• "Do You Wanna Dance" (Bobby Freeman)
Bobby Freeman, *Do You Wanna Dance* (1958), *Best of Bobby Freeman* (1992)
THE BEACH BOYS, *Beach Boys Today* (1965)
Del Shannon, *1,661 Seconds with Del Shannon* (1981)
T. Rex, single (1975), *The Unobtainable T. Rex* (1980)
Ramones, *Rocket to Russia* (1977)

Because Bobby Freeman was a San Francisco performer whose energetic vocals punctuated two R&B dance hits in the late 1950s and mid-1960s, the Dead were long familiar with his greatest hit, "Do You Wanna Dance," which they performed only once, during a third set New Year's Eve jam with THE NEVILLE BROTHERS. There was a rumor afoot for awhile that Garcia, as a teenager, may have played on Freeman's hit single in 1958. When asked about this by Jeff Tamarkin for *Relix* in 1980, Garcia remembered, "I played with Bobby Freeman, but I'm not sure whether it was released. I played on a demo, but I'm not sure if that's the one that was released."

This is still an unconfirmed session as Garcia would only have been fifteen when the single was originally released in 1958, and there is no evidence of Garcia recording with the label on which the record was cut.

Starting out as a teenager, Freeman formed a couple of pop-oriented Bay Area groups, the Romancers and Vocaleers. "Do You Wanna Dance" just missed hitting No. 1 on the R&B charts in 1958 and was one of three hits he enjoyed that year. Six years later, "C'mon and Swim" rode the wave of the dance craze where it became a No. 5 R&B hit. But when "S-W-I-M" fizzled at No. 56 later in the year, so did Freeman. Still, "Do You Wanna Dance" is one classic piece of 1950s pop and a moment of glory that the Dead and the Nevilles evidently never forgot.

12/31/87, Coliseum Arena, Oakland, California

• *Dozin' at the Knick*
GDCD 4025, 1996. Produced by John Cutler and Phil Lesh. Recorded at the Knickerbocker Arena, Albany, New York, March 24–26, 1990.
"Hell in a Bucket," "Dupree's Diamond Blues," "Just a Little Light," "Walking Blues," "Jack-a-Roe," "Never Trust a Woman," "When I Paint My Masterpiece," "Row Jimmy," "Blow Away," "Playing in the Band">"Uncle John's Band">"Lady with a Fan">"Terrapin Station">"Mud Love Buddy

GRATEFUL DEAD

KNICKERBOCKER ARENA

DOZIN' AT THE KNICK

(© Grateful Dead Merchandising, Inc.)

Jam"➤"Drums"➤"Space"➤"The Wheel"➤"All Along
the Watchtower"➤"Stella Blue"➤"Not Fade
Away"➤"And We Bid You Goodnight"➤"Space"➤ "I
Will Take You Home"➤"Goin' Down the Road Feeling
Bad"➤"Black Peter"➤"Around and
Around"➤"Brokedown Palace"

From its Pranksterish title down to its nectar-dripping offerings, *Dozin' at the Knick* is proof positive that the Dead never stopped passing the acid test. There's enough joyful noise on this crisp three-disc set (the fourth in their *Vault* release project) to wake old Rip Van Winkle from his legendary nod. Culled from the band's hot first appearance at the Knick, the release is kind of a composite dream show from the era with a first set drawn from highlights from the entire 1990 Albany run. This is followed by the entire second set from the first night and a bonus taste from the following night's set two. Yet the grafting is a seamless, if not entirely plausible, example of the last glories of the Brent Mydland–era Dead.

- ### *Dragon Fly*/Jefferson Starship
  Grunt BFL 1-0217, 1974.

Finally coming together to form a cohesive group, the Jefferson Starship put together a shimmering album, which soared to numero uno on the charts. Along with David Frieberg and Steve Schuster, Hunter cowrote the lyrics to "Come to Life" on this thoughtful disc.

- ### "Drink Up and Go Home" (Carl Perkins)

This "face-on-the-barroom floor" novelty from Carl Perkins is only known to have been sung by Garcia at one 1970 acoustic show.

8/5/70, Golden Hall, San Diego

- ### *Drive Alive*/NEAL CASSADY/Merry
  Pranksters/WARLOCKS
  Key-Z Productions, 1991.

KEN KESEY made a couple of choice archival tapes available by mail order in the early 1990s, including these musings of Neal Cassady accompanied by the Warlocks with additional music by Garcia.

- ### *Drumming at the Edge of Magic: A Journey into the Spirit of Percussion* (book)/Mickey Hart with Jay Stevens
  268 pp. 100 black and white and 50 color illustrations.
  Selected readings. Discography. HarperCollins,
  1990.

Drumming at the Edge of Magic is a musical audio-biodyssey chronicling Hart's personal musical journeys. The first book written by a member of the Dead, Hart's tome is a personal account of his discovery of "the spirit of the drum"—from "The Big Bang" through the many influences that he has encountered along the way.

An interesting footnote to the drummer's publishing foray was that Hart persuaded HarperCollins to plant two trees in a Latin American rainforest for every tree cut down in the production of his books.

- ### *Drums of Passion—The Beat*/BABATUNDE
  OLATUNJI
  Rykodisc 10107, 1989 (originally released as *Dance to the Beat of My Drum*, Blue Heron BLU 706-1 D, 1986). Produced by Mickey Hart.
  "The Beat of My Drum," "Loyin Loyin," "Ife L'ou L'aiye," "Akiwowo" (a capella), "Akiwowo," "Se Eni A Fe L'Amo - Kere Kere"

In a collection of songs celebrating the evocative power of the drum, Babatunde Olatunji leads a percolating percussion assault of West African instruments. With Carlos Santana *wailing* as guest guitarist on a couple of tracks, the impassioned call-and-response vocals give melodic shape to the intense rhythms driving this worthy, incantatory album.

• *Drums of Passion—The Invocation*/BABATUNDE OLATUNJI

Rykodisc #10102, 1988. Produced by Mickey Hart. Coproduced by Babatunde Olatunji.

"Ajaja," "Sango," "Obe Lgbo," "Kori," "Orere," "Ogun La Ka Alya"

Babatunde Olatunji–lead vocal, ngomo drum, ashiko drum, djembe drum, shekere. Mickey Hart–hoop drum, concussion stick. Sarah Abukusta–vocalist. Sikru Adepoju–talking drum. Iyalu Akanbi–vocalist. Rotimi Byrd–djembe drum. Frank Ekeh–agogo, shekere, vocalist. Marija Especialze–shekere, agogo. Sanga Francis–djembe drum. C. K. Ganyo–bembe drum, djembe drum. Olabisi Hunter–vocalist. Sundiatta Keith–djembe drum. J. Bruce Langhorne–agogo, vocalist. AIRTO MOREIRA–caxixi. Babafunmi Ohene–djembe drum, log drum. Soji Randolph–vocalist. Gordy Ryan–junjun drum, bell, vocals. Carolyn Seibron–vocalist. Ayisha Shabazz–vocalist. Taiwo Shabazz–ashiko drum. Yao Tamakloe–vocalist. Bobby Vega–bass guitar.

Showcasing his lauded multi-rhythm style in a fresh context, Babatunde Olatunji employs his venerable formula by mixing African percussion with jazz and R&B while fueling the careening, expansive tracks that include everything from the human voice to the most exotic instruments from Africa. Teeming, infectious, and deeply spiritual, *The Invocation* is a blend of traditional and contemporary African and Western elements at its best.

• "Drumz" (a.k.a. "Drums"; "Drum Solo"; "Rhythm Devils")/(Hart/Kreutzmann et al.)

Grateful Dead, *Dead Set* (1991), *One from the Vault*/'75(1991), *Infrared Roses* (1991), *Dick's Picks Volume Five*/'79 (1996), *Dick's Picks Volume Six*/'83 (1996), *Dozin' at the Knick*/'90 (1996)

Known by any number of different titles, "Drumz" is the most commonly accepted denotation of the percussion segment of the Grateful Dead second-set rhythm orgy. Deadheads who used "Drumz" as a cue to visit the nearest *pissoir* were missing something special every night. Hart and Kreutzmann were never exactly in the Keith Moon or Ginger Baker school of showboating but their percussion adventures weren't for the faint-of-heart either. It changed nightly and evolved over the course of years to incorporate the sounds and traditions from every corner of the globe and points both upward and downward. Though there was a drum solo incorporated into the early versions of "Good Lovin'," "The Other One," and "Alligator," the formalization of the mid–second set

Mickey Hart, Spartan Stadium, San Jose, California, 4/22/79. (© Ed Perlstein)

"Drumz" presentation didn't really occur until 1976 when Hart rejoined the band for good.

12/12/69, Thelma Theater, Los Angeles

4/21/78, Rupp Arena, Lexington, Kentucky

10/21/78, Winterland Arena, San Francisco

11/10/79, Crisler Arena, Ann Arbor, Michigan

11/29/80, Alligator Alley Gym, Gainesville, Florida

4/24/84, Veterans' Memorial Coliseum, New Haven, Connecticut

9/5/85, Red Rocks Amphitheater, Morrison, Colorado

3/29/87, The Spectrum, Philadelphia

6/6/91, Deer Creek Music Center, Noblesville, Indiana

6/26/94, Sam Boyd Silver Bowl, Las Vegas

- ### *Duino Elegies* (book)/Rainer Maria Rilke
   (translated by Robert Hunter)
   120 pp. Illustrations by Maureen Hunter. Hulogos'i, 1987,

Rainer Maria Rilke's *Duino Elegies* is a collection of poems by one of the most moving and original writers of this century. As with much of Rilke's work, the *Duino Elegies* reflects the central concern of both Rilke's life and art: the achievement of "being," which this most spiritual yet least doctrinaire of modern German poets defined as his most complete attempt "to prepare in men's hearts the way for those gentle, mysterious, trembling transformations, from which alone the understandings and harmonies of a serener future will proceed."

Rilke (1875–1926) was an Austrian writer whose semiautobiographical poetry and prose have gained him a place in the academy and the hearts of all who read him with lines like: "To love is to give light with inexhaustible oil." His verse is characterized by a form of mystic pantheism that seeks to achieve a state of ecstasy in which existence can be apprehended as a whole.

Rilke was born in Prague and traveled widely. For a time he was secretary to the sculptor Rodin.

Breaking down his approach to the nitty-gritty work of translating one of history's most sensitive poets, Hunter told David Gans in 1988, "Well, you can *read* the German and get the cadence and flow of the German. And I tried to approximate the cadence and flow of the German language in it. My German is not strong, and I used other translations, for example, to show me when he moved into the subjunctive tense, or something, and for idiomatic expressions which I might not be familiar with. And I used *Cassell's German Dictionary*, you know, and broke every word I didn't know down and saw all the shades of meaning. It's very, very good—*Cassell's Classical German Dictionary*—because it gives you the meanings of a German word, say, in the 1800s. The shades of

Bill Kreutzmann, Spartan Stadium, San Jose, California, 4/22/79. (© *Ed Perlstein*)

variation you'll find in *Webster's Complete Dictionary* or the *Complete Oxford*, the *shades* of meaning. Which is very valuable, because I found that many of the words had been mistranslated, I felt, by previous translators, that they made Rilke sound more ambiguous than he was. And I felt very often that the wrong shade of meaning was insisted on in earlier translations and just sort of bled on into further translations. So I think I stopped a lot of it with this. That I have offered alternatives to readings which are kind of tried and true at this point and moved on into further translations."

- ### *Duino Elegies/The Sonnets to Orpheus*/(audiotape) Rainer Maria Rilke.
  Translated and read by Robert Hunter
  Hulogos'i Communications, 1993.

This spoken-word reading by Robert Hunter of Rainer Maria Rilke's best known works was released in conjunction with the publication of Hunter's translation of the poet's *Duino Elegies.*

Hunter described Rilke's oral cadences and emotional resonance with the project to David Gans in 1988. "I took what I felt best supported the emotional tone of the elegies. And it's so easy for me to read it, because it's my word choice. But it's Rilke's ideas, not to forget, and those ideas still rock me when I read them. And reading them aloud, which I've done quite a bit of recently in order to prepare for this reading, I find that the meanings become more and more apparent to me, and the interlacing of the meanings throughout the elegies, the grand idea that this is moving towards—I can't read it enough or speak it enough to thoroughly know it, at least at this point. It's still surprising me."

Discussing one of the recording sessions with Gans, Hunter reported, "Last night I went into the studio with Tom Constanten and did, by my own estimation, one hell of a reading of those elegies. Boy, they just *roared* out of me, and Tom was playing Brahms and Chopin and a little bit of Scriabin as background music for it. I think we've got quite a little number here—I'm going to give it away free to public radio, and also make up cassettes and bundle them with the book because I feel that a lot more people will listen to it on their cassette machines than will ever read the book. Don't you? I think that's the appropriate place for poetry. It *should* be read [aloud]. It's only secondhand when it's on the page."

- ### "Dupree's Diamond Blues"
  (Hunter/Garcia/Lesh)
  Grateful Dead, single, *Aoxomoxoa* (1969), *Dozin' at the Knick*/'90 (1996)

Robert Hunter and Jerry Garcia made a little cottage industry out of reinterpreting some of the most venerable songs in the American folk canon and "Dupree's Diamond Blues" is the earliest example of their talents in this area. Hunter himself has said that songs "like 'Dupree' and 'STAGGER LEE' are studied efforts to continue the oral tradition."

And, like some of the songs that sprang from this well, "Dupree's" is based on an actual event. On December 15, 1921, Frank DuPre shot and killed a Pinkerton detective and gravely wounded B. Graham West, Atlanta's comptroller, in the violent wake of a broad daylight robbery in which he absconded with a diamond bauble. But before the dashing twenty-one-year-old South Carolina native met his fate on the gallows the following September, he became something of a *cause célèbre* in the region, a veritable O. J. Simpson of his time. Naturally, DuPre's crime sprang up in folk songs, even as he was waiting in jail to meet his Maker.

Discussing the graphic qualities of the song with Charles Reich and Jann Wenner in 1971, Garcia noted: " 'Dupree' is one of my favorite recorded ones, too; it reminds me of a little cartoon strip, with cartoon characters. It has a banjo in it, a little twelve-string and stuff like that. Texturally, it's really successful to my ears. It does what it's supposed to. It has a little sort of calliope sound where T.C. [Tom Constanten] is playing a *perfect* organ part for it. All that stuff was *there*, it's just a matter of making it work."

A side note regarding the song's composition. As Hunter explained to Leslie D. Kippel and Toni Brown of *Relix* in 1981, "I only wrote one song drunk. That was 'Dupree's Diamond Blues.' I wrote it when I was good and drunk one night. My best writing comes when I am perfectly straight. No beer even . . . for at least three or four days. I do exercises . . . my head is clear . . . I can turn it out."

The Dead are known to have performed "Dupree's Diamond Blues" about a dozen times in 1969 but shelved it until 1977, after which it became a sporadic first-set surprise. The Dead were probably the last touring artists still singing a song about Frank DuPre and warning us that "jelly roll will drive you stone-mad."

3/31/85, Cumberland County Civic Center, Portland, Maine

· *Dupree's Diamond News*
(magazine)

Like *RELIX*, *Dupree's* started out as little more than a Xerox-art freebie by John Dwork and Sally Ansorge Mulvey circulated at Dead shows in 1986. Dwork stayed true to the zine's credo by specifically focusing on "Documenting the Deadhead Experience" while covering other bands (including Phish, Blues Traveler, and Rusted Root) before the Dead disbanded. Even after it became the quarterly, four-color journal it is today, *DDN* adhered to its benevolent and environmentally aware roots by handing out free flyers with recent set lists and excerpts from the magazine at Dead shows.

Dwork got his start as a publisher and archivist with *Dead Beat*, which was put out by the Hampshire College Grateful Dead Society in 1978. In 1986, they joined forces with *Terrapin Flyer*, another early Deadzine, and took to the road.

Carving out a niche for itself as the socially conscious voice of the Deadhead universe, *DDN* supplements set lists and band interviews with articles on environmental activism.

DDN published *Garcia: A Grateful Celebration*, a beautiful 104-page paperbound tribute to Jerry Garcia that included great photos, Robert Hunter poetry, and reflections from the Dead family. In 1997, Dwork was overseeing the production of *The Deadheads' Taping Compendium*, an exhaustive, two-volume in-depth accounting of every Grateful Dead concert, to be published in 1998 by Henry Holt & Co.

Bob Dylan recording *Highway 61 Revisited*, 1965. *(The New York Public Library for the Performing Arts)*

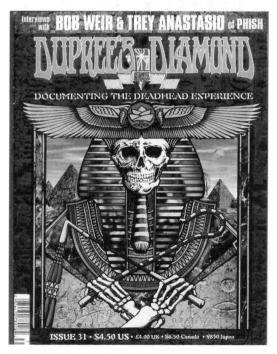

(Pasework/DDN Inc. 1995)

· **Bob Dylan**
Born Robert Zimmerman, May 24, 1941, Duluth, Minnesota

See the entries for his songs: **"All Along the Watchtower," "Ballad of a Thin Man," "Ballad of Frankie Lee and Judas Priest," "Chimes of Freedom," "Dead Man, Dead Man," "Desolation Row," "Don't Think Twice, It's Alright," "Forever Young," "Gotta Serve Somebody," "Heart of Mine,"**

"Highway 61 Revisited," "I'll Be Your Baby Tonight," "It's All Over Now, Baby Blue," "It Takes a lot to Laugh (It Takes a Train to Cry)," "I Want You," "Joey," "John Brown," "Just Like Tom Thumb's Blues," "Knockin' on Heaven's Door," "Maggie's Farm," "Man of Peace," "Quinn the Eskimo," "Mr. Tambourine Man," "Queen Jane Approximately," "Rainy Day Women #12 and 35," "She Belongs to Me," "Shelter from the Storm," "Simple Twist of Fate," "Slow Train," "(Stuck Inside of Mobile with the) Memphis Blues Again," "Tangled up in Blue," "The Times They Are a-Changin'," "Tomorrow Is a Long Time," "Visions of Johanna," "Watching the River Flow," "When I Paint My Masterpiece," "The Wicked Messenger."

- ### Dylan & the Dead
  Columbia OC 45056, 1989. Produced by Jerry Garcia and John Cutler.
  "Slow Train," "I Want You," "Gotta Serve Somebody," "Queen Jane Approximately," "Joey," "All Along the Watchtower," "Knockin' on Heaven's Door"

Admirers of the 1987 six-concert collaboration of these two legends felt that it was a shame that this document didn't adequately reflect the excitement and excellence of those shows. With their common roots in American musical traditions, Dylan and the Dead created a fresh musical vision onstage. This fusion, combining more than fifty years of musical expression, challenged and inspired fans both old and new, distilling the lightning flash and fluid drive of the Grateful Dead with the lyric passion and dark intensity of BOB DYLAN. Only "All Along the Watchtower" sprouts wings and soars amidst this ill-chosen track list.

- ### Bob Dylan's Greatest Hits
  ### Volume 3/BOB DYLAN
  Columbia CK 66783, 1994.

Bob Dylan saturated the market with several products in late 1994 and early 1995, and this volume, despite the inclusion of a fine never-before-released track entitled "Dignity," was undoubtedly the weakest. Critics not only lambasted the release as a crass marketing exploitation to ride the wave of Dylan's newfound Generation X popularity on the heels of his well-received Woodstock II and *MTV Unplugged* performances but derided both the choices on the disc and the haphazard order in which they were presented as well.

"Silvio," the Robert Hunter lyric that includes a backup-vocal track by Garcia, Weir, and Mydland, suffers anew in the harsh light of re-release noon. The song did receive a certain degree of airplay and, unlike some of the other inclusions on the album, is maybe considered a "greatest hit" if not a great song.

(Courtesy of Rykodisc)

- ### Dzintars: Songs of Amber/The Latvian Women's Choir
  Rykodisc RCD 10130, 1990. Produced by Mickey Hart and Jerry Garcia.
  "Blow, Wind, Blow," "Breaking Flax," "The Sun Moves Quickly," "Sleep My Child," "Song of the Wind," "So Silent Is the Ukrainian Night," "The Forest Shook from Dancing," "Orphan Girl in White," "Da Raike Christman Masquerade (Mummery Song)," "Oi Hanuke," "Autumn Landscape," "The Tomtit's Message"

Dzintar is the Latvian word for amber, fossilized pitch turned into a warmly glowing semiprecious stone. Considered very special among Latvians who wear it as jewelry, *dzintar* is a symbol of national identity, representing beauty, openness, and freedom. The Dzintars Choir was founded in 1947 and has become a highly acclaimed professional artistic group under the direction of Imants Cepitis and Ausma Derkevica. The ethereal sound of Latvian music has won them legions of admirers in Europe and the United States.

Amidst *glasnost,* there was a minor rediscovery and renaissance of the folk chorales of Eastern Europe. Hart and Garcia produced this album of traditional and modern songs performed by the Latvian Women's Choir and helped spread the group's magic, which would sound as at home in a concert hall as it would around a campfire.

- *Early Flight*/Jefferson Airplane
  Grunt CYL 1-0437, 1974.

Two tracks featuring Garcia ("J.P.P. McStep Blues" and "In the Morning") found their way onto this beguiling collection of bluesy, druggy, and idealistic leftovers from the Airplane's recorded output.

- **"Early Morning Rain"** (Gordon Lightfoot)
  Singles: Peter, Paul and Mary (1964), George Hamilton IV (1965), Chad and Jeremy (1966)
  Gordon Lightfoot, *Lightfoot* (1966), *Best of Gordon Lightfoot* (1981)
  THE WARLOCKS, *Emergency Crew* demo (1965)
  Judy Collins, *Fifth Album* (1965)
  BOB DYLAN, *Self Portrait* (1970)
  Elvis Presley, *Elvis Now* (1972)

Singer/songwriter Gordon Lightfoot (born November 17, 1938, Orilla, Ontario) gained wide recognition in the mid-1960s when his compositions "For Lovin' Me" and "Early Morning Rain" became big hits for Peter, Paul and Mary. Soon after, Marty Robbins topped the country charts with the Canadian's "Ribbon of Darkness." With an understated style, Lightfoot's tasteful folk arrangements rounded by a gentle burr of a voice were a winning combination.

He began releasing albums in 1966, but it wasn't until *Sit Down Young Stranger* in the 1970s that he scored his first commercial coup and became an in-demand performer. The early 1970s were his, but he hit his peak in 1974 with *Sundown*, which went to Number One as did the title song. A little out of step with perceived commercial trends over the next two decades, his concert appearances in the early 1990s confirmed that he had remained an engaging performer and that his top-notch catalog of originals stand alone.

"Early Morning Rain," perhaps his most recognizable song, tells the simple story of someone who has just seen their love fly away. The Dead's few versions of the song do tender justice to its misty-eyed beauty.

1/7/66, The Matrix, San Francisco

- **"Easy Answers"** (Hunter/BRALOVE/
  Weir/Welnick/Wasserman)
  Rob Wasserman, *Trios* (1994)

"Easy Answers" was the first Grateful Dead song to be released on another artist's album before finding its way to a Grateful Dead disc. "Easy Answers" asks the difficult questions about the intricacies of romantic entanglement with a hint toward the larger issues and the relationships within the family of humanity.

Rob Wasserman described the shaping of the song in the liner notes to his *Trios* album on which the song first appeared: "The night before this session, Bob Weir and I were rehearsing a song idea for our trio with Neil Young. As we were wrapping up he asked me if I wanted to hear another new tune he had been working on. The next day Neil, Bobby, and I were sitting in Neil's ancient vintage Cadillac listening to both songs and we decided to record the newer one from the previous evening, which, needless to say, became 'Easy Answers'! Bobby recorded his lead vocal around midnight. Neil and I wouldn't let him do it over again as we both felt that he had captured the true spirit of a preacher in his late-night delivery. I remember thinking that the song must be pretty good when I saw Neil simultaneously washing dinner dishes at the studio sink and dancing nonstop while he listened to the playback. He commented that my vocal part sounded like a disinterested New Yorker on a street corner using a pay phone while singing the words 'easy answers'!"

6/5/93, Giants Stadium, East Rutherford, New Jersey

▪ "Easy to Love You" (Mydland/Barlow)
Grateful Dead, *Go to Heaven* (1980)

Brent Mydland, despite his detractors who found fault with what they felt was his angry stage presence and repertoire, had a very sweet and sentimental aspect that this song reveals. Unabashedly saccharine, "Easy to Love You" was an uplifting first set love song when the Dead focused on performing it in 1979 and 1980. Ironically, after a ten-year absence from their set lists, the Dead revived "Easy to Love You" for nine performances in the months just prior to Mydland's death in July 1990.

6/8/80, Folsom Field, Boulder, Colorado

▪ "Easy Wind" (Robert Hunter)
Grateful Dead, *Workingman's Dead* (1970)
Robert Hunter, *Live '85* (1985)

Hunter wrote the perfect song for Pigpen when he gave the brash performer this hard-edged blue-collar blues. "Easy Wind" concerns itself with the imagery and toils of a laborer "balling a steel jack hammer" on a road crew. Unlike many of Pigpen's concert songs, "Easy Wind" didn't really lend itself to the vocal improvising talents he was famous for. However, it did open itself up for churning musicianship as the Dead delivered many punchy readings of "Easy Wind" when they featured it in their concerts between 1969 and 1971.

In 1993, Hunter recalled to Blair Jackson the genesis of the swamp rocker via Marin County. "How I wrote 'Easy Wind' was I'd been listening to Robert Johnson and liking Delta blues an awful lot, so I sat down to write down a blues a la Robert Johnson. I played it for Pigpen and he dug it, so he did it. My arrangement was a little bit closer to one of those slippin' and slidin' Robert

Johnson–type songs because it was just me and a guitar. Then when the whole band got a hold of it, it changed a bit, as they always do. Still, a lot of that original style crept over into the band's version."

The song was equally rewarding for the rest of the group. Weir told Jackson that, " 'Easy Wind,' to my way of thinking, was one of our coolest tunes. We didn't play it that much, but I always liked it."

2/27/70, Family Dog, San Francisco
5/15/70, Fillmore East, New York
2/21/71, Capitol Theater, New York

▪ *Eclipse*/HAMZA EL DIN
Rykodisc RACS 0103, 1988. Produced by Mickey Hart. Originally recorded by Hart in 1978.
"Helalisa (Nubian Song)," "The Visitors," "Ollin Arageed," "Your Love Is Ever Young," "Mwashah"

These meditatively paced traditional songs by the Sudanese master of the oud include "OLLIN ARAGEED," the traditional Nubian composition Hamza performed with the Grateful Dead.

▪ *Electric Guitar Quartet*/Electric Guitar Quartet
EGQ Cassettes, 1983.

Tom Constanten's composition "Alaric's Premonition" appears on this *very* obscure album.

▪ *The Electric Kool-Aid Acid Test* (book)/Tom Wolfe
384 pp. Bantam Doubleday Dell.

Though the effect of Tom Wolfe's epic in new journalism had on the masses in the years following the Acid Tests may forever be obscured by the cultural and political fallout of the 1960s, there is little argument that this extraordinary piece of prose helped shatter the walls of traditional reportage. Adopting a style that perfectly reflected its subject matter (there are those that claim an LSD "contact high" can be achieved from randomly reading sections of the book), Wolfe's account of Ken Kesey's vision quest served as a veritable bible of the psychedelic explosion of the late 1960s.

▪ "Electronic Cybernetic Biomusic"
See Seastones

- **"The Eleven"** (Hunter/Lesh)
  Grateful Dead, *Live Dead* (1969), *Two from the Vault/'68* (1992)
  Solar Circus, *Juggling Suns* (1989)

All the excruciating agonies and sublime ecstasies of Grateful Dead music can be heard in "The Eleven," perhaps their most elusive and mercurial composition. Drawn in the awkward time signature of 11/4 (hence the reasoning of the title), the song was difficult to perform and virtually faded from Grateful Dead concerts after 1970. Melodically repetitive but unusually compelling, "The Eleven" was powered by searing instrumental work and a rhythmically contrapuntal device—you could practically hear the band thinking as Garcia would make run after spectacular run up his guitar neck.

Lyrically based on a confluence of traditional roots, the modality seems to at once invoke folk themes of the British Isles, gospel inclinations of release, and "call and response"—the most common element of African tribal music.

Often utilized as the segue coda of "St. Stephen" and prelude catalyst to "Turn on Your Love Light," "The Eleven" was sometimes performed without lyrics. Truly, there isn't an uninteresting version of this highly treasured and sadly missed piece of the Grateful Dead canon.

"The Eleven" made particularly good use of the Dead's drummers. Hart and Kreutzmann chased each other like the great Orobouros, the dragon snake of legend that eternally pursues its own tail. But the ease of the song's groove was not as effortless as it sounded. As Garcia told Blair Jackson in 1988: "We used to do these revolving patterns against each other where we would play eleven against thirty-three beats, or sixty-six beats, and the other part of the band would be tying into that eleven figure. That's what made those things sound like, 'Whoa—what the hell is going on?!' . . . it was thrilling. But we used to rehearse a lot to get that effect. It sounded like chaos but it was in reality hard rehearsal."

In 1981, Garcia told David Gans and Blair Jackson, "When we started working on 'The Eleven' in the late sixties, we'd spend hours and hours just playing groups of eleven beats, to get used to that phrase. Then we started working things out in seven, playing patterns and phrases and licks that were two and three seven-beat bars long. We had to do it! You can't play confidently and

fluidly in those times without really knowing what you're doing. . . .

"It didn't happen overnight, either. It was a long, slow process that started when Mickey first met Alla Rakha. It was the first time he'd ever heard Eastern players, and he was impressed with their level of technical ability in odd times. . . .

"The challenge was, how do you take these meters and translate them to Western body of knowledge. Our music is basically in smaller increments—two and threes and fours. It's harder for Western ears to hear the longer meters."

Lesh, in his 1990 conversation with Blair Jackson, confirmed some of the song's difficulties. "It was really too restrictive, and the vocal part—the song part—was dumb.

"It was really designed to be a rhythm trip. It wasn't designed to be a song. That more or less came later as a way to give it more justification, or something, to work in a rock & roll set. We could've used it just as transition, which is what it was, really."

A bit of Dead trivia concerns the song's lyrical composition: "The Eleven" was originally conceived and rendered by Robert Hunter as a poetic coda for the bard's equally squirrelly lyric, "China Cat Sunflower."

3/16/68, Carousel Ballroom, San Francisco
1/26/69, Avalon Ballroom, San Francisco (*Live/Dead*)
3/1/69, Fillmore West, San Francisco
3/29/69, Ice Palace, Las Vegas
6/13/69, Convention Center, Fresno, California
11/8/69, Fillmore Auditorium, San Francisco
12/30/69, Boston Tea Party, Boston
1/16/70, Springer's Inn, Portland, Oregon

- **Ramblin' Jack Elliott**
  Born August 1, 1931, Brooklyn, New York

An important link between Woody Guthrie (Jack Elliott's dominant influence both in life and in song) and the folk artists of the 1960s and beyond, Ramblin' Jack Elliott has been on the folk scene since the 1940s. A reservoir of folk-blues, cowboy songs, and early country, Elliott is also a legendary spinner of tall tales (most of them true), an archivist, and performer still treasured by old and new admirers.

Born eleven years to the day before Jerry Garcia, Elliott Charles Adnopoz was the son of a Jewish doctor—unlikely roots for one who would come to be more closely associated with the sounds of sagebrush than the liturgical incantations of a Brooklyn rabbi. An early fan of cowboy music, he ran away from home to join Colonel Jim Eskew's rodeo in 1947, calling himself Buck Elliott. Returning East, he attended New York University, where he took up the guitar around the same time he met Woody Guthrie in 1951. As Guthrie's acolyte and torch-bearer, Elliott perfected Guthrie's repertoire and style so perfectly that it reputedly prompted his teacher to ex-claim, "He sounds more like me than I do!"

Guthrie enlisted Elliott for his last recording in 1954 for Moe Asch and the pair remained close during Guthrie's many years of illness. A year later, as Ramblin' Jack, he ventured to Europe, performing Guthrie songs and an additional repertoire that included a sweep of American and country songs with an emphasis on Hank Williams. His continental travels were also significant because his collaborations with British folkies Derrol Adams and Ewan MacColl were among the first major modern transatlantic unions of the folk music of these two countries and their myriad of musical traditions. The journey also resulted in his first recording date as a soloist for Topic, a British folk label.

Returning to the States, Ramblin' Jack was a familiar sight on stages of the major festivals during the folk re-vival of the early 1960s and he recorded prolifically for a variety of labels. Among these were collections of Guthrie songs as well as a mix of traditional songs like "House of the Rising Son," Jesse Fuller's rousing "San Francisco Bay Blues," and such then-new Dylan compo-sitions as "DON'T THINK TWICE, IT'S ALRIGHT."

A senior figure on the landscape of New York folk music, he befriended and guided many young performers such as Dylan, Dave Van Ronk, and Phil Ochs. When Guthrie died in 1967, he appeared with his students and peers at the Guthrie Memorial Concert at New York's Carnegie Hall in 1968. Renewing his friendship with Dylan in the mid-1970s, he toured with Dylan's Rolling Thunder Revue in 1976 and appeared in the controversial Dylan-directed *cinéma vérité Renaldo and Clara.*

Keeping true to his Beat Generation ethos, Ramblin' Jack recorded *Kerouac's Last Dream* in 1984 and though he has nominally faded from the folk circuit, he does regularly embark on low-key tours.

Ramblin' Jack only played with the Dead on two oc-casions but they were both memorable. With members of Traffic (including Steve Winwood), he joined the Dead at the band's November 23, 1970, benefit for the Hell's An-gels at New York's Anderson Theater for a rousing, rootsy, and raw medley of "NOT FADE AWAY" and the Dead's Guthrie special "GOIN' DOWN THE ROAD FEELIN' BAD." At the 1987 New Year's show seventeen years later, he and DAVID NELSON helped the Dead with their encore that night: Dylan's "KNOCKIN' ON HEAVEN'S DOOR."

■ **"El Paso"** (Marty Robbins)
Marty Robbins, single (1959), *Gunfighter Ballads and*
Trail Songs **(1960),** *The Music Never Stopped: The*
Roots of the Grateful Dead **(1965)**
Grateful Dead, *Steal Your Face* **(1976)**

Marty Robbins's star soared in 1959 with the release of "El Paso," one of the biggest country hits ever. At the time of its waxing, story-songs were the trend in country music, and the previous success of his own "Hangin' Tree" may have inspired Robbins to give this formula another try. Reminiscent of the great *corridos* sung in old Mexico, the narrator of "El Paso" sings a tale of the events leading to his own death in the arms of the woman he loves.

In the words of country music historian Bill C. Ma-lone, "Robbins was a singing cowboy born just a few years too late."

Born on September 26, 1925, in Glendale, Arizona, Marty Robbins was one of country music's most consis-tent hitmakers, with records on the country charts every year between 1958 and his death in 1982. It was in the Arizona desert as a young boy that he began worshipping his first heroes, Gene Autry and the Sons of the Pio-neers, two of the genre's most popular acts at the time.

Beginning with gigs in Phoenix-area clubs after his discharge from the navy in 1948, Robbins soon gradu-ated to his own television and radio show, which gave him wide exposure. He was signed to Columbia in 1952 and his first hit was the sanguine "I'll Go on Alone" in 1953. Similar sentimentalities, including "Pretty Words" and "At the End of a Long Lonely Day," earned him the moniker "Mr. Teardrop."

He destroyed that image in 1954 when he recorded and earned a Top Ten hit with country music's first ver-sion of ARTHUR CRUDUP's "THAT'S ALL RIGHT, MAMA," a tune initially recorded by Elvis Presley (and also cov-ered by the Dead). Columbia exploited this idea of using Robbins to record country versions of pop hits, a formula that devolved into more directly teen-oriented material.

Marty Robbins. *(Archive Photos)*

But in 1959, just when it seemed his greatest talents would never be properly nurtured, Robbins had his first success with a Western-inspired composition and theme song to the film *The Hanging Tree*. This was immediately followed by "El Paso," his first international hit.

Describing the origins of "El Paso," Robbins recalled, "I always wanted to write a song about El Paso, because traditionally this is where the West begins. Western stories that I read and stories my grandfather told me inspired me to write it. I went through El Paso three times before I ever wrote the song. I wrote it on Christmas vacation on my way to Phoenix. Had I been born a little sooner, the cowboy life is the kind of life I'd like to have led."

Although a string of hit cowboy ballads followed (including "Big Iron," a song covered by Bob Weir in his band Bobby and the Midnites), Robbins turned away from the oeuvre by the mid-1960s and devoted himself to more conventional pop composition. He did, however, record "El Paso City," a sequel to his most famous song, in 1976.

Heart trouble severely restricted his later musical activity and eventually felled him on December 8, 1982.

The Dead performed "El Paso" regularly since 1970, but it is in the versions from the early seventies in which the song's drama, B movie though it may be, is best portrayed. Though it's one of the few songs the Dead play that doesn't really lend itself to instrumental jamming, Garcia can, nevertheless, be heard passionately soloing behind Weir's vocal lead through the song, adding effective electricity to the drama. Usually a first-set stand-alone, "El Paso" was occasionally tucked into longer jams as a segue linked with "Dark Star."

9/28/72, Stanley Theater, Jersey City, New Jersey
11/19/72, Hofheinz Pavilion, Houston
2/9/73, Roscoe Maples Pavilion, Palo Alto, California
2/24/74, Winterland Arena, San Francisco
6/10/94, Cal Expo Amphitheater, Sacramento, California

- ### *Embryonic Journey*/Jorma Kaukonen and Tom Constanten
  Relix Records RRCD2067, 1995.

What's better than listening to an alternate version of Jorma Kaukonen and Tom Constanten performing "Embryonic Journey"? For those who answered "listening to eleven versions!" this is the album for you. Definitely one of the weirdest (and most obsessive) Dead-related releases ever.

- ### *Emergency Crew* (demo tape)/WARLOCKS
  Recorded May 3, or November 3, 1965, Los Angeles, California.
  "Can't Come Down," "Confusion's Prince," "Walking in the Sun," "I Know You Rider," "Early Morning Rain," "The Same Thing," "Stealin'," "New Minglewood Blues," "Cold Rain and Snow," "Sittin' on Top of the World," "Untitled"

There's very little on the Warlocks demo tape that gave any indication of great things to come. But as a novelty, the recording is an interesting collector's item with its early interpretations of several songs that would stay in the band's repertoire forever.

The Warlocks went into an L.A. studio sometime in 1965 to put down some tracks with hopes of using the material to land a record deal. Not without reason, it fell on totally deaf ears. The group was still transforming from a jug band into an electric combo, and the original material sounds stifled even by mid-1960s standards.

▪ "Empty Pages" (McKernan)

Pigpen only performed his original song at two consecutive August 1971 concerts.

8/26/71, Gaelic Park, Bronx, New York

▪ "Equinox" (Lesh)

Garcia sang lead on this *Terrapin Station* outtake and ripe tape filler. Discussing the song with David Gans in 1977, Bob Weir described its problems. "One tune that took the longest to get was one that we didn't use, another of Phil's originals. It was just too long, the song itself was too long to put on without crowding something else off the record. It was just very long and quite involved, and it was looking to require a good deal of work—you can only put about nineteen minutes per side on a record before you start losing fidelity. Phil's tune was six minutes long or so and it would have put both sides well over that, so we decided to axe it and bring it back some other time."

▪ "Estimated Prophet" (Weir/Barlow)

Grateful Dead, *Terrapin Station* (1977), *Dick's Picks Volume Three*/'77 (1995), *Dick's Picks Volume Five*/'79 (1996), *Dick's Picks Volume Six*/'83 (1996), *The Arista Years* (1996)

Burning Spear, *Deadicated* (1991)

DAVID MURRAY, *DARK STAR (THE MUSIC OF THE GRATEFUL DEAD)* (1996)

The Dead's jangly psychedelic reggae, "Estimated Prophet" is visionary Grateful Dead at its finest. Ironically, the song was written as a tongue-in-cheek snipe at the band's most fanatical, and sometimes threatening, followers.

According to Bob Weir in his 1977 conversation with David Gans, "Essentially, the basis of it is this guy that I see at nearly every backstage door. Every time we play anywhere there's always some guy that's taken a lot of dope, and he's really bug-eyed and he's having some kind of vision. Somehow I work into his vision, or the band works into his vision, or something like that. He's got some rave that he's got to deliver. So I just decided I was gonna beat him to the punch and do it myself. I've been in that space, and I know where he's coming from.

"If there's a point to 'Estimated Prophet,' it is that no matter what you do, perhaps you shouldn't take it all that seriously. No matter what. I don't know how better to say

it than that with the song. It pretty much illustrates a point that's so nebulous as to defy description with prosaic words.

"It's not that one doesn't appreciate the adulation, but some of the importance that people ascribe to what we're doing may be undue, it seems. I'm not entirely sure that a whole lot of good can come from that. It's music and poetry and it's art, and it can do what art can do."

Describing the song's composition, Weir told Gans, "It just sort of occurred to me, that line 'My time comin' any day now.' It occurred to me with the melody, and it took me a long time to reach into that one line and melodic phrase and pull the picture out of who that was talking. Finally it occurred to me that it was this guy that I've seen at the back door and on the street corner, or whatever, who's taken some dope and had a flash or two and is taking it a little too seriously. He seemed like the kind of guy that you might write a song about. I don't know why. It's a signpost, y'know? 'There but for fortune'—like 'Wharf Rat.' That's a real guy, too."

This said, "Estimated Prophet" was snugly nestled in its slot as a second set centerpiece, especially when linked as the first half of a common and highly regarded jam with the Garcia/Hunter "Eyes of the World." With overtones of a coming redemption with California as the designated site of the narrator's release from human bondage, "Estimated Prophet" incorporates notions of spiritual ascension inherent in both Eastern and Western mystical thought. "Estimated Prophet" also includes two very different jams, one an ecstatic explosion in the song's middle and a brooding foray that often led to "Eyes of the World."

Discussing the song's early evolution with David Gans in 1981, Weir remembered: "We didn't have it on the road originally and we went into the studio and tried to put it down—we learned the song, basically, in the studio.

"Then we went and did one weekend in southern California and then came back into the studio and got it in three takes. It was completely cohesive, as opposed to a disheveled mess. . . . I think we only played it twice; that much is all you really need. It's nice to have more, but it makes a world of difference presenting it to people as a piece. Once you present a song from onstage, that's pretty much where it comes together."

As an indication of the kind of group effort that goes into the nuts and bolts of a Grateful Dead song, drummer Bill Kreutzmann once pointed out that "In 'Estimated Prophet' I came up with the idea of putting two seven-beat measures together to make a fourteen-beat phrase. That's a more comfortable length to play with *and* to listen to. It all hangs together because Mickey and I play half-time over it for most of the song, which gives it a natural feel."

Tom Scott, the legendary L.A. reedman, contributed a lyricon solo to the tune's original release. Discussing his response to the final wash, Weir told Gans in 1977: "Keith [Olsen] said, 'I'm going to bring Tom Scott in and see if he wants to do anything on this stuff.' Being familiar with Tom Scott and his work, it sounded like a good idea to me. I didn't know what tunes he had in mind, really. I didn't know there was going to be anything added on 'Estimated Prophet.' As it is, I'm kinda pleased overall with what he did on 'Estimated Prophet'—it's not often I hear one of my tunes all dressed up like that. It sort of tickles me."

Finally, the line in the song "way up the middle of the air" is drawn from "Twelve Gates to the City," the great gospel-blues rave favored by one of Weir's teachers, the REVEREND GARY DAVIS.

5/8/77, Barton Hall, Ithaca, New York
4/19/82, Civic Center, Baltimore
9/5/85, Red Rocks Amphitheater, Morrison, Colorado
12/16/86, Coliseum Arena, Oakland, California
9/15/87, Madison Square Garden, New York
10/18/88, Keifer Lakefront Arena, University of New Orleans
3/29/90, Nassau Veterans Memorial Coliseum, Uniondale, New York
6/14/91, RFK Stadium, Washington, D.C.

▪ "Eternity" (Weir/DIXON/Wasserman)

Other than Bob Dylan and the Beatles, the Dead have covered more of Willie Dixon's tunes than those of any other recording artist. So it was ironic and fitting that Dixon's last known composition, a contemplative meditation on love, mortality, and the possibilities of the beyond, was this simple, sober collaboration with Bob Weir.

Weir described the genesis of "Eternity" with Jon Sievert of *Guitar Player* in 1993. "I met Willie at the Sweetwater [a club in Mill Valley, California] about five years ago or so. Then I met Rob [Wasserman] at the Sweetwater. And then Rob and I joined up and Rob was working with Willie on his *Trios* project and I said, 'Well, I know Willie. I played with him a time or two.' At the first we thought it might be kind of a cool trio for me and

Rob and Willie. We thought we'd at least go down and pursue writing a tune with him. And, as it turns out, I think it was his last major work. Not unfittingly it was called 'Eternity.'

"Here's a story about that. We were working in Hollywood, and I had this chord progression and melody that I wanted to run by Willie to see if he liked it. And he did, so he started dashing off words. He wanted me to run a certain section by him again and stuff like that, and we started working on the bridge. Then he dashes off this sheet of lyrics and hands it to me. Now, I'm really stoked to be working with the legendary Willie Dixon and I'm prepared for about anything. He hands these lyrics to me and I'm reading through them. And they seem, you know, awfully simplistic. Like there wasn't a whole lot to them as I'm reading through them as I'm reading them from the page. But, still, this is my chance to work with the great Willie Dixon and I'll be damned if I'm going to be picky or blow it. Now he wants me to read through it and sing the melody I have and see if they fit. And so I start singing through these lyrics, and that simplicity takes on a whole other dimension. By the time I had sung through them, it's like my head is suddenly eons wide. I can hear what's happening just sort of echoing around in there and I'm astounded by the simple grace of what he has just presented to me. I'm sitting there with my mouth open, literally, and Willie's laughing. He's just sitting there laughing, saying, 'Now you see it. Now you see it. Dat's the wisdom of the blues.' This happened.

"One of the reasons I think he wanted to work with me was to get out of his bag. And he knew that I would take him a little further than the I–IV–V chords, because I don't do much of that. Every now and again, but not that much. I don't know that he knew this but I guess he had a feeling that I was going to pull him out of there a little bit. I think he wanted that. He certainly pulled me out of my bag, because if I started getting out there he'd say, 'That's too much of that jazz, now, that's too much of that jazz. Bring it back down now.' And I'd do that. So it was real meaningful for me to have that guy make me simplify and bring what I'm writing down to earth. I think I may retain some of what I learned in that session. At least, I'm *hoping* that I'll retain it. To know him was to realize that he was a true simple genius in capital letters. Maybe the only one I've ever met. There's just nobody like him. Nobody could write something that simple and have it mean that much. At least I can't."

9/28/94, Boston Garden, Boston

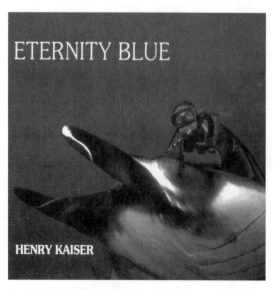

(Courtesy of Shanachie Entertainment)

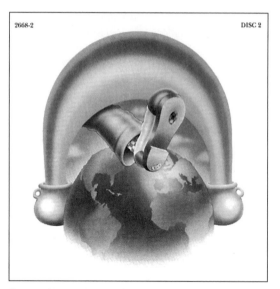

(Courtesy of Warner Bros. Records)

- ### *Eternity Blue*/HENRY KAISER
  **Shanachie 6016, 1995. Produced by Henry Kaiser.
  "Mason's Children," "High Time," "Blues for Allah,"
  "Cold Rain and Snow," "Dark Star">"A Love
  Supreme">"Dark Star," "Blue Eternity,"
  "Brokedown Palace."**

Henry Kaiser's homage to Garcia (partly comprised of outtakes and previously unissued Dead-centric material) explores the Dead's music as fully as any of Kaiser's best. With Coltrane's "A Love Supreme" tucked into the folds of "Dark Star," Kaiser celebrates two of America's foremost improviser/composers and no doubt put a smile on both their faces in Valhalla. With Dead musical family members Tom Constanten and Bob Bralove on board, Kaiser's immensely colorful and curious catalog reveals the truth of his primary artistic tenet: "Improvisation is where the past stops and future begins."

- ### *Europe '72*
  **Warner Bros. 3WX 2668, 1972. Produced by the Grateful
  Dead.
  "Cumberland Blues," "He's Gone," "One More Saturday
  Night," "Jack Straw," "You Win Again," "China Cat
  Sunflower">"I Know You Rider," "Brown-Eyed
  Women," "It Hurts Me Too," "Ramble on Rose,"
  "Sugar Magnolia," "Mr. Charlie," "Tennessee Jed,"
  "Truckin' ">"Epilog," "Prelude">"Morning Dew"**

This crisp, *triple*-album culled from the band's legendary tour of the continent was probably most responsible for establishing the Dead's early popularity with its wide range of musical expression. Containing early definitive vinyl versions of many Grateful Dead standards and a trio of cover tunes, the set also displays extended jazzy instrumental forays. Of the new Dead compositions on the album ("He's Gone," "Jack Straw," "Brown-Eyed Women," "Ramble on Rose," "Mr. Charlie," "One More Saturday Night," and "Tennessee Jed"), Hunter commented to Blair Jackson in 1991, "To me, that material was sort of the kicker followup album to *American Beauty*. Instead, we put out this three-album package that sounds wonderful, but it spread out the material so much we never got to hear what those songs might've sounded like as a package. I personally would've liked to hear those songs on an album of their own."

- ### "Every Time You Go Away" (Darryl Hall)
  Hall and Oates, *Voices* (1980), *Live at the Apollo* (1985)

A unique Grateful Dead one-off performed while backing Hall and Oates at the Rainforest Benefit in 1988.
  9/24/88, Madison Square Garden, New York

- ### *Excalibur*/Tom Fogerty
  Fantasy 9413, 1973.

Tom Fogerty was best known as cofounder of Creedence Clearwater Revival with his more justifiably renowned brother, John. A punchy rhythm guitarist, Tom added zest to both CCR and his live work with Garcia, Saunders, and company. But this, his second solo effort, is not representative of his best work, even backed as it is with the likes of Garcia, Saunders, JOHN KAHN, and Bill Vitt. It wasn't without reason that the Fogerty brothers had a major falling out over John's refusal to allow CCR to record Tom's songs.

▪ "Eyes of the World" (Garcia/Hunter)

Grateful Dead, *Wake of the Flood* (1973), single (1974), *Without a Net* (1990), *One from the Vault* /'75(1991), *Dick's Picks Volume Three*/'77 (1995), *Dick's Picks Volume Six*/'83 (1996), *The Arista Years* (1996)
Freddie McGregor, *Fire on the Mountain: Reggae Celebrates the Grateful Dead* (1996)

Jazzy, flowing, and bright, "Eyes of the World" is another Dead tune that can only be described as visionary. Singing the body electric in the best Whitmanesque sense, the song's lyrics, despite their sometimes embarrassingly hippie-dippy qualities, earnestly suggest that personal and planetary enlightenment are legitimate and attainable goals for mankind. "Wake up to find out that you are the eyes of the world," beckons the song's chorus and with it the hopeful realization that all life is intertwined and interdependent on Spaceship Earth if only humankind can singularly and collectively realize its Utopian potential.

Commenting on the song during his 1986 interview with Robert O'Brian for *Relix*, Hunter admitted: " 'Eyes of the World' was quite mystical and, I think, a very right song for the late sixties and early seventies. Looking back on it now, it's kind of dated . . . it's a song about compassion, as I understand it. Being able to see things from someone else's point of view. It's always a right message, but I think it can be overdone. It can be made corny. Of course there are eternal verities. You can't avoid those too much if you want to want to say something."

2/15/73, Dane County Coliseum, Madison, Wisconsin
9/12/73, College of William and Mary, Williamsburg, Virginia (with horns)
2/23/74, Winterland Arena, San Francisco
6/9/76, Boston Music Hall, Boston
9/12/81, Greek Theatre, Berkeley, California
12/16/86, Coliseum Arena, Oakland, California
3/29/90, Nassau Veterans Memorial Coliseum, Uniondale, New York (with Branford Marsalis)
9/21/91, Boston Garden, Boston

The Grateful Dead, 1972.
(The New York Public Library of the Performing Arts)

▪ "Far from Me" (Mydland)
Grateful Dead, single, *Go to Heaven* (1980), *The Arista Years* (1996)

The angry, unrequited longing of the eternal outsider was a constant theme in Brent Mydland's compositions and "Far from Me" is an early prime example of the artistic ground he most often chose to tread.

Both a classic put-down song and a sober acknowledgment of eternal lost love, "Far from Me" received heavy concert treatment on the heels of the tune's inclusion on the Dead's 1980 *Go to Heaven* LP. The Dead attacked the song's clangy chord changes, awkward bridge, and relative compositional constrictions with zest, slowly developing "Far from Me" into a quiet concert gem complete with poignant backup vocals by Garcia and Weir.

On an arcane note, "Far from Me" was Mydland's most often performed song, with more than seventy renditions in existence.

7/16/88, Greek Theatre, Berkeley, California

▪ "Feedback" (Grateful Dead)
Grateful Dead, *Live/Dead* (1969), *Dick's Picks Volume Four*/'70 (1996)

Before "Space" there was "Feedback."

The Dead always experimented with atonal "serial" aural landscaping in concert. In the late 1960s and early 1970s, before the introduction of higher-tech electronic gadgetry afforded more nimble possibilities, the guitarists would simply turn their instruments toward their amps and attempt to manipulate the torrent of ear-piercing screeches and tortured howls emanating from their Marshalls. Executed near the end of their concerts, "Feedback" was the Dead's trippiest, if sometimes unlistenable, music.

2/14/68, Carousel Ballroom, San Francisco
2/28/69, Fillmore West, San Francisco
5/2/70, Harpur College, SUNY, Binghampton, New York
See also Seastones; "Space"

▪ "Feel Like a Stranger" (Weir/Barlow)
Grateful Dead, *Go to Heaven* (1980), *Dead Set* (1981), *Without a Net* (1990)

Over the years, Weir and Barlow composed a song cycle describing the consummate outsider—a character unable to make meaningful contact with a world that is always spinning away from him, just beyond his grasp. "Lazy Lightning," "Lost Sailor," "Estimated Prophet," and the later "Picasso Moon" are, along with "Feel Like a Stranger," the most prescient in this recurring theme. The sentiments expressed in these songs would also seem to describe the way many Deadheads view their misunderstood position in society. Musically, "Feel Like a Stranger" is a funky romp that majestically opened up for burning, kaleidoscopic improvisation, often early in the Dead's first sets.

9/6/80, State Fairgrounds, Lewiston, Maine
10/12/84, Civic Center, Augusta, Maine
5/3/87, Frost Amphitheater, Palo Alto, California

10/16/89, Brendan Byrne Arena, East Rutherford, New
   Jersey
8/18/91, Shoreline Amphitheater, Mountain View,
   California
3/10/93, Rosemont Horizon, Rosemont, Illinois

- ## "Fennario"
  See "Peggy-O"

- ## *Festival Express* (film)
  Produced by Garth Douglas, 1970–1997.

The Trans Canadian Pop Tour was a legendary weeklong train tour undertaken by an augmenting varying cast of thousands, including the Band, Janis Joplin, Mountain, Traffic, Buddy Guy, Ian and Sylvia, and Great Speckled Bird, for whistle-stop concerts and jam sessions east to west. More than ninety hours of the doings were filmed and surfaced more than two decades later synthesized for this time-encapsuled release of a party to end all parties, which includes the Dead performing "Candyman" and an acoustic version of "Don't Ease Me In." Eddie Kramer, the engineer responsible for the sonically perfect Hendrix recordings, was brought in to add his wizardry to the project.
See also **"Might As Well"**

- ## *Fillmore: The Last Days*/Various artists
  Fillmore 31390, 1972.

The Dead perform "Casey Jones" with the NEW RIDERS and Garcia gives his pedal steel a workout on "Henry" for this triple-LP box set documenting the closing of Bill Graham's fabled venues.

- ## "Fire in the City"/"Your Sons and Daughters" (Jon Hendricks)
  Verve VK-10512, 1967.
  Fire in the City soundtrack (1967)

The Dead backed up the legendary scat-singing progenitor Jon Hendricks for this 1967 studio lark. The songs were part of a soundtrack for the obscure, politically radical film *Fire in the City.*

- ## "Fire on the Mountain" (Hart/Hunter)
  Grateful Dead, *Shakedown Street* (1978), *Dead Set*
     (1981), *The Arista Years* (1996), *Dick's Picks Volume*
     Six/'83 (1996)

Mickey Hart, *Furthur* (1996)
Diga Rhythm Band, *Diga* (1976)
Chalice, *Fire on the Mountain: Reggae Celebrates the*
   Grateful Dead (1996)
THE NEVILLE BROTHERS, *Mitakuye Oyasin Oyasin/All My*
   Relations (1996)
MERL SAUNDERS and the Rainforest Band, *Merl Saunders*
   Live: Still Having Fun (1996)

Not to be confused with the venerable bluegrass breakdown with which it shares the same title, "Fire on the Mountain" has long been established as one of the Dead's keystone jams. A simple two-chord riff, "Fire on the Mountain" had a lengthy and interesting development. It started off as a Diga Rhythm Band percussion exploration entitled "Happiness Is Drumming," but Mickey Hart and Robert Hunter simultaneously constructed an alternate approach to the song, which can only be described as "Acid Rap." The rare, unreleased studio recording finds the band anticipating a trend that predates rap's impact on the mainstream by a decade.

In concert, the song was no less a volatile improvisational vehicle. Usually connected as the back end of its customary linking with the rock-waltz "Scarlet Begonias," "Fire on the Mountain" was a consistently sizzling concert favorite with its extended and explosive jamming for the entire Grateful Dead unit. Garcia in particular often used "Fire" as a musical template for his most extreme guitar experiments where he constantly tinkered with both the tone he got from his instrument and the shapes with which he carved its sounds. Sometimes replicating an astral steel drum, sometimes eclectically electric, Garcia never came close to hitting the bottom of his guitar's deep well.

The song's lyrics don't really make much sense; it's a story of sorts transpiring in a bottom-of-the-barrel gin joint with a "long distance runner" dominating as the vague, mysterious catalyst. Yet, the clarion call of "fire on the mountain" in the song's chorus invokes a mood of apocalyptic portent. The Dead occasionally played off this theme in concert, performing it, for instance, in Portland, Oregon, shortly after Mount St. Helens blew in 1980.

Hunter recalled the lyric's catalyst in *A Box of Rain:* "Written at Mickey Hart's ranch in heated inspiration as the surrounding hills blazed and the fire approached the recording studio where we were working."

Bringing the song full circle, Hart dusted off the early

rap arrangement as a highlight of his Mystery Box sets at the 1996 Furthur Festival.

4/11/78, Fox Theater, Atlanta
9/16/78, Gizeh Sound and Light Theater, Cairo, Egypt
6/18/83, Saratoga Performing Arts Center, Saratoga, New York
7/13/84, Greek Theatre, Berkeley, California
9/15/85, Devore Field, Chula Vista, California
12/28/86, Henry J. Kaiser Convention Center, Oakland, Coliseum
10/14/94, Madison Square Garden, New York
See also **"Happiness Is Drumming"**

▪ *Fire on the Mountain: Reggae Celebrates the Grateful Dead*/Various Artists

Pow Records PWD 7462, 1996. Executive Producers: Judy Cacase and Herb Corsack

"Casey Jones" (Wailing Souls), "Touch of Grey" (Mighty Diamonds), "Catfish John" (Frederick "Toots" Hibbert), "Row Jimmy" (Judy Mowatt), "Uncle John's Band" (Joe Higgs), "Franklin's Tower" (Steel Pulse), "Fire on the Mountain" (Chalice), "Wharf Rat" (Michael Rose), "Eyes of the World" (Freddie McGregor), "Cassidy" (Lasana Bandele), "Good Lovin' " (Dennis Brown)

(Courtesy of Pow Wow Records)

No doubt in part because they share two sacraments (ganja and good music), Deadheads and Rastas have enjoyed more than a bit of commingling. Picking up where *Deadicated* left off, *Fire on the Mountain* successfully brings together two musical traditions, throwing ten and a half Dead tunes into the reggae blender topped off by a half cup of Trenchtown funk. None of the Jamaican artists were familiar with the Dead's music, yet each one of them makes an emotional connection with their chosen song. Check out Michael Rose, Black Uhuru's former lead singer, doing his microtonal melismatic thing on "Wharf Rat," or the I-Threes' Judy Mowatt raising the tabernacle roof with "Row Jimmy," and the power of the Dead's legacy is not hard to fathom.

▪ *Fire Up*/MERL SAUNDERS

Fantasy 9421, 1973. Produced by Tom Fogerty with Merl Saunders.

"After Midnight," "Expressway (to Your Heart)," "Soul Roach," "Benedict Rides," "The System," "Lonely Avenue," "Charisma," "Chock-Lite Pudding"

Merl Saunders–organ, Arp, electric piano, clavinet. Jerry Garcia–lead guitar, vocals. Tom Fogerty–rhythm guitar. JOHN KAHN–Fender bass, electric piano. Bill Vitt–drums. Gaylord Birch–congas. Mike Howell–rhythm guitar. Christopher Parker–drums. Walter Hawkins–lead vocals. The Hawkins Singers (Walter, Tramaine, Lynette, Freddie)–background vocals. Bill Kreutzmann–drums.

Recorded when Garcia and John Kahn were gigging with Merl Saunders, *Fire Up* is a varied disc with a soul-jazz emphasis. Garcia is featured on "Expressway to Your Heart," "Benedict Rides," "The System," "Soul Roach," and a sleepy "After Midnight," which belies the percolations he brought to the tune in concert. "Lonely Avenue," the only live cut included on the album, is the standout here as Saunders and Garcia lead the song to some soulfully funky grooves.

▪ **"First There Is a Mountain"**
See **"Mountain Jam"**

▪ *The Fish*/Barry Melton

United Artists UAS 29908, 1976. Produced by Barry Melton and Dave Charles.

Robert Hunter cowrote and occasionally performed "Jesse James," a fine song appearing on this rare Melton import. "Speed Racer," a minor but pleasant rocker also appearing on the album, was a Melton/Mickey Hart collaboration.

The Flight of the Marie Helena/Robert Hunter
Relix RRLP 2009, 1985.

Following the path he bushwhacked with his conceptualized musical novel *Amagamalin Street*, Hunter recited a seven-part story he described to Blair Jackson as "an adventure. The largest raft the world has ever seen takes off, and then the events of the story are more or less psychic events. It's an allegory about birth, death, and rebirth."

The Flight of the Marie Helena, an extended tone poem cast in Hunter's allusive, mischievously humorous verse, is one of his most ambitious written works. But the spare recording finds Hunter speaking his beautifully crafted voice over his own low-key instrumental backing and has a dreamy quality that may have limited its potential audience.

This was perhaps underlined in a 1987 conversation with William Ruhlman for *Relix:* "It's pretty obvious what the Marie Helena is. It's a microcosm of birth, death, and conscious rebirth, with all of the negatives and all of the positives, and then moves about it all into hopefully a grand dance in which everyone finds their place according to who they are. And I tried putting in as much negative as positive. It's a really rich stew, and I hope legitimately I got to the point of transcendence, which you couldn't do by just saying nice things. You've got to balance everything."

Commenting on his choice of record label, Hunter told Jackson: "What I'm doing with this record is using the power of a small, independent record company, where I know my sales are going to be phenomenally low, that promotion will be zero, distribution next to nothing. Therefore, why try putting out high-power rock & roll records to try to catch the public attention instead of really putting out what I *want?*"

"The Flood"

With Weir leading the charge, this dire song of vague heritage is only known to have been performed at a 1970 gig that fell, appropriately, on the anniversary of the Great Frisco Quake of '06.

4/18/70, Family Dog, San Francisco

John Fogerty
Born May 28, 1945, Berkeley, California

First achieving fame as the lead singer/songwriter and guitarist in Creedence Clearwater Revival, John Fogerty brought a passion to rock that few have delivered. Though he was born and raised in the Bay Area, his music and soul seemed steeped in the Spanish moss of the Mississippi Delta and his songwriting skills spoken in the same rarefied air as CHUCK BERRY, WILLIE DIXON, and Hank Williams.

Fogerty got his start with his brother, Tom, in the late

John Fogerty with the Grateful Dead, Polo Field, Golden Gate Park, San Francisco, 11/3/91. *(Photo: Chris Walklet)*

1950s when they put together the Blue Velvets, undergoing several transformations until signing and recording as the Golliwogs for Fantasy Records in 1964. After first fashioning themselves with a British sound, they were encouraged by Saul Zaentz, Fantasy's new owner, to turn to American roots and change their name to Creedence Clearwater Revival in 1967.

CCR hit paydirt a year later with a Top Twenty hit by reworking Dale Hawkins's "Suzie Q." Fogerty's strident vocals sung over a solid, spare rhythm did for rock music what Booker T. and the MG's did for soul. *Bayou Country*, their 1969 LP, propelled them into the gold record mainstream with "PROUD MARY," while songs such as "Green River," "Down on the Corner," and "Fortunate Son" from other albums were hits as well.

Future albums found the group expanding themes flavor to social and political commentary with a Mississippi Delta. With a reasoned yet impassioned approach, CCR avoided direct comments on obvious pop-music themes and led private, family-oriented lives when not touring. Even before the Dead began handling their own business affairs and booking their own concerts, CCR took control of their own internal bureaucracy. Bill Graham was impressed by their professionalism, once commenting, "This group is the best example of honest businessmen I've met in rock. They are very straightforward."

But artistic differences within the band and increasing difficulty with Fantasy resulted in the band's demise by 1972 and John Fogerty's protracted and bitter absence from the recording biz until the mid-1980s when he returned to form with *Centerfield*.

Fogerty joined the Grateful Dead for a mini-set in the midst of the Bill Graham Memorial Concert on November 3, 1991, at San Francisco's Golden Gate Park where he led the Dead through four of his best-loved numbers: "BORN ON THE BAYOU," "GREEN RIVER," "BAD MOON RISING," and "Proud Mary."

▪ "Foolish Heart" (Garcia/Hunter)
Grateful Dead, *Built to Last* (1989), *The Arista Years* (1996)

"Foolish Heart" was the song from *Built to Last* that was designated by the radio-industry deities as the can't-miss followup hit to the Dead's "Touch of Grey" chartbuster and the tune did receive substantial airplay. But, unlike its antecedent, "Foolish Heart" didn't garner the blockbuster success of "Touch of Grey." However, it developed tremendously in concert with a long, loose jam that arrived at some startlingly intuitive peaks.

Thematically, the song follows the route of many Hunter lyrics that gently attempt to dispense some kind of useful advice in a cryptically playful manner. In this case, the warning is to "never trust your love, my friend, unto a foolish heart." Ironically, as earnest as the lyrics are, its consequences caused Garcia and Hunter to wonder whether the advice was, in fact, correct.

As Hunter commented to Blair Jackson in 1991, "Over the years I've learned what he'll accept and what he'll reject, and what he'll accept is what he can feel speaks for him. Although we did have some problem with 'Foolish Heart,' where he wasn't sure where it was coming from. . . . He trusted me on it. I think it's good advice, but perhaps it's only minimal advice and maybe you don't really need to know this; maybe it's not a world-shaking issue."

In his 1989 interview with Blair Jackson, Bill Kreutzmann remembered the band's excitement when first running through the song. " 'Foolish Heart' is a wonderful song. When Jerry laid that song on us, everyone liked it so much they played everything they knew all at the same time. It was a mish-mash, but we were excited. It was like, 'Settle down, cowboys! Rein 'em in a little!' But after a few times we got the feel for it better. It's evolved nicely."

Discussing the song's openness, Garcia told Steve Peters of *Relix* in 1989, "Nobody is playing any chords. Everybody is playing lines, and they are telling you about the harmonic structure of the tune. What Bob and Brent and Phil are doing is the architecture of the song, it's like an open weave, and it's a style of playing that possibly only the Grateful Dead plays that way really, and it's evolved a little further, partly because of the songs, which generate a kind of openness."

> **3/19/90, Hartford Civic Center, Hartford, Connecticut**
> **6/8/90, Cal Expo Amphitheater, Sacramento, California**
> **9/17/93, Madison Square Garden, New York**

▪ *Foolish Heart*
(video)

When MTV and other music-video outlets screen a Grateful Dead video, it is invariably the endearing

"Touch of Grey" clip that gets the nod. They would do well to spin the sprockets of Gary Gutierrez's equally lighthearted arty vid integrating a lip-synch of the band, stop-motion animation, actual sleight-of-hand magic, and bizarre footage from *Kingdom of the Fairies,* a turn-of-the-century fantasy film by Georges Méliès, a French filmmaker innovator.

· *For Dead Heads*
Round/United Artists SP 114, 1975.

For a period in the early and mid-1970s, the Dead were taking their Deadheads mailing list *very* seriously. Periodically, little GD care packages would pop into our mailboxes with everything from announcements of upcoming concert dates to annual financial accountings to diagrams of the Wall of Sound. Without a doubt, the biggest surprise came in the form of *For Dead Heads,* two 45-rpm singles with each side featuring a cut-off solo project in progress: Garcia's *Old & in the Way,* Hunter's *Tiger Rose,* Lesh's *Seastones,* and Keith and Donna's self-titled duet album.

· "Forever Young" (BOB DYLAN)
Bob Dylan, *Planet Waves*/ (1974), *Before the Flood*
   (1974), *At Budokan* (1978), *Biograph*/'73 (1985),
   ***Bob Dylan's Greatest Hits Volume 3* (1994)**
THE BAND (with Bob Dylan), *The Last Waltz*
   (1978)
JOAN BAEZ, *From Every Stage* (1976)
Hothouse Flowers, single (1993)

"Forever Young" represents something of an oddity in Bob Dylan's officially released output. It is the only song included *twice* on a single album, the underappreciated 1974 LP *Planet Waves.* The first and better known rendition is a slow ode rounding out the A side of the album, while side B leads off with a vitalized arrangement of the song, a jaunty romp with a playful harmonica that almost serves as an antidote for its predecessor.

The tune was conceived in Tucson, Arizona, Dylan remembered. "I wrote it thinking about one of my boys and not wanting to be too sentimental. The lines came to me, they were done in a minute. I don't know. Sometimes that's what you're given. You're given something like that. You don't know what it is exactly that you want but this is what comes. That's how that song came out. I cer-tainly didn't intend to write it—I was going for something else. The song wrote itself—naw, you never know what you're going to write. You never even know if you're going to make another record, really."

Although "Forever Young" was a staple of the Jerry Garcia Band for many years, the Grateful Dead's only performance of the song came during the encore to the free concert in San Francisco's Golden Gate Park celebrating the life and mourning the passing of impresario Bill Graham.

   11/3/91, Polo Field, Golden Gate Park, San Francisco
      (with Neil Young)

· "For the Children of the Eighties" (JOAN BAEZ)
Joan Baez, *Live in Europe: Children of the Eighties*
   (1983)

Just because Joan Baez was having a tough time landing a major record deal in the United States during the late 1970s and early 1980s didn't prevent her from releasing material in other corners of the globe. *Live in Europe: Children of the Eighties* is regarded as the best of several live albums she cut on the Continent around then, mixing old favorites like "Farewell, Angelina" with new originals like "For the Children of the Eighties."

Baez performed "For the Children of the Eighties" with the Grateful Dead at two 1981 shows as an acoustic collaboration.

   12/12/81, Fiesta Hall, County Fairgrounds, San Mateo,
      California

· *For the Faithful*
See *Reckoning*

· "Foxey Lady" (Jimi Hendrix)
Jimi Hendrix, *Are You Experienced?* (1967), *Smash Hits*
   (1971), *Isle of Wight* (1971), *Hendrix in the West*
   (1972), *Band of Gypsies*/'69 (1986), *Live at*
   Winterland*/'68 (1987), *Radio One*/'67 (1989), *Live
   & *Unreleased*/'67 (1989)
Group Therapy, *People Get Ready* (1968)
Booker T. and the MG's, *Soul Limbo* (1968)
The Cure, *Three Imaginary Boys* (1979)
Gil Evans, *The Gil Evans Orchestra Plays the Music of*
   ***Jimi Hendrix* (1988)**

The Dead shared some bills and some private jams with Jimi Hendrix but, somewhat surprisingly, the Dead shied away from the guitar master's catalog. Certainly, some of Hendrix's blues, such as "Hear My Train a-Comin'," would have been interesting challenges for the band. The closest they came was a one-time instrumental jam off one of Hendrix's most recognizable and funky compositions "Foxey Lady."

4/21/69, The Ark, Boston

▪ "France" (Hart/Hunter)
Grateful Dead, *Shakedown Street* (1978)

A loose percussion groove from *Shakedown Street*, "France" never made it to the Dead's concert stage.

Hunter recalled the composition's genesis in *A Box of Rain*. " 'France' was written to tapes of a joyous afternoon Latin jam at Mickey Hart's ranch, the same jam that spawned 'Molly Dee' and 'Northeast by West.' It was recorded by the Dead with abbreviated lyrics and a very different feel."

▪ "Franklin's Tower" (Hunter/Garcia/ Kreutzmann)
Grateful Dead, single, *Blues for Allah* (1975), *Dead Set* (1981), *Without a Net* (1990), *One From The Vault/'75* (1991), *Dick's Picks Volume Three/'77* (1995), *The Arista Years* (1996)
Robert Hunter, *Live '85* (1985), *Box of Rain* (1991)
Steel Pulse, *Fire on the Mountain: Reggae Celebrates the Grateful Dead* (1996)

Grateful Dead songs are filled with mystical locales—regions of Maxwell Parish–esque Utopia that point to an undefined higher calling. "Franklin's Tower" is such a place. Steeped in symbolic imagery, the song paints landscapes and offers timescapes where the four winds blow around a structure that contains a bell with magical properties so powerful that an unnamed brand of salvation may be attained by its ringing. But, like the Arthurian "Sword in the Stone," that ability appears reserved only for the worthy willing to take certain risks.

Hunter, naturally, can't guide us to such a sacred place without sharing some of the advice he'd picked up along the way with such choice Grateful Zenisms as "When you plant ice, you're going to harvest wind" liberally dispensed along the way.

Musically, "Franklin's Tower" is a basic two-chord exercise and, like other similarly simple Grateful Dead

forays, the band brought bright improvisations to the song's performances.

6/9/77, Winterland Arena, San Francisco
1/13/80, Coliseum Arena, Oakland, California
9/11/83, Sante Fe Downs, Sante Fe, New Mexico
4/19/87, Irvine Meadows Amphitheater, Irvine, California
9/25/91, Boston Garden, Boston

▪ *Freedom Chants from the Roof of the World*/THE GYUTO MONKS TANTRIC CHOIR
Rykodisc RCD 20113, 1989. Produced by Mickey Hart.
"Yamantaka," "Mahakala," "#2 For Gaia"

Reprising their initial outing with Hart, TIBETAN TANTRIC CHOIR, the Gyuto Monks conjure some more karma (musical and otherwise) with this release, again not for the faint of heart or casual listener.

▪ *Fresh Tracks in Real Time*/Tom Constanten, Urban Folk Pianist
Tom Constanten Productions, 1989. Produced by Terry Ryan.
"Cold Rain and Snow," "Any Face Card Beats a '10,'" "Hesitation Blues," "Quanto Sia Liet' il Giorno," "Chiclets," "Tabby Cat Walk," "Speaking," "Parallax," "Dark Star," "The Syntax Collector—I. Praalude: The Haight Street Slither, II. That There Old West Is Older Now Than Ever, III. Luder: Licentious Bicentennial Rag, IV. The Green and Gold Take the Cakewalk, V. Postlude: The San Andreas Stomp," "Recombinant Strains—Dejavalse, Land of the Hassled and Free, Claude Greenberg's Springtime Catch."

Typically atypical, this fine collection of solo-piano music is Tom Constanten at an eclectic peak showcasing a couple of familiar standards ("Hesitation Blues" and "COLD RAIN AND SNOW"), a short but gorgeous "Dark Star," interpretations of contemporary composers such as Terry Ryan ("Chiclets"), the Pulitzer Prize winner William Bolcom ("Tabby Cat Walk"), and a bushel of predictably odd originals that tread on everything from Old West saloon ivory tinkling and ragtime to the blues, American pop, and classical. Strange phrasing, false endings, overlapping genres all combine to reveal T.C. at his most playful.

- ## "Friend of the Devil"
(Garcia/Dawson/Hunter)

Grateful Dead, *American Beauty* (1970), *Dead Set*
(1981), *Dick's Picks Volume Five/'79* (1996)

Jerry Garcia and DAVID GRISMAN, *Jerry Garcia/David
Grisman* (1991)

Robert Hunter, *Jack O' Roses* (1979)

Chris Smither, *Another Way to Find You* (1971), *Don't
Drag It On* (1991)

NEW RIDERS OF THE PURPLE SAGE, *Keep on Keepin' On*
(1982)

Tom Constanten, *Nightfall of Diamonds* (1992)

Lyle Lovett, *Deadicated* (1991)

One of the Dead's most recognizable songs, "Friend of
the Devil" has been presented in concert with two dia-
metrically opposed arrangements. During its first incarnation in the early 1970s, "Friend of the Devil" bore a
close resemblance to its spritely, bluegrass-inspired
vinyl companion.

But when the Dead returned to the stage in 1976 after their eighteen-month touring hiatus, the band had effectively transformed the song into a slow, brooding
ballad. This became the standard and seemed set in performance stone especially after it appeared with this
arrangement on the Dead's live *Dead Set* LP. Then, in the
early 1990s, the original version was simultaneously
reestablished so that either rendition was a possibility
from night to night. With this, "Friend of the Devil" became one of the only Grateful Dead songs with such flexibility.

Discussing the song's transformation with David
Gans in 1981, Garcia said, "It's the thing of flashing on
a song from a different point of view. What happened
with that one was that I heard a tape of Kenny Loggins
doing the tune. Loggins and Messina used to do it as a
solo acoustic tune, and he did it as a slow ballad. I heard
a tape of that, and it stuck in my head and I thought,
'Wow, that's a nice way for that song to go. It is a nice
ballad.' It was somebody else's version of the song,
which exposed a character thing to it that I had never no-
ticed before."

Though both Dead arrangements are commercially
available, the *Jerry Garcia/David Grisman* acoustic collaboration again reset the standard. Grisman's mandolin
work on the disc is nothing short of breathtaking.

Hunter's lyrics deserve some investigation here as
well, as he recasts Robert Johnson's haunting "Me and

the Devil Blues" into a spooky chase scene from a Western B movie. A man on the run has made a regrettable
pact from which there is no escape. The two musical
arrangements come into play here as well. In the early,
upbeat version, there is some hope that the storyteller
might escape his fiery fate. The brooding successor,
however, would seem to provide no such redemptive
possibilities.

Remembering the song's composition and his role in
it, John "Marmaduke" Dawson told J. C. Juanis of *Relix*
in 1992, "Hunter and Garcia were trying to come up
with a hook for the song and they weren't having very
much luck, and I said, 'A friend of the devil, is a friend
of mine,' and it just clicked."

Recalling the genesis of the song, Hunter told Jeff
Tamarkin of *Relix* in 1986, "I was playing bass with the
New Riders (although I never did actually get to the
stage with them). We were sitting around practicing one
night and I had 'Friend of the Devil' more or less already
written. I said 'Try this out,' and David Nelson and John
Dawson helped by smoothing out some of the rough
changes. I still have the recording of that evening, and
it's not that much different.

"Then we went down to get some coffee and Marmaduke said, 'It's a real good song but it has that one re-
peating line.' The line was, 'it looks like water but it
tastes like wine,' and he asked me if I could get anything
punchier. I said, 'I got it' and came out with 'A friend of
the devil is a friend of mine.' He said, 'You got it, that's
it.' So I took the tape back to Larkspur house where the
Riders were staying and got up the next morning, and I
heard Garcia listening to the tape. He had that funny
look in his eye. The next thing you know he'd written a
bridge for it, the 'Ann Marie' part. Before that it was the
same melody all the way through. The next thing I knew,
the Grateful Dead had snapped it up, much to the New
Riders' dismay."

Additionally, there is the matter of the phantom
lyrics. As Hunter related to Blair Jackson in their 1988
discussion, "There's a verse to 'Friend of the Devil' that
I do and he [Garcia] doesn't do, which I feel kind of ties
the bow on that song in a certain direction. He's loath to
change something once he feels like it's done, while I'll
tinker endlessly with things, for whatever good it does
me."

That same year, Hunter elaborated on the additional
verse to David Gans: "I may not have given him the

verse at the time when he locked it into concrete in his head. I may have given it to him later and said, 'Here's another verse.' And he had the form—where it should begin, where it should end—formalized at that point. It might open the song up to being a different sort of ellipse than it is. Perhaps. Perhaps he doesn't like the verse, perhaps he's simply being perverse. Check one, check two, check three . . ."

9/20/70, Fillmore East, New York (with DAVID GRISMAN)

5/7/77, Boston Garden, Boston

2/28/82, Oakland Auditorium Arena, Oakland, California

7/2/89, Sullivan Stadium, Foxboro, Massachusetts

▪ "From the Heart of Me" (Donna Godchaux)
Grateful Dead, *Shakedown Street* (1978)

Considering she was a fixture at Dead shows for the better part of a decade, it's astounding to realize how few opportunities Donna Jean Godchaux was given as a lead vocalist. "From the Heart of Me" was one of two originals she sang about two dozen times from 1978 through her departure from the Dead in early 1979.

11/14/78, Boston Music Hall, Boston

▪ *From the Mars Motel*
See *Grateful Dead from the Mars Motel*

▪ "Frozen Logger" (Traditional)
Oscar Brand, *Absolute Nonsense* (1957)
Cisco Houston, *Hard Travelin'* (1958)
Odetta, *At Town Hall* (1964)
The Weavers, *Reunion at Carnegie Hall, Part 2* (1965), *The Best of the Weavers* (1977), *Goodnight Irene* (1994)

A folkie favorite probably derived from the western United States, "Frozen Logger" was sung by Weir and only performed by the Dead at about a half-dozen concerts between 1970 and 1972, sometimes with an acoustic arrangement. It made a special 1985 one-time appearance as a public soundcheck when equipment problems prevented the concert from starting on time.

12/26/70, Legion Stadium, El Monte, California

10/27/71, Onondaga County War Memorial, Syracuse, New York

▪ Jesse Fuller
Born March 12, 1896, Jonesboro, Georgia; died January 29, 1976, Oakland, California

Remembered as a country-blues singer as well as a unique one-man band, Jesse Fuller's classic "San Francisco Bay Blues" influenced many white folk-blues artists of the early 1960s. "BEAT IT ON DOWN THE LINE," a lesser known work, was included on the Dead's debut album and was covered by them in concert throughout their career.

The twelve-string guitar, played with the Piedmont-inspired finger-picking style favored by many Georgia bluesmen, was Fuller's primary instrument. But he was equally renowned playing the "fotdella," a homemade bass that was made with piano strings and played with a foot pedal. When combined with the swish of his cymbals, the wail of his harmonica and kazoo, and the rhythmic scrape of his washboard, Fuller could nearly create the sound of a traditional jug band, an oeuvre near and dear to the heart of the Grateful Dead.

Somewhere during his difficult youth, Fuller learned how to play guitar but he didn't seriously pursue a blues career until he was well into his fifties. Fuller's childhood was spent in extreme poverty. Never really knowing his natural parents, he was raised by a couple who treated him "worse than a dog." He was able to leave that situation by age nine and worked as a cow grazer near Atlanta. After working for slave wages in a lumber camp, Fuller hoboed through the South and West as a young man. He eventually landed work in Los Angeles in the early 1920s as an extra in several films including *The Thief of Baghdad, East of Suez,* and *End of the World.* During the filming of *Baghdad,* he struck up a friendship with the film's star, Douglas Fairbanks, who helped him set up a hot dog stand outside the studio lot.

In the following decades he worked on farms, in the shipyards, and on the Southern Pacific Railroad, which probably inspired the train imagery imbuing many of his songs.

Eventually he moved to the Bay Area where he worked odd jobs, performing at parties and on street corners. Committing himself to music in the early 1950s, he wrote his trademark tune, "San Francisco Bay Blues," in 1954. With his one-man band routine drawing attention, he was discovered in a local bar a year later and shortly thereafter released the album *Folk Blues: Working on the*

Railroad with Jesse Fuller, which included "San Francisco Bay Blues."

As his reputation grew, recording sessions for other labels followed, as well as an extensive and fruitful touring regime that included the college coffeehouse circuit, the famous 1964 Newport Folk Festival, and Europe. Spicing his repertoire with folk and religious numbers, rags, and country blues, Fuller was an extroverted musician who based his performance on a rhythmic style that brimmed with good humor while bespeaking a life of hard work and hard times.

- ### "Funiculi Funicula" (Denza/Turco)
  Grateful Dead, *Dick's Picks Volume Three*/'77 (1995)
  Luciano Pavarotti, *Neapolitan Songs* (1977)

A tune-up number so endearing the Dead actually saw fit to release it. Often mistaken as an Italian folk song, it was actually written by the prolific Luigi Denza (1846–1922) for the occasion of the grand opening of the funicular railway ascending Mount Vesuvius near Naples, Italy, in 1880. Even by today's standards, the publication of "Funiculi Funicula" was a smash hit, selling more than a half a million copies while being translated widely into other languages. G. Turco, a shadowy figure, wrote the lyrics, which tell the story of a young man who attempts to seduce his sweetheart, Nina, by promising her a trip up the tram with its awe-inspiring views of the fiery crater and, in the distance, Spain and France.

The tune has at least two standard sets of English words. The most common of these was written by E. Oxenford and has nothing to do with the original lyrics. C. L. Burnham's more obscure translation is somewhat more faithful to the original. And there are several parodies as well. Though Denza was a director of the London Academy of Music and wrote more than 500 songs, he is best remembered for this memorable ditty.

  6/9/77, Winterland Arena, San Francisco
  4/8/82, Onondaga County War Memorial, Syracuse, New York

- ### FURTHER! Ken Kesey's American Dream (film)
  Produced and Directed by Joan Saffa and Steve Talbot, 1987.

This one-hour documentary on the great American writer and teacher, includes footage from the Acid Tests, the Merry Pranksters, and some quick glimpses of Garcia and the Boys.

- ### Furthur/Various Artists
  Hybrid Records, HY20012, 1996. Produced by Michael Leon, Cameron Sears, John Scher.
  "Spider Fingers" (BRUCE HORNSBY), "Bertha" (LOS LOBOS), "Fire on the Mountain" (Mickey Hart's Mystery Box), "I Need a Miracle" (Ratdog), "Keep on Truckin'" (Hot Tuna), "When the Beatles Hit America" (John Wesley Harding), "Big Mama's Door" (Alvin Youngblood Hart), "Jack Straw" (Bruce Hornsby with Bob Weir), "Knockin' on Heaven's Door" (Ratdog), "Amazing Grace" (Rob Wasserman)

A souvenir of the 1996 "Deadapalooza" tour, *Furthur* compiles samples from most of the artists who made the cross-country whistle-stop road trip (the producers couldn't figure out how to get the Flying Karamazov Brothers or those Samba dancers onto a CD!). The one omission from this otherwise choice compilation would be an example of the rousing all-star jam, which typically capped the evening.

The Furthur Festival

A year after Jerry Garcia's death, former members of the Grateful Dead launched a tour jokingly referred to as "Deadapalooza." Ratdog, co-led by Weir, was on the bus along with Mickey Hart's Mystery Box. Adding to the fun and ceremony were BRUCE HORNSBY, Los Lobos, Hot Tuna, and the Flying Karamazov Brothers. Naturally, a communal jam session ended the concert.

The seven-hour jubilee was named after the destination sign on Ken Kesey's Merry Prankster's bus that put an idealized California on the road. It was the California of fond 1960s memories, where all-American traditions—the blues, country, bluegrass, jazz—were alternately preserved and mixed, bringing together the fatalist wisdom of folk music with the open-ended hedonism of psychedelia. As teenagers danced alongside gray-bearded ex-hippies with cellular phones, Garcia was remembered without mourning. The various performers often worked Dead songs into their sets, drawing waves of applause and sing-alongs. When Hornsby joined Ratdog for a rendition of "Throwing Stones" that reached to a fervent crescendo, Weir's repetition of the lyric "We are on our own" took on a new meaning.

"This festival is gaining consciousness," Hart told the *New York Times* mid-tour. "The musicians are meeting in buses and working stuff out and trying to make the show better. In the Grateful Dead world, we were kept from interacting like this on tour because of the pressures of being the Grateful Dead. This is very refreshing to me and Bob. It's easier. My only gripe is that we don't play long enough."

While it was generally considered that the Los Lobos sets were high points of the Furthur shows, the ex-Dead bandleaders more than held their own with first-class sidemen, if second-rate songs. Though the blues Weir could pull off with the Dead ("LITTLE RED ROOSTER" and "GOOD MORNING LITTLE SCHOOLGIRL") were more like leering bar-band boasts with Ratdog, the band's instrumental stretches moved toward the Dead's supple explorations, particularly when it played "Cassidy" with the piano and guitar catching and extending the other's lines, seeming to ramble but making its way toward jubilant major chords.

Mystery Box, Mickey Hart's percussion-vocal fantasy, allowed the Dead's former drummer to volley cross-rhythms with Giovanni Hidalgo, a master salsa percussionist, and Zakir Hussein, the renowned Indian drummer. As they pursued one another in rumbling bliss, the Mint Juleps, a six-woman vocal group, harmonized Robert Hunter's homilies about love and perseverance. A definite high point of the Mystery Box sets was "Fire on the Mountain," in a old arrangement that featured a rapping Mickey.

The all-star jam session concluding each concert was easily the most Dead-like with various songs tucked into "Playing in the Band" or "Truckin'." David Hidalgo of Los Lobos would briefly summon Garcia's twinkling guitar tone with teasing lines above Weir's undulating rhythm chords, while Jorma Kaukonen brought stoic, searing blues lines to "ALL ALONG THE WATCHTOWER."

Writing in the *New York Times*, Jon Pareles noted, "The concert ended with the central vamp of 'Playing in the Band' drifting toward silence: not a grand finale but a glimmer that will always be rekindled."

▪ "Games People Play" (Joe South)

Joe South, *Introspect* (1968), *The Best of Joe South*
(1990)
Harvey Mandel, *Games Guitars Play* (1970)
The Everly Brothers, *The Everly Brothers Show* (1970)
Georgia Satellites, *In the Land of Salvation and Sun*
(1989)
Jack Jones, *Live at the Sands* (1993)

With Bobby Ace and the Cards from the Bottom of the
Deck (his early sometimes semi-acoustic pickup band that
included Garcia, Lesh, and Hart), Weir turned in a one-off
performance of Joe South's one-hit wonder in 1969.

South was born on February 28, 1948, and by the
time he hit as a solo artist in his very early twenties, he
had just about done it all: country-music DJ, seasoned
sessionman, and producer. His studio sessions included
the electric guitar parts for Simon and Garfunkel's
"Sounds of Silence"; he produced Billy Joe Royal's
quartet of medium hits and a quartet of his own tunes.

"Games People Play" was South's first big solo hit
reaching No. 12 in 1968; it won the Grammy for song of
the year in 1969 and established him as a preachy
straight-talking Southern artist. But after a string of
chartmakers including "Rose Garden," a worldwide
million-selling hit for country singer Lynn Anderson that
was later covered by Elvis and a score of other artists,
South went the way of his name and hasn't been heard
from since.

6/11/69, California Hall, San Francisco

▪ *Garcia*

Warner Bros. BS 2582, 1971 (CD reissue GDCD 4003,
1988).
"Deal," "Bird Song," "Sugaree," "Loser," "Late for
Supper," "Spidergawd," "Eep Hour," "To Lay Me
Down," "An Odd Little Place," "The Wheel"

Jerry Garcia, Polo Field, Golden Gate Park, San Francisco, 6/21/67.
(Photo: Mike Polillo courtesy of Robert Minkin)

Jerry Garcia–guitar, vocals. Bill Kreutzmann–drums. Robert Hunter–lyrics.

Playing every instrument except drums on his solo debut, Garcia displayed his skills on a compelling batch of desperado-rock originals that became tried and true Grateful Dead concert staples. The album also includes a deft and groundbreaking audio collage that anticipates the work of Brian Eno.

Discussing the then-still-in-progress project with Charles Reich and Jann Wenner in 1971, Garcia admitted, "I'm doing it to be completely self-indulgent—musically. I'm just going on a trip. I have a curiosity to see what I can do and I've a desire to get into sixteen-track and go on trips, which are too weird for me to want to put anybody else I know through. And also to pay for this house! . . .

"So far I'm only working with Bill Kreutzmann because I can't play drums. But everything else I'm going to try to play myself. Just for my own edification. What I'm going to do is what I would do if I had a sixteen-track at home; I'm just going to goof around with it. And I don't want anyone to think that it's me being serious or anything like that—it's really me goofing around. I'm not trying to have my own career or anything like that.

There's a lot of stuff that I feel like doing and the Grateful Dead, just by the fact that it's now a production for us to go out and play, we can't get as loose as we had been able to, so I'm not able to stay as busy as I was. It's just a way to keep my hand in, so to speak, without having to turn on a whole big scene. In the world that I live in there's the Grateful Dead, which is one unit which I'm a part of, and then there's just me. And the me that's just me, I have to keep my end up in order to be able to take care of my part of the Grateful Dead."

Garcia, the first studio album to come from the Dead camp since the group's 1970 commercial breakthrough, *American Beauty*, was the peak of his solo career, hitting No. 35 on the Billboard pop chart.

- ### *Garcia* (book)/the editors of *Rolling Stone*
  240 pp. 150 color and black and white photos and illustrations. Rolling Stone Press/Little, Brown and Company, 1995.

Most of the quickie books that hit the shelves in the months following Garcia's death were tasteful affairs. But none came close to *Rolling Stone*'s oversized tome, which reprinted articles from their own archives and a variety of sources, all spiced with rare and choice photos

Jerry Garcia, Orange County Fairgrounds, Costa Mesa, California, 8/4/68. *(The New York Public Library for the Performing Arts)*

evocatively celebrating the man, his music, and his muse.

■ Jerry Garcia

Born Jerome John Garcia, August 1, 1942, San Francisco, California; died August 9, 1995, Forest Knolls, California

"I serve the music," Jerry Garcia was fond of saying, but who could have imagined the scope of that dedication? Perhaps it was destined from his birth when his father decided to name his younger son after Jerome Kern, the suave Broadway composer. José "Joe" Garcia was a Spanish immigrant and jazz clarinetist and bandleader who, before Jerry's birth, was involved in a labor dispute with the local musicians' union, forcing him to abandon playing. Instead he tended bar and eventually opened his own watering hole, the Four Hundred Club. Jerry's mother, Ruth, was of Irish and Swedish descent and worked as a nurse.

Jerry was exposed to Roman Catholicism from birth as well as surrounded by music. José would lull his youngest son to sleep at night by playing clarinet to him. Ruth was an opera fanatic and family gatherings often turned into singalongs. One of his earliest memories was of playing a 78-rpm record over and over until everybody in the house went crazy and distracted him with a toy.

As a five-year-old Garcia was maimed in a freak camping accident when his older brother Clifford (nicknamed Tiff) accidentally cut off the upper half of his middle right finger while the two were chopping firewood. Another mishap took the life of his father, who drowned in a fishing accident in 1948 while Jerry stood onshore. When his mother was then forced to work at the bar full time, Jerry and Tiff were sent to live with her parents for the next five years in San Francisco's working-class Excelsior District. Garcia recalled this period of his life in his posthumous, "anecdoubtal" memoir *Harrington Street*. His grandmother, Nan, was a devotee of Nashville's Grand Ole Opry Saturday-night radio broadcasts and Garcia developed a fondness for the music, particularly the facile, blues-inflected mandolin playing and mournful vocal style of bluegrass founder Bill Monroe. As Jerry Garcia said much later in his life, "See, music was always a part of my life. My grandmother listened to country music and my mother listened to opera. My father was a musician. I was in the middle of music. And nobody was saying this kind of music is bad, nobody was telling me rock & roll was out of tune."

His creative inclinations were recognized early on by his third-grade teacher, a true San Francisco bohemian who pointed him in the direction of the graphic arts. As far as he was concerned, painting was his path to artistic nirvana. But other forms of expression had a strong sway over him as well. When Garcia was ten, he and his brother moved back in with their mother, where she was running a sailors' bar and hotel near the city's waterfront. There Garcia listened to the boozy, fanciful yarns told by the hotel's old tenants.

Artistic inspiration also came from devouring horror comics such as EC comics' *Tales from the Crypt* and films like *Abbott and Costello Meet Frankenstein*, the 1948 comedy-thriller, which his mother took him to see when he was seven. As he recalled in 1995: "I have a general fascination with the bizarre that comes directly from that movie. That was my first sense of, there are things in this world that are really weird, you know? I don't think I knew that before I saw that movie, that there are things that are really weird and there are people who are concerned with them. In some way, that became important to me, and I guess I thought to myself on some level, 'I think I want to be concerned with things that are weird.' I think that seems interesting to me because it seemed like fun. And that is in fact who I am."

His next big musical flash hit when, under Tiff's influence, he became transfixed by the funky rhythms and raw textures of early rock 'n' roll and R&B. The other-worldly sounds of CHUCK BERRY and T-Bone Walker were unlike anything he had ever heard before and he immediately began petitioning his mother for an electric guitar for his upcoming fifteenth birthday. When she bought him an accordion, he demanded they take it to a pawn shop and exchange it. His first axe was a Danelectro guitar, which he tuned until it sounded right, coarsely imitating his new hero, Freddie King.

A textbook teenage underachiever, Garcia ran with a rough crowd and failed school as "a matter of defiance," prompting his mother to move the family down the peninsula to Menlo Park for about three years. But Garcia was also leading a secret life on weekends and during summer, venturing to the California School of Fine Arts in the North Beach section of San Francisco, absorbing the beatnik sensibilities of the neighborhood. "I was going to the art institute on Saturdays and summer sessions," he later remembered. "This was when the beatniks were happening in San Francisco, so I was of that culture. The art school I went to was in North Beach, and in those days the old Coexistence Bagel Shop was open, and the Place, notorious beatnik places where these guys—Lawrence Ferlinghetti, Kenneth Rexroth—would get up and read their poetry."

By the time he was seventeen, though, Garcia had quit school and, for reasons even confounding to him, enlisted in the army ("It was either that or jail," he later quipped)—an attempt to change his life that lasted all of nine months. It was during that stint (which included two court-martials and eight AWOLs) he discovered and began devoting himself to the acoustic guitar he smuggled on base. He met another soldier who played country guitar and got Garcia into finger-picking. "I was just a three-chorder then. I was self-taught and I had never met another guitar player, actually, until I got into the army. Then I met this recruit who played a little bit of finger style and I was totally fascinated by it."

Following his dishonorable discharge, Garcia found his way back to Menlo Park where, while living out of his car, he met Robert Hunter who, coincidentally, just happened to be dwelling in his jalopy after an unequally unfulfilling National Guard stint. Sharing a passion for folk music, canned pineapples, and Stanford coeds, the two were soon thick as thieves and began performing as "Bob and Jerry" at local coffee houses like the Tangent and St. Michael's Alley.

Perhaps the transforming event of Garcia's early adulthood was a car accident he was in that took the life of Paul Speegle, an artist friend of his. Garcia was thrown out of his shoes, through the windshield and landed in a field without a scratch. "That's where my life began," he once mused. "Before then I was always living at less than capacity. I was idling. That was the slingshot for the rest of my life. It was like a second chance. Then I got serious."

Garcia also met Sarah Katz, with whom he formed the short-lived folk duo "Jerry and Sarah" and an almost-as-brief marital union that produced his first daughter, Heather, in 1963.

Attempting to live something of a straight life, Garcia continued to teach guitar while working at Dana Morgan's music store. None of it stopped him from woodshedding with Jorma Kaukonen, DAVID NELSON, Ron "Pigpen" McKernan, and many of the musicians who would forge the San Francisco sound a few years later. Garcia developed a chronic case of bluegrass-itis and

gave up everything else to travel cross country with Sandy Rothman (a local guitar phenom) in search of Bill Monroe and his "high lonesome sound." He bought his first banjo from Bill Kreutzmann, a fifteen-year-old drummer who was also working at Dana Morgan's in Palo Alto. Garcia was soon performing in the area's hottest bluegrass units, the Wildwood Boys, the Sleepy Hollow Hog Stompers, and other acoustic aggregations that included Rothman, Nelson, and Hunter.

The sway of bluegrass was so strong for Garcia that in a 1991 *Musician* magazine interview with Elvis Costello he credited the generally unheralded Scotty Stoneman, (the Coltrane of bluegrass fiddle) with informing his improvisational vision. "Well, I get my improvisational approach from Scotty Stoneman, the fiddle player, who is the guy who first set me on fire. Where I just stood there and don't even remember breathing. He played with the Stoneman family for years; he was just an incredible fiddler. He grew up in bars, and he was a total alcoholic wreck by the time I heard him, in his early thirties playing with the Kentucky Colonels—who used to have Clarence White and Roland White.

"So I went down to hear him the first time, at the Ash Grove in L.A. They did this medium-tempo fiddle tune, like 'Eighth of January,' and it's going along, and pretty soon Scotty starts taking these longer phrases—10 bars, 14 bars, 17 bars—and the guys in the band are just watching him! They're barely playing, going ding-ding-ding, while he's burning. The place was transfixed for like twenty minutes, which is unheard of in bluegrass.

"I'd never heard anything like it. I asked him later, 'How do you do that?' And he said, 'Man, I just play lonesome.' "

Simultaneously, the friendship he was developing with Phil Lesh, a slightly older avant-garde classical composer and jazz trumpeter, led to semiregular appearances on *The Midnight Special*, a folk music show on the Pacifica Foundation's Berkeley radio affiliate, KPFA, and further renown (and paying gigs) in the area.

On New Year's Eve 1963, Bob Weir and a friend were wandering Palo Alto's back streets when they heard a banjo emanating from the music store. It was Garcia, totally oblivious to the fact that none of his students had shown up because it was New Year's Eve and they had better things to do. Too young to get into any of the happening joints, Weir coaxed Garcia into a jam session using the store's instruments, thus sowing the seeds for MOTHER MCCREE'S UPTOWN JUG CHAMPIONS. The jug band with a core trio of Garcia, Weir, and Pigpen, evolved into more of a rock band once the Beatles hit big. "I'm a cinephile," Garcia said once, "and I remember going to see a Richard Lester film one night—*A Hard Day's Night*—and being blown away by the Beatles. 'Hey!' I said to myself. 'This is going to be fun!' The Beatles took rock music into a new realm and raised it to an art form."

Joined by Kreutzmann on drums, they changed their name first to the Zodiacs and then to the Warlocks after enlisting bass player Dana Morgan. As Garcia and crew developed a repertoire of cover tunes from old 45s, they began tearing up Magoo's Pizza Parlor in Menlo Park. In the summer of 1965, Garcia persuaded Lesh to replace Morgan—setting what would become the original lineup of the Grateful Dead. That fall, the Warlocks started performing as the house band for LSD-fueled jubilees hosted by novelist Ken Kesey and the burgeoning band of Merry Pranksters, a free-form anarchist collective concerned with the possibilities of liberating human consciousness. The parties evolved into multimedia shows known as the Acid Tests.

It was during the Acid Tests that Garcia met Carolyn "Mountain Girl" Adams, one of Kesey's flock, and with whom he would form a long relationship and raise two more daughters, Anabelle and Theresa. The events also opened the band's eyes to what a total musical experience could be for an audience and a band. Commenting on those possibilities, Garcia said, "The Acid Tests meant to do away with old forms, with old ideas, try something new. . . . There were no sets. Sometimes we'd get up an play for two hours, three hours; sometimes we'd play for ten minutes and all freak out and split. We'd just do it however it would happen. It wasn't a gig, it was the Acid Tests, where anything was okay. Thousands of people, man, all helplessly stoned, all finding themselves in a roomful of other thousands of people, none of whom any of them were afraid of. It was magic— far-out, beautiful magic."

After Lesh claimed he saw an album by another band calling themselves the Warlocks, Garcia and Company huddled in search of a new moniker, finally stumbling upon the phrase *Grateful Dead* in a randomly opened dictionary. The words referred to a genre of folktales in which a Good Samaritan arranges for the burial of a pen-

Jerry Garcia, Selland Arena, Fresno, California, 1/15/78. (© Ed Perlstein)

niless stranger. At some point thereafter, the Samaritan encounters life-threatening peril and is, himself, aided by the spirit of the man he helped bury, hence "grateful dead." On December 4, 1965, the Grateful Dead appeared under their new name for the first time at a San Jose Acid Test.

Developing a Bay Area following, the Dead paralleled the growth of the San Francisco music scene by playing a mixture of blues, R&B, rock, and country covers and a clutch of period-piece originals all marked by their loose onstage jams. Commenting on the Dead's decision to head into uncharted territory night after night, Garcia mused, "It doesn't help having a set list. There was a time probably in the first couple of years that we were playing when we used to write set lists. But we found that we changed them so often during the course of a show depending on how it felt. The tune would come up that was on the list and we'd say, 'Oh no, this is not the right song for right now. It just isn't right.' We ended up doing that so much that it got to be senseless to write a list. It's just easier to read the situation."

With the Dead, Quicksilver Messenger Service, and Jefferson Airplane leading the charge, the sound of acid rock began to galvanize and spread across America. By the time the band's first album was released on Warner Bros. in January 1967, Garcia's guitar personality seemed set: a bright, optimistic siren, alternately bell-like in its ecstatic humor and frightening in its noir agony. Playing the way a dolphin swims with its school, his guitar lines gliding out, shimmering in the sunlight before blending into the group as if nothing had happened. Like any young guitar gun, Garcia liked to strut the speed in his early stuff. Indeed, as demonstrated on "Viola Lee Blues" or any other of the warp-speed numbers preferred by the band at the time, there was little doubt that the man could play *fast*. But it was speed with spirit, as he made every note (and silence) count and communicate with a totally identifiable yet fresh stamp that would mark his sound as he evolved with the grandeur of a seasoned jazzster.

The next four years were undeniably the Dead's most volatile: they produced a series of albums running the gamut of musical influences earning them a national following that was as rabid as it was curious. Along with releasing the studio experimentations of *Anthem of the Sun* and *Aoxomoxoa*, the in-concert fireworks display of *Live/Dead*, and the stripped-bare acoustic albums *Work-*

ingman's Dead and *American Beauty*, the Dead were constantly on the road, playing 141 shows in 1969 and 145 a year later, garnering a reputation as "the people's band." But while the Dead may have seemed to be the ultimate hippie band, Garcia and the Dead were far more tough-minded than many of the kids who wafted into their shows. The Dead were independent, apolitical, free of self-dramatizing posturing and had an ornery edge that turned out to be one of the secrets to their longevity.

Even though the band had no official leader, Garcia managed to project a casual authority with a stolid, impassive, faintly Buddha-like presence onstage. In conversation he turned out to be a street philosopher with a keen wit and a taste for the absurd. Despite, or perhaps because of, all the drugs, he was a lucid, articulate raconteur and spokesman even though what he was a spokesman for was never exactly clear. In any case, he wisely disavowed the role. Yet he wasn't above truthful pontification or waxing spiritual. As he told Fred Stuckey of *Guitar Player* magazine in 1971, "It could be that music is one of those things left that isn't completely devoid of meaning. Talk—like politics—has been made meaningless by endless repetition of lies. There is no longer any substance in it. You listen to a politician making a speech, and it's like hearing nothing. Whereas, music is unmistakably music. The thing about music is that nobody listens to it unless it's real. I don't think that you can fool anybody for too long in music. And you certainly can't fool everybody. There is no music that everybody likes. Music goes back way before language does. And music is like the key to a whole spiritual existence, which this society doesn't even talk about. We know it's there. The Grateful Dead plays at religious services essentially. We play at the religious services of the new age. Everybody gets high, and that's what it's all about really. Getting high is a lot more real than listening to a politician. You can think that getting high actually did happen—that you danced and got sweaty and carried on. It really did happen. I know it when it happens. I know it when it happens every time."

Elaborating on the notoriety the Dead were receiving as the hippie movement reached full flower power in the peak years of the Vietnam War, Garcia was setting the record straight in regard to the group's mission as early as 1967 with words like these: "We're trying to make music in such a way that it doesn't have a message for anybody. We don't have anything to tell anybody. We don't want to change anybody. We want people to have the chance to feel a little better. That's the absolute most we want to do with our music. The music that we make is an act of love and act of joy . . . we're not telling [anybody] to go get stoned, or drop out. . . . We are trying to make things groovier for everybody so more people can feel better more often, to advance the trip, to get higher—however you want to say it—but we're musicians, and there's just no way to put the idea 'save the world' into music."

The addition of two new bandmates, percussionist Mickey Hart and keyboardist Tom Constanten, enhanced the Dead's mix. While the septet concept did not last long, the critical mass of musicians created an atmosphere of possibility present in few other enterprises, musical or otherwise. These were also the halcyon days of the Garcia/Hunter songwriting collaboration, with the two contributing more songs to the band's repertoire between 1969 and 1974 than at any other period in the band's history.

As the Dead continued to morph through the early 1970s with the departure of Constanten, the temporary exit of Mickey Hart, the arrival of keyboardist Keith Godchaux and his vocalist wife Donna, and the death of Pigpen, Garcia, a self-admitted musical junkie, began to record and tour with other bands, beginning an alternate career as a bandleader. His 1971 gigs with keyboardist Howard Wales resulted in *Hooteroll?*, a lush album of instrumentals. His Monday-night jams with MERL SAUNDERS, another keyboardist, mixed R&B, rock, jazz, and soul and produced the albums *Heavy Turbulence, Fire Up, Live at Keystone*, and scores of hot performances that, to some, rivaled the Dead's for passion and intensity. On a completely different front, Garcia helped form short-lived acoustic splinter groups: the Great American String Band and the popular OLD & IN THE WAY, an influential 1973 bluegrass band that helped reignite interest in that genre. At the same time, Garcia established himself as a tireless studio musician who, over the years, contributed his signature licks to albums for artists as diverse as the Jefferson Airplane, Link Wray, DAVID GRISMAN, BOB DYLAN, Kitaro, THE NEVILLE BROTHERS, BRUCE HORNSBY, KEN NORDINE, and ORNETTE COLEMAN.

Garcia, a smashing solo album released in 1972, featured Garcia playing every instrument except drums and introduced a half-dozen tunes that became a part of the Dead's quickly growing repertoire. His second solo effort (also titled *Garcia* but referred to by Deadheads as and eventually retitled *Compliments of Garcia*) added to his own solo band's musical well.

Throughout all this, the Grateful Dead continued to tour relentlessly (including Europe in 1972 and 1974), release albums, start their own record label, and develop "the Wall of Sound," an enormous sound system with giant banks of speakers. Because of the system's excessive cost and time involved with transportation and set-up, it began driving the long, strange trip into the ground. Calling what turned out to be a temporary halt to touring, the Dead played and filmed a string of "farewell" concerts at San Francisco's Winterland Arena in October 1974 and entered a hiatus phase that was anything but laid-back. Along with inaugurating the Jerry Garcia Band with tours and recordings, Garcia holed up in the editing studio shaping the 150 hours of raw footage from the Winterland gigs that were eventually released as *The Grateful Dead Movie* in 1977.

Reunited with a rejuvenated Mickey Hart, the Dead were back on the road in spring 1976 with a bang, following the release of the popular and widely lauded *Blues for Allah* album; they only gained steam with the next year's *Terrapin Station*. The band and Garcia picked up where they left off, settling into a touring regime and performing template they would pretty much stick to for the next two decades. In addition, Garcia augmented his Dead tours with sojourns with the newly incarnated Jerry Garcia Band and whatever studio project came along. He made a couple of underheralded solo albums, *Reflections* (1976) and the extraordinary *Cats Under the Stars* (1978), which provided the Garcia Band a choice repertoire in its many following incarnations.

Although firmly established as a topflight national act, the Dead were in dire financial straits brought on by the debt incurred producing *The Grateful Dead Movie*, the boondoggle of establishing Grateful Dead Records, journeying to Egypt for their famous show there, and meeting the payroll of an extended workforce. Additionally, the continued lack of a hit record kept the band on the road for much of the year.

Making a final attempt to act like a typical commercial rock 'n' roll band, the Dead dismissed the faltering Godchauxs, hired a new keyboard player, Brent Mydland, and released *Go to Heaven* in 1980, never missing a beat. Clearly juiced by Brent's energy, the Dead entered something of a golden age in the early 1980s, sticking to the road, introducing new songs, and gaining legions of new fans on their performance legacy alone. By the mid-1980s, they were playing football stadiums to satisfy their millions of followers.

Never comfortable with being tagged as a hippie nostalgia revue, Garcia told Chris Vaughan of *Spin* in 1987, "The Grateful Dead is always in the process of becoming something . . . depending on the tune or what's going on in the rest of this culture. We are of this time, of this society, so everything that happens touches us."

But all was not well within the Dead's family as was evidenced by Garcia's ballooning weight and drug problem. In 1985 he was arrested in San Francisco's Golden Gate Park for possession of cocaine and heroin—he got off with a community service sentence and a stint in rehab temporarily cleaning up his act. The deleterious effects of years of physical neglect caught up with him big time in July 1986 when he fell into a life-threatening diabetic coma. Garcia regained consciousness after several days and entered into a period of extended convalescence that kept the band off the road until the following spring.

Putting the episode into context, Garcia told *Spin*, "This illness changed me, but then so did LSD. So did going to Egypt. I've had about a dozen totally life-altering experiences. They're kind of before-and-afters. There was the me before I went to Egypt, and then there's the me since I've been to Egypt. . . . When I was in the hospital, the only thing I could think about was, 'Man, if I get out of here, I'm gonna play every chance I get.' The worst thing about being in the hospital was not being able to play."

The coma may have been brought on by his persistent weight problems, and perhaps by his history of drug use. Garcia compared the coma, in which he seemed to be "involved in some kind of incredible struggle," to a psychedelic experience.

Who could have imagined that by the end of 1987, the Dead would become media darlings, rising from the ashes with a high-profile tour with Bob Dylan and *In the Dark*. The Top 10 album spawned a chart-topping single, "Touch of Grey," which vaulted the band, Deadheads, and Garcia into the national spotlight. The result was a huge increase in the band's following and, therefore, increased problems with crowd control. The gypsy following of Deadheads, vendors, drug dealers, and ticketless fans sometimes became too much for certain communities and resulted in the banning of the Dead from some of their more cherished venues including Red

Rocks Amphitheater in Morrison, Colorado, and Berkeley, California's Greek Theatre. Meanwhile local police and the Drug Enforcement Agency cracked down on Deadheads with a vengeance that bordered on the draconian.

In the late 1980s, Garcia also returned to acoustic music. After a short solo tour with JOHN KAHN, the Garcia Band bassist, in 1986, Garcia re-formed the Black Mountain Boys with Sandy Rothman on banjo, David Nelson on guitar, and David Kemper on drums for concerts in San Francisco and a record-breaking run at New York's Lunt-Fontanne Theater in 1987. What made those concerts extra special was Garcia's two-pronged attack: He opened the show with the acoustic band and returned for an extended electric set with the Garcia Band.

In 1991, Garcia started playing with mandolinist DAVID GRISMAN and recorded the acoustic duo album *Jerry Garcia/David Grisman* and the 1993 collection *Not for Kids Only*. The interest in pursuing an album of songs for children may have been inspired by Garcia fathering a fourth daughter, Keelin, in 1988, by his companion in the late 1980s and early 1990s, Manasha Matheson. In addition, Garcia released his first electric solo album in almost a decade, the double-disc *Jerry Garcia Band*, a live recording featuring some of the group's most searing work.

"Soloing can be like a bead game," Garcia said of his lead-guitar approach. "That's the intellectual part of it. It's like these are things that I can string together that will work. I prefer not to be that cerebral about it but I'll do that in a pinch if I feel like there's a complete absence of flow. Sometimes there's an absence of ideas, and then I just play. Sometimes the way to get to that other space is to exhaust your thinking.

"Somewhere along the way, the idea of the value of the negative space, the value of the silence, and the value of the holes and the fascination with dynamics, and what each note is doing became more interesting. So I got concerned with the personality of each note rather than the thrust of an idea. If you listen to the old tapes you can hear ideas being played with that you don't ever hear again. Sometimes that's me doing things consciously and sometimes you get lucky. Sometimes you hit a vein."

Meanwhile Garcia was rededicating himself to the graphic arts, with nationwide art shows that led to a line of J. Garcia neckties based on his paintings, which sold briskly at upscale department stores such as Bloomingdale's. (Concurrently, Ben & Jerry's made its gastronomic mark with a popular addition to American dessert palates: Cherry Garcia ice cream.) Discussing the corollaries between his artistic pursuits, Garcia mused, "I don't find many corollaries between painting and songwriting. The way I approach art is really reflexive. I start and something emerges. In a sense that's the way I write songs but it's really more like playing, it's more like improvising. Something starts to emerge and I begin to go after it.

"I rarely start painting or drawing with an idea. I almost never have an idea. My idea is to make something happen on the paper. That's as far as it goes. And then things come out and I just go with them. Composing for me is more trial and error. I try different ideas and some other voice enters in, which says, 'That's good. That isn't.' It's a process where you are dividing ideas out. I think in art it isn't like that. It would be more like maybe sculpting, where you're taking things away *and* leaving something. For me, songwriting is more like sculpting. It's eliminating ideas.

"Sometimes when I play I have a strong visual image. My original orientation was as a visual artist, so sometimes music is very visual to me, and I tend to play toward that, too. It just has to do with going from a flurry of notes into shaping the notes more carefully and it has to do with that those things are like forms.

"Sometimes I see notes as forms that are pointed at one end and diffused at the other. Or round at one end and sharp or shiny. There's lots of texture and form to them the way I imagine them. I see them in perspective sometimes; they're like moving away from me. That's kind of like an underwater sort of thing. It's like when fish are swimming away from you. The notes are kind of like that. I think there are other people who have actually succeeded in doing something like that better than me, and so it's something I don't chase after. If I had another lifetime . . ."

While the untimely death of Brent Mydland in 1990 didn't knock the band off its schedule (he was replaced by Vince Welnick), Garcia's continued bad personal habits did. Shortly after turning fifty in 1992, Garcia's failing health once again forced the temporary postponement of Grateful Dead concert activities. Diagnosed with exhaustion and a congested heart, Garcia was ordered to quit smoking, eat better, exercise, and fly right. He took these recommendations to heart and went on a health

Jerry Garcia, Greek Theatre, University of California at Berkeley, 9/13/81. *(© Ed Perlstein)*

kick, losing sixty pounds, tapering his cigarette intake, and resumed scuba diving, a passion he had developed after his first health crisis in 1986.

Discussing the effect scuba diving had on his well-being, Garcia said, "I don't think my diving experiences have influenced the music in any direct way. It's influenced a lot of things in my life because it kind of takes up some of the space that drugs left insofar as it's like going to a different world. And physically, it's good for you. But it satisfies that thing of going to space. You're in a place where there's no gravity and you're surrounded by a whole raft of interesting life forms, many of which are interactive. You can't go to the forest and pet raccoons but you can go into the water and pet eels and octopuses. You can touch 'em. I love 'em, I *love* 'em. I've done things I would've never believed I was capable of doing by diving."

The band was back in action by December 1992 and in 1993 was ranked as the highest grossing concert attraction in the United States. In 1994, the Grateful Dead were inducted into the Rock and Roll Hall of Fame, and

Jerry Garcia, Oakland Coliseum, 12/92. *(Robert Minkin)*

while Garcia did not attend the ceremony, his colleagues made the trip and brought a life-sized cardboard cutout of him to stand in his place. Less than a month later, Garcia resurfaced when he married Deborah Koons, a filmmaker, on Valentine's Day.

"I like a night that's seamless," Garcia pointed out late in life. "Every once in a while when I've been playing a lot and the band's really warm and everything is going good, I can step out of myself, and it's like the guitar is playing itself and there's no process involved. It's not like thinking, 'Now I have an idea and I'm going to execute it.' There's none of that—it just flows. I try to go to that place. Sometimes I hit the wall and sometimes I suddenly find myself way beyond it. But I find that if I struggle I tend to stay pretty much where I am. It's kind of a thing of releasing some amount of your control. It's like saying, 'I am not going to be in control of this music. I'm just going to let it happen.'

"It's a difficult thing to describe. It's a little like driving a car, and you're having wonderful thoughts and you're having ideas. Like you're riding somewhere thinking something, and somebody's driving the car—some part of you is paying attention and making it go places but another part of you is someplace else en-

tirely. It's a little bit like that insofar as some other part of your consciousness is dealing with the thing of making the music happen, and you're almost like a spectator. Sometimes in that space, I go 'Wow! Listen to that! That was cool.'"

The Dead's thirtieth year on the road, 1995, began in typical fashion with spring and summer tours (the latter included an opening set by Bob Dylan). Garcia found time to contribute a couple of covers to the soundtrack of the quirky New York film, *Smoke*: Jerome Kern's "Smoke Gets in Your Eyes" and Jerry Butler's "Cigarettes and Coffee." It was during the summer tour, however, that things began to go terribly wrong. A gate-crashing incident in Indiana in July forced the cancellation of a show, and at a Missouri campsite several nights later dozens of Deadheads were injured, some critically, when a weak structure collapsed during a thunderstorm. Of equal seriousness was a death threat Garcia received, and his obvious musical and physical struggles onstage as the "tour from hell" wound to a close.

Still unable to shake the web of addiction, Garcia checked himself into the Betty Ford Clinic in Rancho Mirage, California, but stayed only two weeks, leaving for home to celebrate his fifty-third birthday. Persuaded by his wife and friends to stick with the treatment, he began a residency at the Serenity Knolls facility in Marin County. Tired and ailing, Garcia was discovered comatose and without a pulse during a routine bed check at around 4 A.M. on August 9 and, after attempts to revive him failed, was pronounced dead within a half-hour.

The response to Garcia's passing was overwhelming, surpassed only by the outpouring following John Lennon's murder in 1980 and Elvis's death in 1977. Radio stations played Grateful Dead music nonstop, online computer services were jammed, impromptu wakes formed across the country, and public statements mourning the loss were made by everybody from President Bill Clinton to Bob Dylan. San Francisco Mayor Frank Jordan ordered flags lowered to half-staff and flew a tie-dyed flag from City Hall. Going on with his scheduled show that night with his band Ratdog in New Hampshire, Bob Weir told his grieving audience, "Our departed friend, if he proved anything to us, he proved music could make sad times better" before launching into a heart-rending and soul-baring performance.

A private gathering for family, friends, and band members on August 11 at St. Stephen's Episcopal

Church in Belvedere, California, was followed two days later by a public memorial at San Francisco's Golden Gate Park. Resembling a New Orleans funeral procession, it helped begin the healing for the thousands of Deadheads who attended. Garcia's ashes were later scattered in the Pacific Ocean off the San Francisco coast and in India's Ganges River.

It is difficult to determine exactly when or how Jerry Garcia crossed the ill-defined frontier from musician to icon. He certainly never endorsed the media's portrayal of him as a cultural symbol or wished to be anybody's guru, aspiring merely to be a "competent" musician. That humbleness is exactly why Garcia's legacy is overwhelmingly positive. Grateful Dead tours became a late twentieth-century American institution—a mobile Chautauqua of music, communion, cross-generation joy, and the occasional traffic jam. For every show that imploded into noodling mediocrity, there were two or three that showered Deadheads with beneficent rock & roll pixie dust. A century from now people may wonder what the fuss was all about when they come to know the band only via recording. After all, the Dead's most original creation was the gestalt of their concerts—the group's being and purpose, the belongingness that enveloped their audience making it as central to their music as their very voices and instruments.

■ *Garcia: A Signpost to a New Space*
(book)/Jerry Garcia, Charles Reich, and Jann Wenner 260 pp. 50 black and white photographs. Straight Arrow Books, 1972.

Along with Tom Wolfe's *The Electric Kool Aid Acid Test* and Hank Harrison's *The Dead Book*, this uncensored and unexpurgated book (comprised of two *lengthy* interviews with Garcia) was among the first glimpses many Deadheads had of the man. Waxing cosmic, philosophical, and mundane while giving his inquisitors a glib history of his roots and sensibility, this is vintage Captain Trips at his tricksterish extreme.

■ "Gathering Flowers for the Master's Bouquet" (Marvin E. Baumgardner)
The Stanley Brothers, *Clinch Mountain Bluegrass*/'59 (1994), *The Complete Columbia Stanley Brothers* (1996)

"A lot of the songs we do are hymns, songs of a religious nature, so we're gonna include one here tonight. And this is one of the real old ones," said Ralph Stanley, introducing this sweet, mysterious song favored by the Stanley Brothers in the late 1950s, which deals loosely with angels delivering righteous souls to Heaven. The Dead are only known to have performed an acoustic version of "Master's Bouquet," with Garcia on vocals, at one 1969 concert.

12/26/69, McFarlin Auditorium, Southern Methodist University, Dallas

■ "Gentlemen, Start Your Engines"
(Mydland/Barlow)

The late 1980s were a fertile songwriting period for keyboardist Brent Mydland. Four of his songs appeared on the Dead's *Built to Last* album, but he performed a few others that did not make it onto the disc. "Gentlemen, Start Your Engines" was one of these, a slow-burning paean to alcoholic excess that was road-tested at a couple of concerts in 1988. The bluesy, hard-rock flavored composition also featured a space-cum-jazz break in the middle that showed some interesting, if untried, potential.

Lyricist JOHN BARLOW described the song's impetus to Blair Jackson in 1988: "The difference between an alcoholic and a normal drinker is that whereas a normal drinker gets to a certain point and thinks, 'Well, that's enough. I just said something weird,' the same little voice in the back of an alcoholic's head says, 'GENTLEMEN, start your engines!' When other people are starting to question their judgment, that's when *you* decide the race is on."

6/26/88, Civic Center, Pittsburgh

■ "Get Back" (The Beatles with Billy Preston)
The Beatles, single "Don't Let Me Down" (b/w/) (1969), *Let It Be* (1970)
Paul McCartney, *Tripping the Light Fantastic* (1990)
Elvis Presley, *Elvis Aron Presley* (1980)
Rod Stewart, single (1978)

"Get Back" was credited to "The Beatles with Billy Preston," making Preston the only musician to officially share label billing with the Beatles at their request. Preston, one of many known as the "Fifth Beatle," met the Fab Four in Hamburg in 1962. Seven years later, George Harrison saw Preston perform at a Ray Charles show in London. Renewing his friendship with the keyboardist, George brought Preston over to the Beatles' Apple Studios where the group was recording. Impressed by his ivory tinkling and winning personality, they invited Preston to spend the next two weeks recording and filming with them on their "Get Back" project.

After its release, Preston said, "I didn't even know until the record was out that they had put my name on it. It was something that I could have never asked for or no manager could negotiate, just something they felt for me."

"Get Back" was a Paul McCartney tune, but it had gone through exhaustive transformation and rehearsal before the final mix. Intended as a satire on the British immigration laws, the song originally included such controversial lines as "Don't dig no Pakistanis taking all the people's jobs."

When the early drafts of "Get Back" began to circulate via bootleg several years later, McCartney took his share of unjustifiable flak for writing a racist song. In defense of McCartney, it is apparent from listening to all of the song's unreleased versions that he was making a political comment, taking the powers-that-were to task for their rigidity regarding immigration and naming names such as MP Enoch Powell and Edward Heath. The working titles of "Get Back," including "Commonwealth Song" and "White Power," further support Paul's tongue-in-cheek diatribe as progressive satire.

The Dead's only performance of "Get Back" was a sloppy affair led by Bob Weir nearly eighteen years to the day of the Beatles notorious rooftop concert presentation of the song above the Abbey Road studio.

1/28/87, Civic Auditorium, San Francisco

▪ *Gimme Shelter* (film)/Directed by David Maysles, 1970.

All of the promise and hope of the 1960s collapsed on itself one brittle December afternoon in 1969 at a free concert headlined by the Rolling Stones at Altamont Speedway outside San Francisco. On the advice of the Grateful Dead the Stones had hired members of the Hell's Angels as security for the show. While the band was playing "Under My Thumb" a young black person was stabbed to death in front of the stage by members of the motorcycle gang. *Gimme Shelter* is a brilliant documentary that captures the generation's worst bad trip with the coldest of eyes.

Garcia and Lesh appear briefly in a scene shot at the San Francisco heliport when they first hear about the events of the cruel day.

▪ "Gimme Some Lovin' " (Muff and Steve Winwood/Spencer Davis)
Spencer Davis Group, *Gimme Some Lovin'* (1967)
Ike and Tina Turner, *In Person* (1969)
Traffic, *Welcome to the Canteen* (1971)
Dave Mason, *Certified Live* (1976)
Great White, *Once Bitten* (1987)
Thunder, *Back Street Symphony* (1990)
Terry Reid, *The Driver* (1991)
The Blues Brothers, *The Definitive Collection* (1992)

A megahit in the U.S. and the U.K., "Gimme Some Lovin' " was written by Stevie Winwood when the prodigal keyboardist for the Spencer Davis Group was a mere sixteen years of age. The song has an infectious beat and ecstatic organ hook that helped establish the Hammond B-3 organ as a legitimate rock instrument.

"Gimme Some Lovin' " was one of a couple of covers Phil Lesh and Brent Mydland worked up together in 1984 after discovering that their vocal talents blended well. When the Dead broke out the song for the first time during the Halloween gigs at the Berkeley Community Theater that year, Lesh said: "I heard that famous roar comin' back at us when we started that. I've heard it for the Grateful Dead, and I've heard it for other groups, but that was the first time I ever heard it while I was singin' lead!"

Lesh obviously had fun singing this high-energy crowd pleaser when the Dead were performing it between 1984 and 1990. Upon losing Mydland's vocal harmony, the Dead all but dropped "Gimme Some Lovin' " from the set lists after his tragic death.

6/30/85, Merriweather Post Pavilion, Columbia, Maryland
7/15/88, Greek Theatre, Berkeley, California

▪ "Gloria" (Van Morrison)
Them, single, *(The Angry Young) Them* (1965), *Them Featuring Van Morrison* (1972)
Van Morrison, *The Best of Van Morrison* (1990), *A Night in San Francisco* (1994)
Shadows of Knight, *Gloria* (1966), *Ge-El-O-Are-I-Ay* (1985)
Blues Magoos, *Electric Comic Book* (1967)

Tangerine Zoo, *Tangerine Zoo* (1968)

Electric Prunes, *Mass in F Minor* (1968)

Jimi Hendrix, *Polydor Box Set* (1980)

Patti Smith, *Horses* (1975)

The Residents, *The Third Reich and Roll* (1977), *Nibbles* (1979)

Eddie and the Hot Rods, *Teenage Depression* (1977)

13th Floor Elevators, *Fire in My Bones* (1985), *Demos Everywhere/'66* (1987)

MC5, *Live '72 Kick Copenhagen* (1987)

"Gloria" wasn't just a garage-band staple, it virtually invented the genre when the song was released by the great Belfast-based group Them in 1965. Van Morrison wrote the song when he was lead singer for Them and he has continued to perform it over the years. A tad gimmicky, the high point of "Gloria" is when the desired girl in question's name is literally spelled out: "And her name is G! . . . L! . . . O!," etc.

Though they did it now and again as the Warlocks, the Dead didn't begin performing "Gloria" until 1981, when Bob Weir debuted it and some other oddities during a bizarre concert at Amsterdam's famous hash bar, the Melk Weg (Milky Way) on his thirty-fourth birthday. After that the Dead performed the raveup some half-dozen times, usually as an encore.

10/16/81, Melk Weg, Amsterdam

11/1/85, Richmond Coliseum, Richmond, Virginia

1/26/93, Oakland Coliseum, Oakland, California (with Carlos Santana)

■ Donna Godchaux
Born August 22, 1945, Muscle Shoals, Alabama

As the only female musical member of the Grateful Dead, Donna Godchaux, along with her husband, keyboardist Keith, symbolized the sound and image of the band in the 1970s. With her winning stage presence and strident vocals, Donna seemed to capture the imagination of many female Deadheads, who identified with her at the height of the women's liberation movement of the early and mid-1970s.

Donna Jean Thatcher was raised in the R&B hotbed of Muscle Shoals, Alabama, where the likes of Aretha Franklin and Sam Cooke cut the albums that defined the genre in the 1960s. As a teenager, Donna was a member of Southern Comfort, a vocal group that regularly recorded in and around the local studio scene. They scored professional success when Percy Sledge's "When

Donna Godchaux, Lindley Meadows, Golden Gate Park, San Francisco, 9/28/75. (© ED PERLSTEIN)

a Man Loves a Woman" (on which they lent background vocals) hit No. 1 on the *Billboard* pop charts. When Elvis Presley heard their recording of "Suspicious Minds" some years later, he brought the group to Memphis to wax it and several other tunes with him.

After additional Muscle Shoals session work with the likes of Lynyrd Skynyrd, Little Feat, and the Rolling Stones, Donna gave up music and moved to the Bay Area in 1970. She met her future husband Keith, dropped acid, and saw the Dead all in the course of a few days upon arriving in the region, forever shifting her destiny. About a year later, they approached Garcia and were soon hired to enhance the band that, with Pigpen's failing health, was in need of reinvigoration.

Donna's tenure with the band officially commenced on March 25, 1972, at New York City's Academy of Music, sharing vocals on "HOW SWEET IT IS," and although she joined the band on their tour of Europe that spring, it wasn't until the autumn that she began to fully emerge as a backup presence or lead vocalist. But as Donna's confidence increased, her soulful upper-range harmonies melded with Weir's tenor cowboy lilt taking the band's repertoire to new levels of expression. Songs such as "Looks Like Rain" and much of the material from Weir's solo debut *Ace*, on which she appeared, developed powerfully onstage. A couple of cover songs she brought to the band (the gospel-influenced "TOMORROW IS FOREVER" and the brassy "YOU AIN'T WOMAN ENOUGH") fit in nicely with the Dead's presentations of Americana.

Additionally, she and Keith became integral members of the Garcia Band in the mid- to late 1970s and almost stole the show on perhaps Garcia's best solo album, *Cats Under the Stars* (1978). Donna's impeccable work in the studio is clear in the Dead's string of releases during the era: *Blues for Allah, Terrapin Station,* and *Shakedown Street.* Paradoxically, her efforts in concert were terribly uneven—she could make or break "Playing in the Band" with an off-key holler. While some of these problems may have been caused by improper monitor support onstage, they became increasingly hard for the other musicians, and by early 1979, the Godchauxs and the rest of the group mutually agreed to end their musical relationship.

The duo joined Ghosts, a Marin County bar band that developed an intense local Northern California following. But after Keith was killed in a July 23, 1980, car accident, Donna devoted herself to Christianity, religious music, a new husband, David McKay, a bassist and pastor, and her two sons, Zion and Kinsman.

▪ Keith Godchaux

Born July 19, 1948, Concord, California; died July 23, 1980, Marin County, California

Long after his reign as the Dead's preeminent keyboardist of the 1970s had ended, Keith Godchaux may still be the most underappreciated contributor to the Dead's musical legacy. An intuitive pianist with instincts as firmly rooted in the jazz idiom as in classical, Keith could, at his frequent best, be the glue that held together many a jam during one of the band's most explorative stages.

Godchaux was born and raised in suburban San Francisco. He took lessons in classical piano for five years as a child but as a teenager branched to country, rock, and Dixieland as well as cocktail jazz in a trio that worked the local lounge circuit.

The circumstances leading to Keith joining the Grateful Dead were nothing short of miraculous. After deciding that the Dead would benefit from his stylings, he and his wife, vocalist Donna Godchaux, approached Jerry Garcia at a Garcia-Saunders gig offering his services. Coincidentally the Dead were casting for a key-

Keith Godchaux, backstage at Robertson Gym, Santa Barbara, California, 2/27/77. (© Ed Perlstein)

board player to augment the ailing Pigpen, and Garcia invited Keith to the next rehearsal. He was hired after a two-day audition.

Keith commenced performing with the Dead on October 19, 1971, at the Northrup Auditorium in Minneapolis, Minnesota, which was the first stop on a short Midwest/Northeast tour. Tapes of these first shows, including the superlative October 31, 1971, Ohio Theater gig in Columbus (which appears on *Dick's Picks Volume Two*), clearly demonstrate just how quickly Godchaux caught on, sounding as if he had been playing with the band for years.

In the years that followed, Godchaux's elastic flexibility helped propel the Dead into what was easily their jazziest era. With only a single drummer to contend with (this was during Mickey Hart's performing hiatus), the Dead were able to cut those musical corners with ease, and Godchaux's relaxed, lyrical touch added a majesty to music begging for expansion. Chameleon-like in his ability to find the perfect style to fit the song, Godchaux could add Bachian touches to "China Doll," Jerry Lee Lewis on "Around and Around," Scott Joplin on "Brown-Eyed Women," or be a Thelonious Monk clone during the Dead's outside voyages.

When not touring with the Dead, Keith and Donna

toured with a late-1970s version of the Garcia Band and with their own group, which recorded one *very* unsuccessful, bordering on embarrassing, eponymous disc in 1975.

With the return of Mickey Hart to the Dead's recording and touring fold in 1975, Godchaux's percussive-heavy approach and insistence on playing only the piano often clashed with the tonal coloration of the band's overall sound. This, combined with an increasingly dour attitude, heavy (even by Grateful Dead standards) hard-drug use, and marital problems with Donna (exacerbated by years on the road and the challenges of parenthood) resulted in the mutual decision by all parties that the destiny of the Grateful Dead would be best served by their resignations.

Landing with the Ghosts, a hot Marin County bar band, the Godchauxs seemed rejuvenated by the pleasures of the small-scale venues at which the group appeared. But the darkness did not totally disappear from Keith, who was killed in a car accident less than a year later near his home, a few days after his thirty-second birthday.

▪ Goin' Down the Road: A Grateful Dead Traveling Companion (book)/Blair Jackson
322 pp. 35 photos. Harmony Books, 1992.

As publisher, chief cub reporter and Edward R. Murrow of *The Golden Road*, Blair Jackson had the pick of the litter when compiling his indispensable book drawn from the pages of that "Mother of all Grateful Dead fanzines." Interviews with most of the band members comprise the bulk of the book, with the Donna Godchaux and dual Garcia/Hunter powwows taking center stage. But there is something here for everybody, including Steve Silberman's probing article on "Cowboy NEAL" CASSADY, Blair's "roots" research of some of the Dead's most well-worn cover material, and a history of the Dead's musical evolution by way of reviewing the "primal" concert tapes from each year.

▪ "Goin' Down the Road Feelin' Bad"
(Traditional)
Singles: Sam Collins (1931), Mrs. Etta Baker (1956)
Grateful Dead, *Grateful Dead* (Skull & Roses), (1971),
    One from the Vault /'75 (1991), *Dick's Picks Volume Two*/'71 (1995), *Hundred Year Hall*/'72 (1995),

Dozin' at the Knick/'90 (1996)
Woody Guthrie, single (1940), *Library of Congress Recordings* (1988), *The Music Never Stopped: Roots of the Grateful Dead* (1995)
ELIZABETH COTTEN, *Folksongs and Instrumentals* (1958)
Chet Atkins, *Chet Atkins* (1967)
Delaney and Bonnie & Friends, *To Bonnie from Delaney* (1970)
Dead Ringers, DEAD RINGERS (1993)
Don Nix, *Back to the Wall* (1994)

"Goin' Down the Road Feelin' Bad" is an integral song of both black and white musical traditions since at least the 1920s. Though most experts agree that it is of rural black folk origin, "Goin' Down the Road" was popular in the Appalachian Mountains during the 1920s and a favorite among destitute farmers during the Dust Bowl flight from the south-central U.S. The thematic elements of the song suited the Depression worldview well, with a "seen better times but I'm gonna see them again" sensibility.

"Going where the water tastes like wine," one of the song's favored lines, may reference the wedding at Cana where Jesus created one of his first miracles. When the host's wine ran out, Christ turned the water into wine.

Because the song traveled with Okies across America, changing often, Garcia sang a hybrid version of the song that would seem to rely most heavily on Woody Guthrie's well-known rendition, though Garcia said he learned the song from Delaney Bramlett of Delaney and Bonnie during the Dead's trans-Canada train tour in the summer of 1970.

The Dead broke out "Goin' Down the Road" later that year, playing it hundreds of times after that. But the song's prime was in the early 1970s when it was neatly tucked in the middle of the driving "Not Fade Away." Those "Not Fade Away">"Goin' Down the Road Feelin' Bad">"Not Fade Away" medleys were primal and fluid, encompassing much of what made Dead shows the stuff of legend. Though the song's inclusion in Dead shows waxed and waned after that, it always showcased the band's ability to turn a bleak tune into an optimistic anthem of triumph over adversity.

4/28/71, Fillmore East, New York
11/7/71, Harding Theater, San Francisco
2/17/73, Auditorium, St. Paul, Minnesota
9/26/81, War Memorial Auditorium, Buffalo, New York

9/17/82, Cumberland County Civic Center, Portland, Maine

6/25/91, Sandstone Amphitheater, Bonner Springs, Kansas

■ *The Golden Gate Gypsy Orchestra of America and California, a.k.a. The Traveling Jewish Wedding*

Rykodisc RCD 10105, 1988. Produced by Mickey Hart.

"Kalinka," "Tumbalalaika," "Tov L'Hodot," "Hana'ava Babanot," "Joshua's Yiddishe Momme," "Oylupnuv Obrutch," "Cuando el Rey," "Hungarian Dance #5," "Trepak," "Guitara," "Svetyet Myesats," "Monti's Czardas"

Arella Barlev–vocals, tambourine. Gloria Itman Blum–vocal, tambourine. Robert Blum, M.D.–accordion, synthesizer bass, piano. Barry Blum, M.D.–balalaika, contrabass, balalaika, dumbek. Joshua David Burk–violin. Liya Kushnitaskaya Hoefling–vocal, tambourine. Douglas Gerstein, M.D.–guitar, maracas. Nathan Segal–guitar, flute, voice, casio, sound effects. Aubrey Swartz, M.D.–vocal, drums. Clark Welsh–balalaika, domra. Roberta Wollons, Ph. D. –accordion, balalaika. David Wise, Ph. D.–bouzouki, Spanish flute, contrabass, balalaika, piano, vocal.

Despite the cult of Deadheads who took to wearing "Jews for Jerry" buttons on their lapels, Mickey Hart was the only performing member of the Grateful Dead with a documented Jewish heritage. It was only natural then that he turned his attention to traditional Jewish music as part of his world music offerings with Rykodisc.

The Golden Gate Gypsy Orchestra of America (a.k.a. the Traveling Jewish Wedding) awakens the dormant Jewish spirit in any listener whether Jewish or not. The itinerant troupe is comprised of doctors, teachers, engineers, and accomplished musicians who sing and play music together wherever people come to celebrate. Violin, balalaika, guitar, and accordion resonate with heavenly singers from Russia, Israel, and Mill Valley, California. Formed in 1976 by friends from Marin County and San Francisco who grew up with a passion for Yiddish, Russian, and Gypsy music, the group has an eclectic gig slate that included concerts, weddings, bar mitzvahs, and festivities throughout California.

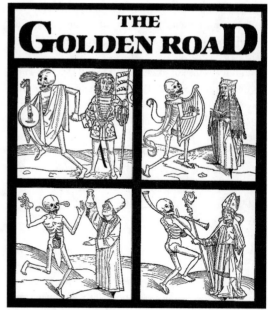

(Courtesy of Blair Jackson)

Capturing some tastes from the Gypsy's musical menu, this album is part of the renaissance of the old country's musical traditions, as if the golden days of the Yiddish Theater have come back to life through these committed musicians.

■ *The Golden Road*
(magazine)

The pinnacle of Grateful Dead fanzines, *The Golden Road* was an important, galvanizing publication during its reign from 1984 through 1993. The zine was the brainchild of Bay Area journalists Blair Jackson and Regan McMahon and was inaugurated in the winter of 1984 as a mail-order-only quarterly that slowly evolved into an annual whopper.

From the start, Jackson and McMahon gave *The Golden Road* a humble design aesthetic and down-home style that brought forth archival photographs, concert reviews, informed letters, Blair's "Roots" column investigating the sources of the Dead's cover songs, interviews with band members and the Grateful Dead family members at-large, reasoned gossip, irreverent but good-spirited satire, and special features such as in-depth articles on Neal Cassady and Pigpen.

Most importantly, Jackson's academic but fun touch lent an air of respectability and scholarship to the band that had been long neglected by mainstream rock critics.

▪ "The Golden Road (to Unlimited Devotion)" (MCGANNAHAN SKJELLYFETTI)

Grateful Dead, *Grateful Dead* (1967), *What a Long Strange Trip It's Been* (1977)

"The Golden Road (to Unlimited Devotion)" was the very first song that listeners heard when they plunked their turntable needles (remember those?) on the A side of the Dead's debut disc. Strangely and unintentionally prophetic in its description of the enthusiasm with which many Deadheads would later approach their relationship with the Grateful Dead, "The Golden Road," with its Yellow Brick Road allusion and Oz-like beckoning, captured the unbridled energy of Haight-Ashbury's Summer of Love.

Garcia told Blair Jackson in 1991 that: "'Golden Road' was our effort at nailing down some of that feeling. I guess. That was sort of a group writing experience before Hunter was with us. We kept it simple."

As a performance vehicle, however, the song did not fare as well as some of the other material on *The Grateful Dead,* as there are only three known live versions, all from 1967.

3/18/67, Winterland Arena, San Francsico

▪ "Good Golly Miss Molly" (Robert Blackwell/John Marascalo)

Little Richard, *Little Richard 2* (1958), single (1968), *20 Classic Cuts* (1986)
The Valiants, single (1959), *Rockin' from Coast to Coast*/'59 (1996)
Jerry Lee Lewis, *Live at the Star Club, Hamburg 1964* (1964), *The Session* (1973), *Live at the Vegas International* (1973)
Swinging Blue Jeans, single (1964), *Hippy Hippy Shake* (1993)
Mitch Ryder, *Sock It to Me!* (1967), *La Gash* (1992)
Creedence Clearwater Revival, *Bayou Country* (1968)
The Cowsills, *The Cowsills in Concert* (1969)
The Everly Brothers, *The Reunion Concert* (1983)
Meat Puppets, *Duck and Cover* (1990)
The Sonics, *Here Are the Ultimate Sonics* (1992)
Hasil Adkins, *Look at That Caveman Go!* (1993)

In a collaboration with John Marascalo and Richard "Bumps" Blackwell, his producer at Specialty records, Little Richard had a Top 10 hit with "Good Golly Miss Molly" in February 1958. After the Swinging Blue Jeans

revived the tune with a schmaltzy (and heavily criticized) reworking, Mitch Ryder and the Detroit Wheels breathed new life into "Good Golly" when they fused it with Ryder's "Devil with a Blue Dress On."

It was to Ryder's sound the Dead pay homage in their three 1987 performances of the medley led by Brent Mydland.

9/16/87, Madison Square Garden, New York

▪ "Good Lovin' " (Arthur Resnick/Rudy Clark)

Olympics, single (1965), *All-Time Greatest Hits!* (1991)
Grateful Dead, single, *Shakedown Street* (1978), *The Arista Years* (1996)
Rascals, *The Young Rascals* (1966), *Time Peace* (1968), *In Retrospective* (1992)
Dave Clark Five, *Satisfied with You* (1966)
The Kingsmen, *15 Great Hits* (1966)
It's a Beautiful Day, *Live at Carnegie Hall* (1972)
The Residents, *The Third Reich and Roll* (1977), *Nibbles* (1979)
Dennis Brown, *Fire on the Mountain: Reggae Celebrates the Grateful Dead* (1996)

Both the Olympics and the Rascals had hits with "Good Lovin' " in the mid-1960s, so it was still pretty fresh in audiences' minds when the Dead debuted it in 1969. But the Pigpen vehicle (Garcia briefly sang lead when the Dead first trotted the song out in 1969) was about as different from its predecessors as Jack Daniel's is from Bazooka bubble gum. Lewd, crude, and stewed, the Dead transformed this three-chord special into the best of their hoodoo rock, with the musicians trading licks like a tight bop outfit. Pigpen was the centerpiece of the Dead's early versions of "Good Lovin'" and his nasty vocal improvisations rank with the best of his libido-driven exploits.

Weir overhauled and resurrected the affair some years after Pigpen's death in 1973 and the Dead's 1978 *Shakedown Street* version still receives considerable radio airplay. Used primarily as a show-ending showstopper, Weir made "Good Lovin'" all his own, even subtly referencing Pigpen in the song's vocal testifyin' rap: "Like a friend of mine used to say . . . "

10/4/70, Winterland Arena, San Francisco
4/17/71, Dillon Gym, Princeton University, Princeton, New Jersey
10/12/84, Civic Center, Augusta, Maine

"Good Morning, Little Schoolgirl"

(John Lee "Sonny Boy" Williamson)

Sonny Boy Williamson, single (1937), *Complete Recorded Works, Vols. 1–5* (1990)

Andrew "Smokey" Hogg, single (1947)

John Lee Hooker, *The Folk Blues of John Lee Hooker* (1959)

Grateful Dead, *Historic Dead*/'66 (1972), *Grateful Dead* (1967), *Two from the Vault*/'68 (1992)

Junior Wells, *South Side Jam* (1967)

Muddy Waters, *Folk Singer* (1964), *I'm Ready* (1978)

The Yardbirds, *Crossroads* (1964), *Five Live Yardbirds* (1965), *For Your Love* (1965)

Paul Butterfield Blues Band, *What's Shakin'* (1965)

Ten Years After, *Ssssh* (1969), *Recorded Live* (1973)

Johnny Winter, *Johnny Winter* (1969), *Johnny Winter And* (1971), *Live* (1971), *The Johnny Winter Collection* (1988)

Heavy the World, *Reunion* (1987)

Van Morrison, *A Night in San Francisco* (1994)

Huey Lewis and the News, *Four Chords and Several Years Ago* (1994)

Pigpen's debt to Sonny Boy Williamson is evidenced nowhere as strongly as it is in his salacious cover of the classic blues master's "Good Morning, Little Schoolgirl." This venerable standard has been recorded many times and with several different melodies.

The first modern master of the blues harp, John Lee "Sonny Boy" Williamson (born March 30, 1914, in Jackson, Tennessee) is credited with transforming the instrument from a simple, down-home accouterment used mainly for novelty twist and light jug-band riffs, to an essential part of the early Chicago blues sound. Known to bluesologists as "the first Sonny Boy" or "Sonny Boy I" because he preceded another famed blues harpist (Aleck "Rice" Miller who chose the moniker in reverence—and sly self-promotion), Sonny Boy Williamson pioneered the harmonica-led small-combo format that defined the Chicago blues idiom in the 1940s.

Teaching himself how to play at an early age, he was a competent enough harp player in his mid-teens to travel with the likes of Sleepy John Estes, Big Joe Williams, Robert Nighthawk, and "Homesick James" Williams, his underheralded cousin, during the Depression. The twenty-three-year-old Williamson settled in Chicago in 1937 and quickly became *the* desired sessionman recording for the Bluebird label. Recording often with Big Joe Williams, who played a rough-edged nine-string guitar, Williamson transformed his harp style and singing from the country sound he developed while hoboing through the South to one which fired the small units that Bluebird was waxing at the time. By the time World War II was in full swing, Williamson had recorded and performed with guitarists such as Tampa Red and Big Bill Broonzy and had established himself as a mainstay on the city's blues landscape as its preeminent and deeply respected harmonica player.

Despite the handicap of a "slow tongue" (a speech impediment that made his words slur, which he cleverly worked into his style to create an alluring drag), Williamson was also a talented vocalist as well as a cunningly bawdy songster. "Good Morning, Little Schoolgirl," recorded when he was still in his country phase, and "Stop Breaking Down" were easily his most popular tunes, becoming a part of the blues lexicon.

It was his harmonica playing, however, that will forever secure him a place in the blues pantheon. The electrification of all instruments, including his harmonica, in 1945, added an extra dimension to the aggressive, urban blues and allowed Williamson to undertake his most breathtakingly inspired mouth organ feats. Before he was murdered as he walked home from a club date on Chicago's South Side in 1948, the victim of an ice-pick attack, Sonny Boy Williamson had left a mark on the blues that was guaranteed to remain well past the millennium.

It is the pre-electric 1937 Williamson and well-known 1947 version of "Good Morning, Little Schoolgirl" by Smokey Hogg on which the Dead clearly modeled their earthy interpretation. Pigpen, with his early interest in the genre, was undoubtedly familiar with Hogg's recording of "Schoolgirl," as well.

Though relatively obscure, especially in comparison to his cousin LIGHTNIN' HOPKINS, Hogg was a journeyman Texas blues guitarist and singer with a prolific recording career. Born in 1914, Hogg was influenced by the likes of Big Bill Broonzy and Blind Lemon Jefferson. His father taught him the guitar and as a youth he played informally with Babe Turner, better known as "The Black Ace," at various East Texas venues. His first session in 1937 for the Decca label in Dallas sparked what would become a twenty-year recording career, in which Hogg contracted with a variety of labels.

As did other Texas bluesmen who went to California during World War II, Hogg built a West Coast fan base following his discharge from the army. With his coarse, country-blues vocals and guitar figures, Hogg also had a hit with the song "Long Tall Mama" in 1948. Despite the success of "Long Tall Mama" and "Schoolgirl," Hogg spent the last years of his life as a musician playing jukes, rent parties, and picnics in Texas and California until his death in 1960.

"Schoolgirl" was another Grateful Dead blues special credibly resurrected by Weir in 1992 for a few surprise performances. Ace also included the old stomp in his shows with Rob Wasserman and Ratdog.

> **11/11/67, Shrine Exhibition Hall, Los Angeles**
> **4/12/69, Fillmore West, San Francisco**
> **8/21/93, Autzen Stadium, Eugene, Oregon (with Huey Lewis)**

▪ "Goodnight Irene" (LEADBELLY)

> **Leadbelly, single (1933), *The Legend of Leadbelly/'39* (1976), *Midnight Special* (1991), *Goodnight Irene* (1996)**
> **The Weavers, *Goodnight Irene* (1949), *The Weavers at Carnegie Hall* (1956), *Best of the Weavers* (1987)**
> **Jerry Lee Lewis, *Jerry Lee Lewis* (1959)**
> **Nat King Cole, *Ramblin' Rose* (1962)**
> **Little Richard, *Little Richard Is Back* (1965)**
> **Jimi Hendrix and Little Richard, *Together/'64-65* (1970)**
> **Mississippi John Hurt, *The Last Sessions* (1972)**
> **Leon Russell, *Hank Wilson's Back* (1973)**
> **Ry Cooder, *Chicken Skin Music* (1976)**
> **Alex Harvey, *Penthouse Tapes* (1976)**
> **Raffi, *The Corner Grocer* (1979)**
> **Brian Wilson, *A Vision Shared* (1988)**
> **Maureen Tucker, *Life in Exile* (1989)**
> **The Chieftains, *Another Country* (1992)**
> **Lawrence Welk, *American Favorites* (1996)**

The most famous song from one of America's treasured bluesmen, Leadbelly's "Goodnight Irene" helped put him and the genre on the map. Though there is some debate among Leadbelly scholars and biographers regarding his authorship of "Goodnight Irene," the song has endured as an American standard.

The first recording of "Goodnight Irene" was made by Leadbelly for the Library of Congress archives while he was serving time in a Louisiana state penitentiary during the mid-1930s. The Weavers, with Gordon Jenkins's Orchestra, brought it to the general public with their hit in the 1950s

Garcia recalled the song's early influence on him in a 1991 discussion with Blair Jackson and Robert Hunter. "[Burl Ives] was maybe the main popular folk voice of that time, a guy who did folk and kids' stuff. The Weavers, too. I remember being really impressed as a kid by their versions of 'Goodnight Irene,' 'So Long It's Been Good to Know You.' I don't think of those kinds of songs as direct influences, but they probably were in a way because they were a part of American culture."

A line from the song, "Sometimes I get a great notion to jump in the river and drown" was excerpted and shorthanded by KEN KESEY for the title of his second novel, *Sometimes a Great Notion*. Kesey was part of the festivities on New Year's Eve in 1981 when Garcia led the Dead into their only performance of the classic. Garcia covered "Goodnight Irene" more than forty times sans Dead between 1976 and 1988.

> **12/31/83, Civic Auditorium, San Francisco**

▪ "Good Times" (Sam Cooke)

> **Sam Cooke, single, *Ain't that Good News* (1964), *The Man and His Music* (1986)**
> **The Rolling Stones, *Out of Our Heads* (1965)**
> **Aretha Franklin, *I Never Loved a Man (the Way I Love You)* (1967)**
> **Phoebe Snow, *Phoebe Snow* (1976)**

Sometimes confused with Mydland's "Good Times" (a.k.a. "Never Trust a Woman") or the many songs entitled "Let the Good Times Roll," Sam Cooke's "Good Times" was a surprisingly rousing Grateful Dead cover from 1988 to 1994.

A natural show opener in which Garcia, Weir, Mydland, and later Vince Welnick traded the lead vocal chores, Garcia also wrote the lyrics to the verse he sang: "It might be six o'clock, it might be eight / Don't matter if it's gettin' late / We gonna make the band play one more song / Get in the groove if it takes all night long . . ."

Cooke's "Good Times" hit No. 11 on the pop charts in 1964 but the Dead were probably equally aware of the Stones' version released a year later.

> **7/17/89, Alpine Valley Music Theater, East Troy, Wisconsin**

▪ *Go to Heaven*

> **Arista AL5-8181, 1980. Produced by Gary Lyons.**
> **"Alabama Getaway," "Far from Me," "Althea," "Feel**

Like a Stranger," "Lost Sailor," "Saint of Circumstance," "Antwerp's Placebo (the Plumber)," "Easy to Love You," "Don't Ease Me In"

Condemned as a slick and unsuccessful attempt to crack the mainstream, this well-recorded but under-rehearsed album contains decent but raw versions of many tunes that made the long haul with the Dead, including "Feel Like a Stranger," "Althea," and "Saint of Circumstance" as well as one that had gone the distance from their jugband days, "Don't Ease Me In."

Not all members of the band were thrilled with the final result, either. As Weir related to Blair Jackson in 1985, "My major reservation with that record had nothing to do with him [producer Gary Lyons]. I just felt that we didn't have good, mature material when we recorded it. Some of it we'd never even played live."

◾ "Gotta Serve Somebody" (BOB DYLAN)

Bob Dylan, *Slow Train Coming* (1979), *Dylan and the Dead* (1989), *Bob Dylan's Greatest Hits Volume 3* (1994)

Dead Ringers, DEAD RINGERS (1993)

Booker T. and the MG's, *That's the Way It Should Be* (1994)

Judy Collins, *Judy Sings Dylan Just Like a Woman* (1994)

Of all the right-angle turns Bob Dylan has taken in his catalytic career, none had such widespread and flabbergasting effects as his acceptance of Jesus Christ as his savior and his musical embrace of gospel rock evident on his 1979 album, *Slow Train Coming.*

The events leading up to this transformation are steeped in the mystique of Dylan lore. During his grueling world tour in 1978, Dylan claims he was visited by Jesus in a Phoenix hotel room. After the tour, Dylan took off the first five months of 1979 and "went to Bible school." Upon returning to the studio in May, it was with the production team that included a fresh attitude and the legendary Jerry Wexler.

"Gotta Serve Somebody" was an early composition in Dylan's born-again period. The song is essentially a list of everybody from ambassadors to boxing champs to thieves to doctors who Dylan suggests should pay heed to a Christian God. He also playfully includes himself through a variety of aliases (Zimmy, Timmy, R. J., and Ray) and references the domed mansion he was then building for himself in Malibu.

Ironically, critics seemed to forget that Dylan's work had always been rooted in religious symbol. It was a further irony that "Gotta Serve Somebody," Dylan's best-known song from this phase, was not originally planned for inclusion on *Slow Train.* As Wexler began putting together sequences for the album, "Gotta Serve Somebody" did not appear.

But, according to Dylan: "I had to fight to get it on the album, it was ridiculous."

To bring the irony full circle, Dylan won the Grammy Award for Best Male Rock Vocal and performed the song at the 1980 awards ceremony.

It was also somewhat surprising when "Gotta Serve Somebody" and "SLOW TRAIN COMING" popped up on the 1987 Dylan/Dead set lists, given the Dead's eschewal of religious proselytization. Still, both songs were rendered with force during this brief redisplay of the tunes.

7/26/87, Stadium, Anaheim, California

◾ Bill Graham

Born January 8, 1931, Berlin, Germany; died October 25, 1991, Vallejo, California

When it comes to rock impresarios, there was Bill Graham and then there was everybody else. Truly, his life story is the story of rock. But it is also one of rags to riches in the archetypal tradition of Horatio Alger, with the Holocaust, the Korean War, the Borscht Belt, Haight-Ashbury, Hollywood, Woodstock, and Live Aid thrown in for good measure.

Born Wolfgang Grajonza at the peak of Weimar Germany and just two days before the unexpected death of his father from a blood infection, the boy was sent out of Germany on a Red Cross transport by his mother when he was just nine years old when the Nazis began to enforce stricter regulations on Jewish communities. As a young refugee who left most of his family behind, Grajonza eventually made his way with hundreds of other young war orphans to American soil. Separated from his family and not speaking English, Wolfgang was sent to a Pleasantville, New York, temporary housing facility sponsored by the Jewish Foster Home Bureau, which sought to find adoptive families for these children.

Adopted by the Ehrenreich family in the Bronx, Billy Grajonza learned English and worked with his foster brother Roy to lose his accent. Still, being German and Jewish made him the object of derision from the neighborhood bullies instilling even more tenacity and fight in the boy. Gaining acceptance with his acculturation, he became a New Yorker by the end of his first year in the States. Within a couple of years, he also became a jazz and Latin-music devotee, attending dances at the Palladium and Apollo Theater to hear bands like Cab Calloway, Xavier Cugat, and Tito Puente.

Picking the name William Graham from the phone book because the pronunciation of his surname was habitually butchered, the eighteen-year-old attended Brooklyn College but, even though he was not yet an American citizen, he was drafted into the United States Army. Graham became an artillery spotter in the Korean War and was eventually awarded a Bronze Star. Though his foster parents died soon after his discharge, Graham reunited with his five surviving natural sisters, who were allowed to come to America. He also became an American citizen at the legal age of twenty-one.

Graham had worked as a singing waiter at Grossinger's, the famed Jewish Catskill Borscht Belt resort as a teenager and briefly resumed working there. But he also tried his hand at other menial jobs, such as cab driving, crisscrossing the country between California and New York living by a whim and a prayer. Along the way, Graham dabbled in acting, even studying for a time with Lee Strasberg at the influential Actors Studio in New York. When a stab at character acting in Hollywood resulted in rejection partially based on his Jewish appearance, Graham returned to the Bay Area where he

Bill Graham. *(The New York Public Library of the Performing Arts)*

became involved with the San Francisco Mime Troupe, the progressive, politically radical theater company that continues to thrive.

No longer interested in becoming an actor himself, Graham became involved as the unofficial business manager for the Troupe. He hung posters, promoted shows, drove trucks, and did all the odd jobs and grunt work that no one else really wanted to do but that needed to be done. Since he was someone bereft of roots and displaced by the terrible consequences of history, it is easy to fathom why the Mime Troupe's highly political sense of community and call to a higher purpose appealed to Graham. Here was a group of people attempting to engender a better society through expression of art as they saw it with no compromises . . . and no money.

A suave opportunist with canny chutzpah and soul, Graham made his management skills apparent from the get-go. When a member of the Troupe was arrested during a performance that was dubbed as obscene, Graham (not totally unprepared for this possibility) orchestrated a wave of public sympathy that resulted in judicial leniency and, better still, free publicity for the Mime Troupe.

Coincidentally, one of the first dance concert benefits Graham organized for the Mime Troupe was also the WARLOCKS' first billing as the Grateful Dead. The success of the benefit led to others and soon he was doing regular business with the Dead, Frank Zappa, and Grace Slick and the Great Society. The events seemed to fill a need in the growing youth culture as a place to commune and/or hang out while listening to the great music that was coming out of the burgeoning scene.

Correctly sensing the larger picture, Graham left the Mime Troupe to begin presenting events full time, always doing as much grunt work as it took to make them happen. Whether it meant sweeping the stage or refilling the always-present barrel of apples at the Fillmore (the first of three permanent venues to host what became Bill Graham Presents), the bustling promoter was always everywhere at once presiding over everything, famed clipboard in hand.

Graham didn't merely work, he became famous for that work—especially the little flourishes, the final touches that capped the evening off in style. Wanting his events to be special and perfect for audiences and performers alike, he provided musicians with hotel suites, catered food, and dressing room flowers while giving his

customers some of the wildest double (and triple) bills in music history, such as the Dead and Miles Davis, Woody Herman opening for the Who, and Buddy Rich leading off for Ten Years After. The man who presented the last public appearances of Lenny Bruce, Groucho Marx, and the Sex Pistols was also the man who served a complete Thanksgiving dinner for 5,400 at the Band's "Last Waltz" at San Francisco's Winterland in 1978, and who ran down the block to fetch Otis Redding a 7-Up after another exhausting Fillmore gig. He presented new bands like Santana, the Allman Brothers, and the J. Geils Band and treated them as well as he treated Miles, the Dead, or Jimi Hendrix. He doled out respect and he expected (and received) it in return.

As the economics of rock music changed, so did Graham. He became the father of the megaconcert, producing shows in ever larger sites and establishing large arenas and even stadiums as viable venues.

Of the many bands he booked and befriended, his bond with the Dead was the deepest. It was Graham whom the band approached when they decided to undertake their 1978 Egyptian adventure and it was Graham who could be seen scurrying up and down Forty-seventh Street in Manhattan as he oversaw Garcia's 1987 Broadway shows at the Lunt-Fontanne Theater.

Graham also had the last laugh on Hollywood as he was tapped for the odd appearance on the big screen—Francis Ford Coppola's *Apocalypse Now!* and *The Cotton Club* among them.

In many respects, there were no new frontiers for Bill Graham to conquer. He had taken a ragtag group of bands playing for peanuts in funky Bay Area dance halls and molded that scene into one of nothing-less-than-international proportions and significance. So, it was appropriately ironic that on the rainy, stormy evening of October 25, 1991, a helicopter carrying Graham, his companion Mellis Gold, and pilot Steve Kahn crashed into a Pacific Gas and Electric Company transmission tower along Highway 37 near Vallejo, California, as the trio was returning from a Huey Lewis and the News concert at Graham's Shoreline Amphitheater in Mountain View, California.

A week later, an all-star cast of Fillmore graduates and others honored the three with a free afternoon concert in San Francisco's Golden Gate Park. The Dead were joined by JOHN FOGERTY and Blues Traveler's John

Popper for part of their vital set, which concluded with "Sunshine Daydream," the coda of Graham's favorite Dead tune, "Sugar Magnolia."

■ *Grateful Dead* (a.k.a. "Skull and Roses" or "Skull Fuck")
Warner Bros. 2WS 1935, 1971. Produced by the Grateful Dead.
"Bertha," "MAMA TRIED," "BIG RAILROAD BLUES," "Playing in the Band," "The Other One," "ME & MY UNCLE," "BIG BOSS MAN," "ME & BOBBY MCGEE," "JOHNNY B. GOODE," "Wharf Rat," "NOT FADE AWAY">"GOIN' DOWN THE ROAD FEELING BAD"
MERL SAUNDERS–organ on "Bertha," "Playing in the Band" and "Wharf Rat."

The stripped-down, five-man Grateful Dead combine original and cover material on this popular live double album that still sounds fresh. Highlights include an embryonic "Playing in the Band," a searing "Big Railroad Blues," the modal "The Other One," the mournful, gospel-infused "Wharf Rat," and a propulsive "Not Fade Away">"Goin' Down the Road Feeling Bad" medley.

Garcia was evidently pleased with the result. As he told Charles Reich and Jann Wenner in 1971, "It's *us*, man. It's the prototype Grateful Dead. Basic unit. Each one of those tracks is the total picture, a good example of what the Grateful Dead really is, *musically*. Rather than 'This record has a sort of a country, light acoustics sound,' and so on—like for a year we were a light acoustic band, in somebody's head. The new album is enough of an overview so people can see we're like a regular shoot-em-up saloon band. That's more what we are like. The tracks all illustrate that nicely. They're hot.'"

■ *Grateful Dead* (film)
Produced and directed by Robert Nelson, 1967.

Given the Dead's experimental roots, it is appropriate that their first formal cinematic documentation was achieved by the respected avant-garde filmmaker Robert Nelson.

The seven-and-a-half-minute, 16mm no-budget film was made in early 1967 and, with its jagged collage aesthetic, captures a taste of the humor, mystery, and disorientation of the psychedelic experience through quick cuts, prismatic imaging, close-ups, wide-angle shots, color and black and white images, inversion, negative images, out-of-focus photography, double exposures, and slow- and fast-motion sequences. Intriguing as it is frustrating, *Grateful Dead* has the choppy look of a period-piece light show and even contains a few light-show shots. Yet, even three decades down the pike, Nelson's touch still seems fresh.

Instrumental portions drawn from the sessions that produced the Dead's first album provide the soundtrack for the film, but this is anything but a glorified promotional video.

The Dead in a scene from Robert Nelson's film, *Grateful Dead. (The New York Public Library for the Performing Arts)*

Nelson first encountered the Dead in the mid-1960s when they were still the WARLOCKS. He met Phil Lesh through his work with the San Francisco Mime Troupe, with whom he had made a couple of films. Around the same time, the filmmaker attended a Jefferson Airplane show and was impressed with the possibilities of San Francisco's new music scene. When Nelson received a grant from the Belgium Film Archive in 1966, he decided to approach the Dead about using them in a film. As Nelson told Blair Jackson in 1985, "It was all very low-key. They were just starting to happen, so I called them up and said, 'Look I have to make this film. Can I come over to the practice studio?' They said 'sure' and that was that. Things were much simpler then."

Utilizing a number of different locations, Nelson shot the Dead at their rehearsal space, at the Russian River, where the band can be seen goofing around in a canoe, and at a couple of Bay Area dance concerts. Nelson also filmed what he believes was the Dead's first TV appearance right off the screen and used it in the film. The film ends with its longest shot of a scary-looking Pigpen sitting next to an empty bottle of Southern Comfort.

In exchange for their services, the Dead were given a print of the finished product, which they soon screened at a couple of concerts. The Belgium Film Archive apparently thought highly of *Grateful Dead* as it won an award at a Belgian film festival later that year. After that it all but disappeared, save for the odd screening at the local art house.

Nelson retained the rights to the film for many years but eventually sold it to the band. As he later said to Blair Jackson in 1985: "I was in financial trouble and I needed money so I decided to sell the rights to the movie. I called Garcia up and asked him if he wanted to buy my film. I didn't really know what it was worth or how much to ask for it, so I just came up with the figure of eleven thousand dollars. Garcia said, 'No problem, man.' At that point I didn't know whether I asked too much or too little for the film. When the check came in the mail a few weeks later I discovered Jerry had sent me fifteen thousand dollars. Now that's what I call class!"

▪ *The Grateful Dead*

Warner Bros. WS 1689, 1967. Produced by Dave
    Hassinger.
"The Golden Road (to Unlimited Devotion)," "Beat It on
    Down the Line," "Good Morning, Little Schoolgirl,"

(Courtesy of Warner Bros. Records)

"Cold Rain and Snow," "Sitting on Top of the World," "Cream Puff War," "Morning Dew," "New, New Minglewood Blues," "Viola Lee Blues"

Though the Dead's commercial debut is a speedy effort featuring many tunes that never left their voluminous set-list rotation, Garcia's Freddie King–style solo on "Viola Lee Blues" is cited as the album's lost classic.

Remembering the band's entrée into the record biz, Garcia told Charles Reich and Jann Wenner in 1971 that "At that time we had no real *record* consciousness. We were just going to go down to L.A. and make a record. We were completely naive about it. We had a producer whom we had chosen—Dave Hassinger—and were impressed by him because he'd been the engineer on a couple of Rolling Stones records that we liked the sound of; that was as much as we were into record-making.

"So we went down there and, what was it we had, Dexamyl? Some sort of diet-watchers speed, and pot and stuff like that. So in three nights we played some hyperactive music. That's what's embarrassing about that record now, the tempo was way too fast. We were all so speedy at the time. It has its sort of crude energy, but obviously it's difficult for me to listen to it; I can't enjoy it really. . . .

"But in reality, the way we played was not really too much different from the way that record was. Usually we played tunes that lasted a long time because we like to play a lot. And when you're playing for people who are dancing and getting high, you can dance easy to a half-hour tune and you can even wonder why it ended so soon. So for us the whole time thing was weird 'cause we went down there and turned out songs real fast—less than three minutes, which is real short.

"It was weird and we realized it. The first record was like a regular company record done in three nights, mixed in one day. It was done on three track, I believe—it wasn't even four track—Studio A in L.A., an imposing place, and we really didn't much care about it while we were doing it. So we weren't surprised when it didn't quite sound like we wanted it to.

"It's hard for me to go back to the past in terms of the music because for me it's a continuum and to stop it at one of those points it's got . . . to me it always looks un-developed and not quite working. Which in fact it was."

Grateful Dead: A Photofilm

(film)/Directed by Paul McCartney, produced by Paul McCartney, Linda McCartney, and Robert Montgomery, 1996.

Inspired and armed with just four rolls of photographs, Paul McCartney orginated a new venture in cinemato-graphic art—a Photofilm. His nine-minute movie of the Grateful Dead in concert and at ease is the result of many hours spent imagining and experimenting with how still photography could be made to move and morph and complement a celebrated soundtrack of the sixties.

Grateful Dead: A Photofilm began when McCartney was studying contact sheets of photographs that his wife Linda had taken of the Grateful Dead during 1967–68. Then living in New York, Linda had photographed the band in concert in Central Park and at their Haight-Ashbury digs. She had, however, just four rolls of film from each shoot.

McCartney noted how, before the vogue of using a motordrive, Linda had taken successive shots of Bob Weir in an attempt to get a portrait. Caught by the whimsy of how the series of stills might look if flipped rapidly in sequence and motivated by his wish to cele-brate the Dead of that era, he began to create—spurred, too, by a sudden memory of his childhood.

"When I was a kid, recovering from an illness, I had a strange experience when by concentrating on a photo-graph in a newspaper I seemed to be able to make it

move," McCartney recalled. "Looking at these pictures, I got that feeling again and I thought that I could maybe make these four rolls more interesting by making a film of the Dead at a time of which not much footage exists."

McCartney began storyboarding the one-hundred-forty stills, which were then filmed in a variety of styles on a rostrum camera at his direction—or, as he put it, "filmed to my grocery list." The film was then loaded into a computer so that McCartney could oversee the digital edit: shortening, lengthening, speeding, slowing, and morphing the sequence of stills so that the band members seem to be moving. Other times the camera slowly pans across faces in a magnified crowd photo, stopping at the most interesting characters: a man in a trilby who looks like an undercover agent; a woman who seems a bit overimbibed.

McCartney's handwritten titles and credits create a moody, hyptnotic period piece. "That's It for the Other One," "New Potato Caboose," and "Alligator" from the Dead's *Anthem of the Sun* play sans vocals for the length of the film.

Though the film has prompted some to accuse Mc-Cartney of cashing in on Garcia's death (which was a year before the short was released), he had begun work-ing on the film long before then. "I heard on the news that Jerry had died and I thought, 'Oh no, I was just about to show the film to him,'" McCartney said. "I'd been in correspondence with him, because he was a painter and I thought he'd like this. Unfortunately, I missed him. I suppose it has become a little bit of a trib-ute to Jerry because of it."

Grateful Dead Comix

A nifty idea that never really took off, *Grateful Dead Comix* suffered from the same heavy-handedness of MTV by providing a visual when perhaps none was ever called for. Eight installments were published over the course of the early 1990s. The project did have some high points, although, including Moebius's "Terrapin Station, Part I," Tim Truman's rendering of Hunter's never-performed "Eagle Mall," and some slices of Grateful Dead history such as the Woodstock debacle. Criticism of the enterprise centered on the notion that interpretations of Dead songs are very personal and the graphics may not match one's inner gestalt—much in the same way MTV can forever set a song in graphic stone.

• Grateful Dead Family Album

(book)/Jerilyn Brandelius
256 pages. Illustrated with color and black-and-white
photos, drawings, and graphic art. Warner Books,
1989.

Jam-packed with 256 pages of Grateful Dead fun stuff, Jerilyn Brandelius's informal family scrapbook contains more than five hundred photos (most previously unpublished), article snippets, band quotes and personal reminiscences from the clan-at-large. A veritable silver mine of Dead ephemera, the "album" is arranged in a loose chronological arc from the band's prehistory through the late 1980s. It includes extracts of old *Dead Head* newsletters, poster reproductions, and memorabilia mostly hinged around the touchstone events and hodgepodge acquaintances from their long strange trip: childhood snaps, Kesey, the Acid Tests, the Warlocks, Europe '72, Egypt, the closing of Winterland, Bill Graham, etc., etc., etc. Though not much new ground is cov-

(Courtesy of Zosafarm Publications)

ered here, Brandelius's loving touch can be felt on each, very different, page.

• Grateful Dead Folktales (book)/edited by

Bob Franzosa
Zosafarm Publications, 1989.

While some Deadheads are dimly aware that the term *grateful dead* also denotes a cycle of obscure but archetypally ripe folk tales from many cultures, Bob Franzosa took this underdocumented aspect of Dead scholarship and published one of the more important tomes to inform Grateful Dead culture.

Compiling thirteen stories in the genre from as many cultures around the world, Franzosa's collection is the first volume of its kind devoted specifically to grateful dead folktales. His sharp, insightful introduction about the stories offers exactly the kind of historical background about the form and content of the legends he selected that they deserve.

Franzosa, a mathematician and researcher at the University of Maine, became interested in grateful dead folktales in the early 1980s after reading *The Grateful Dead*, a long out-of-print book from the turn of the century that contained brief synopses of about one hundred grateful dead tales. Already a fan of the band, Franzosa's curiosity was piqued, so he began a vision quest to collect as many of the stories as possible leading to countless hours in the libraries of the University of Maine and Harvard.

The diverse selection on which he eventually settled are drawn from as far west as Iceland and as far east as Persia with stops in Scandinavia, the British Isles, France, Spain, Poland, Russia, Italy, Greece, and Israel featuring enough heroism, villainy, treachery, and true love to make the biggest summer blockbuster seem tame.

• Grateful Dead from the Mars Hotel

Grateful Dead Records GD 102, 1974. Produced by
Grateful Dead.
"U.S. Blues," "China Doll," "Unbroken Chain," "Loose
Lucy," "Scarlet Begonias," "Pride of Cucamonga,"
"Money Money," "Ship of Fools"
Ned Lagin–synthesizer on "Unbroken Chain." John
McFee–pedal steel on "Pride of Cucamonga."

The Dead had worked out their recording methodology by the time they went into the studio to cut *Mars Hotel*,

GRATEFUL DEAD FROM THE MARS HOTEL

(© Grateful Dead Merchandising, Inc.)

rehearsing extensively beforehand. Even when they were actually in the process of laying down tracks for *Mars Hotel*, they would rehearse at Studio Instrument Rentals across the street from Ron Hallee's recording studio where they were cutting the album. They rehearsed all the tunes for about a month before actually recording them, so they were nearly fully arranged.

The strategy worked. Unveiling five new Garcia/Hunter songs, all of which became concert keepers, *Mars Hotel* was a crisp, artistic (if not commercial) success. "Scarlet Begonias" showed off the Dead's instrumental magic, even in the studio; "China Doll" revealed another shade of the introspective Hunter; "Loose Lucy" reflected the good ol' Grateful Dead; "Ship of Fools" served as a potent political assessment at the height of the Watergate era; and "U.S. Blues" still comes off as a hip State of the Union address. The songs were better live of course, but given the Dead's constant battle with studio endeavors, the album does justice to even its sole clunker, the Weir/Barlow "Money Money." Additionally, "Unbroken Chain," one of two songs composed by Phil Lesh and his old friend Bobby Petersen, became the stuff of Deadhead obsession.

For the trivia-obsessed, the Mars Hotel was a bluelight, skid-row dive in San Francisco's Mission District where Jack Kerouac slept a few off (he references it as a site of debauchery in his novel *Big Sur*), and a clip of the hotel being razed is included in *The Grateful Dead Movie*. Additionally, the psychedelic calligraphy on the

back of the album spells out "Ugly Rumors"—a humanitarian spoof of the phrase "Ugly Roomers" that referred to the transient residents of the flop house. Finally, the band considered shipping bars of soap (Mars Bars) with promotional copies of the album.

▪ *Grateful Dead Hour*
(radio program)

There have been Grateful Dead radio programs broadcast locally since the 1970s but there is only one nationally syndicated *Grateful Dead Hour*. One didn't have to go to every Dead show or even ever see the band to keep up on the group and their music. For those preferring to tape the band in the comfort of their own living rooms, there is still a radio show to suit the occasion. Host David Gans, author of *Playing in the Band: An Oral History of the Grateful Dead* and *Conversations with the Dead*, is a writer, editor, musician, and all-around friend to all Deadheads.

Typically, the show is an audio kaleidoscope of sorts, featuring a mixture of high-quality concert tapes, interviews with band members and associated figures, an eclectic sampling of the Dead's source music, up-to-date concert information and other news, and Gans's offbeat sound montages. Describing himself more as a "scholarly facilitator than an entertainment purveyor," Gans told Richard Gehr of *Newsday* in 1989, "What I'm doing is highly unusual in the world of intellectual property—for the Dead to give away unpublished stuff on the air every week is pretty cool."

Originating as *The Deadhead Hour* at San Francisco's KFOG in 1984, the weekly program, not surprisingly, found a waiting audience in the Dead's home turf. Already a ten-year veteran of Dead concerts, Gans took the reins in 1985 and slowly built an empire that included scores of affiliates from coast-to-coast, dispensing the band's legacy like some cybernetic town crier. Though he has a vast and varied collection of concert tapes as well as access to the Dead's own vaults, the only restriction placed on Gans was that he not broadcast entire sets. Instead, he uses the hour to offer a kind of community resource to Deadheads aware that the Dead scene isn't merely the music.

▪ *The Grateful Dead Movie* (film)/Produced
by Eddie Washington, directed by Jerry Garcia and Leon Gast, and animation by Gary Gutierrez, 1977.

"U.S. Blues," "GOIN' DOWN THE ROAD FEELING BAD," "Eyes of the World," "Stella Blue," "He's Gone," "MORNING DEW," "One More Saturday Night," "Truckin'," "Sugar Magnolia," "Playing in the Band," "Casey Jones," "It Must Have Been the Roses," "JOHNNY B. GOODE"

When the Dead announced they were going to retire after a final, five-night stand at San Francisco's Winterland in October 1974, they had the wherewithal to arrange a five-camera shoot to catch all the emotion and energy of this electrically charged event.

The band, of course, only took an extended sabbatical during which time Garcia holed up in an editing studio to turn out one of the best rock concert films ever produced. When it was released in 1977, *The Grateful Dead Movie* was the definitive up-to-that-moment musical, historical, social, and cultural perspective on the band and Deadheads.

In addition to its well-recorded and -selected track list, the movie features music sometimes mixed with added subtlety so that when a specific band member appears in a close-up, his instrument is separated and slightly amplified as a method of coloring his contribution to the jam. Other features include short but candid offstage glimpses of Garcia, Lesh, Kreutzmann, Weir, and Barlow; a wild tour through the backstage catacombs; a healthy dose of mid-1970s Deadhead culture; a compact, visual history of the band; and some of cinema's most legendary animation in the form of Gary Gutierrez's stunning work that opens the film.

Filmmaking had interested Garcia since the early 1960s when he spent time working on soundtracks at the Stanford University Communications Department. With his background in the visual arts, he was drawn to the notion of a Grateful Dead movie. In discussing the Dead's decision to film all five nights of the Winterland run with Steve Weitzman of *Relix* in 1977, Garcia explained, "When we decided we weren't going to perform anymore, our farewell show, so to speak, was five days at Winterland. It was after we got back from our second trip to Europe—October '74. About a month before the Winterland dates I got the idea that it would be a neat idea to be able to film it, just because I didn't know if we were going to perform in that kind of a situation again. And that five nights in a place would at least give us the possibility, numerically anyway, that we would have one or two really good nights. In about two or three weeks

the whole production thing came together to make the movie.

"At first we thought, let's just make a record of the idea, and I wanted it to look good. I wanted it to be really well filmed but I didn't really know a lot about film when the idea got under way, but when it was time for the show to start, we had about nine camera crews and a lot of good backup people, good lighting people, and the whole thing was already on its way to happening. It was chaotic but well organized in spite of the relatively short preproduction time we had. After the five days were over—and during that time I involved myself mostly with the music, I didn't really get into the film part—we had a couple hundred thousand feet of film in the can. So then it was, What's going to happen with this? Originally, we were thinking in terms of what about a canned concert. Would something like that work? Could we send out a filmed version of ourselves? Then, after getting involved and interested in the movie as a project, I started looking at the footage and the concert stuff and I felt that there was a *movie* there. A movie in the movie sense rather than a movie in the concert sense."

Garcia and the band's soundman DAN HEALY took the film to Burbank Studios to mix the soundtrack, painstakingly synching the footage with the music. After editing the film down to a final length of 131 minutes, Garcia had once again learned a craft through trial-by-fire, describing the experience as "two years of incredible doubt."

Saying the film "redeems the genre" of rock movies, Robert Christgau's *Village Voice* review pointed out that "The ignorant person who reviewed it for the *Times* complained that the film doesn't probe, which it certainly doesn't. It wouldn't be a Dead film if it did. What it does is lay out enough information for anyone who is genuinely curious to find out what the Dead are really about. The ticket hassles and awkward bodies, the spaced-out gibberish and inspired nonsense, the music with all its high and lows—they're all here. In fifty years, when people want to know what a rock concert was like, they'll refer to this movie. But all they'll find out is what a Dead concert was like. It's not the same thing—not the same thing at all."

■ ***Grateful Dead: The Official Book of the Deadheads*/Edited by Paul Grushkin. 216 pages. Hundreds of color and black and white photos, Deadhead drawings, poems, letters,**

(Courtesy of Plunderphonics/John Oswald)

doodles, and graphic art. Foreword by Jerry Garcia. Quill Books, 1983.

Lovingly assembled from crates full of correspondence the band collected over the years, this is the first book by, about, and for Deadheads. Letters, artwork, reviews, and the fun-lovingly obsessed are bared in this time-warp between covers. An added bonus is the first semi-authoritative concert listing ever available in the days before *DeadBase*.

- *Grayfolded*/**Grateful Dead and John Oswald**
  Plunderphonics Swell/Artifact 1969–1996. Reproduced by John Oswald 1995.
  Part I: *Transitive Axis*: "Novature (Formless Nights Fall)," "Pouring Velvet," "In Revolving Ash Light," "Clouds Cast," "Through," "Fault Forces," "The Phil Zone," "La Estrella Oscura," "Recedes (while we can)"; Part II: *Mirror Ashes*: "Transilence," "73rd Star Bridge Sonata," "Cease Tone Beam," "The Speed of Love," "Dark Matter Problem/Every Leaf Is Turning," "Foldback Time"

One man plunders what another man spills! Sifting through twenty-five years of the Dead's "Dark Star" performances and employing his "plunderphonic" methods—editing, overlapping, manipulating—to the tapes, John Oswald assembled an extended, time-warped psychedelic jam that is meticulously hallucinatory. On *Transitive Axis*, the first installment, Oswald flashed his technique by rearranging and essentially creating new

Grateful Dead music from numerous versions of "Dark Star" recorded between 1968 and 1993.

The fourth CD in Oswald's plunderphonics series, *Grayfolded* (pronounced Grateful Dead) was created by the Canadian composer, whose 1989 *Plunderphonic* CDs were destroyed at Michael Jackson's dictum after Oswald had, without permission, rearranged Jackson's song "Bad" as "Dab" for one of the CD's tracks. (Oswald had also altered the image of Jackson's anatomy on the CD cover so that he resembled a white woman.) Oswald sought and received permission this time around from Phil Lesh, who gave him access to the Dead's tape vault.

According to Lesh, Oswald "approached a mutual friend about doing something with Grateful Dead music. And I enjoyed his sense of humor on the *Plunderphonic* CD and was interested to see what would happen if he did a whole CD of one song."

"It's always interesting applying very unusual techniques to very conventional music," Oswald told *Rolling Stone* in 1994. "The thing everybody hears over the years is that the Dead don't come across on record. You have to get the experience, and 'Dark Star' is the epitome of that experience . . . in an hour on record, we travel a lot farther than we do in a normal concert."

Oswald defines the word *plunderphonics* as making new songs by deconstructing well-known recordings. *Plexure*, the third CD in the series, featured pieces credited to amalgamations such as Marianne Faith No Morrissey, Ozzy Osmond, and Sinéad O'Connick Jr., all of whom were sampled without permission.

The technology ultimately allows Oswald to perform such sleight-of-hand maneuvers as, for instance, display a twentysomething Jerry Garcia performing a duet with a fiftysomething Jerry Garcia, sustaining single words for up to a minute, and transferring keyboard lines among the myriad of instrumentalists who have passed through the band.

Rather than being put off by the manipulation of their favorite music, Deadheads seemed to take to the release. As one Internet posting read: "This is not like any 'Dark Star' you've heard before. It's more like the one you wish the Dead will play next time."

Indeed, Lesh agreed, saying, "If anything, the CD will suggest new ways that we can work together."

Mirror Ashes, Oswald's followup, doesn't fare quite so well. While *Transitive Axis* relied heavily on layering of sounds, *Mirror Ashes* is marred by an overdose of tape echo, preludes, and repeats of source material, and ineffective speed alterations. An example of his good intentions gone awry can be experienced in the "Cease Tone Beam" passage in which he manipulates the speed to stretch a short "Space" performance into a just plain dull twelve-minute exercise in endurance. One wonders about the inclusion of the unfolded "Feelin' Groovy" jam from the famed February 13, 1970, show: rather a cop-out from a man whose bread and butter is regurgitating this stuff into a new form altogether. After all, these shenanigans were what prompted sales of this disc in the first place. And the Dead released the "Dark Star" from this concert as part of *Dick's Picks Volume Four* less than a year later. One is left wishing that Oswald had spent more time on the hints of "St. Stephen," "Morning Dew," "Stella Blue," "Eyes of the World," and "The Other One" that sneak in during the adventure.

The bonus of the package were Rob Bowman's excellent and extensive liner notes. With in-depth interview quotes from Garcia, Lesh, and Hunter about the composition and soul of "Dark Star," Bowman put together a piece of journalistic prose that rivals the music he wrote about. Also included in the release is a visual map outlining the multitude of "Dark Star"s used in the production of both discs.

▪ Great American String Band

In 1974, Garcia launched a short-lived successor to OLD & IN THE WAY. The Great American String Band included Garcia on banjo, DAVID GRISMAN on mandolin, Richard Greene on fiddle, and two newcomers to the Dead scene: Taj Mahal on bass and David Nichtern on guitar and vocals. The group played a nifty assortment of bluegrass, country blues, rock, and Tin Pan Alley but only performed from April through July before folding.

▪ "Greatest Story Ever Told" (a.k.a. "The Pump Song") (Weir/Hunter/Hart)
Bob Weir, *Ace* (1972)
Mickey Hart, *Rolling Thunder* (1972)
Grateful Dead, *Dead Set* (1981), *Dick's Picks Volume Six*/'83 (1996)

If the Grateful Dead could compose a song around the gyrations of a temperamental electric fan like they did with "Bertha," why not a water pump? In fact, the spunky beat underlying "Greatest Story Ever Told" was not only inspired by such a pump, but a recording of said device was actually used on the version of the song released on Mickey Hart's *Rolling Thunder* album.

As Weir recounted to David Gans in 1981, "That one started out with a rhythm guitar lick. It actually started out with a pump that Mickey had—he recorded the pump and told me to write a song. I ran the pump tape and built a chord structure around it. Mickey suggested that I pattern the song after 'Froggy Went a-Courtin' and He Did Ride.' So I sort of patterned the melody after that. Was it Mickey who suggested it, or Hunter, or me? I forget. Hunter responded: 'Froggy went a-courtin' and did he ride.' Well, 'Moses come ridin' up on a guitar' was about as close as Hunter could get. . . . I liked 'quasar' better. In fact, I think I supplied that word."

"Greatest Story" was one of the few songs on which Weir collaborated with Robert Hunter and despite the pair's previous creation of several Dead classics ("Sugar Magnolia" and "Playing in the Band"), the match was not an easy one. As Hunter related on the specifics of "Greatest Story," "Weir didn't want to sing 'Moses come ridin' up on a guitar,' so I changed it to 'quasar.' He thought that was great, but I subsequently thought, "Wait—*quasar* doesn't fit the song in any way. *Guitar* is a wooden image; it fits the textures."

"I have a tendency not to write the sort of things Weir wanted in his songs at that time. He wasn't looking for the telling phrase, the really apt combination of words to fire off a thought or an emotional process; he was more interested in water color, the textures of the words."

"I called the song 'Greatest Story Ever Wrote,'" said Weir. "I don't know how it got changed to 'Greatest Story Every Told.' Must have been a clerical error on the album copy."

Filled with biblical allusion and allegory, "Greatest Story Every Told" unintentionally shares the same title as the 1965 George Stevens cinematic schlock extravaganza about the life of Christ starring Charlton Heston. Additionally, *The Greatest Story Ever Told: A Tale of the Greatest Life Ever Lived* was a bestselling book by Fulton Oursler in 1949, which rewrote the story of Jesus's life in the idiom of modern popular fiction.

Onstage, "Greatest Story Every Told" developed splendidly. The earliest 1971 renditions bear a stronger resemblance to the syncopated version on Hart's album. But, within a year, the rhythm had been loosened and the jam elongated to allow the sublime incorporation of the "St. Stephen" theme into its peak moments. Over the course of time, the Dead reined the song back in to a spunky first-set cannonball.

9/28/72, Stanley Theater, Jersey City, New Jersey
12/28/79, Oakland Auditorium, Oakland, California
4/24/84, Veterans' Memorial Coliseum, New Haven, Connecticut
3/25/91, Knickerbocker Arena, Albany, New York

"Green, Green Grass of Home" (Curly Putnam)

Porter Wagoner, *On the Road* (1966)
Jerry Lee Lewis, *The Greatest Live Show on Earth* (1965), *Country Songs for City Folk* (1966)
Tom Jones, *Green, Green Grass of Home* (1966)
Johnny Cash, *Johnny Cash at Folsom Prison* (1968)
JOAN BAEZ, *David's Album* (1969)
Elvis Presley, *Elvis Today* (1975)
John Otway, *Stiff Box Set/'78* (1995)
Flying Burrito Brothers, *Dim Lights, Thick Smoke and Loud, Loud Music* (1987)
Goodbye Mr. Mackenzie, single (1990)
Bill Bare, *Best of Bill Bare* (1994)

Like Merle Haggard's "Sing Me Back Home," which the Dead commonly covered in the early 1970s, "Green, Green Grass of Home" is a melancholy lament about a condemned prisoner. Because it was only included in about a half-dozen shows in the summer of 1969, it is much coveted and sought-after song by collectors.

Porter Wagoner had a Top 5 country hit with "Green, Green Grass" in 1965, but it was penned by Curly Putnam, one of the most respected songwriters in country music to have emerged in the 1960s. Born Claude Putnam Jr. on November 30, 1930, in Princeton, Alabama, the son of a sawmill worker, Curly grew up on a mountain named for his family. After briefly attending Southern Union College and spending a four-year hitch in the U.S. Navy, Putnam also worked in a sawmill, attended trade school, and sold shoes. All the while he was honing his skills on the steel guitar, playing in several bands, actively writing and singing. By 1960, he had charted his first hit when "The Prison Song" reached the Top 30.

He continued selling shoes for another three years and, even after moving to Nashville to join Tree Publishing as a staff writer, worked for a clothing company until his big break. That came in 1965 with his first major country hit and one of his biggest, "Green, Green Grass

of Home." Two years after Wagoner's success with the song, Tom Jones of all people had a smash with "Green, Green Grass," taking it to Top 15 on the U.S. pop charts and No. 1 in the U.K. Those credentials not only allowed Putnam to quit his job in the garment industry but to carve out a choice place for himself as a much-desired hit provider for the biggest country names of the past three decades: Dolly Parton, Charlie Rich, Tanya Tucker, and George Jones. With a résumé like that, it is no wonder that he was inducted into the Country Songwriters' Hall of Fame in 1975 for his work in Nashville.

The story behind Putnam's composition of "Green, Green Grass of Home" is the stuff of Trivial Pursuit. While watching television one evening in 1965, Curly Putnam saw the 1950 move *The Asphalt Jungle*, starring Marilyn Monroe and Sterling Hayden, and was impressed by the scene in which criminal Hayden (who had been shot) struggles to go home and see his farm one last time. The house was located on a hill surrounded by "green, green grass." It took Putnam about two hours to write the song.

While demand for Putnam's songs tapered off during the late 1980s, he rallied with "Cafe on the Corner," a Top 5 hit for Sawyer Brown in 1992.

7/12/69, New York State Pavilion, Flushing Park, Queens, New York

▪ "Green Onions" (Jones/Cropper/ Steinberg/Jackson)

Booker T. and the MG's, *Green Onions* (1962)
Michael Bloomfield and Al Kooper, *Live Adventures* (1969)
Johnny Thunders, *Diary of a Lover* (1983), *In Cold Blood* (1983)

Booker T. and the MG's, the Stax house band and the definitive sixties Southern-soul R&B unit, made their name with the help of this definitive funk instrumental, which the Dead played as a one-off novelty in 1988. Garcia also covered it a couple of times with his own group in 1978.

The Stax-Volt house band was in full operation by 1962 and consisted of Booker T. Jones on keyboards, Al Jackson on drums, Lewis Steinberg on bass, and Steve Cropper on guitar. Augmented by the Mar-Keys (later the Memphis Horns), the Stax revolution was just about to coalesce. As the legend goes, it was while waiting for a session to commence that the band section began jamming on a blues that, unbeknownst to them, an engineer caught on tape and eventually titled "Behave Yourself." Deciding that it was good enough to release, the group quickly worked up a riff that Jones and Cropper had been messing around with. "Green Onions" was the result and the eventual hit.

According to Cropper, "I knew when we cut 'Green Onions,' I said, 'Shit, this is the best damn instrumental I've heard in I don't when.' I knew we had a winner there." In recalling the genesis for the song's intriguing title, he elaborated, "We were trying to think of something that was as funky as possible. I think Lewis Steinberg was the one that said, 'Well, the funkiest thing I ever heard of was onions.' To him they were funky because they were stinky."

6/30/88, Silver Stadium, Rochester, New York

■ **"Green River"** (JOHN FOGERTY)
Creedence Clearwater Revival, *Green River* (1969), *Live in Europe* (1974), *Creedence Chronicle* (1976), *The Concert/'70* (1980)

A true hit among several from Creedence Clearwater Revival's album of the same title, "Green River" was performed by the Dead once with its author, at the Bill Graham memorial concert.

11/3/91, Polo Field, Golden Gate Park, San Francisco

■ **David Grisman**
Born March 23, 1945, Hackensack, New Jersey

So how did a nice Jewish boy from suburban New York wind up as a late-twentieth-century King of Bluegrass? David Grisman didn't just reinvent bluegrass in his own image, he invented a musical brand of distinct American form: "Dawg Music," a unique hybrid sound mixing jazz, swing, folk, blues, and country. For more than three decades, Grisman has left his mark on acoustic music through his association with some of the greatest players to pick up an instrument, while managing to defy categorization.

Grisman began as a bluegrass mandolin player, working with Red Allen, Don Stover, and others. Greatly influenced by mandolin superstar Jethro Burns, Grisman grew up in suburban Passaic, New Jersey, playing piano as a youngster. By the time he hit high school, though, he was a confirmed folkie and formed his first bluegrass band with a couple of pals while still in high school. Playing mountain music required the proper name, so

David Grisman. *(Photo: Jay Blakesberg courtesy of Acoustic Disc)*

they took the name from a local Jersey landmark and called themselves the Garrett Mountain Boys. "The first thing that struck me was the banjo, but I actually thought the mandolin was the most unusual instrument," remembered Grisman. "I liked it because no one played it."

An interested teacher at his school was the cousin of Ralph Rinzler, the mandolinist with the Greenbriar Boys and a pivotal figure in the burgeoning bluegrass musical style. Rinzler became Grisman's guru and passed on his wealth of folklore and technique to the eager acolyte. Discussing Rinzler with Nano Riley of *Organica* magazine in 1994, Grisman said, "He's responsible for my education. He was the most influential folklorist of the century."

In 1961 Grisman cut his first record with the Even Dozen Jug Band, which included some others who would go one to enjoy acclaim later in the decade as well: Maria Muldaur, John Sebastian, Stefan Grossman, and Steve Katz.

Grisman slowly acquired a taste for bluegrass (and the chops necessary to perform it), and his epiphany came the day Rinzler and he heard Bill Monroe perform in Rising Sun, Maryland. As Grisman told J. C. Juanis of *Relix* in 1991, "When I heard that voice coming out of a body, I was converted right there."

An added bonus to the show was his introduction to bluegrass as interpreted by Frank Wakefield, a mandolinist in the Monroe vein. Venturing backstage, he went to mandolin heaven and never came back when he encountered Monroe and Wakefield playing duets.

In 1963, with Monroe and Wakefield as his new idols, Grisman sought Wakefield out by venturing to Washington, D.C., with his mandolin and Wollansack tape machine because he heard that the mandolinist and Red Allen were playing at a bar there. Feeling a bit responsible for the boy who seemed a bit out of his element, Wakefield took Grisman under his wing and brought him home that night, where he and Allen jammed in the kitchen while Grisman let the tape roll.

Soon after, Grisman notched his first credit as a producer with Wakefield and Allen. As he told Juanis: "Red had just sold a tape of ten songs to Moe Asch at Folkways Records, and when I heard the songs I felt that they had better material. So I called Moe out of the blue and told him that they had a lot better stuff, and he gave me a budget for three hours of studio time. I got Bill Keith, who is a great banjo player, and Fred Weiss on bass to cut six tunes at a place called Q Studios in New York. That was my first job as a producer and resulted in *Red Allen and Frank Wakefield*."

Back in New York, Grisman was making a local name in folk music circles with the Even Dozen Jug Band working the Hootenannies in Greenwich Village and Carnegie Hall. Connecting with a network of other young players who shared a similar musical vision, Grisman helped put together the New York Ramblers, a pickup band that won the Union Grove Fiddlers Competition in North Carolina in what Grisman describes as the biggest thrill of his life. It was at the festival where Grisman first crossed paths with a wild-haired banjo picker by the name of Jerry Garcia, who passed the hot licks test Grisman casually threw his way. As Garcia told John Carlini of *Guitar* magazine in 1991, "We bumped into each other at Sunset Park, Pennsylvania, I think, in the parking lot. I was traveling the South with Sandy Rothman, and we were recording and meeting guys in bluegrass bands. We were hungry bluegrass nuts from the West Coast, where bluegrass never finds its way. Actually, we were accompanying the Kentucky Colonels at that time in the early sixties; were part of their tour across the United States. They were ending up in Boston, but we went south to Alabama and Florida, and came up through Georgia. So we'd just gotten to Pennsylvania after being on the road for three to four weeks; I got out of the car, and Grisman was walking across the parking lot with kind of a long coat on and a mandolin case. I introduced myself, and we started talking, maybe picked a few tunes or something."

A couple of years later, Grisman visited the Bay Area and encountered the Warlocks and was, upon his return to New York, responsible for garnering the band their first national press in *Sing Out!* in which he was quoted as describing the first rock & roll band to combine bluegrass and folk music.

After an abortive stab at rock with Earth Opera, an electric band that included Peter Rowan, Grisman moved to the Bay Area. After Grisman attended a Grateful Dead and Jefferson Airplane softball game, Garcia invited the unemployed mandolinist to the *American Beauty* sessions, where he graced "Friend of the Devil" and "Ripple."

Grisman's only appearance with the Grateful Dead in concert came in conjunction with the release of *American Beauty* when he shared the stage at the September 20, 1970, gem of a Fillmore East concert for an acoustic set that included, "Uncle John's Band," "Deep Elem Blues," "Friend of the Devil," "Big Railroad Blues," "Dark Hollow," "Ripple," "To Lay Me Down," "Truckin'," "Rosalie McFall," "Cumberland Blues," "New Speedway Boogie," and "Brokedown Palace."

In the early 1970s Grisman began composing instrumental pieces in earnest, the first of which, "Cedar Hill," has been a keeper in his repertoire. But composing was just one ingredient in Grisman's larger vision: an all-instrumental band that would galvanize the disparate elements of the fractured bluegrass tribe. The first step was the Great American String Band, a short-lived unit with guitarist-fiddler Richard Greene, which, after Greene left to join Loggins and Messina, gave birth to the David Grisman Quintet with the incomparable Tony Rice on guitar.

Muleskinner, a side project with Greene, Clarence White, Peter Rowan, and Bill Keith resulted in a popular neo-bluegrass album in 1974 and led to his best known bluegrass band, Old & in the Way, with Garcia, who, during the group's all-too-short 1973 comet-like flash across the musical landscape, tagged the mandolinist with the nickname "Dawg."

While Garcia rejoined the Dead and focused on forming the Jerry Garcia Band, the acoustic sound of Grisman's quintet, in all its evolutions and revolutions, carved a place for itself at jazz, folk, and bluegrass festivals that continues to the present day. While the personnel has transformed through the years, Grisman maintains the exciting acoustic style that has become his signature. In the ensuing years, Grisman developed a dense repertoire of acoustic instrumentals that stretched his genre's boundaries into a sound that fused bluegrass and jazz with his own diverse sensibilities and extraordinarily nimble talent.

Sounding like an updated version of Django Reinhardt's and Stephane Grappelli's mid-1930s Quintet of the Hot Club of France, the David Grisman Quintet's eponymous debut album in 1977 is representative of Dawg music at its finest, almost single-handedly launching an acoustic-music revival. The David Grisman Quintet became to bluegrass and modern American acoustic music what Art Blakey's Jazz Messengers were to jazz, a training ground for the up-and-coming young turks and a bully pulpit for Grisman to strut his stuff with everyone from Rob Wasserman to the great Grappelli.

Throughout, Grisman's mandolin playing developed into a light, highly melodic style as opposed to the guttural, heavy chord chopping often heard in traditional bluegrass work. He also avoided overuse of vibrato, another trademark of bluegrass mandolin picking that is usually overdone, particularly on ballads. Energetic but not hard-driving, Grisman's power as an instrumentalist comes through complex melodic variations and the excitement generated by his invention.

Recording for a number of labels and in many capacities through the mid-1980s (including session work for Bonnie Raitt, Dolly Parton, and James Taylor), Grisman became fed up with the larger record companies when MCA demanded that he submit his masters for prerelease approval. In 1988, he decided to form his own record label, aptly named Acoustic Disc, with a couple of friends. Grisman issued his own and other acoustic-oriented recordings in the late 1980s.

Since then, Acoustic Disc has released several albums annually that sound as good as being there—so exquisite are the recording techniques employed by Grisman and Bob Dennison, his longtime engineer. Some of the more notable examples include *Mandolin Master of Brazil* by Jaco do Bandolim, *Czech It Out* from Czechoslovakian mandolinist and Grisman protégé Radim Zenkl, *The Kitchen Tapes* from those informal Frank Wakefield sessions in the early 1960s, *Songs Our Fathers Taught Us* (a collection of Jewish music with folk and Klezmer giant Andy Statman), *Dawgwood* (a Grisman Quintet outing featuring some Grisman numbers and Django classics), and the two studio reunions

with Garcia in the 1990s, *Jerry Garcia/David Grisman* and *Not for Kids Only*.

While publicizing the latter two discs, Garcia and Grisman showed up on *Late Night with David Letterman* in September 1993 for a wonderful turn on "Friend of the Devil."

Perhaps Grisman's most ambitious project was *Tone Poems*, a duet album recorded with Tony Rice in 1994. In this one remarkable disc, Grisman gathered together seventeen vintage mandolins, seventeen vintage guitars, and, with Rice, recorded seventeen old and new compositions, including such classics as "Wildwood Flower." Symmetry or what? *Tone Poems II*, a followup album recorded with Martin Taylor in 1995, matched the first release lick for stunning lick.

The 1992 recipient of the Rex Foundation's Ralph J. Gleason Award, Grisman summed up his acoustic vision and philosophy best when he said, "I don't think you can be a complete musician playing electric. There are some great practitioners of electric music like B. B. King, but acoustic separated the men from the boys. You can develop a sound on an acoustic instrument. An electric tone has no character. It's not human—it's only a pickup you're hearing. When the lights go out, there will be only acoustic music."

■ *Gypsy Cowboy*/NEW RIDERS OF THE PURPLE SAGE
Columbia KC 31930, 1972.

The New Riders invited Donna Jean Godchaux to their *Gypsy Cowboy* recording session and her vocals appear on two tracks, "She's No Angel" and "Long Black Veil."

■ The Gyuto Monks Tantric Choir

Encountering the chants of the Dalai Lama's personal choir is to confront a ritual beyond music, ceremony, or conventional religion. Rather, it is to glimpse the innermost core of what it means to be human. Contrary to a common assumption that a single voice cannot sing a multinote chord, each Gyuto Monk does so. Imagine the transcendental mix of melody, rhythms, and unearthly overtones when twenty monks sings these chords in unison.

Describing the effect the Dalai Lama's personal choir has on just about anybody who encounters these profoundly spiritual men, Mickey Hart told Richard Price of *BAM* magazine in 1988, "The vibrations draw you in, and then your imagination takes over. And once you're released from your ego, your preconceptions of music, the power, the magic, will affect you differently. You should feel very calm, very centered, and you might think higher thoughts. This is certainly music to travel by. If you really want transportations-transmutations music, this is it. This will alter your consciousness. Their main thrust is vibration—vibration possibly being at the origin of creation."

That's no joke. What the Gyuto Monks present on-stage, on albums, and in temples is not to be messed with. At once awe inspiring and downright scary, it is hard not to catch a glimpse of the friendly and wrathful deities lurking in the background of our own personal mandalas while experiencing this uncompromising music.

Buddhism is a religion based upon the teachings of Buddha in the sixth century B.C. after he experienced enlightenment leading to a profound understanding of the human condition. Buddhism spread through Asia in the following centuries and was introduced into Tibet from the seventh to eleventh centuries, where the religion transformed a rough-and-ready culture into a gentle, monastic, contemplative, and creative nation. The teachings, or tantras, studied by many Tibetan Buddhists are the most advanced, subtle, esoteric forms of all Buddhist teachings, providing specific techniques for mastering all life energies and death confrontation.

Originating in the fourteenth and fifteenth centuries, the multiphonic voice technique of the Gyuto Monks was devised by Tsong Khapa, the founder of the Gyuto University. Tsong, an artist, philosopher, scientist, and religious reformer, is said to have received revelations of the deep and resonant voice used in this practice. It was then expanded by the members of the monastery in the ensuing centuries. With the Chinese occupation of Tibet in 1959, the Dalai Lama fled the Gyuto Monastery with many of his followers, which included nearly nine hundred practicing monks. As the end of the century approaches there are fewer than one hundred monks in exile in Northern India practicing this ancient and mystical form of yoga and meditation.

The Gyuto Monks are celibate practitioners of Mahayana Buddhism, a socially (as opposed to self-) oriented form. Termed a "yoga of the imagination," it involves the total revisioning of reality for all humans away from fear and self-centeredness to personal connectedness with all that exists. Sound, they believe, can communicate and bring into being this more heavenly vision—that the sound of a chorus in expression of the Buddha comes *through* them, not from them, and that the listener (consciously or not) is enfolded in the sound and is inevitably enlightened.

At the musical core of the monks' technique is the incredible feat they can achieve by singing a three-note major chord. Through their training they have reshaped their vocal cavity in such a way that overtones not normally audible can resonate intensely enough to be heard, with each singer's harmony joining with the slightly varying vibrations of the other singers' harmonies, creating endless shifting waves of unfathomable sounds.

Fittingly, the monks joined the Dead for one of the band's last "Space" jams at Shoreline Amphitheater on June 2, 1995, almost as if they were assisting Jerry Garcia's spirit into its next realm.

See also **Tibetan Tanric Choir** *also* **Freedom Chants from the Roof of the World.**

Merle Haggard, Sahara Hotel, Las Vegas, 2/13/76. *(Archive Photos/Fotos International)*

▪ Merle Haggard
Born April 6, 1937, Bakersfield, California

The life of Merle Haggard is woven into the fabric of the American mythos. The grinding poverty of his hardscrabble upbringing, his fated stint in jail, his numerous falls from grace and comebacks are the stuff of legend and artistic sainthood. His musical breadth of vision is remarkable in its synthesization of Lefty Frizzell, Bob Wills, Dixieland jazz, and most importantly, Woody Guthrie, establishing him as a custodian of country music's rich past.

Displaced Okies from the small town of Checotah, Haggard's parents, like thousands of other Dust Bowl refugees, were driven from their land by the ravaging drought and depression of the mid-1930s and headed west in search of a better life in California. In true *Grapes of Wrath* style, they found living conditions dire and jobs few (they actually lived for a time in a converted boxcar), faring better after Haggard's father got a job with the Sante Fe Railroad. But his premature death ended this brief period of prosperity when Haggard was nine. Though his devoutly Christian mother "tried to raise" him better, as he put it in "MAMA TRIED," he soon became wayward.

His father's death led to troubled teenage years with its usual symptoms: unruliness, running away from home, delinquency, reform school, crime, and a couple of visits to the pokey. The second and most serious of these visits was a two-and-a-half-year stint in San Quentin for armed robbery, but it was a turning point in Haggard's life. His interest in country music was renewed when he saw Johnny Cash perform at the big house and he vowed to turn his life around.

After Haggard's release in early 1960, he worked for his brother digging ditches and as an electrician while dabbling in country music onstage on the Bakersfield bar and club scene. Wynn Stewart, a pioneer of honkytonk, hired him to play in his backup band and it was with him that Fuzzy Owen heard him play and signed him to his Tally record label. "Sing Me a Sad Song," Merle's first solo hit in 1963, was followed by a minor duet hit with Bonnie Owens on "Just Between the Two of Us." Bonnie was married to Buck Owens, Bakersfield's other major country star, at the time but soon left him to marry Haggard and join his road show.

Haggard's shot to fame began with his versions of a couple of tunes by Liz Anderson—"(My Friends Are Gonna Be) Strangers" and "I'm a Lonesome Fugitive"—in 1966 and 1967, a deal with Capitol and the popular string of songs about being on the run and life in prison, two of which the Dead covered: "SING ME BACK HOME" and "Mama Tried." When Capitol "revealed" Haggard's past, it only spurred his popularity.

Defining and redefining his public identity as the "poet of the working man," Haggard wrote many songs about the lives of blue-collar workers in America testifying his commitment to honoring and remembering the broad musical and social Southwest tradition of country music in an era when many Nashville stars had forgone their past in search of pop hits.

Though his recording career has been spotty since the 1980s, he has continued to have some notable success. *Pancho and Lefty*, a 1983 album he recorded with Willie Nelson, yielded the No. 1 title track (written by Townes Van Zandt, covered by Dylan, and introduced to the pair by Haggard's daughter) and he scored the odd chart hit while touring with one of the tightest country revues on Earth, stubbornly performing his own brand of country balladry. As he mingles with the dust of the past while blazing into the future, Haggard is still carving a permanent place for himself in the pantheon of American country music.

▪ "Handsome Cabin Boy" (Traditional)
Jerry Garcia and David Grisman, *Shady Grove* (1996)

The Dead only played one pensive instrumental version of this song, an old sea chantey in the gender-bending mold of "JACK A ROE," at a 1993 show in Maryland, perhaps as a testament to that state's seafaring history. Garcia and Grisman learned "Handsome Cabin Boy" off an album of sea songs and chanteys called *Blow Boys Blow*

and featured it in their acoustic shows of the early 1990s.

3/17/93, Capital Centre, Landover, Maryland

▪ "Happiness Is Drumming" (Mickey Hart)
Diga Rhythm Band, *Diga* (1976)

Before the Dead sang the lyrics for "Fire on the Mountain," this two-chord rumba was a one-concert instrumental exercise.

6/28/76, Auditorium Theater, Chicago
See also **"Fire on the Mountain"**

▪ *Harbor Lights* / BRUCE HORNSBY
RCA, 1993.

After leaving his band the Range with barely any public notice, Hornsby recorded this well-performed album of good-hearted, if unmemorable, songs. With an all-star cast including BRANFORD MARSALIS, Pat Metheny, Phil Collins, Bonnie Raitt, and Jerry Garcia, *Harbor Lights* sees Hornsby taking the chops he always had and honed during his Dead gigs at the time, and applying them to adult-contemporary radio. Garcia plays guitar on "Pastures of Plenty" and "Passing Through" on the album.

▪ "Hard to Handle" (Redding/Jones/Isabell)
Otis Redding, *The Immortal Otis Redding* (1968), *The Best of Otis Redding* (1984)
Grateful Dead, *History of the Grateful Dead, Vol. 1 (Bear's Choice)* (1973)
Toots Hibbert, *Toots in Memphis* (1988)
Black Crowes, *Shake Your Money Maker* (1990)

The late, great Otis Redding cowrote and performed this driving soul classic. But as treasured and influential a performer as he was, the Dead's versions of the superfunky "Hard to Handle" may have had even Otis on his hands and knees pleading for mercy.

Who knows what direction Otis Redding's music would have taken had he not been killed in a plane crash at the height of his fame in 1967? The gently affecting "Dock of the Bay," his last hit, pointed away from the take-no-prisoners soul ballads with which he'd gained international acclaim . . . and "respect."

Redding, the son of a minister, was born on September 9, 1941, in Dawson, Georgia. He first sang in church and dreamed of a professional career but he was painfully shy. In what has to rate as one of the oddest

Otis Redding. *(Archive Photos/Frank Driggs Collection)*

breaks in show business, Redding got his chance to audition for a Stax big shot after chauffeuring another band to Memphis. When the other singers failed to rise to the occasion, Redding was summoned and impressed the label with "These Arms of Mine," which was waxed. It hit the R&B Top 20 and made Otis a local star. When he followed that up with "Pain in My Heart," his classic slow ballad showcasing his histrionic approach, he joined other popular groups on the chitlin circuit.

Guided by Phil Walden, a white Southerner who later assisted THE ALLMAN BROTHERS BAND, Redding established his rep in 1964 and 1965 with a series of hits that displayed the tight call-and-response interplay of voice and horns that became his signature. One of these, "I've Been Loving You Too Long" (co-written with Jerry Butler) remains a most moving and complex love song (for soul or anywhere else) and was Redding's first Top 30 pop hit.

He did well with "Respect" in 1965 (even though Aretha Franklin put a lock on the song a couple of years later) but really began hitting his stride with a string of raucous, uptempo songs that exemplified his use of a stuttering technique to signify the overwhelming pressure of emotion on the singer. Redding also had the un-

canny ability to take undistinguished ballads such as "Try a Little Tenderness" and transform them into pew-rocking testaments worthy of the most impassioned fire-and-brimstone spewing stump preacher.

His choice to cover the Rolling Stones' "Satisfaction" won him a 1966 European tour and legions of fans on the continent, but it wasn't until his volcanic performance at the Monterey Pop Festival in 1967 that he made a similar impact on white American teenagers.

Redding seemed on the verge of assuming the mantle of Ray Charles when the Fates decided to have their way with him. En route to a Midwestern gig on December 10, 1967, Redding and all but one aboard a private twin-engine Beechcraft were drowned in an icy lake near Madison, Wisconsin, after their plane encountered trouble in heavy fog.

Ironically and inevitably, the elegiac "Dock of the Bay" reached No. 1 on the pop charts a month after his death and will always serve as Otis Redding's epitaph.

A swaggering vocal platform for Pigpen to really strut his stuff, and an open groove that consistently allowed his band mates to reach peaks of exploding musical ecstasy, "Hard to Handle" was perhaps the Dead's most combustible vehicle in 1969, 1970, and 1971. At some point the Dead began incorporating the "St. Stephen" theme in their molten renditions of the tune. An air guitarist's special.

The band revived "Hard to Handle" twice during their 1982 New Year's run with blues legend Etta James performing the vocals.

4/22/71, Municipal Auditorium, Bangor, Maine
8/6/71, Hollywood Palladium, Hollywood, California

■ ***Harrington Street*** (book)/Jerry Garcia
Delacorte Press, 1995.

Harrington Street came from Garcia's memories of his childhood on this street in San Francisco's Excelsior district. As he describes his publishing lark in the book's introduction: "It's AUTO-APOCRYPHA, full of my ANECDOUBTS. Like things to do with my relatives, my family, the block I grew up on, the things that scared me (animals), the discovery of fire, you know, things like that. I've written to age ten. I talk to myself, sort of remember things about my family, things they told me, things I think I heard."

Like in a Garcia guitar solo, ideas, images, and themes are introduced and repeated, falling back on themselves, resonating with components. For instance, an early childhood memory of being thrown into a swimming pool dovetails with his father's accidental death by drowning and his own later obsession with scuba diving. Much of the look of the book has a submerged, watery quality as if the reader were gazing at a fluorescent bed of coral.

But the book is also a revealing glimpse into Garcia's difficult early years and the odds he had to overcome to find himself. As a last testament to his admirers, *Harrington Street* stands as a warm, personal farewell from him to us.

Jerry Garcia left a legacy in pictures as well as music as is evident in the book's montage containing images either sketched and scanned or generated electronically by the author/artist using Adobe Photoshop and Fractal Painter software. Every element of the book—the text and the more than two hundred images—was provided by Garcia in electronic form, which sped production and facilitated a timely printing just eight weeks after his death.

▪ Mickey Hart

Born Michael Hart, September 11, 1943, Brooklyn, New York

Mickey Hart's visit to Spaceship Earth as one of our master drummers sometimes seemed to have been preordained. Hart's path in life was passed down to him from his parents, Lenny and Leah Hart, who were champion drummers in the 1930s and 1940s. Though his father left home before Mickey was born, his mother encouraged her son's seemingly inherited rhythmic passions by supporting him with drum lessons through high school. Obsessively and passionately devoting himself to his kit, Hart discovered Gene Krupa's 1938 drum solo on "Sing, Sing, Sing," from the famous album *Carnegie Hall Jazz Concert* and tried matching the great jazz drummer lick for lick.

Hart dropped out of high school to join the air force in early 1960. While stationed in Spain, Mickey continued to pursue the drum, and was exposed to martial arts through a man who became his first mentor, a judo instructor named Pogo who taught Hart deep, single-minded focus.

Hart moved to California after his discharge in 1965 to join his estranged father who had invited him to work at Hart Music, his Bay Area drum store. Renaming the store Drum City at Mickey's suggestion, they became the nexus of San Francisco's drum community, holding drum clinics and developing friendships with the hide beaters passing through town. When the Count Basie Big Band performed at the Fillmore Auditorium in 1967, Hart attended to check out Basie's ace drummer Sonny Payne and was introduced to the Dead's drummer Bill Kreutzmann. Sharing a bottle of scotch, the two became swift "drum brothers," hitting the city's streets that night and trading rhythms on parked cars.

Shortly after, Kreutzmann invited Hart to sit in with the Grateful Dead at the September 29, 1967, show at San Francisco's Straight Theater for a legendary "Alligator">"Caution" jam that reportedly lasted two hours! Embracing with the other musicians after the concert, Hart was immediately invited to join the Dead as their second drummer, and from then on, his rhythmic complexity and exotic instrumental approach redefined electric ensemble music.

With Hart onboard, the Dead entered their most adventurous phase exploring and tinkering with a set that fluidly ran the gamut of "Dark Star," cowboy songs, Pigpen-heavy R&B and back again often within the twinkling of an eye. Hart can be heard everywhere on these old tapes, adding texture and counterpoint as the music careened from mind-blown town to mind-blown town.

Along the way, Hart recommended his father to the band as their business manager. But when it was discovered that Lenny was embezzling receipts in 1970 (he eventually served time in prison), Hart decided to take a leave of absence in 1971, though no one in the Dead held him personally, fiscally, or karmicly responsible. For a while the drummer hibernated at his ranch in Novato, California, nursing his pain and sorting out his confusion over the fallout for this very personal and artistic crisis. Aided by a stipend from the Dead (who still considered him a member of the band and musical brother) and an advance from Warner Bros. for a three-record solo deal, Mickey built a state-of-the-art sixteen-track studio that became the nexus for much musical activity in the ensuing years and the wellspring for many albums, including *Rolling Thunder* and *Diga* as well as the soundtrack for Francis Ford Coppola's *Apocalypse Now!*

Hart began edging back into the Dead's performing and recording ensemble by appearing at the final show at Winterland before the band took a hiatus in October 1974 and taking part in the *Blues for Allah* LP a year later. When the Dead resumed touring in 1976, there was Hart right next to Kreutzmann as though he had never left.

In a band of reluctant overachievers, Hart stretched himself as thin as one of his timpani skins upon his formal return to the Dead. In addition to his drumming chores with the Dead, Hart's activities included overseeing the restoration of the Smithsonian Institute's voluminous Folkways archive, researching music's salutary effects on the elderly, and producing a series of ethnic recordings. He also coauthored two books published by HarperCollins, *Drumming at the Edge of Magic* and *Planet Drum*.

As the executive producer of "The World," Rykodisc's ongoing project to record indigenous music from ancient cultures around the world, the drummer indulged himself and provided this quirky but growing market niche with an eclectic geographic aural smorgasbord. By collecting the musics of India, Egypt, Tibet, the South Pacific, New Guinea, Eastern Europe, Africa, and North America under the umbrella of a single company,

Hart has taken giant steps in preserving the history of Planet Earth's all-too-quickly disappearing tribal heritage.

"I've been making remote recordings since 1967 with my Nagra all over the world. It was a hobby that got out of hand," Hart said in 1993. "And then I realized that this music is falling off the edge of the world. If we don't preserve it now, kids will never get a chance to hear what their ancestors sounded like.

"These are sacred songs," Hart continued, "and it's difficult to record them because these ceremonies have been guarded so carefully. They are not public events."

In the spring of 1992, prior to the Dead's three-night stand in Washington, D.C., Hart and the boys hosted official Washington at the Great Hall of the Library of Congress to introduce *The Spirit Cries*, an album of indigenous recordings from cultures threatened by the ever-encroaching technologically based society.

In the summer of 1991, Hart put his mouth where his tom-toms are by speaking before the U.S. Senate's Special Committee on Aging. Addressing the beneficial ef-

Mickey Hart. *(Photo: Bill Scott courtesy of Rykodisc)*

fects drumming could have on the elderly when practiced in drumming circles, Hart urged the committee to consider some of the large population of musicians in the United States as possible candidates in presenting this form of nonverbal communication to many of the older people who spend their days in nursing homes. Hart suggested that some of the benefits would include an immediate reduction in feelings of loneliness and alienation through interaction with each other and heightened contact with the outside world.

"Instead of watching television for hours every day," Hart testified, "older people would have direct exposure to younger people from the outside community."

As part of the Grateful Dead's dynamic drumming duo with longtime collaborator Kreutzmann, Hart developed a clear sense of the group's connection with the community.

"Beneath the core of all this lies another kind of reality and that's what music is all about: to bring people together," Hart said. "It doesn't matter whether it's for entertainment or if it's sacred music. Music is synonymous with bringing people together. In some cultures the words for 'music' and 'bringing people together' are the same. It does the same thing."

Describing the people the Grateful Dead brought together, Hart said, "Deadheads are creating their own Grateful Dead myth. We certainly didn't create them. They created themselves and they did a great job at it. And they've been creating us and reinventing us over and over again. That's the great thing about being reborn—every night you have the chance of creation. That's a great ability and a great privilege. It constantly keeps reinventing itself all the time. That's why it stays fresh. Without that ability to shed one's skin, you're history: you cannot evolve as a person or a people."

Musing on the ritualistic component to the Dead's musical and cultural function in society, Hart commented, "Without music our rituals would be pretty dry. Music is one of our greatest inventions as a people. Can you imagine a world without music? It's hard to imagine. We seem to have that need as a people, as a species. We are a music-making kind of people. There is no culture without music, without some kind of organized sound. Every culture uses music for transformative power.

"There are certain shamanic overtones in performance to what we do. The Grateful Dead are really involved in a shamanistic performance at times: 'seat-of-the-pants shamanism,' as Jerry calls it. We do try to transcend and we use music as the auditory driver just as a shaman would use rhythm, repetition, redundancy for trance inducing. We use the same techniques but louder and with many more people.

"We have to learn these rituals. It's something that we haven't been given so we're sort of stumbling into all of this as twentieth-century men and women. We're learning the archaic techniques. We've been cut off from the past. Civilization has cut us off effectively. We're rediscovering our roots as a species by employing these archaic techniques.

"Grateful Dead is a very unique happening. It was born at a very unique time in our history. There will never be another Grateful Dead and [no one will ever] do what the Grateful Dead does. They'll do their own version of transcendence but the Grateful Dead is unique unto itself. There never was anything like it before nor do I think will there ever be anything like it. Not better or worse but just in its unique power to transcend. It's not technique we're talking about. It's the spirit world that the Grateful Dead addresses."

Given that the band was, in fact, germinated out of the LSD-informed community of San Francisco's Haight-Ashbury in the mid-1960s, Hart never shied away from discussing how psychedelic substances influenced the band's original vision. "Psychoactive drugs played an important part in the development of Grateful Dead music. It allowed us to explore this territory. It gave us a road map to the imagination and to say, 'It's legal to do this musically. Let's go here. Let's play loud. Let's play long. Let's play different.' Psychoactive drugs allowed us to explore all of these alleys that led us on. Some of them were dead ends but with full force we went on that road together.

"You don't have to take acid every day or every week or every month or every year to know the experience. The Grateful Dead certainly embodies the freedom that psychedelics provide. We don't take psychedelics and play together anymore. That's not what we do now. It's just a different version of it."

From the beginning, nearly every Grateful Dead show included an extended percussion jam in which Hart and Kreutzmann communed in free-form improvisations that have long since broken every rule of the drummer's defined role in rock 'n' roll.

Of performing with the Grateful Dead, Hart said, "I try to forget as much as I can. The whole idea is to get everything out of your mind and not worry about what's going to happen and be in the 'now'—be in the moment. If you can be in the moment, the chance of greatness is there, it's at your door. If you're re-creating something then you are a great re-creator. Some people like to create, some people like to re-create. It's risky, it's dangerous. You wouldn't want to do it for a living unless you're in the Grateful Dead or some place where it's expected of you. They expect me to go out there and experience what we all sound like collectively because it's a thing of the moment. We're all creating something very individual. We're creating something from nothing just for that night. When the music stops, they go, we go but it was created for us: whoever was there. It was a certain interaction that created that thing. That's why the Deadheads take this so personally because it's their invention as well as ours. And we created something very unique, never to happen again. That's a great work of art. Sometimes when we play good and they happen to be there and it all happens and we all start heating up—it's magic. They call it magic but it's really a coming together of souls trying to raise consciousness and to try to have fun in this not so fun world. It's an important ingredient in the make-up of the youth of America: the ability to have fun without hurting themselves or other people and having deep fun. To throw themselves totally into what they're doing and not worry about getting busted, not worry about someone stepping on their face. Let themselves go so they can fly, so their imagination can soar. There are very few places where you can do that. We're having a conversation. The Grateful Dead is a thirty-year-old conversation. We are the dance band for the Millennium."

Interested listeners will have a hard time choosing from the dizzying range of Hart's output for additions to their music libraries. Hart appears on most of the Grateful Dead's officially released albums but his contributions to these are probably best heard on *Anthem of the Sun, Live/Dead, Blues for Allah, Terrapin Station, Dick's Picks* volumes three, four, five, and six; *Two from the Vault, Hundred Year Hall,* and *Infrared Roses.*

In addition, Hart has released many solo and collaborative albums with and without the Grateful Dead's participation, including: *Rolling Thunder, Diga Rhythm Band, Dafos, Rhythm Devils* (the *Apocalypse Now!* sessions), *At the Edge, Music to Be Born By,* and the Grammy Award-winning *Planet Drum.* And, in the wake of Garcia's death, Hart reinvented himself more dramatically than any other Grateful Dead member with the re-

lease of *Mystery Box*, a pop-soul-percussion group featuring lyrics by Robert Hunter, which toured as a main attraction of the Furthur Festival in 1996.

For the even more adventurous, Mickey's multiplying productions on Rykodisc include GYUTO MONKS TIBETAN CHOIR, *Freedom Chants;* Sarangi: *The Music of India; The Music of Upper and Lower Egypt,* Babtunde Olatunji's *Invocation* and *The Beat; He's All I Need, The Golden Gate Gypsy Orchestra: The Traveling Jewish Wedding, Dzintars: The Latvian Women's Choir, The Spirit Cries, Around the World,* and *Eclipse,* music from the Sudanese oud master HAMZA EL DIN.

Following Garcia's passing, Hart threw himself into Mystery Box, a percussion-vocal group featuring the lyrics of Robert Hunter which released an album in the summer of 1996 and toured at the Furthur Festival. As Hart told the *New York Times,* "There really is life after the Grateful Dead. I've been in the Grateful Dead my whole life. It's had its ups and downs and it has taken almost all of my time. Now that the Grateful Dead isn't there, it opens up a whole other set of possibilities."

Mickey Hart's Mystery Box

Rykodisc RCD 10338. Produced by Mickey Hart, 1996.
"Where Love Goes (Sito)," "Full Steam Ahead," "Down the Road," "The Sandman," "Look Away," "Only the Strange Remain," "Sangre de Cristo," "John Cage Is Dead," "The Last Song"
Mickey Hart—vocals, drums, claps, timbales, high crystal percussion, beam, castanets, cowbell, gourd, guiro, udu, chains, wine glasses, devil chasers, synthesizer, berimbau, cymbals, bells, angklungs, dumbek, prepared piano, noise, metal saw high-hat, surdo. Robert Hunter—lyrics. Mint Juleps (Debbie Charles, Elizabeth Charles, Julie Isaac, Debbie Longworth, Marcia Charles, Sandra Charles)—vocals. Giovanni Hidalgo—bongo, timbales, cowbell, congas, metal percussion, bata, guiro, bell springs. ZAKIR HUSSAIN—dholak, shekere, duggi tarang, djembe, madal, metal percussion, finger snaps, dimri. Sikiru Adepoju—talking drum. Habib Faye—bass guitar. Jeff Sterling—synthesizers, Burundi drums, low bamboo, synthesizer strings, door stoppers, prepared piano sequence. BABATUNDE OLATUNJI—background vocal. AIRTO MOREIRA—split bamboo on sleigh bells, caxixi. springs, percussion, clacker. BRUCE HORNSBY—accordion, background vocals. Bob Weir—guitar. Robin Millar—marimba.

Taro Hart–drums. Mark Smith–bass guitar. Graham Wiggins–didjeridoo. THE GYUTO MONKS TANTRIC CHOIR–**vocals. Robin Millar–sine bass, computer vocal. Habib Faye–bass guitar.**

And now for something completely different! Mickey Hart gathers his Planet Drum tribe for a series of group compositions that add up to the percussionist's most accessible solo album. The first release of new music by former Grateful Dead members following Jerry Garcia's death, *Mystery Box* is a deft conglomeration of myriad styles and works as a kind of open letter to Deadheads and the world at large assuring all that the music will never stop. Gospel, soul, funk, disco, rap, hip-hop, and metal are some of the more modern genres informing this percussion-heavy offering, and Hart sounds downright Tom Waitsian in his dark reading of Robert Hunter's sharp lyrics that hearken back to the Zen-trickster sensibility of albums like *Workingman's Dead*. But it is the Mint Juleps who steal the show here, taking Hunter's words to another sphere altogether and adding the heart to this pop record with an edge.

He described the project to Mark Rowland of *Musician* in 1996. "Being the Grateful Dead, you live in your own world. So you don't really get to meet other people and mix it up. When I started this, I knew approximately where it was going—guitarless sound, mostly tuned percussion, bass and five or six parts on top, and with Robert Hunter's words—but it was kind of like, unchar-

tered seas. Like going for the New World, you know? Cause we knew there was a new world out there.

"I threw myself into the music. When Jerry died I walked into the studio and started playing and finishing the record, and I never came up for air."

The music of Hart's new band is quite different from the American-roots musical journeys of the Grateful Dead. The product of four years of precision work (he spent two and a half weeks just preparing a piano with small percussive objects for the album's tribute to John Cage), the emotional centerpiece of the album is "Down the Road," in which Hart gently speaks over the soulful cooing of the Mint Juleps about a strange sound he hears coming from the sky: "It sounded like Garcia, but I couldn't see the face. Just the beard and glasses and a smile in empty space."

The material was the surprise hit of the 1996 Furthur Festival, stealing many shows with its crisp warmth.

▪ Hart Valley Drifters
See **Mother McCree's Uptown Jug Champions**

▪ Dan Healy

You can't have a rock concert without amplification and Dan Healy, the Dead's former audio wiz who virtually invented (and reinvented) their always state-of-the-art sound system, was as important to them as the "sixth man" is to any pro basketball squad. But, unlike any other rock techie, Healy was constantly manipulating the sound during a concert—performing, if you will, with the musicians.

Uncharacteristically for a man whose life would be intertwined with sophisticated technology, Healy was raised in Garberville, a rural community in Northern California, in a family that included an intriguing mix of danger and art—his father was a nightclub owner and slot-machine racketeer and his grandfather was a folksinger. While his peers in grade school were out playing baseball, Healy was teaching himself how to use a soldering iron to wire together a couple of turntables and a transmitter, putting his own neighborhood pirate radio station on the air.

Moving to San Francisco after dropping out of high school in 1963, Healy took odd jobs at KSFO and Commercial Recorders—living on a houseboat in Larkspur. Healy had known John Cippolina of the Quicksilver Messenger Service since they were kids and went to see the lead guitarist with his band in June 1966 at the Fillmore. But when Healy arrived, the Dead were onstage and unable to play because Phil Lesh's amplifier had broken down. Pressed into action, Healy fixed the amp but was unimpressed with the Dead's sound system. Challenged by Garcia and Lesh to improve upon it, Healy delivered a month later what was up to that time the best rock sound system, forging a unique partnership that would last the better part of the next three decades.

Soon the Dead, at Healy's behest, were recording during the graveyard shift at Commercial Recorders and while Top 40 AM radio shied away from the tapes because the band had yet to sign a record deal, word started to spread when Healy played the reels on his late-night radio gig, marking the dawn of free-form FM radio.

After several years on the road with the Dead, Healy's talents as a producer lured him away from the Dead and from late 1969 until early 1971 he was at the helm for albums from artists as diverse as the Charlatans, Mother Earth with Tracy Nelson, Dr. John, Quicksilver Messen-

ger Service, and Junior Parker. But when he crossed paths with the Dead at a December 1971 show at the Felt Forum in New York City, he was horrified at the atrocious state of the band's sound and promptly rejoined.

Working with Owsley (the Dead's early benefactor and sound technician), Healy's major project over the course of the next several years was the research, development, and implementation of the Wall of Sound, a mammoth speaker system that towered above the band onstage in 1973 and 1974 and which eventually drove the Grateful Dead to financial disaster but made crystalline concert sound available in a fashion that has rarely been equaled. Healy's colleagues in sound formed a veritable kibbutz of radical technological innovation that pursued the possibilities of audio in a matter not dissimilar to the manner in which the Dead chased the lost chord.

Perhaps more than any single member of the Dead's organization, Healy was responsible for the existence of high-quality concert tapes, as he allowed budding tapers

The Wall of Sound, 1973.
(Archive Photos/The Platt Collection)

to patch into the soundboard, dispensed advice as to how to obtain optimum results, and helped establish and formalize the tapers' section in 1984.

By the time Healy inaugurated the Dead's *Vault* series in 1991 (what became a duo of archival releases), he had become a cult figure among Deadheads with adherents as passionate as those that claimed "Jerry is God!" So it was with some degree of shock when Healy abruptly left the band in 1994 reportedly due to a contract dispute.

▪ *Heart of Gold Band Live*
Relix RRLP 2020.

See ***Double Dose***

▪ "Heart of Mine" (BOB DYLAN)
Bob Dylan, *Shot of Love* (1981), *Biograph* (1985)

"Heart of Mine," a ragged but sweet love song from Bob Dylan's overlooked *Shot of Love* album, is filled with wise advice and cold realities of romantic attraction with twists on cliché lines like "You can play with fire but you'll get the bill" that only Dylan can pull off with a straight face. The official release of the song sounds like a first take with Bob plunking the piano keys and Ron Wood helping out on guitar.

In his liner notes to *Biograph*, Dylan recalled, "Well, I had somebody specific in mind when I wrote this, somebody who liked having me around. That's just a guitar song, you know. I think we lost the whole riff on it, though, on the record. I recorded it a couple of different ways, and the original way I didn't use for some reason."

Dylan has intermittently performed the song since its 1981 release, and it was with the Dead that one of those revivals took place.

5/87, Club Front, San Rafael, California (Bob Dylan rehearsal)

▪ *Heart's Desire*/HENRY KAISER **Band**
Reckless, 1990.

With Tom Constanten joining in, this superlative eighteen-cut release is a versatile adventure reflected in its eclectic mix of material including a major-league "Dark Star."

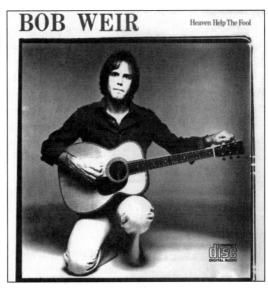

(Courtesy of Arista Records)

▪ *Heaven Help the Fool*/Bob Weir
Arista AB 4155, 1978. Produced by Keith Olsen.
"Bombs Away," "Easy to Slip," "Salt Lake City," "Shade of Grey," "Heaven Help the Fool," "This Time Forever," "I'll Be Doggone," "Wrong Way Feelin'"
Bob Weir–guitars, vocals, background vocals. David Foster–keyboards. Bill Champlin–keyboards. Nigel Olsson–drums. Waddy Wachtel–guitars. Dee Murray–bass. Tom Kelly, Carmen Twilly, Lynette Gloud–background vocals. Mike Porcaro–bass. David Paich–keyboards. Mike Baird–drums.

Right down to its Richard Avedon cover photo, this altogether too-slick, over-produced Weir release shrouded a collection of pretty good songs. A testament to the album's strengths and staying power is that several of the selections ("Bombs Away," "Easy to Slip," "Shade of Grey") became integral inclusions in Weir's various solo tours. Additionally, "Heaven Help the Fool" and "Salt Lake City" were briefly treated by the Dead.

▪ "Heaven Help the Fool" (Weir/Barlow)
Bob Weir, Heaven Help the Fool (1978)

The title track of Bob Weir's slick L.A. studio album is one of his most sophisticated and inward-looking songs from the late 1970s, with Weir playing the part of the materialistic playboy who begins to notice that the fast track isn't all it's cracked up to be.

"Heaven Help the Fool" has been a constant in the set lists of Weir's different bands over the years, but the Dead only briefly performed it as a segue instrumental during their 1980 acoustic revival. The Dead never adopted anything else from the *Heaven Help the Fool* album and, even when it was performed by Weir and keyboardist Brent Mydland, it was only as a spare instrumental coloration. Though other band members joined in sporadically, it never received the attention of the full ensemble.

10/6/80, Warfield Theater, San Francisco

▪ *Heavy Turbulence*/MERL SAUNDERS

Fantasy 8421, 1971. Produced by Tom Fogerty with Merl Saunders and Brian Gardner.

"My Problems Got Problems," "The Night They Drove Old Dixie Down," "Save Mother Earth," "Imagine," "Welcome to the Basement," "Man-Child"

Merl Saunders–keyboards, vocals. Jerry Garcia–lead guitar, vocals. Tom Fogerty–rhythm guitar, vocals. JOHN KAHN–bass. Bill Vitt–drums. The Hawkins Singers (Edwin, Walter, Tramaine, Lynette, Freddie, Carol)–background vocals. Eddie Moore–drums, saw. Kenneth Nash–percussion. Bob Drew–alto saxophone. The Tower of Power Horns–reeds.

Many of the musicians on this album could often be found jamming together in and around the Bay Area, so it's not surprising they ended up playing one another's recording sessions. But while Garcia's guitar is on every track here, *Heavy Turbulence* is a Merl Saunders disc and not a wall-to-wall Garcia showcase, though he takes a good crack at "My Problems Got Problems," sings lead on "The Night They Drove Old Dixie Down," and wails under some unnecessary studio vamping on "Man-Child."

▪ "Hell in a Bucket" (Weir/Barlow)

Grateful Dead, *In the Dark* (1987), *The Arista Years* (1996), *Dick's Picks Volume Six/'83* (1996), *Dozin' at the Knick/'90* (1996)

The Grateful Dead producing a song with S&M biker-chick allusions? Hard to fathom but true, "Hell in a Bucket" playfully toys with the risqué in a catchy, fun-loving way. Often used as a show-opening jump starter, Weir's wail was one of several *In the Dark* selections to garner heavy FM airplay long after the peak of the album's 1987 popularity.

The song's confident chorus "May be going to hell in a bucket, but at least I'm enjoying the ride" captured the plucky apocalyptic angst of the Reagan era, the last years of the Cold War as we knew it, and was a fitting credo to a typical Deadhead's worldview.

A final note on the song concerns the song's authorship. David Gans suggested the lyric "sipping champagne from your boot" that Weir eventually replaced over John Barlow's "kissing the toe of your boot."

8/22/87, Calaveras County Fairgrounds, Angel's Camp, California

▪ *Hell's Angels Forever, Forever Hell's Angels* (film)/Directed by Richard Chase, Kevin Keating, and Leon Gast, 1983.

A superficial, quasi-documentary portrait of the Hell's Angels (some parts of it even come off as a recruiting film), *Hell's Angels Forever* is redeemed only by some brief footage of the Jerry Garcia Band performing at a benefit for the notorious motorcycle gang. Amazingly, the film was, according to *Variety*, the fourth top-grossing film of the week ending December 12, 1983, behind *Terms of Endearment, A Christmas Story,* and *The Big Chill.* Codirector Leon Gast had worked in the same capacity with Garcia on *The Grateful Dead Movie* in the mid-1970s and, in 1997, won an Oscar for *When We Were Kings,* a documentary about the 1974 Muhammad Ali–George Foreman heavyweight championship fight in Zaire.

▪ "Help Me Rhonda" (Brian Wilson)

THE BEACH BOYS, *Beach Boys Today!* (1965), *Summer Days (and Summer Nights)* (1965), *The Very Best of the Beach Boys* (1983)

Beach Boys Today! and *Summer Days,* the summer albums for 1965, hinted at Brian Wilson's increasing musical sophistication and eccentricity, including "Help Me Rhonda," one of several hits for the band that year.

"Help Me Rhonda" made an appearance at only one Dead show, when the boys were joined by the Boys, the Beach Boys that is, at the famous Fillmore East concert during the Dead's final run at that fabled venue.

4/27/71, Fillmore East, New York

▪ "Help on the Way" (Garcia/Hunter)

Grateful Dead, single, *Blues for Allah* (1975), *Without a*

Net (1990), *One from the Vault* /'75 (1991), *Dick's Picks Volume Three*/'77 (1995)

Notions of salvation and deliverance waiting just around the corner are a constant theme in Grateful Dead music and this dense, jazzy piece poetically explores these inclinations in words and sound. Forever joined at the musical hip with "Slipknot!" and "Franklin's Tower," "Help on the Way" slipped in and out of the Dead's playlists since its 1975 debut possibly because of its inherent musical complexities.

> 8/4/76, Roosevelt Stadium, Jersey City, New Jersey
> 4/17/83, Brendan Byrne Arena, East Rutherford, New Jersey
> 4/21/84, Civic Convention Hall Auditorium, Philadelphia
> 6/14/91, RFK Stadium, Washington, D.C.
> 9/25/91, Boston Garden, Boston

■ "Here Comes Sunshine" (Garcia/Hunter)
Grateful Dead, single, *Wake of the Flood* (1973), *Dick's Picks Volume One* /'73 (1993)

"Here Comes Sunshine" is the Grateful Dead at their sublime Beatlesque pinnacle. This lush, incredibly beautiful, and powerfully positive song was dudlessly displayed more than thirty times during its 1973 debut. Really and truly, there wasn't a bad one in the batch. Capped by a soaring jam stretching from here to eternity, "Here Comes Sunshine" was sadly shelved for almost twenty years after a single performance in 1974.

It was at Vince Welnick's well-intentioned instigation that "Here Comes Sunshine" returned to a semi-regular slot in the band's concerts. Welnick had begun performing the song with his occasional spare-time band, the Affordables, and after they opened for the Garcia Band, Garcia expressed a desire to do it again. However, the dusted-off version, though still triumphant, was only a shade of its former self.

The definition of "Primal Dead," "Here Comes Sunshine" found the band intuiting and complementing one another in a continual, centrifugal state of "becoming"—reemerging and reinventing themselves with each and every luscious lick. A gem of a song.

According to Robert Hunter's comments in *A Box of Rain*, the lyrics were inspired by "remembering the great Vanport, Washington, flood of 1949, living in other people's homes, a family abandoned by father; second grade."

> 2/9/73, Roscoe Maples Pavilion, Palo Alto, California
> 2/17/73, Auditorium, St. Paul, Minnesota
> 3/21/73, Memorial Auditorium, Utica, New York
> 12/19/73, Curtis Hixon Hall, Tampa, Florida (*Dick's Picks Volume One*).
> 7/20/94, Deer Creek Music Center, Noblesville, Indiana

■ *Here Goes Nothin'* /Zero
Relix RRCD 2030, 1987.

Donna Jean Mackay (formerly Donna Godchaux) appears briefly on this rare Zero album, singing lead on a song entitled "Showboat."

■ *The Hero's Journey: The World of Joseph Campbell* (film)

Garcia, Hart, and Mydland contributed to the soundtrack of this film about Joseph Campbell, the mytho-historian who forged a unique friendship with the Grateful Dead shortly before his passing.

■ *He's All I Need* /San Quentin Mass Choir
Grateful Dead Records/Rex Foundation GDCD39042, 1992. Produced by Mickey Hart.
"I'm on the Lord's Side," "Only a Look," "He Watches Over Me," "Take Care of Me," "He's All I Need," "You Can Make It If You Try," "Tribute"/"Storm Clouds Rising," "The Bible," "Amazing Grace," "He's All I Need (Reprise)"

On the high spiritual plane, Hart produced a hit gospel record titled *He's All I Need* notable because it was performed by the fifty-voice San Quentin Mass Choir comprised entirely of inmates and correctional officers from the infamous prison in Marin County.

"It began with the GYUTO MONKS," Hart said, speaking of the troupe of Tibetan Buddhist monks with whom the drummer has long been involved. "The monks were here on tour in the late 1980s and passed by San Quentin prison and worried, 'What's going on here?' They felt a funny vibration and they stopped the van and were told that there were 6,500 trapped souls in there. They got out and did a 'puja,' a Tibetan Buddhist ceremony, a prayer, and expressed a desire to go in and relieve some of the stress there in the form of a musical offering in the prison.

"So we arranged it through the Rex Foundation (the charity organization associated with the Grateful Dead).

They went in and sang for the choir and the choir sang for them. There was this flower growing in there. So the Rex Foundation gave me some funds to record them.

"As we started to work with them over several months of rehearsing, the Christian guards started coming off the walls. Little by little they started joining the choir and soon the guards and prisoners were singing sacred songs in the chapel. All of a sudden the choir started getting *big*.

"They really did an incredible thing. They created incredible art under such adverse circumstances. You have to overcome a lot to make joyous music in San Quentin."

▪ "He's Gone" (Garcia/Hunter)
Grateful Dead, *Europe '72* (1972), *Dick's Picks Volume One /'73* (1993), *Dick's Picks Volume Five/'79* (1996)

"He's Gone" originally referenced the band's dismal experience with Lenny Hart, their one-time manager and Mickey Hart's father. The tune's opening lyric says it all: "Rat in drain ditch, caught on a limb." After that, the dirge developed into a more gospel-influenced elegy and was often used by the band to mourn the passing of such revered individuals as Bob Marley, Irish freedom fighter Bobby Sands, and their own Ron "Pigpen" McKernan. As Hunter told Blair Jackson in 1991; "Later it became an anthem for Pigpen, and it's changed through the years. These songs are amorphous that way. What I intend is not what a thing is in the end."

8/21/72, Berkeley Community Theater, Berkeley, California
6/22/73, P.N.E. Coliseum, Vancouver, British Columbia, Canada
12/1/79, Stanley Theater, Pittsburgh
10/9/84, Centrum, Worcester, Massachusetts
12/2/92, McNichols Sports Arena, Denver

▪ "He Was a Friend of Mine"
(Traditional/BOB DYLAN)
LEADBELLY, single (1935)
Smith Casey, *Afro-American Blues and Game Songs/'39* (1978)
James "Iron Head" Baker, *The Ballad Hunter Vol. 5/'43* (1982)
Bob Dylan, *Bootleg Series Vols. 1–3/'62* (1992)
David Van Ronk, *Inside David Van Ronk* (1962)

Eric Von Schmidt, *The Folk Songs of Eric Von Schmidt* (1963),
The Byrds, *Turn! Turn! Turn!* (1966), *The Best of the Byrds Vol. II* (1972), *Monterey International Pop Festival* (1992)
The Washington Squares, *The Washington Squares* (1987)

The roots of the mournful "He Was a Friend of Mine" are somewhat curious. The song was recorded for, but did not appear on, Bob Dylan's Columbia debut album, *Bob Dylan*. But when he was interviewed by Robert Shelton for the liner notes to the record, Dylan mentioned that his own version was an adaptation of a song he'd learned from a Chicago street singer named Blind Arvella Gray. Supporting this is the original copyright filed by Dylan that indicates it is a traditional composition with supplemental lyrics.

Elsewhere, it is reported that the source for "He Was a Friend of Mine" is a traditional Southern prison song entitled "Shorty George," which was recorded by Leadbelly in 1935 and by some penitentiary singers for the Library of Congress. It was from those Library of Congress cuts that Eric Von Schmidt taught himself the tune. Von Schmidt, an early influence on and colleague of Dylan's, claimed credit for teaching the song to Dylan and had this to say to Anthony Scaduto, Dylan's first biographer, regarding their mutual folk explorations: "He was very impressed by that concept of being able to take the black expression in that kind of song and being able to sing it. He wasn't at that time quite able to handle material that related to the blues, and he was still feeling around for a way to do that."

Dylan seems to agree with this astute observation in the liner notes to his second album, *The Freewheelin' Bob Dylan*: "I don't carry myself yet the way that Big Joe Williams, Woody Guthrie, Leadbelly, and Lightnin' Hopkins have carried themselves. I hope to be able to someday, but they're older people . . ."

Despite the fact that "He Was a Friend of Mine" didn't make it onto Dylan's first album, he did perform it often in Greenwich Village folk clubs. In turn, his version was adopted as a standard by other local folkies including Dave Van Ronk, who included his own recasting of the song on his 1963 LP. Von Schmidt also recorded the song and it was probably from the both of them that it was passed down to Roger (then Jim) McGuinn, who later brought it to the Byrds and recorded its most famous release in 1966 as a tribute to the late President Kennedy.

The Dead's ragged but right performances of "He Was a Friend of Mine" in the late 1960s have an air of distinct personal loss about them and fit right in with the death-theme songs that were a constant aspect of their concert presentations.

5/3/69, Winterland Arena, San Francisco

5/24/69, Seminole Indian Village, West Hollywood, Florida

12/12/69, Thelma Theater, Los Angeles

• "Hey Bo Diddley" (BO DIDDLEY)

Bo Diddley, single (1957), *Bo Diddley* (1958), *Bo Diddley's Beach Party* (1964), *Roadrunner* (1964)

The Crickets, *Bobby Vee Meets the Crickets* (1961)

Kenny Rogers, *Kenny Rogers and the First Edition* (1970)

Bob Seger, *Smokin' O.P.'s* (1972), *Live Bullet* (1976)

Jimi Hendrix, "Untitled French Compilation" (1975)

Maureen Tucker, *Playin' Possum* (1982), *Life in Exile After Abdication* (1989)

Ron Wood and Bo Diddley, *Live at the Ritz* (1987)

The Everly Brothers, *Rock & Roll Odyssey* (1990)

It takes gumption to write a song, name it after yourself, and get away with it. But that's exactly what Bo Diddley did in 1957. Set to his signature ("shave 'n' a haircut, two bits"), four-beat "Not Fade Away" rhythm, the Dead performed the send-up five times between 1972 and 1986, including one with the raucous author himself in 1972 during a wild, four-song first set in which they covered a number of primeval rock & roll classics.

3/25/72, Academy of Music, New York (with Bo Diddley)

8/26/72, Berkeley Community Theater, Berkeley, California

• "Hey Jude" (Lennon/McCartney)

The Beatles, *Hey Jude/'68* (1970)

Paul McCartney, *Tripping the Light Fantastic* (1990)

Jazz Crusaders, *Powerhouse* (1968)

Wilson Pickett, *Hey Jude* (1969)

The Everly Brothers, *The Everly Brothers Show* (1970)

Smokey Robinson and The Miracles, *Four in Blue* (1970)

The Temptations, *Puzzle People* (1970)

Elvis Presley, *Elvis Now* (1972)

Shadows, *Midnight Shadows* (1982)

In the violent summer of 1968, Paul McCartney wrote this tender ballad for Julian Lennon, who was depressed after the failure of his parents' marriage. Originally conceived as "Hey Jules," the song changed as McCartney and John Lennon put the finishing touches on it in early August. The official release is augmented by a forty-piece orchestra, many of whom were also enlisted to sing on the song's extended coda.

For the biblically curious, Jude was one of the Twelve Apostles. Also called Thaddeus, he is believed to be the author of the Epistle of Jude in the New Testament. He was venerated in the Middle Ages, but his cult suffered as his name became confused with that of Judas Iscariot, Christ's betrayer. For centuries no one would invoice him for anything—hence his willingness to help people even in the most desperate situations. Jude was martyred with arrows, or javelins, or on a cross.

Running more than seven minutes, "Hey Jude" is not only the longest single track in the Beatles' canon, it is one of popular music's most venerable hits, selling nearly eight million copies between its release in 1968 and 1972. The single was so popular, in fact, that the album on which it later appeared outsold both *Sgt. Pepper's Lonely Hearts Club Band* and *The Beatles* (the White Album).

With a raw Pigpen vocal lead, half-hearted and evidently unrehearsed versions of "Hey Jude" showed up at a couple of spring 1969 Dead shows. But sixteen years later, with Brent Mydland singing, the band dusted off the famous finale and paired it with Traffic's "DEAR MR. FANTASY" as a popular late-second-set offering. After Mydland's passing in 1990, the "Dear Mr. Fantasy">"Hey Jude" tandem was permanently shelved.

3/22/90, Copps Coliseum, Hamilton, Ontario

• "Hey Little One" (Burnette/Vorzon)

Dorsey Burnette, single (1960), *Greatest Hits* (1969)

J. Frank Wilson and the Cavaliers, single (1965)

Glen Campbell, single, *Hey, Little One* (1968)

Garcia is only known to have sung Dorsey Burnette's bubblegum ballad at one 1966 show, but its author is one of teen pop's lost icons. Dorsey Burnette (born December 28, 1932) grew up in Memphis and was weaned on country music. As soon as he could drive a car and had some change in his pocket he began driving all the way to Nashville every Saturday night to go to the Grand Ole Opry, which he had been listening to on the radio since he was a child. He formed a band with his older (and ultimately more successful) brother Johnny in the 1950s, playing an Elvis-inspired brand of music in the Rock 'n' Roll Trio. They recorded a clutch of regionally successful singles for Decca in 1956 and 1957 that, with their fuzzy-tone guitar sound, energetic vocals, and slapping bass, compare well to the classic Sun Records rockabilly of the same era. Unable to compete with Presley, the trio broke up in 1957 and Johnny Burnette went on to become a teen idol in the early 1960s with hits like "You're Sixteen" and "Dreamin'."

Dorsey Burnette made the charts with "Hey Little One" and "Tall Oak Tree" in 1960. In 1968, Burnette's close friend Glen Campbell turned out a single of "Hey Little One" that went platinum. But his brother's death in a 1964 boating accident left Burnette emotionally scarred for years.

A fixture on the L.A. music scene throughout the balance of the 1960s and the 1970s, his talents as a singer and a writer caught the attention of country fans as he placed fourteen songs on the national charts. It was in Southern California where he died in 1979 of a heart attack.

3/25/66, Trouper's Hall, Los Angeles

■ **"Hey Pocky Way"** (a.k.a. "Hey Pocky A-Way")
(Traditional)
The Meters, *Rejuvenation* (1974), *Fire on the Bayou*
    (1975), *Mardi Gras in New Orleans Vol. II* (1965),
    Best of the Meters (1975)
Wild Tchoupitoulas, *Wild Tchoupitoulas* (1975)
THE NEVILLE BROTHERS, *Fiyo on the Bayou* (1981),
    Treacherous (1988)
Aaron Neville, *Mardi Gras Party* (1991)
Irma Thomas, *Simply the Best: Live!* (1991)

From time to time, the Dead have delved into the rich cultural history of New Orleans to retrieve some suitable cover material. In all probability it was the Neville Brothers, who played with the Dead many times starting in the mid-1980s, who pointed them towards "Hey Pocky Way." Actually, it was the Meters, a cherished Crescent City–based funk/rock band that included Art Neville, who first set this old Mardi Gras street chant to music. Later, when Neville was forming the Neville Brothers, he brought a few Meters numbers into their repertoire, "Hey Pocky Way" included. A good example of what the authentic Mardi Gras "Indian" chant

sounded like can be gleaned from a version on the early records of the Wild Tchoupitoulas, an embryonic version of the Nevilles.

Brent Mydland sang the song with the Dead when they started playing "Hey Pocky Way" in 1987, but it disappeared from their concerts after his death in 1990.

4/30/88, Frost Amphitheater, Palo Alto, California
3/28/90, Nassau Veterans Memorial Coliseum,
    Uniondale, New York

■ **"Hideaway"** (Freddie King)
Freddie King, *Let's Hide Away and Dance Away with
    Freddie King* (1961), *Hide Away* (1969), *Just Pickin'*
    (1989), *Hide Away: The Best of Freddie King* (1991)
John Mayall and the Bluesbreakers, *Bluesbreakers*
    (1966)
Electric Blues, *Underground* (1967)
Eric Clapton, *History of Eric Clapton* (1972)
Cream, *Live Cream Vol. 2* (1972)

Garcia always credited Freddie King (born Freddie Christian, September 3, 1934, in Gilmer, Texas) with be-

Freddie King. *(The New York Public Library for the Performing Arts)*

ing a huge influence on his early approach to the guitar and rightly so. Garcia does sound like a King clone on old WARLOCKS tapes, and "VIOLA LEE BLUES," the show-stopping finale on the Dead's debut disc, sounds like the kind of solo this linchpin of the modern blues guitar could do in his sleep.

Remembering the effect King had on his early playing, Garcia told Charles Reich and Jann Wenner in 1971, "I think Freddie King is the guy I learned the most volume of stuff from. When I started playing electric guitar the second time, with the Warlocks, it was a Freddie King album that I got almost all of my ideas off of, his phrasing really. That first one, *Here's Freddie King*, later it came out as *Freddie King Plays Surfin' Music* or something like that, it has 'San-Ho-Zay' on it and 'Sensation' and all those instrumentals."

Those who had the good fortune to catch a Freddie King concert saw a mighty figure who, at more than six-and-a-half-feet tall, could dominate a bandstand like his searing, aggressive solos dominated a group of rare homogeneity: the blues-rock instrumental.

Because he moved to Chicago with his family when he was a teenager, King absorbed the styles at both ends of Highway 61 and developed a style noted for its technical brilliance. He began recording for obscure labels in the 1950s but it wasn't until he hooked up with Sonny Thompson, a pianist and King Records A&R man, that King's work began to gain popularity.

He scored a series of rhythm and blues hits with "Have You Ever Loved a Woman," "The Stumble," and "Driving Sideways" in the early 1960s, which were later covered by the likes of Eric Clapton and John Mayall.

It was King's instrumentals in this era that brought him his greatest fame and spread his influence far and wide. "Hideaway," easily his most recognizable instrumental composition, reached No. 29 on the *Billboard* pop charts in 1961 and ranks among the most popular blues instrumentals ever waxed. Named for a noted Chicago blues club, Mel's Hideaway Lounge, "Hideaway" showcased King's twangy sound, technical prowess and inventiveness in forging infectious musical hooks sifted from blues, rock, and R&B.

As his work began to impact the British blues scene, King undertook a fierce recording and touring slate that may have hastened his early passing of a heart attack and bleeding ulcers after being taken ill during a club performance in Dallas, Texas, on December 28, 1976.

The Dead only performed "Hideaway" at a couple of concerts some eighteen years apart.

11/7/71, Harding Theater, San Francisco
6/21/89, Shoreline Amphitheater, Mountain View, California

- ## "High Time" (Garcia/Hunter)
  Grateful Dead, *Workingman's Dead* (1970), *What a Long Strange Trip It's Been* (1977), *Dick's Picks Volume Four/'70* (1996)
  HENRY KAISER, *ETERNITY BLUE* (1995)

A wise wastrel dispenses hard-earned advice in this somber reworking of "Murphy's Law" from *Workingman's Dead*. "Nothing's for certain, it can always go wrong / Come on in when it's raining, go on out when it's gone" is one of several aphorisms the storyteller offers in "High Time," which reads like an introduction to the Dead's school of hard knocks. The whole mood and setting of the song reeks with the atmosphere and morning-after sentiment of a turn-of-the-century western brothel during a deluge.

"High Time" was a concert regular since its introduction in 1969 and appeared in nearly every context: an acoustic folk song, a first-set pace slower, and as a second-set downshift. It is particularly effective as one of Garcia's world-weary testaments.

3/20/70, Capitol Theater, Port Chester, New York
6/9/76, Boston Music Hall, Boston
3/24/81, Rainbow Theater, London
11/1/85, Coliseum, Richmond, Virginia
9/26/93, Boston Garden, Boston

- ## "Highway 61 Revisited" (BOB DYLAN)
  Bob Dylan, *Highway 61 Revisited* (1965), *Real Live* (1984)
  Bob Dylan and THE BAND, *Before the Flood* (1975)
  Johnny Winter, *Second Winter* (1969), *Captured Live* (1976), *The Johnny Winter Collection* (1988), *Bob Dylan: The 30th Anniversary Celebration Concert* (1993)
  Terry Reid, *Terry Reid* (1969)
  P J Harvey, *Rid of Me* (1993)

Highway 61 linked southern blacks with the northern cities of the Midwest. It brought impoverished rural families to urban opportunity and the country blues to Chicago and Detroit. The ribbon of highway extends from the Gulf of Mexico to Duluth, Minnesota, and became the poetic road that allowed Bob Dylan to unite his contemporary vision of the American musical landscape on one of his most profound albums, *Highway 61 Revisited*.

In its original pressing, this ringing blues shuffle is spurred by a police car whistle while his crack studio band races to keep up, paced by the drumming and flavored with Mike Bloomfield's stinging bottleneck guitar. The lyrics are informed by a range of traditions that include everybody from the mumbo jumbo of the blues liturgy to Lord Buckley, the neglected, visionary jazz comedian-storyteller who is an overlooked influence on the development of Dylan's early aesthetic.

"Highway 61 Revisited" has often been visited by Dylan during his career and was performed at three of his 1987 concerts with the Grateful Dead with an arrangement regarded by Dylanists as one of the better treatments of the song.

> **7/19/87, Autzen Stadium, Eugene, Oregon (with Bob Dylan)**

■ "Hi-Heel Sneakers" (Robert Higgenbotham)

> **Tommy Tucker, single (1964), *Vintage Collectibles*/'64 (1987)**
> **Garcia/Saunders/Kahn/Vitt, *Keystone Encores Vol. 2*/'73 (1988)**
> **Stevie Wonder, single (1965)**
> **Ike and Tina Turner, *Live! The Ike & Tina Turner Show* (1965)**
> **The McCoys, *Hang on Sloopy* (1965)**
> **Jerry Lee Lewis, *The Greatest Live Show on Earth* (1965)**
> **Everly Brothers, *Beat and Soul* (1965)**
> **Ramsey Lewis, *Greatest Hits*/'66 (1973)**
> **Elvis Presley, single (1968), *Elvis Aron Presley* (1980), *Reconsider Baby* (1985)**
> **Jose Feliciano, *All-Time Greatest Hits*/'68 (1988)**
> **Street, *Street* (1968)**
> **CHUCK BERRY, *Chuck Berry '75* (1975)**
> **Paul McCartney, *Unplugged—The Official Bootleg* (1991)**
> **Johnny Rivers, *Totally Live at the Whisky-a-Go-Go* (1995)**
> **Reunion Blues Band, *Back Home to Clarksdale* (1996)**

"Hi-Heel Sneakers" was written by Robert Higgenbotham and recorded by him under the name Tommy Tucker in 1964, reaching No. 11 on *Billboard*'s pop chart. Higgenbotham was born on March 5, 1934, in Springfield, Illinois, and was a Golden Gloves boxer in the early 1950s before turning to music. Starting out as a clarinetist, Higgenbotham switched to piano and made quite the name for himself in the Midwest, even working for a spell in the band of jazzman and multireed instrumentalist wunderkind Rahsaan Roland Kirk (a true American visionary if there ever was one!).

But it was after his move to Asbury Park, New Jersey, in the early 1960s that he began to gain a following singing and recording his own songs, signing a contract with the Checker R&B label and scoring hits with "Hi-Heel Sneakers" and "Long Tall Shorty" in 1964. Mysteriously, Higgenbotham died of poisoning in 1982.

Garcia sang this funky and funny strut with the Dead at a few shows in the late 1960s and took it to his own bands some years later.

> **5/7/69, Polo Field, Golden Gate Park, San Francisco**

■ *The Hippie Temptation*
(television special)

What do you get when you get Harry Reasoner digging his double-square heels into the Haight-Ashbury sod? Why this biased, laughable indictment of hippiedom, of course. Complete with the *de rigueur* predictably lame simulated LSD-trip sequence that looks like a *Dragnet* reject, the *60 Minutes*–style exposé does include a revealing interview with Garcia (looking for all the world like Boy George's demented older brother), Lesh, Weir, Rock Scully, and Danny Rifkin as well some choice footage of the Dead playing "Dancin' in the Streets" in Golden Gate Park's panhandle. But wouldn't you know it, just as the jam starts to kick in, Reasoner uses this as a cue to begin obnoxiously pontificating on the bankrupt state of the youth culture.

■ *Historic Dead*

> **MGM-Sunflower SNF 5004, 1972. Produced and engineered by Robert Cohen.**
> **"Good Morning Little Schoolgirl," "Lindy," "Stealin'," "The Same Thing"**

This semi-legal disc stood as a granny snapshot of the Dead's 1966 electric dawn until the proliferation of good quality tapes became widely and commonly traded.

See also **Vintage Dead** *and* **The History of the Grateful Dead**

▪ *The History of the Grateful Dead*

Pride-MGM PRD 0016. Produced by Robert Cohen and
Peter Abram.

"Dancing in the Streets," "Lindy," "Stealin'," "It's All
Over Now, Baby Blue," "I Know You Rider," "In the
Midnight Hour," "It Hurts Me Too"

Squeezing every ounce of material out of their questionable endeavor, MGM released this compilation disc collecting the meat of their two previous efforts.

See also **Historic Dead** *and* **Vintage Dead**

▪ *The History of the Grateful Dead*

(book)/William Ruhlmann

96 pp. Large format, color and black and white
photographs throughout, large color poster,
discography, index. Gallery Books/W. H. Smith
Publishers, Inc., 1990.

This oversized, coffee-table wanna-be should have been
published as a magazine at a fraction of its sticker price.
Still, William Ruhlmann's on-the-money prose and rare
selection of photos are important for collectors.

▪ *History of the Grateful Dead Vol. 1 (Bear's Choice)*

Warner Bros. BS 2721, 1973.

"Katie Mae," "Dark Hollow," "I've Been All Around This
World," "Wake Up Little Susie," "Black Peter,"
"Smokestack Lightning," "Hard to Handle"

Sometimes criticized as an uninspired live outing culled
from two otherwise fabulous February 1970 Fillmore
East concerts, this mix of acoustic and electric performances has many incendiary moments. At the very least,
the Grateful Dead's ninth album is a good representation
of what the band's unplugged sets were all about at the
time. Pigpen's raveup of Otis Redding's "Hard to Handle" and the ensuing guitar fireworks show how the Dead
could take R&B to the edges of the stratosphere and
back with astonishing grace. Supporters of the album
point to this air-guitar special as reason alone to take the
plunge.

The album's title references Owsley Stanley (a.k.a.
Bear) who recorded the shows and chose the tracks for
inclusion on the album. Though not to every Deadhead's
taste, the acoustic/electric mix serves as an aural snapshot of this fertile Grateful Dead era and emphasizes a
lesser-known side of the band at the time it was released

(three years after its original recording). It also represents the Dead's first attempt at an archival release.
With Pigpen heavily represented, the album was also a
fitting tribute to the Dead's frontman who had passed
away only months before the album appeared.

Deadheads who came into the fold some years after
might be a little surprised at how relaxed and engaging
the band's stage presence is. Pigpen endears the crowd
with his bluesy manner, Weir plays the role of ringleader
during the acoustic set, and Garcia actually speaks, ban-
tering with Weir between songs. The album is also unusual in its lack of original material. "Black Peter," the
Garcia/Hunter ballad, is the only homegrown Grateful
Dead track on the album.

The album's cover art unveiled two archetypal Grateful Dead icons: the lightning-bolt skull and the dancing
bear.

▪ Holland-Dozier-Holland

Brian Holland–born February 15, 1941, Detroit,
Michigan. Lamont Dozier–born June 16, 1941,
Detroit, Michigan. Eddie Holland–born October 30,
1939, Detroit, Michigan.

If you grew up near a radio during the 1960s, the songs
of Brian Holland, Lamont Dozier, and Eddie Holland
probably provided the soundtrack for your formative
years. The many hits written and produced by this Motor
City trio for the Supremes, Marvin Gaye, the Four Tops,
and other artists in Berry Gordy's Motown stable are still
often just a turn of the FM dial away.

After unsuccessful solo stabs in the late 1950s and
early 1960s, the songwriting team came together under
Gordy's aupicies after Eddie Holland had a hit with
"Jamie," which cracked the Top 30 in 1962. From 1962
through 1968 the Holland-Dozier-Holland legend became familiar to pop fans, appearing under the title of
songs on their favorite discs.

First paired with Martha and the Vandellas, for whom
the trio wrote "Heat Wave" in 1964, the songwriters had
their greatest hits with the Supremes. The insistent
"Where Did Our Love Go?" in 1964 inaugurated a run
of six chart-toppers in the next three years including
"Baby Love," "Stop! In the Name of Love," "You Can't
Hurry Love," "The Happening," and "You Keep Me
Hanging On," which was later a 1968 hit for Vanilla
Fudge in 1968.

The front-line Motown artists benefiting from later
Holland-Dozier-Holland material were the Isley Broth-

ers ("This Old Heart of Mine" in 1966), the Four Tops ("I Can't Help Myself," "Reach Out and I'll Be There," "It's the Same Old Song," and "Bernadette," all of which hit No. 1), Marvin Gaye ("Can I Get a Witness," "You're a Wonderful One" and "HOW SWEET IT IS [to Be Loved by You]," which was later a Garcia Band staple), and the Vandellas ("Nowhere to Run" and "Jimmy Mack").

A two-year battle with Gordy over royalties resulted in an acrimonious split with Motown and the founding of their own Invictus and Hot Wax labels where they produced songs with biting social agendas such as Freda Payne's antiwar "Bring the Boys Home" and Honey Cone's "Want Ads" in 1971. But additional lawsuits led Dozier to break up the partnership two years later.

Success, however, seemed to stick. Dozier had solo hits with a couple of singles and cut three critically acclaimed albums: *Right There* in 1976, *Peddlin'* in 1977, and *Bittersweet* in 1979. During the 1980s, he produced and wrote for artists as diverse as Aretha Franklin, Ben E. King, Simply Red, Eric Clapton, Phil Collins, and Yes's Jon Anderson. The Holland brothers occasionally made forays into the studios and briefly reunited with Dozier to write for the Four Tops.

The Rock and Roll Hall of Fame recognized their immense contribution to American song by inducting them in 1990. The Grateful Dead briefly shared a couple Holland-Dozier-Holland's songs with Deadheads: "How Sweet It Is" and "ROAD RUNNER."

■ *Home, Home on the Road*/NEW RIDERS OF THE PURPLE SAGE
Columbia PC 32870, 1974. Produced by Jerry Garcia.

This enjoyable, if standard live album was Dave Torbert's last with NRPS and includes Robert Hunter's "Kick in the Head."

■ *Honor the Earth Powwow: Songs of the Great Lakes Indians*
Rykodisc RCD 10199, 1991. Produced by Mickey Hart.
"Grand Entry Song," "Intertribal Dance Song," "We're the People," "Sneak-Up," "Winnebago Army Song," "Intertribal Dance Song," "Ojibway Air Force Song," "Intertribal Dance Song," "Intertribal Dance Song"
Little Otter Singers, Lco Soldiers' Drum, Smokeytown Singers, Bad River Singers, Winnebago Sons, Bear Claw Singers, Three Fires Society Singers

Mickey Hart's state-of-the-art recording captures a Native American powwow in Northern Wisconsin. Stripped of all pretense, the wailing and trilling voices create a charged atmosphere celebrating the spiritual dimension of life and humanity's connection to the earth.

(Courtesy of Alan Douglas Productions)

■ *Hooteroll?*/Howard Wales and Jerry Garcia
Douglas KZ 30859, 1971. (Re-release Rykodisc RALP 0052, RACD 10052, 1987.) Produced by Alan Douglas and Doris Dynamite.
"Morning in Marin," "Da Bird Song," "South Side Strut," "Up from the Desert," "DC-502," "One A.M. Approach," "Uncle Martin's," "Evening Ranch"
Jerry Garcia–guitar. Howard Wales–organ, piano. JOHN KAHN–bass. Curly Cook–rhythm guitar. Bill Vitt–drums. Michael Marinelli–drums. Ken Balzall–trumpet. Martin Fierro–saxophone, flute.

Garcia and Bay Area keyboardist Howard Wales hooked up for an all-too-short collaboration at a few local clubs in the early 1970s and a winter 1972 visit to the Northeast. The pair was evidently inspired to commit their jazzy efforts to vinyl, Garcia's first non-Dead release, as *Hooteroll?* But both the results and the reaction to the outing were mixed.

In his 1978 interview with Jon Sievert of *Guitar Player* magazine, Garcia described the process of working with Wales. "With Howard we never had tunes; Howard would just play through tremendously extended changes. That developed my ear because I had nothing to go on. I didn't even know what key we were in. Here were all these extended chords coming out, and I really had to be able to hear a correspondence somewhere. MERL [SAUNDERS] helped me improve my analytical ability and to understand more about how substitution chords work in standard musical forms. Howard was a great in-between there, because his playing was so outside and totally unpredictable."

Reporting on a Garcia-Wales Academy of Music gig in the *New York Times,* critic Don Heckman wrote, "Playing a slow blues on Friday night's first show, Garcia slipped in and out of the time with an almost rhythmic swing. On the rock-based numbers, he modified his sound and his articulation, and used the wah-wah pedal superbly (and—unlike many guitarists—almost casually). When Garcia left the Wales group on its own, the quality level dropped. Wales has mechanical technique to burn, and he obviously delights in providing an energetically physical display of prowess, but the net result too often was sound for its own sake."

Alternately, Patrick Carr pointed out in the *Village Voice,* "Jerry played four numbers with the whole band, beginning with the uptempo, chompy picking of 'Uncle Martin's' and ending with a conventional electric blues, the most successful of their collaborations. Apart from that and 'One A.M. Approach,' a delightful harmonious dreamy blend of organ and guitar alone, the cohesiveness of the unit was not impressive. Jerry seemed distinctly out of place in a band that leans more towards jazz than rock, and who have it all down tight together while he has the status of an occasional visitor, not usually present for rehearsals. When Jerry returned for an encore that only a few appreciative customers seemed to want, they all cooked together very nicely. The music was mostly good but the evening had the distressing character of a nonevent. I hear it was different at the late show."

Though there is a somewhat repetitive quality to its overall conception, *Hooteroll?* has many stunning moments—especially in the ecstatically frenzied plateaus the pair reach on "South Street Strut."

Commenting on *Hooteroll?* during his 1971 chat with Charles Reich and Jann Wenner, Garcia critiqued the unusual album. "It came out pretty successfully. It could have come out better. It could've come out *really* fine, in

Sam "Lightnin'" Hopkins. (ARCHIVE PHOTOS/FRANK DRIGGS COLLECTION)

my opinion. I'm talking about the way it fell together, 'cause none of their material was written or anything. We either worked it out in the studio or it was totally improvised, like 'South Side Strut' is just a jam, it's a thing which just happened, with all those changes and horn parts, we did it all live. It was very loose, but the results of it came out remarkably sophisticated."

▪ Sam "Lightnin'" Hopkins
Born March 15, 1912, Centerville, Texas; died January 30, 1982, Houston, Texas

Lightnin' Hopkins was more than a true giant in blues history cutting an imposing figure on the Texas blues scene and setting the standard for post-war down-home blues. He was a force of nature. In a career that spanned six decades, Hopkins, in all likelihood, made more recordings than any other blues artist, leaving his mark not only on countless country bluesmen across the land but also many of the younger urban-blues stylists. A prolific songwriter, a master raconteur, and a convincing performer, Hopkins's guitar style, with its ragged rhythms and carefree collection of meter and structure was anything but conventional. Remarkably durable and authentic, he carried his songs with his dry, sagebrush-scratched vocals. Making up verses as he went along, Hopkins often improvised with wit and humor in studio and onstage. After Blind Lemon Jefferson, T-Bone Walker, and, perhaps, Albert Collins, no Texas blues-man has had as much impact on the state's blues legacy as Hopkins. No doubt about it, Lightnin' was the real thing.

Learning the guitar from his older brother Joel, also a blues musician, Sam Hopkins met and performed with Blind Lemon Jefferson at a country picnic when he was just eight years old. This was a defining moment for the young boy, leaving a profound mark on him and strengthening his desire to become a blues musician. By the time he was in his early teens he was accompanying Texas Alexander, his popular blues vocalist cousin, at house parties and picnics and traveling the East Texas circuit.

These were the years of wandering for Hopkins, per-forming off and on with Alexander through the 1930s, playing in workers' camps or for country parties. His move to Houston led to a precarious life of fights, vio-lence, backbreaking jobs, and time for an undetermined offense at Big Brazos Penitentiary.

He reunited with Alexander upon his release, per-forming on Houston street corners, in small clubs and the occasional juke joint or party gig in Mississippi and other southern states.

But it wasn't until an Aladdin Records talent scout discovered the duo in Houston and offered them a recording contract in 1946 that Hopkins's fortunes brightened. But when Alexander didn't follow up on the offer, Hopkins cut his first songs in Los Angeles later that year not with his cousin but with Wilson "Thunder" Smith, a Houston pianist. How that sat with Hopkins is unclear, but the debut session did result in the acquisi-tion of his famous moniker when he was given the nick-name "Lightnin'" and Aladdin billed the team as "Thunder and Lightnin'" on its first releases.

His first taste of success came with "KATIE MAE," which became a hit in the Southwest and a Pigpen cover more than two decades later when the Dead's de facto bluesman played it solo during the band's acoustic sets in 1970.

Hopkins recorded prolifically until the mid-1950s when the more sophisticated blues coming out of Chicago caught the fancy of the blues record-buying public. Lightnin' lived off his local reputation until 1959

when he was rediscovered by ethnomusicologists Mike McCormick and Sam Charters, who turned Hopkins into a "folkloric" artist and one of the key figures of the blues revival, filling the gap left open by the absence of Big Bill Broonzy and the station of the mythical "last blues singer alive."

Lightnin' lived the part too. For although he seemed to be everywhere (festivals, concerts, colleges, and clubs from coast to coast) he developed into a true cipher, mysteriously disappearing into the murk of East Texas between engagements. All along, Hopkins kept on recording for practically any label that would pay him cash up front for records of electric country blues and boogie for the black R&B market or acoustic guitar records for the folk market. Between 1959 and 1966 he recorded intensively but irregularly for more than ten different companies, at times recording as many as three records in a single week.

His concerts and session work revealed a continuing freshness in his material. His songs might hark back to Blind Lemon or they might deal with the latest-breaking news. Whether traditional or topical, acoustic or elec-tric, whether recording solo or with a small combo, Hop-

Bruce Hornsby with Vince Welnick (background), Shoreline Amphitheater, Mountain View, California, 5/91. (Robert Minkin)

kins was a natural: a master musician, singer, and blues poet and storyteller.

Hopkins's simple, traditional interpretation of the blues influenced a number of white folk-blues artists. By the late 1960s, his appeal had even begun to pour over into rock territory. He headlined over the Jefferson Airplane at one Bay Area concert and opened for the Dead at a couple of October 1966 Fillmore shows. Pigpen must have thought he had died and gone to heaven.

Hopkins developed a large European following as well, but because he feared flying, his engagements there were few and he progressively limited himself to local Houston performances. Contributing to the soundtrack of the movie *Sounder* in 1972, he also appeared in a number of blues documentaries continuing to maintain his traditionalist blues style, even though interest in his brand of country blues had, by the late 1970s, practically evaporated.

Hopkins was inducted into the Blues Foundation's Hall of Fame two years before his death of cancer in 1982.

▪ Bruce Hornsby
Born November 25, 1954, Williamsburg, Virginia

Bruce Hornsby was to the Dead what any great relief pitcher is to a World Series champ, the indispensable bridge between disaster and salvation. And when Hornsby joined the band for an eighteen-month stretch beginning in September 1990, the Dead were on the ropes. Brent Mydland had just died, a huge European tour was set and they were breaking in Vince Welnick as the new, full-time keyboardist. But Hornsby was well primed for his Grateful Dead experience, having jammed with the Dead a half-dozen times between 1988 and 1990, impressing the boys with his aggressive playing, sensitive ear, and gonzo sense of musical adventure.

Hornsby was raised in Williamsburg, Virginia in a musical family in that combination college town and tourist center. He discovered jazz and the blues in high school and was introduced to the Dead by his older brother John and became a Deadhead after the famous September 1973 shows in his hometown in which the band performed a free concert at William and Mary College just because they were having so much fun.

After the Hornsby brothers put together Bobby Hi-Test and the Octane Kids, a local pickup band specializing in Dead covers, Bruce pursued formal jazz training at the Berklee College of Music in Boston, Massachusetts, and the University of Miami, becoming a devotee of jazz pianists Bill Evans, Herbie Hancock, and McCoy Tyner. There followed years playing in bars and sending demo tapes to record companies. In 1980, the brothers Hornsby (who had become songwriting partners) moved to Los Angeles where they spent three years writing for 20th Century Fox and met Huey Lewis, who would eventually produce and record Bruce and his band the Range.

The Way It Is, their 1986 debut album on RCA, featured Hornsby's characteristically melodic right-hand piano runs and stayed on the charts for nearly eighteen months, selling two million copies and garnering a Grammy award for Best New Artist. *Scenes from the Southside*, his second album, was not as successful but did produce "THE VALLEY ROAD," a Top 10 single he later performed with the Dead. His talents as a songwriter were also recognized by the pop music elite like Don Henley, who tapped Hornsby for his hit "The End of the Innocence."

Hornsby broke away from his signature sound and moved into other areas with *A Night on the Town* in 1990 and *Harbor Lights*, his first album without the Range, three years later. By the time of his 1995 *Hot House* album release, Hornsby had successfully abandoned the conventional pop-rock, three-to-four minute structures that had dominated his songwriting, turning toward an open-ended fusion, showcasing his musical skills in an impressive exercise that also served as a nod to his bebop idols.

Hornsby's formal association with the Dead commenced in the summer of 1988 when he opened for and jammed with the band at an Ohio concert, impressing Phil Lesh with his interpretations of Charles Ives and garnering a first-set invite to give his touch on accordion to "Sugaree" and "(Stuck Inside of Mobile with the) Memphis Blues Again." That fall he was the opening act at the Dead's Rainforest Benefit concert at New York's Madison Square Garden. When the Range opened for the Dead at a pair of consecutive July 1989 shows at Washington, D.C.'s, RFK Stadium, Hornsby again made cameos. Two weeks before Mydland's death on July 26, 1990, Hornsby joined the band in Raleigh, North Carolina, for an extended concert appearance that really road-tested his accordion chops as he hung tough on some of the Dead's most wide-open material: "Bird Song" and "Playing in the Band."

LEROY CARR and **SCRAPPER BLACKWELL**

(© R. Crumb/Shanachie Entertainment)

Hornsby was, naturally, one of the names Deadheads tossed around following Mydland's death as a possible replacement so it was really no surprise when he became an onstage fixture for the next year and a half, seated firmly behind a grand piano and leading the band into a new era alongside Vince Welnick, who got the nod as the Dead's permanent keyboardist.

■ *Hot House*/BRUCE HORNSBY
RCA 66584, 1995.

Garcia's final appearance on record to come out during his lifetime was his lead guitar work on "Cruise Control," a track from Bruce Hornsby's homage to bebop.

■ "How Long, How Long Blues"(Traditional)
Singles: Ida Cox (1925), Blind Lemon Jefferson (1928), Gladys Bently (1928), Willie Jackson (1928), Jed Davenport (1929), Reverend A. W. Nix (1930), Sam

Collins (1931), Kokomo Arnold (1935), Amos Easton (1935), Bill Gaither (1936), Pete Johnson (1939), the Varsity Seven (1940)
Alberta Hunter, *Young Alberta Hunter*/'21 (1991)
Leroy Carr, *The Blues: A Smithsonian Collection*/'28 (1993)
Tampa Red, *It's Tight Like That, 1928–42*/'28 (1976)
LEADBELLY, *The Legend of Leadbelly*/'43 (1976)
Lonnie Donnegan, *Lonnie Donnegan Showcase* (1956)
Jimmy Rushing, *The Essential Jimmy Rushing* (1957)
Alexis Korner, *R&B from the Marquee* (1962)
Ella Fitzgerald, *These Are the Blues* (1963)
B. B. King, *Confessin' the Blues* (1966)
Hot Tuna, *Acoustic* (1970)
Big Joe Turner and T-Bone Walker, *Basses of the Blues* (1980)
Big Joe Turner, *Best of Joe Turner* (1980)
Lou Rawls, *Spotlight On . . . Lou Rawls* (1996)

Though the Dead, with Garcia singing lead, are only known to have performed "How Long Blues" as an acoustic cover at three shows in the summer of 1970, the song and its popularizer, Leroy Carr, were a galvanizing force in the blues during the late 1920s and early 1930s. Carr was a pianist and with his partner, guitarist Scrapper Blackwell, helped give the blues a more polished, urbane edge during his short life.

Carr was born on March 27, 1905, in Nashville, Tennessee, and grew up in Indianapolis; he was barely thirty years old when he died there on April 29, 1935. But in that time he became one of the top blues stars of his day, composing and recording two hundred sides including "How Long Blues," "Prison Bound Blues," and "Blues Before Sunrise."

Carr taught himself how to play and quit school to begin a life of travel that included a stint in the circus, a hitch in the army, bootlegging, and a career as a house-party institution. His recording career didn't begin until he met Blackwell in 1928 when they cut "How Long Blues" for the Vocalion label. The song instantly became a best-seller, leading to an incredible seven-year run. "How Long Blues" was one of the first million-selling blues records, and Carr and Blackwell had to record the song four different times in less than a year because the master copy—from which the records were pressed—kept wearing out.

A heavy drinker and carouser, Carr was also a bootlegger, whose fondness for his product led to his death of acute alcoholism but not before leaving behind a vast catalogue of blues which influenced many pianists who followed him in the pre–World War II period.

After the Dead's first three 1970 outings of "How Long Blues" it made a surprise re-appearance in 1989 when Spencer Davis joined the Dead at a wild and woolly Los Angeles show at which Dylan later made an extended cameo.

7/14/70, Euphoria Ballroom, San Rafael, California

- ### *How Sweet It Is*/Jerry Garcia Band
    Arista 14051, 1997. Produced by John Cutler and Steve Parish.
    "How Sweet It Is (To Be Loved by You)," "Tough Mama," "That's What Love Will Make You Do," "Someday Baby," "Cats Under the Stars," "Tears of Rage," "Think," "Gomorrah," "Tore Up Over You," "Like a Road"

Recorded at San Francisco's Warfield Theater in 1990, this choice set features the usual mix of Garcia/Hunter originals, cover songs, and Dylan as Garcia talks his way through the lyrics before burning a hole in the melodies with molten solo after molten solo.

(© Grateful Dead Merchandising, Inc.)

- ### "How Sweet It Is" (HOLLAND-DOZIER-HOLLAND)
    Garcia/Saunders/Kahn/Vitt, *Keystone Encores Vol. 2*/ '73 (1988)
    Jerry Garcia Band, *Live* (1991), *How Sweet It Is* (1997)
    Marvin Gaye, *The Motown Story* (1964)
    Junior Walker and the All Stars, single (1966)
    James Taylor, *Gorilla* (1975)

The Dead only played this AM radio special at the crazed Big Apple show in 1972, which featured a surprise set with Bo Diddley, but it holds the distinction of being the song most often performed by the Jerry Garcia Band with in excess of four hundred renditions catalogued.

3/25/72, Academy of Music, New York

- ### "Hully Gully" (Smith/Goldsmith)
    Olympics, single (1960), *Cruisin'* (1960), *All-Time Greatest Hits* (1991)
    Dovells, single (1962)
    B. B. King, *Easy Listening Blues* (1962)
    THE BEACH BOYS, *Beach Boys Party!* (1966)
    Ike and Tina Turner, *Feel Good* (1972)
    The Beatles, *Live in Hamburg* (1977)

Bob Weir's thirty-fourth birthday was one for the ages as the Dead let him pull out *all* the stops. The band included no less than three major surprises in their acoustic and electric concert at the Melk Weg, Amsterdam's famed hash bar: the first "Love Light" since Pigpen's passing, the first "Gloria" since the WARLOCKS, and a one-time-only performance of the early 1960s oddity "Hully Gully," a song about (among other things) a dance.

10/16/81, Melk Weg, Amsterdam

- ### *Hundred Year Hall*
    Grateful Dead Merchandising, Inc. GDCD 4020, 1995. Produced by John Cutler and Phil Lesh; tape archivist, Dick Latvala; Liner notes by Robert Hunter. Recorded April 26, 1972, Jahrhundert Hall, Frankfurt, West Germany.
    "Bertha," "ME AND MY UNCLE," "NEXT TIME YOU SEE ME," "China Cat Sunflower"➤"I KNOW YOU RIDER," "Jack Straw," "BIG RAILROAD BLUES," "Playing in the Band," "TURN ON YOUR LOVE LIGHT"➤"GOING DOWN THE ROAD FEELIN'

BAD," "One More Saturday Night,"
"Truckin' ">"Cryptical Envelopment (The Other
One)">"Comes a Time">"Sugar Magnolia"

A truly incredible live recording, *Hundred Year Hall* not only gives *Europe '72* a run for its money but every other officially released Grateful Dead recording as well. Drawing on the bulk of a Frankfurt concert from their 1972 Continent-storming excursion, this double CD is paced very much like a standard Dead show from the era as it commences with shorter, familiar songs and slowly builds to exalted, exploratory medleys.

"Playing in the Band" is a particular standout here with an *intense* jam that should be bottled. The raison d'être of the album is the instrumental foray that follows "Love Light," a jam that hints at "Cumberland Blues," "Good Lovin'," and "Not Fade Away" before finally settling into "Goin' Down the Road." Other highlights include "Bertha," "Next Time You See Me," "China">"Rider," "The Other One," and "Sugar Mag."

This was the first *From the Vault* project following DAN HEALY's departure from the band a couple of years earlier and, in deference to their differences, the band wisely chose to give the release a title that bore no resemblance to the series that had been spearheaded by their former soundman.

A final delight are Robert Hunter's liner notes, written twenty-two years and two days after the concert, which put the music and the tour into unique historical and personal perspective.

Robert Hunter
Born June 23, 1941, Arroyo Grande, California

Just as Rodgers had Hammerstein, Brecht had Weill, and Lerner had Lowe, Jerry Garcia had Robert Hunter. But, curiously, the wordsmith of one of the most prolific songwriting duos in twentieth-century American music is little known outside the Grateful Dead sphere—and Robert Hunter seems to like it that way or at least accept it. Though not in the same reclusive league as J. D. Salinger or Thomas Pynchon (with whom he shares some aesthetic concerns), the band's bard is more interested in crafting lyrics in the confines of his study than being seen at the Hard Rock Cafe or lecturing on Yeats at U.C. Berkeley. Not exactly what one would expect from the

Robert Hunter, 11/30/77. (© Ed Perlstein)

man who's best known for contributing the line "What a long strange trip it's been" to the national phraseology.

The invisible cog in the Dead's creative machinery, Hunter cherished his anonymity while turning the words to just about every great Dead song one can conjure while crafting a vision of the Old West, at once mythic and believable, while slipping in philosophical aphorisms richly applicable to everyday life. Synthesizing a range of influences into his cosmic word blender (Dylan, Shakespeare, LEADBELLY, *Zap Comix*, Taoist simplicity, fractured psychedelia, metaphorical agility, tales of hard-luck working stiffs, cartoonish whimsy, from-the-heart love songs), his oeuvre includes scores of songs, and though each one of them can stand alone, most strive to address (though not necessarily answer) the Big Questions.

What's more, Hunter accomplished this in a manner so attuned to Jerry Garcia's personality that the transference seemed organic. As he once quipped, "I remember introducing a girlfriend to Jerry back when I was twenty-one or so. And after she met him she said to me, 'It's hard to know where he leaves off and you begin.'"

But Hunter's wisdom was hard won. Probably more than any other member of the Grateful Dead, his early childhood was distinctly hard-scrabble, bordering on the desperation experienced by many of the characters in his songs. His father was an itinerant electrician, owned a motorcycle, and had a great affection for freedom. As Hunter told Bob Sarlin in 1971, "My dad was sort of a soldier-of-fortune-type dude. He was a good hustler. He could go into a grocery store without any money and talk his way into two bags of groceries. I remember we'd be driving along in the old panel truck and we'd drive by a bar—he was an electrician too—and the neon signs would be out. So we'd park in the parking lot and he'd go up there and do a few things with the wires and the sign would be on, and then he'd go in and drink up his pay. And we'd sit out there in the car.

"What would happen was, my dad would meet somebody in a bar and get to be pals, like that, and the next thing we knew, me and my mother and my brother would be up and moved into this fellow's house and then my dad would split. He'd kind of park us there, and then we'd have to make do with the family he'd park us with."

Relocating to the Bay Area, Hunter's mother remarried a man who prided himself on his intellectuality. Perhaps the spirit of both men can be perceived as an influence on Hunter's song-poems with the characters inhabiting them being cut out of the same fabric as his father while the philosophical musings coloring his lyrics are inspired by his stepfather.

Living in San Francisco from the fourth through the seventh grade, Hunter's family moved to Palo Alto where he attended high school before studying drama at the University of Connecticut for a year. He moved back to Palo Alto after a six-month National Guard hitch in Oklahoma and, his curiosity piqued by Aldous Huxley's *The Doors of Perception*, volunteered for the same psychedelic research project at the V.A. hospital in Menlo Park in which Ken Kesey was involved.

Immersing himself in the peninsula's folk scene, Hunter first crossed paths with Jerry Garcia at a local production of *Damn Yankees* at Palo Alto's Commedia Theater in 1960. Soon the two were neighbors of sorts, living out of their cars scraping together meals of canned pineapple and performing in a series of acoustic groups that included everything from a duo to the legendary bluegrass and jug bands that were the nucleus of the Grateful Dead: the Hart Valley Drifters, the Thunder Mountain Tub Thumpers, and the Wildwood Boys.

As the Warlocks were transmuting into the Grateful Dead, Hunter had relocated to New Mexico but was coaxed back to the musical fold by Garcia after sending the guitarist lyrics to what became "Alligator," "China Cat Sunflower," and "St. Stephen." When he whipped together some lyrics for "Dark Star" immediately upon his return at a rehearsal, it became obvious to all concerned that the band had found its wordsmith.

The early collaborations between Hunter and company were distinctly obtuse as evidenced by the mostly extreme poetic whimsy of *Aoxomoxoa* in 1969. But with *Workingman's Dead* and *American Beauty*, Hunter seemed to settle into his role with a song cycle that seemed to emanate from a bygone, sepia-toned America where characters living on the edge are illuminated by the storyteller's lamp while in the folds of epiphany. But Hunter also crafted love songs, which, like Dylan before him, fall completely outside the previous boundaries of pop music as he sings to women as equals—no vulgar condescension emanating from the tip of his quill.

Dylan's influence on Hunter may be overstated yet the two have certainly been mining similar strains of creative gold especially regarding their use of colloquialisms to present sophisticated statements—more concerned with survival than revolution. Probably the most apparent similarity between the two is their methodology

Michael McCLURE

DEAD POET ROBERT HUNTER

Tom Constanten

AN EVENING OF POETRY & PIANO
INTRODUCING NEW YORK POET KATIE JOHNTZ
SATURDAY, MAY 19, 1990 · 8 P.M.
130 KANE HALL · U of W · ROETHKE AUDITORIUM
TICKETS $12.50 *TICKETMASTER 628-0888* & HUB TICKET OFFICE
FREDERICK & NELSON · TOWER RECORDS/VIDEO

(Author's collection)

of filtering archaic forms into a modern sensibility, troubadours whose lyrics can take on a multitude of shades and meanings. Maybe the ultimate tribute paid to Hunter was by Dylan himself who recorded a couple of later Hunter compositions ("Silvio" and "The Ugliest Girl in the World") and has performed three others ("Friend of the Devil," "West L.A. Fadeaway," and "Alabama Getaway").

During his early years with the Dead, Hunter kept a mysteriously (and tantalizingly) low profile, preferring to "own his own face," after seeing the downside to celebrity firsthand. The first glimpse in-the-know Deadheads had of Hunter was on the cover of *Workingman's Dead* as he stood among his bedraggled band mates in a Depression-era setting.

With the release of *Tales of the Great Rum Runners* in 1974, his debut solo album, Hunter began to emerge in the public sphere. *Tiger Rose*, an even stronger followup a year later, may have prompted Hunter to hit the road

giving his fans the chance to experience his poetry straight from its maker as he mixed old favorites with the dusky gems on his solo albums. *Jack o' Roses*, a 1979 studio release, was a pretty fair example of his live shows at the time and included an extended presentation of the "Terrapin Station Suite."

But soon Hunter's albums took on a novelistic tone, constructed as song cycles with interrelated characters and themes. *Promontory Rider* (1982), *Amagamalin Street* (1984), *Flight of the Marie Helena* (1986), *Rock Columbia* (1986), and *Liberty* (1987) were all released on the Relix label, which allowed the artist to pursue his muse without the constraints imposed by a typically insensitive record-company weasel looking more for platinum-selling pap than for eternal artistic diamonds.

In all, Hunter has himself released a dozen solo efforts and, while they and his concert performances are compelling, his words achieved a mythic quality when sung by Garcia on a good night.

Much of Hunter's time in the late 1980s and early 1990s was spent in pursuit of literary rather than recorded gold. After translating German poet Rainer Maria Rilke's *Duino Elegies* and *Sonnets to Orpheus*, Hunter hunkered down to produce three volumes of his own works. While *A Box of Rain* (Viking, 1990) largely consisted of printed lyrics from all of his and the Dead's commercial releases, *Night Cadre* (Viking, 1992), a neosymbolist lyric; *Idiot's Delight* (Hanuman Books, 1992), a study in symmetry; and *Sentinel*, a Rilkesque exercise, displayed the poet's ability to explore a variety of literary settings.

One of the more overlooked aspects of the demise of the Grateful Dead following Garcia's death was the future of Hunter's lyrics in a performance setting. But his contribution to *Mickey Hart's Mystery Box* and that unit's subsequent tour as part of the Furthur Festival in the summer of 1996 seemed to open up new landscapes of possibility for the poet. Hunter tended to pursue such avocations in seclusion, avoiding interviews or even having his picture taken. But a funny thing happened after Garcia died: Hunter became the Web master of the Dead's home page on the Internet, posting his journal entries online while answering hundreds of queries from the Dead's coterie.

"People are mourning the passing of the Grateful Dead as they knew it," he told Mark Rowland of *Musician* in 1996, "but resolving to hold together as Deadheads because they understand that the real thing that happened was not the music, it was the community. And that still exists.

"It is therapy in terms of filling the space for me. I've always been on the periphery of things; they've been Jerry's fans or Bob's fans or Phil's fans, not my fans. I'm exercising my skills as a writer, and if I lose my motivation for five minutes, all I have to do is open my e-mail. But for now I'm setting aside symbols for straight communication."

Reflecting on his collaborative legacy, Hunter recalled words Jerry once spoke to him: "I created one half of the universe and you created the other."

▪ Zakir Hussain
Born March 9, 1951, Bombay, India

Learning the tabla at the knees of a master (his father, Allah Rakha), Zakir Hussain is now the most widely recognized and recorded tablaist in the world. Usually content to lend dynamic support as a sideman, his all-too-few efforts as a session leader are usually in world-music fusion groups.

Mickey Hart met Hussain at the Ali Akbhar School of Music in the early 1970s and the two men formed an immediate bond. Hussain was a founding member of DIGA, an all-percussion group cofronted by Hart and fusion drummer Billy Cobham, which performed and recorded in the mid-1970s. Concurrently, Hart recorded Hussain and Chautasia, India's classical-flute master, performing a delicate raga, which was released by Rykodisc under Hart's "The World" series in 1990.

Two of Hussain's better recordings follow both traditional and world beat directions. *Magical Moments of Rhythm*, a series of excerpts recorded live in the United States and subcontinent, focuses on Hussain's astonishing mastery of the tabla's complex rhythms. *Zakir Hussain and the Rhythm Experience* is world music the way it should sound, weaving the rhythms of India, Cuba, Africa, the Middle East, and Indonesia.

Given their long association, it is somewhat odd that Hussain only performed with the Grateful Dead at one show, August 8, 1982. For that appearance at the Alpine Music Center in East Troy, Wisconsin, Hussain jammed through "Drumz" and "Space" before finding himself along for the ride on a particularly propulsive "The Other One."

- **"I Ain't Superstitious"** (WILLIE DIXON)
  Willie Dixon, *I Am the Blues* (1970), *The Chess Box* (1988), *Essential Blues, Vol. 2* (1996)
  Howlin' Wolf, *London Howlin' Wolf Sessions* (1970), *Change My Ways* (1977), *The Chess Box* (1991), *Blues Masters, Vol. 6* (1993)
  Jeff Beck, *Truth* (1968)
  Lonnie Brooks, *Bayou Lightning* (1979)
  Megadeath, *Peace Sells . . . But Who's Buying* (1986)
  Savoy Brown Blues Band, *Shake Down* (1987)
  Rod Stewart, *Storyteller* (1989)

Willie Dixon wrote this voodoo blues for Howlin' Wolf, whose rough growl fit the lyrics like a glove. Fittingly, Weir introduced "I Ain't Superstitious" on Halloween in 1984 but only performed it a half dozen times through the middle of 1985 when it was usually paired with another Dixon tune, "DOWN IN THE BOTTOM."

  4/3/85, Providence Civic Center, Providence, Rhode Island

- **"(I Can't Get No) Satisfaction"**
  (Jagger/Richards)
  The Rolling Stones, *Out of Our Heads* (1965), *Still Life* (1982), *Flashpoint* (1991)
  Otis Redding, *Otis Blue* (1966), *Live in Europe* (1967), *Otis Redding in Person at the Whisky-a-Go-Go* (1968), *Monterey International Pop Festival*/'67 (1970)
  The Kingsmen, *15 Great Hits* (1966)

Billy Preston, *The Wildest Organ in Town* (1966)
Aretha Franklin, *Aretha Arrives* (1967), *Live at the Olympia* (1968)
Blue Cheer, *Outside Inside* (1968)
Bohemian Vendetta, *Bohemian Vendetta* (1968)
Jimi Hendrix, *Birth of Success*/'65 (1970)
Mountain, *Avalanche* (1974)
The Troggs, *Troggs* (1975), *Live at Max's Kansas City* (1981)
The Residents, single (1976)
Eddie and the Hot Rods, *Teenage Depression* (1977)
Devo, *Q: Are We Not Men? A: We Are Devo!* (1978), *Hot Potatoes! The Best of Devo* (1993)
Rob Wasserman, *Trios* (1994)

"I'd woken up in the middle of the night, thought of the riff and put it straight down on tape. In the morning . . . I played it to Mick and said, 'the words that go with this are, I can't get no satisfaction.'"

That, according to Keith Richards, was the birth of rock's most quintessential anthem in Tampa, Florida, in early May 1965. Originally envisioned as a folk protest song for the Rolling Stones' *Out of Our Heads* album, that's how "Satisfaction" sounded when they cut it at Chess Records on May 10.

Just two days later, the band was back in the studio, dramatically altering the song. The most famous three-note riff in rock was patented by Richards on a Gibson fuzz box while Mick Jagger, in a half-spoken tone that veered from mockery to anger, turned in a career-making performance.

Although rock scribe Robert Palmer called Jagger's stinging lyrics "a quasi-Marxist critique of consumerism," the first thing Richards reportedly did with his royalties was buy a Bentley.

The WARLOCKS included "Satisfaction" in their set lists but after the Grateful Dead the song wasn't touched until it was pulled out of the hat as an encore in November 1980 at the Hollywood Sportatorium in Florida. Thereafter, it popped up several dozen times as an encore or second-set closer.

In his 1981 interview with David Gans, Weir remembered the song's Dead baptism, saying that it "just came up one night . . . one of those little clouds of madness that drifted across the stage. I don't think we'll do 'Gloria' that often, but we may do 'Satisfaction' every now and again, because when I really feel like doing 'Satisfaction' it's because I'm feeling pretty ringy. Oftentimes that means I'm going to come up with something to say in the end bit. . . . We have never done that one remotely the same twice, and obviously we've never ever rehearsed the song."

6/24/84, Saratoga Performing Arts Center, Saratoga, New York

Idiot's Delight /(book)/Robert Hunter
136 pp. Hanuman Books, 1992.

Poetry may not be everyone's first passion, but Robert Hunter is no ordinary poet. Known primarily for his timeless lyrics for the Dead and the San Francisco music family at large, Hunter wrote this long poem specifically for the palm-sized format of Hanuman's books. *Idiot's Delight* centers around one man's meditation on "hunger, desire, and mortality." Hunter has room here for more than one LP's worth of lyrics. Thus the poem goes into far more detail than most songs can and offers plenty of twists and turns.

Weaving an immense tapestry of images both concrete and imagined and words that can be specific or not, Hunter tells a story that revolves around an *Alice in Wonderland*–style dinner party where the host ". . . provides one / thimbleful of / Idiot's Delight / to enable digestion."

With appetite and hunger used as a metaphor for human emotion and desire, Hunter leads the reader through a maze of thoughts and feelings, scattering gems of wisdom and humor along the way.

Another Hanuman publication worth tracking down is *SAVED! The Gospel Speeches of Bob Dylan*, just for the pure novelty.

If I Could Only Remember My Name /David Crosby
Atlantic SD 7203, 1971.

This San Francisco scene Hall of Fame guest-star album includes contributions from all Grateful Dead members, the Airplane, Quicksilver, Santana, CSNY, and others in a good and still-relevant release.

David Crosby is joined by Garcia, Lesh, and Kreutzmann on "Cowboy Song" (allegedly performed at a December 22, 1970 Dead show) while Garcia takes the lead-guitar duties on "Song With No Words" and "Tamalpais High." Garcia once commented that his pedal steel work on "Laughing" captured the sound he was most happy with from that instrument. Hart and Kreutzmann play throughout the disc but, as no track-by-track credits are included, it is impossible to pinpoint their exact musical whereabouts.

The disc's crowning glory is "What Are Their Names," a powerful and angry finger-pointer written by Crosby, Garcia, Lesh, Neil Young, and Mike Shrieve, who all turn in trippy but solid performances.

Of his contribution to this classic piece of hippieana, Garcia is quoted in Crosby's autobiography as saying, "As far as being personally satisfied with my own performances, which I rarely am, he's gotten better out of me than I get out of myself."

"If I Had the World to Give"
(Garcia/Hunter)
Grateful Dead, *Shakedown Street* (1978)

This saccharine piece of Garcia/Hunter album filler didn't even begin to cut the mustard during its trio of airings around the time of its vinyl release.

11/20/78, Cleveland Music Hall, Cleveland

"I Fought the Law" (Sonny Curtis)
Bobby Fuller Four, *Bobby Fuller Memorial Album '66* (1966), *The Best of Bobby Fuller* (1981), *Bobby Fuller Tapes, Vol. 2* (1984)
The Clash, *The Clash* (1977), *Clash on Broadway* (1991)

Dead Kennedys, *Give Me Convenience or Give Me Death* (1987)
Bryan Adams, *Live! Live! Live!* (1988)
Nitty Gritty Dirt Band, *Not Fade Away* (1992)
Mary's Danish, *American Standard* (1992)
The Stray Cats, *Rock Tokyo* (1992)
Hank Williams Jr., *Rock Your Socks Off* (1994)

This piece of pop music madness was performed by the Dead as a ragged and downright giddy surprise encore exclusive during their last three tours.

Ex-Cricket Sonny Curtis wrote "I Fought the Law," but it was Bobby Fuller, a man with a full-blown case of Buddy Holly-itis, who made the song famous. Like Holly, Fuller was a Texan and somewhat of an anomaly in the mid-1960s with his Strat and brash, full sound that may have sounded like Buddy if he had survived another decade or so.

Fuller was born in Baytown, Texas, on October 22, 1943, and cut his stage chops in El Paso in the early 1960s. He moved to California soon after and toyed with surf music before connecting with producer Bob Keene. Keene tapped Fuller's rocking, tuneful, and infectiously joyous sound and showed the singer/songwriter to be a worthy inheritor of early rock & roll and rockabilly traditions without sounding self-consciously revivalist.

"I Fought the Law," an in-your-face plaint of another born loser, cracked the Top 10 in 1966 and made Fuller an overnight star. He was not able to enjoy the limelight for long as he died under mysterious circumstances in a parked car in Hollywood later that year.

9/17/93, Madison Square Garden, New York

▪ "If the Shoe Fits" (Phil Lesh/Andrew Charles)

The penultimate (and uncharacteristically bitter) Phil Lesh song introduced by the Dead in the summer of 1994, "If the Shoe Fits" worked against type as a kiss-off song and was performed well into 1995.

7/2/94, Shoreline Amphitheater, Mountain View, California

▪ "I Got a Mind to Give Up Livin'" (Alan Toussaint)
Paul Butterfield Blues Band, *East-West* (1966)

A Grateful Dead one-shot performed with Boz Scaggs and John Cipollina at a Vietnam Vets benefit, "I Got a Mind to Give Up Livin'" was written by Alan Toussaint,

a musical diplomat hailing from New Orleans. Toussaint was born on January 14, 1938, and grew up in Gert Town, the German neighborhood in the Crescent City where Buddy Bolden, the luminous jazz cipher, was said to enjoy blowing his coronet at the century's turn.

With his inherently funky piano work heavily influenced by his city's ivory masters (Professor Longhair, Huey "Piano" Smith, and Fats Domino, with a lethal touch of Ray Charles), Toussaint helped fashion a fresh, vital New Orleans R&B sound for the early 1960s. After first earning a vaunted rep as a sessionman, Toussaint moved into A&R work and quickly proved himself to be the ultimate behind-the-scenes Svengali on the Big Easy scene. The early to mid-1960s were undoubtedly the busiest time in his career as he tirelessly wrote, arranged, produced, and performed on dozens of R&B hits, his rolling keyboards vital to the spell cast on virtually all of them.

After sharing the Meters with the rest of the still-recovering planet, Toussaint slowly began to step out as a frontman. Though his low-key vocals may have prevented him from achieving the same degree of commercial success he produced for others, Toussaint's superb compositions have been covered by everyone from Herb Alpert and the Tijuana Brass and Glen Campbell to Robert Palmer, the Band, Three Dog Night, and Bonnie Raitt. He has also been tapped by filmmakers like Louis Malle, for whose New Orleans–based *Pretty Baby* he provided the musical supervision in 1978. In a surprise move, he appeared with Ruth Brown in the 1987 stage presentation of *Staggerlee*.

One of these days we'll have a special Alan Toussaint wing of the Smithsonian. Until then, we'll just have to settle for the music he continues to leave us.

5/28/82, Moscone Convention Center, San Francisco

▪ "I Got My Mojo Workin'" (Preston Foster)
Muddy Waters, single (1956), *Muddy Waters at Newport* (1961), *Muddy Waters* (1964)
Ann Cole, single (1957)
Zombies, *The Zombies* (1965), *The Collection* (1988)
Bill Cosby, *Bill Cosby Sings* (1966)
Shadows of Knight, *Ge-El-O-Are-I-Ay* (1985)

"I Got My Mojo Workin'" was one of Muddy Waters's big hits. But this furious piece of blues was composed by Preston Foster, who penned the song for the even more obscure Ann Cole. Cole and Waters had toured together, during which she ended her set with the song. But when Waters added his own lyrics and recorded it under his own name, Chess Records was forced to withdraw the single from the stores and press it with the correct credit when threatened with a lawsuit.

The Dead first showed off this old blues stomp when they tucked it into the middle of a great 1977 "Dancin'" jam as an instrumental. But it was upon their return from Egypt that they aired it out as both a Weir vocal lead and instrumental for a trio of October 1978 Winterland concerts.

4/22/77, The Spectrum, Philadelphia

10/21/78, Winterland Arena, San Francisco (with Lee Oskar on harmonica)

▪ "I Hear a Voice Callin'" (Traditional)

Although the Dead are only known to have turned in three acoustic performances of this bit of high-lonesome country gospel, it stands as an unusually effective, if a tad off-key, stab in a direction not often explored by the group.

5/15/70, Fillmore East, New York

▪ "I Just Wanna Make Love to You"

(WILLIE DIXON)

Muddy Waters, *Chess Masters* (1954)

The Rolling Stones, *England's Newest Hit Makers* (1964)

Cold Blood, *Cold Blood* (1964)

Van Morrison, *It's Too Late to Stop Now* (1974)

ETTA JAMES, single (1961)

Foghat, *Foghat* (1972), *Live* (1977), *The Best of Foghat* (1991)

Of all the Willie Dixon songs in the Dead liturgy, "I Just Wanna Make Love to You" is the one approached most casually. Before Garcia began singing it at his last tours in 1995, the Dead were only known to have performed it on two previous occasions and those were some eighteen years apart. The song shows up on one very early 1966 tape with Pigpen handling the vocals and again in 1984 when Mydland sprang it out of a typically hot "Samson & Delilah." Perhaps as a declaration to his newly betrothed, Garcia lit into it again, though somewhat less convincingly if not sincerely, a few months before his passing in 1995.

Dixon's recognizable boast was originally recorded by Muddy Waters for the Chess label in 1954. Compared to the Dead's uptempo reading, Waters's version is considerably slower and possesses a smoldering sensuality.

In Willie Dixon's autobiography, *I Am the Blues,* the maestro had this to say about one of his most famous and oft-covered gems: "The average person wants to brag about themselves because it makes that individual feel big. . . . These songs make people want to feel like that because they feel like that at heart. They just haven't said it so you say it for them.

"Like the song, 'I Just Wanna Make Love to You,' a lot of time people say this in their minds or think it. You don't have to say it but everybody knows that's the way you feel anyway because that's how the other fella feels. You know how you feel so you figure the other fella feels the same way because his life is just like yours."

10/8/84, Worcester Centrum, Worcester, Massachusetts

2/21/95, Delta Center, Salt Lake City

▪ "Iko Iko" (Traditional)

Sugar Boy Crawford, *Mardi Gras in New Orleans Vol. II* (1954)

Larry Williams, *Creole Kings of New Orleans* (1957)

The Dixie Cups, *Chapel of Love* (1964), *Mardi Gras in New Orleans Vol. II* (1965), *The Music Never Stopped: Roots of the Grateful Dead/'64* (1995)

Dr. John, *Gumbo* (1972)

THE NEVILLE BROTHERS, *Fiyo on the Bayou* (1981)

Belle Stars, *Belle Stars* (1982)

Cyndi Lauper, single (1989)

Ringo Starr, *Ringo Starr and His All-Starr Band* (1990)

Buckwheat Zydeco, *Choo Choo Boogaloo* (1994)

The roots of "Iko Iko" are probably older than any other in the Dead's songbook. It certainly has a fascinating, complex, and lengthy history. Surely based on African call-and-response chants, "Iko Iko" is thought to have arrived in the Americas with the first slaves. In their rituals before the Middle Passage, indigenous Africans would don ceremonial leaves as part of their celebrations. In North America white plantation owners who used slaves banned the practice when it was initially displayed. But, by the late 1700s, whites were slowly intrigued with black tribal ritual, soon allowing the slaves to re-create their celebrations at Congo Square in New Orleans one day a week while the ruling class watched.

With the passage of time, the blacks began forming Mardi Gras "tribes." The leaves were replaced by feath-

The Dixie Cups. *(Archive Photos/Frank Driggs Collection)*

ers, evidently due to the influence of the Seminoles and other Native American tribes, some of whom, ironically, even owned slaves. Along with hard partying, the Mardi Gras tribes used their celebration days to fight each other. For many obvious reasons, the empowered gentry prohibited the fighting in 1890s as the battles mutated into style wars with sometimes violent results.

The Dead's version of "Iko Iko" includes lyrics drawn from two separate Mardi Gras chants. But the basic gist of the words is in the idiom of the "dozens-playing" peculiar to New Orleans, a brand of verbal one-upmanship specific to the language and mores of African-American culture. The meaning of "Iko Iko" is somewhat more speculative, but, along with various sexual interpretations, it is commonly thought to be a bastardization of "hike-o" because, after all, the Indian tribes would hike all day on Mardi Gras day to inspect the haberdashery of the other groups participating in the festivities.

"Iko Iko" was first recorded under the title "Jock-O-Mo" by Big Easy native James "Sugar Boy" Crawford in 1954. According to Crawford, he decided to create a simple tune to accompany his favorite street chants after years of hearing them on Mardi Gras. But even Crawford admitted that he never had any idea exactly what the words to his regional hit meant.

Probably the best known version of "Iko Iko" was by the Dixie Cups, a New Orleans girl group in 1965. The Dixie Cups had a fluke Top 20 national hit with "Iko Iko" when their producers, LEIBER AND STOLLER, secretly turned on the reel-to-reel when the trio was using the tune as a warm-up.

It wasn't until the late 1960s, however, that New Orleans began to significantly impact the mainstream. Undoubtedly and ironically, it was a white musician from New Orleans calling himself Dr. John the Night Tripper who achieved this. The former Mac Rebennack, with his somewhat contrived image—complete with feather gowns and a stage show that included singers and dancers that wreaked havoc with the spirit of the Louisiana Bayou—caught the fancy of the music-listening and concert-going public with his rock & boogie trick or treats. More importantly, he had the likes of the Rolling Stones, Paul Simon, Paul McCartney, and many others sitting up and taking notice. Dr. John's success allowed the arguably more legitimate home-grown talent to emerge. By the late 1970s first the Meters, and then throughout the 1980s and early 1990s, the NEVILLE BROTHERS became the city's most recognizable acts.

The Dead performed two distinctly different arrangements of "Iko Iko." When they first began performing the song in 1977 and on through the last years of the decade, it had a sensuous and swampy groove that lent itself to easy segue action in the band's second sets. But by 1984, it had been reinvigorated with an accelerated beat and often used to open concerts, which got their audiences on their feet and dancing posthaste. Also visited briefly during the Dead's 1980 acoustic sets, "Iko" was ritually employed at the Dead's annual Mardi Gras concerts, sometimes with members of the Neville Brothers sitting in.

One final note: "Iko Iko" often appears misspelled for still undetermined reasons as "Aiko Aiko" on tapers' cassette boxes.

4/11/78, Fox Theater, Atlanta
8/10/82, Fieldhouse, University of Iowa, Iowa City
11/2/84, Berkeley Community Theater, Berkeley, California
3/18/95, The Spectrum, Philadelphia

- ## "I Know You Rider" (Traditional)
  Grateful Dead, *Vintage Dead*/'66 (1970), *Europe '72*

(1972), *Without a Net* (1990), *Hundred Year Hall*/'72 (1995), *Dick's Picks Volume Four*/'70 (1996)
Tom Constanten, *Nightfall of Diamonds* (1992)
The Big Three, *The Big Three* (1963)
Hot Tuna, *Acoustic* (1970)
Mountain Bus, *Sundance* (1971), *Splashdown* (1975)
The Seldom Scene, *Live at the Cellar Door* (1974)
The Byrds, *Never Before* (1989)
Erica Wheeler, *From That Far* (1992)

"I Know You Rider," a traditional black song, was already a century old when the Warlocks began playing it at their early concerts in 1966. After shelving it for a few years, the Dead paired it with the spunky "China Cat Sunflower" on the receiving end of a brilliant medley that served them well in the following decades.

Historically, the song has transmuted with verses and melodies added and subtracted through space and time. The Dead themselves even toyed with the melody, arrangement, and lyrics before settling on a version they felt comfortable with. Paradoxically, few recordings of "I Know You Rider" exist in comparison to other, less prescient compositions.

"Rider," the song's direct object and nemesis, exists in the murk of the antebellum South. Generally, the term arises in the early blues to describe a difficult woman (or a man, if a woman is singing). But there is some evidence suggesting that "rider" was colloquial for a prison guard who oversaw prison workers while on horseback. The term did sneak into some prison blues songs, perhaps as a code word that the guards wouldn't understand. This might suggest that the song's roots are far more ancient than previously suspected. This type of linguistic codification was commonly employed by black slaves working on the plantations to communicate without tipping "Massa" off as to the nature of their conversation.

10/4/70, **Winterland Arena, San Francisco**
5/16/72, **Radio Luxembourg, Luxembourg**
8/27/72, **Old Renaissance Fairegrounds, Veneta, Oregon**
5/19/74, **Memorial Coliseum, Portland, Oregon**
9/29/80, **Warfield Theater, San Francisco**
8/28/81, **Long Beach Arena, Long Beach, California**
6/15/85, **Greek Theatre, Berkeley, California**
10/18/89, **The Spectrum, Philadelphia**
3/18/93, **Capital Center, Landover, Maryland (with Bruce Hornsby on accordion)**

▪ "I'll Be Your Baby Tonight" (BOB DYLAN)

Bob Dylan, *John Wesley Harding* (1968)
The Hollies, *Hollies Sing Dylan* (1969)
Emmylou Harris, *Gliding Bird* (1969)
Linda Ronstadt, *Hand Sown—Home Grown* (1969)
Robert Palmer, *Don't Explain* (1990)
RAMBLIN' JACK ELLIOTT, *Me & Bobby McGee* (1996)

John Wesley Harding shocked the music industry (and Dylan's adherents) when it was released in early 1968. Not only was it his first official release since his much-discussed (and debated) "motorcycle accident" nearly two years before, the album was a total about-face from the psychedelic impressionism that had marked his previous three efforts, *Bringing It All Back Home*, *Highway 61 Revisited*, and *Blonde on Blonde*. As much provocation as his electrification had caused when he commenced performing rock & roll at the Newport Folk Festival in 1965, the somber, light acoustic strains heard on *John Wesley Harding* spun almost as many heads.

Yet the album managed to be highly influential both because of the superb quality of the writing and in the ways it anticipated the many major changes that were about to transpire in popular music, particularly the rise and success of Joni Mitchell; Jackson Browne; and Crosby, Stills, Nash and Young. Even the Dead were bitten by the bug as heard in the releases *Workingman's Dead* and *American Beauty* in 1970.

In "I'll Be Your Baby Tonight," Dylan toys with the clichés of simple love. The message seems to say "forget philosophy and ideology and settle for life's simple pleasures." In closing an otherwise dark album, this sweet song points ahead to Dylan's new vistas in *Nashville Skyline*.

Writing about the song in the liner notes to *Biograph*, Dylan mused, "There's not too much to say about this . . . maybe it was tongue in cheek, I don't know. It's just a simple song, a simple sentiment. I'd like to think it was written from a place where there is no struggle but I'm probably wrong . . . sometimes you may be burning up inside but still do something that seems so cool and calm and collected. Maria Muldaur called me soon after this album came out, said she recorded it. Actually, it could have been written from a baby's point of view—that's occurred to me."

The Dead's only performances of "I'll Be Your Baby Tonight" were with Dylan during their 1987 gigs giving

Garcia an excuse to redisplay his skills on the pedal steel.

> **7/4/87, Sullivan Stadium, Foxboro, Massachusetts (with Bob Dylan)**

■ "I'll Go Crazy" (James Brown)

James Brown, *Live at the Apollo* (1963), single (1966)

Pigpen is only known to have sung this JB special at one very early Dead show.

> **1/7/66, The Matrix, San Francisco**

■ "I'm a Hog for You" (LEIBER & STOLLER)

Coasters, *Coasters Greatest Hits* (1959), *50 Coastin' Classics* (1992), *The Very Best of the Coasters* (1994)

Otis Redding and Carla Thomas, *King & Queen* (1967)

Clifton Chenier, *Live at the St. Marks* (1971), *Out West* (1972), *King of the Zydeco at Montreux* (1975), *60 Minutes with the King of Zydeco* (1986)

Canned Heat, *One More River to Cross* (1973)

Living Earth, *Living Earth* (1988)

The Nighthawks, *Rock This House* (1993)

Pork, *Strip* (1994)

Hitmakers Leiber and Stoller wrote this down and dirty ditty for the Coasters, who had some commercial success with the tune in 1959. It was a piece of natural raunch for Pigpen, but the Dead are only known to have performed "Hog for You" a few times in 1966 and once in 1971.

> **3/25/66, Trouper's Club, Los Angeles**
> **4/6/71, Manhattan Center, New York**

■ "I'm a King Bee" (Slim Harpo)

Slim Harpo, single (1957), *Rainin' in My Heart* (1961), *The Best of Slim Harpo* (1989), *I'm a King Bee* (1989)

Rolling Stones, *England's Newest Hit Makers* (1964)

Frank Marino and Mahogany Rush, *Live* (1978)

Muddy Waters, *King Bee* (1981)

Family, *He Was She Was You Was We Was* (1982)

Imperial Pompadours, *Ersatz* (1982)

Louisiana blues maestro Slim Harpo recorded his best known tune, "I'm a King Bee," as the A-side of his hit debut single in 1957 for Excello Records. The song has a strange and uncanny history, written while driving on the highway with his wife. Once, while heading to Virginia, the two passed some beehives and Harpo began singing, "I'm a king bee, buzzin' around your hive." As was her practice, Harpo's wife jotted down the lyrics on her ever-present legal pad for later compilation and development at home.

Along with Lightnin' Slim, with whom he regularly performed and recorded, Slim Harpo was among the flame-bearers of Louisiana swamp blues, virtually defining the idiom in the 1950s and 1960s. With a raw yet smooth-flowing beat and musky roots aura, Harpo's distinctive quality was achieved with his guitar, harmonica, and nasally vocals helping establish him as one of Excello's bestselling recording artists.

Born James Moore on January 11, 1924, in Baton Rouge, Louisiana, Harpo began his career in the 1940s as "Harmonica Slim." Over the next decade he built a reputation playing a circuit that included juke joints, parties, and picnics before getting the chance to accompany Lightnin' Slim on a 1955 Excello recording session.

But it wasn't until the Rolling Stones release of "King Bee" in 1964 that Harpo's reputation reached new prominence. The Stones went on to reference Harpo's big 1966 hit "Baby Scratch My Back" in their own "Stray Cat Blues" as well as create a virtual doppelgänger of Slim's "Shake Your Hips" on *Exile on Main Street*, their timeless 1972 album.

The success of "Baby Scratch My Back" resulted in a major commercial breakthrough for Harpo: opening for the Godfather of Soul James Brown, at Madison Square Garden in 1966. All of this allowed Harpo to attain gigs at rock venues including New York's Fillmore East and L.A.'s Whisky-a-Go-Go.

Harpo died of heart failure in 1970, a year the Dead were concentrating on "I'm A King Bee" as a vehicle for Garcia's burgeoning abilities on slide guitar and, of course, for Pigpen's vocal talent in bringing out the sensuous innuendo in the double-entendre-steeped composition. Weir resurrected "King Bee" for a buzzed L.A. audience in December 1993 and then again several months later in Atlanta.

> **11/19/66, Fillmore Auditorium, San Francisco**
> **2/28/69, Fillmore West, San Francisco**
> **11/8/69, Fillmore Auditorium, San Francisco**

■ "I'm a Man" (Spencer Davis)

Spencer Davis Group, *I'm a Man* (1967)

Providing perfect period-piece instrumentation with the composer onstage, the Dead only performed this popular rocker at one 1989 gig.

> **12/10/89, Great Western Forum, Los Angeles (with** BRUCE HORNSBY **on accordion and Spencer Davis on guitar, and vocals)**

■ "(I'm a) Road Runner"

(HOLLAND-DOZIER-HOLLAND)

Jr. Walker and the All Stars, *Shotgun* (1965),
  Roadrunner (1966), *Greatest Hits* (1982)
Zombies, *Begin Here* (1965), *The Collection* (1988)
Humble Pie, *Smokin'* (1972)
KINGFISH, *Kingfish* (1976)
Chris Spedding, *1977 Hurt* (1977)
Peter Frampton, *I'm in You* (1977)

Weir broke out this Holland-Dozier-Holland nifty and apropos ditty at two East Coast spring-tour shows in 1986.

> **3/31/86, Providence Civic Center, Providence, Rhode Island**

■ *In Concert* (television program)

One of the Dead's more bizarre national-television forays was their 1991 appearance on Don Kirschner's canned concert program. In exchange for being allowed to dispense a hefty chunk of Rainforest propaganda (no small feat on a network program), the Dead churned out a decent dose of music from their June 17, 1991, show at Giants Stadium, including "Eyes of the World" and "Saint of Circumstance."

■ "I Need a Miracle" (Weir/Barlow)

Grateful Dead, *Shakedown Street* (1978), *The Arista Years* (1996)
Ratdog, *Furthur* (1996)

Visionary poet William Blake once wrote, "The path to wisdom is laid with excess." If Blake were alive today he would no doubt appreciate the similar sentiments expressed in this Weir/Barlow existential paean to over-the-top living. This hard-rockin', hard-livin' rant found its place at Dead concerts, materializing out of "Space" and signaling the final rush to the last phase of the show. It was also paired effectively with "Bertha" as a first set closer in the early 1980s.

Ticketless Deadheads took the song to heart, incorpo-rating the title on their sandwich boards before shows with such slogans as "I Need a Miracle Ticket" begging entree to their paradise.

> **1/11/79, Nassau Veterans' Memorial Coliseum, Uniondale, New York**
> **6/24/84, Saratoga Performing Arts Center, Saratoga, New York**

(© Grateful Dead Merchandising, Inc.)

■ *Infrared Roses*

Grateful Dead Merchandising Inc. GDCD 40142, 1991.
  Produced by BOB BRALOVE.
I. "Crowd Sculpture," "Parallelogram," "Little Nemo in
  Nightland"; II. "Riverside Rhapsody,"
  "Post-Modern Highrise Table Top Stomp,"
  "Infrared Roses"; III. "Silver Apples of the Moon,"
  "Speaking in Swords," "Magnesium Night Light";
  IV. "Sparrow Hawk Row," "River of Nine Sorrows,"
  "Apollo at the Ritz"
Willie Green III—kick snare hat on "Post-Modern
  Highrise Table Top Stomp." BRUCE HORNSBY—piano
  and synthesizers (strings, vibes) on "Silver Apples
  of the Moon." BRANFORD MARSALIS—tenor and soprano
  saxophones on "Apollo at the Ritz."

The labor-of-love pet project of stage techie and MIDI maestro Bob Bralove, this tape spliced collage documents the Dead at their most far-out: the free-form, lyricless "Drums" and "Space" segment of their concerts. This dense and challenging (but often beautiful) music

(Courtesy of Arista Records)

(1974), *American Soul Man* (1987)
Grateful Dead, *Vintage Dead /'66* (1972)
Billy Preston, *The Wildest Organ in Town* (1966)
Booker T. and the MG's, *And Now!* (1966)
Mitch Ryder and the Detroit Wheels, *Breakout . . . !!!*
(1966), *All Mitch Ryder's Hits* (1967)
Chocolate Watch Band, *No Way Out* (1968)
The Flat Earth Society, *Walleec* (1968)
The Rascals, *Time Peace* (1968)
Paraffin Jack Flash Ltd., *Paraffin Jack Flash Ltd.* (1968)
Ben E. King, *Rough Edges* (1970)
The Chambers Brothers, *Time Has Come* (1971)
Cross Country, single (1973)
Roxy Music, *Flesh and Blood* (1978)
B. B. King, *Six Silver Strings* (1985)
Tina Turner, *Live in Europe* (1988)
The Commitments, *The Commitments* (1991)
Mary Wells, *Dear Lover* (1995)
The Lady of Rage, *Eargasm* (1996)

owes a lot more to Sun Ra than Sun Records. Dead lyricist Robert Hunter handled the task of titling each sound segment.

In the Dark

Arista AL-8452, 1987. Produced by Jerry Garcia and John Cutler.
"Touch of Grey," "Hell in a Bucket," "When Push Comes to Shove," "West L.A. Fadeaway," "Brother Esau," "Tons of Steel," "Throwing Stones," "Black Muddy River"

After a seven-year studio hiatus, the Dead struck literal and figurative pay dirt with *In the Dark*. Fusing the style of their old material ("When Push Comes to Shove"), puckish whimsy ("Touch of Grey"), apocalyptic desperation ("Throwing Stones"), elegiac world-weariness ("Black Muddy River"), and rock & roll ("Hell in a Bucket") with incendiary musicianship throughout the Top 10 album, the Dead finally captured the imagination (and pocketbooks) of mainstream America.

"In the Midnight Hour" (Wilson Pickett/Steve Cropper)

Wilson Pickett, *In the Midnight Hour* (1965), *The Exciting Wilson Pickett* (1966), *A Man and a Half: The Best of Wilson Pickett* (1992), *Live in Japan*

"The Wicked Pickett," "The Midnight Mover," or just plain "bad"—whatever one chooses to call Wilson Pickett—the blustering, rhythmic style of soul-funk he intro-

Wilson Pickett. *(Archive Photos/Frank Driggs Collection)*

duced made him, along with Otis Redding, the best-known soul star of the mid-1960s.

Pickett was born on March 18, 1941, in Prattville, Alabama, and his story is nearly identical to dozens of other musical greats of postwar America: a rural Southern childhood, a move to the industrial north with his family, a background in gospel, and acclaim in rhythm and blues. In Pickett's case, Detroit was the city in which he landed, and the Falcons the group with which Pickett's apoplectic lead tenor caught the attention of enthusiastic, if modest, audiences.

A deal with Capitol Records followed, as did a couple of false starts. It was only when producer Jerry Wexler sent Pickett down to the Stax studio in Memphis that he hit a geyser. Teamed with Stax legend guitarist Steve Cropper, he began turning out the riffs that would be Pickett's ticket to glory.

"Midnight Hour," one of their earliest efforts, has an amusing little history. Before Pickett arrived in Memphis, Cropper began doing a little homework on his incoming guest by scouring out the singer's gospel recordings in the local record shops. He discovered that Pickett enjoyed doing a little ad lib at the end of every song. The day Pickett arrived they started writing and finished "In the Midnight Hour" in about an hour. With Cropper's stinging riffs, "Midnight Hour" became the leitmotif for every white soul band that followed.

A string of equally compelling hits, such as "Mustang Sally," followed and Pickett's stage show was matched in power only by Redding and James Brown. Though he was not able to ride the crest of stardom through the decades, his live act was still smoking in the late 1980s. But by the mid-1980s, troubles with substance abuse landed him in trouble with Johnny Law.

The Dead always seemed to have a lot of fun covering Wilson Pickett's most famous gift to pop culture in the dozens of performances of the tune that spanned the breadth of their career. With Pigpen leading the charge, the band laid into many crazy readings of "Midnight Hour" that saw the band turn the straight-ahead evil bit of funk-soul into a Mobius Strip of Sound. A natural for a Weir resurrection, "Midnight Hour" returned as a surprise selection in 1982, often popping up at the band's New Year's Eve concerts.

9/3/67, Dance Hall, Rio Nido, California

4/29/71, Fillmore East, New York

8/22/87, Calaveras County Fairgrounds, Angel's Camp, California (with Carlos Santana)

■ "In the Pines" (Traditional/LEADBELLY)

Lizzie Abner, *English Folksongs from the Southern Appalachians* by Cecil Sharp (1917)

Singles: Dock Walsh (1926), Peg Leg Howell (1929)

Leadbelly, *The Legend of Leadbelly/'39* (1976), *Where Did You Sleep Last Night/'44* (1996)

Pete Seeger, *American Favorite Ballads* (1958)

Kentucky Colonels, *Long Journey Home* (1964)

Clifford Jordan, *Clifford Jordan* (1965)

Dave Van Ronk, *Dave Van Ronk Sings Ballads, Blues & a Spiritual* (1959)

Gene Clark, *Two Sides to Every Story* (1977)

The Oak Ridge Boys, *Ozark Mountain Jubilee* (1983)

Annette Zalinskas, *Poison Love* (1986)

Bill Monroe, *Live at the Opry* (1989), *In the Pines* (1993), *The Music of Bill Monroe* (1994)

Sandy Rothman & Steve Pottier, *Bluegrass Guitar Duets* (1991)

Merle Travis and Mac Wiseman, *Great American Train Songs* (1993)

Nirvana, *Unplugged in New York* (1994)

Dolly Parton, *Heartsongs* (1994)

A widely known country blues also known as "Black Girl" or "Where Did You Sleep Last Night" among literate folkies, this eerie tune often attributed to Leadbelly (whose version the Dead's most closely resembled) about a wandering love with overtones of violence is only known to have been sung by Garcia at one early Grateful Dead show.

Actually, "In the Pines" dates back to at least the 1870s and its appearances in such a wide variety of repertoires only dimly suggest its complex history. Researching the song for a 1970 dissertation, Judith McCulloh found 160 different versions, a finding that raises a question: Why does a song like "In the Pines" endure and permutate so insistently? The answer may be that its essence is not a specific or even a musical style but the kind of intensely dark emotion that, as is the case with much American music, survives longer in popular memory than does treacly sentiment.

"In the Pines" probably had its origins in the southern Appalachians, where it is still passed on as part of an oral tradition. Dolly Parton once noted that "The song has been handed down through many generations of my family. I don't ever remember not hearing it and not singing it. Any time there were more than three or four songs to be sung, 'In The Pines' was one of them. It's easy to play, easy to sing, great harmonies, and very emotional. The perfect song for simple people."

Norm Cohen, in the 1981 book *Long Steel Rail: The Railroad in American Folksong*, notes that "In the Pines" has three frequent elements, not all of which always appear. There is the chorus "in the pines," a stanza about "the longest train I ever saw" and another verse in which someone is decapitated by a train.

"The longest train" section probably began as a separate song, which merged with "In the Pines," referencing in some renditions to "Joe Brown's coal mine" (see: "Beat It Down the Line"). "The Georgia line" may date its origins to Joseph Emerson Brown, a former Georgia governor, who operated coal mines in the 1870s. The earliest printed version was four lines and a melody compiled by Cecil Sharp in 1917 in Kentucky. After another variant mentioning the train accident was recorded by a folk collector onto cylinder in 1925, commercial hillbilly recordings of "In the Pines" and "The Longest Train" began appearing.

For all its complicated history, the meaning of "In the Pines" may be even more blurry, a vast continuum of different varieties of misery and suffering. As James Leisy wrote in his 1966 book, *The Folk Song Abecedary:* "This unique, moody, blues-style song from the Southern mountain country is like a bottomless treasure box of folk-song elements. The deeper you dig, the more you find."

Though the basic elements of the song remain similar from version to version, the context can be altered with just a few words. It may be a husband, a wife, or even a parent whose head is "found in the driver's wheel" and whose "body has never been found." Men and women and sometimes wayward adolescents flee into the sordid pines, which serve as a metaphor for everything from sex to loneliness and death. The "longest" train can kill or give one's love the means to run away or leave an itinerant worker stranded far from his home.

7/17/66, Fillmore Auditorium, San Francisco

▪ "I Second That Emotion" (Smokey Robinson/Al Cleveland)
Smokey Robinson and the Miracles, single (1967), *Greatest Hits, Vol. 2* (1968), *Live!* (1969), *The Very Best of Smokey Robinson* (1995)
Garcia/Saunders/Kahn/Vitt, *Keystone Encores Vol. 2*/'73 (1988)

Japan, single (1982, 1987)
Jose Feliciano, *Jose Feliciano* (1985)
Tammy Wynette, *Without Walls* (1994)
Manhattan Transfer with Smokey Robinson, *Tonin'* (1995)

Smokey Robinson and the Miracles had a huge crossover hit with this Baby Boomer favorite for Motown in 1967. It shot to No. 1 on the R&B charts and No. 4 on the pop charts. Smokey Robinson and the Miracles were an essential element in the success of Motown Records. Not only was the group one of the label's top acts, but Robinson himself was Berry Gordy's right-hand man—songwriting, producing, and discovering new talent. While such compositions as "I Second That Emotion," "The Tracks of My Tears," and "The Tears of a Clown" made him a revered popular songwriter of the twentieth century, his ethereal tenor was equally renowned as one of the most expressive voices in music.

Born William Robinson on February 19, 1940, in Detroit, Michigan, Smokey Robinson was still in high school when he formed the Miracles with vocalists Pete Moore, Bobby Rogers, Ron White, and Claudette Rogers, whom he later married.

When Gordy formed Motown in 1959, it was the Miracles who provided his first big pop hit with Robinson's "Shop Around" a year later. As the Miracles began turning out the hits over the next decade, Robinson began to write and produce for many artists on Motown's growing roster, his first success coming with Mary Wells in 1962. But when the Beatles covered and recorded Robinson's "You've Really Got a Hold on Me" and Mary Wells did "My Guy" in 1963 and 1964 respectively, his songwriting credentials were set in stone.

As the popularity of Smokey Robinson and the Miracles continued through the late 1960s and early 1970s, Robinson provided hit songs for the likes of the Temptations, the Four Tops, the Supremes, and Marvin Gaye.

Despite some great versions of this R&B chestnut, Garcia only sang "I Second That Emotion" a half-dozen times in April 1971 with the Grateful Dead but went on to include the masterpiece as a Garcia Band concert perennial.

4/29/71, Fillmore East, New York

▪ "It Hurts Me Too" (Tampa Red)
Elmore James, *Golden Hits* (1957), *The Great Elmore James* (1971), *History of Elmore James* (1972), One

Way Out (1994), *Elmore James Memorial Album* (1967), *The Sky Is Crying* (1993), *King of the Slide Guitar* (1994)

Grateful Dead, *Vintage Dead/'66* (1970), *Europe '72* (1972)

CHUCK BERRY, *In Memphis* (1967)

Savoy Brown, *Blue Matter* (1969)

BOB DYLAN, *Self Portrait* (1970)

Hound Dog Taylor, *Hound Dog Taylor and the Houserockers* (1971)

Nicky Hopkins, *Jamming with Edward* (1972)

Mike Bloomfield and John Hammond, *Triumvirate* (1973)

Eric Clapton, *Crossroads* (1974), *From the Cradle* (1994)

Foghat, *Stone Blue* (1978)

Junior Wells and Buddy Guy, *Pleading the Blues* (1979)

Sonny Rhodes, *Just Blues* (1985)

Kenny Neal, *Hoodoo Moon* (1994)

Freddie King, *King of the Blues* (1995)

Tracy Nelson, *Blues Live from Mountain Stage* (1995)

Buddy Guy, *A Tribute to Elmore James* (1996)

"It Hurts Me Too" was closely associated with Elmore James and it was his version of the song with which the Dead were undoubtedly familiar when they commenced performing the slow, aching blues in 1966. Though he didn't cut his first record until 1952 when he was thirty-four years old, Elmore James is arguably the first great electric-blues slide guitarist whose approach and style influenced *everyone*.

Born Elmore Brooks to a sharecropping family on January 27, 1918, in Richland, Mississippi, he taught himself blues rudiments on a one-string homemade guitar and his sound never lost that raw primitivism. While still a teenager, he began playing in the Mississippi Delta juke joints, where he met Robert Johnson. Though Johnson died a year later, the legendary King of the Delta Blues left a lasting impression on James, who incorporated Johnson's slide guitar technique as the primary element in his own style.

Around this time, James befriended harpist Sonny Boy Williamson, with whom he began performing and recording haphazardly.

After serving with the U.S. Navy in the Pacific during

Elmore James (*right*), with Sunnyland Slim (*left*) and Homesick James (*center*), Chicago, 1950s. *(Archive Photos/Frank Driggs Collection)*

World War II, James returned to Delta country and formed one of the earliest electric blues bands in 1945. Simultaneously, Muddy Waters was doing the same thing at the northern end of Highway 61 in Chicago.

James recorded "Dust My Broom" for the Mississippi-based Trumpet Records in 1952, and his gnarly presentation helped the song become the fledgling label's first hit and one of the biggest records on the R&B charts that year. The success of "Dust My Broom" led to other recording offers and, eventually, a move to Chicago. Recording for Meteor Records, James formed a Windy City band with the gimmicky handle, the Broomdusters.

"Dust My Broom" turned out to be a blessing and a curse for James. While its success ensured his continuing viability as a recording artist, it also encouraged subsequent recording directors to request more-or-less transparent reworkings of this piece. In the long run, these variations may have belied James's potential range and impact.

Returning periodically to the Delta enabled James to stay aligned with the region's rougher-hewn music and, quite accidentally, make an artistic bridge between the urban and rural blues.

Possibly because he recorded for relatively obscure labels and because of the perceived homogeneity of his songs, Elmore James never achieved the widespread popularity enjoyed by Muddy Waters in the postwar blues era. Consequently, his reputation was limited to Chicago and the Mississippi Delta during his lifetime.

Still, the slide guitarist persevered, recording some of his most influential tunes in the last few years of his life. "The Sky Is Crying," recorded in 1959, and 1961's "Done Somebody Wrong" were later covered and recorded by Jimi Hendrix and the ALLMAN BROTHERS BAND, respectively.

Ironically, James was still at his peak when a massive heart attack killed him in 1963 just as young whites were beginning to discover the treasures of Chicago's electric blues.

"It Hurts Me Too" was, however, shaped and introduced by Tampa Red, another charismatic blues giant. But like the dozens of blues slide-guitar greats, only a handful—James, Muddy Waters, and Robert Johnson—left a lasting mark on the tradition by creating immediately recognizable, if widely imitated, instrumental styles. One of Chicago's earliest blues stars, Tampa Red was billed as "The Guitar Wizard" during his heyday in the 1920s and 1930s, with stunning slide work on his

steel National guitar showing why he earned his title.

Born Hudson Whitaker (or Woodbridge) on January 8, 1904 (or circa 1903), in Smithville, Georgia, it was his red hair and family's eventual move to Tampa, Florida, that earned him his nickname. Tampa Red had already developed his slide-guitar technique by the time he moved to Chicago sometime in the mid-1920s, playing on street corners for spare change while working in small clubs. It wasn't until his partnership with pianist Georgia Tom Dorsey in 1928 that his career took shape and took off with "It's Tight Like That," a double-entendre blues that initiated what became known as "the hokum sound," which featured light, airy melodies and sentimental or humorous lyrics. Selling thousands of copies, Georgia Tom and Tampa Red performed extensively as the Hokum Boys from Chicago to Memphis while continuing to record. But Dorsey became disillusioned with the blues and became a gospel musician around 1930.

Tampa Red's thirty-year career produced hundreds of sides: hokum, pop, jive, and, of course, the blues. His classic compositions ("Anna Lou Blues," "Black Angel Blues," "Crying Won't Help You," "It Hurts Me Too," and "Love Her with a Feeling") reveal the deeper side of one Chicago's blues mainstays. During his prime, Red could be seen in any one of a wide variety of venues: down-home juke joints, the streets, the vaudeville theater circuit, and the Chicago club scene. Meanwhile, his apartment became something of a salon for bluesmen during the 1930s.

But, as the bigger-sounding electric-blues bands began to overshadow Tampa Red's quainter style, the ravages of his long-standing drinking problem began to take their toll and he slowly faded from the spotlight, eventually going into permanent retirement in 1962. He died in Chicago on March 19, 1981, the same year he was inducted into the Blues Foundation's Hall of Fame.

Pigpen sang "It Hurts Me Too" with the Dead, who performed it as a veritable Elmore James doppelgänger. This allowed their vocalist–mouth harpist to accentuate the agonized theater of the song more passionately on-stage.

4/6/71, Manhattan Center, New York
4/17/72, Tivoli Concert Hall, Copenhagen

▪ "It Must Have Been the Roses" (Robert Hunter)
Grateful Dead, *Steal Your Face* (1976), *Reckoning*

The lonely narrator ruminating on lost love and/or missed opportunity is a fairly constant Hunter concern, as this wistful ballad portrays. Roses, Hunter's prized symbol, are the enchanting talisman that first brought the song's participants together and are the Proustian madeleine that brings for the singer a torrent of bittersweet memory and feeling.

Although the song is often credited as a Garcia/Hunter composition, the guitarist credited his songwriting partner as the melody maker.

In his 1978 interview with David Gans, Hunter described the process of creating the song as "straight transmission," claiming that he "sat down to write a song that would be perfect for Butch Waller's bluegrass band, High Country."

A concert regular since 1974, "It Must Have Been the Roses" saw action in both sets and was a natural for the Dead's 1980 acoustic presentations.

1/15/78, Selland Arena, Fresno, California

▪ **"It's All Over Now"** (Bobby and S. Womack)
The Valentinos, single (1964)
The Rolling Stones, *12 x 5* (1964)
Alex Taylor, *With Friends and Neighbors* (1971)
J. Geils Band, *Full House* (1972)
Ry Cooder, *Paradise & Lunch* (1974)
Johnny Winter, *Captured Live* (1976)

Though "It's All Over Now" is usually associated with the Rolling Stones, this song was actually written and first recorded by Bobby Womack. But despite overdue recognition, Womack was a catalyst on the evolution of black music in the 1970s and 1980s. Absorbing gospel music from his father and soul from Sam Cooke, Womack became one of the first black artists to impact British rock, as evidenced by the Stones' treatment of "It's All Over Now."

Womack was born March 3, 1944, in Cleveland, Ohio. As a boy, his father, Friendly Womack, organized his sons into the Womack Brothers Gospel Quartet. The group followed Cooke's lead into secular music and Memphis, changing their name to the Valentinos and recording with Cooke's own Sar label. They quickly established themselves with Bobby Womack's "Looking for a Love" in 1962 and "It's All Over Now" in 1964.

By the end of the year, Cooke was dead, suspiciously murdered in a Los Angeles motel room, and Womack received pandemic disapproval by marrying the singer's widow.

Since then, Womack has never been out of the loop. Over the years he has been successfully associated with talent as diverse as Wilson Pickett, the Mamas and the Papas, JANIS JOPLIN, Sly Stone, the Crusaders, and Teddy Pendergrass. In 1986, he reunited with the Rolling Stones, appearing on *Dirty Work* and producing a solo album for Ron Wood.

Interestingly, "It's All Over Now" was the first tune the Stones recorded in the U.S. and the site they chose for the event wasn't accidental—Chess Studios was where anybody who was anybody in Chicago cut wax.

"It's All Over Now" is a spunky, got-done-wrong-by-a-woman but having-the-last-laugh song and fit well into Weir's first-set repertoire. The early, ragged versions of the song in 1969 and 1970 featured some tight harp playing courtesy of Pigpen.

9/16/78, Gizah Sound and Light Theater, Cairo, Egypt
8/28/82, Oregon County Fair Site, Veneta, Oregon

▪ **"It's All Over Now, Baby Blue"** (BOB DYLAN)
Bob Dylan, *Bringing It All Back Home* (1965), *Biograph* (1985), *The Music Never Stopped: Roots of the Grateful Dead* (1995)
Grateful Dead, *Vintage Dead /'66* (1970)
JOAN BAEZ, *Farewell, Angelina* (1965)
Tom Constanten, *Morning Dew* (1993)
Them, *Them Again* (1966)
Chocolate Watch Band, *The Inner Mystique* (1967)
Thirteenth Floor Elevators, *Easter Everywhere* (1968)
The Byrds, *Ballad of Easy Rider* (1969)
Judy Collins, *Judy Sings Dylan Just Like a Woman* (1994)

Bidding farewell to a woman, the political left, and his own youthful folly, Dylan crafted a song for the ages with "It's All Over Now, Baby Blue." The song seems to depict a cold world where all perceived certainties are certainties no longer. Everything you know is wrong.

The Dead performed some peppy yet fragile arrangements of the tune as early as 1966. But within a couple of years they had returned to a dirge-like rendition similar to Dylan's and found that it was a natural encore choice.

4/6/82, The Spectrum, Philadelphia

■ **"It's All Too Much"** (George Harrison)
The Beatles, *Yellow Submarine* **(1969)**
Journey, *Look in the Future* **(1976)**
Steve Hillage, *Live Herald* **(1979)**

George Harrison originally called this song "Too Much" when the Beatles started recording it in May of 1967. Harrison sang lead vocals with John Lennon and Paul McCartney adding the backup vocals and hand clapping. A week later the title of the song was changed and a bass clarinet and trumpets overdubbed onto the track. At the time of its recording, the number was more than eight minutes in length, but was later edited down.

"It's All Too Much" was written for the *Yellow Submarine* movie and is one of the songs featured on the film's soundtrack. A shorter version, with one of the verses taken out, can be found on the soundtrack album that was released almost two years after Harrison wrote it.

James Brown, 1965. *(Archive Photos/Frank Driggs Collection)*

As with most of the Beatles' songs introduced into their very late repertoire, Vince Welnick brought this lush and trippy gem to the Grateful Dead in 1995.

3/26/95, The Omni, Atlanta

■ **"It's a Man's, Man's, Man's World"**
(Brown/Jones/Newsome)
James Brown, *Live at the Apollo* **(1963),** *It's a Man's, Man's, Man's World* **(1966),** *Live at the Apollo, Vol. 2, Part 2* **(1968),** *Sex Machine* **(1970),** *Star Time* **(1991)**
Ray Charles, *Ray's Mood* **(1966)**
MC5, *Live '69* **(1988),** *Live '69/'70* **(1991)**
The Residents, *The White Single* **(1984)**
Sara Hickman, *Equal Scary People* **(1989)**
Ice Cube, *AmeriKKKa's Most Wanted* **(1990)**
Countess Vaughn, *Countess* **(1992)**
Concrete Blonde, *Walking in London* **(1992)**
Van Morrison, *A Night in San Francisco* **(1994)**
Cher, *It's a Man's World* **(1996)**
Irma Thomas, *Sweet Soul Queen of New Orleans* **(1996)**

Whether billing himself as "The Godfather of Soul," "Soul Brother Number One," or "The Hardest Working Man in Show Business," James Brown played the most significant role in the consequence of post–World War II black American music and entertainment.

Directly derived from such gospel models as Reverend Julius Cheeks of the Sensational Nightingales, Brown's hoarse, gravelly shriek opened the doors for the likes of fellow soul shouters, like Wilson Pickett and Otis Redding. In addition, his tight, heavily orchestrated records with their mesmerizing rhythms and repetitive lyrics, were the cornerstone of the later funk movement led by Sly and the Family Stone and George Clinton's Parliament and Funkadelic ensembles.

James Brown was also a powerful and potent social commentator with an unsubtle approach to incorporating his philosophies (political and otherwise) into song. This thread of activism that ran through his work from "Say It Loud—I'm Black and I'm Proud" in 1968 and "King Heroin" in 1972 to "Living in America" in 1986, reflected the experience of black America.

Another element in Brown's resilience was his ability at controlling both his artistic and business careers—a fact not lost on later superstars Michael Jackson and Prince who demanded, and received, the same.

Like the great artists throughout history, Brown's relevance to modern musical and social trends was apparent in the late 1980s when his songs were heavily sampled by a new generation of hip-hop artists.

Finally, Brown's stage show virtually reinvented pop theater. With the expertly trained backing group led by Alfred "Pee Wee" Ellis, Brown would leap, dance, gyrate, and crawl across the stage on his knees and "collapse," only to be revived when wrapped in a regal cape.

James Brown was born May 3, 1933, in Barnwell, South Carolina, and raised by an aunt. His family moved to Augusta, Georgia, when he was quite young and it was there that he misspent most of his youth. A childhood marked by a struggle for survival forced him to work as a shoeshine boy when he was in grade school. He ran with a tough crowd and developed a bad reputation with the local police by the time he reached his teens. Predictably, he found himself in the kind of trouble that accompanies situations of desperation and landed in prison after a conviction for petty theft in 1949.

Released in 1953 after four years, Brown joined the Gospel Starlighters, an Atlanta-based group. By 1955, they had changed their name and their act. The Famous Flames transformed themselves into an R&B group and had a Top 10 hit with "Please, Please, Please." In 1958 "Try Me" initiated a string of Top 10 hits on the R&B charts that included "I'll Go Crazy" in 1960, "Night Train" in 1962, and "Prisoner of Love" in 1963.

Live at the Apollo, recorded in 1962, represented a major turning point for Brown, selling an unprecedented (for a live album by an R&B artist) number of copies and documenting what had become the western world's most dramatic and highly choreographed stage presentation. Brown's later *Live at the Apollo Vol. II* is even more legendary.

By the end of the 1950s and through the mid-1960s, Brown was considered R&B's king and, with the Famous Flames, he was the hottest act in the field. Brown's dominance in R&B allowed him to abandon the grind of one-nighters in dilapidated theaters and matchbox clubs while sharing the bill with a half dozen other acts. Now he could sell out large concert halls all by himself and deliver de rigueur marathon concerts to predominantly black audiences.

After renegotiating his contract with King Records in 1965, giving him complete artistic control, Brown released a string of innovative pop hits through 1967, including "Papa's Got a Brand New Bag," "I Got You (I Feel Good)," "It's a Man's, Man's, Man's World," and "Cold Sweat." These recordings found the Famous Flames shaping and sharpening their funk sound to perfection, even introducing a Latin flavor into the short, chopping, repetitive phrases.

The black-power movement had made earnest gains by 1968 and James Brown stayed right in step with its evolutionary and revolutionary aspects. He fashioned slogans for the movement such as "Say It Loud—I'm Black and I'm Proud" *and* intervened to prevent ghetto riots after the assassination of Reverend Martin Luther King, Jr. Mixing his broiling funk sound with lyrics that were sometimes folksy nonsense, sometimes blatantly sexual, Brown continued churning out the hits throughout the 1970s. "Get Up I Feel Like Being a Sex Machine," "Hot Pants," and "My Thang" were probably his best known songs of the decade. During those years he also moved into films, providing the soundtracks for *Black Caesar* and *Slaughter's Big Ripoff* in 1973 and acting in *Come to the Table* the following year.

In the early 1980s, Brown began to fall out of favor with black American popular culture, displaced by younger funk, hip-hop, and rap artists to whose artifice he replied with "Rap Payback." But in 1986 his oddly patriotic "Living in America" and theme to *Rocky IV* renewed his successful pop standing.

But the James Brown story took a bizarre turn in 1988 when he was sentenced in an Aiken, South Carolina, courtroom to six years in prison for leading police on a two-state car chase three months earlier. After serving a year and a half in prison, Brown was released in a work-release program and soon reclaimed his turf on the circuit.

Brown's explosive three minute version of "It's a Man's, Man's, Man's World" is right, tight, lean, and mean. Additionally, its accompanying string arrangement influenced much of the soul music that followed it.

Relating the song to his own life, Brown once said: "Well, now, I got to believe my own song, 'It's a Man's World.' It's a man's world, yes. But it wouldn't be nothin' without a woman or a girl. I just ain't found the *right* one yet."

The Dead covered "It's a Man's, Man's, Man's World" about a dozen times in 1970 in a version that was about as loose as Brown's original was taut. The arrangement included some strained background vocals but their jam was an exploratory and spacey voyage.

5/2/70, Harpur College, SUNY, Binghamton, New York

■ **"It's a Sin"** (Zeb Turner/Fred Rose)
Singles: Eddy Arnold (1947), Marty Robbins (1969)
Elvis Presley, *Something for Everybody* **(1961)**
George Jones, *George Jones Sings of His Country*
Cousins **(1962)**
George Thorogood, *Bad to the Bone* **(1982)**
Pet Shop Boys, *Actually* **(1987)**
Willie Nelson, *Just One Love* **(1995)**

Zeb Turner and Fred Rose wrote "It's a Sin" for Eddy Arnold, who had his first hit with the song in 1947.

Garcia handled the vocals and Pigpen the mind-eating harp on this old country blues at about eight Dead shows from 1966 through 1969 and the theme was vamped on at one 1974 concert. A rare chestnut.
2/23/66, The Matrix, San Francisco

■ **"It Takes a Lot to Laugh (It Takes a Train to Cry)"** (BOB DYLAN)
Bob Dylan, *Highway 61 Revisited* **(1965),** *Bootleg*
Series, Vol. 1-3 **(1991)**
George Harrison with Bob Dylan, *Concert for*
Bangladesh **(1971)**
Leon Russell, *Leon Russell and the Shelter People*
(1971)
Garcia/Saunders/Kahn/Vitt, *Live at the Keystone*
(1973)
Bloomfield/Kooper/Stills, *Super Session* **(1968)**
Phluph, *Phluph* **(1968)**
Blue Cheer, *New Improved* **(1969)**
The Earl Scruggs Review, *The Earl Scruggs Review*
(1973)
The Heart of Gold Band, *Double Dose* **(1984)**

Dylan began working on this song, originally entitled "Phantom Engineer," in June 1965, completed it within a month, and included it on his corner-turning LP *Highway 61 Revisited*. Like many of the tunes on that album, the song is a moody blues expressing feelings in a string of disconnected impressions. "It Takes a Lot to Laugh" also contains hints of apocalyptic and sexual frustration.

Dylan, for his part, has never strayed far from the tune. Since he performed it in his notorious electric set at the Newport Folk Festival in July 1965, it has hardly missed a tour (or reinterpretation) right up to and including his triumphant performance at Woodstock '94.

Though the Dead rarely performed "It Takes a Lot to Laugh," displaying it at a couple of 1973 summer mega shows before reintroducing it as a 1991 treat, Garcia kept this classic in his band's concerts for years. Keith and Donna Godchaux also played the song in their 1975 band, with Keith singing lead and Garcia sitting in on occasion.
6/10/73, RFK Stadium, Washington, D.C. (with the
ALLMAN BROTHERS BAND and MERL SAUNDERS)

■ **"I've Been All Around This World"**
(Traditional)
Louis "Grandpa" Jones, single (1947)
Grateful Dead, *History of the Grateful Dead, Vol. 1*
(Bear's Choice) **(1973),** *Reckoning* **(1981)**
Jerry Garcia Acoustic Band, *Almost Acoustic* **(1989)**
Dave Van Ronk, *Inside Dave Van Ronk* **(1962)**
Joe Val and the New England Bluegrass Boys, *Cold*
Wind **(1983)**

The earliest recorded version of this dire traditional folk song in which the narrator returns to town to settle some old scores, was cut by Grandpa Jones. Born Louis Marshall Jones October 20, 1913, in Niagra, Kentucky, the banjo and guitar player aged right into his makeup. His nickname was supposedly given to him by a fellow hillbilly crooner when Jones was in his mid-twenties, and the geezer image stayed with him for the rest of his career. With Merle Travis and the Delmore Brothers he formed the influential Brown's Ferry Four. Jones joined the Grand Ole Opry after World War II and he appeared there regularly for decades, often with his wife Ramona. The last of the Uncle Dave Macon school of banjo picking and folksy but cornpone entertaining style, Jones was also a regular on the popular television program *Hee Haw*. He was inducted into the Country Music Hall of Fame in 1978.

The Dead first trotted out "All Around This World" as an acoustic number in December 1969 and presumably performed it in their 1970 acoustic sets although the evidence for more than the February 14, 1970, Fillmore West show that wound up on *Bear's Choice* is slim. Ten years later it returned when the Dead briefly recommenced performing acoustically and remained as a sometimes revisited chestnut by Garcia during his occasional acoustic forays in the intervening fifteen years.
12/26/69, McFarlin Auditorium, Dallas
9/29/80, Warfield Theater, San Francisco

- **"I've Got a Tiger by the Tail"** (Buck
Owens/Harlan Howard)
Buck Owens, *I've Got a Tiger by the Tail* (1965)
Porter Wagoner, *On the Road* (1966)
Ray Charles, *Country & Western Meets Rhythm & Blues*
(1966)

Dwight Yoakam's musical great-grandpappy, otherwise known as Buck Owens, may have retired from performing in 1992 but he left a mark on country music that promises to last another millennium. The creator of the Bakersfield Sound who turned out twenty-six consecutive No. 1 hits in the 1960s, Owens was equally well known as a cohost of television's long-running bit of hokum *Hee Haw*, as well as a music publisher and manager of talent.

Alvis Edgar Owens was born August 12, 1929, in Sherman, Texas, and raised by his sharecropping family. The hardscrabble road that was Route 66 led Owens from his birthplace to Arizona, where he learned mandolin and guitar as a child, becoming a professional musician in his teens. His family followed Route 66 once again and landed in Bakersfield, California, where Buck formed the Schoolhouse Playboys. He made his first sessions for Capitol on records by Wanda Jackson, Sonny James, and Faron Young, eventually signing with the label. The floodgates opened when he scored a hit with "Second Fiddle" in 1959. His formula was the hard, rhythmic edge that was later emulated by Merle Haggard, another Bakersfield denizen (who coincidently married Owens's ex-wife).

After some pointedly patriotic songs in the 1970s, Owens's star in the recording industry began to fade, although he maintained his *Hee Haw* gig until 1986. His career came full circle in 1988 when he released *Hot Dog!*, which included a poignant duet with Yoakam, "The Streets of Bakerfield."

Disguised as the Weir cover band Bobby Ace and the Cards from the Bottom of the Deck, the Dead performed Owens's well-known 1965 hit "I've Got a Tiger by the Tail" at one 1969 gig.

6/11/69, California Hall, San Francisco

- **"I've Just Seen a Face"** (Lennon/McCartney)
The Beatles, *Rubber Soul* (1965), *Help!* (1965)
Wings, *Wings over America* (1976)

Leon Russell and the New Grass Revival, *The Live*
Album* (1981)
The Dillards, *Mountain Rock* (1990), *There Is a Time*
(1991)
Paul McCartney, *Unplugged (The Official Bootleg)*
(1991)

Paul McCartney composed "I've Just Seen a Face" for the Beatles movie *Help!* during the same three-hour session that produced his screaming rocker "I'm Down" and classic "Yesterday," making this folk-rock song's discreet assurance even more remarkable. The song became one of McCartney's Auntie Gin's favorites when he was composing it, hence the working title of the song was "Auntie Gin's Theme" (which was the title of the instrumental version of "I've Just Seen a Face" when it was later recorded by the George Martin Orchestra).

Undercover as Bobby Ace and the Cards from the Bottom of the Deck, the Dead performed this infectious Beatles' gem at one 1969 gig.

6/11/69, California Hall, San Francisco

- **"I Want to Tell You"** (George Harrison)
The Beatles, *Revolver* (1966)

One of three George Harrison compositions to make its way to the *Revolver* album, "I Want to Tell You" first found life as a late-entry Grateful Dead cover in the summer of 1994 with Garcia handling the lead vocals, trotting it out a half dozen times primarily as a second set segue. "I Want to Tell You" was hinged around the Beatles' superb harmonies and, as with many a Harrison love song, failed communication is the order of the day. Throughout the Beatles' career, Harrison rarely wrote a straightforward love song: all his portrayals of romance were surrounded in misunderstanding and the dreadful prospect of boredom.

7/19/94, Deer Creek Music Center, Noblesville, Indiana

- **"I Want You"** (BOB DYLAN)
Bob Dylan, *Blonde on Blonde* (1966), *At Budokan*
(1978), *Dylan & the Dead* (1987)
Hollies, *Hollies Sing Dylan* (1969)
Sophie B. Hawkins, *Bob Dylan: The 30th Anniversary*
Celebration Concert* (1993)

The last song cut for Dylan's still-resonant LP *Blonde on Blonde*, "I Want You" was finished in the Nashville hotel room where Dylan stayed while recording the record. Dylan had taught Al Kooper the piano part and Kooper played it over and over while the author worked out the final lyric.

In its original release, the song has a lilting melody, a fine harmonica solo, and an intriguing guitar line by Nashville sessionman Wayne Moss. "I Want You" captures the irrepressible feeling of new love reflected in a fresh moment when Dylan stumbles on a line someone else would have edited out. Yet with Dylan, the little slip works to the song's advantage.

By 1978 Dylan had drastically altered "I Want You," transforming the song into a wistful torch song for his 1978 Elvis-style world tour.

Dylan performed "I Want You" at two of his 1987 summer concerts with the Grateful Dead keeping closer to the original, country-flavored arrangement.

7/4/87, Sullivan Stadium, Foxboro, Massachusetts (with Bob Dylan)

▪ "I Washed My Hands in Muddy Water" (Joe Babcock)
Singles: Stonewall Jackson (1965), Johnny Rivers (1966), Charlie Rich (1966)
Elvis Presley, *Country Memories* (1978)

Stonewall Jackson had a No. 8 C&W hit with Joe Babcock's "I Washed My Hands in Muddy Water." Garcia handled the vocals for this gospel-influenced, Grateful Dead one-timer at a Big Apple shindig in 1971.

12/5/71, Felt Forum, New York

▪ "I Will Take You Home" (Mydland/Barlow)
Grateful Dead, *Built to Last* (1989), *Dozin' at the Knick*/'90 (1996)

Without a doubt Brent Mydland's most tender moment, "I Will Take You Home" is a soft lullaby that could be alternately applied to a child or a long-lost love. Many Deadheads fondly remember Mydland singing this song with his young daughter on the piano seat beside him.

10/21/88, Reunion Hall, Dallas
4/1/90, The Omni, Atlanta

▪ "Jack a Roe" (Traditional)

Grateful Dead, *Reckoning* **(1981),** *Dozin' at the Knick/'90* **(1996)**

Tom Paley, *Folk Songs from the Southern Appalachians* **(1953)**

Jean Ritchie, *Songs from Kentucky* **(1956)**

Peggy Seeger and Ewan MacColl, *Two-Way Trip* **(1961)**

JOAN BAEZ, *In Concert Part 2* **(1963),** *Rare, Live and Classic* **(1969)**

BOB DYLAN, *World Gone Wrong* **(1993)**

Jerry Garcia/DAVID GRISMAN, *Shady Grove* **(1996)**

The tale of a woman who disguises herself in a man's attire in order to carry out a heroic deed is as old as any in the folk tradition, and "Jack a Roe" may be the most enduring of this venerable strain of songs. Legends of what historians call "The Maiden Warrior" can be traced to ancient Greece. However, the song we know as "Jack a Roe" is probably only about two or three centuries old and derives from the troubadours of the British Isles.

The song's history in North America is equally ripe, with permutations of the melodrama appearing in states with such diverse folk traditions as Missouri, Kentucky, North Carolina, and Virginia. Known alternately as "Jack the Sailor," "Jack's Gone a-Sailing," "Jack Munro," "Jackaro," "Jack-a-Roe," and even "Jack the Farmer," many of the United States versions share similar plot lines and language, though there are regional differences with some containing more or less of the story than the others. And, as is customary in the oral tradition, versions were often localized to make them more intimate to specific audiences.

The Grateful Dead adaptation stays fairly close to the earliest known versions of the song and is basically an accelerated variation of the well-known Joan Baez renditions. The daughter of a wealthy London merchant is in love with "Jack the Sailor" despite having many worthy suitors. When Jack ships off to an unnamed war in a distant unnamed land, she attempts to join him—enlisting by cloaking herself in manly garb. Though she is met at the recruiting office by doubt, she gives her name as "Jack A. Roe" and is signed up. Arriving at the turmoil after a horrific battle, she finds her love and secures a doctor to heal him. By the song's end the couple is married and the storyteller offhandedly proposes the same to an enchanted listener. There is some confusion regarding the meaning "A Roe" in the song's title, with the notion of it being a bastardization of "a rogue" being the most common.

An infrequent but always shockingly welcome first-set Garcia cover, "Jack a Roe" was included in Dead shows since 1977, its favored renderings in its 1980 acoustic version. Garcia also trotted out the chestnut several dozen times between 1977 and 1992 in various guises with his many side bands.

11/20/78, Cleveland Music Hall, Cleveland, Ohio
9/30/80, Warfield Theater, San Francisco
12/28/88, Coliseum Arena, Oakland, California

■ *Jack O'Roses*/Robert Hunter

Dark Star DSLP 8001, 1979 (Reissue: Relix RRLP 2001, 1980).

"Box of Rain," "Reuben and Cherise," "Talkin' Money Tree," "Friend of the Devil," "Delia DeLyon and Stagger Lee," "Lady of Carlisle," "Book of Daniel," "Terrapin: a. 'Lady With A Fan,' b. 'Terrapin Station' c. 'Ivory Wheels'/'Rosewood Track,' d. 'Jack O' Roses,' " "Prodigal Town"

Robert Hunter's legitimacy as a recording artist evolved by leaps and bounds from his first efforts in the mid-1970s through the present day. A turning point in this growth, *Jack O'Roses* was a well-received and performed effort.

Mixing Grateful Dead favorites with several of his own gems, the record finds Hunter in top form interpreting the selections with the intangible qualities of musician and poet. A couple of the tunes, "Friend of the Devil" and the complex "Terrapin" suite, offer extended verses to those known and cherished by Deadheads. "Terrapin," in particular, fleshes out the familiar song cycle to include characters and scenarios that draw on American folk, blues, English balladry, and Grateful Dead mythology: Peggy-O, Stagger Lee, and Delia De-Lyon are a few of those who make cameos in Hunter's epic song.

Finally, both the song and the character "Jack O' Roses," assume the same mysterious role as Bob Dylan's tricksterish "Jack of Hearts," an elusive catalyst to the unfurling events described in this highly conceptualized and sharply executed outing.

■ "Jack Straw" (Weir/Hunter)

Grateful Dead, *Europe '72* (1972), *What a Long Strange Trip It's Been* (1977), *Hundred Year Hall*/*'72* (1995), *Dick's Picks Volume Seven*/*'74* (1997)
Robert Hunter, *Live '85* (1985), *Box of Rain* (1991)
BRUCE HORNSBY and the Range, *Deadicated* (1991)
Bruce Hornsby (with Bob Weir), *Furthur* (1996)

A score-settling revenge song of loyalty gone awry and dramatic derring-do, "Jack Straw" stands as one of the Grateful Dead's more theatrical songs. Despite the very un-P.C. lyric that bookends "Jack Straw" ("We can share the women, we can share the wine"), the song conveys an Old West spirit with its desperado, on-the-lam plot.

Of the negative interpretation the lyric has received, Hunter explained to Blair Jackson in 1988, "Well, I think that people have often believed that the character in 'Jack Straw' who says 'We can share the women, we can share the wine' is expressing my personal sentiments, which is not the case. I heard a lot from feminist groups about that one when it first came out. If you really look at what happens in that song, you'll see it's a situation that ends in tragedy. It's a dialogue between two people, and here's the outcome of the various attitudes which Shannon is mouthing off in the song."

But the hero of the song's title also has antecedents in fourteenth-century British history. Jack Straw is the name of a character in the Great Rebellion of 1381 in England. At that time the serfs rebelled, burned the masters' manors, and marched on London. They seized that town, demanding that they be set free and given land. Jack Straw was among the names of the movement's reputed spokespeople. The King went to the mob, and, in writing, granted their demands. The peasants then returned to what they thought were now their farms. The King and nobles then formed an army, killed those rebel leaders they could identify, and returned the peasants to serfdom. However, the song's plot line is even vaguer than this arcane slice of history. For although there is a story being played out here, the events that inform the desperation of the picaresque characters are never revealed.

A multi-tempoed composition, "Jack Straw" easily shifts between moods and is highlighted by a vital jam leading to the song's conclusion. Part of this effect is aided by the trading off of lyrics by Weir and Garcia accentuating the song's inherent drama. Like several of the Dead's earlier compositions, this dynamo reached full flower in the 1980s as a show-stopping show opener.

4/17/72, Tivoli Concert Hall, Copenhagen
9/20/78, Giants Stadium, East Rutherford, New Jersey
4/22/79, Spartan Stadium, San Jose, California
1/13/80, Coliseum Arena, Oakland, California
10/10/80, Warfield Theater, San Francisco
10/20/84, Carrier Dome, Syracuse, New York
7/2/88, Oxford Plains Speedway, Oxford, Maine
12/12/92, Coliseum Arena, Oakland, California

■ Etta James
Born January 25, 1938, Los Angeles, California

"Rage. You can hear it in my music. It's always been there. I had it when I was a little kid. I have it now," wrote Etta James in her 1995 autobiography, *Rage to Survive*. The title was perfect for the no-holds-barred story that neither apologized for nor glorified the life of one of popular music's true divas.

James came by her attitude through the school of hard knocks with a childhood that was a social worker's worst nightmare. Born Jamesetta Hawkins to a disturbed teenage mother and a nameless father, she was passed around among relatives and family friends whose ethnic backgrounds were so varied that she grew up straddling just about every racial boundary that existed.

Johnny Otis discovered the sixteen-year-old James fronting an all-girl vocal trio. An individual stylist who alternately growls and purrs her songs, she hit pay dirt while still a teenager with her "Roll with Me Henry," a 1950s feminist response to Hank Ballard's sexy "Work with Me Annie." While James hit the R&B tour circuit, Georgia Gibbs's cover "Dance with Me Henry" made its way to the pop mainstream in what James called a "Suzy Creamcheese version."

It was when James signed with Chess Records in the 1960s that she really hit her stride, putting twenty-four crossover hits on the charts between 1960 and 1970. Her range and delivery of material such as "All I Could Do Was Cry" and "At Last" presaged the soul music explosion to come.

After suffering a long, slow decline partially due to bad business dealings and drugs, Etta mounted a comeback in the late 1970s that has gone the distance.

It was near the height of her return to acclaim that she opened for and joined the Dead during their 1982–83 New Year's run, turning in encore sets with the band that included a long-gone "Hard to Handle," "Love Light," "Midnight Hour," and her own signature soul-belter, "Tell Mama."

■ *James and the Good Brothers*/James and the Good Brothers
Columbia CS 30889, 1971.

Even Garcia's guest appearance couldn't save this disc from obscurity.

■ "Jerry Garcia"
(asteroid)

When Jerry Garcia joined Bach, Coltrane, and Muddy Waters at the Great Jam Session in the Sky, few could imagine how literal that would come to be. In November 1995 the International Astronomical Union approved a request to name asteroid 4442 after the rock star who had died the previous August.

The suggestion came from Simon Radford, an astronomer at the National Radio Astronomy Observatory in Tuscon, Arizona, and his colleague Ed Olszewski of the University of Arizona's Steward Observatory. "I've enjoyed his music for a long time," said Radford. Under the IAU rules, however, only the discoverer of an asteroid can name it, and neither Radford or Olszewski had a spare asteroid to name.

So they turned to Tom Gehrels of Kitt Peak National Observatory, who has been systematically scanning the heavens for asteroids. He offered 4442, which he discovered on September 14, 1985. "Jerry Garcia" is about 160 kilometers across. "It seemed like a good tribute to his memory," said Radford.

■ *Jerry Garcia/David Grisman*
Acoustic Disc ACD2, 1991. Produced by Jerry Garcia and DAVID GRISMAN.
"The Thrill Is Gone," "Grateful Dawg," "Two Soldiers," "Friend of the Devil," "Russian Lullaby," "Dawg's Waltz," "Walkin' Boss," "Rockin' Chair," "Arabia"
Jerry Garcia—acoustic guitar. David Grisman—mandolin. Jim Kerwin—bass. Joe Craven—percussion, fiddle

Garcia's committed return to acoustic work came full flower on this collaboration with his old colleague and fine-fretted friend, David Grisman. Along with Jim Kerwin's bass and Joe Craven's percussion and fiddling contributions, the stellar renditions of a wide range of music are exquisitely and soulfully executed, setting new standards for the artists and the songs.

The concept for the album began in the summer of 1990 when the two bumped into each other at a party. After a couple of jam sessions at Grisman's cozy home studio in Mill Valley, California, they knew they had the makings of a record. The tape machines started running the first day they got together and there was very little rehearsing per se. Over the course of eight months and two dozen sessions, the pair recorded twenty-six tunes.

One of the pieces, an instrumental called "Grateful Dawg," could well have been the album's or the band's title in its allusion to the two featured musicians. Grisman, it should be known, has long referred to his own particular brand of music (a fusion of bluegrass, jazz, folk, and classical) as "Dawg Music." Indeed, the entire album is a psychic amalgamation of the Garcia-Grisman aesthetic.

The combo blends each of the songs into this vision. B. B. King, Irving Berlin, Hoagy Carmichael, and traditional folk tunes are mixed and filtered through purposeful intuition. The album also includes a few covers, a definitive "Friend of the Devil" and an ambitious, atmospherically jazzy "Arabia." Perhaps the only thing missing from the disc is the wonderful Garcia-Grisman interpretation of Miles Davis's "SO WHAT," an outtake from the album that was performed by the group in their all-too-rare concert performances in the early 1990s.

Discussing the birth of the album, Grisman told John Carlini of *Guitar* magazine in 1991, "One thing led to another, and then last year the Grateful Dead gave me an award. They established a music award a few years ago called the Ralph J. Gleason Award. So, sometime last year I got a phone call that I got this check, and that I'd been awarded this prize, and I found out that Jerry was the culprit who nominated me, so I called him up to thank him, and said, 'Hey, why don't we get together and play sometime?' We made a date, he came over, walked in, and he immediately said, 'What we should do is make a record, 'cause that'll give us something to focus on.'

"So, that day, I called up my engineer and said, 'Hey, can you come over?' I didn't tell him who was here. He just came over, and we started recording. Every time we got together, we'd record, and of course, there's a lot of loose tape of us just trying stuff out. Finally, I said to Jerry, 'When do you want to start?' And he said, 'Now!' "

Jerry Garcia Band

Any group would consider itself fortunate to have a twenty-year run, play joints like Madison Square Garden, and enjoy the type of success experienced by Garcia's "other band." The formalization of the Jerry Garcia Band was typically informal. Garcia had been playing bar gigs with MERL SAUNDERS, JOHN KAHN, Tom Fogerty, and various other Bay Area musicians since the early 1970s. Discussing the band's early days in a 1983 MTV interview with Nina Blackwood, Garcia recalled, "What happened was that when we were home and the Grateful Dead weren't working, I would get hot to play, so I started going to these Monday night jam sessions that they used to have at this club in San Francisco called the Matrix. I started going down there and playing. That's where I met Merl Saunders and I started playing with him on a regular basis. I met John Kahn there, and we started playing for maybe a year on every Monday night. It was very casual, and it gradually turned into something a little more formal, and so on, until now. This really just comes from my wanting to play a lot."

Loosely known as Garcia and Saunders (or vice versa), the culmination of the flavor of their gigs is reflected on the double LP *Live at Keystone* and a couple of Saunders albums, *Fire Up* and *Heavy Turbulence*. These engagements presented a way for Deadheads to catch Garcia up close and personal since the Dead had hit the big time by 1973, playing civic centers and hockey rinks instead of auditoriums with their unwieldy Wall of Sound PA system, Garcia was all too quickly coming to the sobering realization that success can often suck. But the Garcia-Saunders union was an antidote to the big hassles; their relative spontaneity and small scale provided a welcome contrast to the long-range planning that the Dead had been forced into.

When the Dead hung it up for a couple of years in late 1974, Garcia and Saunders had achieved enough coherence to take to the road with Kahn on bass, drummer Ron Tutt, and Martin Fierro on flute and sax. Consisting of freewheeling jams, a typical Garcia-Saunders gig favored songs from their albums spiced with liberal doses of Dylan, nascent Garcia/Hunter compositions, loads of

R&B, and a reservoir of blues. Much in the manner of the Dead, the band would enter "Space" near the end of its shows but encores were a rarity.

For Grateful Dead–starved heads, a shot of Garcia was better than nothing at all, even if the dynamics of the band were sometimes a trifle lackluster. But for a man who loved playing (and needed the bread performances provided), Garcia had found a vehicle to fill the artistic and financial void left by the Dead's hiatus.

Renaming themselves LEGION OF MARY in 1975, the last incarnation of the Garcia-Saunders combo made its final regional swings throughout the United States. While tapes of these shows reveal a flexible and searing group, complaints of "too little Jerry" were common at the time. Still, when he played those CHUCK BERRY licks on "Let It Rock," passionately bellowed the sendup for "The Harder They Come," or traded fiery fours with Saunders from their R&B grab bag, one was reminded that he was a virtuoso.

But, by late 1975, Garcia and Saunders parted ways, Martin Fierro left, and a major overhaul of this touring package was under way. When Nicky Hopkins, the respected session man most recently of Quicksilver, took over the piano chair, the first unit calling itself the Jerry Garcia Band hit the road. New songs were learned, old songs were rearranged, and the overall emphasis went from jazzy meandering to rock & roll boogie. Borrowing songs such as "Sugaree" from the Dead songbook, reviving the old Drifters classic "Money Honey," and featuring Hopkins on a few instrumental pieces, this first incarnation of the band bearing Garcia's name ended up being short-lived.

Hopkins was an excellent studio player but an increasingly unreliable onstage presence whose ego may have prevented him from accepting a subordinate role in someone else's band. Hopkins had played with the likes of the Rolling Stones and John Lennon and seemed to suffer from swollen-headitis during his tenure with the burgeoning Garcia Band. Still, the aggregation did leave its mark and is represented by four tracks on Garcia's *Reflections* album including "Catfish John" and "Tore Up Over You," which are remembered as the concert highlights at the time.

The decision to name a band after himself was probably not an easy one. After attempting to form a leaderless collective patterned after the Dead, Garcia became,

Jerry Garcia Band (Jaclyn LaBranch and Gloria Jones, vocals), OAKLAND COLISEUM, 10/31/92. *(Robert Minkin)*

despite his avowed distaste for the limelight, that most dreaded of all stations in life: the boss.

Before the Dead resumed touring in mid-1976, Garcia re-formed his unit by turning to his Grateful band mates Keith and Donna Godchaux for the piano and vocal parts and hit the road in support of *Reflections*. This quartet (Garcia, Kahn, and the Godchauxs) were the basic JGB for the better part of the next three years. Keith Godchaux was in his prime, and a typical concert would feature two pros trading licks on some classic tunes bolstered by Donna Godchaux and, for a stretch, Maria Muldaur, Kahn's wife.

This was a watershed period for the Garcia Band with scads of new material introduced to the repertoire including: "The Way You Do the Things You Do," the Stones' "Moonlight Mile," Clapton's "Lonesome and a Long Way from Home," Dylan's "Knockin' on Heaven's Door," and much of the material from *Cats Under the Stars*, one of Garcia's strongest solo albums, released in 1978.

But the same problems facing the Dead at the time (i.e., Keith and Donna Godchaux) were also affecting the Garcia Band. Shows began to drag, the music's drive began to wane as did the enthusiasm of his fan base. One New York City concert, in fact, failed to sell out.

Abandoning his own band for the better part of 1979, Garcia reunited with Merl Saunders in Reconstruction, a group with a harder, funkier edge that included Kahn on bass, Gaylord Birch on drums, Ed Neumeister playing trombone, and Ron Stallings on tenor sax and vocals. While some new covers were introduced ("Dear Prudence," "Strugglin' Man," and his own "Deal"), it was essentially business as usual with the group mining much of the material they had covered in the early part of the decade.

Ready to rebuild the Garcia Band from the ground up, Garcia and Kahn began with a couple of streamlined quartets that carried them through the end of 1980. When they took to the road again in 1981, it was with new musicians and new arrangements. Old reliables like "The Harder They Come" and "Midnight Moonlight" were played at breakneck tempo and experiments began with two keyboardists and a pair of backup vocalists. Between late 1981 and mid-1983, no less than four lineups were billed as the Garcia Band, with Billy Kreutzmann even signed up for a stretch in 1982. In addition, Garcia and Kahn began performing some all-acoustic duet concerts. But as the decade wore on, the lineup

pretty much settled into a reliable coalition that included Melvin Seals on organ, David Kemper on drums, and a couple of never-say-die backup singers, Jackie LaBranch and Gloria Jones.

Discussing the state of the band with Rip Rense of *Mix* magazine in 1987, Garcia said, "We've been learning lots of different material lately. That's the main thing. The band has just been playing so well. Melvin is just a monster keyboard player, and everyone in the band has been really loving it. It's taken a long time to dial it in—a lot of personnel changes. It started off with my own theory about a four-piece band—that you can make a lot of music with just four pieces, provided everyone is thinking conceptually the same way. With four pieces, you can play and still hear everything. It's like a string quartet or something like that; it's conversational. So the band is starting to really *play*. It works.

"It took a long time before I started playing with Melvin to get that thing of being able to make that tran-

(Author's collection)

sition from background to foreground without any loss of energy. It used to be that I could play a solo and go back to playing rhythm and feel the energy fall out. It makes you play stiff. But Melvin has this thing of being able to play really wide. He can support a solo no matter what the intensity is, or conversely, no matter how sensitive it is. He really listens and is able to maintain that sense of energy. So the changes from instrumental parts to singing parts, etc., are all smooth. Melvin is able to cross all that stuff. Effectively, he's like an orchestra, in terms of what he's able to provide for me to play against."

But if there was flexibility within the band's personnel, new songs were harder to come by until Garcia began fashioning some Hunter compositions for his own. Soon songs such as "Valerie" and "Run for the Roses" joined "Gomorrah," "Rhapsody in Red," "Mission in the Rain," and "Reuben and Cherise" as fodder to help create a distinct yet familiar aura of Garcia Band shows. Additionally, an exploration of Dylan's songbook upped the ante for the performers and audience alike with "When I Paint My Masterpiece," "Simple Twist of Fate," and "Knockin' on Heaven's Door" colored in ways that would have impressed even their author. Dylan's "Tangled Up in Blue" along with the Garcia/Hunter "Deal" became bona fide showstoppers.

■ *Jerry Garcia Band*

Arista 18690-2, 1991. Produced by Jerry Garcia, JOHN KAHN, and John Cutler.

"The Way You Do the Things You Do," "Waiting for a Miracle," "SIMPLE TWIST OF FATE," "Get Out of My Life," "My Sisters and Brothers," "I Shall Be Released," "Dear Prudence," "Deal," "Stop That Train," "Señor (Tales of Yankee Power),"
"Evangeline," "The Night They Drove Old Dixie Down," "Don't Let Go," "That Lucky Old Sun,"
"TANGLED UP IN BLUE"

Jerry Garcia–guitar/vocals. John Kahn–bass. Melvin Seals–organ/keyboards. David Kemper–drums. Jackie LaBranch–vocals. Gloria Jones–vocals.

Garciaheads had been pining a long time for a live Jerry Garcia Band album and the results were well worth the wait. A juicy cross-section of R&B, soul, Dylan, the Beatles, pure rock & roll, gospel, avant-garde, and original material, the album captured Garcia's most enduring unit at a performance peak.

(Courtesy of Arista Records)

■ *J. Garcia: Paintings, Drawings and Sketches* (book)/Jerry Garcia. Edited by David Hinds.

96 pages. Approximately 70 prints of watercolors, pen-and-ink drawings, and sketches. Berkeley: Celestial Arts, 1992.

Before plunging himself into the musical and cultural maelstrom of the Grateful Dead, Jerry Garcia was an art student at the San Francisco Art Institute. Despite his career choice, Garcia never stopped doodling and grew progressively more serious about his hobby in the late 1980s.

Much like a Dead show, Garcia's humble art book includes an array of execution and emotion: translucent, sloppy, light, and heavy. Whether or not his name is ever mentioned in the same breath as the Impressionists (or the Marvel Comics crew) is something for history to decide. But this collection shows promise above and beyond the celebrity artists who periodically cashed in on their notoriety to hawk their wares. Some of the most appealing works include the more rooted pen-and-inks such as "Paris in the Rain," "Zoot," and "South of the Border."

True to form and to his credit (and unlike much of the contemporary art scene), Garcia said this about his collection: "I hope that nobody takes them too seriously."

- ### "Joey" (BOB DYLAN/Jacques Levy)
  #### Bob Dylan, *Desire* (1975), *Dylan & the Dead* (1987)

Not only was "Joey" regarded as one of Bob Dylan's most puzzling songs when it was released on the popular *Desire* album, its revival by Dylan when he teamed up with the Grateful Dead eleven years later was met with even greater skepticism. This is, after all, a song about Joey Gallo, a ruthless New York City mobster. Dylan pulls off this dusky jewel with his sly mastery, though, delivering the song like an eye-witness confidant with a colloquial-steeped, "from me to you" authenticity as if the song were a conversation transpiring on a Little Italy stoop.

Dylan was living in New York's Greenwich Village in the summer of 1975, hanging out at his old haunts, reuniting with old friends, meeting new ones, and routinely closing the neighborhood watering holes with many a boozy jam session.

One of his running buddies was Jacques Levy, a doctor of psychology, steeped in Jungian thinking, with whom Dylan had become acquainted about a year before. Levy was a theatrical handyman and the director of *Oh! Calcutta*, the risqué Broadway show. But he was also a seasoned lyricist and, after a chance meeting, Dylan suggested a casual collaboration.

Dylan had already begun working on "Isis," probably the best song on *Desire*, and the two worked on and finished it in one night. They agreed to continue the process but, when New York became a little claustrophobic, they retired to eastern Long Island for a few weeks in August and banged out a reported fourteen songs. Levy ended up collaborating with Dylan on every *Desire* selection except "Sara," Dylan's highly personal and revealing parting song to his wife. At one point Levy suggested Joey Gallo as a subject because he had known the hip hood during the last year of his life in 1972.

After the release of *Desire*, "Joey" was heavily criticized for its perceived glorification of organized crime. Even New York's radical press came out with their knives sharpened on this one with headlines such as "Wake Up Dylan, Joey Gallo Was No Hero," scolding the recording artist.

Part of the confusion, no doubt, stemmed from the fact that the album's most notorious song upon its release was "Hurricane," the finger-pointing invective that protested the wrongful conviction and imprisonment of middleweight boxing contender Rubin "Hurricane" Carter and his friend John Artis. "Joey," it was argued, seemed to cheapen the powerful political possibility contained in "Hurricane."

The scribes, of course, missed the point of the song, which was consistent with Dylan's obsession with the social pariah, a bill which Joey Gallo fit to a tee. He read Nietzsche in jail and was, according to the song, "Always on the outside / Of whatever side there was." Gallo alienated his "family" contacts even further by his friendship with blacks "'Cause they seemed to understand / What it's like to be in society / With a shackle on your hand."

Many Dylanists still hate this song but it has actually improved with age and Dylan's retooling of "Joey" with the Grateful Dead was the first step in this direction. Before his 1987 collaboration with them, Dylan had never performed the song and although it didn't translate particularly well at the large stadium venues where it was performed, its revival evidently inspired the singer/songwriter as he has kept it as an on-again, off-again inclusion in his post-Dead concert presentations.

5/87, Club Front, San Rafael, California (Dylan/Dead rehearsals)

7/12/87, Giants Stadium, East Rutherford, New Jersey (with Bob Dylan)

- ### "John Brown" (BOB DYLAN)
  #### Bob Dylan, *Broadside Ballads Vol. 1* (1963), *MTV Unplugged* (1995)

One of the many surprises of Bob Dylan's union with the Grateful Dead was the reappearance of so many of his forgotten masterworks. "John Brown," regarded as perhaps the best of these surprises, is a bitter antiwar tract attacking the concept of war heroes. Written during the very early days of the U.S. military involvement in Vietnam but filled with the aura of *Johnny Got His Gun*, Dalton Trumbo's World War I–era novel, "John Brown" tells the story a young man—a boy really—who leaves home at his parents' urging to fight on an unnamed foreign shore for an unknown cause. His parents, particularly his mother, express their pride at his decision and boast of his exploits to their friends and neighbors. But the mother is sobered when she goes down to meet her son at the train station upon his return only to find him crippled, blind, and maimed. He bitterly tells her that when he went to battle he saw that his enemy's face "looked just like mine" before dropping his worthless medals into her hand.

7/12/87, Giants Stadium, East Rutherford, New Jersey

■ **"Johnny B. Goode"** (CHUCK BERRY)

Chuck Berry, single (1958), *Chuck Berry Is On Top* (1959), *Live at the Fillmore Auditorium* (1967), *The London Chuck Berry Sessions* (1972), *The Collection* (1988)

Grateful Dead, *The Grateful Dead* (1971), *Dick's Picks Volume Five/'79* (1996)

THE BEACH BOYS, *Beach Boys Concert* (1964)

Jerry Lee Lewis, *Greatest Live Show on Earth* (1965), *The Return of Rock* (1965)

Johnny Winter, *Second Winter* (1969), *Johnny Winter, And* (1971), *Live* (1971)

Jimi Hendrix, *Hendrix in the West* (1971), *Jimi Plays Berkeley* (1975)

Elvis Presley, *From Memphis to Vegas* (1970)

Equals/Eddy Grant, *Equals Rock (Around the Clock) Vol. 1* (1973)

Dr. Feelgood, *Stupidity* (1976)

Elton John, *Victim of Love* (1979)

The Sex Pistols, *The Great Rock n' Roll Swindle* (1979)

Shadows, *Live at Abbey* (1982)

Peter Tosh, *Mama Africa* (1983)

Judas Priest, *Ram It Down* (1988)

Not only was Chuck Berry one of the avatars of postwar America, his most famous song, "Johnny B. Goode," is about rock & roll stardom. Recalling the genesis of his signature song, Berry wrote in his 1987 memoir: "One song had its birth when the tour first brought me to New Orleans, a place I'd longed to visit ever since hearing Muddy Waters's lyrics, 'Going down in Louisiana, way down behind the sun.' That inspiration, combined with little bits of Dad's stories and the thrill of seeing my black name posted all over town in one of the cities they brought the slaves through, turned into the song 'Johnny B. Goode.'

"Leonard Chess took an instant liking to this song and stayed in the studio coaching us the whole time we were cutting it. I'd guess my mother has as much right to be declared the source of 'Johnny B. Goode' as any other contender in that she was the one who repeatedly commented that I would be a millionaire someday. She con-

stantly proclaimed she knew I would become lucky in my life and urged me on to get an education (which I fumbled around with until I was grown) to aid me in maintaining that fortune that I would likely come into.

"Johnny in the song is more or less myself, although I wrote it intending to be a song for Johnny Johnson. I altered the predictions that my mother made of me and created a story that paralleled it. It seems easy, now that it's been around so long, that it only took a period of about two weeks of periodic application to put the lyrics together. When I worked on 'Drifting Heart' it took almost four months and it scarcely sold twenty copies.

"It is obvious that a story that brings a subject from out of the boondocks to fame and fortune is more dramatic than one out of midtown to somewhere crosstown. 'Rags to riches' even sounds more attractive than 'fortune to fame.' It was with this in mind that I wrote of a boy with an ambition to become a guitar player, who came from the least of luxury to be seen by many, practicing until the listener believes he has all but made it to the top as the chorus prompts him like his mother's encouraging voice, 'Go Johnny Go.'

"The gateway to freedom, I was led to understand, was somewhere 'close to New Orleans' where most Africans were sorted through and sold. I had driven through New Orleans on tour and I'd been told my great grandfather lived 'way back up in the woods among the evergreens' in a log cabin. I revived the era with a story about a 'colored boy name Johnny B. Goode.' My first thought was to make his life follow as my own had come along, but I thought it would seem biased to white fans to say 'colored boy' and changed it to 'country boy.'

"As it turned out, my name was in lights and it is a fact that 'Johnny B. Goode' is most instrumental in causing it to be. I have many times said and now again say 'Thanks' though I could never voice it loud enough to equal the appreciation that so many people have claimed to have enjoyed from something that I created. I imagine most black people naturally realize but I feel safe in stating that NO white person can conceive the feeling of obtaining Caucasian respect in the wake of a world of dark denial, simply because it is impossible to view the dark side when faced with brilliance. 'Johnny B. Goode' was created as all other things and brought out of the modern dark age. With encouragement he chose to practice, shading himself along the roadside but seen by the brilliance of his guitar playing. Chances are you have talent. But will the name and the lights come to you? No! You have to 'Go!'"

Weir started singing "Johnny B. Goode" in early 1971, and it quickly settled into a rip-roaring encore selection, closing out nearly three hundred Grateful Dead concerts.

6/22/73, P.N.E. Coliseum, Vancouver, British Columbia

4/27/77, Capitol Theater, Passaic, New Jersey

▪ Janis Joplin

Born January 19, 1943, Port Arthur, Texas; died October 4, 1970, Hollywood, California

For all her talent and charisma, there was enough despair in Janis Joplin's life to fill a couple of lifetimes. "To sing the blues you gotta live the blues" is an old saw, but Janis did in spades. Hailing from East Texas, Janis ventured to San Francisco in 1963 to sing, soon hooking up for infrequent gigs with Jorma Kaukonen. After three years of frustration, she returned to Austin to sort out her life and even briefly gave up singing and considered marriage. But when word reached her that the Bay Area band Big Brother and the Holding Company were auditioning female singers, Joplin was lured back.

With Big Brother, Joplin immediately won audiences with her intensity and aching vulnerability. In 1968 *Cheap Thrills*, right down to its R. Crumb cover, caught on immediately with classic performances of "Piece of My Heart," "Summertime," "Combination of the Two," and "Ball and Chain." The album sold a million and helped cement San Francisco as the nexus of American youth culture.

But despite fronting a *hot* band (the guitar interplay of Big Brother's Sam Andrew and James Gurley could proudly stand alongside the Dead's triumvirate at the time), Joplin departed for a solo career, releasing *I Got Dem Ol' Kozmic Blues Again Mama* in 1969 and assembling the Full Tilt Boogie Band for a followup album. But Janis's monster drug and alcohol addiction quickly caught up with her and she was found dead at Hollywood's Landmark Hotel of an accidental heroin overdose. *Pearl*, an album recorded with her new band, was released shortly after her passing and along with its intense version of Kris Kristofferson's "ME AND BOBBY MCGEE" became No. 1 hits.

As with any performer of Joplin's stature, her mystique has continued to grow over the years and while the level of the mythologizing may never reach Elvis-like

Janis Joplin, Shea Stadium, New York, 8/6/70.
(Archive Photos/Russell Reif)

levels (her skills, though considerable, are not quite on par with a Bessie Smith or a Billie Holliday), the legacy she left on her two known taped performances of "Turn on Your Love Light" with Pigpen and the Grateful Dead made their mark on that song, Deadheads, and tape collectors.

"Jordan" (Traditional)

Stanley Brothers, *For the Good People* (1961), *Clinch Mountain Bluegrass* (1994)
Emmylou Harris, *Roses in the Snow* (1980)
Garrison Keillor, *Garrison Keillor and The Hopeful Gospel Quartet* (1992)
The Isaacs, *Our Style* (1993)
Laurel Canyon Ramblers, *Rambler's Blues* (1995)

The Dead only played this country gospel number a handful of times in their 1970 acoustic sets. As a performance tool, it represented one of the few examples of the Dead engaging in group harmony, with no individual really taking a lead vocal.

The Stanley Brothers popularized "Jordan" in the late 1950s and early 1960s and it was picked up on by the early version of the Black Mountain Boys, the bluegrass band that included Jerry Garcia, Sandy Rothman, and DAVID NELSON a few years later. Rothman later suggested that the Black Mountain Boys learned the song from the Stanley Brothers record *For the Good People.*

Along with Bill Monroe and Lester Flatt and Earl Scruggs, the vocal and instrumental duo Stanley Brothers set the style of early bluegrass. Born in the late 1920s, Ralph and Carter Stanley were reared in Virginia's Clinch Mountains where many luminaries of folk and country & western music (including the Stoneman Family and the Carter Family) were spawned. Their mother, a talented singer and musician, taught her sons vocal harmony almost as soon as they could talk and saw to it that they learned to play instruments. Ralph took up the banjo while Carter specialized in the guitar. Although the region is lesser known for its contribution to bluegrass, the Clinch Mountains produced many of the genre's greats of the post–World War II period.

But unlike most of their musical neighbors, the Stanley Brothers strayed far from home, if not the "lined-out" hymns of the local Baptist church. Their raw, emotional harmonies were the very definition of that high lonesome

(Courtesy of Vangard Records)

sound associated with bluegrass that passed into the music's syntax. While still teenagers, the boys entertained at local events and, in 1945, began appearing at clubs in Bristol, Virginia. Receiving high marks, they became regulars on the Farm and Fun Time radio show broadcast on WCYB in Bristol on which they remained for a good part of the 1950s.

Working with various small ensembles, the Stanley Brothers made their first small label recordings in the late 1940s with material that ranged from old mountain songs to selections from the Bill Monroe catalogue.

After moving to Raleigh, North Carolina, they were signed to Columbia by Art Satherley, an Englishman known for his pioneering work in the development of blues and hillbilly talent of 1920s and 1930s. The Columbia sides, recorded between 1949 and 1952, were more rough-hewn than Monroe's and possessed a primitive power that stands alone. "A Vision of Mother," "Lonesome River," and "The White Dove" are just three of dozens of examples of the Stanley Brothers' contribution to white American soul.

Carter Stanley developed his lead-singing skills during a short spell with Monroe's group, recording with the bluegrass patriarch in 1951. The brothers reunited soon after and were signed to Mercury where they exchanged their plaintive style for a hot, fast-moving approach. Alan Lomax described bluegrass as "folk music in overdrive" and the Stanley Brothers' work of the mid-1950s was certainly that. But the quality of their musicianship could not compete with the rock & roll explosion that left traditional music by the wayside.

As their career suffered, the Stanley Brothers moved to record labels of lesser impact and were forced to make musical compromises. At one point, record company pressure forced them to de-emphasize the fiddle and mandolin and highlight the guitar, which was played as a lead rather than rhythm instrument by some of their great finger-pickin' collaborators, including George Shuffler and Bill Napier.

Thanks to the folk revival of the late 1950s and early 1960s, bluegrass enjoyed a modest revival and the Stanley Brothers found themselves on the road, making personal appearances in forty-two states. These gigs included everything from country fairs to college concerts, major folk festivals and coffee houses, including several dates at the West Coast temple of folk, the Ash Grove in Los Angeles.

Their reputation grew beyond the borders of the United States and, as part of a folk caravan, they played for appreciative European audiences in England, Switzerland, Germany, Sweden, and Denmark in 1965.

But life on the road took its toll and possibly contributed to Carter's death in 1966.

Ralph continued to record and perform through the 1970s, putting together bands of younger musicians and keeping the bluegrass flame lit for the next generation of artists and audiences.

As the Stanley Brothers legend grew, their influence could be heard in the traditionally inclined musicians of the modern era who turned to their repertoire in the 1980s. Chris Hillman, a former member of the Byrds, and Emmylou Harris recorded Ralph's "The Darkest Hour Is Just Before Dawn" in 1980 and BOB DYLAN recorded and began performing the Stanley Brothers' haunting "Rank Strangers to Me" in 1987.

5/2/70, Harpur College, SUNY, Binghamton, New York

- ### *Jubilation*/Rowans
  Asylum 7E 1114, 1977.

Mickey Hart can be found on this, the Rowans' penultimate release.

- ### "Just a Little Light" (Mydland/Barlow)
  Grateful Dead, *Built to Last* (1989), *The Arista Years* (1996), *Dozin' at the Knick*/'90 (1996)

Brent Mydland's talent and maturity as a songwriter were considerably sharpened by his collaborations with JOHN BARLOW in the late 1980s. "Just a Little Light" provided Mydland with an upbeat song that countered much of his dour work quite well.

4/1/90, The Omni, Atlanta

- ### "Just Like Tom Thumb's Blues" (BOB DYLAN)
  Singles: Gordon Lightfoot (1965), West (1968)
  Bob Dylan, *Highway 61 Revisited* (1965), *Bob Dylan's Greatest Hits Vol. 2* (1971)
  Judy Collins, *In My Life* (1967), *Living* (1972)
  Frankie Miller, *Once in a Blue Moon* (1973)
  Neil Young, *Bob Dylan: The 30th Anniversary Celebration Concert* (1992)
  Barry McGuire, *Anthology* (1993)
  Nina Simone, *The Essential Nina Simone* (1993)

When discussion of Dylan's great songs arises among fans and scholars alike "Just Like Tom Thumb's Blues" is seldom mentioned. Yet it is an extraordinarily brilliant portrait of a sad, empty night in a Mexican border town (always good artistic fodder) and a man whose life and career are in tatters. Reminiscent of Orson Welles's sinister film noir *Touch of Evil*, "Just Like Tom Thumb's Blues" is a moody, shadowy composition studded with great lines, dark wit, and massive literary references.

Predictably, Dylan's many versions of the song varied tremendously over the years. From the woozy studio take to his soul-baring live outing with THE BAND in 1965 to his jaunty send-ups in 1978 and beyond, "Just Like Tom Thumb's Blues" retains a biting theatrical edge.

Phil Lesh started performing "Just Like Tom Thumb's Blues" with the Grateful Dead in 1985 and enjoyed inserting "San Anselmo" in the verse that reads, "I'm going back to New York City." Lesh's cover of the song is of particular note in that it was the first tune Phil field-tested as a lead vocalist since 1974 when vocal chord injuries stopped the bass player from singing safely for many years.

4/1/85, Cumberland County Civic Center, Portland, Maine

9/22/88, Madison Square Garden, New York

John Kahn

Born 1947, Memphis, Tennessee; died May 30, 1996, Mill Valley, California

Other than his mates in the Grateful Dead, Jerry Garcia logged in more onstage time with bassist John Kahn than any other single musician, the one constant in all the permutations of the Jerry Garcia Band. More importantly, Kahn (or "Freebo," as he was known in his busy 1970s session days) was associated with virtually every side project of Jerry Garcia's for twenty-five years—an important ally in such projects as *Compliments of Garcia, Cats Under the Stars, Shakedown Street, Run for the Roses,* and *Old & in the Way.*

Kahn grew up in Beverly Hills, California, and went to school with future show-biz types such as Richard Dreyfuss, with whom he studied drama. After turning to music in grade school and dabbling in rock as a high school student, Kahn discovered the jazz of Bill Evans, Scott LaFaro, ORNETTE COLEMAN, and John Coltrane, prompting him to take up the string bass and even a bit of symphonic composition. He attended the University of Southern California for a semester, coming to the Bay area in late 1966 to enroll at the San Francisco Conservatory of Music.

As the energy in San Francisco became increasingly focused on rock 'n' roll, Kahn traded in his upright for an electric bass and fell through various scenes that included gigging with Top Forty cover bands, jam sessions with Steve Miller, and an offer from Mike Bloomfield to join his band with Al Kooper for a collaboration that became *The Live Adventures of Mike Bloomfield and Al Kooper* album. By then, Kahn had absorbed the essence of a variety of bassists including the unsung heroes of R&B, Motown, and Stax (Duck Dunn, Chuck Rainey, and Jerry Jermott) as well as Paul McCartney, and, of course, the bass god of jazz, Charles Mingus.

Kahn continued to work with Bloomfield in a series of little bands that toured and recorded over the course of the next couple of years. Kahn also collaborated with Bloomfield on such film scores as *Steelyard Blues* and began an artistic and romantic relationship with the singer Maria Muldaur, which lasted many years.

Kahn met Garcia in 1972 when Bill Vitt, Bloomfield's drummer at the time, dragged him down to a Monday night session at the Matrix, a now-defunct San Francisco club where Garcia and organist Howard Wales were experimenting in jazzy instrumental jams. For the next six months, the group woodshedded at the spectacularly underattended gigs. When Wales tired of the situation, Kahn enlisted MERL SAUNDERS, whose touch immediately took the music in new directions and helped the nascent group establish a local but dedicated following. As the Saunders and Garcia unit began branching out with East and West Coast tours, Garcia invited Kahn to join OLD AND IN THE WAY, the bluegrass band he was forming with David Grisman and Peter Rowan. Those experiences pretty much joined Garcia and Kahn at the hip when the Dead were not on tour.

When Saunders and Garcia transmuted into the LE-

GION OF MARY and then the various permutations of the Jerry Garcia Band, Kahn was there augmenting a sound that transformed and evolved along with the music. In the mid-1970s, Kahn started his own jazz-influenced band called Reconstruction, which at first included Garcia, but because the group wanted to work while their lead guitarist was on tour with the Dead, Kahn engaged some other people to fill the spot, most notably former Moby Grape leadman Jerry Miller.

Whether it was providing a jazz-like drive to those earlier ensembles, complementing Nicky Hopkins's Chopin-like approach during his tenure with the band in the mid-1970s, relaxing gospel-style with Keith and Donna Godchaux when they joined the group, coshaping the unit as it forged through the 1980s and into the 1990s, providing a producer's stewardship to the various Jerry Garcia Band releases and a usually unacknowledged role in the Dead's *Shakedown Street*, or enduring the string of grueling one-nighters when touring, Kahn naturally assumed the role of a silent partner in Garcia's pet projects.

With a cig dangling from his lips, the tall, angular Kahn took on the persona of a cool-cat hipster, sharing the stage with Garcia upwards of eleven hundred times and performing more than four hundred different songs.

In the months after Garcia's death, Kahn became active with the newly re-forming Old & in the Way and the John Kahn Band featuring members of the last Jerry Garcia Band with Ho Kim on guitar.

Tragically, Kahn died of "undetermined causes" at his California home less than a year after Garcia's passing; heart disease and narcotics may have been contributing factors in his demise.

Henry Kaiser

Born September 11, 1952

A preeminent interpreter of Grateful Dead music, Henry Kaiser didn't start playing the guitar until he was twenty years old. Because he had been exposed to the Dead in concert and on record since his early teens, many of his musical values developed from unconsciously emulating the Dead. By the time he first attempted to play any Dead music in 1987, he was a prolific member of the Bay Area music scene and globally recognized as a leader of the "second generation" of free improvisers who came of age in the 1970s. His earliest musical inspirations were Derek Bailey, an avant-garde English

guitarist, and Captain Beefheart's many guitarists, but Kaiser went on to absorb the subtle string textures of the American blues stylists and traditional music of Asia.

Kaiser's first recordings were a combination of solo projects and spontaneous groupings with other adrenalized improvisers like Fred Frith, the ROVA Saxophone Quartet, pianist Greg Goodman, and vocalist Diamanda Galás. Unearthing many new and unconventional electric guitar techniques, Kaiser's restless creativity combined his innovations with a strong sense of logic and concise development often aided by state-of-the-art high-tech devices.

When he began returning to the Dead's music in the mid- to late-1980s, he had already played on sixty or seventy albums of material that had nothing to do with the Dead's, and most of the music he has recorded since has nothing to do with the Dead's. *Those Who Know History Are Doomed to Repeat It* in 1989 and *Heart's Desire* a year later contained, among other things, versions of "Dark Star," helping the Dead acquire a legitimacy in the New Wave, which they had never really enjoyed before. Aligning himself with Tom Constanten in a touring group that performed his Dead-heavy material, Kaiser developed a following in the Deadhead community but never performed with the Dead, though he did form friendships and record with Garcia, Weir, and Vince Welnick. Kaiser was, along with David Gans, a producer of *The Music Never Stopped: The Roots of the Grateful Dead*, a release that collected many of the original versions of songs the Dead later covered and *Eternity Blue*, a personal appreciation celebrating Jerry Garcia.

- **"Kansas City"** (LEIBER & STOLLER)
  Singles: Little Willie Littlefield (1952), J. T. Adams and
    Shirley Griffith (1961)
  Wilbert Harrison, *Cruisin' 1959* (1959)
  Muddy Waters, *The Best of the Blues Singers* (1960)
  James Brown, *Live at the Apollo* (1963), *Live at the
    Apollo, Vol 2, Part 1* (1968)
  Alexis Korner, *At the Cavern* (1964)
  Fats Domino, *Getaway with Fats Domino* (1965)
  The Beatles, *Beatles for Sale* (1964), *Beatles VI* (1965),
    Live at the Star Club, 1962, Vol. 1 (1977), *Live at the
    BBC* (1994), *Anthology 1* (1995)
  Little Richard, *The Fabulous Little Richard* (1959)
  DAVID BROMBERG, *Wanted Dead or Alive* (1974)
  Albert King, *Born Under a Bad Sign* (1967), *Albert Live*
    (1977)

Michael Bloomfield, *If You Love These Blues, Play 'Em as You Please* (1977)

Paul McCartney, *Choba B CCCP* (1991), *Paul Is Live* (1993)

Dirty Dozen Brass Band, *Jelly* (1993)

Various Artists, *The Best of Kansas City* (1994)

The Dead only performed "Kansas City" at two shows on their fall 1985 East Coast tour (reportedly in honor of baseball's Royals, who had just won the World Series), but it is a song steeped in controversy. Leiber and Stoller, the hit songwriting team, are generally credited with authorship. But Little Willie Littlefield has laid claim to it as well, charging that after recording a tune called "K.C. Loving," he sold the song's rights to Leiber and Stoller who went on to make back their investment many times over from the many recordings of the song.

"Kansas City" knocked around for a few years before finally hitting pay dirt when Wilbert Harrison had a No. 1 hit with the song in 1959 when it spent an impressive twelve weeks in the Top 40.

11/5/85, The Centrum, Worcester, Massachusetts

▪ "Katie Mae" (SAM "LIGHTNIN'" HOPKINS)

Lightnin' Hopkins, single (1947), *It's a Sin to Be Rich* (1972), *The Complete Aladdin Session* (1991), *Mojo Hand* (1993), *The Rising Sun Collection* (1995)

Grateful Dead, *History of the Grateful Dead, Vol. 1 (Bear's Choice)* (1973)

Arthur "Big Boy" Crudup, *Mean Ole Frisco* (1962)

Pigpen was sometimes coaxed into doing his solo Delta-blues thing when the Dead were including an acoustic set in their marathon, three-set 1970 concerts. Pig's heartfelt but endearingly self-conscious renditions of this Lightnin' Hopkins nugget stole many a show as well as the Dead album on which it appeared.

3/20/70, Capitol Theater, Port Chester, New York

4/3/70, Field House, University of Cincinnati, Cincinnati, Ohio

▪ "Keep on Growing" (Eric Clapton/Bobby Whitlock)

Derek and the Dominoes, *Layla and Other Love Songs* (1970)

Sheryl Crow, *Boys on the Side* soundtrack (1995)

Eric Clapton and Bobby Whitlock cowrote "Keep on Growing" for *Layla and Other Love Songs*, the monumental and excruciatingly bittersweet blues-rock album by Clapton's pseudonymous Derek and the Dominoes project. Some of Clapton's best blues-guitar work was featured on the album, inspired by his then-unrequited love for Patti Harrison, the wife of his best friend, Beatle George Harrison. An added dimension of the sessions was Clapton's growing heroin habit and self-confidence problem that resulted, in part, from the pressure put on him by his adoring fans who insisted that he was, indeed, "God." Finally, there was the presence of Duane Allman in the studio to further galvanize the sessions, which produced some of the most moving rock and blues-rock guitar work ever. "Key to the Highway," "Why Does Love Have to Be So Sad?," and "Layla" (cited by some critics as the greatest guitar song in rock history) are just a few of the tunes that lit up a scorching two-record set.

Like most of Clapton's group efforts, Derek and the Dominoes was short-lived and *Layla* was their only studio album. After just a few Allman-less gigs, Clapton returned to Great Britain and fought his personal problems before emerging two years later to resume his solo career.

"Keep on Growing" is one of the more optimistic songs on *Layla* and its Phil Lesh–sung cameo during the Dead's twentieth-anniversary summer in 1985 was an appropriate acknowledgment of this milestone.

6/30/85, Merriweather Post Pavilion, Columbia, Maryland

▪ "Keep Your Day Job" (Garcia/Hunter)

Grateful Dead, *Dick's Picks Volume Six*/'83 (1996)

Many Deadheads despised this advisory when it was included, all too often, in the band's early-1980s concerts. In fact, according to Robert Hunter's notes in *A Box of Rain*, "This song was dropped from the Grateful Dead repertoire at the request of fans. Seriously."

The song, with its explicit message in the title, isn't quite the travesty of its reputation and was a decent, if half-baked and overplayed, set closer. The basic gist of the song, found in its chorus, is to "Keep your day job / Until your night job pays."

10/30/83, Marin County Veterans Auditorium, San Rafael, California

■ *Keith and Donna*

Round RX 104, 1975.

"River Deep, Mountain High," "Sweet Baby," "Woman Make You," "When You Start to Move," "Showboat," "My Love for You," "Farewell Jack," "Who Was John," "Every Song I Sing"

Jerry Garcia—guitar. Additional session musicians.

Keith and Donna Godchaux brought many good things to the Grateful Dead during their long tenure with them in the 1970s but their solo album was not one of them. It's pretty safe to say that if they were not members of the Grateful Dead at the time, this weak album would never have been released.

Maybe the best thing about this album is Garcia's artistic contribution. Garcia provided drawings representing the thoughts of the Godchauxs' son Zion, whose picture was used for the cover.

■ Ken Kesey

Born September 17, 1935, La Junta, Colorado

It is sometimes easy to overlook the literary tradition that informed the roots of the Grateful Dead. And, if there is one person who symbolizes this in the Dead's universe, that would have to be novelist Ken Kesey, whose magic continues to challenge America with characters who confront all the madness of a polluted society. A brawling storyteller who could be a character from one of his own books, Kesey has been a key figure in the cultural history as he helped lead the revolution that forever altered the nation's consciousness. It was at his Electric Kool-Aid Acid Tests where this caped and costumed crusader dispensed a brand of "Made in America" transformation that could only have happened in California during the 1960s.

Kesey was reared in a westerly mobile family that ended up in Oregon when his father gained employment with the Eugene Farmers Cooperative. A small-town Baptist boy who listened to his Granny Smith's Bible stories, young Ken loved to entertain with his own magic shows that included ventriloquism and hypnosis. When he was a teenager, Kesey was a local hero excelling as a scholar-athlete, distinguishing himself as both a champion wrestler and as thespian and artist. But while his wrestling won him a scholarship to the University of Oregon, he continued to pursue his dramatic muse. It was during his junior year in 1956 that he wed Faye Hixby, his high-school sweetheart, to whom he remains married.

When he graduated in 1957 with a Woodrow Wilson Fellowship to the Graduate School of Creative Writing at Stanford University, the bubble-bursting Beats were catching the eye of the budding novelist. While enrolled in Malcolm Cowley's demanding writing workshop, Kesey found himself surrounded by like-minded souls including future literary luminaries Larry McMurtry and Robert Stone. But none of that could prepare him for what awaited just around the corner.

In 1960 the Federal Government hired Kesey to become one of the volunteers to be a human guinea pig on the effects of the "psychotomimetic" drugs that were being researched. Psilocybin, peyote, LSD-25, morning-glory seeds, and other drugs were all administered at the Veterans Hospital in Menlo Park.

Not surprisingly, samples of the drugs were "liberated" from the facility and found their way to Perry Lane, the Bohemian enclave in Palo Alto where Kesey resided. The milieu that was spawning around Perry Lane inspired *The Zoo*, an early (still unpublished) novel that pitted a selfish, freedom-loving protagonist against looming societal obligations and responsibility.

While dabbling in the coffeehouse, teahead, post-Beat Bay Area scene by day, Kesey took a job as a paid orderly during the graveyard shift at the same Veterans Hospital where he had been volunteering. It was during this time that Kesey began shaping *One Flew over the Cuckoo's Nest*, a novel centering around what is perhaps his greatest literary character, the fast-talking Randle McMurphy, an individualist who stands opposed to the authoritative, mechanical, and destructive forces of society's witless, spirit-eating machine. This darkness was embodied in the book by Big Nurse Ratched, a character Kesey fashioned after his own real-life scuffles and confrontations with orderlies and nurses in charge of the ward where he worked. The book's own individuality is also shaped by its sole narrator, a mute Native American named Chief Broom, who Kesey invented during an experience with peyote. Ultimately, *Cuckoo's Nest* operates on several profound levels but most of all, it has a vast, hard-hitting allegory in which redemption is attempted by a cosmic-giggling fool who takes on the sins of the world as its jester-savior.

Almost as soon as it was published in 1962, the book became wildly popular and appeared on Broadway in a stage adaptation starring Kirk Douglas a year later. In

1975, the film version, directed by Milos Forman and starring Jack Nicholson, was released, winning six Academy Awards.

Sometimes a Great Notion, published in 1964, represented an about-face for Kesey, who, with magnificent, Faulkneresque sweeps, set his family-oriented, rambling novel in the familiar logging country of Oregon. As in *Cuckoo's Nest*, Kesey champions a character who relishes swimming upstream. In this case, it's Hank Stamper, patriarch of a wildcat family of loggers who refuse to go on strike, bucking a system that includes a powerful union and old neighbors alike. With literary sleight-of-hand that includes merging and telescoping time, shifting viewpoints, and cinematic artifice, Kesey manages to focus on the family's plight while exploring the dueling natures within himself.

By the time the book was finished, Perry Lane was a memory, bulldozed by developers, and the Keseys safely nestled in a log home bought with the profits from *Cuckoo's Nest* in nearby La Honda, California. The new digs became a kind of floating party-pad-cum-philosophers-round-table where kindred spirits congregated and brainstormed. These included the likes of Allen Ginsberg (whose poem "First Party at Ken Kesey's with Hell's Angels" memorialized the scene in Beat verse) and that champion of verbal spontaneity, Neal Cassady.

Calling themselves the "Merry Pranksters," Kesey,

NEAL CASSADY, and their small tribe of visionaries embarked on a 1964 prank from which we are all still recovering. Diagnosing America as a soulless prison, the Pranksters decided to share the righteous fun they were having with the rest of the country. Thus, the pioneering cross-country "bus" trip was conceived with the New York World's Fair as a kind of loose destination. The Pranksters purchased and painted a 1939 International Harvester school bus with shocking swirls of color, wired it for sound, tagged the heap "Furthur," and, with Cassady at the helm, took off to help America find itself.

Beginning to experiment with artistic strictures, Kesey employed his entire aesthetic arsenal (magician, dramatist, and orator) in his approach to the adventure, shaping it into a kind of multimedia novel. Four years later, Tom Wolfe's masterful piece of "New Journalism" captured the spirit of the trip and the era with *The Electric Kool-Aid Acid Test*, in which Kesey is the subject cast (as Kerouac had done to Cassady before him) as the mischievous, picaresque charismatic with a joyously twisted brand of salvation on his mind.

Surely, La Honda was unique in the cultural history of the United States, for it was there that the eyes of the countercultural hurricane was centered, where the Beat 1950s merged and mingled with the ethos of the 1960s. The LSD-spiked venison-chili parties that Kesey casually held in Palo Alto were turning into something far

Ken Kesey with author, Central Park, New York City, 8/91.
(Photo: Elaine Beery)

more grandiose: the Acid Tests. These events, now fueled by "Electric Kool-Aid," initiated the earnest exorcism of America's stifling, gray-flannel conformity and rigid, artificial *Ozzie and Harriet* worldview in a bacchanal of liberation and common sensual experiences.

Providing the soundtrack for these happenings were the WARLOCKS, who had been hanging around Kesey's scene since the Perry Lane days. But the Acid Tests were not about music. Rather they were a galvanizing community force in their unconscious coalescing of the new, electro-visionary way of being stirring in the Bay Area.

But the shenanigans were not lost on the local authorities, who busted Kesey on marijuana charges in early 1966. He fled to Mexico, bouncing around underground for a spell before returning home and digging the Acid Tests in disguise before he was finally nabbed by the cops. After Kesey served five months in a California prison, Kesey and Faye pulled up the family stakes and bought the farm in Pleasant Hill, Oregon, where he still lives.

Running the family business, a creamery, Kesey was said to have "given up writing" and be "waiting for the millennium." While these crackpot tendencies were overplayed, there was no doubt that the revolution, at least as far as he was concerned, was better waged by a return to a spare, rigorous, and austere life. This is not to suggest that he had, in fact, totally turned his back on literary pursuits. Along with helping Stewart Brand in the creation of The *Last Whole Earth Catalog* in 1971, Kesey toyed with *Over the Border,* a screenplay which dealt, in Marvel Comics fashion, with his fugitive days in Mexico following Devlin Deboree, his novelistic alter ego who is driven to life's cliff edge by society's material madness. The cinematic extravaganza was published a couple of years later in *Kesey's Garage Sale,* a kind of collage grab bag produced with fellow Pranksters Ken Babbs and Paul Foster. Clearly inspired by Brand's vision, the pastiche contains a forward by Arthur Miller and serves as a compendium of writing, inspiration, and other sources. Additionally, Kesey and Babbs's self-published *Spit in the Ocean,* a sporadic arts magazine with stories that eventually appeared in *Demon Box,* a 1986 collection of Kesey's short stories.

During the 1980s, Kesey slowly reemerged in the coterie of Beat and post-Beat writers, and in the artistic community with appearances at various literary forums. At a 1982 conference at the University of Oregon honoring the quarter-century anniversary of the publication of *On the Road,* Kesey called Kerouac the "Paul Bunyan of the Beats," adding that the footloose writer was instrumental in the consciousness transformation in America and other countries in his blend of religions to produce a "fourth world," which was neither capitalist nor communist but founded on Beat values of love, mercy, and beatitude, tempered with spontaneous humor and hope.

A year of tragedy for the writer, however, was 1984, when his son Jed (a champion wrestler like his father) was killed in a traffic accident involving his school wrestling team's bus. But two years later, Kesey was back on his feet and on the road promoting *Demon Box* with his other son Zane and the Thunder Machine, a space-age musical contraption always seemingly in progress. Part drums, part harp, part horns, and part washtub bass, the Thunder Machine made occasional onstage appearances with the Dead, played by Kesey and various other Pranksters.

In 1986, Kesey cranked out *Last Go Round,* a screenplay about the 1910 Pendleton Round-Up based on the true story of two cowboys, one black and one white, meeting in a classic showdown straight out of *High Noon.* Kesey and Ken Babbs turned the cinematic treatment into a novel, which was published in 1993.

A creative-writing course Kesey taught in 1987–88 at the University of Oregon resulted in a group novel entitled *Caverns.*

The Further Inquiry followed in 1990. A sprawling, four-color, multimedia extravaganza featuring a flip-book movie sequence of Neal Cassady jiving around, this "unbook" takes the form of a scripted drama with Cassady standing trial in a futuristic courtroom as inquisitors attempt to determine the effect the accused had on the nation's heart and soul.

A year later, Kesey's stab at children's book writing was met with widespread acclaim with the publication of *The Sea Lion,* an allegorical tale dealing with ecological and spiritual respect. The bigger news that year was the release of *Sailor Song,* Kesey's first full-length novel since *Sometimes a Great Notion.* Set sometime in the near future after a terrifying 1994 devastation of the Pacific northwest coast, the book received mixed reviews but did reveal the artist flexing his chops with breezy aplomb.

"I'd rather be a lightning rod than a seismograph" may be Kesey's most famous quote and could well serve as his epitaph. Indeed, just like the characters who populate his novels, Kesey was never content sitting on life's sidelines just watching the parade. Rather, he fashioned himself more like a drum major at the front of the line, marching to his own wild beat. As the millennium approached, he (along with his son Zane and daughter-in-law, Stephanie) started another family business, selling archival materials and documentation (video, audio and otherwise) of the Pranksters' quests, various ephemera, and the coolest Dead family T-shirts this side of 1972. Additionally, "Twister," a multimedia, tactile, vertigo-heavy event featuring video projection, lasers, and high-tech sound began making the rounds, extending (just like the old Acid Tests) the possibilities of expression once again.

As for the bus, Kesey (helped by friends and family) restored, repaired, and repainted the 1939 International Harvester that the Merry Pranksters used for their 1964 cross-country trip. After he and friends displayed the new-look roadster at a couple of Eugene Dead shows in the summer of 1990 (and a final prank in which they attempted to pass off a different, appropriately stained bus to the Smithsonian Institute), Furthur came to its final resting place in the sheep meadow on Kesey's farm, where it has been rusting away (complete with a cardboard skeleton in driver's seat) ever since.

Keystone Encores, Vol. 1

Fantasy MPF-4533/FCD 7703-2, 1988. Produced by MERL SAUNDERS and JOHN KAHN.

"I SECOND THAT EMOTION," "One Kind Favor (SEE THAT MY GRAVE IS KEPT CLEAN)," "Money Honey," "Merl's Tune"

Merl Saunders—organ. Jerry Garcia—electric guitar. John Kahn—bass. Bill Vitt—drums.

See also **Live at Keystone** and **Keystone Encores, Vol. 2**

Keystone Encores, Vol. 2

Fantasy MPF-4534, 1988/FCD 7703-2. Produced by MERL SAUNDERS and JOHN KAHN.

"HI-HEEL SNEAKERS," "MYSTERY TRAIN," "It's Too Late (She's Gone)," "HOW SWEET IT IS"

Fifteen years after the release of *Live at Keystone*, the dual release of *Keystone Encores* served as a potent chaser for admirers of the former. Following the formula set down in the original double album, this very tight quartet easily handles the blues ("One Kind Favor"), R&B ("Hi-Heel Sneakers"), Motown ("I Second That

Emotion"), and Elvis ("Mystery Train") with funky grace and fluid chops.

The one common complaint with the *Keystone Encores* releases was the sentiment that they should have been packaged as a combined offering because the individual packaging smacked of profiteering.

See also **Live at Keystone** and **Keystone Encores, Vol. 1**

▪ *kicks joy darkness* / Kerouac / Various Artists
Rykodisc RCD 10329, 1997. Produced by Jim Sampas.

Robert Hunter's scat-sung snatch of a section entitled "Have you ever seen anyone like Cody Pomeray? . . . " from Jack Kerouac's unwieldy opus *Visions of Cody* joins more than two dozen wonderfully off-the-wall homages to the Beat bard on this niche tribute album. Other notables appearing here include Hunter S. Thompson, Allen Ginsberg, Johnny Depp, Patti Smith, Joe Strummer, Lenny Kaye, Jeff Buckley, Eric Anderson, Eddie Vedder, and John Cale. In true *On the Road* spirit, Hunter recorded his spot while driving in his car, accompanying a tape of Kerouac reading aloud.

▪ Kingfish

In the years following the explosion of the San Francisco sound, the Bay Area became a Mecca for musicians from points north, south, east, and west. By the mid-1970s, its reputation for creativity and musical experimentation

Kingfish. *(The New York Public Library for the Performing Arts)*

had attracted an abundance of exceptionally talented musicians. It was in this ripe atmosphere that Matthew Kelly, a harp player, guitarist, and singer/songwriter, and bassist-vocalist Dave Torbert, his long-time musical companion, decided to join forces to form the group Kingfish.

Both musicians had strong ties to the Dead over the years. Kelly had occasionally played harp with the band and also contributed to *Wake of the Flood* and *Shakedown Street* and Torbert played bass on a number of Dead classics, including "Box of Rain." Torbert was an early member of the NEW RIDERS OF THE PURPLE SAGE.

At Torbert's request, Kelly periodically gigged with the New Riders. The two had played together in various bands dating back to the 1960s and had developed close relationships as both friends and musical associates. Kelly's roots were firmly imbedded in the classic blues; he had toured with legends such as T-Bone Walker and Champion Jack Dupree. But just as he was becoming fully incorporated into the Riders' lineup, Torbert surprised everybody when, right at the height of his success with NRPS (following the release of *Panama Red*), he decided that he needed to get back to his musical roots and quit the band.

Kelly and Torbert continued to collaborate and, while working on a Bay Area anthology album that comprised a collection of San Francisco all-stars (including Garcia, Weir, Nicky Hopkins, members of the New Riders, Quicksilver, the Airplane, Moby Grape, and many others), they felt compelled to venture forth and start Kingfish. With an original lineup consisting of Kelly, Torbert, lead guitarist Robbie Hoddinott, drummer Chris Herold, and keyboardist Mick Ward, the newly formed band went immediately to Alaska, where they wrote, performed, and literally woodshedded, trying to define their new material and sound. But when Ward was killed in a car accident soon after their arrival, the disheartened band was sent reeling. After many auditions to replace him, no one suitable could be found so, instead, they continued to gig as a quartet.

After they came back from Alaska, they started playing local Bay Area clubs and managed to stir up a bit of a following. Bobby Weir heard about them, checked out their gigs, and started sitting in. As luck would have it, the Dead had just agreed to shut down shop for a spell and Weir ended up joining Kingfish. This very conveniently put an end to their search for a keyboard player as Weir managed to fill the position very nicely on guitar.

Weir and Kelly were certainly no strangers, having grown up together as kids and even played on the same football team in junior high school. By the summer of 1974, the newest Kingfish lineup was complete and in place and, with the notoriety of Weir and Torbert, the band got off to a flying start.

Kingfish had a sound all its own. Sure there were the obvious Dead and NRPS comparisons, but for the most part, Kingfish had a funkin', rockin' R&B flavor. With the release of their self-titled 1976 debut album and the radio exposure of songs like "Hypnotize" and "Jump For Joy," the group found itself on the road opening for the era's marquee attractions: the Eagles, Elton John, Eric Clapton, Lynyrd Skynyrd, and Aerosmith. But it wasn't long before they were headlining themselves.

Between their premiere show in November 1974 in San Anselmo, California, and their final Hempstead, New York, gig in August, 1976—about seventy concerts down the highway—Kingfish had performed in six states with an obvious California emphasis.

The group made a second LP in 1977 with Weir, who then returned to the Dead on a more full-time basis later that year.

Discussing the difficult responsibilities of playing in a second touring and recording band, Weir told David Gans in 1977 that "I never really found just exactly what I was going to be doing with Kingfish. The problem was that I didn't spend enough time with them. I had the Grateful Dead's various projects, records, movies, and, in the end, touring. That left me very little time to devote to Kingfish, so I never really homed in on what my place was in that outfit and what that outfit was really up to. I was just beginning to get a handle on what Kingfish was all about, and then came a Grateful Dead tour, and a lot of movie work, and it just became impossible. . . .

"It was fun when it was happening. It just wasn't happening that much. It must have drove them all bonkers sitting on their hands."

Kingfish did go on without him, signing with Jett Records, which was distributed by CBS. A couple of albums followed, as did numerous Weir-less tours, but the band was to have some major setbacks in the ensuing years, the most crushing of which was Torbert's death from a heart attack at age thirty-three in 1983. After a falling out with Jett, Kelly and Weir formed the All New Kingfish Review in 1984. With lead guitarist Garth Webber, keyboardist Barry Flast, bassist David Margen, and drummer Dave Pepper the group played a few shows in the fall of that year and, with Steve Evans on bass and the addition of vocalist Anna Rizzo, a score of 1986 concerts as Kingfish with Bob Weir.

Though the bulk of the material utilized in these latter-day shows relied on Kingfish staples, the band did serve as both an alternative showcase and rehearsal tidal pool for songs Weir was performing with or would eventually slip into Grateful Dead concerts, including "Throwing Stones," "DAY TRIPPER," "I AIN'T SUPERSTITIOUS," "DOWN IN THE BOTTOM," "SPOONFUL," "MAN SMART, WOMAN SMARTER," "DESOLATION ROW," "Victim or the Crime," "WANG DANG DOODLE," and "WILLIE AND THE HAND JIVE."

Since then, Kelly has maintained the Kingfish name and stayed on the road with a number of fairly impressive lineups throughout the years and, in the mid-1990s, he joined Weir and bassist Rob Wasserman to form Ratdog.

Reminiscing on the many roads Kingfish had traveled, Kelly once remarked, "In retrospect, we realize that many mistakes were made in the way in which our business affairs were handled. However, from a musical and creative perspective, things were, for the most part, pretty good. Especially when we played live. The original Kingfish band definitely had a very special chemistry that seemed to work exceptionally well."

Kingfish/Bob Weir

Round-UA RX 108 RX-LA565-G, 1976 (Relix RRLP 2005). Produced by Dan Healy and Bob Weir.

"Lazy Lightnin'," "Supplication," "Wild Northland," "Asia Minor," "Home to Dixie," "Jump for Joy," "Good-Bye Yer Honor," "Big Iron," "This Time," "Hypnotize," "Bye and Bye"

Bob Weir—guitar, vocals. Dave Torbert—bass, vocals. Mathew Kelly—guitar, harp, vocals. Robby Hoddinott—lead guitar, slide. Chris Herold—drums, percussion. J. D. Sharp—string synthesizer on "This Time," "Lazy Lightning," and "Hypnotize." Pablo Green—vocals on "Hypnotize." Anna Rizzo—additional vocals. Barry Flast—additional vocals, piano. Jim Sanchez—additional drums. Steve Evans—additional bass.

Kingfish was the fun and polished band fronted by Bob Weir in the 1970s and early 1980s. Their self-titled first album gave a good, if raw, studio example of the band's

musical range and capabilities. Reggae, country, rock, and Dead music are the order of the day with "Lazy Lightning" and Marty Robbins's "Big Iron" seen as the standouts.

Kingfish in Concert

King Biscuit Flower Hour Records 70710-88006-2, 1995. Executive producers–Barry Ehrman, Steve Ship, Evert Wilbrink. Recorded April 3, 1976, at the Beacon Theater, New York.

"Mystery Train"›"Muleskinner Blues," "Juke," "Jump Back," "Battle of New Orleans," "Goodbye Your Honor," "Big Iron," "I Hear You Knockin'," "All I Need Is Time," "Around and Around," "C.C. Rider," "Home to Dixie," "Hidden Charm," "Bye and Bye," "Promised Land," "Lazy Lightning"›"Supplication," "Jump for Joy," "Asia Minor," "New Minglewood Blues," "One More Saturday Night"

Bob Weir—rhythm guitar, vocals. Dave Torbert—bass, vocals. Mathew Kelly—guitar, harp, vocals. Robby Hoddinott—lead guitar, slide. Chris Herold—drums, percussion.

This performance was originally taped for the *King Biscuit Flower Hour* in 1976 at a sold out Beacon Theater show in New York City and mixes the material from the group's debut album with a few Grateful Dead perennials. The "Biscuit," as it is fondly referred to by its devotees, was one of *the* great radio concert shows of the

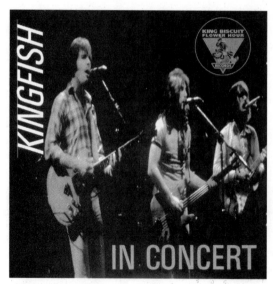

(Courtesy of BMG Records)

1970s and 1980s. They started a label of their own name in 1995, and some of the best shows were released on CD. But unlike the shows that aired for an hour, the discs featured the concerts in their entirety, with digitally remixed sound. Of the initial half dozen releases, a two-disc Kingfish set captured Kingfish in a scorching mood evidenced by a dynamite "Lazy Lightning">"Supplication" that can stand proud next to any Grateful Dead version.

▪ "Knockin' on Heaven's Door" (BOB DYLAN)

Bob Dylan, *Pat Garrett and Billy the Kid* (1973), *At Budokan* (1978), *Dylan and the Dead* (1987), *The 30th Anniversary Celebration Concert* (1993), *Bob Dylan's Greatest Hits Volume 3* (1994), *MTV Unplugged* (1995)

Bob Dylan and THE BAND, *Before the Flood* (1974)

Jerry Garcia Band, *Run for the Roses* (1982)

Eric Clapton, *There's One in Every Crowd* (1975), *Timepieces Vol. II* (1979), *Just One Night* (1984)

Kevin Coyne, *In Living Black & White* (1977)

Green on Red, *The Lost Weekend* (1992)

The Alarm, *Spirit of '76* (1986)

Randy Crawford, *Rich and Poor* (1989)

Guns n' Roses, *Use Your Illusion II* (1991)

Dead Ringers, DEAD RINGERS (1993)

Ratdog, *Furthur* (1996)

Dylan "acted" in and composed a perfect soundtrack for *Pat Garrett and Billy the Kid,* Sam Peckinpah's gem of a Western. Oddly, a hit emerged from the album, the hymn-like "Knockin' on Heaven's Door," which received substantial airplay in the summer of the film's 1973 release. Dylan said that he wrote the song specifically for the powerful scene in which the town sheriff (Slim Pickens) dies in his wife's (Katy Jurado) arms.

Jerry Garcia's metaphoric interpretation of the "Knockin' on Heaven's Door" suited his own band's and Grateful Dead shows since the mid-1980s as a perfect encore selection. The Garcia Band visited the song nearly two hundred times between 1973 and 1994.

7/12/87, Giants Stadium, East Rutherford, New Jersey (with Bob Dylan)

▪ Bill Kreutzmann
Born May 7, 1946, Palo Alto, California

From the start, Bill Kreutzmann's drumming has served both as a rhythmic anchor around which Garcia and company could weave their harmonic tapestries and as an emotive river seeking its own course.

Like Mickey Hart, his Grateful Dead brother in percussion, Kreutzmann was playing with rhythm at a very early age, keeping beat on an Indian tom-tom for his

Bill Kreutzmann, Max Yasgur's Farm, Bethel, New York, 8/16/69.
(Archive Photos)

mother, a dancer who taught at Stanford University. Love of music and his devotion to the drums commenced in earnest when, as a twelve-year-old, he began his first formal studies with a local drum teacher who, after giving him the standard half-hour lesson, would let the boy loose on his set for hours because all Kreutzmann owned at that point was a pair of sticks.

Buying a used Ludwig set from an ad for $250, Billy began practicing at his Arizona prep school after his father sent him his rig to help him keep his spirits up. Instead of joining the high school band when he returned to matriculate closer to home, Kreutzmann linked up with the Legends, a local rock & roll unit that played at the rough and tumble YMCA dances. But he was also peeking in on Garcia, Pigpen, and, occasionally, Bob Weir honing their licks at the Tangent, one of Palo Alto's hepper joints.

Gravitating to the Crescent City music of Fats Domino, Kreutzmann clocked in loads of listening time and gave himself a musical education in record stores at the height of the record booth era when patrons could spin discs in soundproofed rooms.

It was when he began working at the same music store as Garcia that he was enlisted as the drummer for his and Pigpen's new electric-blues and rock band, the Zodiacs. As the band morphed into first the Warlocks and then the Grateful Dead, Kreutzmann was always low-key on the high seat, developing the loose, airy style of a seasoned jazzman, with a fluidity that often acted as a catalyst, propelling the music in unexpected and sometimes ecstatic directions.

No doubt this was aided by the arrival of Phil Lesh in 1965 who turned Kreutzmann on to Elvin Jones, the incomparable jazz drummer who burned up John Coltrane's quartet in the early 1960s. Mickey Hart's arrival in 1967 also opened the doors of world percussion to the eager student. With Kreutzmann and Hart chasing each other in dense rhythmical environments, the Dead entered what was arguably their most experimental phase in the late 1960s—handling even the most complex time signatures with fire and grace.

The introduction of simpler songs into the Dead's early 1970s repertoire, combined with Hart's four-year hiatus from the band, allowed Kreutzmann again to settle into a single drummer role in which his musical maturity helped the band turn all the corners during their jazziest period in 1973 and 1974.

Never one to showboat with the gaudy but lifeless

Bill Kreutzmann (far right) powering the band, 1972. *(The New York Public Library for the Performing Arts)*

drum solo, Kreutzmann always preferred to accent the ensemble. It was only when Hart returned to the fold in 1975 that the second set extended drum jam between the two began to formalize and evolve into a rhythmic tapestry incorporating instruments and traditions from across the globe.

The drummer's 1984 pickup band Billy Kreutzmann's All-Stars included DAVID NELSON on lead guitar, Larry Murphy Sr. on fiddle, and Larry Murphy Jr. on bass. Playing a small clutch of California dates that winter, the unit's kick-ass two-set shows drew from a predictable sweep of material: Bill Monroe's "Sitting Along in a Blue Light," the Stones' "Dead Flowers," CHUCK BERRY's "You Never Can Tell," and some New Riders' chestnuts.

Go Ahead, another short-lived Grateful Dead spinoff band, which toured in the mid-1980s, included Brent Mydland on keyboards and Kreutzmann on drums. Describing his experiences with the unit, Kreutzmann told Blair Jackson in 1988, "When I was in Goathead—that's what I like to call Go Ahead—the other guys in the band wanted me to do a drum solo, but I just didn't dig it; it didn't feel right.

"I really enjoyed playing the music, and I liked the musicians . . . but I didn't like eatin' other people's smoke and smelling booze and seeing fights and all that stuff that happens in places like that. But also it was too much trying to work in two bands. It didn't give me enough time to do things by myself and with my family."

As the Dead's gentleman farmer, Kreutzmann was happy to hole up for weeks on end at his rustic Mendocino County ranch, with his wife and his dogs and horses and, after Garcia's passing, was rumored to have moved to Hawaii to pursue a passion for scuba diving that threatened to send the drummer into early retirement. Kreutzmann had devoted himself to the sport since 1985 when he and Garcia took lessons and became certified divers, often traveling to such remote locales as Palau and Truk in Micronesia, the Gigedo Islands located some 460 miles off Mexico's Coast and the Galápagos Archipelago, a province of Ecuador, more than 600 miles west of the mainland. While these adventures took Kreutzmann to some of the world's most pristine environs, he gave (along with Bob Weir) his wholehearted support to Coral Forest, an organization dedicated to the preservation of one of the planet's largest and most biologically complex ecosystems—the coral reefs, which are faced with a multitude of environmental threats. The

organization's efforts to stem the tide of destruction included public education; support of research and scientific analysis into ecological dangers; pressure on corporations and development agencies to establish and adhere to measures to protect reefs; and outreach programs to divers and dive shops. As Kreutzmann was quick to point out in the *Grateful Dead Almanac,* "Divers have to understand that we are part of the problem." Taking a page out of Garcia's neckwear line which benefited environmental concerns, Kreutzmann devised a line of "Grateful Diver" products to support Coral Reef's work.

The Kreutzmann who made the most noise in the late 1980s and early 1990s was Justin, a Bay Area filmmaker and the drummer's son. At sixteen he directed *The Making of the "Touch of Grey" Video,* a best-selling video about the creation of the Dead's megahit video of their blockbusting single. After playing small, behind-the-scenes roles in *In the Dark, Built to Last, Without a Net,* and *The Jerry Garcia Band Live,* Justin directed Garcia and mandolinist David Grisman in a fanciful video of B.B. King's "The Thrill Is Gone," from their Grammy-nominated acoustic release. In the fall of 1991, the younger Kreutzmann coproduced *Backstage Pass,* a six-song, thirty-five-minute video journey through the Dead's history.

Jim Kweskin and the Jug Band
Jim Kweskin, born July 18, 1940

Jim Kweskin's Jug Band included Bill Keith, Geoff Muldaur, Maria D'Amato (later Maria Muldaur), and several others. They came out of the Cambridge, Massachusetts folk scene in 1963 with a combination of oldtimey country, bluegrass, and ragtime music, single-handedly reviving the jug band genre and inspiring Garcia, Weir, Pigpen, and the Bay Area music crowd to form their own jug bands. The fad never really caught on in either coast in a big way, but provided the future Grateful Dead members with a taste of the musical fun they would continue to seek.

Kweskin's units followed the recipe that had long composed the jug-band gumbo: washboards, kazoos, novelty songs, and general hilarity. The unselfconscious efforts resulted in some of the decade's most delightfully foolish music. Though the jug band craze was short, its whimsical style set the stage for much of the American popular music that followed.

"La Bamba" (Traditional; Ritchie Valens/William Clausen)
Ritchie Valens, single (1959, 1962, 1966, 1979, 1987), *Ritchie Valens* (1959), *The Ritchie Valens Story* (1993), *Rockin' All Night* (1995)
HARRY BELAFONTE, *Belafonte Returns to Carnegie Hall* (1960)
Neil Diamond, *The Feel of Neil Diamond* (1966)

Blues Image, *Open* (1970)
NEW RIDERS OF THE PURPLE SAGE, *OH, WHAT A MIGHTY TIME* (1975)
Los Lobos, *La Bamba* soundtrack (1987), *Just Another Band from East L.A.* (1993)
Richie Cole, *Popbop* (1987)
Red Grammer, *Red Grammer's Favorite Sing Along Songs* (1993)

Ritchie Valens. *(Archive Photos)*

Ritchie Valens's "La Bamba" was not only enjoying a renaissance of mammoth proportions when the Dead snuck it into the middle of "Good Lovin'" for a quartet of shows in September 1987, it was the No. 1 song in the country.

The inclusion of "La Bamba" made sense on several levels. The popularity of "La Bamba" was a direct offshoot of the highly regarded Valens bio-pic *La Bamba* in which the Tex-Mex band Los Lobos performed the soundtrack. Garcia's own Spanish heritage, his admiration of Los Lobos, and the song's close similarity to "Good Lovin'" may have prompted him to suggest "La Bamba" as a timely novelty.

Though it first gained popularity in Mexico's Vera Cruz region right after World War II, the precise lineage of "La Bamba" is difficult to trace. The lyrics concern a dance called La Bamba and the flirtation that ensues when it is displayed. It lingered as a kind of Tex-Mex garage band favorite for more than a decade when Southern California teen idol Ritchie Valens cut it in 1959 just before his death in the Clear Lake, Iowa, plane crash that also killed Buddy Holly and the Big Bopper on February 3, 1959; the day, according to Don McLean's "American Pie," the music died.

The story of how Valens came to record "La Bamba" is typical of the ephemeral and serendipitous nature of pop music. He was strumming a Latin rhythm one day and singing along when his producer, Bob Keene, asked him about the catchy riff. When Valens replied that it was a Mexican folk song to which he didn't know the words, the two tracked down Valens's aunt, who wrote down the lyrics for them. But Valens still had to be persuaded to record it as a rock & roll song.

That diffidence followed Valens his entire life (which commenced on May 13, 1941, in Pacoima, California, a Los Angeles suburb). Aside from "La Bamba," Valens is mostly remembered as a singer who successfully mingled rock with Mexican-American music. Of Mexican-American heritage himself, Valens formed a band in high school called the Silhouettes and was already toying with his musical alchemy.

In 1958, when he was seventeen years old, Valens signed with Keene's Del-Fi label and released "Come On, Let's Go," which became a minor hit later that year. It was his next single, combining "La Bamba" with "Donna," a mournful teen ballad about his girlfriend, which broke artistic and commercial ground. A double-sided million seller in 1959, both songs had different

and wide-ranging influences on everybody from the Crickets and the Isley Brothers to the Mormon Tabernacle Choir. For a great peek at the Valens legacy, *La Bamba*, the 1987 film starring Lou Diamond Phillips, is a must.

9/23/87, The Spectrum, Philadelphia

▪ "Lady Di and I" (JOAN BAEZ)

A tongue-in-cheek comment on the Royal Family as salient today as it was when it was written around the time of the media event wedding of Prince Charles to Lady Diana in 1981. Baez led the Dead through the tune at two of their three December 1981 pairings.

12/30/81, Oakland Auditorium Arena, Oakland, California

▪ "Lady with a Fan"

See "Terrapin Station"

▪ "L'Alhambra" (Garcia/Hunter/Kreutzmann)
Grateful Dead, *Terrapin Station* (1977)

This bright, spritely instrumental nestled in the folds of the Dead's *Terrapin Station* album was performed at but one 1977 concert. According to Hunter's notes in his collection of lyrics, *A Box of Rain*, it was "written to a Moorish setting composed by Mickey Hart that eventually evolved into a wordless melodic segment of 'Terrapin Station.'"

3/18/77, Winterland Arena, San Francisco

▪ *Late Night with David Letterman* (television program)

Garcia and Weir made a few appearances on *Late Night*, sitting in with Paul Schaffer's hot studio band and engaging in some playful banter with David Letterman. The first of these appearances was in 1982, with two acoustic numbers, "DEEP ELEM BLUES" and "THE MONKEY AND THE ENGINEER," getting the performance nod. A second appearance in 1987, while shamelessly plugging *In the Dark*, was memorable not only for the music and typically glib interview, but for the parlor trick whereby Weir orchestrates Garcia's "levitation." Truly weird.

▪ *Last Days of the Fillmore* (film)
Directed and produced by Richard D. Heffron, 1972.

This little celluloid slice of history documents the scene swirling around the closing of Bill Graham's fabled Fillmore West and stars the tempestuous impresario as himself. With performances from some of the era's great and forgotten acts (including Santana, Jefferson Airplane, Cold Blood, and It's a Beautiful Day), the Dead's inclusion in the final wash is a mite disappointing. Their badly filmed and poorly edited sequence zeroes in on Garcia and Weir and virtually ignores their band mates. Also frustrating are the song selections ("Casey Jones" and "JOHNNY B. GOODE") from the otherwise choice July 2, 1971, concert. Where are the outtakes?

The film also includes a shot of Garcia noodling on the pedal steel in rehearsal with the NEW RIDERS OF THE PURPLE SAGE and a glimpse of the Dead holding court backstage.

▪ "The Last Time" (Jagger/Richards)
The Rolling Stones, *Out of Our Heads* (1965), *Through the Past Darkly (Big Hits Vol. 2)* (1969), *Stone Age* (1971)
The Who, *Who's Missing*/'66 (1987)

"The Last Time" was among the first singles pressed bearing the songwriting credit Mick Jagger/Keith Richards on the label; it was also the first Stones single to secure a No. 1 spot on the British charts and was a major confidence boost to the brash, young band. Partially based on an early-sixties gospel song with the same title by the Staples Singers, "The Last Time" begins with a characteristic Stones riff that cuts right through the song with lyrics emphasizing Jagger's relationship-threatening ultimatum. A new spitefulness was beginning to shade the group's vision and they wore this song like a badge.

When the Dead broke out the Stones classic in February 1990, rumors immediately began flying that the band was on the verge of imminent breakup. Not only did this prove not to be the case, the Grateful Dead developed "The Last Time" with spooky aplomb in the years that followed. Weir's lead vocals progressively broke down from self-assured to apoplectic.

> **8/21/93, Autzen Stadium, Eugene, Oregon (with Huey Lewis on harmonica)**

▪ "Lazy Lightning" (Weir/Barlow)
Grateful Dead, *Dick's Picks Volume Three*/'77 (1995)
KINGFISH, *KINGFISH* (1976), *KINGFISH IN CONCERT*/'76 (1995)

"Lazy Lightning" was one of the earlier Weir/Barlow compositions that can be viewed in the context of their song cycle describing the aloof and confused outsider fruitlessly trying to connect. "Feel Like a Stranger," "Picasso Moon," and "Easy Answers" are a few songs in this ilk that followed. "Lazy Lightning" is a jazzed-up riff, providing interesting jams and intricate ensemble interplay. Linked with its sister coda, "Supplication," "Lazy Lightning" was a welcome if infrequent first-set chop-loosener from 1976 until 1984, when it was surprisingly dropped out of the Dead's rotation.

Along with "Estimated Prophet," "Money Money," and "Supplication," "Lazy Lightning" is one of several songs written in cycles of seven beats. When David Gans asked Weir about this potentially awkward time signature in 1977, the guitarist said: "I like it, because you can get the 'best of three, best of four' if you play it right . . . three then four, four then three, two then two then three—whatever. Break it up however you like. It gives you a chance to get two different rhythmic feels happening at the same time, and you can play them against each other to interesting effect."

> **7/18/76, Orpheum Theater, San Francisco**
> **11/2/77, Field House, Seneca College, Toronto**
> **12/28/82, Oakland Auditorium Arena, Oakland, California**

▪ "Lazy River Road" (Garcia/Hunter)

The late 1980s was an unusually fallow period for the Garcia/Hunter collaboration. But when the two reconvened in the early 1990s, they did so with a vengeance, hashing out a number of noteworthy pieces. "Lazy River Road," more than any of them, harks back to the spirit of their earlier stylings in its attempt to recall the days of yore through the wistful eyes of the gracefully aging narrator who finds himself in love once again. A pleasing mid-tempo ramble and low-key musing, "Lazy River Road" has that early twentieth-century folk sensibility found in the Dead's typical first-set songs such as "Brown-Eyed Women" and "Ramble on Rose."

Discussing the song's development with Jon Sievert of *Guitar Play* in 1993, Garcia recalled, " 'Lazy River Road' is an interesting example. When we started working on that, I wasn't sure if it was going to be a shuffle or what. It's the kind of song that can go any numbers of ways, because stylistically it's wide open and you can phrase it *any* way. I was trying all kinds of things when I was writing it on the keyboard. It wasn't until we actually started to try to work on it that it started to get a rhythmic feel. The one that we've got for it seems real natural for it now, although it feels to me like it's starting to be wanting to pick up the tempo a little bit. It might have a slightly different feel but it's somewhere around where it ought to be. The song does what it seems to want to do."

4/1/95, The Pyramid, Memphis, Tennessee

▪ Leadbelly

Born Huddie Ledbetter, January 15, 1888, Shiloh, Louisiana; died December 6, 1949, New York City

With a biography as intriguing as his moniker, Leadbelly, more than any other black folk-blues artist of his era, shared black America's vast musical riches (and social suffering) with the rest of the country. The "King of the Twelve-String Guitar" would live a life that included

hopeless poverty, two murder convictions, two incredible pardons, and a musical career that would extend from the bustling street corners, juke joints, and prisons of Texas and Louisiana, to the coffeehouses of Greenwich Village and the studios of Hollywood, from a jail cell on Rikers Island to the inauguration of a president. In the process, he helped preserve a folk legacy that became a significant part of this nation's cultural treasury.

A short but massive man, Leadbelly was born and raised in rural Louisiana to hardworking sharecropper parents. His nickname could have been derived from any one or a combination of sources: a corruption of his surname, his physical strength, a buckshot wound and/or his sexual prowess. Though little is known about Leadbelly's early life, he left home as a youth and wandered through Louisiana and East Texas, meeting up and performing with Blind Lemon Jefferson around 1915. Leadbelly, who was already a competent practi-

Leadbelly (Huddie Ledbetter) .
(Photo: James Chapelle courtesy of Smithsonian Folkways Records)

tioner of the mandolin, piano, and accordion, settled on the twelve-string guitar as his instrument of choice, probably having heard its rich, ringing sound from the Mexican musicians who often played in Texas saloons and bordellos. Developing a delightful rhythmic guitar style in which he imitated the walking bass figures then commonly employed by the barrelhouse pianists on Fanin Street (Shreveport, Louisiana's, notorious red-light district), Leadbelly became a fixture in the area's nightspots.

But Leadbelly's explosive temper and frequent run-ins with the law landed him in Texas's Huntsville Prison Farm after being convicted of killing a man in an argument over a woman in 1917, and six years were added to his sentence when he attempted escape. A shrewd prisoner, Leadbelly used his musical talents to avoid the cruel work details and was, astoundingly, able to wrangle a pardon from Texas governor Pat Neff in 1925 after composing a song he wrote to him pleading for freedom. Part of the song went like this: "If I had the gov'ner / Where the gov'ner has me / Before daylight / I'd set the gov'ner free."

Returning to the Lake Caddo district of his youth, Leadbelly was arrested five years later for assault with intent to murder and sent to Louisiana's Angola Prison Farm. It turned out to be a turning point in the minstrel's life because in 1933 he was discovered by father and son folklorists John and Alan Lomax who, on a trip collecting songs from prisoners, recorded him for the Library of Congress. The Lomaxes, struck by Leadbelly's powerful voice, guitar style, and wide knowledge of rural black folk songs, petitioned Louisiana governor O. K. Allen to pardon Leadbelly. Their valuation of Leadbelly's ability and songs that Leadbelly himself wrote as pleas for his release, secured another pardon into John Lomax's care in 1934 and a launch upon the concert halls and folk-song circles of the East Coast as the torchbearer of the riches of black song.

Commencing to record 200 additional pieces for the Library of Congress, Leadbelly began that last phase of his life in New York City where he was a welcome favorite among left-leaning white folksingers of the 1930s and 1940s in an early example of radical chic. He became friends and musical partners with Woody Guthrie and Pete Seeger and black bluesmen Sonny Terry and Brownie McGhee, performing with them at hootenannies and union halls, often in support of progressive causes. His involvement with politics and his relocation to New York separated him from his rural Southern roots but the opportunity to prolifically record, if not capitalize, on hundreds of sides for the Library of Congress, Folkways records, and a slew of other labels forever place his legacy in the landscape of American song.

More a songster than a traditional blues singer, Leadbelly played the blues, spirituals, pop, and prison songs, as well as dance tunes and folk ballads. With his unmistakable whoops and hollers, driving guitar, and storytelling, he became a high profile, if barely successful, performer. He did not sell many records and constantly lived on the brink of poverty.

A move to Hollywood in the mid-1940s did little to improve his economic station and, after an unsuccessful trip to Paris in 1949, where he had hoped to build a European following, he was diagnosed with Lou Gehrig's disease, which quickly destroyed his muscular system. By the end of the year, he was dead.

Leadbelly's stature has only grown in the half century since his passing. His music was absorbed by succeeding generations of troubadours who passed on his brilliance to their audiences. His acclaim reached new heights with the aid of *Leadbelly*, the uniformly excellent 1976 bio-pic by Gordon Parks, which starred Walter Mosely (later of *Magnum P.I.* fame) in the title role. And, in 1988, Columbia Records released *Folkways: A Vision Shared*, which contained renditions of Leadbelly and Guthrie songs by such artists as BOB DYLAN, Bruce Springsteen, Taj Mahal, and Brian Wilson. The record's net profits went to purchase the Folkways catalog for the Smithsonian Institution. A shoo-in for the Blues Foundation's Hall of Fame, to which he was inducted in 1986, Leadbelly became a member of the Rock and Roll Hall of Fame in 1988 as one of the music form's chief pioneers. For the ultimate inside scoop on the songster, *The Life and Legend of Leadbelly*, by Charles Wolfe and Kip Lornell, is a must.

Of the many songs closely associated with him, some of the more famous—"Midnight Special," "Rock Island Line," "Cotton Fields," "Good Morning Blues," and the blues ballad "Boll Weevil"—have been recorded and covered repeatedly. Influenced by Guthrie and the other New York–based folksingers, Leadbelly wrote songs that carried strong political messages such as "Scottsboro Boys" and "Bourgeois Blues."

The Dead performed three of Leadbelly's songs, "DEATH LETTER BLUES," "ROBERTA," and "GOODNIGHT IRENE," easily the maestro's most popular song.

■ "Leave Your Love at Home"/(Lola Jean Dillon)

After playing till breakfast on New Year's Day, 1972, the Dead were back on the Winterland stage the night after. Weir used the opportunity to break out the one-time only version of "Leave Your Love at Home."

1/2/72, Winterland Arena, San Francisco

■ Legion of Mary

Garcia had been jamming and recording with organist MERL SAUNDERS for years before they finally decided to name their group Legion of Mary in July 1974. The original lineup included Garcia on guitar and vocals, Saunders on organ and vocals, JOHN KAHN on bass, Martin Fierro on tenor saxophone, flute, and percussion, and Paul Humphrey on drums. Ron Tutt replaced Humphrey on drums the following winter.

Though they played the vast majority of their hundred-plus gigs in the Bay Area, the unit did periodically venture to the East Coast, South, and Midwest.

When visiting New York for a clutch of shows in April 1975, Garcia was pleased by the quality of his band, telling John Rockwell of the *New York Times*, "We're more on the relaxed than the hurried side of the metronome. We get a nice conversational quality in our music."

Garcia also cleared up some of the mystery involving the name of his new band in his discussion with Rockwell. "Legion of Mary got its name by default. There's a billion-member—or is it million?—Catholic organization called the Legion of Mary. They came by with all these pamphlets, but they've been really good humored about it, and so far we haven't gotten any threats."

Like the Dead, the Legion of Mary presented a broad range of music. Covering Dylan ("Tough Mama"), R&B ("HOW SWEET IT IS"), reggae ("The Harder They Come"), good time rock & roll ("Tore Up over You"), and a handful of originals ("Mississippi Moon"), the group played many blistering shows and laid the foundation for the later Jerry Garcia Band.

In a conversation with Blair Jackson, Saunders jokingly recalled the band's first trip to Southern California: "We came off the plane in San Diego, and this porter is looking at us very strangely as we got into the limo. He said, 'Oh, my God, what kind of band is this? You've got a hippie [Garcia], a black guy [Saunders], a white guy [Kahn], an Indian [Fierro], and a super fly [Humphrey, who enjoyed attiring himself in flashy colors]. "We got a good laugh at that!"

During their April 1975 run at New York City's Bottom Line, the group had another memorable encounter. According to Saunders: "I will never forget when we played the Bottom Line in the spring of 1975. We did three shows in three days, and the place was jam packed. We were playing and the audience was just freaking out, and all of a sudden we hear all the noise stop. We hear an 'oooh,' and we see a flash go by into the dressing room. We look at each other because we didn't know who went in there. When we went into the dressing room John Lennon was sitting there. We were shocked. He came to thank us for doing his number 'Imagine,' on my album *Heavy Turbulence*. I had done the first cover version of his song. Lennon wrote 'Imagine' in 1971 and the record had just come out that September. I was at Fantasy Records that fall with Garcia, Tom Fogerty, John Kahn, and Bill Vitt to record my album. This guy at the studio had a promotional copy of the record. I listened to 'Imagine' and thought it was gorgeous, so I wanted to do an instrumental cover version of it. This was before 'Imagine' became a hit. I let Garcia hear the song and he said, 'It's a neat song, let's do it.'"

A partial list of songs performed by the Legion of Mary: "HI-HEEL SNEAKERS," "Expressway," "He Ain't Give You None," "Wonderin' Why," "I SECOND THAT EMOTION," "It's Too Late," "ROAD RUNNER," "THAT'S ALL RIGHT, MAMA," "It's No Use," "The Harder They Come," "The Night They Drove Old Dixie Down," "After Midnight," "Leave Your Hat On," "That's What Love Will Make You Do," "HOW SWEET IT IS (TO BE LOVED BY YOU)," "Think," "Last Train," "Lala," "MYSTERY TRAIN," "Lonely Avenue," "Someday Baby," "Neighbor, Neighbor," "Sittin' in Limbo," "My Funny Valentine," "Going, Going Gone," "Tough Mama," "Freedom Jazz Dance," "That's the Touch," "System," "Albany Rag," "Till The End of the World," "Reggae Woman," "LET IT ROCK," "My Problems Got Problems," "Blue Montreux," "Desilu," "Bossa Martin," "When the Hunter Gets Captured by the Game," "Are You Lonely for Me," "Tore Up over You," "Finders, Keepers," "Dynamite," "Soul Roach," "Mississippi Moon," "Every Word You Say," "All by Myself," "THE WICKED MESSENGER," "I'll Take a Melody," "Flute Thing," "Favella," "It Hurts So Bad"

4/19/75, Oriental Theater, Milwaukee, Wisconsin

See also **Jerry Garcia Band**

▪ Leiber and Stoller
(Jerry Leiber–born April 25, 1933, Baltimore, Maryland. Mike Stoller–born May 13, 1933, Belle Harbor, New York)

The old coin, "irony rules," is probably in no more evidence than in the success of Leiber and Stoller. White boys wonderstruck by black music, they are among the most inventive R&B and rock 'n' roll songwriters and producers to emerge in the 1950s and 1960s, whose work was covered by everyone from Elvis to the Coasters and the Drifters to the Grateful Dead.

Born on the East Coast but reared in Los Angeles, where their parents moved as part of the great post–World War II migration, Jerry Leiber and Mike Stoller were introduced in 1950 by Lester Sill of Modern Records, who released their first recorded composition, "Real Ugly Woman" by Jimmy Witherspoon, in 1951. Their first R&B hit, Charles Brown's "Hard Times" in 1952, was followed by more than twenty artists (including Lucky Millinder, Esther Phillips, and Big Mama Thornton) cutting their songs over the next two years. "Hound Dog," the song recorded by Thornton, became an even bigger hit when Presley got ahold of it in 1956, a recording that led Leiber and Stoller to write the score for the King's 1957 movie *Jailhouse Rock*. The wheel had come full circle for them: Jewish guys who wrote black songs for a white boy who sang like a black man.

But it was upon setting up the Spark label with Sill in 1954 and signing the Robins that they began to make their mark as production revolutionaries. Moving to New York, they used the Robins as protégés for their "playlets" (Leiber's term for the songs whose humorous lyrics read like stories). The success of "Riot in Cell Block # 9," "Smokey Joe's Café" and "Framed" led Atlantic to buy the label, rename the Robins as the Coasters and hire Leiber and Stoller as independent producers (among the first in the business) to work with Ruth Brown ("Lucky Lips"), Joe Turner ("The Chicken and the Hawk"), and LaVern Baker ("Saved"). With their subterranean ambiance, bluesy speech-song and wise-guy attitude, these songs are quintessential early Leiber and Stoller.

Many of the these songs were written in explosive

bursts that Stoller once described as "spontaneous combustion." As he told Stephen Holden of the *New York Times* in 1995, "I'd be hanging on the piano and Jerry would be yelling and pacing. It all happened at once."

They repeated the formula with the Drifters—who had already recorded some of their songs—and began to spread themselves across the pop spectrum. The Drifters scored with "Under the Boardwalk," Ben E. King had a hit with "Stand By Me," the Cheers had their fifteen minutes of teen-pop idolatry with "Black Denim Trousers," Perry Como catapulted to the top of the charts with "Dancin'," and Peggy Lee, the jazzy torch singer did the same, with "I'm a Woman."

With carefully preplanned productions, some songs were given up to sixty takes with much editing to achieve the desired, surprisingly spontaneous sounding effect with their assistant and acolyte Phil Spector, who later took this method to its ultimate extremes. Saying "We don't write songs, we write records," they relied on Brill Building songwriters and their own production vision to transform the public's conception of an LP as merely a collection of singles into something more akin to a unified artistic whole.

Though they never matched the heights of their earlier work, Leiber and Stoller stayed at the forefront of the music business for the next three decades, working with a cross section of American musicians as diverse as T-Bone Walker, the Dixie Cups, Procol Harum, and Doc Pomus. Showered with awards from every musical Hall of Fame imaginable during the late 1980s, Leiber and Stoller will be remembered as the ones who took R&B from the ghetto into the mainstream, creating pop classics that transcended musical and racial categories. *Smokey Joe's Café,* a Broadway revue of their greatest hits, had a successful run in the mid-1990s.

The Dead took on a few Leiber and Stoller songs, mostly in the early days. "I'M A HOG FOR YOU," "RIOT IN CELL BLOCK #9," and "SEARCHIN' " were all briefly tackled in the late 1960s and early 1970s, while "KANSAS CITY" made a couple of surprise appearances in 1985.

Summing up their success, Mr. Leiber told the *New York Times* in 1995, "I don't know why, but we really didn't believe that there was any longevity to rock & roll. Cole Porter and Irving Berlin, they wrote standards. We might write some hits, but they weren't going to be standards."

Phil Lesh

Born Phillip Chapman Lesh, March 15, 1940, Berkeley, California

The eccentric in a group of verifiable eccentrics, bassist Phil Lesh's roots in the bohemian avant-garde run deep. When he was four years old he experienced his first musical epiphany while listening to a radio broadcast. As he told Hank Harrison in 1972, "I got this huge hit from the Brahms Symphony when I was four years old. Brahms First Symphony, conducted by Bruno Walter and the New York Philharmonic sometime in 1944. My grandmother said, 'Phillip, come listen to the nice music on the radio. I walked over and sat down next to my grandmother (who I dearly loved—anything to be next to my grandmother). And wooow! This fucking thing comes out of the radio and knocks my head off. I have never been the same since. But dig this irony: Six years later, when I was ten, my violin teacher took me to hear the same conductor performing the same symphony in San Francisco."

When he hit his mid-teens, Phil caught the jazz bug, took up the trumpet, and switched from a high school in El Cerrito (where the marching band quickly wore thin) to Berkeley High School because it offered advanced

Phil Lesh, Polo Field. Golden Gate Park, San Francisco, California, 6/21/67. (Photo: Mike Pollilo courtesy Robert Minkin)

courses in harmony. (On a trivial note, the earliest extant example of a Grateful Dead member's recorded legacy are three Stan Kenton–style big-band jazz arrangements Lesh put together for his high school ensemble.)

He got his professional start in music as a "cool" jazz trumpeter in the late 1950s before edging into Stockhausen-inspired composition in the 1960s while studying with modernist composer LUCIANO BERIO. This association culminated in "Foci for Four Orchestras," a dainty piece requiring a mere 123 musicians and four conductors to perform. "You learn more in one semester hanging around someone like Berio than you would if you were to study and listen to lectures for five years under someone else," Lesh once commented.

Lesh became discouraged with composing, however, because there was no place for his pieces to be publicly presented and little recognition came to him as a result of his work. "There seems to be a kind of establishment in the academic world. You have to have a certain set of credentials in order to achieve anything, and the politics of it are pretty intense. I was at a musical dead end, so I just stopped being a musician," Lesh commented to *Guitar Player* magazine in 1977.

A fan of all kinds of music, Lesh first encountered Garcia playing banjo at Kepler's Bookstore, a famed Palo Alto hangout, and invited him to perform on *The Midnight Special* radio show on Berkeley's Pacifica affiliate, KPFA, where Lesh worked as an engineer.

Melting easily into the pre-hippie Haight-Ashbury scene of the early 1960s, Lesh drove a U.S. Postal Service truck to earn his keep and embraced the boho community when he experienced another musical epiphany: BOB DYLAN's "Subterranean Homesick Blues" and the Beatles' film *A Hard Day's Night*.

One spring evening in 1965, Lesh was invited to a party down the Peninsula to see Garcia's new electric band, the earliest version of the Warlocks, at Magoo's Pizza Parlour. When he couldn't stop dancing, he knew that he had found bliss. As Lesh recalled in a 1977 *Guitar Player* interview, "At the time, they weren't quite to the point of playing out. They were just rehearsing at Dana Morgan's, the local music store. Anyway, I mentioned to Jerry Garcia that I would like to learn the electric bass and maybe join a band. From there, we immediately moved on to a totally different subject. Three weeks later, I came down to hear a gig that they were doing. Jerry sat me down in a corner and said, 'Now you are going to play bass for the band,' I said okay. He really didn't know what he was in for."

Lesh practiced more with the group than on his own because he felt that he could get his chops down better if he had to keep up with and receive input from the other musicians. "We spent an awful lot of time practicing in the back of Guitars Unlimited in Menlo Park—about four hours a day."

Lesh was listening mainly to jazz when he joined the Warlocks, favoring the likes of John Coltrane and Miles Davis and admitting a strong influence from Scott La-Faro, who had made his mark with Ornette Coleman's early bands but was killed in a car accident in his early twenties. But, being a modern composer, he was attracted to the music of Karlheinz Stockhausen as well, saying, "Electronic music always seemed like the logical thing to me. It was always easy for me to hear it as music. I gather it is not that easy for just anybody."

Lesh's first bass, which he bought at age twenty-five, was a Gibson EB-O. "It was terrible. It had telephone poles for strings."

Although he had never picked up an electric bass before first playing with the Warlocks in 1965, the tall, elfin composer quickly revolutionized the instrument and complemented Garcia's solos from the get-go. With his background in jazz, classical composition, and experimental electronic music, Lesh helped lay the groundwork for the instrument's future that would be realized in the likes of Jack Casady, Jaco Pastorius, and Stanley Clarke. Blair Jackson once compared Lesh's approach to the dancing elephants from *Fantasia*, Disney's classic animation. Indeed, Lesh seemed to defy musical gravity in his simultaneity and contrapuntality as his explorations of the Dead's exponentially increasing repertoire helped define the sound of the band.

Lesh immediately set about turning on his band mates to the work of innovators from Coltrane to Charles Ives. Ives was a particularly strong influence, because his music had so many elements occurring simultaneously within it: Folk tunes and hymns collide with Civil War marching songs while pastoral visions of Thoreau's America superimpose upon thunderous cacophony. When a cowboy song emerged from the depths of a "space" jam at a Dead concert or a Sonny Boy Williamson blues dissolved into screeching atonality, the bit of Ives Lesh brought to the Dead was strongly evident.

As the band edged into sustained group composition in the late 1960s, Lesh was at the fore, leading the charge on the seriously experimental *Anthem of the Sun*

Phil Lesh, Spartan Stadium, San Jose, California, 4/22/79. (© Ed Perlstein)

album, collaborating with Garcia and Hunter on the *Aoxomoxoa* project, and singing the leadoff tune on *American Beauty,* his beloved "Box of Rain."

Lesh was also the band's able high-octave background singer until the long-term acute vocal-chord damage he sustained by crooning incorrectly put his singing on the shelf in 1974. It would be nearly a decade before the injury had healed itself and Lesh would resume his lead and background vocal duties—this time singing within his proper range.

Blessed with perfect pitch, Lesh was always at the vanguard of the Grateful Dead's unrelenting explorations into (and obsessive fussing with) state-of-the-art sound systems. In addition to urging the band along in their MIDI quests, Lesh went to the extreme of redesigning his own instrument. In the mid-1970s, he started performing with "The Godfather," a Guild Starfire bass that he had crammed with electronics. In 1982, when he commissioned a six-string bass with one string tuned a fifth higher than the normal bass and one string a fifth lower, Lesh refined and developed this unusual axe with the intensity of some modern-day Merlin of the lower registers.

As the band's senior member, Lesh never acquired a taste for the trappings of rock stardom, preferring to retreat from the rigors of Dead tours to enjoy the fruits of domestic life with his wife and two sons. But, like his band mates, he always kept a few irons in the musical fire. Starting in the late 1980s, Lesh cohosted Rex Radio with Gary Lambert, showcasing "out there" jazz and contemporary classical music. The monthly radio program was broadcast on KPFA, Berkeley, California's Pacifica Radio affiliate. At the same time, Lesh's efforts with the Dead's Rex Foundation resulted in several sizable grants to composers toiling in the back eddies of highbrow obscurity.

Commenting on the choice of composers who benefited from Rex, Lesh told the *New York Times* in 1994 that "They are all outsiders, and I guess, despite our success, we're outsiders, too. These guys take no prisoners. They are not writing down to anybody. They are not trying to be comprehensible. I'm sure there is a certain vicariousness for me in giving these grants. If I were out there, I'd hope there was somebody like me out there."

Under Phil's guidance, the foundation spent more than $100,000 commissioning and recording works by avant-garde composers including Robert Simpson, Michael Finnissy, and Richard Barrett. Through Lesh,

Rex has also helped revive the work of Havergal Brian, a British composer who had only one of his thirty-two symphonies recorded before he died in 1972. "Phil Lesh has been key in sparking interest in Brian's music," said David J. Brown, vice president of the Havergal Brian Society. "His money allowed us to record some of his music and show there was an audience for it. Now the Marco Polo label is recording all of his symphonies."

As Lesh told the *London Chronicle* in 1991, "composers tend to be tied to the academic world. The younger ones who are not—minimalists and neo-romantics—don't interest me at all. The Rex Foundation deals with environmental concerns—the rain forests—and human need, like cancer clinics and senior citizen homes. I went in and argued that we should do something for music."

In the spring of 1994, Lesh lived out a longtime dream when he appeared as a guest conductor for the Berkeley Symphony as part of that orchestra's annual Celebrity Conductor benefit concert. While most of the evening's other wannabe Toscaninis led the orchestra through the classical jukebox, Lesh tackled two of the most challenging compositions in twentieth-century music: the "Infernal Dance" from Igor Stravinsky's *Firebird* suite and Elliott Carter's "A Celebration of Some 100 x 150 Notes." Lesh described the experience as "exhilarating and terrifying," and though he was typically self-critical of his performance, it gave his admirers a taste of what Maestro Phil's life might have been like had he not taken a little career detour some three decades earlier.

Following Garcia's passing, Lesh helped organize a program of West Coast experimental music with Michael Tilson Thomas, director of the San Francisco Symphony. Two of the concerts featured an unlikely Grateful Dead reunion—Lesh, Mickey Hart, Bob Weir, and Vince Welnick—augmenting performances of compositions from the likes of John Cage, and Steve Reich and Henry Cowaall. As Lesh related to Mark Rowland of *Musician* in 1996, "Michael's idea was to celebrate the work of the pioneers in the field and also to demonstrate how their ideas had filtered into the mainstream of music at large—in that sense, the Grateful Dead were as much West Coast and as experimental as anybody. He felt that our inclusion was in some way a logical step, to deal with the vernacular end of the experimental tradition."

■ "Let It Be Me" (Curtis/Delanoe/Becaud)
Jill Corey, single (1957)

Everly Brothers, single (1960), *The Fabulous Style of the Everly Brothers* (1960), *Reunion Concert* (1983)

Jerry Butler, *He Will Break Your Heart* (1960), *The Best of Jerry Butler* (1987), *The Ice Man* (1992)

Herb Albert and the Tijuana Brass, *The Lonely Bull* (1962)

Carla Thomas, *Comfort Me* (1966)

Nancy Sinatra, *How Does That Grab You* (1966)

Billy Vera and Judy Clay, *Storybook Children* (1967)

Glen Campbell and Bobbie Gentry, *Glen Campbell and Bobbie Gentry* (1969)

BOB DYLAN, *Self-Portrait* (1970)

Elvis Presley, *On Stage February 1970* (1970), *Walk a Mile in My Shoes* (1995)

The Voices, *The Voices of East Harlem* (1971)

Willie Nelson and MERLE HAGGARD, *Pancho & Lefty* (1982)

Little Milton, *Age Ain't Nothing but a Number* (1983)

Indigo Girls, *Rites of Passage* (1992)

Lawrence Welk, *A Musical Anthology* (1992)

Julio Iglesias, *Crazy* (1994)

The Dead (headlining as Bobby Ace and the Cards from the Bottom of the Deck) only performed this song, first made famous by the Everly Brothers, at one 1969 semi-acoustic show.

"Let It Be Me" was written by Pierre Delanoe and Gilbert Becaud in 1955 under the French title "Je t'Appartiens" and was first recorded that year by Becaud. Mann Curtis wrote English lyrics and Jill Corey introduced the song in an episode of the TV series *Climax*. Her recording peaked at No. 57 on Billboard's Pop charts. But it wasn't until the Everly Brothers recorded the song that it became a hit, reaching No. 7.

6/11/69, California Hall, San Francisco

■ "Let It Grow (Weather Report Suite Part 2)" (Weir/Barlow)

Grateful Dead, *Wake of the Flood* (1973), single (1974), *Without a Net* (1990), *Dick's Pick's Volume One/'73* (1993), *Dick's Picks Volume Seven* (1997)

One of the Dead's most enduring compositions, "Let It Grow" served the band well wherever it popped up in concert—either as a late-first-set dynamo or as second-set segue fodder. At once evoking both the humanity of a Brueghel landscape and the flamenco stylings of the Spanish musical tradition, "Let It Grow" has also been interpreted on a political level as a veiled plea for legalization of the cultivation and use of cannabis. "Let It Grow" is a buoyant piece of music, capped by a syncopated jam that expanded in breadth and complexity with the Dead's own evolution. Alternately, such lines as "the love of the women, work of man" have been chided as chauvinist.

9/15/73, Providence Civic Center, Providence, Rhode Island

3/23/74, Cow Palace, Daly City, California

6/18/74, Freedom Hall, Louisville, Kentucky

7/18/76, Orpheum Theater, San Francisco

9/11/83, Sante Fe Downs, Sante Fe, New Mexico

6/14/85, Greek Theatre, Berkeley, California

2/14/86, Henry J. Kaiser Convention Center, Oakland, California

4/30/88, Frost Amphitheater, Palo Alto, California

3/10/93, Rosemont Horizon, Rosemont, Illinois

■ "Let It Rock" (CHUCK BERRY)

Chuck Berry, *Rockin' at the Hop* (1959), *Chuck Berry Twist* (1962), *The Collection* (1988)

Jerry Garcia, *Compliments of Garcia* (1974)

Savoy Brown, *Street Corner Talking* (1971)

This lesser-known Berry paean to hard work and even harder living was a Garcia Band staple in the mid-1970s but only unveiled at one Dead show.

6/23/74, Jai-Alai Fronton, Miami

■ "Let Me Sing Your Blues Away" (Keith Godchaux/Robert Hunter)

Grateful Dead, single, *Wake of the Flood* (1973)

Considering he was with the Grateful Dead for the better part of a decade, it is somewhat surprising that keyboardist Keith Godchaux didn't contribute more songs to the band's repertoire. Perhaps his retiring demeanor predisposed him to being content with merely fulfilling his role as a musician rather than a composer. Whatever the reason, he barely left his mark on the Grateful Dead catalog. Judging by his sole contribution to this realm, "Let Me Sing Your Blues Away" was a promising and freshly hopeful if a tad hokey stab at songwriting, especially coming from one of the band's gloomier participants. Though it is easily the weakest entry on the Dead's well-regarded *Wake of the Flood* album, this piece of rock honky-tonk has aged well since its six performances in September 1973.

9/21/73, The Spectrum, Philadelphia

■ *Liberty*/Robert Hunter
Relix RRLP-RRCD 2029, 1988. Produced by Robert Hunter.
"Liberty," "Cry Down the Years," "Bone Alley," "Black Shamrock," "The Song Goes On," "Do Deny," "Worried Song," "Come and Get It," "When a Man Loves a Woman."
Robert Hunter–guitar, vocals. Jerry Garcia–guitar. Michael White–bass. David Mann–drums. Rick Meyers–piano, vocals, Roland S50 Sound Sampler.

Robert Hunter was on a roll in the latter half of the 1980s, churning out songs for the Dead and putting together a series of albums that were as hard-to-find as they were pleasing for Relix Records.

Discussing the songs with Blair Jackson in 1988, Hunter said, "Some of them are from the collection of seventeen lyrics that I got together for the Dead right before they made *In the Dark*. Of the songs on this record, I'd given the Dead 'Liberty,' 'Bone Alley,' and 'Black Shamrock.' From the collection of lyrics I gave them they took 'Black Muddy River' and 'When Push Comes to Shove,' and Dylan took 'Silvio' and 'Ugliest Girl in the World.' So it was a fairly successful batch."

"When a Man Loves a Woman" should not be confused with the classic 1966 Calvin Lewis–Andrew Wright song of the same title. According to Hunter's notes in *A Box of Rain*, he was unaware of the existence of the other song when he wrote the piece.

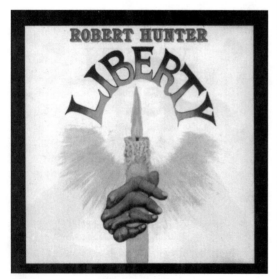

■ "Liberty" (Garcia/Hunter)
Robert Hunter, *Liberty* (1988)

Garcia reshaped Robert Hunter's paean to individualism in 1993 when it became a concert regular, primarily in the encore slot. The song is full of comic-book imagery that falls in on itself in typically Grateful Dead ways. The narrator, in his declaration of self no matter the cost, likens himself to a rock looking for shade, a river running upstream, a tree that chops itself down, and a bed that stays unmade.

"Liberty" is also a statement of devotion, charting the lengths the poet is willing to go to prove his love. A quirky mixture of stylings, "Liberty" is alternately cartoony and passionate—R. Crumb mingled with Baudelaire—and one of the Dead's better compositions from the early 1990s. With its iconoclastic pride, "Liberty" captured the essence of the decade just as "U.S. Blues" and "Touch of Grey" had been perfect songs for their eras.

5/26/93, Cal Expo Amphitheater, Sacramento, California

■ *The Light of the Spirit*/Kitaro
Geffen 24163, 1987. Produced by Mickey Hart.

A vaunted New Age musician and composer, Kitaro's style is the epitome of the contemplative, melodic music most closely associated with this movement. Ironically, this Japanese native taught himself to play electric guitar in high school—inspired by Otis Redding's pulsating R&B. By the early 1970s Kitaro formed the Far East Family Band and released a pair of progressive-rock albums.

But after meeting the innovative German synthesist Klaus Schulze during a 1972 trip to Europe, Kitaro changed his direction. Building his first synthesizer, Kitaro began experimenting with the kind of unusual sounds that fans of the Dead's "space" jams would appreciate. *Astral Voyage*, his debut album, quickly developed a cult following and led to a gig producing the first of several soundtracks for *Silk Road*, a Japanese television documentary series that ran for five years.

As his reputation grew through the release of several *Silk Road* albums, Kitaro landed a deal with Geffen Records in 1986, which brought his music to a wider Western audience by re-releasing his earlier work and giving him the support to expand his scope in many ways.

It was at this juncture that Kitaro hooked up with Mickey Hart for *The Light of the Spirit,* an album that featured American musicians. This gave the disc slightly more of an ensemble feeling than his usual one-man productions. It was nominated for a Grammy Award in the Best New Age Performance category in 1987. Hart spoke of Kitaro's music to William Ruhlmann for *Relix* in 1987. "His music appeals to such a unique sensibility. It's very private music. It appeals to a very private place. It's his vision of some natural soundscape. He's painting a soundscape and it allows you to look into yourself and it's very reflective. In this music, he has something very important he's saying, he's just not a casual musician out there. He has a vision and he knows how to interpret it, and he's a twentieth-century man who knows electronics. So this makes him very adept at translating and that's a part of music, it's translating your field, your soundscape. You have to look at your world, your sound world, and a musician interprets this world. He's not addressing everything. He's not addressing dance music. He's not disco. It's very specific. Some musics take all of that into consideration, but his doesn't. He lays it in a very narrow, specific place."

As Kitaro told Ruhlmann during the same interview: "From the standpoint of my own growth as a human being and as a musician, my music at any given point in my career has always been a sum total of who I am. It just flows from me and it's the result of all the people I've met, all the experiences I've had. It's the sum total of all those things I bring to bear on composition at any given point, and as my experiences grow and I meet more people and I expand my own understanding and knowledge of the world around me, it's reflected in my music."

Kitaro made his first live tour of North America that same year and sold more than two million albums in the United States alone. This was all quite a leap for a man who was accustomed to creating music in the privacy of his home studio near Japan's Mount Fuji.

Quite naturally, Kitaro's style changed, becoming more theatrical and assertive while retaining a certain level of simplistic purity. By the early 1990s, he was showing renewed interest in the rock and pop that had originally brought him to music.

■ **"Lindy"** (Traditional)
   Grateful Dead, *Historic Dead/'66* (1973), *The History of the Grateful Dead/'66* (1972)
   Memphis Jug Band, *Double Album/'28* (1990)

JIM KWESKIN AND THE JUG BAND, **Jim Kweskin and the Jug Band (1963)**

A WARLOCKS and early Dead-show rarity, "Lindy" was derived from the Memphis Jug Band's "Lindbergh Hop," a folk celebration of Charles Lindbergh's monumental transatlantic flight.

12/1/66, The Matrix, San Francisco

■ **"Little Red Rooster"** (WILLIE DIXON)
   Willie Dixon, *I Am the Blues* (1970), *20 Blues Greats* (1987), *The Chess Box* (1988)
   Howlin' Wolf, *The Best of Howlin' Wolf* (1960), *Poor Boy* (1965), *Super Super Blues Band* (with Muddy Waters and BO DIDDLEY) (1968), *The Howlin' Wolf Album* (1969), *London Howlin' Wolf Sessions* (1970), *The Music Never Stopped: Roots of the Grateful Dead* (1995)
   Grateful Dead, *Dead Set* (1981)
   Sam Cooke, single (1963), *Sam Cooke's Night Beat* (1963), *The Rhythm and the Blues* (1995)
   The Rolling Stones, *The Rolling Stones Now* (1965), *Big Hits (High Tide & Green Grass)* (1966), *Love You Live* (1977), *Flashpoint* (1982)
   The Doors, *Live in Europe* (1968), *Alive She Cried* (1983), *In Concert* (1991)
   Luther Allison, *Love Me Mama* (1969), *Live In Paris* (1995)
   Big Mama Thornton, *Jail* (1975)
   Otis Rush, *Lost in the Blues* (1977)
   Big Joe Duskin, *Cincinnati Stomp* (1979)
   Misunderstood, *Golden Glass* (1984)
   Lucky Peterson, *Ridin'* (1984)
   Jesus and Mary Chain, *The Sound of Speed/'88* (1993)
   The Persuasions, *Right Around the Corner* (1994)
   Sugar Blue, *In Your Eyes* (1995)

The late Willie Dixon gave the best description of the roots of his oft-covered song, "Little Red Rooster," when in 1983 he told Blair Jackson, "On farms, there always seems to be an animal that has the spotlight on it—it makes trouble, chases everything, messes around, but also keeps life going. In this particular instance, it was a rooster that kept everything upset. One day, the red rooster comes up missing, nobody can find him, and they learn that the barnyard is too quiet without him. I wrote it as a barnyard song really, and some people even take it that way!

"People try to pretend that the blues have a lot of sexual things involved, and they say that's bad. I say the blues is about the facts of life. If there are things about sex, well, everything that fly, crawl, walk, or swim is involved in sex one way or another. But with a lot of songs, it's just the way people think that makes 'em see sex in everything."

One has to take Dixon's comments with a grain of salt. Certainly, he must have known that a rooster is commonly called a "cock."

"Little Red Rooster" is a vibrant and sexually charged Chicago blues no matter who the performer. Howlin' Wolf cut it first, but in whatever form the song has been fashioned, the vivid image of the "Little Red Rooster too lazy to crow for days" takes center stage.

The WARLOCKS are said to have enjoyed playing this chestnut and after bringing the provocative number back into the fold in 1980, "Little Red Rooster" served as one of Bob Weir's stable of first-set blues covers.

7/16/88, Greek Theatre, Berkeley, California

7/31/88, Laguna Seca Recreation Area, Monterey, California (with David Hidalgo)

4/2/89, Pittsburgh Civic Center, Pittsburgh

▪ "Little Sadie" (Traditional)

Charlie Poole and the North Carolina Ramblers, *Charlie Poole and the North Carolina Ramblers* (1993)

Cliff Carlise, *Old Timey 1 & 2* (1965)

Doc Watson and Clarence Ashley, *The Original Recordings of 1960–1962* (1995)

Doc Watson, *The Vangard Years* (1995)

BOB DYLAN, *Self-Portrait* (1970)

Trees, *On the Shore* (1970)

DAVID GRISMAN, *Early Dawg* (1985)

Garcia sang this old folk song of Southern lineage during a few of the Dead's 1969 and 1970 acoustic sets. It made a one-night acoustic return for the October 31, 1980, Radio City concert and the odd appearance at Garcia's acoustic shows from 1982 through 1988.

2/13/70, Fillmore East, New York

▪ "Little Star" (Bob Weir)

Weir briefly introduced this lyrical instrumental jam (a.k.a. "Bob Star") at three 1983 concerts.

4/16/83, Brendan Byrne Arena, East Rutherford, New Jersey

▪ *Live at Keystone*/Saunders, Garcia, Kahn, Vitt

Fantasy F 79002, 1973; CD reissue FCD 7701 & FCD 7701-1, FCD 7701-2. Produced by Saunders, Garcia, Kahn, Vitt.

"Finders, Keepers," "Positively 4th Street," "The Harder They Come," "IT TAKES A LOT TO LAUGH, IT TAKES A TRAIN TO CRY," "Space," "It's No Use," "THAT'S ALL RIGHT, MAMA," "My Funny Valentine," "Someday Baby," "Like a Road"

MERL SAUNDERS–organ. Jerry Garcia–electric guitar. JOHN KAHN–bass. BILL VITT–drums. DAVID GRISMAN–mandolin on "Positively 4th Street."

If anything, the funky rhythm and bluesy music this cool combo cut at a famed Frisco club in 1973 has gotten better with age. Like the best Grateful Dead concerts, it mixes many oeuvres, filtering them through the strengths of the individual musicians and the group as a whole.

The unit takes on Dylan ("Positively 4th Street" and "It Takes a Lot to Laugh"), reggae ("The Harder They Come"), jazz ("Finders, Keepers"), blues ("It's No Use"), American songbook ("My Funny Valentine"), Elvis ("That's All Right, Mama"), and even atonal music ("Space") with confidence and fluidity.

See also **Keystone Encores, Vol. 1** and **Keystone Encores, Vol. 2.**

▪ *Live/Dead*

Warner Bros. 2WS 1830, 1969. Produced by the Grateful Dead and Bob Mathews and Betty Cantor.

"Dark Star">"St. Stephen">"The Eleven">"TURN ON YOUR LOVE LIGHT," "DEATH DON'T HAVE NO MERCY," "Feedback">"AND WE BID YOU GOODNIGHT"

The early Grateful Dead at their live, blistering best. Three sides of this two-record set interweave beatific avant-garde improvisation ("Dark Star"), quirky time signatures ("St. Stephen">"The Eleven"), and down-home rhythm & blues ("Turn on Your Love Light") in a seamless medley praised as one of the Dead's finest performances.

Future Patti Smith guitarist Lenny Kaye, writing in a February 1970 *Rolling Stone*, asserted, "*Live/Dead* explains why the Dead are one of the best performing bands in America, why their music touches on ground that most other groups don't even know exists."

Waxing positive on the Dead's fourth album, Garcia

(Courtesy of Warner Bros. Records)

told Charles Reich and Jann Wenner in 1971, "It's good. It has 'Dark Star' on it, a real good version of it. We'd only recorded a *few* gigs to get that album. We were after a certain sequence to the music. In the sense of it being a serious, long composition, musically, and then a recording of it, it's *our* music at one of its really good moments."

The Dead used a sixteen-track machine to record the album at San Francisco's Avalon and Carousel Ballrooms without a mixing console, correctly assuming that the shortest path from microphone to tape would yield the cleanest recording. With that stroke of ingenuity, *Live/Dead* became the first live record ever made with sixteen-track equipment.

■ *Live! Fillmore West, 1969*/Country Joe and the Fish and Friends
Vangard VCD 139/140-2, 1996.

Twenty-seven years after the event comes one of the final concerts by a major, major-league acid-rock band of the 1960s—Country Joe and the Fish. Though the group only recorded a few albums, they created one of the era's enduring sounds.

The group's appearance in the movie *Woodstock* has ensured that their image and music found international currency but, for fans of the period, any new album adds substantially to their meager catalog.

That the finally issued album is brilliant is a very good bonus indeed. Drawing on the best of their wild psychedelic blues, *Live! Fillmore West, 1969* comprises five extended tracks followed by a typically superextended jam of over thirty-eight minutes on the melancholy melodic "Donovan's Reef" where the band is joined by Steve Miller, the Airplane's Jack Casady and Jorma Kaukonen, and the Dead's Garcia and Hart.

■ *Live '85* /Robert Hunter
Relix RRLP 2016, 1985.
"Jack Straw," "It Must Have Been the Roses," "Franklin's Tower," "Easy Wind," "Promontory Rider," "Amagamalin Street," "Boys in the Barroom," "Red Car," "Sweet Little Wheels"

A strong collection of Hunter signatures, uncommon selections, and rarities marred only by some repetitive flanger guitar effects and the exclusion of some of his chestnuts ("Box of Rain" and "Mason's Children") that made his shows so riveting at the time.

■ *Live n' Kickin'* /KINGFISH
Jet-UA JT-LA732-G, 1977 (Reissue: Accord SN 7128).
"Goodbye Your Honor," "Juke," "Mule Skinner Blues," "I Hear You Knockin'," "Hypnotize," "Jump for Joy," "Overnight Bag," "Jump Back," "Shake and Fingerpop," "Around and Around"
Bob Weir–guitar, vocals. DAVE TORBERT–bass vocals. Mathew Kelly–guitar, harp, vocals. Robby Hoddinott–lead guitar, slide. CHRIS HEROLD–drums, percussion.

In an effort to establish their own identity in the post-Weir Kingfish era, the rhythm guitarist's parts were toned down in the release of this able live album.

Commenting on why he was mixed out of certain tracks, Weir explained to David Gans in 1977 that Kingfish "wanted to establish themselves as Kingfish without me, and they only had a tape with me to work with. They couldn't erase me completely, because I was in the drum track. Otherwise, I think they would have, and covered by doing another guitar part in my register. If I was playing or singing a pivotal part, they left that in."

■ *Living with the Dead* (book)/Rock Scully with David Dalton
Little, Brown, 1996.

Though Rock Scully's "snort and tell" memoir isn't the *Jerry Dearest* Deadheads feared, it does soberly and humorously give an insider insider's glimpse of the acid-rock wars by a grunt in the trenches who lived to remember most of it . . . or was that some of it?

▪ *Living with the Dead* (audio book CD)/Rock
Scully with David Dalton
Time Warner Books 2-523717, 1995 .

One for the "Is this *really* necessary?" column, Rock Scully's book as a spoken-word release is only useful for the anal completist, the sight impaired, or the just plain frivolous.

▪ "Long Black Limousine" (George/Stovall)
Gordon Terry, *Square Dance Party* (1962)
Glen Campbell, single (1962)
Jody Miller, *The Best of Jody Miller* (1973)
Elvis Presley, *From Elvis in Memphis* (1969)
J. D. Crowe and the New South, *Somewhere Between* (1982)
Bobby Bare, *The Best of Bobby Bare* (1994)
Wynn Stewart, *California Country* (1995)

While Bobby George was stationed in the Air Force in West Germany in 1954, he overheard a wife telling her husband that she wished she was rich so she could ride in a long black limousine. The phrase stayed with him and in 1962 he and Vern Stovall wrote "Long Black Limousine," which was first recorded by Gordon Terry for RCA. Later that year Glen Campbell also recorded the song. Neither version charted. Jody Miller had the first and only chart recording of "Long Black Limousine" in 1968 when it reached No. 73 on the country chart. Elvis recorded the song in early 1969 and released it later in the year.

Weir handled this tune at five Dead shows, mostly as an acoustic set job, between December 1969 and June 1971.

6/21/71, Château d'Herouville, France

▪ *Long Live the Dead* /Billy and Terry Smith
K-Tel Records, 1996.

Considering Garcia's at-the-hip ties to bluegrass, a country-music tribute to the Dead made sense. Too bad the Smiths' innocuous acoustic versions of Grateful Dead perennials barely warrant a second listening.

Their versions of "Truckin' " and "Friend of the Devil" may go over in a coffeehouse but the bland arrangements make this release particularly painful, a half-step away from what you might expect a Muzak version of a Dead song to sound like.

▪ "Look over Yonder's Wall" (Jazz Gillum)
Jazz Gillum, single (1946)
ARTHUR "BIG BOY" CRUDUP, *Mean Ole Frisco* (1962)
Elmore James, *The Sky Is Crying*/'61 (1993)
PAUL BUTTERFIELD BLUES BAND, *Paul Butterfield Blues Band* (1965), *Monterey International Pop Festival*/'67 (1992), *Blues with a Feeling* (1993)
HARRY BELAFONTE, *Don't Stop the Carnival* (1991)
Jimmy Johnson, *I'm a Jockey* (1995)
Eddie Taylor, *Bad Boy* (1995)

The position of a partially disabled man who has not been drafted into military service but takes advantage of his station to entertain lonely married women inspired many postwar blues, and "Look over Yonder's Wall" is probably the most famous. From Jazz Gillum's imagination, if not his experience, the song has been transposed from one war to another until Vietnam and remains a Chicago blues-bar standard.

Born William McKinley Gillum September 11, 1904, in Indianapolis, Mississippi, Jazz Gillum was, next to John Lee "Sonny Boy" Williamson, the most popular and in-demand harmonica sessionman during the 1930s. As both a leader and sideman, his high, reedy sound meshed perfectly on dozens of hokum sides on the Bluebird label.

The Dead are only known to have performed "Yonder's Wall" at a couple of shows in 1966 and 1968.

10/9/68, The Matrix, San Francisco (Mickey and the Hartbeats with Paul Butterfield and Elvin Bishop)

▪ "Looks Like Rain" (Weir/Barlow)
Bob Weir, *Ace* (1972)
Grateful Dead, *Without a Net* (1990), *Dick's Picks Volume Five*/'79 (1996)

A stray-cat lullaby, "Looks Like Rain" is Weir's melancholy lament to a departed lover—the impending storm casting a bittersweet gloam over the entire mood of the song. Starting in 1972, the band utilized "Looks Like Rain" well in both sets of their concerts where some

Deadheads claim its magical effects prompted the heavens to open up and drench particularly warm outdoor summer shows with a much-needed deluge. And, typical of many Weir songs, it contains a rant that serves as much as musical theater as it does as rain dance. Weir always delivered with the song, but his sublime duets with Donna Jean Godchaux are truly airborne.

6/29/76, Auditorium Theater, Chicago
5/13/77, Auditorium Theater, Chicago
7/6/86, RFK Stadium, Washington, D.C.
10/30/90, Wembley Arena, London

- ## "Loose Lucy" (Garcia/Hunter)
Grateful Dead, single, *From the Mars Hotel* (1974)

One of the Dead's most badassed originals, "Loose Lucy" is a song from the other side of the tracks. There's not much of a story here, simply a down-and-dirty funky litany of the Job-like woes encountered by a spurned but upward-looking lover. The narrator gets laid, drunk, and mugged but still comes to the surface for more abuse.

The Dead retired "Loose Lucy" for sixteen years after its punchy debut outings in 1973 and 1974. The later versions, though essentially identical to the earlier arrangements, have a raw, metallic edge.

5/19/74, Memorial Coliseum, Portland, Oregon
1/25/93, Coliseum Arena, Oakland, California

- ## "Loser" (Garcia/Hunter)
Jerry Garcia, *Garcia* (1972)
Grateful Dead, *Dead Set* (1981)
Cracker, *Kerosene Hat* (1994)

"Loser" is one of the Dead's most quintessential testaments to desperation and chance. Transpiring over the course of a high-stakes poker game, the narrator, a broke and flim-flamming wastrel, cons some coin from the woman by his side while attempting to coax a marked card (the Queen of Diamonds) to fill an inside straight. Though it is never disclosed whether he is successful in his attempt, the cards and karma seem forever stacked against him.

As Garcia once commented about the song's subject to David Gans, "Like sometimes I sing that song 'Loser' and it's a self-congratulatory asshole. Sometimes it's an idiot. The lyrics have the guy an idiot, but the idiot's version of himself is, 'Hey, I'm great!' I can ride that either way and there's lots of shading in between where it's both

those things at the same time. I love it when a song is ambiguous like that."

Musically tinged by the country blues, the slinky "Loser" perfectly reflects the dusty, gaslit mood of the tragic stage. You can practically smell the stale cigar smoke, the cheap perfume, and the rancid beer while sitting under a flickering gaslight as a honky-tonk piano player comps in the background.

As a first-set Garcia spike, the Dead have crafted this song in concert with masterful interpretations since 1971.

12/29/77, Winterland Arena, San Francisco
7/18/82, County Fairgrounds, Ventura, California
11/2/84, Berkeley Community Theater, Berkeley, California
5/23/93, Shoreline Amphitheater, Mountain View, California

- ## "Lost Sailor" (Weir/Barlow)
Grateful Dead, *Go to Heaven* (1980)

Commonly paired with its sister song "Saint of Circumstance" in its early years of performance, "Lost Sailor" disappeared from Dead concerts by 1986. Thematically, the song fits into Weir's large song cycle of a metaphorically and, in this instance literally, lost sailor, hopeful but fruitless in his attempt to touch the shore of life. The allegories are quite clear as the boat of the subject described in the song is tossed by an unforgiving and soulless sea. The song's ever-shifting rhythms and melody also reflect the ocean's fickleness, shifting easily between dead calm and typhoon.

Filled with vivid nautical and seafaring lore, "Lost Sailor" has one lyric misheard and therefore misinterpreted by Deadheads who think the sailor in question is looking for the "Dark Star" when, in fact, the orb for which he searches is Sirius, the "Dog Star."

4/6/82, The Spectrum, Philadelphia

- ## "Louie Louie" (Richard Berry)
Richard Berry, single (1956), *12 Flip Hits* (1959), *Great Rhythm and Blues Oldies Vol. 12* (1977)
The Kingsmen, single (1963, 1964, 1981), *Louie, Louie: The Kingsmen in Person* (1964), *Louie, Louie: Greatest Hits* (1987)
Paul Revere and the Raiders, single (1963), *Here They Come!* (1965)
THE BEACH BOYS, *Shut Down Vol. 2* (1964)

Otis Redding, *Pain In My Heart* (1964)

The Kinks, *Kinksize* (1965), *Kingdom* (1966)

Standells, *The Standell's in Person at P.J.'s* (1965)

The Troggs, *From Nowhere . . . The Troggs* (1966)

Beau Brummels, *Beau Brummels '66* (1966)

Sand Pipers, *Guantanamera* (1966)

West Coast Pop Art Experimental Band, *The Legendary Unreleased Album* (1966)

Mongo Santamaria, *Hey, Let's Party* (1967)

Frank Zappa, *Uncle Meat* (1968)

Toots and the Maytalls, *Funky Kingston* (1973)

Iggy and the Stooges, *Metallic K.O.* (1976)

Flamin' Groovies, *Slow Death* (1972), *Still Shakin'* (1976)

John Belushi, *Animal House* (soundtrack) (1978)

Stanley Clarke and George Duke, *The Clarke/Duke Project* (1981)

Barry White, *Beware* (1981)

Maureen Tucker, *Playin' Possum* (1982)

Johnny Thunders, *In Cold Blood* (1983)

Motorhead, *No Remorse* (1984)

Black Flag, *Who's Got the 10 1/2* (1986)

The Cult, *Lil' Devil/Zap City* (1987)

Paul Shaffer, *Coast to Coast* (1987)

Michael Doucet, *Cajun Brew* (1988)

Iggy Pop, *American Caesar* (1993)

Various Artists, *The Best of "Louie Louie"* (Rhino Records Compilation) (1993)

Pretty Things, *A Whiter Shade of Pale* (1994)

"Duh duh duh. Duh duh. Duh duh duh. Duh duh."

A song so embedded in the western psyche that Dave Marsh wrote an entire book about the all-time garage-rock classic. Of course, Marsh's longtime antipathy towards the Grateful Dead may have precluded him from mentioning their late-1980s versions of the song, which transformed "Louie Louie' into a sexy snake dance.

"Louie Louie" has the kind of life story that rock & rollers pay publicists good money to invent and represents rock at its most sublime . . . and ridiculous. The most insistent riff in rock history, a dirty song or a bizarrely endurable hit, the song's still-mysterious (for their incomprehensibility) lyrics so excited the imagination of the FBI that J. Edgar Hoover became personally involved in investigating the rumors of its salaciousness. And who would suspect that this song whose musical substance is little more than three chords and a cloud of dust has so deeply penetrated the subconscious of a generation? More than 1,200 legitimate "Louie Louie" records exist—by artists ranging from Patti Smith and Frank Zappa to Sounds Orchestral and Julie London.

Richard Berry holds a permanent place of honor in the history of rock 'n' roll if for no other reason than that he was the original writer and performer of "Louie Louie" (itself based on "El Loca Cha Cha" by Rene Touzet). Berry was born April 11, 1935, in Extension, Louisiana, moving to California as a child and becoming an important if secondary figure of the early- and mid-1950s R&B Los Angeles area, performing and recording with the Flairs and as a solo act. He demonstrated his versatility with ballads, novelty songs, and even some Little Richard–style send-ups. His knack with deep-voiced, comic material was a clear forerunner of the Coasters and, in fact, he was the uncredited lead singer on LEIBER AND STOLLER'S "RIOT IN CELL BLOCK #9," recorded by the Robins, later to mutate into the Coasters. Berry also made an uncredited vocal appearance as Etta James's deep-voiced sparring partner on one of the biggest R&B hits of mid-1956, "Roll with Me, Henry,"

After he wrote and recorded "Louie Louie" in the late 1950s, Berry's recording career petered out, though he remained an active performer. In the early 1960s, several Northwest bands rediscovered "Louie Louie" as a cover song and scored sizable, if regional, hits. When the Kingsmen of Portland, Oregon, cut the song in 1963, it took off soaring all the way to No. 2 on the national charts.

Undoubtedly, much of the song's reputation as a "blue" codification was spawned by the garbled vocal track laid down by lead singer Jack Ely. As rumors began circulating that "Louie Louie" contained lascivious lyrics (specifically the "F-word"), the FBI and the FCC both investigated the song—going as far as slowing down the record in an attempt to decipher the words and calling on Ely and Berry to testify. When some radio stations balked at spinning the single, sales of "Louie Louie" only increased. In all, more than 12 million copies of the song have sold worldwide.

The Kingsmen disbanded five years later but had a few minor hits in that time, including "Little Latin Lupe Le" and "The Jolly Green Giant." An unsuccessful comeback attempt was made with an altered lineup in 1973.

"Louie Louie" was like a cat with nine lives, gaining increasing popularity with succeeding generations of youthful Americana, inspiring parades, all-day radiothons, and campaigns to adopt it as the official song of the State of Washington. There was a happy ending for Berry: in the late 1980s he regained the rights to his song that he had lost many years before.

The Dead are known to have performed "Louie Louie" during at least one 1966 show, but their half dozen slithery readings of the classic in the late 1980s will be fondly remembered for their shock value alone.

"Duh duh duh. Duh duh. Duh duh duh. Duh duh."

4/9/89, Freedom Hall, Louisville, Kentucky

▪ *Love in the Valley of the Moon* /Norton
Buffalo
Capitol 11625, 1977. Produced by Norton Buffalo.

Mickey Hart contributed his percussion talents to a couple of tracks on the first solo album by Norton Buffalo, a Bay Area harmonica ace who was best known for his work with Steve Miller and Commander Cody.

▪ "Love the One You're With" (Stephen
Stills)
Stephen Stills, *Stephen Stills* (1970)
Crosby, Stills, Nash and Young, *Four Way Street*
(1971)
Isley Brothers, single (1971)
Rufus, *Rufus* (1973)
THE NEVILLE BROTHERS, *Live on Planet Earth*
(1994)

Stephen Stills made a surprise two-show cameo with the Dead in 1983 and led the band through one of his most famous songs.

4/17/83, Brendan Byrne Arena, East Rutherford, New
Jersey

▪ "Lucifer's Eyes" (JOAN BAEZ)

Another Joan Baez gem performed at two of the Dead's December 1981 gigs with her, "Lucifer's Eyes" is not known to have been otherwise recorded by its composer.

12/12/81, Fiesta Hall, San Mateo, California

▪ "Lucy in the Sky with Diamonds"
(Lennon/McCartney)
The Beatles, *Sgt. Pepper's Lonely Hearts Club Band*
(1967)
Elton John, single (1974)

Contrary to psychedelic legend, the inspiration for "Lucy in the Sky with Diamonds" came from Julian Lennon. When the four-year-old returned home from nursery school with a painting, his father, John Lennon, asked what he had depicted, Julian answered, "It's Lucy in the sky with diamonds."

But since the song's primary initials coincide with those of the drug LSD, which was at its controversial apex at the time of the song's release, several radio stations banned the record, concerned that it was advocating use of the drug.

While Lennon had previously admitted taking "the sacrament," it was his early love of Lewis Carroll's *Alice in Wonderland* books that were at least an equal source for the song's admittedly trippy lyrics.

Paul McCartney confirmed this when he later recalled the song's composition. "We did the whole thing like an *Alice in Wonderland* idea, being in a boat on the river, slowly drifting downstream and those great cellophane flowers towering over your head. Every so often it broke off and you saw 'Lucy in the Sky with Diamonds' all over the sky. This Lucy was God, the big figure, the white rabbit. You can just write a song with imagination on words and that's what we like."

Despite the song's enduring popularity, Lennon was never really satisfied with the Beatles' version asserting that the group didn't play well on the *Sgt. Pepper's Lonely Hearts Club Band* cut. However, Lennon dug Elton John's cover of "Lucy in the Sky with Diamonds"—once even agreeing to play guitar and sing backing vocals with Elton at New York's Madison Square Garden.

Vince Welnick brought this late addition to the Dead's repertoire to the band and established it as a quick crowd favorite in 1994.

5/23/93, Shoreline Amphitheater, Mountain View,
California

M

(Courtesy of Verve Records)

■ **"Mack the Knife"** (Blitzestein/Brecht/Weill)

Lotte Lenya and Bruckner-Ruggberg Orchestra,
   Threepenny Opera (1928)
Louis Armstrong, *Singin' 'n' Playin'* (1959)
Bobby Darin, single (1959), *The Ultimate Bobby Darin*
   (1988), *Mack the Knife* (1991)
Ella Fitzgerald, *Live in Berlin* (1960)
Duke Ellington, *New Mood Indigo* (1964)
Liberace, *Best of Liberace* (1972)
Secret Affair, *Business as Usual* (1982)

Frank Sinatra, *L.A. Is My Lady* (1984)
Sting, *Lost in the Stars: The Music of Kurt Weill* (1985)
Psychedelic Furs, single (1987)
Mario Bauza, *My Time Is Now* (1993)

The sole, raggedy-ass Grateful Dead cover of this cherished piece of business from *Threepenny Opera* is redeemed only by its high-camp fudge factor when the band killed some time early in a 1981 show because the equipment gremlins caused a delay in the usual proceedings.

"Mack the Knife" was composed by Germany's Kurt Weill who relentlessly searched for music and words that would directly affect and address his contemporaries. With the poet Bertolt Brecht, Weill had a big hit with the *Threepenny Opera* in 1927 in representing Berlin's society onstage and mirroring it back on itself. In doing this, they invented what has been called the "educational opera" and took political satire to a peak that has rarely been rivaled. With music based on the style of the cabaret theater, developing a richness never heard before and with modern harmonies and progressions that anticipated the freedom of bebop by a generation, Weill and Brecht left a legacy for the ages and the sages.

Weill eventually fled Germany when the Nazis burned his music and attacked his publishing house but he landed on his feet in the United States, becoming one of Broadway's most popular composers and paving the way for the likes of Leonard Bernstein and *West Side Story*.

"Mack the Knife" is without a doubt Brecht and Weill's most popular composition and, in the words of critic Peter Keepnews, "has found its way into the act of practically every lounge singer in America (no small feat for a song celebrating the exploits of a cold-blooded killer)."

For a sure-bet life-altering experience, the interested listener should make a bee-line to Ella Fitzgerald's live version recorded in Berlin during the mid-1960s. Fasten seatbelts and put on your oxygen masks!

11/30/81, Hara Arena, Dayton, Ohio

▪ "Maggie's Farm" (BOB DYLAN)
Bob Dylan, *Bringing It All Back Home* (1965), *Bob Dylan's Greatest Hits, Vol. 2* (1971), *Hard Rain* (1976), *At Budokan* (1978), *Real Live* (1984)
Specials, *The Singles Collection/'75* (1991)
Hot Tuna, *Live at Sweetwater* (1992)

When Bob Dylan upped the ante on rock music by plugging in his electric guitar at the 1965 Newport Folk Festival, he began his earth-shattering set with "Maggie's Farm." Because of that single event it has become perhaps his most personal protest song, one that he has returned to and reinvented many times.

In '65 Dylan wasn't going to continue being simply a gifted folkie playing for a select, and sanctimoniously purist, circle. In 1976, his Rolling Thunder Revue medicine show barnstormed the country and flew in the face of conventional rock touring. Even in 1978, when he transformed his catalogue into a glitz-fest complete with Vegas-influenced arrangements and an Elvis-inspired big band behind him, "Maggie's Farm" was still front and center confounding the most die-hard Dylan fans. In 1984, on the heels of his well-received *Infidels* album, which even his toughest critics begrudgingly hailed as yet another comeback success, the song was again recast as a smirking rock rave.

Throughout, "Maggie's Farm" was a symbol for Dylan's highly static, oil-and-water, right-angular career. He wasn't about to work on Maggie's Farm or fulfill any of the expectations of his audience, his management, or the corporate interests behind him not because he hasn't wanted to but because he couldn't even if he did want to. He has simply never been that kind of artist.

Despite its many incarnations in Dylan's storied and stormy career, it was never cast as a bluegrass vehicle. Yet the Grateful Dead's version of "Maggie's Farm" (with

and without Dylan) owes more to that oeuvre than any other. The Dead's arrangement, which sounds remarkably like their own blue-collar testament "Cumberland Blues," was first worked up for their 1987 shows with Dylan but continued to get an airing out several times a year after that. The Dead's version is also notable because it was one of their few songs in which Garcia, Lesh, Weir, and the keyboardist alternated on the vocal leads.

Appropriately, the Dead performed the song during their 1987 appearance on the Farm Aid III television simulcast.

7/19/87, Autzen Stadium, Eugene, Oregon (with Bob Dylan)
1/25/93, Oakland Coliseum, Oakland, California

▪ "The Main Ten (Playing in the Band)" (Mickey Hart)
Mickey Hart, *Rolling Thunder* (1972)

"The Main Ten" is an alternate title for the Grateful Dead anthem, "Playing in the Band." It appeared with this title, referencing the number of beats in the song's time signature on Mickey Hart's debut solo album and was performed, lyricless, at five Dead shows in 1969 and 1970.

11/8/69, Fillmore Auditorium, San Francisco
See also **"Playing in the Band"**

▪ *The Making of the "Touch of Grey" Video* (film)
Directed by Justin Kreutzmann; produced by Debra Robina and Justin Kreutzmann. 1987.

An all-access pass to a film set that gives new meaning to the term "skeleton crew," *The Making of the "Touch of Grey" Video* takes the viewer on location for the shooting of the first-ever Grateful Dead video.

Justin Kreutzmann, drummer Bill Kreutzmann's son, gives a behind-the-scenes look at the intricate machinations that went into creating the Dead's popular video, which skillfully interspersed the excitement of a live Dead show with footage depicting eerily accurate "Dead Ringers" standing in for the band.

The film was a surprise top-seller when released on videocassette and includes the entire, unedited version of the *Touch of Grey* video.

▪ "Mama Tried" (MERLE HAGGARD)
Merle Haggard, *Okie from Muskogee* (1970)

Grateful Dead, *Grateful Dead* (1971), *Dick's Picks Volume Six*/'83 (1996)

The Everly Brothers, *The Everly Brothers Show* (1970)

Merle Haggard never served "life without parole" as the chorus of "Mama Tried" attests. But he has lived a troubled life with his share of run-ins with the law and his songs reflect that hardbitten ethos.

Weir began singing "Mama Tried" as one of his first-set cowboy songs in 1969 and it represents one of the Dead's most often-performed songs.

7/31/71, Yale Bowl, New Haven, Connecticut

6/11/76, Boston Music Hall, Boston

12/28/79, Oakland Auditorium Arena, Oakland, California

6/17/92, Coliseum, Charlotte, North Carolina

■ *Manhole*/Grace Slick
Grunt BFL 1-0347, 1974.

Robert Hunter contributed the lyrics and David Freiberg the music to "It's Only Music," on this Grace Slick solo effort. According to Hunter's notes in *A Box of Rain*, "It's Only Music" was "set to the same changes as 'I Heard You Singing,' which appears on both *Tales of the Great Rum Runners* and Quicksilver's final album, *Solid Silver*. Freiberg and I got value for money out of these flexible changes."

■ "Mannish Boy" (a.k.a. "I'm a Man")
(London/Morganfield/ McDaniels)
BO DIDDLEY, **single (1955),** *Roadrunner* **(1964),** *Hey . . . Bo Diddley in Concert* **(1986)**

The Who, *My Generation* (1965), *Who's Missing*/'65 (1987)

Muddy Waters, *The Real Folk Blues* (1966), *Hard Again* (1977), *Muddy Mississippi Waters Live* (1979), *Risky Business* soundtrack (1984)

THE BAND with Muddy Waters, *The Last Waltz*/'76 (1978)

The Yardbirds, *The Yardbirds Featuring Eric Clapton* (1964), *Five Live Yardbirds* (1965), *For Your Love* (1965), *Having a Rave Up* (1965), *Live Yardbirds Featuring Jimmy Page* (1968), *The Very Best of the Yardbirds* (1991)

Jimi Hendrix and Curtis Knight, *Flashing* (1967)

Jimi Hendrix, *Birth of Success*/'64 (1970), *Live & Unreleased*/'67 (1989)

Yellow Payges, *Yellow Payges* (1968)

The Rolling Stones, *Love You Live* (1977)

Paul Butterfield, *The Legendary Paul Butterfield Rides Again* (1986)

WILLIE DIXON, *20 Blues Greats* (1987)

Iggy and the Stooges, *Death Trip*/'73 (1987)

Hank Williams Jr., *The Bocephus Box* (1992)

Inspired by the "Hoochie Coochie Man" of Willie Dixon and Muddy Waters, Bo Diddley cut his first sides and made his first mark with "I'm a Man." Waters responded immediately with "Mannish Boy." Both cuts inspired more than one hundred covers of the two similar blues, proclaiming (among other things) the sexual feats of their authors.

The Dead's only known version was inspired by Diddley and their impromptu set with him in 1972.

3/25/72, Academy of Music, New York

■ "Man of Peace" (BOB DYLAN)
Bob Dylan, *Infidels* (1983)

After three gospel-infused albums in as many years, Dylan's zealous embrace of born again Christianity began to wane in 1982. When he returned to the studio a year later, he seemed intent on making a first-rate record and, working with Mark Knopfler of Dire Straits, who had produced *Slow Train Coming*, Dylan did just that.

But CBS got behind the new album, *Infidels*, as they hadn't for any other Dylan effort in years, hoping to signify a comeback for the singer/songwriter whose reputation had suffered because of his religious presentation.

Ironically, *Infidels* seemed to herald Dylan's move towards Orthodox Judaism. A photograph on the album sleeve shows Dylan touching soil on a mountaintop overlooking Jerusalem. Naturally, speculation was renewed that he was re-exploring his Jewish roots, although it has been suggested that it might have been site inspection for William Blake's New Jerusalem that was being portrayed in the photograph and on the vinyl.

In fact, Dylan had devoted considerable time in 1983 at Chabad Lubavitch, the Brooklyn, New York–based Hasidic sect that incorporates music as a central aspect of its rituals and group life. Concurrently, he was photographed wearing a yarmulke and prayer shawl at the bar mitzvah of his son Jesse at the Wailing Wall in Jerusalem's Old City.

But, as if to downplay his interest in any singular system or ideology, Dylan was ever ready to confuse his true stance by saying that "all these political and religious labels are irrelevant." At the same time he referred to the born-again phase as "part of my experience. When I get involved in something, I get totally involved. I don't just play around."

Regardless of the master's deft ability to be pinned down, with *Infidels* he was once again seen as a social diagnostician of America's failing spiritual health. The *New York Times* said the album's "incendiary political rants, quasi-biblical tirades and surreal love songs capture the apocalyptic mood of the moment with shuddering immediacy."

Of all the songs on *Infidels*, the one that finds Dylan still in high-stump preacher mode spewing fire, brimstone, and maybe a touch of cock & bull (as well as rock & roll) is his bluesy, finger-pointer "Man of Peace." And if the lyrics of the song are unimaginative, Dylan's singing is daring and caustic. In "Man of Peace," Dylan warns of Satan's many disguises, from thief and joker to the chief of police and the Führer.

"Man of Peace," though performed well at three of the Dylan/Dead shows in '87, never made it past that brief collaboration and into the Dead's regular concert repertoire. Too bad, as Garcia would have done well by it.

7/4/87, Sullivan Stadium, Foxboro, Massachusetts (with Bob Dylan)

■ "Man Smart, Woman Smarter" (Norman Span and King Radio or David Miller, a.k.a. D. Klieber)

The Brute Force Steel Band, *Music to Awaken the Ballroom Beast* (1950s)

HARRY BELAFONTE, *Calypso* (1956), *All the Greatest Hits, Vol. 2* (1987)

Robert Palmer, *Some People Can Do What They Like* (1976)

Rosanne Cash, *Right or Wrong* (1973)

The Carpenters, *Passage* (1977)

C. J. Chenier, *Too Much Fun* (1995)

Harry Belafonte's 1956 *Calypso* was wildly popular and was one of the earliest Caribbean-influenced records to make broad inroads in the United States. "Man Smart, Woman Smarter," one of the album's standout tunes, contains some proto-feminist sentiments that surely won the hearts of female Deadheads and is a nice counter to the few Dead tunes that have been interpreted or misinterpreted as being chauvinist.

Belafonte probably learned the tune from Antigua's Brute Force Steel Band's peppy instrumental on their Cook Records album, *Music to Awaken the Ballroom Beast*. Calypso is generally associated with Jamaica but is thought to have been refined on Trinidad before it reached Jamaica. Dating in its crudest form to the late eighteenth century, calypso is still found on most Caribbean islands.

The Dead's version is quite different from Belafonte's in its emphasis on rhythm and a truncation of the lyrics. Belafonte sings "Man Smart, Women Smarter"—as he does everything on the record—with a rich brogue, and includes many verses not found in the Dead's. As such, Belafonte's rendition relies more on the song's story, which involves a romance and the birth of a child that may or may not be the narrator's. Brent Mydland and Bob Weir handled the lead vocals on the song commencing in 1981, duties taken over solely by Weir after Mydland's death in 1990. The Dead performed nearly two hundred versions of the song.

7/2/81, The Summit, Houston

9/11/85, Henry J. Kaiser Convention Center, Oakland, California

7/15/88, Greek Theatre, Berkeley, California

■ *Marrying Maiden*/It's a Beautiful Day

Columbia CS 1058, 1970. Produced by Brent Dangerfield.

Marrying Maiden makes a game effort at rekindling the spark found on the debut disc of the early San Francisco psychedelic band It's a Beautiful Day, helped along by Garcia's banjo on "Hoedown" and his pedal steel on "It Comes Right Down to You."

■ Branford Marsalis

Born August 26, 1960, Breaux Bridge, Louisiana

Late in their career the Grateful Dead had the opportunity to invite four excellent saxophonists to perform with them. But while their unions with Clarence Clemons, ORNETTE COLEMAN, and DAVID MURRAY resulted in fine textural meldings of reedman and ensemble, it was their five concerts with tenor saxophonist Branford Marsalis in the 1990s that brought the music to unmatched heights, perhaps defining true "acid jazz" once and for all.

As a member of jazz's best-known family, Branford Marsalis's first instrument was alto sax, and it was on that instrument that he won a spot in that venerable spawning ground for would-be greats in 1981: Art Blakey's Jazz Messengers. But within a year he joined his brother Wynton's band and switched (a la Coltrane) to tenor and soprano. The group's extensive national and international tours through 1985 won critical plaudits and commercial fanfare.

Marsalis eased out of his brother's band and began leading his own unit while also touring and collaborating with Sting (gaining his brother's temporary ire) on a string of albums: *The Dream of the Blue Turtles*, *Bring on the Night*, *Nothing Like the Sun* and *The Soul Cages*.

To all his endeavors, including his year-long stint as the leader of the new *Tonight Show* band, Marsalis brought his swooping, huge tone, supple phrasing, and witty licks (with links to Wayne Shorter, Sonny Rollins, Coleman Hawkins, and Ben Webster) while developing his own voice.

All of his considerable powers were at full force during the five concerts at which he appeared with the Grateful Dead. The match was so good that the Dead saw fit to include the second song they ever played together ("Eyes of the World") on their *Without a Net* release. Thereafter, Marsalis's appearances with the Dead were concert-long affairs and demonstrated his comfort with everything from Dylan to "Dark Star."

Describing Marsalis's March 29, 1990, Grateful Dead baptism at the Nassau Coliseum, Eric Pooley wrote in *New York* Magazine, "The band began the simple, undulating melody of a 1971 Garcia tune called 'Birdsong,' and the guitarist started to play genial host to the jazzman. Smiling above his white beard, Garcia danced a little shuffle, guided Marsalis through the changes, and gave him some room to play. Soon Marsalis's soprano sax and Garcia's bell-like guitar were somersaulting through the upper reaches of the audible spectrum—trading licks, chiming together—while Lesh's bass lines bounded around in the depths. The entire band seemed galvanized by Marsalis's presence, and the crowd—even those who had, like, no idea who the dude with the horn *was*—settled down for a night of exploration."

Lesh discussed his indirect influence on Marsalis's first collaboration with the Dead in 1990 with Blair Jackson. "I've been a fan of his for some time. I heard him and his brother when they were playing with Art Blakey, and I've sort of followed both of their careers, separately and together," Lesh said. "We were going to

connect in Albany originally, but that didn't work out because he was leaving the stage there around the same time we were. So when we got to New York we told him to come on over. Then the next day we found out he wanted to bring his horn! I was totally surprised. 'Branford wants to play with *us*? Great!'"

His union with the Dead also led to collaborations with BRUCE HORNSBY, including an interesting gig indeed: performing "The Star-Spangled Banner" at the 1992 NBA All-Star game.

True to the classy economy of his music and heart, Marsalis had this to say upon Garcia's passing: "There is not a sentence in the world that could respectfully do justice to the life and music of Jerry Garcia."

▪ Jim Marshall
Born 1936

Photographer Jim Marshall could be as outspoken as many of his subjects. In the introduction to *Shooting Stars*, his seminal 1973 photography tome, Marshall said: "Photographers are on the lowest fucking rung on whatever levels there are in the music business. They're the first ones someone tries to hassle on any level. And the people who hassle you the hardest are the first ones to ask for your photographs too—usually for free."

Since the early 1960s, Marshall's photographs have been the most in-demand and valued images of the counterculture.

David Gahr, one of Marshall's most accomplished peers, said that Marshall "is the best live music photographer this country has ever seen."

Born in Chicago and raised in San Francisco's Fillmore district, Marshall photographed the world's preeminent jazz, country, folk, blues, and rock musicians, as well as such bohemian notables as Allen Ginsberg, Lenny Bruce, and Lord Buckley. A history of modern music, Marshall's sensitive portraits and performance shots perfectly captured the spirit of each subject.

Marshall's foray into photography began in 1960 when he put a down payment on his first Leica MS, hung out in the North Beach coffeehouses, meeting and shooting jazz legends Thelonious Monk and John Coltrane. Within two years, Marshall relocated to New York's Greenwich Village at the peak of the folk music craze, photographically documenting the club scene, recording sessions, and the streets.

Garnering album cover work from many record companies and with over 500 to his credit, Marshall also worked for individual artists such as Bob Dylan and took occasional assignments for the likes of *LOOK* and the *Saturday Evening Post*.

By the middle of the decade, Marshall was back in San Francisco as an established photographer. He later commented on the move, saying, "The timing was unbelievable on my part. I was just in two places at the right times—there with my camera."

It was a shrewd decision. By 1965, all the world's musical attention had turned to rock and San Francisco was the music's mecca. Marshall gained the trust of the local bands, including the Grateful Dead, and they all wanted his pictures. Bill Graham, the late impresario and venue owner, was so impressed with Marshall's work that he gave the photographer unlimited stage access.

The only lensman granted backstage access at what was the Beatles' last United States gig (at San Francisco's Candlestick Park in 1966), Marshall went on to be named the chief photographer at Monterey Pop, Woodstock, and the 1972 Rolling Stones tour.

There are many who claim that any frame on any contact sheet by Jim Marshall is superior to the best print of some of his colleagues. The immense evidence includes current and departed musical heroes such as Santana, Joan Baez, Jimi Hendrix, Janis Joplin, Miles Davis, Duane Allman, and, of course, the Dead.

Putting his art in context, Marshall said, "Too much bullshit is written about photographs and music. Let the photograph be the one you remember . . . let it become part of your life—a part of your past to help you shape your future. But most of all, let the music and the photograph be something you love and will always enjoy."

Mars Hotel

See Grateful Dead from the Mars Hotel

"Mason's Children" (Garcia/Hunter)
Grateful Dead, *Dick's Picks Volume Four*/'70 (1996)
Living Earth, *Living Earth* (1988)
HENRY KAISER, *THOSE WHO KNOW HISTORY ARE DOOMED TO REPEAT IT* (1988), *ETERNITY BLUE* (1995)

A tapers' favorite and a *Workingman's Dead* outtake, "Mason's Children" was long thought by many Deadheads to be an allegorical treatment of the plight of Ken Kesey and the Merry Pranksters and the Dead's relation-

ship with them. But, according to Hunter's notes in *A Box of Rain*, the song was "dealing obliquely with Altamont."

Garcia said to Blair Jackson in 1986; "'Mason's Children' was an *almost* song. I guess it's got a famous underground reputation, but really it never quite collected itself into a song. I never was that happy with the lyrics."

The song was only played a handful of times by the Grateful Dead in 1969 and 1970 but was successfully revived on disc and in concert by one their best interpreters, avant-garde guitarist Henry Kaiser.
12/28/69, International Speedway, Hollywood, Florida
1/10/70, Golden Hall, Community Concourse, San Diego
2/14/70, Fillmore East, New York (*Dick's Picks Volume Four*)

"Matilda" (H. Thomas/Belafonte/M. Thomas)
HARRY BELAFONTE, *Belafonte at Carnegie Hall* (1959), *Belafonte '89* (1989)
Bolivor, *Yellow Bird* (1991)

Garcia worked this jaunty Caribbean skip, a little, lilting love plea, into a few second sets in 1994 and 1995.
3/29/95, Omni, Atlanta, Georgia

"Maybe You Know" (Brent Mydland)

Mydland introduced this jilted lover's lament at five April 1983 shows and that's where it stayed until exactly three years later when it reappeared for a surprise second-set swan song.
4/20/83, Providence Civic Center, Providence, Rhode Island

Ron "Pigpen" McKernan
Born September 8, 1945, San Bruno, California; died March 8, 1973, Corte Madera, California

Anyone who had the experience of seeing Ron "Pigpen" McKernan rise from his Hammond B-3 organ, swagger across the stage, heroically pull himself up to the microphone and commence belting a torrid "TURN ON YOUR LOVE LIGHT" while the band percolated behind him will likely take that fearsome, show-stopping, jaw-dropping sight to the grave—the tie-dye memories slowly fading to sepia.

Pigpen *was* scary. Easily the most frightening looking member of a gruesome looking crew with his shitkicker motorcycle boots, buck knife, and lethal key chains

Ron "Pigpen" McKernan, New York City, 1967. *(The New York Public Library for the Performing Arts)*

swinging from his belt buckle, frayed denim jacket perched on his broad shoulders, a pirate's bandana wrapped casually around his bearded head, a clutch of geraniums sprouting just so from behind his ear, and various hoodoo charms scattered across his burly frame, Pigpen was a vision and a half to behold—as perfect a creation as Michaelangelo's David. There could only be one of them.

But belying that tougher than tough exterior was a tender soul with a heart of gold, whose role in the formation of the Grateful Dead was key—the grounding, soulful force in an outfit always threatening to spin off its axis.

Pigpen had the blues in his blood. His father, Phil McKernan, was a Berkeley DJ from the mid-1940s to the mid-1950s who spun hep 78 rpm discs under the colorful moniker Cool Breeze. With his father's huge record collection always handy, the young Ron spent countless hours absorbing the likes of LIGHTNIN' HOPKINS, Big Joe Turner, and the Coasters. His family's move to Palo Alto's eastern fringes, a working class, checkerboard community not to be confused with the pristine environs

associated with Stanford University, was also important in informing McKernan's worldview as he moved easily between an ever-widening group of friends, both black and white.

By the time he met Jerry Garcia at age fourteen, he had cultivated his biker image, developed a taste for cheap wine, groomed himself for high school expulsion, become expert in the blues, and picked up the rudiments of blues piano and guitar. When he took up the harmonica, he became known as "Blue Ron" in the black community but was soon christened "Pigpen" after the equally scruffy character in Charles Schulz's *Peanuts* comic strip.

Hanging around and jamming at parties and Peninsula coffeehouses with Garcia, Robert Hunter, DAVID NELSON, Jorma Kaukonen, and Jack Casady, Pigpen became a local attraction with his LIGHTNIN' HOPKINS style and ability to improvise blues lyrics to order. As the jugband craze was dying out, it was Pigpen who pushed Garcia into forming an electric band modeled after the Rolling Stones. Through the primordial stages of the Grateful Dead, from MOTHER MCCREE'S UPTOWN JUG CHAMPIONS and the ZODIACS to the WARLOCKS, Pigpen was there with his bag of blues and R&B covers: Elmore James's "IT HURTS ME TOO," Junior Parker's "NEXT TIME YOU SEE ME," Lightnin' Hopkins's "AIN'T IT CRAZY," and marathon versions of "MIDNIGHT HOUR" that found Pigpen in high-stump preacher mode with salty raps mixing James Brown, Wilson Pickett, Otis Redding, W. C. Fields, and Lord Buckley.

The early years of the Grateful Dead were easily their most blues-based and Pigpen was omnipresent and, in many respects, the leader of the band, who was making sure promoters came forth with payment after a gig and dealing with the nuts and bolts of the operation when the others were too far gone in the psychedelic ozone to care. A sizable chunk of the crowd in the first few years was always comprised of those who came to see Pigpen and his backup band.

In his 1984 conversation with David Gans, Mickey Hart fondly recalled his old friend: "Pigpen was the *musician* in the Grateful Dead. When I first met the Grateful Dead, it was Pigpen and the boys. It was a blues band, and Pigpen played blues harp."

On the Dead's eponymous debut album, Pigpen's solid organ playing and stomping sendup of Sonny Boy Williamson's "GOOD MORNING LITTLE SCHOOLGIRL" showcased both his and the Dead's ability to explore and develop a solid groove. Pigpen was never a stellar key-board player yet his raw funk did help establish the band's earliest sound. When he retired his Vox organ in favor of the warmer Hammond B-3, his instrumental work took on a richness and soulfulness injected into tunes such as "DEATH DON'T HAVE NO MERCY."

It was as the first album was making the rounds that the Dead began performing "Alligator," Pigpen's first collaboration with Robert Hunter, which developed into a tour de force for musicians and vocalist alike. A true hero of the Haight, Pigpen was the Dead's ace in the hole, the guy whose stage persona carried such a wallop and who could always be counted on to get the crowd off. But Pigpen is remembered as a reluctant performer, one who needed immense prodding (from both his cohorts and the bottle) before taking the stage. Additionally, it is questionable how effective a performer he would have been as the Grateful Dead juggernaut rolled into the sta-dium era as his one-on-one, mind-touching soul man vi-brations might have been lost before crowds of seventy thousand. But at the old Fillmores and small theaters across the land which the Dead frequented in the late 1960s and early 1970s, Ron McKernan was the Holy See of psychedelic blues vocals. With his cocksure de-livery, words tumbling out of the corner of his mouth, a well-worn hat perched just so as he stopped the show with another testifyin' "Love Light," Pigpen added an el-ement of real danger to the Dead's already ugly and rough-hewn, though relatively flowery, presence.

As Hart recalled, "He'd get down on his knee, and he'd bring that audience right up. He'd talk right to ya, you know. He *played*, so hard."

But when Mickey Hart and Tom Constanten joined the group in the late 1960s, stretching the music to places and spaces unknown, Pigpen's role in the Dead diminished somewhat, evidenced by his lack of involve-ment in the *Aoxomoxoa* project. This was music that re-quired rehearsal, never one of Pigpen's stronger suits, and an appreciation for the avant-garde, which, given his penchant for roots music, was never exactly his cup of tea either. Socially, Pigpen set himself somewhat apart from the rest of the band as well. Even when the band was living communally at 710 Ashbury Street, Pigpen enjoyed entertaining his own coterie that included Hell's Angels, blues musicians, and barflies.

As a septet, the Dead's music burned on all cylinders, but never so brightly as when Pigpen delivered his greatest versions of "Turn on Your Love Light" or some

of the newer tunes he was adding to his arsenal: Otis Redding's "HARD TO HANDLE," the Rascals' "GOOD LOVIN'," Howlin' Wolf's "SMOKESTACK LIGHTNING," or Robert Hunter's boisterous "Easy Wind."

The Dead's turn to acoustic performance after the release of *Workingman's Dead* in 1970 gave Pigpen a chance to trot out Lightnin' Hopkins's "KATIE MAE" as a solo, dobro vehicle. An added treat in the electric sets that year was his cover of James Brown's brooding "IT'S A MAN'S, MAN'S, MAN'S WORLD" in the band's electric sets.

Pigpen's drinking was finally catching up with him and even though he didn't touch alcohol for the last year and a half of his life, his liver disease continued its cruel progression, forcing him to cut down on touring. Despite his dwindling presence at Dead shows, Pigpen contin-ued to contribute material that fit well with the band's changing repertoire. Pigpen showed off "Chinatown Shuffle," a Hunteresque rumba, and "Two Souls in Com-munion," a dark ballad, on the Dead's Europe '72 Tour, which turned out to be the bluesman's last road trip. With Keith and Donna Godchaux now firmly on board, the die was pretty much cast for at least a temporarily Pigpen-less Grateful Dead.

Mickey Hart again revealed how Pigpen's life and art would ultimately contribute to his downfall. "He was the blues; he lived it and he believed it and he got caught in that web and couldn't break out. And it killed him. He was just living the blues life, you know. Singin' the blues and drinkin' whiskey. That's what all those blues guys did. That went along with the blues."

While the band resumed their heavy performance schedule upon returning home in the summer of 1972, Pigpen settled in to put together an album of solo mate-rial. But the European adventure had had a deleterious effect on his health and he began to slowly fade away. Completely alone and unable to travel, Pigpen seemed resigned to death. Going to the piano, he sat down and composed a few tunes. "Bluebird gonna fly/blackbird gonna fly" he repeated over and over with tears in his eyes. Feeling tired, he turned in for a nap but never woke up.

Perhaps Phil Lesh articulated the sympathies of Deadheads everywhere when he said, "If I could have one wish in the world, it would be that Pigpen was still with us. I think it's safe to say we *all* miss Pigpen."

Fittingly the greatest testimony to the fallen icon is his grave marker at Alta Mesa Memorial in Palo Alto, which reads: "Pigpen Was and Is Now Forever One of the Grateful Dead."

▪ "Me and Bobby McGee" (Kris

Kristofferson/Fred L. Foster)

Kris Kristofferson, *Kristofferson* (1970), *Me and Bobby McGee* (reissue) (1971)

Grateful Dead, *Grateful Dead* [Skull and Roses] (1971)

Roger Miller, *King of the Road/'69* (1992)

Gordon Lightfoot, *The Best of Gordon Lightfoot* (1981)

JANIS JOPLIN, *Pearl* (1971), *Janis Joplin's Greatest Hits* (1973)

Bill Haley and His Comets, *Rock Around the Country* (1971)

Jerry Lee Lewis, *The "Killer" Rocks On* (1972), *Live* (1989)

Willie Nelson, *Sings Kris Kristofferson* (1979)

Waylon Jennings & Willie Nelson, *Waylon and Willie* (1978)

RAMBLIN' JACK ELLIOTT, *Me and Bobby McGee* (1996)

The Dead sometimes enjoyed breaking out tunes that were enjoying widespread popularity at the time and, for a spell in the early 1970s, "Me and Bobby McGee" was one of their most endearing. Weir sang "Me and Bobby McGee" as one of his country numbers for the night, keeping its reading closer to Kristofferson's tender original than Janis Joplin's better-known, posthumously released, barrelhouse arrangement.

Kris Kristofferson, a Rhodes Scholar, groundbreaking country music legend, film star, and political activist, has cut a large swath since his birth (June 22, 1936 in Brownsville, Texas). Since he was the son of a two-star general, Kristofferson's childhood was that of a typical army brat, moving from place to place in a pat-

Kris Kristofferson in a 1972 publicity shot from the film *Cisco Pike.* *(ARCHIVE PHOTOS)*

tern that probably contributed to the disjointed feelings about life that he often addresses in his songs.

Spending some of his boyhood in the South, Kristofferson gained an affinity for country music, but his early inclinations were more literary than musical. His intellectual and athletic skills served him well at Pomona College in Claremont, California, where he received a Rhodes Scholarship to Oxford University in England in the late 1950s, most likely the only country music star to gain admittance to that esteemed institution. Renamed Kris Carson and marketed unsuccessfully as a "genuine American rock & roller" by the shameless pop impresario Larry Parnes, Kristofferson became disgusted with the business, returned to the United States in 1960 and joined the army for a five-year hitch spent mostly in Europe.

While sweeping the floors as a custodian at Nashville's Columbia Records studio upon his discharge, Kristofferson became a pilot, flying crews to oil rigs in the Gulf of Mexico.

Commenting on the genesis of "Me and Bobby McGee," Kristofferson remembered, "I had just gone to work for Combine Music. Fred Foster, the owner, called me in and said, 'I've got a title for you: "Me and Bobby McKee."' Bobby was a secretary in Boudleaux Bryant's office, but I thought he said, 'McGee.' He said, 'How's that grab you?' I said, 'How's what grab me?' Foster said, 'The song title. Go write it.' I thought there was no way I could ever write that, and it took me months of hiding from him. One day I was driving between Morgan City and New Orleans. It was raining and the windshield wipers were going. I started coming out with Baton Rouge and other places I was working at the time. I took an old experience with another girl in another country. I had it finished by the time I got to Nashville. That song probably turned more audiences on to me than any other song I ever had."

He was just about take a construction job when Roger Miller recorded "Me and Bobby McGee" to finally put Kristofferson on the map. Within a year, Johnny Cash pushed him onstage at the Newport Folk Festival, which led to a recording deal with Foster. That same year, Sammi Smith had a big hit with his "Help Me Make It Through the Night," an unusually forthright love song for the era. But it was Janis Joplin's version of "Bobby McGee," recorded just before her tragic death in 1971, that helped catapult Kristofferson into pop stardom.

With his five-year marriage to folk-pop warbler Rita Coolidge, Kristofferson took on the trappings of a leftist folk hero campaigning eloquently for progressive causes. Though he became increasingly absorbed with a film career that kept him on location (*Pat Garrett and Billy the Kid* in 1974, the notorious bomb *Heaven's Gate* in 1981, and John Sayles's highly acclaimed *Lone Star* in 1996 are three of his more notable efforts), Kristofferson returned to singer/songwriting and recording in the mid-1980s with releases that included superior collections of bitter songs about contemporary America.

12/15/71, Hill Auditorium, Ann Arbor, Michigan

▪ "Me & My Uncle" (John Phillips)

Grateful Dead, *Grateful Dead* [Skull and Roses] (1971), *What a Long Strange Trip It's Been* (1977), *Hundred Year Hall/'72* (1995), *Dick's Picks Volume Four/'70* (1996), *Dick's Picks Volume Five/'79* (1996), *Dick's Picks Volume Seven/'74* (1997)
Judy Collins, *The Judy Collins Concert Album* (1964)

It may surprise even the hardest core Deadhead to discover that the Grateful Dead performed "Me & My Uncle" more than any single song in their vast repertoire. But "Me & My Uncle," a B movie cowboy Bob Weir cover about a cunning but sympathetic double-dealer, was firmly enshrined in the Dead's set list as early as 1966.

John Phillips of the Mamas and the Papas takes the songwriting credit for "Me & My Uncle" but apparently never recorded it himself. Weir said he learned the song from "a hippie named Curly Jim" who may have been Curly Jim Cook of A.B. Skhy, a long-gone Bay Area group. Weir may also have cribbed "Me & My Uncle" from the live Judy Collins record whose slower version of the song was widely heard in the mid-1960s.

Some of the Dead's most surprising versions of the song were when they tucked it into the murkiest depths of "The Other One" in the early 1970s. Later it was commonly paired with any one of several cowboy selections in Weir's first-set rockabilly double-dip.

12/5/69, Fillmore West, San Francisco
12/1/71, Boston Music Hall, Boston
3/26/72, Academy of Music, New York
12/12/73, The Omni, Atlanta
5/9/87, Laguna Seca Recreation Area, Monterey, California
6/8/94, Cal Expo Amphitheater, Sacramento, California

▪ "Mercy of a Fool" (Garcia/Hunter)

A *Terrapin Station* outtake and popular piece of tape-filler, this almost-song could have shaped up into something special but ended up on the cutting-room floor instead.

▪ "The Merry-Go-Round Broke Down"
(Cliff Friend and Dave Franklin)
Bill Coleman, *Bill Coleman* **(1938)**
Dick Jurgens, *Dick Jurgens and His Orchestra* **(1937),**
    Who Framed Roger Rabbit **soundtrack (1988)**

Creating an art form out of dealing with temperamental equipment, the Grateful Dead often used this piece of Depression-era pap as a downtime exercise.

▪ "Mexicali Blues" (Weir/Barlow)
Bob Weir, *Ace* **(1972)**
Grateful Dead, *Steal Your Face* **(1976),** *Dick's Picks*
    Volume Seven/'74 **(1997)**

The border town binge is not an uncommon subject for great art as evidenced by Charles Mingus's highly stylized, conceptual album *Tijuana Moods* and the masterful Orson Welles film *Touch of Evil.* Though "Mexicali Blues" doesn't quite reach these lofty heights, it nonetheless captures the spirited pathos of the jaded adventurer who barely escapes the consequences of his drinking and underage whoring.

With a tip of the hat to Marty Robbins and Tex-Mex polkas, Bob Weir and John Barlow crafted a morning-after confessional to end all morning-after confessionals that regularly filled the band's first set "cowboy song" slot beginning in 1971 and was performed more than four hundred times.

"Mexicali Blues" is notable in Grateful Dead history as it marked the first collaboration between Weir and Barlow. Because Weir and Robert Hunter's aesthetic and methodology were at odds, the rhythm guitarist recruited Barlow, his old prep-school partner in anarchy.

Barlow remembered the invitation in his 1982 conversation with David Gans. "Bobby said, 'Well, you write poetry—you might try your hand at writing lyrics.' I wasn't doing anything else, so I did try my hand. I'm not sure Hunter was too enthusiastic about there being another Grateful Dead lyricist, but on the other hand, he did tell me rather pointedly to take Weir *with his bless-*

ing. So I sort of made up some things that sounded like lyrics. The first one was 'Mexicali Blues,' and I was just *stricken* when I heard what kind of setting he'd chosen for it. I turned out to be okay after I got over the initial shock."

2/24/74, Winterland Arena, San Francisco
6/8/77, Winterland Arena, San Francisco
10/27/84, Berkeley Community Theater, Berkeley,
    California
3/17/94, Rosemont Horizon, Rosemont, Illinois

▪ "Mexican Hat Dance"

A tune-up specialty in the early 1970s, this popular refrain added spice to the often interminable downtime between songs.

9/28/72, Stanley Theater, Pittsburgh

▪ Mickey and the Hartbeats

In the fall of 1968, about a year after Mickey Hart had joined the Dead as their second drummer, he and Bill Kreutzmann joined Garcia and Lesh for regular jam sessions at the Matrix, a notorious San Francisco hippie haunt. Often joined by such local luminaries as rock-blues guitarist Elvin Bishop or bassist Jack Casady, the loose aggregation investigated some of the Dead's more improvisationally open spaces such as "Dark Star" and "The Other One" with a good dose of the blues thrown in for good measure. While some of the impetus to form the group seems to have been a response to Weir and Pigpen's unwillingness and/or inability to push the musical envelope in a jazz-like ensemble setting, all concerned missed the dynamics of playing together and the Hartbeats were disbanded.

▪ "Might as Well" (Garcia/Hunter)
Jerry Garcia, *Reflections* **(1976)**

In the early summer of 1970, the Dead were joined by a number of bands on a four-city whistle-stop tour of central Canada, traveling by chartered rail. The libertine exploits while en route from show to show have become the stuff of rock legend.

Remembering the escapade in *A Box of Rain,* Hunter wrote, "In the early seventies a train was leased for a trip across Canada, stopping in major cities to throw music festivals. On board were Delaney and Bonnie, Ian and Sylvia, THE BAND, JANIS JOPLIN, the Grateful Dead,

Charlebois, the NEW RIDERS, and various other acts that boarded from time to time. Everyone agreed we had just about the time of our collective lives in the week of non-stop music and partying. Nearing her last days, Janis, for one, wished aloud that the ride would never have to stop."

Steeped in locomotive lore, "Might as Well" mentions just about every style of American music and connects it with a specific component of the runaway train that dispenses good times wherever it goes. It is a tempered but rollicking account of that wild ride that the Dead used primarily as both a show opener and first-set closer after its introduction to the repertoire in 1976.

6/19/76, Capitol Theater, Passaic, New Jersey
8/29/83, Silva Hall, Eugene, Oregon
6/17/91, Giants Stadium, East Rutherford, New Jersey

Mikel
(newsletter)

Mikel flyer and sticker. *(Author's collection)*

Michael Linah took the meaning of the phrase "writing with your feet" to new levels with the crude but vital labor-of-love newsletter produced between August 1982 and the fall of 1986, when he died of cancer.

Linah, who shared the same birthday as Garcia (August 1, 1942), made his living as a bridge-tournament director and was widely respected among his peers in that field for his encyclopedic knowledge of the laws of bridge. The former MIT student handed out the idiosyncratic but informed Xeroxed pamphlet at Dead shows and, for the price of a dozen SASEs, subscribers would receive the newsletters at their home mailboxes along with colorful, venue and date-specific stickers featuring the "dancing skeleton" or the "ramblin' rose" iconography Deadheads grew to know and love.

Enthusiastic, humane and fun, *Mikel* embodied the Deadhead spirit by including set lists, tour schedules, press clips, surveys, bulletin boards, breezy commentary, and personal statements from the publisher.

Steve Miller
Born October 3, 1943, Milwaukee, Wisconsin

One of the few products of the San Francisco Renaissance to achieve true pop stardom, Steve Miller has proved himself to be a most durable musician in a career that has spanned three decades with a style genially mixing blues and mainstream rock.

The son of a jazz- and blues-loving doctor, Miller actually hailed from Milwaukee, Wisconsin, by way of Texas and Chicago. By the time he and the nucleus of his group (which included Boz Scaggs) moved to San Francisco in the mid-1960s they had developed a huge word-of-mouth following and, after their performance at the Monterey Pop Festival in 1967, were signed by Capitol for a then-unheard-of $50,000 advance that included full artistic control of their record releases.

Blues fanatics who dabbled in psychedelia (instead of the other way around), the Steve Miller Band was a well-oiled machine that proved to be a consistent hitmaker. From *Children of the Future* in 1968 through *Fly Like an Eagle* in 1976, there seemed to be hardly a month that passed when a Steve Miller song wasn't omnipresent on the radio.

After a couple of quiet years that saw him retire to Oregon where he built a studio, Miller returned to form with *Circle of Love* in 1981 and the next year's *Abracadabra* with its catchy title track that sold a million and reached Number One. Though Miller's recording work began a sloppy and desultory slide over the course of the next decade, he did re-form his band and open for the Grateful Dead at a string of stadium concerts in the summer of 1992. Miller jammed with the Dead during six of the shows on a generous selection of tunes that included "SPOONFUL," "The Other One," "MORNING DEW," "BABA O'RILEY," "TOMORROW NEVER KNOWS," "One More Saturday Night," "I Need a Miracle," "Standing on the Moon," "KNOCKIN' ON HEAVEN'S DOOR," "IKO IKO," "GOOD MORNING LITTLE SCHOOLGIRL," "ALL ALONG THE WATCHTOWER," "TURN ON YOUR LOVE LIGHT," "MIDNIGHT HOUR," and "West L.A. Fadeaway."

■ "Mission in the Rain" (Garcia/Hunter)
Jerry Garcia, *Reflections* (1976)

Though it had been a regular highlight of many Jerry Garcia Band shows since the mid-1970s, the Dead only performed "Mission in the Rain" at five concerts in June 1976. Still, it is one of the Garcia/Hunter gems—the poignant rumination of a lost soul searching for the answers to himself in San Francisco's rough-edged and rain-soaked Mission District. One lyric, in particular, seems to sum up the narrator's sad state of affairs: "All the things I planned to do I only did halfway / Tomorrow will be Sunday born of rainy Saturday."

Down but not out is the order of the day, but, as always, we are left in doubt as to the wanderer's fate.

Garcia can sing virtually any Hunter lyric and make it sound as if he was speaking from actual experience and "Mission in the Rain" is a prime example. As he told Blair Jackson in 1991, "I don't feel like I'm inhabiting the characters, but I do feel like I'm inhabiting their *world*. I don't really very often relate to the characters in the song. I don't feel like, 'Okay, now this is *me* singing this song.' Occasionally Hunter writes me an autobiographical song, like 'Mission in the Rain,' which is a song that *might* be about me . . . it's autobiographical, though I didn't write it."

6/29/76, Auditorium Theater, Chicago, Illinois
11/11/82, Felt Forum, New York (Jerry Garcia Band)

■ "Mississippi Half-Step Uptown Toodleoo" (Garcia/Hunter)
Grateful Dead, *Wake of the Flood* (1973), *Steal Your Face* (1976), *Without a Net* (1990), *Dick's Picks*

Volume One/'73 (1993), *Dick's Picks Volume Seven/'74* (1997)

Faintly echoing the title and classic jazz sensibility of Duke Ellington's "East St. Louis Toodleoo," this warm and rousing composition endured as a Grateful Dead standard. And, typical of many Dead songs, it portrays a character born to lose but pluckily persevering nevertheless, as its opening lines attest: "On the day that I was born, Daddy sat down and cried."

"Mississippi Half-Step" is actually two songs in one, fused with a lilting coda that describes the hero's release from the past and entry to a bright but unsure future "Across the Rio Grand-eo, across the lazy river."

A Dead perennial since 1972, "Half Step" found its place as a subdued early-concert inclusion and was performed well over two hundred times.

12/2/73, Boston Music Hall, Boston
4/8/79, Veteran's Memorial Coliseum, Jacksonville, Florida
8/31/85, Manor Downs, Austin, Texas
4/19/87, Irvine Meadows Amphitheater, Irvine, California
9/16/91, Madison Square Garden, New York

■ "Mona" (Ellas McDaniels)
BO DIDDLEY, single (1957), *His Greatest Sides* (1989)
The Rolling Stones, *The Rolling Stones Now!* (1965)
Quicksilver Messenger Service, *Happy Trails* (1969)
J. J. Cale, *5* (1979)
NRBQ, *RC Cola and a Moon Pie* (1986)
DINOSAURS, *Dinosaurs* (1988)
Matt Kelly, *Wing and a Prayer* (1989)

Quicksilver Messenger Service were the best-known San Francisco messengers of Bo Diddley's hit, but the Dead performed "Mona" with its author at a famed 1972 concert. Eighteen years later, Weir handled the vocals at one of the concerts following the death of Bill Graham at which Gary Duncan, one of Quicksilver's old guitarists, joined the band.

3/25/72, Academy of Music, New York

■ "Money Money" (a.k.a. "Finance Blues")
(Weir/Barlow)
Grateful Dead, *From the Mars Hotel* (1974)

"Money Money" didn't last long as a Grateful Dead concert song and with good reason. Misogynistically describing a parasitical and golddigging woman, it alienated many Deadheads, female *and* male. This reaction was probably compounded by its release at the height of the Women's Liberation Movement of the 1970s. Still, its rocking tongue-in-cheek humor has not sufficiently dated it and, in fact, "Money Money" can be viewed in the tradition of the put-down song so common in the blues. In comparison to some songs from the blues lexicon, "Money Money" seems quaint.

Remembering the response from his partners during his 1977 interview with David Gans, Weir remembered: "Well, a couple of people in the band didn't like the little story in that song, which—though tongue-in-cheek—they didn't think it was as funny as I thought it was. Didn't think it was funny at all. So we just put that one away."

Commenting on how the best intentions can sometimes go awry, lyricist John Barlow admitted to David Gans in 1982, "I had the notion of 'Money Money' as a Mose Alisony kind of jive blues. It came out sounding like Mose Alison done by Grand Funk Railroad. I was really upset by that for a while and refused to write lyrics without hearing the music first. I got stubborn and decided that my judgment regarding what the music meant was better than Weir's judgment regarding what words meant. That was kind of a silly attitude. The way it works best, I think, is when both of us are trying to develop something together and it gets done that way."

5/19/74, Memorial Coliseum, Portland, Oregon

▪ "The Monkey and the Engineer" (JESSE FULLER)

Jesse Fuller, *The Lone Cat* (1958)
Grateful Dead, *Reckoning* (1981)

A humorous song of "tragedy narrowly averted," this Jesse Fuller original chronicles the shenanigans that transpire when a simian stows away on a train locomotive. A shaggy-dog story set to song, "The Monkey and the Engineer" was a regular Bob Weir inclusion in the Dead's 1970 and 1980 acoustic sets.

2/14/70, Fillmore East, New York
10/4/80, Warfield Theater, San Francisco

▪ Airto Moreira
Born August 5, 1941, Itaiopolis, Brazil

Arguably the most important and famous percussionist to emerge from Brazil, Airto Moreira was already a seasoned musician by his teens, having worked professionally since he was just six years old accompanying on tambourine or shaker an old man who played button accordion at German and Polish weddings to which they sometimes traveled six hours on horse to perform.

Describing his musical awakening in Mickey Hart's book, *Drumming at the Edge of Magic,* Airto remembered, "I was born in 1941 in a small village in southern Brazil. When I was only a few months old, I began making erratic physical movements that alarmed my mother. Concerned that I might have some strange disease, my mother went to grandmother, and while they were discussing me I suddenly began twitching and rocking. 'See,' my mother said, 'there, he's doing it now.' My grandmother watched me intently and then she stood and crossed the room and turned off the radio. I immediately stopped rocking. I'm told my grandmother then turned to my mother and exclaimed, 'Oh my God! We've got another musician in the family.'"

Also a student of guitar and piano, he became a familiar figure in Brazil's nightclubs and spent three years on that circuit. He later worked with and then co-led a group with Hermeto Pascoal. Collecting scores of instruments during his extensive travels throughout South America, Moreira left Brazil for the United States with his wife FLORA PURIM in 1968. He joined Miles Davis two years later and received instant, widespread acclaim. After a brief stint with the jazz trumpeter Lee Morgan in 1971, Airto was a founding member of Weather Report, the influential and enormously popular jazz-rock fusion band, and the first incarnation of Return to Forever several years later.

The most in-demand percussionist of the 1970s, Airto led his own bands, worked in Purim's groups, and recorded with jazz saxophone greats Julian "Cannonball" Adderley and Stan Getz among many others.

Airto's association with the Grateful Dead kicked off when Mickey Hart invited the percussionist and his wife to collaborate on the *Apocalypse Now!* recording project. Thereafter, the duo became a surprise and welcome addition to nine spirited jams (four of those New Year's Eve shows) with the band from 1980 through 1993, including a February 11, 1989, appearance featuring their daughter Diana.

Though he hasn't been as active in the 1980s and 1990s, Airto still appears on many albums, paving the way for the inclusion of unusual Latin instruments and sounds into the jazz lexicon.

■ "Morning Dew" (Bonnie Dobson)

Bonnie Dobson, *Bonnie Dobson at Folk City* (1962), *Hootenanny With Bonnie Dobson* (1963), *Bonnie Dobson* (1969), *Troubadours of the Folk Era, Vol. 1* (1992), *The Music Never Stopped: Roots of the Grateful Dead* (1995)

Grateful Dead, *Grateful Dead* (1967), *Europe '72* (1972), *Two from the Vault/'68* (1992), *Dick's Picks Volume Three/'77* (1995), *Dick's Picks Volume Seven/'74* (1997)

Tim Rose, *Tim Rose* (1968), *Morning Dew* (1983)

Lulu, *To Sir with Love* (1967), *From Crayons to Perfume* (1994)

Jeff Beck, *Truth* (1968)

The Damnation of Adam Blessing, *The Damnation of Adam Blessing* (1968)

Group Therapy, *People Get Ready* (1968)

Frantic, *Conception* (1970)

THE ALLMAN BROTHERS BAND, *Duane and Gregg/'68* (1973), *Dreams* (1989)

Bonnie Dobson. *(The New York Public Library for the Performing Arts)*

Devo, *Smooth Noodle Maps* (1990)

Beck, Bogert and Appice, *Live in Japan* (1973)

Episode, *Put Yourself in My Place/'67* (1987)

Tom Constanten, *Morning Dew* (1993)

Oracle, *Oracle* (1994)

Toni Brown, *Blue Morning* (1996)

One of the earliest and most powerful antinuclear message songs, "Morning Dew" was a Grateful Dead concert regular since 1967. Bonnie Dobson, a Canadian singer/songwriter, wrote the song during a run at the Ash Grove, a famed Los Angeles folk club, in 1961. While staying at a friend's home, she was shaken into writing "Morning Dew" following an overwrought discussion on the possible consequences of the atomic bomb after a screening of *On the Beach*, the thoughtful 1959 film about nuclear annihilation.

Composed in the form of a conversation between the last man and the last woman in a post-apocalyptic landscape, "Morning Dew" poses a series of bleak suggestions as the two people slowly realize that there is nothing left on the planet: no flowers, no children, no sounds, no morning dew.

There has been some confusion and ill-will in the wake of Dobson's original composition regarding the credit (and royalties) she came to share with Tim Rose. Rose approached Dobson through her agent saying that he wanted to record the song but that he wished to slightly alter a lyric. Naively, Dobson signed a new contract that wrote in Rose as colyricist without first insisting on approving the lyric. The change amounted to nothing more than switching the chorus from "Take me for a walk in the morning dew" to "Walk me out in the morning dew."

To add insult to injury, Rose never gave Dobson any credit after popularizing "Morning Dew" to the point where he was the sole lyricist listed on some recordings of the song. Dobson, however, still collects 75 percent of the song's royalties and is on record as saying that she likes the Grateful Dead's "Morning Dew."

The Dead's rendition of the song has transformed significantly since its earlier outings where it was played at a faster pace and with a slightly programmed, off-kilter rhythm. By the early 1970s it had evolved into a mournful dirge imbued with portent and emotion. Filled with dense, building, and spiraling solo work by the entire Grateful Dead ensemble, "Morning Dew" provides

Garcia with the ultimate world-weary song to sink his vocal teeth into.

11/10/67, Shrine Exhibition Hall, Los Angeles

5/2/70, Harpur College, Binghamton, New York

4/29/71, Fillmore East, New York

5/18/72, Civic Hall, Rotterdam, the Netherlands

5/8/77, Barton Hall, Ithaca, New York

4/15/82, Providence Civic Center, Providence, Rhode Island

6/18/83, Saratoga Performing Arts Center, Saratoga, New York

7/12/87, Giants Stadium, East Rutherford, New Jersey

5/13/92, Giants Stadium, East Rutherford, New Jersey

3/17/94, Rosemont Horizon, Rosemont, Illinois

■ *Morning Dew*/Tom Constanten

Relix Records RRCD2063. Produced by Tom Constanten & Leslie D. Kippel, 1993.

Jorma Kaukonen–guitar on "Embryonic Journey"

"Morning Dew," "Lather," "It's All Over Now, Baby Blue," "Boogie Woogie Blues," "Mountains of the Moon," "Overture," "The Affair of Rue de Lourcine," "Cattle Call," "Pastime Rag #4," "Four Horrications: 'Dejazz,' 'Unchained Seranade,' 'Brook Waves Bachwelle,' 'Dejavalise,'" "Parallax," "Sonatina," "Alaric's Premonition," "Les Baricades Mistereieuses," "Sonata in G Minor, K. 4," "Hesitation Blues," "John Barleycorn Must Die,"

"The Fat Angel," "I've Just Seen A Face," "Embryonic Journey"

Another collection from T.C.'s magic bag of musical tricks, *Morning Dew* leans on Constanten's original material more so than his other solo efforts, yet he makes even the oldest standards, such as "Hesitation Blues," seem like his own.

■ Mother McCree's Uptown Jug Champions

In early 1962, about a year after they first met, Jerry Garcia and Robert Hunter worked in a series of folk-country-bluegrass bands circulating among such favored long-gone venues as the Tangent and St. Michael's Alley in Palo Alto, the Boar's Head in San Carlos, the Off Stage in San Jose, the Jabberwock in Berkeley, and some fly-by-night coffee houses in San Francisco's bohemian North Beach.

These groups were fairly fluid, changing personnel and names in short order. But there were some notable aggregations including the Thunder Mountain Tub Thumpers (Garcia, Hunter on bass, mandolinist Ken Frankel, Joe Edmiston), the Asphalt Jungle Boys (Garcia, Hunter, Bob Mathews on jug, Dave Parker on washboard, and John "Marmaduke" Dawson on guitar and vocals), the HART VALLEY DRIFTERS (Garcia, Hunter, guitarist DAVID NELSON, and dobroist Norm Van Mastricht) who snagged first prize at an amateur bluegrass contest at the 1963 Monterey Folk Festival, and the Black Mountain Boys (Garcia, Nelson, and Hunter, who was later replaced by Eric Thompson and then by Sandy Rothman).

The Wildwood Boys—the renamed the Hart Valley Drifters—were the earliest documented Garcia-Hunter unit leaving behind a couple of spirited recordings. But it was as Mother McCree's Uptown Jug Champions, the bluegrass predecessor to the Warlocks, that the earliest formal incarnation of the Grateful Dead can be traced. Garcia, playing bass, had previously jammed with Pigpen and Bill Kreutzmann in the Zodiacs, an itinerant East Bay garage band predating Mother McCree's. Joining Garcia was Weir on guitar, Pigpen on harmonica and guitar, Bob Mathews (the Dead's future recording engineer) on guitar, Dave Parker on washboard and kazoo, Tom Stone on fiddle, and Marshall Leicester on guitar.

Placing this unit in their traditional context and recalling the confusing quality of their group, Garcia said,

"Jug band is essentially country music in that it is rural. It was mostly a result of musicians not having enough money to buy fancy instruments. So they bought kazoos and used whatever was around.

"Our jug band was complete and total anarchy. Just lots and lots of people in it, and Pigpen and Bob and I were more or less the ringleaders. We'd work out various kinds of musically funny material. It was like a musical vacation to get onstage and have a good time."

Weir's recollections are an equal testament to the fun-loving mayhem of the loose-knit band. "I really couldn't play guitar at all, so I got relegated to jugs and washtub bass—which I also couldn't play at all, but they figured if anybody had to start from scratch it probably ought to be me.

"The next day I got a washtub and a broom handle and a piece of string and a bunch of different kinds of jugs and showed up at the next rehearsal. God knows how, but I figured out how to play them all. I could make notes happen with a washtub bass . . . and the jug, too.

"We became really popular around the mid-Peninsula area—had work just about every weekend.

"All the time we were getting started, we were really happy playing jug band music. And we were getting real good at it. But after we got to be pretty tight, we started wondering what we were going to do. People started quitting the band, to go away to school or this or that, and at one point Garcia left on a tour of the South to study bluegrass music. By the time he got back a couple of months later, we didn't know what we were going to do. Re-forming the jug band wasn't it.

"About that time the Beatles started to become popular. Garcia had been playing in rock & roll bands all along—guitar and bass, whatever was required of him—to bolster his income. We started kicking around the idea of maybe firing up electric guitars and playing some blues, Chicago-style or Jimmy Reed–style or whatever."

Soon after, they traded in the kazoos for electric guitars and the WARLOCKS were born.

- ## "Mountain Jam" (Donovan Leitch/ALLMAN BROTHERS)
  Donovan, *Donovan in Concert* (1968), *Donovan's Greatest Hits* (1969)
  The Allman Brothers Band, *Eat a Peach* (1972), *Live at Ludlow's Garage/'70* (1990)

Donovan wrote and recorded "First There Is a Mountain" as a whimsical ditty. But it was the Allman Brothers who lit some atomic firecrackers under the song and launched it into the galaxy. Their sweet, mammoth improvisation, which they retitled "Mountain Jam," was to the Allmans what "Dark Star" was to the Dead.

Though there are only a couple of versions of the Dead performing "Mountain Jam," both are memorable. In 1970, the Dead pulled a surprise version out of the middle of a second-set medley and, in 1973, they joined members of the Allman Brothers and the Band during the second encore of the monster Watkins Glen gig in upstate New York.

11/6/70, Capitol Theater, Port Chester, New York

7/28/73, Grand Prix Race Course, Watkins Glen, New York

12/31/73, Cow Palace, Daly City, California (Allman Brothers with Jerry Garcia)

- ## "Mountains of the Moon"
  (Hunter/Garcia/Lesh)
  Grateful Dead, *Aoxomoxoa* (1969)
  Tom Constanten, *Morning Dew* (1993)
  Dead Ringers, *DEAD RINGERS* (1993)

Melodically inspired by the English ballad and the waltz, "Mountains of the Moon" is a cryptic Grateful Dead song. This was Hunter at his allegorically arcane peak, crafting a symbolic tale set in a magical land. Sharing a similar title and theme, the song was probably partially influenced by "Mountains of Morn," a British music-hall number set to the tune of "Bendemeer's Stream," a classic Irish folk song.

Unlike the locales of personal mythos in which Hunter would later place his stories (i.e. "Terrapin Station" or "Franklin's Tower"), though, "Mountains of the Moon" can at least be found on a map. The actual Mountains of the Moon comprise a rugged range in Western Uganda. Still, this song does not seem to be continent or even planet specific, transpiring in a realm where a Hobbit would be just as comfortable as a Vulcan.

"Mountains of the Moon" is about as close to an *I Ching* hexagram as a Grateful Dead song can get. The story here, if there is one, concerns the unsuccessful bid by a destitute suitor to win the matrimonial hand of a respected family's daughter. But that loose plot is really only the thin onion skin of the song's intangible meanings. If anything, "Mountains of the Moon" concerns itself with the perseverance of the human spirit no matter what obstacles confront it. In this regard, the song can be seen as exploring the themes Hunter later returned to with the more realized "Terrapin Station."

But "Mountains of the Moon" does draw on the mythology of ancient Greece. In Greek mythology, Electra (the woman in the song who is courted) was one of the seven daughters of Atlas. The daughters were pursued by Orion, the lusty hunter, but escaped after the gods took pity and changed them into stars, now known as the Pleiades. Electra is the Seventh Pleiad, a very dim, dark star, said to be lost or in hiding.

Another lyric in the song, "hey the laurel," also references Greek mythology where the laurel represents the nymph Daphne. Daphne was pursued by Apollo, the sun god. She prayed to her own goddess for escape and was transformed into a laurel tree.

Melodically, "Mountains of the Moon" is a rich and lovely composition at once bittersweet and strident, neatly mirroring Hunter's haiku.

In his 1971 conversation with Charles Reich, Garcia said, " 'Mountains of the Moon' is still one of my favorites of the ones I've ever written. I thought it came off like a little gem. On the record as it is now, I've dropped a lot of the junk off it. It sounds more like what I hoped it would when we recorded it."

Hunter wasn't as pleased with his lyrical contribution to the song. As he told Blair Jackson in 1988: "I've written up the lyrics for most of our songs, compiling them, and I still can't overcome the need to change lines that I've never liked. So I changed them, and I have an asterisk on the line and then an appendix which has the line as it was recorded. For example, in 'Mountains of the Moon' there's the line: 'Twenty degrees of solitude, twenty degrees in all, all the dancing kings and wives assembled in the hall' . . . 'Twenty degrees in all'? Hmmm. I don't think so. It doesn't mean much. So I've changed it to 'Twenty degrees of solitude, a fiddler grim and tall, plays to dancing kings and wives assembled in the hall.' I think that's much better. When I wrote it originally [for *Aoxomoxoa* in 1969] we were in a pressured recording situation, I knew it was weak, but I just didn't have the time to fix things I wasn't entirely happy with."

There are only a few surviving examples of the Dead performing "Mountains of the Moon," usually as an acoustic prelude to "Dark Star." Listening to these recordings, the ensemble shedding its wooden instruments one-by-one and donning their electric axes for an amplified adventure of "Dark Star."

A final note on the song—the early pressings of *Aox-*

Jerry Garcia sharing licks with Dickey Betts on "Mountain Jam," Grand Prix Racecourse, Watkins Glen, New York, 7/27/73. *(Photo: Richard Berner)*

omoxoa included a full vocal-chorus coloring "Mountains of the Moon." Again, this is a route that was also followed with the later "Terrapin Station."

Many Deadheads suggested that the Dead would have done well in bringing back "Mountains of the Moon," perhaps as an encore. But, alas, that was not to be.

3/1/69, Fillmore West, San Francisco

■ **"Mr. Charlie"** (McKernan/Hunter)
Grateful Dead, *Europe '72* (1972), single (1973)

Cut out of the same voodoo cloth as their earlier "Alligator," "Mr. Charlie" is the bad-ass challenge of a wronged rounder finally doling out his revenge. In the blues idiom Mr. Charlie is a common character, usually taken to mean the field foreman who keeps the plantation slaves in line—sort of the blues song equivalent of an Uncle Tom.

Musically, "Mr. Charlie" is a funky, high-spirited bounce with an R&B-heavy groove. But its roots lie firmly in the blues of rural black America represented by any one of a number of compositions with the same title and theme. LIGHTNIN' HOPKINS, for example, recorded a song called "Mr. Charlie" when Pigpen was still blowing through the wrong end of his harmonica.

12/14/71, Hill Auditorium, Ann Arbor, Michigan
4/17/72, Tivoli Concert Hall, Copenhagen

■ **"Mr. Tambourine Man"** (BOB DYLAN)
Bob Dylan, *Bringing It All Back Home* (1965), *Bob
**   Dylan's Greatest Hits* (1967), *At Budokan* (1978),**
**   *Biograph* (1985)**
George Harrison, Bob Dylan, et al., *Concert for
**   Bangladesh* (1971)**
The Byrds, *Mr. Tambourine Man* (1965), *The Byrds
**   Greatest Hits* (1967), *Untitled* (1970)**
Judy Collins, *Fifth Album* (1965)
Barbarians, *Are You a Boy or Are You a Girl* (1965)
Duane Eddy, *Duane Eddy Does Bob Dylan* (1966)
Stevie Wonder, *Down to Earth* (1967)
William Shatner, *The Transformed Man* (1968)
Beat Street Band, *Psychedelic Songs of the '60s* (1989)
Cliffs of Doneen, *The Dog Went East and God Went West
**   * (1991)**

One of Dylan's most celebrated and enduring statements, "Mr. Tambourine Man" is a monumental lyric poem about the artist's search for transcendence. The song is concerned with feeling—its nature and whether to surrender to it or control it with humor or toughness. Naturally, Dylan was angered when "Mr. Tambourine Man" was criticized as being a "drug song" after its initial release and the popularity it received through both the Byrds' and Judy Collins's covers. Less hysterical reaction correctly evaluated it as an invocation to the singer/songwriter's muse for inspiration and the freedom that it brings.

Alternately, Dylan has cited Federico Fellini's film *La Strada* and Bruce Langhorne at a recording session with a giant tambourine as direct inspiration for "Mr. Tambourine Man."

In a 1968 *Sing Out!* interview, Dylan commented on the song's elusive core: "There was one thing I tried to do which wasn't a good idea for me. I tried to write another 'Mr. Tambourine Man.' It's the only song I tried to write 'another one.' But after enough going at it, it just began bothering me, so I dropped it. I don't do that anymore."

As if beckoned by the song's own mercurial qualities, Dylan has returned to "Mr. Tambourine Man" several times over the years, most notably with the up-tempo 1978 big band versions replete with a flute accompaniment and his mid-1990s acoustic renditions during what was known as his Never Ending Tour. His one performance of it with the Grateful Dead, however, seemed like an afterthought.

7/26/87, Stadium, Anaheim, California

■ **"Mud Love Buddy Jam"**

See "Your Mind Has Left Your Body"

■ **David Murray**
Born February 19, 1955, Berkeley,
**   California**

The Dead always paid a lot of lip service to jazz. But it was only in the late 1980s and 1990s that they were really able to parlay any substantial or noteworthy collaborations into musical gold. Yes, there was the early studio work with scat master Jon Hendricks and the '73 tour with the mini-horn section of Martin Fierro and Joe Ellis spicing some of the *Wake of the Flood* material, but a true crossover musical experience was yet to be.

While Ornette Coleman may have been the most important jazz musician to perform with the Grateful Dead, it was tenor saxophonist and bandleader David Murray (along with their Branford Marsalis collaborations) who represented the music's next generation and a key alignment of worlds in the Dead's final years.

Born and raised in the East Bay, Murray is a true product of the Oakland-Berkeley area's rich and diverse cultural mix and was exposed to gospel, R&B, rock, funk, and, obviously, jazz, which he studied with Phil Hardyman in Berkeley High School's vaunted music program, absorbing the modes of such tenor sax heroes as Ben Webster, Paul Gonsalves, Coleman Hawkins, Sonny Rollins, and John Coltrane. Never comfortable in merely rehashing the sounds of the masters, Murray made their innovations the launching pad for his own mold-smashing style on tenor sax or bass clarinet and running the gamut from shimmering, octave-crashing pyrotechnics to gorgeous lyricism.

When Murray moved to New York in the mid-1970s, he resolved to continually push himself and forged alliances with members of the first generation of great "outside" jazz musicians, including drummers Billy Higgins, Andrew Cyrille, Milford Graves, and the late Ed Blackwell, and pianists Don Pullen, John Hicks, and Randy Weston.

Equally comfortable in a variety of settings, Murray (who attended the same high school as Phil Lesh) has risen to the top of the jazz world on the strength of his playing, composing, arranging, hustle, and more than a little well-deserved recognition. With a nod to Sonny Rollins, Murray's playing is as much steeped in the church as in R&B. Whether it be as a member of the esteemed World Saxophone Quartet, leading the hottest octet this side of Tadd Dameron's early 1950s ensemble, big bands, or the smallest combos, plaudits have followed Murray, leaving little doubt that he is among the most formidable jazz musicians of the late twentieth century.

Hooking up with the Dead through his involvement with Bob Weir and Taj Mahal and their work on a piece of musical theater based on Negro League and Major League baseball pitching legend Satchel Paige, Murray studied the Dead's September 21, 1993, Madison Square Garden gig and joined them the following evening for a first-set-ending exploration of "Bird Song" and a classic second-set jam that included "Estimated Prophet," "Dark Star," "Wharf Rat," "Throwing Stones," and "Love Light."

Two months later, Murray shared the same Garden stage with the Garcia Band for a workout on that band's standard fare of Garcia originals and R&B chestnuts.

Of his experiences playing with the Dead, Murray enthusiastically told G. Ove Lyons of *Dupree's Diamond News*, "The thing about the Dead that hit me the most was how relaxed they were onstage! I mean, they have their own internal system hooked up where they can talk to each other while they're playing. That's incredible! Their relaxation level was like they were playing in their own living room. The crowd was out there, and they were hollering and screaming, but these guys are like in an inner circle of their own. It's really wonderful the way they have it set up. They have their own aura about them, and their own concept. They have their own thing, and it sounds that way. I was just trying to get into it. Jerry Garcia, I mean this cat is like playing with James 'Blood' Ulmer [an avant-funk, New York–based guitarist]. He's got his own concept of playing, and once you open your ears up to it, you can learn things."

Murray was equally amazed by the response from Deadheads. "I'll tell you one thing, man. When I played at MSG with the Dead, I have never received so much adoration and response from the wildest stuff I play. The wilder I went on the sax, the more they were into it. I have never had that kind of response. I do that stuff on a jazz stage, and people start looking around and getting up to go the bathroom, while I'm working and sweating my butt off. The Deadheads are so attentive and reactionary, they are like the perfect audience. I would like to have a set audience just like that. They really believe in those guys up there onstage. I mean, you can see that these people are dedicated. People do that in Europe. They will drive two or three hundred miles to see my shows. But these people supersede that by ten thousand miles. Their machine is so wonderful, and plus, all the cats are beautiful people. I am a Berkeleyite, and they made me feel real comfortable. The appreciation of the Deadheads is unsurpassed; they're the best audience in the world!"

After Garcia's passing, Murray began working up octet and big-band jazz arrangements of some Dead tunes, which he field-tested at his weekly New York City gig at the Knitting Factory in the winter of 1996. That spring he released *Dark Star: The Music of the Grateful Dead*, a tribute album that included "Dark Star," "Shakedown Street," and "China Doll."

■ *Music to Be Born By*

Rykodisc RCD 0112-2, 1989. Produced by Mickey
Hart.
"Music to Be Born By"
Taro Hart–heart. Mary Holloway–heartbeat
environment. Mickey Hart–surdo. Steve
Douglas–wooden flute.

One of Mickey's most unusual efforts was *Music to Be
Born By*, an album that mixed a recording of his son's in
utero heartbeat with a building and diminishing percussion score to facilitate the birthing experience.

Speaking of the album's practical use, Hart reported
in 1993, "I have files filled with pictures and testimonies. I have maybe a thousand letters and pictures of
babies born to this music. The parents talk to me as if I
were their gynecologist. They put me right there. They
tell me the most intimate details of their birthing. Most
cultures have birthing music: music to be born by. We
don't. We lost that ritual."

■ *Music for the Gods—The Fahnestock South Sea Expedition: Indonesia*

Rykodisc RCD 10315, 1994. Produced by Mickey Hart
and Alan Jabbour.
"Taboehgan," "Serkarinotan," "Pedat," "Genderan,"
"Pemoengkah," "Kerejing," "Laghoe Dindang,"
"Merakngila," "Gambang," "Kecak," "Abimenijoe,"
"Gambangan," "Dendang Gendis"

It's difficult to determine which is more amazing: the
rare music on this collection or the story behind its
recording.

Gamelon, a specific style of music indigenous to the
South Pacific, employs conches, rattles, congas, and,
most uniquely and hypnotically, gongs to produce
sounds that soothe and transport. Like many musics
from the nether reaches of the planet it has recreational
and spiritual functions.

The true tale that produced *Music for the Gods* reads
like a Hollywood nail biter. In 1934 two American
brothers, Bruce and Sheridan Fahnestock, traveled to
what is now Bali in Indonesia to record and document
the native music. That first expedition resulted in failure
as they lost much of their original tape. But, several
years later, they were given a second chance when President Roosevelt hired them to use their music collecting
as cover for a reconnaissance mission to see if the
Japanese had come close to important Allied strongholds in the South Pacific during World War II.

That second attempt was an anthropologic bonanza
but a personal tragedy. The brothers collected hours of
the gamelon but Bruce Fahnestock was killed when a
U.S. plane destroyed the ship he was on, mistaking it for

Balinese dancers with gamelon gong, circa 1941. *(Courtesy of Rykodisc)*

a Japanese vessel. Returning to the States, Sheridan Fahnestock locked the tapes away and never pulled them out again before his death in 1965. Twenty years later, his widow Margaret, realizing their historic importance, donated the collection to the Library of Congress in 1986.

The collection eventually came to Mickey Hart's attention through his work with the Library of Congress. With his crack audio team, Hart cleaned up the fading acetate tape and made the fifty-year-old gamelon orchestra sound fresh.

Discussing his affinity for gamelon, Hart told Roger Len Smith of *Relix* in 1995: "I've been a gamelon fan since I was a kid. I listened to all of it from the Folkways collection and my mom played it unknowingly in our living room. She was into that, and so I thought the whole world listened to this stuff. I was listening to pygmies and treefrogs and all kinds of sounds of the world that I was calling 'music' at that time and my mother was calling music. *Diga* was my stab at twentieth-century gamelon. It's about tuned percussion, but grouping, playing in groups. That's what the gamelon is all about, it's about community . . . Their instruments are made for themselves to communicate with sacred dimensions. That's what it's for, and it's also a way to symbolize their community, that they all work together, they all play together, they dance together, they sing together. They commune together. There's power there."

▪ "The Music Never Stopped"
(Weir/Barlow)
Grateful Dead, single, *Blues for Allah* (1975), *One from the Vault* /'75 (1991), *Dick's Picks Volume Three*/'77 (1995)
Joe Gallant and Illuminati, *The Blues for Allah Project* (1996)

Chock-full of self-reference to the Dead's nineteen-month touring hiatus in the mid-1970s, "The Music Never Stopped" is a Dead anthem sung by Weir with the same oom-pah fervor he brought to "Playing in the Band" with its sharp dynamics and surprising spaces for some of the band's best jamming.

One of the lyrics, "They're a band beyond description, like Jehovah's favorite choir," seems to be an apt description of the Grateful Dead.

5/7/77, Boston Music Hall, Boston
1/15/78, Selland Arena, Fresno, California

(Courtesy of R. Crumb/Shanachie Entertainment)

9/10/83, Sante Fe Downs, Sante Fe, New Mexico
9/15/87, Madison Square Garden, New York
7/17/89, Alpine Valley Music Center, East Troy, Wisconsin
9/25/91, Boston Garden, Boston

▪ *The Music Never Stopped* (book)/Blair Jackson
260 pp. 75 black and white photos. Pull-out family tree. Delilah Books/Putnam, 1983.

Blair Jackson's baptism in authorship still stands as the authoritative history of the Grateful Dead from their early childhoods through the early 1980s. Musician profiles, discographical analysis, the Acid Tests, concert tape recommendations, and social and musical histories are spiced with choice photos and flavored by Blair's insightful prose.

The Music Never Stopped: Roots of the Grateful Dead/Various Artists
Shanachie Records, 1995. Produced by HENRY KAISER and David Gans.
"Rain and Snow" (Obray Ramsey), "MAMA TRIED" (MERLE HAGGARD), "IKO IKO" (Dixie Cups), "SAMSON & DELILAH" (REVEREND GARY DAVIS), "BIG RAILROAD BLUES" (CANNON'S JUG STOMPERS), "EL PASO" (Marty Robbins), "IT'S ALL OVER NOW, BABY BLUE" (BOB DYLAN), "SPOONFUL" (Charlie Patton), "The Red Rooster" (Howlin' Wolf), "THE PROMISED LAND" (CHUCK BERRY), "Don't Ease Me In"

(Henry Thomas), "Big Boss Man" (Jimmy Reed), "Turn On Your Love Light" (Bobby "Blue" Bland), "Morning Dew" (Bonnie Dobson), "Not Fade Away" (Buddy Holly), "Goin' Down This Road Feelin' Bad" (Woody Guthrie), "I Bid You Good Night" (The Pindar Family with Joseph Spence)

This is a valuable exploration of the Dead's all-American roots, and the producers' loving and erudite touch is all over this disc. Including Obray Ramsey's "Rain and Snow," Bobby "Blue" Bland's "Turn On Your Love Light," Cannon's Jug Stompers playing "Big Railroad Blues," and Bob Dylan's "It's All Over Now, Baby Blue," this stuff can get very esoteric, yet it's fascinating to hear how these songs sounded before the band put them into the Dead mill.

The beginning of what could and should be a multidisc project, *The Music Never Stopped* was the first compilation in which Dylan had ever allowed one of his songs to be included. Additionally, the wonderful R. Crumb cover illustration was done in exchange for a stack of old 78 records from the president of Shanachie.

▪ *The Music of Upper and Lower Egypt*
360 Degrees Records 102, 1988. (CD and cassette reissue: Rykodisc 10106.) Produced by Mickey Hart. "Nugumi," "Allah," "The Bride," "The Groom," "Ya Rab Taba," "Manami (My Dream)"

Recording these tracks during the Dead's 1978 tour of Egypt, Mickey Hart captured the folk musics of Egypt for posterity. With their rich melodies affected by the country's historical global location, traditional Egyptian music was influenced by the culture of Pharaonic, Coptic, and Islamic heritages, as well as the more recent Mameluk Kingdoms and subsequent colonial and revolutionary era. Each epoch left its mark on the character and form of the Egyptian folk music. While the ethnomusical map of Egypt is divided primarily into four sections (the Mediterranean, the urban music of Alexandria and Cairo, the Nile region, and the area near and around the Aswan dam), Hart's release focuses on the Aswan region, where the vestiges of ancient Nubia reflect the life of its people.

▪ "My Babe" (WILLIE DIXON)
Little Walter, single (1955), *Best of Little Walter* (1958), *Boss Blues Harmonica* (1972), *The Essential Little Walter* (1993)

LIGHTNIN' HOPKINS, *Swarthmore Concert* (1964)
Spencer Davis Group, *First Album* (1965)
BO DIDDLEY and Muddy Waters, *Super Blues* (1967)
Elvis Presley, *Elvis Aron Presley* (1969), *Elvis In Person* (1970)
Foghat, *Fool for the City* (1975)
Roy Buchanan, *My Babe* (1980)
The Fabulous Thunderbirds, *T-Bird Rhythm* (1982)
WILLIE DIXON, *The Chess Box* (1988)
James Cotton, *Take Me Back* (1989)
John Mayall, *Cross Country Blues* (1994)
Luther Allison, *Live In Paris* (1995)

In 1955, Little Walter's intelligent adaptation of Willie Dixon's "My Babe" became the first Dixon song to top the R&B charts and it was undoubtedly his version of the song that inspired Garcia to include it at an unusual 1970 concert featuring several rarely and never-played again selections. Some bluesologists cite "This Train," the old Negro spiritual formalized by Sister Rosetta Tharpe in the 1940s, as Dixon's inspiration and model for "My Babe."

11/8/70, Capitol Theater, Port Chester, New York

▪ "My Baby Left Me" (ARTHUR CRUDUP)
Arthur Crudup, single (1950)
Elvis Presley, single (1956), *Elvis Recorded Live on Stage in Memphis* (1974), *This Is Elvis* (1981), *Reconsider Baby* (1985)
Creedence Clearwater Revival, *Cosmo's Factory* (1970)
Phil Ochs, *Gunfight at Carnegie Hall* (1971)
Dave Edmunds, *Get It* (1977)
Danny Gatton, *Cruisin' Deuces* (1993)

The Dead's only performance of this song made famous by the very young Elvis was at a 1986 Rex Foundation show when it was paired with "THAT'S ALL RIGHT, MAMA," another tune made famous by the King and written by Arthur Crudup.

4/18/86, Berkeley Community Theater, Berkeley, California

▪ "My Brother Esau" (Weir/Barlow)
Grateful Dead, *In the Dark* (1987)

Call this song "*The Big Chill* Meets the *Five Books of Moses*." Drawing on biblical allusion to create political allegory, "My Brother Esau" is a direct commentary on the fallout of the social effects of the 1960s (Vietnam in particular) as it charts the fates of two brothers. Esau, according to the Old Testament, sold his birthright to his twin brother Jacob for some pottage. Weir and Barlow picked up on the legend's theme of unconsidered hastiness in recasting their own late twentieth-century model for Esau.

As Weir told Blair Jackson in 1985, "['Esau'] is an allegory about what happened to members of our generation where one brother went off and fought a war and one brother stayed home and more or less minded the store, and then the subsequent events and developments of that. There's a real specific Biblical allegory in that story. I think Barlow and I might try to rework it so it's not quite so obscure. Without damaging the imagery, it might have a little more punch if it were a little easier to understand. I don't know—maybe it's better to let it roll around the subconscious and let it ring bells or not if people are open or not."

An *In the Dark* semi-outtake (it was included on the CD and cassette-tape releases as well as the B side of the "Touch of Grey" single but not the LP), Weir performed this effective tune about alienation more than one hundred times in the mid-1980s before it unexpectedly, and sadly, dropped out of the Dead's concert repertoire in 1987.

8/20/83, Frost Amphitheater, Palo Alto, California

■ Brent Mydland

Born October 21, 1952, West Germany; died July 26, 1990, Lafayette, California

Brent Mydland's path to the Grateful Dead was as unlikely as his band mates. An army brat who was born in West Germany but raised in Concord, California, a San Francisco suburb, Mydland's rise in professional music was through the East Bay rock ranks. After a stint as the keyboardist with Batdorf and Rodney, a local folk-rock group, Mydland joined a country rock group called Silver that recorded for Arista, the Dead's label. It was during that stint that he caught Bob Weir's attention and was hired to join the Bob Weir Band in 1978. Coincidentally, the Dead were in the process of reorganizing without Keith and Donna Godchaux, the husband and wife keyboard and vocal duo who had marked the band's identity during the 1970s. Mydland was invited to audition for the band and soon joined.

Though the switch to Mydland may have been a bit of a quick fix for the Dead, the young gun proved himself

immediately, reinvigorating the band's sound from the opening notes of his first Dead show on April 22, 1979, at San Jose's Spartan Stadium. With a keyboard rack that included a Hammond B-3 organ, Mydland added a soulful Jimmy Smith–like funkiness that had been missing from the band since the Pigpen era and his high, unvarnished harmonies, original songs, and pungent choice of covers established the Dead as a very new band when the new decade approached.

Discussing Mydland's early days in the band with David Gans in 1982, Mickey Hart confided, "He had the chance of becoming one of us. I wondered, for a while—I was the hardest critic, in a way. He didn't have the passion at first. Then his attitude and his playing changed, and he relaxed.

"God, he must have been intimidated, playing with the Grateful Dead. . . . He was seeing so many inconsistencies around him in the music. He was used to playing music that had a beginning, a middle, and an end—that repeated, and had bridges and stuff. And people who wouldn't forget lyrics, and they'd play it the same way every time. It killed him! He probably thought every bar was another mistake or two. Until he saw the beauty in it, I couldn't see the beauty in him. He knows now, and I really like him. I think his playing is really nice. He's a better player than when he started with the Grateful Dead, and he's doing more with what he had. But it was strange at first."

As Mydland settled into his role, it became apparent that he was the perfect synthesis of all who had preceded him on the job. Trained on piano since age seven and honed on fusion gigs and L.A. studio dates, he had chops that rivaled Constanten's and Godchaux's, while playing with a sense of drive and urgency that evoked memories of Pigpen. Moreover, Mydland wasn't afraid of music technology. His synth parts were clean, tight, and timbrally refreshing, lending a contemporary sheen to such late-vintage Dead albums as *Go to Heaven* and *In the Dark*. One only had to look at Garcia grinning at Mydland while edging close to the keyboardist during a jam in the late 1980s to see what a strong effect he was having on the music.

Mydland certainly had his detractors who took exception to the darker sides of this complicated person, but the vitality he brought to the band during the 1980s was undeniable. Mydland was primarily a colorist whose full palette of aural colors were brought forth with a jazz sensibility that shifted easily from rock to bop to blues to honky-tonk even incorporating occasional Bachian flourishes into the band's ballads and raveups. Describing his musical role to Blair Jackson in 1987, Mydland said, "Well, the Grateful Dead is already full of rhythm instruments, so a lot of the times it's better to lay back, let the rhythm happen, and just color it. A lot of people kind of put me down for it, but I feel like I'm pretty much there to color, more than paint the picture to start with. Sometimes I feel like it's open enough that I can do both, and I *should* do both."

His background singing added a coziness to already warm songs and his lead vocals gave Garcia and Weir a break in a way they hadn't experienced since the days of Pigpen. Among the more notable cover songs Brent introduced at concerts were "HEY POCKY WAY," "DEVIL WITH A BLUE DRESS," "GOOD GOLLY MISS MOLLY," and a "DEAR MR. FANTASY">"HEY JUDE" medley that topped off many a second set.

Mydland's own songs ranged from the tender ("Easy to Love You" and "I Will Take You Home") to the bitter ("Far from Me" and "Don't Need Leave Love No More") and the raucous ("Good Times"). And on a given night,

his songs could be the sleeper of a Dead show. While his detractors also pointed to what they feel was a heavy-handed misogynist streak in some of his songs, the overall range of his contribution to the band's repertoire would seem to dispel that notion. After all, there are any number of other songs that were performed by the band that could be described as lascivious at best and downright sexist at worst—not many decried Pigpen for his expert renderings of "GOOD MORNING LITTLE SCHOOLGIRL" when the bluesman trotted out the Sonny Boy Williamson classic piece of raunch in the late 1960s.

Mydland's sensitivity toward his role and persona was never far from the surface; he complained that even after he had joined and begun touring with the Dead, many audience members thought Keith Godchaux was still playing the keyboards. But his band mates were always most supportive as supremely evidenced in his four song contributions to their 1989 *Built to Last* LP.

Mydland truly hit his stride in the late 1980s and his last tours in the fall of 1989 through the summer of 1990 were among the Dead's greatest. Reportedly a tortured soul, Mydland was the subject of ugly rumors in the

Brent Mydland, Brendan Byrne Arena, East Rutherford, New Jersey, 10/16/89. *(Robert Minkin)*

Deadhead community that his drug abuse might necessitate his dismissal from the band. Sadly, his personal demons finally caught up with this enigmatic artist who died of a speedball (a morphine and cocaine combination) at his home on July 26, 1990.

▪ "My Own Fault"
B. B. King, *Live at the Regal* (1964)
B. B. King and Bobby Bland, *Together for the First Time . . . Live* (1974)
Johnny Winter, *Johnny Winter And* (1971), *Live* (1971)

Garcia is only known to have sung this Chicago blues of unknown authorship at one very early Dead show.
12/1/66, The Matrix, San Francisco

▪ "Mystery Train" (Phillips/Parker)
Junior Parker, single (1953)
Garcia/Saunders/Kahn/Vitt, *Keystone Encores Vol. 2/'73* (1988)
Elvis Presley, single (1955), *Rock 'n' Roll No. 1* (1956), *For LP Fans Only* (1959), *From Memphis to Vegas*

(1969), *The Sun Session* (1976), *Elvis Aron Presley* (1980), *The Complete Sun Sessions* (1987)
Paul Butterfield Blues Band, *Live* (1971)
Lloyd Cole, single (1988)
THE NEVILLE BROTHERS, *Brother's Keeper* (1990)
The Stray Cats, *Choo Choo Not Fish* (1992)
KINGFISH, *KINGFISH IN CONCERT*/'76 (1995)

The Dead only played this early rock classic, a Garcia bar-band favorite, at a wild show that featured an easy half-dozen surprises.

Before being a hit for Elvis (as well as the title of Jim Jarmusch's rave of a film in 1991), "Mystery Train" was a small success for Junior Parker, who composed it in 1953 with Sam Phillips and released it on Sun Records that same year. Parker is thought to have been inspired by an old Celtic ballad popularized by the Carter Family.
11/8/70, Capitol Theater, Port Chester, New York

∎ *Graham Nash/David Crosby*/Graham
Nash/David Crosby
Atlantic SD 7220, 1972. Produced by Graham Nash,
David Crosby, and Bill Halverson.

Among the first CSNY spin-off projects, *Graham Nash/David Crosby* features Garcia, Lesh, and Kreutzmann on "Wall Song," which was allegedly performed by the Dead on December 22, 1970, though no tape of the concert has yet surfaced. Garcia also played pedal steel on "Southbound Train."

∎ *Neal Cassady Drive Alive*
Key-Z Production, 1965; 1990.

Sixty minutes of wall-to-wall Neal Cassady on a verbal joyride through his life, his cars, his women, and the lessons he learns along the way. Released by KEN KESEY, featuring some Jerry Garcia, this cassette was accompanied by a transcription book for the Cassady-impaired and photos of Cowboy Neal. Recommended for both the beginner and the fanatic.

∎ "Neighborhood Girls" (Suzanne Vega)
Suzanne Vega, *Suzanne Vega* (1985)

Suzanne Vega's surprise two-song appearance with the Dead during the watershed Rainforest Benefit at Madison Square Garden in 1988 caught many Deadheads off guard. With her personal, folk-hued compositions, predictable arrangements, and at-the-time star power, she seemed an unlikely choice to share the stage with the band at the heavily hyped, environmentally correct, fund-raising event. As it turned out, it was Garcia's admiration of Vega's craft that drew her briefly into their circle.

Vega was born on August 12, 1959, in Santa Monica, California, but grew up in New York City. After graduating from the High School of Performing Arts (of *Fame* fame) she attended Barnard College and began attracting attention with her performances at the folk clubs in the Village. By 1984 she had a record deal with A&M and a modest-selling self-titled debut album a year later.

"Luka," a song about child abuse on her second album, *Solitude Standing*, became a surprise hit single, reaching No. 3 in 1987. This success allowed Vega to experiment with less precious music forms on her subsequent albums, including a contribution to a Philip Glass project. She has yet to regain the marquee status of her earlier exploits.

"Neighborhood Girls," a spiffy, New Wave jump, didn't give the Dead much elbow room to show their stuff but is an interesting display of the band playing this type of music.

9/24/88, Madison Square Garden, New York

∎ David Nelson

David Nelson is a veteran of the San Francisco Bay Area music scene whose musical pedigree places him squarely in the middle of the psychedelic-cowboy family tree. Nelson was not only there when it began, he was there before it began. In 1962, he played with Jerry Garcia and Robert Hunter in the Wildwood Boys, years before there even was the Grateful Dead. In 1969, at the peak of the San Francisco psychedelic renaissance, Nelson and John Dawson formed the NEW RIDERS OF THE PURPLE SAGE, a group that included Jerry Garcia on pedal steel guitar. The NRPS were one of the most popular country-rock bands of the late sixties and seventies. It was Nelson who sang their biggest hit, "Panama Red," a certifiable counterculture anthem that earned them a gold record.

Over the course of four decades, Nelson has remained an active player on the San Francisco music scene. He lent his distinctive guitar styling to several of the Grateful Dead's most memorable and critically acclaimed albums, including such classics as *American Beauty* and *Workingman's Dead*. He performed with the Good Old Boys, which included bluegrass legends Don Reno, Chubby Wise, and Frank Wakefield. Their 1975 album, *Pistol Packin' Mama*, was produced by Garcia. And, in 1987, David was called on by Garcia, once again, to perform as a member of the Jerry Garcia Acoustic Band. Their fall tour included a string of eighteen sold-out shows at Broadway's Lunt-Fontanne Theatre, breaking box-office records by selling out in a matter of hours. The CD *Almost Acoustic* was released from these shows.

All of Nelson's past glory should not overshadow the fact that he is currently making some of the best music of his career. The David Nelson Band pairs him with a group of musicians who share his love of a spontaneous and highly conversational style of playing, and gives him the opportunity to stretch out in any number of directions—from tight, concise country-rock tunes through easygoing rock & roll, to extensive improvisational excursions. As always, Nelson's guitar work remains nimble and straight to the point, his clear, distinctive voice loaded with character. The music features his original compositions, many cowritten with Grateful Dead lyricist Robert Hunter, as well as some chestnuts from David's past with the Dead, NRPS, and the Jerry Garcia Acoustic Band.

His band features himself on electric and acoustic guitar and vocals; Bill Laymon (NRPS) on bass and vocals; Barry Sless (KINGFISH, Cowboy Jazz) on electric and pedal steel guitar; Mookie Siegel (Kingfish) on keyboards, accordion, and vocals; and Arthur Steinhorn (NRPS, Cowboy Jazz) on drums. Collectively, they are the David Nelson Band, seasoned veterans with decades of experience on the road.

Nelson has managed the seemingly impossible—with this band, he remains true to his musical vision and integrity over several decades without becoming outdated in the process. The David Nelson Band plays fresh music in cynical times, proving once again the power of music to transcend, overcome, and just plain entertain.

Over the years, Nelson performed with the Dead at a couple of 1969 concerts and as an encore guest at the 1987 New Year's Eve show.

■ "Never Trust a Woman" (a.k.a. "Good Times" or "Good Times Blues") (Brent Mydland) Grateful Dead, *Dozin' at the Knick*/'90 (1996)

Misogyny was a semi-constant theme in Brent Mydland's work. But while some of these expressions tended to exhibit themselves in acidic mean-spiritedness, "Never Trust a Woman," at least, demonstrated a rare humorous and raunchy aspect missing in many of his songs. In fact, this straightahead blues fit the same bill as many Pigpen tunes like "Next Time You See Me."

Mydland relied on "Never Trust a Woman," also known as "Good Times," as one of his first set standbys, adding a little scat vocalese to his later readings of his twelve-bar put-down.

8/31/81, Aladdin Theater, Las Vegas
5/3/87, Frost Amphitheater, Palo Alto, California

■ The Neville Brothers
Aaron Neville, born January 24, 1941, New Orleans, Louisiana; Art Neville, born December 17, 1938, New Orleans, Louisiana; Charles Neville, born December 28, 1939, New Orleans, Louisiana; Cyril Neville, born January 10, 1950, New Orleans, Louisiana

A musical institution even older than the Grateful Dead, the Neville Brothers were New Orleans's best-kept secret until just about the time the group began to open and occasionally jam with their Bay Area counterparts in 1986.

Long before gaining their much-deserved and widespread fame, the Neville Brothers formed the nucleus of Allen Toussaint's studio band in the 1960s and early 1970s that was funk before funk had a name.

Long before that, they were already local music heroes. Art and Aaron's recording career began when they were still in high school. As members of the Hawketts, a Crescent City vocal group, they scored a novelty R&B hit with "Mardi Gras Mambo" in 1954, a song with hypnotic rhythms, which became one of the signature tunes associated with the city's debauched spring rite.

Though Art and Aaron joined different bands, how all four brothers passed through the Meters, the Wild Tchoupitoulas, and other outfits to form their own family band would defy even the most dedicated ethnomusicologist or genealogist. After surviving the flop of an eponymous album in 1978 they came out with *Fiyo on the Bayou,* a brilliant updating of New Orleans R&B, which included strains of Cajun, rock and reggae on standards ranging from "HEY POCKY WAY" to "Sitting in Limbo." There began a string of wildly popular albums and tours that garnered the attention and adoration of everyone from the Dead to Linda Ronstadt (with whom Aaron briefly teamed up), marking a rise that left them chic but still funky.

The Nevilles were a natural choice to open for the Dead's celebrated Mardi Gras shows of the late 1980s and 1990s, yet 1986 was the only set of gigs at which the New Orleans crew appeared. They did, however, open for and jam with the band for six other New Year's Eve and summer shows through 1989.

• "New New Minglewood Blues" (Noah Lewis)

Singles: CANNON'S JUG STOMPERS (1928), Noah Lewis Jug Band (1930)

Grateful Dead, *Grateful Dead* (1967), *What a Long Strange Trip It's Been* (1977), *Shakedown Street* (1978), *Dead Set* (1981), *Dick's Picks Volume Five/'79* (1996)

KINGFISH, *KINGFISH IN CONCERT/'76* (1995)

This song has a fascinating history reflecting the transforming powers of the folk idiom. Geographically, the song references Ashport, Tennessee, just north of Memphis, where there was a sawmill and box factory called Minglewood. The area, with its concomitant hardscrabble townsfolk, eventually became known as Minglewood.

Noah Lewis, one of the great early musicians to come out of Memphis, toiled for a time at the factory, but it was his harmonica and compositional work with Cannon's Jug Stompers (and later his own jug bands) for which he is remembered. Aside from being the main writer of "New Minglewood Blues," Lewis was also responsible

for a couple of other songs covered by the Grateful Dead: "VIOLA LEE BLUES" and "BIG RAILROAD BLUES."

With Lewis on board, CANNON'S JUG STOMPERS first recorded "Minglewood Blues" in 1928. However it is the 1930 Noah Lewis Jug Band recording (retitled "New Minglewood Blues") that bears a closer similarity to the Dead's swampy arrangement.

It's the brash boast of a take-no-prisoners scoundrel on the prowl; this stranger who was "born in the desert, raised in a lion's den" is a self-employed woman stealer.

Bob Weir twice rearranged and retitled the song as "New New Minglewood Blues" and "All New Minglewood Blues" in its two incarnations in the Dead domain, where it was performed more than four hundred times. Weir has had particular fun with one lyric. Where the original mentions the "Memphis girls" who best be on guard when the wandering rogue antihero of the song comes to town, the guitarist inserts a city-specific locale for the action. So, depending where the Dead performed, the lyric became "Austin girls," "Big Apple fillies," "German girls," "Lone Star fillies," or even (gulp!) "Valley girls."

4/26/69, Electric Theater, Chicago

10/14/76, Shrine Auditorium, Los Angeles

4/16/78, Civic Center, Huntington, West Virginia

11/10/79, Crisler Arena, Ann Arbor, Michigan

8/20/83, Frost Amphitheater, Palo Alto, California

12/5/92, Compton Terrace Amphitheater, Chandler, Arizona

• "New Orleans" (Frank Guida/Joe Royster)

Gary U.S. Bonds, *Dance Till Quarter to Three with U.S. Bonds* (1960)

Neil Diamond, *The Feel of Neil Diamond* (1966)

The Kingsmen, *15 Great Hits* (1966)

DR. JOHN, *In The Night* (1985)

With his gruff, expressive voice gracing a series of infectious and influential dance records of the early 1960s, Gary U.S. Bonds is as well known for his early exploits as he is for a couple of Bruce Springsteen–produced tracks he laid down in the early 1980s.

The son of a college professor and music teacher, Bonds (born Gary Anderson on June 6, 1939 in Jacksonville, Florida) was raised in Norfolk, Virginia, and sang in the church choir before gravitating to doo-wop. In 1960, while singing with the Turks, a local group, he caught the ear of Frank Guida, a record store owner turned producer and label owner, who made the young man an offer he couldn't refuse.

Guida was a master at hype and novelty. The year before he had made a small fortune with "High School U.S.A." in which he had recorded a studio band performing twenty-eight versions of the song, each listing different high schools for different urban centers. He leased the music to Atlantic and it made the Top 30. It should have come as no surprise to Gary Anderson when Guida suggested he change his name to U.S. Bonds in a scam designed to garner extra airplay for their first release by disc jockeys mistaking it for a public service announcement.

With his engineer and songwriting partner, Joe Royster, Guida had perfected a canned "live" sound by producing a rough, muzzy effect through a primitive use of tape echo and phasing at a time when pop records were sounding annoyingly smooth.

Their studio machinations were rewarded with "New Orleans," a classic that combined rock raunch with Bonds's impassioned, scorched soul-singing setting the stage for much that would follow.

As Guida related the history of the song to Blair Jackson in 1984, "Believe me, it wasn't easy writing 'New Orleans'! To begin with, I had totally different chord progressions originally. Black musicians, as well as my vocalist, Gary Anderson, all thought this white cat was off his rocker! None of them had any faith the song would make it. This was understandable, because it was in no way similar to the R&B sounds that abounded through the South at that time.

"I was greatly influenced by West Indian music and, in particular, its *rhythms*. Joe Royster, my cowriter, who wrote part of the lyrics, was a country & western aficionado. Thank God Joe always tried to do what I asked of him. Other people were always fighting me tooth and nail, but I suppose that's the price you pay to be in charge.

"'New Orleans' was and still is the bedrock of most rock music. I think most music people who are honest, such as Bruce Springsteen, Isaac Hayes, and the whole British conglomerate, if truly pressed, would attest to that fact."

Weir took a few, too infrequent stabs at "New Orleans" in 1970 and reprised it for a surprise encore outing with the Band at the 1984 Solstice show benefiting Wavy Gravy's Seva Foundation.

6/21/84, Kingswood Music Theater, Maple, Ontario, Canada

- ## "New Potato Caboose" (ROBERT M. PETERSEN/Lesh)
  Grateful Dead, *Anthem of the Sun* (1968), *Two from the Vault*/'68 (1992)

"New Potato Caboose" was perhaps the Dead's first truly gorgeous original song, a Gerard Manley Hopkins–like inscape poem ripe with visionary power and naturalistic allusion.

Weir sang "New Potato Caboose" with the Dead when they performed it from 1967 through 1969, giving it the pure and innocent treatment warranted by its lush and crystalline lyrics.

The words were written by Lesh's friend Bobby Peterson, an all-too-often unheralded contributor to the Dead's canon. Peterson later gave Lesh "Pride of Cucamonga" as well as the beloved but rarely performed "Unbroken Chain."

In concert, "New Potato Caboose" sprang into ecstatic jamming that made it a much sought-after tune by tape collectors, who wondered why it never made a comeback. It deserved one.

11/11/67, Shrine Exhibition Hall, Los Angeles
2/3/68, Crystal Ballroom, Portland, Oregon
2/14/68, Carousel Ballroom, San Francisco
8/24/68, Shrine Exhibition Hall, Los Angeles (*Two from the Vault*)

- # New Riders of the Purple Sage

The New Riders of the Purple Sage began as a loosely constructed offshoot of the Grateful Dead. Founding members John "Marmaduke" Dawson and DAVID NELSON had connections with the Dead dating to the early 1960s. Nelson first hooked up with the then-struggling banjo player named Jerry Garcia as well as his bass player in their early bluegrass bands, Robert Hunter. Together they performed in the Wildwood Boys and the Black Mountain Boys, and, with Dawson, MOTHER MC-CREE'S UPTOWN JUG CHAMPIONS.

By the decade's end, the Grateful Dead were household names in acid rock but were on the brink of changing direction. When Garcia returned to acoustic, country-flavored roots and began playing pedal steel he contacted Dawson and Nelson and the New Riders were born. The band's name, incidentally, was chosen by Nelson and

Hunter after the 1912 novel by Zane Grey, the famous western novelist.

Probably the first glimpse of things to come was the June 6, 1969, gig at San Francisco's California Hall by the band calling itself Bobby Ace and the Cards from the Bottom of the Deck which found Garcia, Weir, Lesh, Hart, and Constanten performing with Dawson and Nelson. The New Riders made their official debut at the Family Dog later that summer with a lineup that included Nelson, Dawson, Garcia, Lesh, and Hart.

In his 1971 interview with Fred Stuckey of *Guitar Player* magazine, Garcia recalled the formation of the band. He said, "I got my pedal steel. Marmaduke—John Dawson—had this gig down the Peninsula playing in coffee houses. He was getting into writing songs, and he'd written five or six songs that I thought were pretty neat. They were all like simple country songs, simple construction. I could understand enough about the pedal steel to play along with simple stuff. I thought, wow, this is the perfect chance for me to be able to get into the pedal steel. You know, I'll just play unobtrusively along behind Marmaduke as he's singing his folk songs. So I went down there and set up my pedal steel in the corner and slowly proceeded to try and learn how to play it. I had a pretty good idea in my head of what I wanted it to sound like, but I didn't have any chops down. Pretty soon it started to sound pretty good, and a couple of other friends who were around here sort of fell into the scene. And pretty soon we had a little band."

Discussing his quest with the pedal steel, Garcia told Stuckey: "What I'm doing with the steel is I'm going after a sound I hear in my head that the steel has come the closest to. But I have no technique on the steel . . . I'm really a novice at it. I'm trying to duplicate something that's in my head."

Seven years later, Garcia described his New Riders and pedal-steel experience with Jon Sievert of *Guitar Player*, saying, "I haven't played it much for quite a while, though I played it pretty steadily for about four years. I really got into it, but it became an either/or situation: I found it very hard to play half the night with a pedal steel and a bar in my left hand and then switch to

The New Riders of the Purple Sage and the Grateful Dead, McMahon Stadium, Calgary, Alberta, 7/3/70. Left to right, Jerry Garcia, David Nelson, Phil Lesh, Bob Weir, John "Marmaduke" Dawson. *(Photo: Steve Slomka courtesy of Joseph Slomka)*

straight overhand guitar. The difference between a solid finger configuration and a moving arm, wrist, and fingers was too great. It was painful to the muscles. It got to where I couldn't play either of them very well, and I realized it just wouldn't work. I don't consider myself a pedal steel player, and I'm always embarrassed to see that I've placed in the *Guitar Player* poll."

In its earliest incarnation, the New Riders were essentially a Grateful Dead spinoff band with Garcia on pedal steel and banjo, Lesh on bass, and Hart playing drums. But within a couple of years, Buddy Cage replaced Garcia on pedal steel, Dave Torbert took over the bass slot and ex–Jefferson Airplane drummer Spencer Dryden began playing drums for the New Riders.

Billing some of their tours in 1970 as "An Evening with the Grateful Dead and the New Riders of the Purple Sage," the groups created an American musical review spanning jug band music, country, bluegrass, gospel, Pigpen's blues, folk tunes, Dead originals, and, of course, a good dose of the band's extended improvisations. Indeed, after all was said and done, Garcia would have spent some six or seven hours onstage with both units.

As Dawson remembered these gigs in his 1992 conversation with J. C. Juanis of *Relix*, "We'd come out before the Dead's set and completely freak out the hippies who weren't ready for country music—but we turned them around."

Eventually the New Riders became a self-contained unit and began touring and recording independently of the Dead, although the two bands remained close and shared the same stage on and off over the next few years. Despite some serious downs, the NRPS never went away and remain a vital, tireless bar and festival band to this day.

▪ *New Riders of the Purple Sage*/NEW

RIDERS OF THE PURPLE SAGE

Columbia C 30888, 1971.

"I Don't Know You," "Whatcha Gonna Do," "Portland Woman," "Henry," "Dirty Business," "Glendale Train," "Garden of Eden," "All I Ever Wanted," "Last Lonely Eagle," "Louisiana Lady"

An album for anyone who appreciates the Dead's sagebrush country-rock includes the original configuration of the NRPS with Garcia, Lesh, and Hart joining David Nelson and John Dawson on an ornery collection.

▪ "New Speedway Boogie" (Garcia/Hunter)

Grateful Dead, single, *Workingman's Dead* (1970), *What a Long Strange Trip It's Been* (1977)

Directly referencing the Altamont apocalypse, "New Speedway Boogie" is one of the Dead's darker numbers, calling into question everything Haight-Ashbury had once symbolized. More specifically, Hunter wrote in *A Box of Rain* that the song was "written as a reply to an indictment of the Altamont affair by pioneering rock critic Ralph J. Gleason."

When the Dead released and first began performing "New Speedway Boogie," the hippie movement had been turned on its ear: categorized, co-opted, manipulated, and preyed upon from both within and without.

The song's opening, "Please don't dominate the rap, Jack, if you got nothing new to say" would also seem to comment on the profiteering charlatans who had strongarmed their way into the community. Additionally, the line "I don't know but I've been told in the heat of the sun a man died of cold" points a finger at the bloody events that transpired at Altamont.

But, in discussing "New Speedway Boogie" with Charles Reich and Jann Wenner in 1971, Garcia admitted, "I think that that song's an overreaction, myself. I think that it's a little bit dire. Really, the thing that I've been seeing since Altamont is that periodically you have darkness and periodically you have light, like the way the universe is in the yin/yang symbol. There's darkness and light and it's the interplay that represents the game that we're allowed to play on this planet. Just the fact that there are two opposing elements in the universe is the grace of that cosmic game that we're allowed to dick around here, you know, on the planet."

He was a bit more enthusiastic when discussing the song's genesis. "That particular album [*Workingman's Dead*] has some *really* beautiful songs on it. They came out like gold or something. 'New Speedway Boogie' is one of those miracle songs. It's one of those 'once-through' ones. The words were just *so* right, that it was immediately apparent, just bam! It came out right. Simple and straight-ahead."

The Dead often performed "New Speedway Boogie" semi-acoustically in 1969 and 1970 after which it fell out of their rotation for more than two decades. The song was happily reintroduced in 1991 and was performed as either a first-set stand alone or a linking device in the band's more bluesy second-set jams.

9/20/70, Fillmore East, New York

10/15/94, Madison Square Garden, New York

■ **"Next Time You See Me"** (Earl
Forest/William G. Harvey)
Grateful Dead, *Hundred Year Hall*/'72 (1995)
Little Junior Parker, *Blues Man* (1957)
James Cotton, *Cut You Loose!* (1968)
Matt Kelly, *Wing and a Prayer* (1989)
Eric Clapton, *Slowhand* (1977)

Also known as "Lied, Cheated" or "Wrong-Doing Woman," Pigpen sang this haughty put-down song many times in the early 1970s. The Dead had two distinct arrangements of the song, a driving, uptempo rendition and a somewhat rarer and moodier take sung as a duet with Garcia.

12/12/69, Thelma Theater, Los Angeles

5/6/70, Kresge Plaza, M.I.T., Cambridge, Massachusetts

2/21/71, Capitol Theater, Port Chester, New York

■ ***Night Cadre*** (book)/Robert Hunter
Viking, 1991

Hunter's first book of verse bears little resemblance to his work with the good ol' GD. Yet the personal from-me-to-you tone of the collection will strike the heart chord of every admirer of this sculptor of words.

■ ***Nightfood***/Brian Melvin's Nightfood
Global Pacific Records/Columbia ZK 40733, 1988.
Produced by Brian Melvin and Steven D. Epstein.
"Sexual Healing," "Fever," "CIA," "Dania," "Did You Hear That Monie (Grandpa Monroe)," "Mercy Mercy Mercy," "Bahama Mama," "J.P.'s Shuffle," "Miles' Mode"
Brian Melvin–drums, percussion, vocals. Bob Weir–guitar, vocals. JACO PASTORIUS–bass. Curtis Ohlson–bass, vocals. Vernon Black–guitar. Norbert Stachel–saxophone. Jan Fanucci, Rose Gaines, Lori Taylor–vocals. MERL SAUNDERS–organ. Andy Narell–steel drums. Jon Davis–Synthesizer. Rick Smith–tenor and soprano saxophone. Tim Hyland–trumpet. Craig Kilby–trombone. Keith Jones–bass. Paul Mousavi–guitar. Bill Keaney–congas, bongos. Thomas Hass–saxophone. Butch Lacy–synthesizer. Jens Melgaard–bass. Thomas Blachman–drums.

Dedicated to bass legend Jaco Pastorius, who plays on this eclectic collection of standards and originals (and who passed away shortly after the album's waxing), Bob Weir takes center stage on several of the disc's more recognizable covers, including "Fever" and "Sexual Healing." Melvin's slick studio album coalesces a range of music (R&B, calypso, jazz, and soul) and an all-star cast adds enormously to this earnest if slightly superficial outing.

Some of the album was recorded at Weir's state-of-the-art home studio. Recalling Weir's enthusiasm, Melvin told Blair Jackson in 1988, "He was just incredibly generous and helpful all the way. He knows a lot about working in the studio, and when he'd get going it was hard to stop him. When he gets into something he bites in big.

"Of course he was a big fan of Jaco. They had tremendous mutual respect for each other. It's funny, because Jaco's daughter is a Deadhead! You know, at times Jaco could play more music than everyone in the band put together. He was just in a different class. He's going to go down in history as one of the heavy prophets in music. I mean, he changed music, molded how people think and play. But what's great is that he was good at every style, so that when Bob wanted to play 'C.C. Rider' or 'Midnight Hour' Jaco was into it. He knew 'em all! It's not like Bob and Jaco were going to play 'Teen Town' [a revered Pastorious Weather Report composition] together. But when you extract a common denominator from talented musicians and throw away the egos, great music can be made. And that's what happened when Bob and Jaco got together."

■ ***Nightfall of Diamonds***/Tom Constanten
Relix Records RRCD2046, 1992. Produced by Tom Constanten.
"Cold Rain and Snow," "Play the Game," "Wildflowers," "Ashokan Farewell," "Dejavalse," "Graceful Ghost," "Whiter Shade of Pale," "Friend of the Devil," "Boris the Spider," "Dejavalentino," "Oriental," "Butterfly Rag," "Chopped Liver," "Fake Fur Elise," "Speaking," "Prelude in E Flat, Op. 23 #5," "I Know You Rider," "Goin' Home," "Dark Star," "And We Bid You Goodnight"
HENRY KAISER–guitar on "Goin' Home" and "Dark Star."

Tom Constanten's appealing blend of solo-piano versions of GD songs, odd covers of folk and rock 'n' roll, classical interpretations, and originals is well represented on this appealing tapestry in sound. Capped off by a "Dark Star" right out of a black hole, Constanten's record treats the listener to tastes of the Rolling Stones ("Goin' Home"), the Who ("Boris the Spider"), Rachmaninoff, Chopin, and Garcia while proving once again why he is the western hemisphere's most revered saloon-playing modernist.

▪ "Nobody's Fault but Mine" (Traditional)

Grateful Dead, *Dick's Picks Volume One* /'73 (1993)
Blind Willie Johnson, *Complete Recordings of Blind Willie Johnson* /'27 (1993), *The Gospel Sound* /'27 (1994), *Dark Was the Night* /'27 (1995), *Roots of Rap* /'27 (1996)
Sister Rosetta Tharpe, *Complete Recorded Works* /'40 (1993)
Mance Lipscomb, *Texas Sharecropper and Songster* (1960)
The Staples Singers, *Freedom Highway* (1965)
Paul Butterfield, *Better Days* (1973)
Walter "Wolfman" Washington, *Out of the Dark* (1988)

BLIND WILLIE JOHNSON

(Courtesy of R. Crumb Shanachie Entertainment)

Led Zeppelin, *Nobody's Fault but Mine* (1990), *No Quarter—Unleaded* (1994)
Nina Simone, *The Blues* (1991)
Dread Zeppelin, *5,000,000* (1995)
Dixie Stompers, *Stock Yard Strut* (1995)

Despite a long history of being often recorded by a variety of blues singers and gospelists, the plaintive "Nobody's Fault but Mine" is most closely associated with Blind Willie Johnson, an intriguingly mysterious and mercurial Texas street singer. Like Robert Johnson, Blind Willie Johnson left a minuscule recorded legacy— only thirty songs are known to exist. Yet his influence and reputation is broad.

Johnson was a coarse-throated interpreter of spirituals who occasionally used the blues idiom to spread the gospel. While accounts of his birthdate range as widely as 1890 to 1902, he grew up in Marlin, Texas, and was blinded with lye by his stepmother during a fight with his father sometime between the ages of three and seven. Like other bluesmen in the prewar period, Johnson earned his living as a busker, singing on Texas street corners, where he perfected his virtuosity as a slide guitarist using his pocketknife to create perfect accompaniments to his scary, emotion-charged voice. He became a Baptist preacher, married in 1927 and relocated to Dallas, where he testified with his wife and recorded a batch of songs that ultimately became classics for Columbia: "Motherless Children Have a Hard Time," "Let Your Light Shine on Me," and "Jesus Make Up My Dying Bed." Primarily Baptist spirituals, his compositions also include "If I Had My Way I'd Tear That Building Down," later rearranged, refined, and retitled by Reverend Gary Davis and, even later, covered by the Dead as "SAMSON AND DELILAH."

Johnson recorded thirty tracks between 1927 and 1930 but never committed any of his songs to tape again, preferring to make his living by playing the streets of small-town Texas. Johnson's death is something of a bizarre footnote in the blues mythos. After his house in Beaumont burnt to the ground in 1947, he slept in the ashes of its remains, contracted pneumonia, and died after the local hospital refused to admit him, assuming he was uninsured because of blindness.

With Garcia on the pained vocals, the Dead only performed "Nobody's Fault" several dozen times over a three-decade span starting in 1966, often as an instrumental segue nestled in the folds of their looser second sets.

5/17/74, P.N.E. Coliseum, Vancouver, British Columbia

▪ Ken Nordine

Born April 13, 1920, Des Moines, Iowa

"Word jazz" poet and commercial voice-over deity Ken Nordine's basso profundo has been regularly heard on Chicago radio for more than three decades. Nordine first hooked up with the Dead for their 1990 New Year's Eve bash, working with Gary Lambert, David Gans, and Dan Healy on the national radio broadcast of the show.

The band's devotion to Nordine's unique brand of dark and light poetic whimsy led to two recordings on Grateful Dead Records: *Devout Catalyst* and *Upper Limbo*, a project with his own Chicago group.

Nordine's delivery is instantly recognizable from his long-running television ads for Levi's jeans and Taster's Choice coffee. These lucrative promotional spots have enabled the robust, silver-maned grandfather to finance a four-decade fine-tuning of word jazz, Nordine's experimental, inquisitive spiels set to sampled sound effects and cocktail-hour music.

Nordine describes his free-form verbal riffing as something he does "just to see where the mind will take you." The genre hit its stride in 1957–58 when Nordine's four LPs of spoken word for Dot Records charted high, paralleling the zooming popularity of the Beat Generation.

Growing up as part of a musical family in Des Moines, Iowa, Nordine studied violin as a boy. But, after puberty lapsed and his voice changed, he realized that his true calling was on the radio. After an undergraduate stint on the University of Chicago's radio frequency doing "far-out stuff nobody ever heard," he got his first job, making fifteen dollars a month as a gopher for WBEZ—the Chicago station that now carries his NPR show.

After stops in Bay City, Michigan, and Palm Springs, Florida (where he created a daily infomercial for the local exterminating company which featured characters like "Rigor Mortis" and "Terrence Termite"), he landed back in Chicago during World War II. For a while he worked long shifts on war-update programs until the grind got to him and he decided to test the free-lancing waters. Giving up a then-cushy annual $18,000 income, Nordine, now a newlywed, hit the panic button when his take-home pay nose-dived to $1,250 a year and he scuf-

fled to do anything he could: slide shows, instructional films, and even acting.

But he was also experimenting with the embryonic version of word jazz on Monday and Tuesday nights at the Leia Loa, a neighborhood tavern with a Hawaiian theme. Along with a few musician friends, Nordine established a little scene at the joint while developing an enthusiastic local following as he made up stories on the spot or took a poem and used it as a diving board to "swim around in a pool of where I wanted to take it."

The 1957 publication of Jack Kerouac's *On the Road* dragged the world of the San Francisco and Greenwich Village poets into the national consciousness, and suddenly every youth-driven venue needed versifying hepcats for entertainment with a dash of enlightenment. When Dot records had Nordine narrate "The Shifting Whispering Sands," a piece Nordine described as "Pat Boone-ish," they had a surprise hit on their hands.

When approached for a follow-up, Nordine suggested his word jazz repertoire, igniting the four album bonanza that yields such pieces as "Reaching into In," a vintage slice of Nordine in which he fiddles with the doorknobs of perception, and "Hunger Is From," a trinket's worth of musing on late-night refrigerator raids, complete with crunching celery stalks.

But while traveling similar verbal fringes as the Beats, Nordine had virtually no contact with them, opting for a curious dismantling of situations and preconceptions in a friendlier, childlike way that was the flip-side of the angst in Ginsberg's *Howl*. A recording he worked on with Lawrence Ferlinghetti of Robert Shure's "Twink" concerned itself with a pair of windshield wipers that go back and forth with each other, but never actually kiss.

The acclaim of word jazz resulted in the high point of Nordine's career: an invitation to Hollywood to record a track to accompany a tap-dancing Fred Astaire on a network variety show.

Back in Chicago, the Wordman from Wonderland settled into the commercial work for which he became ubiquitous as well as an extended stretch of award-winning late-night TV shows on which he simply read great literature into one camera lens, tackling the likes of Kafka, Dostoyevsky, and Balzac.

Concurrent with his initiation as a Grateful Dead collaborator was his occasional work with producer Hal Wilner on the 1988 *Stay Awake* Disney tribute album, a contribution to *A Chance Operation*, a 1993 John Cage tribute album, and a cassette-length personification of the colors of the spectrum specifically produced with children in mind. He capped off his relationship with the Grateful Dead when he joined them onstage during "Drumz" at the Rosemont Horizon outside of Chicago on March 11, 1993, for a recitation of two songs associated with his Grateful Dead detour, "Flibberty Jig" and "Island."

Nordine's work lands somewhere between dreaming and ordinary consciousness: undoubtedly an amusing place to spend a lifetime.

▪ "Not Fade Away" (Charles Hardin/Norman Petty)

Buddy Holly, *From the Original Master Tapes* /'57 (1985), *The Chirping Crickets* (1958), *The Music Never Stopped: Roots of the Grateful Dead* (1995)
Grateful Dead, *Grateful Dead* (Skull & Roses) (1971), *Dick's Picks Volume Two* /'71 (1995), *Dick's Picks Volume Five* /'79 (1996), *Dozin' at the Knick* /'90 (1996), *Dick's Picks Volume Seven* /'74 (1997)
The Rolling Stones, *England's Newest Hit Makers* (1964), *Big Hits (High Tide & Green Grass)* (1966), *Got Live If You Want It* (1966)

Buddy Holly. *(The New York Public Library for the Performing Arts)*

Phil Ochs, *Gunfight at Carnegie Hall* (1970)
Steve Hillage, *Motivation Radio* (1977), *Six Pack* (1979)
Stephen Stills, *Throughfare Gap* (1977)
Arthur Brown, *Speaknotech* (1982), *The Complete Tapes of Atoya* (1984)

The original rock & roll misfit nerd, Buddy Holly led a short life but his voluminous and infectious legacy is still felt. The polite, bespectacled Texan merged country and R&B styles to develop new song forms while exuding a quiet charisma that served as an interesting alternative to Elvis.

Born Charles Hardin Holley September 7, 1939, in Lubbock, Texas, Buddy grew up listening to the radio while learning piano and guitar. He began putting bands together as a teenager and was opening shows for Presley and cutting singles before he was twenty. After initially meeting with commercial failure, Holly formed a new band and traveled to Clovis, New Mexico, to record at producer Norman Petty's studio.

Petty was not overly fond of rock 'n' roll and encouraged the Crickets (the name the band chose for itself during these sessions) to soften their sound. The rest is history as "That'll Be the Day" emerged from the desert and became a No. 1 hit. Holly and Petty continued to experiment in the studio, utilizing different forms of echo ("Peggy Sue"), double-tracking ("Words of Love"), and close-miking techniques that became industry norms.

Never a big hit, "Not Fade Away" was cowritten by Holly and Petty, and it appeared on the B side of the more popular "Oh Boy" on Petty's Coral label in 1957.

Holly's death at the age of twenty-two in a February 3, 1959, plane crash with Ritchie Valens and the Big Bopper (J. P. Richardson) at Clear Lake, Iowa, is the stuff of American legend and tragedy.

The Dead's performances of "Not Fade Away" (there were more than five hundred of them) have taken this primal rock classic in many different directions. Probably the best of these were in the early 1970s when they formulaically jammed the exciting song into "Goin' Down the Road" and back into "Not Fade Away," complete with Bob Weir primal screaming the reprise into out-of-control, voice-losing oblivion. By the latter part of the decade, "Not Fade Away" had been transformed into an incendiary and monolithic jam session that sometimes incorporated riffs from "The Eleven." But, as the song gained a certain tribal call-and-response popularity amongst Deadheads at concerts, the band pared it down once more to where it more closely resembled the arrangement by the Rolling Stones or even the Buddy Holly original (with shades of doo-wop) than their earlier interpretations.

2/11/70, Fillmore East, New York

9/19/70, Fillmore East, New York

4/28/71, Fillmore East, New York

11/7/71, Harding Theater, San Francisco

6/10/73, RFK Stadium, Washington, D.C. (with the ALLMAN BROTHERS BAND and MERL SAUNDERS)

9/10/74, Alexandra Palace, London (*Dick's Picks Volume Seven*/'74 [1997])

5/8/77, Barton Hall, Ithaca, New York

9/3/77, Raceway Park, Englishtown, New Jersey

3/28/81, Grughalle, Essen, West Germany (with Pete Townshend)

2/11/86, Henry J. Kaiser Convention Center, Oakland, California (with the NEVILLE BROTHERS)

(Courtesy of Acoustic Disc)

David Grisman and Jerry Garcia. *(Photo: Gary Nichols courtesy of Acoustic Disc)*

9/18/88, Madison Square Garden, New York
6/20/91, Pine Knob Music Theater, Clarkston, Michigan

■ *Not Fade Away: The On-Line World Remembers Jerry Garcia* (book) / Edited by David Gans.

Thunder's Mouth Press, 1995.

This instant book with a heart retrieved the Internet homages to Jerry Garcia in the digital wake of his passing. While not essential to the Deadhead library, Gans's book portrays a broad tapestry of remembrance and emotion that captures the sober vitality of those terrible days.

■ *Not for Kids Only* / Jerry Garcia and DAVID GRISMAN

Acoustic Disc ACD-9, 1993. Produced by David Grisman.
"Jenny Jenkins," "Freight Train," "A Horse Named Bill," "Three Men Went A-Hunting," "When First Unto This Country," "Arkansas Traveler," "Hopalong Peter," "Teddy Bear's Picnic," "There Ain't No Bugs on Me," "The Miller's Will," "Hot Corn, Cold Corn," "A Shenandoah Lullaby"

While *Not for Kids Only* may not be as mind-boggling as some earlier Garcia/Grisman collaborations, this project is just as intriguing. Through a collection of traditional American folk tunes—most of them originating in the southeastern United States—Garcia and Grisman follow in the same vaunted tradition of Woody Guthrie, Burl Ives, and Raffi with an offering of natural music, not processed kiddie muzak. While most of the songs easily fall into the "milk and cookies" category, at least one of the songs—"When First Unto This Country"—found its way into the set lists of their all-too-rare performances in the late 1980s and early 1990s. Campfire sing-along music at its best.

Placing the offering in context, Garcia said, "This is a reaction to the revisionist approach to children's songs. We've gone poking around in the traditional stuff for songs that don't want to be changed. We'd like to introduce them to kids the way they are and let them be."

All proceeds from the publishing of this music went towards assisting the families of children who suffered from catastrophic illnesses.

■ "No Time to Cry"

SISTERS OF MERCY, *First & Last & Always* (1985)
MERLE HAGGARD, *1996* (1996)

This nearly forgotten song of still-undetermined authorship is known to have been performed at one very early Dead show.

12/1/66, The Matrix, San Francisco

O

- **Ocean Spirit** (video)
  Produced by Bill Kreutzmann, 1995.

It's an open secret that Bill Kreutzmann's love of scuba diving was perhaps even greater than drumming with the Grateful Dead. This passion was marvelously documented in this video odyssey featuring extraordinary undersea footage, original music and environmental insights. As he told *Grateful Dead Almanac* in 1994, his goal was to make not a straight documentary, but what he called a "really entertaining adventure film, with a strong, clear environmental message."

- **"Oh Babe, It Ain't No Lie"** (ELIZABETH COTTEN)
  Elizabeth Cotten, *Negro Folk Songs and Tunes*
      (1958)
  Grateful Dead, *Reckoning* (1981)
  Jerry Garcia Acoustic Band, *Almost Acoustic*
      (1989)

Garcia probably did as much as anybody to bring proper recognition to Elizabeth Cotten. Not only did he sing "Oh Babe, It Ain't No Lie" at the Dead's 1980 acoustic sets, he performed her well-known "Freight Train" with his other bands.

Fittingly, "Oh Babe, It Ain't No Lie" has a charming history. It seems that when Cotten was a little girl residing in Chapel Hill, North Carolina, she was punished for something she didn't do by a woman named Miss Mary who took care of the Cotten kids. While she was lying in bed one night not long after, the words and then the melody came to her. She enjoyed singing it on the porch much to the enjoyment of Miss Mary who never did find out that the song was about her.

Reportedly, the Dead recorded the song for their *Reckoning* album to send a little royalty money Cotten's way as her "Shake Sugaree" was a primary influence on Garcia and Hunter for their own "Sugaree."
  9/29/80, Warfield Theater, San Francisco

- **"Oh Boy"** (Buddy Holly)
  Buddy Holly and the Crickets, single (1957), *The*
      Chirping Crickets* (1958), *Complete Buddy Holly
      (1979), *Buddy Holly Collection* (1993)
  Phil Ochs, *Gunfight at Carnegie Hall* (1970)

While the Dead only played surprise renditions of Buddy Holly's exuberant Top 10 hit at two concerts in 1971 and 1981, they also rehearsed the number with Bob Dylan in 1987.
  4/6/71, Manhattan Center, New York

- **Oh, What a Mighty Time** / NEW RIDERS OF THE
  PURPLE SAGE
  Columbia PC 33688, 1975. Produced by Bob Johnston.

Garcia kept his pedal-steel chops fresh by contributing to three tracks on this mediocre NRPS outing: "Oh, What a Mighty Time," "Layin' My Old Lady," and the R. B. Greaves hit "Take a Letter, Maria."

"Okie from Muskogee" (MERLE HAGGARD)

Merle Haggard, *Okie from Muskogee* **(1970)**
Phil Ochs, *Gunfight at Carnegie Hall* **(1970)**

The Dead's one performance of Merl Haggard's "Okie from Muskogee" was arguably the playful highlight of their famous set with the BEACH BOYS during their last guest-filled run at the Fillmore East. Haggard's tongue-in-cheek recording of "Okie from Muskogee," a song defending the conservative virtues of small-town America against the vices of hippiedom, along with the more directly patriotic "The Fighting Side of Me," made Haggard President Nixon's favorite country singer and an object of hate to many. Though Haggard has refused to be drawn into making political statements over the years, this populist edge remained a constant feature of his work.

"Okie from Muskogee" was inspired when Haggard's drummer Roy Burris spotted a road sign for Muskogee during a tour through Oklahoma and commented: "I bet the citizens of Muskogee don't smoke marijuana." Part of the fallout of the song was the many loony parodies it spawned including the Youngbloods' "Hippie from Olema."

4/27/71, Fillmore East, New York

Babatunde Olatunji

Born April 7, 1927, Ajido, Nigeria

Master drummer and world beat patriarch Babatunde Olatunji came to the United States to study medicine in 1950. But when a musical group of African expatriates he formed to combat homesickness congealed, Olatunji soon became one of the first African musicians to make a major popular impact on the American market. *Drums of Passion*, his 1959 debut album, stayed on the charts for several years, an amazing accomplishment for a record comprised of traditional drumming and chanting. The album's success and Olatunji's high-profile popularity in the early 1960s contributed to John Coltrane's interest in African traditions. Fittingly, Coltrane's last gig was held at Olatunji's cultural center in Harlem in 1967.

Mickey Hart, an early devotee of Olatunji, eventually became a brother in rhythm with the master drummer in the early 1980s and invited him to join the Dead for the 1985 New Year's Eve Show. Hart went on to produce two Olatunji albums for Rykodisc, *The Beat* and *The Invoca-*

Babatunde Olatunji. *(Courtesy of Olatunji Music)*

tion. Thus commenced a seven-show union between Olatunji and the Dead's drummers, which carried beyond a final onstage 1993 meeting to Jerry Garcia's Memorial Gathering on August 13, 1995, at San Francisco's Golden Gate Park, where, fittingly, he led the New Orleans–style funeral drum procession and eulogizers in bidding farewell to "our friend, Jerry Garcia."

Old & in the Way

Like a comet shining brightly for too brief a spell, Old & in the Way made an all too short appearance in the bluegrass universe. During nine months of 1973, it went like it came, leaving its mark on musical history with a mere eighteen club dates, four concerts, three school performances, a radio show, and a bluegrass festival. A lucky few saw them; those slow on the draw wouldn't have a second chance. Comprising Jerry Garcia on banjo, mandolinist DAVID GRISMAN, Peter Rowan or DAVID NELSON on guitar, and either Vassar Clements or Richard Green on violin, the group disbanded before the year was out so its members could go back to work on other musical projects. Luckily a few of the gigs were recorded, bringing the music back to life with all the enthusiasm and zeal that caught the band at its best. The music is alive, vibrant, and fresh. With a mix of free-spirited musical virtuosity, they worked hard at achieving their own unique approach to bluegrass music.

After Garcia, David Grisman, and Peter Rowan decided to form the band, things happened quickly. Garcia recruited John Kahn (from his own electric band) on upright acoustic bass. It was an exciting project for old friends, and Old & in the Way was born. Rehearsals started, songs were chosen, gigs booked, and Owsley came on board as a sound recorder. Grisman invited Richard Greene to play fiddle, and when he couldn't make it, John Hartford sat in. The *coup de maître* came with their first and only East Coast tour when the boys contacted the legendary Vassar Clements in Nashville and asked if he'd come and play. In a matter of days he arrived at the first gig in Boston and brought the music to another plateau, indeed.

Grisman recalled the genesis of the string band in a 1991 *Guitar* magazine interview with John Carlini. "We got together over at Jerry's house just to play bluegrass, because once you're a bluegrass picker, I think it's in your blood. So, we got together in the living room a few times. You know Jerry, if he thinks something is worth doing, he'll just take it out there right away, which is good. He said, 'Let's play some gigs,' and he had the gigs

lined up! We started playing in clubs, and then he booked a tour. It was a real informal thing. We played five gigs on the East Coast and we called up Vassar Clements and said we needed a fiddle player. We were sitting around, and Peter said he knew Vassar's phone number, so hey, what the hell! And he agreed to do the tour."

Similarly, in 1978 Garcia told Jon Sievert of *Guitar Player* magazine, "That band was like scratching an itch I'd had for a long time. I got very much into playing five-string banjo early on but was very frustrated insofar as never really having a *good* band to play with. Bluegrass is band music, and I've always loved that aspect. In fact, that's what I like best—band music rather than solo music. Playing with Old & in the Way was like playing in the bluegrass band I'd always wanted to play in. It was a great band, and I was flattered to be in such fast company. I was only sorry that my banjo chops were never what they had been when I was playing continually, though they were smoothing out toward the end."

Garcia pinpointed the group's lightning in a bottle when he spoke with Greg Jones and Andrew Pickard of *Banjo Newsletter* in 1992. "Well, the band reflected my taste in music perfectly," he said. "That was to say that

Old & in the Way, Culpepper Music Bluegrass Festival, 1973. Left to right, David Grisman, Jerry Garcia, Peter Rowan, and Vassar Clements. *(Photo by Nobuharu Komoriya)*

everybody in the band played the same style of blue-grass. We all had kind of the same feeling. The band had a certain bounce to it. It had a certain kind rhythmic feel that you don't hear too much in bluegrass. It had a swing to it, a groove, that was really nifty. It was really neat. Everybody understood how it worked in the band. Everybody could feel it. It had a lot to with David's ability to read rhythm, and his way of supporting it. But the thing is that we were all coming from the place so it was a perfect balance of styles. Vassar has a way of playing forward but Grisman's rhythm has a way of pushing the fiddle forward. So when the band was cookin' it was just—it was relentless. I mean it was a really, powerful musical organization."

A band of unique revelers on and off stage, they energized each other. Kahn's brilliant dry wit and om-nipresent bass; Rowan's singing and songwriting; Gris-man's unwavering quest for perfection; Vassar's faultless playing, pipe clenched tightly between his teeth; Gar-cia's huge heart and determination to conquer the banjo (his first instrument of expertise), an instrument he had-n't seriously touched in years. Garcia delighted in the challenge of trading licks with Grisman and Vassar and made the banjo his constant companion.

The notes kept coming and they were all special. Each gig had its own personal signature. One night the band was playing for Garcia's adoring fans in New Jersey, and the next day they were in Culpepper, Virginia, for the bluegrass fans of Grisman, Rowan, and Clements. Both audiences and musicians alike were challenged to figure out who was who and what was what. But it was never a problem as the music spoke to everyone . . . and still does!

▪ *Old & in the Way*/OLD & IN THE WAY
Round Records, RX 103, 1975 (CD reissue Rykodisc RCD 10009, 1986).
"Pig in a Pen," "Midnight Moonlight," "Old and in the Way," "Knockin' on Your Door," "The Hobo Song," "Panama Red," "Wild Horses," "Kissimmee Kid," "White Dove," "Land of the Navajo"
Jerry Garcia–banjo, vocals. DAVID GRISMAN–mandolin, vocals. Peter Rowan–guitar, vocals. Vassar Clements–fiddle. JOHN KAHN–acoustic bass.

Recorded live at San Francisco's Boarding House on October 8, 1973, *Old & in the Way* was largely responsible for the enthusiastic bluegrass revival of the mid-1970s

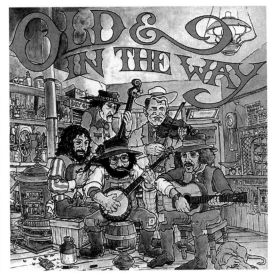

(Courtesy of Rykodisc/Sugar Hill Records)

in that it exposed a whole new audience to this brand of acoustic music.

Writing in the album's liner notes, David Grisman wrote on the band's genesis and inspiration: "I first met Peter Rowan on the school grounds at Union Grove, North Carolina in 1963. The following year, Garcia and I crossed paths in the parking lot at Sunset Park in West Grove, Pennsylvania. Back then, we were all on a quest, searching out that 'high lonesome sound' of Bill Monroe, Flatt and Scruggs, the Stanley Brothers, and other idols (Vassar among them). The music on this disc, recorded live at a gig, embodies the spirit of that original Blue Grass quest, and a genuine affection for that superlative acoustic blend of banjo, guitar, fiddle, mandolin, string bass and voice(s). We hope you dig."

Though some hard-core bluegrass aficionados enjoyed turning up their noses at the band, Old & in the Way played a genuine and sincere brand of the oeuvre exemplified on this recording.

See also **Old & in the Way** *and That High Lonesome Sound*

▪ "Ollin Arageed" (HAMZA EL DIN)
Hamza El Din, *Eclipse* (1988)

Though the Dead's musical presentations during their monumental 1978 journey to Egypt were admittedly overwhelmed by the sheer set and setting of the venue and event, their onstage collaborations with the legendary Nubian oudist Hamza El Din and his troupe are regarded as the undisputed highlights of this strangest of trips.

According to the liner notes of Hamza's *Eclipse* disc, "Ollin Arageed" is "A Nubian percussion performance, played for a person only once in a lifetime—at the celebration of his first wedding—the rhythm composed of three different beats on the tar, accompanied by a melodic handclapping, feet beating on the ground, and, traditionally, singing and the noise of women's jewelry in their soft movements to those rhythms."

During the Dead's concerts at the Pyramids, Hamza's group opened. "Ollin Arageed," a soft, entrancing polyrhythm with a vocal ensemble overlaying the beat, served as the point of the concert where the Dead slowly joined and eventually replaced the Nubian musicians onstage. The deep musical and mystical wells that are the Grateful Dead were readily apparent as they sounded both ancient and modern at the same time while conjuring the spirits of the desert.

Hamza subsequently reunited with the Dead during several shows and explored "Ollin Arageed" more.

> **9/16/78, Gizeh Sound and Light Theater, Cairo, Egypt**
> **10/21/78, Winterland Arena, San Francisco**

■ "Ol' Slew Foot" (Traditional)
Doc Watson, *Old Timey Concert* (1967)
Johnny Cash, *The Junkie and the Juicehead Minus Me* (1974)

Weir probably learned this chestnut off of Doc Watson's record and sang it at seven 1969 concerts when the band was entering its major country phase. Though the song worked well as a stand-alone, even opening up a couple of shows, it could also materialize out of a long jam.

> **6/21/69, Fillmore East, New York**

■ *One from the Vault*
Grateful Dead Merchandising Inc., GDCD 40142, 1991.
Produced by DAN HEALY. Recorded August 13, 1975, at the Great American Music Hall, San Francisco.
"Help on the Way">"Slipknot!>"Franklin's Tower," "The Music Never Stopped," "It Must Have Been the Roses," "Eyes of the World">"Drums," "King Solomon's Marbles," "AROUND & AROUND," "Sugaree," "BIG RIVER," "Crazy Fingers">"Drums">"The Other One," "Sage and Spirit," "GOIN' DOWN THE ROAD FEELING BAD," "U.S. Blues," "Blues for Allah"

Dan Healy, soundboard wizard and the band's longtime erstwhile "seventh man," inaugurated the Dead's ongoing archival project with this searing but commonly bootlegged 1975 concert at San Francisco's elegant Great American Music Hall.

Noted for its excellent fidelity and enthusiastic performances of classic and soon-to-be classic Grateful Dead concert standards, *One from the Vault* also contains the rarely played "Blues for Allah," which was left off many of the illicit pressings of the recording. This was the third of only four Dead shows during an extended hiatus from touring between October 1974 and June 1976 but they were raring to go after putting their *Blues for Allah* album in the can and hot as hell on this night.

See also **Two from the Vault**

■ "One More Saturday Night" (Bob Weir)
Bob Weir, *Ace* (1972)
Grateful Dead, *Europe '72* (1972), *Without a Net* (1990), *Hundred Year Hall/'72* (1995)
KINGFISH, *KINGFISH IN CONCERT/'76* (1995)
DAVID MURRAY, *DARK STAR (THE MUSIC OF THE GRATEFUL DEAD)* (1996)

Weir's paean to CHUCK BERRY, "One More Saturday Night" has been a frequent encore rave since its 1971 debut. The song, with a few exceptions, became a ritual inclusion whenever the Dead performed on a Saturday. A favorite lyric in the tune concerning the president of the United States cranking up the old Victrola and putting on his rockin' shoes has been amended since Ronald Reagan to include the name of the current chief executive.

> **7/18/72, Roosevelt Stadium, Jersey City, New Jersey**
> **4/30/88, Frost Amphitheater, Palo Alto, California**
> **10/27/90, Zenith, Paris**

■ *One More Saturday Night* (film)
Columbia Pictures, 1986.
Saturday Night Live writing team and Deadheads Al Franken and Tom Davis's screwball comedy was highlighted by Garcia's soundtrack production.

■ One More Saturday Night: Reflections with the Grateful Dead, Dead Family, and Dead Heads

(book)/Sandy Troy

284 pp. 30 color illustrations with over 150 black and
white photographs and graphic designs. St.
Martin's Press, 1991.

Though Sandy Troy's nonessential oral history frequently borders on the fringe, there are some special highlights with such behind-the-scenes characters as Owsley and Mountain Girl.

■ One Step Beyond/Chocolate Watch

Band

Tower, 1968. Produced by Ed Cobb.

One of the more obscure Garcia sessions, *One Step Beyond* included his stand-in for Mark Loomis, the Chocolate Watch Band's lead guitarist, who had allegedly overindulged in certain still unknown substances and was unable to play his parts on one of the album's tracks, "Devil's Motorcycle."

■ "Only a Fool" (Mydland)

Not much is known about this Mydland-sung dirge that materialized only once in the midst of a 1984 second-set New Haven jam.

4/23/84, Veterans' Memorial Coliseum, New Haven,
Connecticut

■ "The Only Time Is Now" (Warlocks)

THE WARLOCKS, *Emergency Crew* demo (1965)

Of the several not-even-passable originals the Dead recorded for their demo disc, "The Only Time Is Now" was at least an attempt to sound halfway Beatlesque.

1/7/66, The Matrix, San Francisco

■ "On the Road Again" (Traditional)

Grateful Dead, *Reckoning* (1981)

Memphis Jug Band, *Double Album/'28* (1990)

Canned Heat, *Boogie with Canned Heat* (1968),
Canned Heat Cookbook (1970), *Let's Work Together*
(1989)

Barry Goldberg, *Two Jews' Blues* (1969)

"On the Road Again," a picaresque shuffle in the Delta tradition is sometimes credited to Floyd Jones, an underrated influence on the post–World War II Chicago blues scene. But the song, given its coverage by the

(Courtesy of R. Crumb/Shanachie Entertainment)

Memphis Jug Band, has its roots in at least the 1920s if not earlier.

Weir sang this frolic at least as early as 1966 with the Dead but didn't revive it until the band's 1980 acoustic sets. Thereafter it survived as a rare first set inclusion through 1984.

10/30/80, Radio City Music Hall, New York

8/10/82, Field House, University of Iowa,
Iowa City

■ "Operator" (McKernan)

Grateful Dead, *American Beauty* (1970)

Not to be confused with the Jim Croce hit of the same title or any one of a number of operator songs in a similar vein, Pigpen's "Operator" is a folksy country reel with the blues imagery of the American night. Complete with a campy jug-band intro, there are only four known performances of "Operator" and the last of these is the best. Interestingly, the Dead take liberties with the standard twelve-bar verse form of traditional blues to create a thirteen-bar structure that is accomplished so smoothly and effortlessly that no sense of lopsidedness or awkwardness is felt.

11/8/70, Capitol Theater, Port Chester, New York

■ "The Other One" (a.k.a. "Quadlibet for
Tenderfeet") (Weir/Kreutzmann)

Grateful Dead, *Anthem of the Sun* (1968), *Grateful Dead*
(1971), *One from the Vault /'75* (1991), *Two from the
Vault /'68* (1992), *Dick's Picks Volume One/'73*
(1993), *Hundred Year Hall/'72* (1995), *Dick's Picks
Volume Four/'70* (1996), *Dick's Picks Volume
Five/'79* (1996), *Dick's Picks Volume Six/'83* (1996)

Grateful Dead/John Oswald, GRAYFOLDED
(1995)

HENRY KAISER, *Those Who Know History Are Doomed to Repeat It* (1988)

Joe Gallant and Illuminati, THE BLUES FOR ALLAH PROJECT (1996)

"Quadlibet for Tenderfeet," or "The Other One," as it is now more commonly known, was the Grateful Dead's primary primal psychedelic modal-musical voyage with its introduction in 1967.

Performed well over five hundred times, "The Other One," like "Dark Star," was the exploratory jumping-off point to places and spaces unknown. Sometimes driving, sometimes atonally out there but always intense, "The Other One" is based, as are several of the Dead's most propulsive compositions, on a simple two-chord construction of which the band never tired.

In concert, "The Other One" went through many incarnations. Its earliest renditions were taut but relatively compact explosions. In 1969 and through the early 1970s, "The Other One" was substantially elongated to include a marathon drum solo and some of the Dead's most dynamic musicianship. These versions would often and surprisingly blend into and out of cowboy songs such as "Me & My Uncle" and unexpectedly emerge in the midst of the farthest out jams. By the late 1970s, through the 1980s and right up to the end, "The Other One" returned to its earlier form as a hot but relatively concise firebomb.

Lyrically, "The Other One" is on the same astral plane as "Dark Star," though perhaps somewhat more grounded. In the first verse, a Spanish woman hands the narrator a rose imbued with mystical properties so strong they induce a reality-altering, transpersonal experience that reveals a deep, unspoken truth. The second verse, which materializes out of the plastic elastic instrumental, references both the Merry Pranksters' magic bus and its hipster-shaman driver, "Cowboy NEAL" CASSADY, who permanently takes the singer away through the looking glass. It is with these Peter Pan–like allusions that the song's timeless mood is forever set.

Garcia described the song's staying power to David Gans when he said, "It's wide open and it's got a great drive to it; those triplets. It's one of those things that you can still take anywhere. There's no way for it to get old. I

Jerry Garcia, Roosevelt Stadium, Jersey City, New Jersey, 8/1/73. *(Photo: Richard Berner)*

don't really relate to the lyrics, exactly; I relate to the way it sounds. And it sounds modern."

Describing his approach to performing "The Other One," Mickey Hart told David Gans in 1982 that "The thing about 'The Other One' that was so thrilling was that it had all these climaxes at this incredible rate—and it was already at a very strong pace. Kreutzmann and I started to do this phasing trip, where we'd split the band in half—or two and four, and so on. We'd do threes against five, against fours. . . . We called it 'going out.' "It was totally spontaneous, but the idea was to *go out*. It was important to not go out too soon; we had a tendency to go out too fast. We had to find out where it was a little better before we went out, because when we threw the ones away—the basic beats . . . you have to really know where they are. That was our experiment in rhythm, in polyrhythm."

11/11/67, Shrine Exhibition Hall, Los Angeles
5/3/69, Winterland Ballroom, San Francisco
2/13/70, Fillmore East, New York
5/2/70, Harpur College, Binghamton, New York
12/1/71, Boston Music Hall, Boston
5/3/72, Fairgrounds, Lille, France
11/22/72, Municipal Auditorium, Austin, Texas
6/18/74, Freedom Hall, Louisville, Kentucky
10/2/77, Paramount Theater, Portland, Oregon
10/21/78, Winterland Arena, San Francisco
11/29/80, Alligator Alley, Gainesville, Florida
4/6/82, The Spectrum, Philadelphia
6/16/85, Greek Theatre, Berkeley, California
5/7/89, Frost Amphitheater, Palo Alto, California
2/24/93, Coliseum Arena, Oakland, California
5/16/93, Sam Boyd Silver Bowl, Las Vegas

▪ *The Other Side of This*/AIRTO MOREIRA

Rykodisc RCD 10207, 1992. Produced by Mickey Hart.
"Endless Cycle," "Tumbleweed," "Back Streets of Havana," "Healing Sounds," "The Underwater People," "Old Man's Song," "Hey Ya," "When Angels Cry," "Dom Um (A Good Friend)," "Street Reunion," "Mirror of the Past," "Sedonia's Circle," "Terra e Mar"

Airto Moreira–vocals, the Beast, bata, hand claps, water bottle, wooden flute, Brazilian tambourine, djembe, caxixi, stomping, tree branches, surdo, shakers, cowbell, rattles, bull roarer, chimes, bird calls, berimbau, triangle, nose flute, Brazilian rain stick, conch shell, water sounds, didjeridu, African

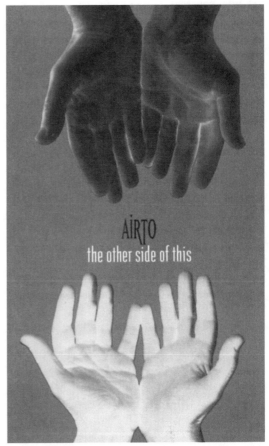

(Courtesy of Rykodisc)

black flute, African rattles, Chinese balls, hollow bamboo blown on water. Mickey Hart–wood, stomping, vocals, shakers, rattles, Tibetan bowl. ZAKIR HUSSAIN–tabla, wood. BABATUNDE OLATUNJI–wood. Kitaro–wood, stomping, vocals. T. H. "Vikku" Vinayakram–ghatam. Frank Colon–bata, shekere, lead vocals. Giovanni Hidalgo–bata, cowbell, shekere, vocals. Diana Moreira–vocals, hand claps, stomping. Dr. Verna Yater–vocals. FLORA PURIM–stomping, vocals. Caryl Ohrbach–stomping, vocals, frame drum. Rose Solomon—stomping, vocals. Cheryl McEanney–stomping, vocals. Sedonia Cahill–frame drum and vocals. Justine Toms—frame drum and vocals. Margaret Barkley–tar and vocals. Leah Martino–frame drum and vocals. Amarita Blain–frame drum and vocals. K. C. Ross–frame drum and vocals. Jana Holmer–frame drum and vocals.

The Other Side of This marked a new direction for Airto Moreira as both a percussionist and composer. An intense and rhythmic percussion album, this Mickey Hart production challenges the listener and establishes Moreira as a musical treasure the entire planet should cherish.

As Hart wrote in the album's liner notes, "With this album, Airto is again pushing the limits of what is thought of as 'music.' As these recordings will reveal, he has transcended musical boundaries just as he did when he came to the United States from Brazil twenty-five years ago. He is tapping a new and powerful source of energy that takes the listener to another place."

■ *OutSides*/Tom Constanten

Tom Constanten Productions, 1990. Produced by Terry Ryan.

"Dejavalse," "Rondo Passo (preview)," "Overture, the Affair of Rue de Lourcine," "Claude Greenberg's Springtime Catch," "Sonatina," "Bugsy," "Fandango Maltallado," "The Disco Delius Banjo Bash," "Uptown Boy," "Sonata Desaxificata: I. Encodex Punctillious, II. Apocryphal Awry, III. Rondo Pazzo," "The Unspeakable Pact of Mohair and Slim Salabim," "Let It Ring," "Prelude," "Ma fin est mon commencement," "Alaric's Premonition, a Gothic fugue en rondeau on a theme by J. Garcia," "Rondo Pazzo (reprise)," "Electronic Study #3"

T.C.'s efforts at self-production continued with *OutSides* with music drawing from a much wider palette of colors and styles than his first offering, *Fresh Tracks In Real Time*. *OutSides* finds the gifted pianist exploring new contemporary musical territory. Of note to Deadheads: Constanten's "Electronic Study #3," which closes side two, is the original piece that was used in *Anthem of the Sun*, portions of which were included between "The Other One" and "New Potato Caboose."

- **"Pain in My Heart"** (Otis Redding/Phil Walden)
Otis Redding, *Pain in My Heart* (1964)
The Rolling Stones, *The Rolling Stones No. 2* (1965)

This slow, aching ballad was a minor hit for a little-known but big-voiced Southern soul singer named Otis Redding in 1963. Despite the writing credits, the song was based on "Ruler of My Heart," which was originally penned by Naomi Neville (alias Allen Toussaint) and first recorded by Irma Thomas. But in Redding's hands the song became a classic, showcasing his histrionic, baroque approach and helping establish Redding as one of the most popular artists on the black touring circuit of the South.

Redding's coauthor on the song was Phil Walden, who guided his career from the beginning. Walden, a white Southerner, went on to manage other soul stars and set up Capricorn Records for which THE ALLMAN BROTHERS BAND recorded.

The Rolling Stones' cover of "Pain in My Heart" brought the song to a wider audience, but the Dead were probably aware of both versions when Pigpen sang the song a couple of times with the band in 1966.

7/16/66, Fillmore Auditorium, San Francisco

- ***Panther Dream*** (book)/Bob and Wendy Weir
Hyperion, 1991.

The Weirs' first stab at children's books was a major score. With its overt but noncloying eco-correct agenda, *Panther Dream* tells a symbolic story of a young boy's walk through a sometimes threatening jungle. In this pointed coming-of-age tale, he learns of life's most important lessons: respect.

In *Panther Dream*, Bob Weir and his sister Wendy have given us a young protagonist, Lokuli, who lives in a small farming community in the heart of the African rain forest. Although desperate for meat, the villagers will not hunt in the dense rain forest, for they believe the forest is haunted by evil spirits. Though forbidden by all except his grandmother, Lokuli ventures into the forest alone to find meat for the village.

Observing the flora and fauna, Lokuli is unaware that a black panther stalks him, watching his every move. The narrative is rich and even eloquent in the details of the rain forest: "There is no breeze. The air is hot and humid. The mass of shaded green is broken only by slats of light filtering down through the trees to the forest floor. The whir of cicadas and the buzz and scrape of insects penetrate the stillness."

Wendy Weir's lush illustrations, framed by liana vines, portray a village and forest habitat teeming with vegetation, people, and creatures of all sorts.

Coming with the best of intentions, *Panther Dream* exudes a concern for the fragile ecology of the African rain forest. Proceeds from sales fund reforestation and education projects in Africa.

As Weir told Greg Cahill of *Pacific Sun* in 1991, "The point of the book is to help get kids in touch with the environment of the rain forests, even though they can't actually reach out and experience it. If we can impart this kind of awareness to them then maybe—just maybe— they'll grow up with this feeling of interconnectedness. In the interim perhaps they'll hammer their parents and get *them* to do something about the issue."

The Weirs selected Africa as the setting for the story because most of the media attention has focused on the plundering of the South American rain forests, while neglecting other tropical regions including America's own Hawaiian rain forests.

In 1991, *Panther Dream* was named the Notable Children's Trade Book in the Field of Social Studies by the Joint Committee of the Children's Book Council and the National Committee of Teachers of Social Studies.

▪ *Panther Dream/Panther Dance*/Bob and Wendy Weir

Virtual Sound 56282-0, 1991.

"Panther Dream," "Panther Dance"

Bob Weir–guitar, synthesizer. Jules Beckman–bass, drums, percussion. Paul Giacomantonio–harp, drums, wind driver. Rob Wasserman–six-string electric upright bass.

The cassette-tape companion to Bob and Wendy Weir's ecologically correct book features Bob reading the story on the A side and leading a small band through an atmospheric evocation of the African rain forest on the flip side.

▪ *Papa John Creach*/Papa John Creach

Grunt/RCA FTR 1003, 1971.

Papa John Creach (born May 1917, Beaver Falls, Pennsylvania) cut one of the more unusual figures onstage with the Jefferson Airplane, Starship, and Hot Tuna through the 1970s. By the time he joined the groups with his electrified violin, the short, wiry, and mercurial musician was already in his early fifties and a veteran of minstrelsy, vaudeville, burlesque, and the blues. As an African American, his enlistment in the Airplane marked one of the first notable racial integrations of a nationally renowned act. The Airplane broke up in 1972 but soon reorganized and relaunched as Jefferson Starship with Creach on board through their million-selling *Red Octopus* album in 1975.

Along the way he began releasing solo albums, *Papa John Creach* being the first. More of a Jefferson Airplane family album than a solo endeavor, *Papa John Creach*

was one of several LPs in a flurry of releases by the Airplane itself and several of its offshoots on their own Grunt label. Each of these albums featured several members of the loose aggregation informally dubbed PERRO (the Planet Earth Rock & Roll Orchestra). All the Bay Area music heavies, including Garcia, make cameos on the platter but the final wash sounds more like the Airplane of the period with Creach's electric violin mixed to soaring levels.

Creach continued to release solo albums through 1992, two years before his death of heart failure at the age of seventy-six.

▪ "Parchman Farm" (Bukka White)

Bukka White, *The Complete Bukka White* (1994)

Mose Allison, *Local Color* (1957)

John Mayall, *Blues Breakers* (1966)

Blue Cheer, *Vincebus Eruptum* (1968), *The Beast Is Back* (1985)

Johnny Winter, *About Blues* (1969)

Hot Tuna, *Pair of Dice Found* (1990)

Cactus, *Cactology* (1996)

Booker T. Washington "Bukka" White's classic "Parchman Farm" is a country-blues classic covered by a number of bands including the Dead when they performed it at one known early concert.

Born November 12, 1909, in Houston, Mississippi, Bukka White was a traditional Delta blues singer and slide guitarist whose rough vocals and sharp guitar riffs defined his style's primitivism. A true blues originator, White made most of his recordings in the 1930s but did not receive proper acclaim until his "rediscovery" in the early 1960s when the folk-blues revival of the era hit. Though he died on February 26, 1977, in Memphis, Tennessee, he lived long enough to see his repertoire and indigenous Delta approach considered alongside the likes of Charley Patton and Robert Johnson.

White's father, a railroad worker and semiprofessional musician, taught him how to play guitar, and White graduated from parties and juke joints to the minstrel life, playing for tips and spare change as he drifted about the South. Though he cut some blues and religious numbers for the Victor label in 1930, he was unable to survive as a full-time musician and turned to professional baseball in the Negro Leagues as well as doing a stint as a boxer.

The low life caught up with him in 1937 when he was

arrested and sent to prison for allegedly shooting a man. Amazingly, he jumped bail and made it to Chicago where, while not exactly lying low, he recorded two songs for Vocalion, before he was nabbed and sent to Parchman Farm, the notorious Mississippi Big House.

Parchman Farm was everything its legend prepared him for: set amidst broiling flat fields worked by convicts under the discipline of the whip, the brick-oven cell blocks bred riots and radiated an Abandon All Hope menace. Parchman: The name alone still sends shivers up the spines of Mississippians and was the spectral enforcer of the harsh police-state-like system of the poor of both races (including Elvis Presley's father) who labored in its hell within the hell of sharecropping misery, the theme of the many convict blues it inspired.

But his two years at Parchman Farm did not break Bukka White. He continued to play music for the entertainment of his fellow inmates and even recorded a couple of songs for Alan Lomax and the Library of Congress.

White continued to perform and record shortly after his release in 1940 but by the end of the decade, with the country blues falling out of favor, Bukka had settled in Memphis where he worked as a common laborer and rarely performed.

When he was "rediscovered" and recorded by two University of California Berkeley students (folk-blues guitarist John Fahey and blues aficionado Ed Dawson in 1963), White was still a vital musician. His best work features a percussive, down-home approach to the country blues accentuated by his National guitar and full-throated vocals that employed spoken or chanted passages. Both talents were probably best on his train songs, which combined talking blues and train sounds emanating from his resonaphonic guitar.

The song made one very early appearance in the Dead's repertoire.

1/7/66, The Matrix, San Francisco

▪ "Passenger" (Phil Lesh/Peter Monk)
Grateful Dead, single, *Terrapin Station* (1977), *Dead Set* (1981), *The Arista Years* (1996)

Phil Lesh and his friend Peter Monk wrote "Passenger," but it was Weir and Donna Godchaux who sang the high-geared song in concert. Lyrically obscure, "Passenger" is open to interpretation. The gist of the poetry, however, would seem to finger us all as passengers in the mysterious and joyous cycle of life. Politically and personally,

"Passenger" deals with alienation. Hearts turn cold and the passage of time freezes the good intentions of the seeker into a tomb of the malnourished soul. Thus a realm is entered where every man must fend for himself.

A concert powerhouse, "Passenger" was, aside from "Feedback," about as close to heavy metal as the Grateful Dead got. Even Lesh admitted, "The only reason I made up 'Passenger' was that I wanted the guitar players to play with a little raunch."

The band frequently performed the tune from 1977 through 1981 when it mysteriously dropped out of their rotations; a sorely missed number.

1/15/78, Selland Arena, Fresno, California

▪ *Peace on Earth*/Country Joe McDonald
Ragbaby Records RAG 1019, 1989.

Hart and Weir lent a hand on two tracks from this album by their old partner in anarchy, Joe McDonald.

▪ "Peggy-O" (Traditional)
Ewan MacColl, *Scots Folk Songs* (1956)
BOB DYLAN, *Bob Dylan* (1962)
JOAN BAEZ, *In Concert Vol. 2* (1962)
Judy Collins, *Golden Apples* (1963)
Simon and Garfunkel, *Wednesday Morning 3 A.M.* (1966)
The Journeymen, *Capitol Collector's Series* (1992)

Also known as "Fennario," "Peggy-O" tells the tragic story of a young woman who loses her beloved captain to the horrors of battle. Perhaps because of its implicit antiwar sentiment, "Peggy-O" attracted the likes of Bob Dylan, Joan Baez, Judy Collins, Simon and Garfunkel, and the Grateful Dead. Predictably, Dylan's snarling early version had a harder, angrier edge while the Dead's arrangement stuck closer to the sweeter melodies of the Baez and Collins versions. But it is in that dichotomy that the power of the song lies. The incredibly sad tale is juxtaposed with an equally tender melody.

Baez went to great lengths to unearth much of what we know about the song's extensive lineage. According to the *Joan Baez Songbook*, "Cecil Sharp discovered several versions of this ballad in the Southern Appalachians on his collecting trips during the First World War, though it seems to have disappeared from the American tradition since that time. It is still extremely popular in Scotland as 'The Bonnie Lass Fyvie-O' and was earlier known in England as 'Pretty Peggy of Derby.'"

"Peggy-O" was introduced as a regular first-set Garcia ballad in 1973 and was exhibited at more than 250 Dead shows through 1995. Garcia also trotted it out as a Garcia Band rarity in the early 1980s.

> **5/9/77, War Memorial Auditorium, Buffalo, New York**
> **4/16/78, Civic Center, Huntington, West Virginia**
> **11/10/79, Crisler Arena, Ann Arbor, Michigan**
> **11/2/84, Berkeley Community Theater, Berkeley, California**
> **3/27/86, Cumberland County Civic Center, Portland, Maine**
> **3/10/93, Rosemont Horizon, Rosemont, Illinois**

▪ Robert M. (Bobby) Petersen

Born 1936; died 1987

Bobby Petersen may be the most overlooked member in the Grateful Dead's extended artistic commune. The author of "New Potato Caboose," "Pride of Cucamonga," "Revolutionary Hamstrung Blues," and "Unbroken

Bobby Petersen. *(PHOTO: DAVID COLARDO)*

Chain" did not leave much of a visible wake, rather a sharp undertow. An old friend of Phil Lesh's, Petersen led a road life that rivaled his sometime-companion Neal Cassady's and published two volumes of poetry (*Far Away Radios* and *Alleys of the Heart*) that should grow in importance with the passage of time.

Described by Lesh as a "mad beatnik poet" and "a road *pirate*," Petersen was born of a solid middle-class background in Klamath Falls, Oregon. But he caught the Beat Generation bug and, in the 1950s, hopped freight trains, played jazz saxophone, attended San Mateo College, served time, practiced freedom, and was a bridge between the beats and the San Francisco rock era. A self-educated man, Peterson absorbed the lore of the West including its local and natural history allowing him to create a body of poetic work that was a testimony of culture in transformation. As Robert Hunter wrote in the forward to the posthumously published *Alleys of the Heart*, "This is not a light poet you hold in your hands. His aim is true. He will take you somewhat deeper than is comfortable, if you enter his lines rather than flipping through them."

▪ *Petulia* (film)/Directed by Richard Lester, 1968.
Starring George C. Scott and Julie Christie.

The Dead's brief appearances in *Petulia* by Richard Lester (the acclaimed and innovative director of *A Hard Day's Night*, *Help!*, and a couple of the *Superman* flicks), are probably the most interesting parts of this quirky muddle of a film, though some cineastes insist that it is a hip, insightful portrayal of contemporary relationships.

Petulia concerns itself with a wealthy but batty San Francisco waif (Julie Christie) and her strange seduction of a successful doctor (George C. Scott). She propositions Scott the first time they meet even though her husband is within view. Later, she shows up at his apartment with a stolen pawnshop tuba. She is, as Scott so observantly points out, "a kook."

As Lester zigzags his film through the flashbacks and flashforwards of cinematographer Nicholas Roeg's startling images, we watch the jigsaw puzzle pieces of *Petulia* come together to form a capsule of upper-class love in the 1960s.

The Dead perform "VIOLA LEE BLUES" early in the film and later appear in a scene as observers on the street after a woman is assaulted by her boyfriend. JANIS JOPLIN with Big Brother and the Holding Company also make a brief performance cameo.

▪ "Phil's Earthquake Space" (Lesh)

On the seventy-sixth anniversary of the Great San Francisco Earthquake of '06, Phil Lesh created a one-time, one-man cacophonous re-creation of that watershed disaster.

4/18/82, Hartford Civic Center, Hartford, Connecticut

▪ "Picasso Moon" (Weir/Barlow/BRALOVE)
Grateful Dead, *Built to Last* (1989)

One of the Dead's most fully realized compositions, "Picasso Moon" was a late addition to the Weir/Barlow song cycle of "Misfit Power" at its extreme. But, where the predecessors to "Picasso Moon" find the narrator at odds with his aloof predicament, this song is a personal call to action and transformation. Picasso's moon illuminates a path, however dim, to enlightenment and redemption. Weir sings the song with an unnerving desperation as if his entire life depends on the answers hidden within the moon's mysterious glow—pursued by both angels and demons at their play in his invocation of the orb's magical properties.

The song went through some typically Weir circumnavigations before the final arrangement was set. He had originally written the tune for another set of lyrics but Brent Mydland had independently composed the music for those lyrics. According to Weir's 1989 interview with Blair Jackson that meant it was time to begin again. He said, "So I took the music and went on a vision quest—I went on a good, long bicycle ride is what it amounted to, and in the middle of it, I came up with what I wanted the song to be about."

In 1993, Weir gave Jon Sievert of *Guitar Player* a more nuts-and-bolts description about how the song fell into place. "On 'Picasso Moon,' for instance, I found that I could fret both the sixth string and the first string with my pinky finger. I arch it over the rest of the fingerboard so I've got this sound that's a lot like one of Keith Richards's weird five-string tunings. With the high string way up there it gives a chord sort of a searing quality. It took a little bit of work, but that kind of stuff pops out and there are happy little surprises, that give you enough joy to come up with a melody that has some life to it. Also, when you're in that joyous space you can bond the melody with the lyric and see where the lyric needs adjustment or whatever."

10/16/89, Brendan Byrne Arena, East Rutherford, New Jersey

5/27/93, Cal Expo Amphitheater, Sacramento, California

▪ *Pistol Packin' Mama*/The Good Old Boys
Round/UA RX 109 RX-LA597-G1975; Grateful Dead Merchandise GDCD 4012, 1991. Produced by Jerry Garcia.
"Ashes of Love," "Here to Get My Baby Out of Jail," "Long Gone," "Dim Lights, Thick Smoke," "Deep Elem Blues," "Pistol Packin' Mama," "Banjo Signal," "Toy Heart," "Leave Well Enough Alone," "Too Wise Special," "On Top of Old Smokey," "Barefoot Nelly," "Don't You Hear Jerusalem," "Glendale Train"
DAVID NELSON—guitar, vocals. Frank Wakefield—mandolin, vocals. Don Reno—banjo, vocals. Chubby Wise—fiddle. Pat Campbell—bass.

Fresh from his "New Grass" experience with OLD & IN THE WAY, Garcia kept his skills as a producer sharp. In this classic bluegrass album he guides some of the genre's most respected practitioners through a number of standards, some of which would show up in his own Almost Acoustic band's concerts more than a decade later.

▪ *Planet Drum* (book)/Mickey Hart and Frederic Lieberman
HarperCollins, 1991.

A smashing anthropo-sociological layman's exegesis of the drum's art and function throughout world history and culture, *Planet Drum* was Mickey Hart's pictorially heavy followup to his autobiographical *Drumming at the Edge of Magic*. With more than 350 photographs and illustrations, the book captures and illuminates the global primacy of percussion and provides a stunning pictorial map of the world beat. Ranging from the Big Bang to the present, from Mesopotamia to Bunker Hill, *Planet Drum* is a celebration of percussion in every form known to man.

Planet Drum was written with Dr. Frederic Lieberman, an ethnomusicologist and professor at the University of California at Santa Cruz, and D. A. Sonneborn, an ethnomusicologist, teacher, composer, and writer.

As Hart told Blair Jackson in 1990, "The first book is sort of the preface to the second book. The second book is really the lumber I gather. It's the anaconda; the time line. All the pearls, all the ornaments, all the jewels I picked up on the search for the Holy Grail."

▪ *Planet Drum*

Rykodisc RCD 10206, 1991. Produced by Mickey Hart.

"Udu Chant," "Island Groove," "Light over Shadow," "Dance of the Hunter's Fire," "Jewe," "The Hunt," "Temple Caves," "The Dancing Sorcerer," "Bones," "Lost River," "Evening Samba," "Iyanu," "Mysterious Island"

Mickey Hart–bass drum, snare drum, hoop drum, tambourine, triangles, "Beam," bomboo indio with split bamboo, drum set, vocals, body percussion, rain stick, Earth drum, clackers, bones, balafon, bell, gourds, grand dumbec, gourds. Sikiru Adepoju–cowbell, duggi tarang, dundun, bell, gudugudu, djembe, bell. ZAKIR HUSSAIN–udu drum, balafon, tablas, madal, dholak, naal, bells, taya, dundun, shaker, bell, duggi tarang, conch shell. AIRTO MOREIRA–tamanco, bird calls, conch shell, claps, chimes, vocals, caxixi, rattles, Chinese cymbal-throwing, snare drum, metal spring, toms,

(Courtesy of Rykodisc)

Mexican donkey jaws, cowbell, cuica, flute, djembe, shakers, slit gongs, conch shell, voice/breath, berimbau, cymbals, wood blocks, floor tom, metal percussion, bass drum, tom toms, tambourine,

Planet Drum: Flora Purim, T. H. "Vikku" Vinayakram, Sikiru Adepoju, Zakir Hussain, Mickey Hart, Babatunde Olatunji, Airto Moreira. *(Photo: John Werner courtesy of Rykodisc)*

bamboo with brushes, bird whistles, body percussion, nose flute. BABATUNDE OLATUNJI–djembe, congas, shekere, vocals, ashiko, ngoma, body percussion, shaker, bell, clapping. FLORA PURIM–vocals, wind chimes, seagulls. Frank Colon–shekere. Giovanni Hidalgo–shekere, congas, bata. Caryl Ohrbach–shaker. T. H. "Vikku" Vinayakram–ghatam, jew's-harp. Bruce Langhorne–vocals, body percussion. Gordy Ryan–body percussion. Molonga Casquelord–vocals. Jeff Sterling– udu drum.

A sparkling all-percussion marathon with plenty of muscle and deep grooves featuring many of the world's master musicians is loosely tied to Mickey Hart's book of the same title.

■ **Planet Earth Rock and Roll**/Paul Kantner
RCA AFL1-4320. Produced by Scott Mathews and Ron Nagle, 1983.

A high-concept, sci-fi epic rock opera with a musical cast of thousands (well, dozens anyway) includes Kantner's "The Mountain Song," which is based on a melody line of Garcia's from an unreleased 1970 session. Garcia shares a writing credit on the tune.

■ **Playboy After Dark** (television program)

In 1969, the Dead visited "Playboy After Dark," Hugh Hefner's casually forced chat and variety show that featured the requisite curvaceous females and live music. Along with exciting versions of "St. Stephen," "Mountains of the Moon," and "Turn on Your Love-light," the appearance was notable for both Garcia's serape and his spacey rap with a clueless Hefner.

For a glimpse at some of the antics that went down on the fringes of the production, check out Rock Scully's *Living with the Dead.* Hefner came *this* close to getting dosed.

■ **"Playing in the Band"** (Weir/Hart/Hunter)
Grateful Dead, *Grateful Dead* (Skull and Roses) (1971), *What a Long Strange Trip It's Been* (1977), *Dick's Picks Vol. 1/'73* (1993), *Hundred Year Hall/'72* (1995), *Dozin' at the Knick/'90* (1996), *Dick's Picks Volume Seven/'74* (1997)
Bob Weir, *Ace* (1972)

A triumphant rock anthem recalling the great marching band music of turn-of-the-century America, "Playing in the Band" was one of the Dead's most often played songs, transforming and metamorphosing with the group nearly six hundred times in concert since 1971. While the earliest versions stay very close to the "Skull and Roses" release, by early 1972 the Dead had begun to tentatively test the song's fluidity and at year's end it had developed into an extended modality, as spacey and tight as anything the Dead performed. It remained in the musical ozone through 1974 as the Dead began experimenting with its qualities as a segue device often linking it with its musically similar "Uncle John's Band." In the late 1970s and throughout the 1980s and 1990s it retained its function as an exploratory tool though, like "The Other One," it began to once again compress in length, intensity, and focus.

In the 1980s, the Dead began breaking up the song, going so far as to start the tune one night and finish it on the next—sometimes in a different city altogether.

The lyrics of "Playing in the Band" contain some interesting (and evidently tongue-in-cheek) messianic overtones: a blameless narrator keeps his head above the fray of human turmoil with the easy excuse that he was "just playin' in the band."

As Hunter told Jeff Tamarkin of *Relix* in 1986, "That was written the same day as 'Greatest Story Ever Told,' which was written to the sound of a pump, by the way. Mickey had a beat for it and laid down some rhythm tracks, then asked me to write some lyrics for it. I wrote the lyrics, then Weir came around and wrote a guitar part for it. I wasn't certain it was going to be a Grateful Dead song . . ."

12/15/71, Hill Auditorium, Ann Arbor, Michigan
4/29/72, Musikhalle, Hamburg, Germany
5/26/72, The Strand Lyceum, London
11/22/72, Municipal Auditorium, Austin, Texas
12/31/72, Winterland, San Francisco
9/21/73, The Spectrum, Philadelphia
11/17/73, Pauley Pavilion, Los Angeles
12/2/73, Boston Music Hall, Boston
5/21/74, Edmondson Pavilion, Seattle
6/19/76, Capitol Theater, Passaic, New Jersey
12/31/76, Cow Palace, Daly City, California
5/17/77, Memorial Coliseum, Tuscaloosa, Alabama
6/8/80, Folsom Field, Boulder, Colorado
10/16/81, Melk Weg, Amsterdam
4/14/82, Civic Center, Glens Falls, New York

6/25/85, Blossom Music Center, Cuyahoga Falls, Ohio

3/29/87, The Spectrum, Philadelphia

5/26/93, Cal Expo Amphitheater, Sacramento, California

- ## *Playing in the Band* (book)/David Gans and
  Peter Simon. Foreword by Phil Lesh.
  191 pp. St. Martin's Press, 1985.

Taking the Studs Terkel approach, David Gans lets the Dead tell their own story. This must-have volume (studded with photographic gems thoughtfully collected by Peter Simon) gives an insider's view of the band's real and musical history from the cats who lived and played it.

- ## *Powerglide*/NEW RIDERS OF THE PURPLE SAGE
  Columbia KC 31284, 1972.

Despite the fact that Buddy Cage had joined the New Riders of the Purple Sage as their full-time pedal steel player and the overt connection with the Dead had softened by the time *Powerglide* was released, Garcia and Kreutzmann's appearance on the album may have helped it crack the Top Forty. Garcia can be heard playing banjo on "Sweet Lovin' One" and "Duncan and Brady," and piano on "Lochinvar." Kreutzmann's percussion is evident on "I Don't Need No Doctor" and "WILLIE AND THE HAND JIVE," the Johnny Otis hit the Dead would cover many years later.

- ## "Prisoner Blues" (Traditional)

An informal unit calling itself MICKEY AND THE HART-BEATS enjoyed jamming at the Matrix, a hip coffeehouse in San Francisco during the fall of 1968. Featuring the likes of Jerry Garcia, Mickey Hart, Phil Lesh, Elvin Bishop, and Jack Casady, the Hartbeats toyed around with a few expansive Dead tunes, spontaneous groove improvisations and several covers. "Prisoner Blues," a self-explanatory lament of unknown origin, was performed at a couple of these loose Matrix gigs. The Hartbeats' version does bear a resemblance to "Prison Bound Blues," one of Leroy Carr's best compositions, which was originally recorded in 1928 and inspired countless versions from Big Bill Broonzy to Muddy Waters.

10/30/68, The Matrix, San Francisco

- ## "The Promised Land" (CHUCK BERRY)
  Chuck Berry, *You Never Can Tell* (1964), *St. Louis to Liverpool* (1964), *Chuck Berry's Golden Decade Vol. 2* (1964), *The Music Never Stopped: Roots of the Grateful Dead* (1995)
  Grateful Dead, *Steal Your Face* (1976), *Dick's Picks Volume Five*/'79 (1996)
  THE BAND, *Moondog Matinee* (1973)
  Elvis Presley, *Promised Land* (1974)
  KINGFISH, *Kingfish in Concert*/'76 (1995)

It is ironic that one of the greatest road songs in popular Americana was written in jail. But it was in the Federal Medical Center at Springfield, Missouri, that Chuck Berry found himself in 1962—convicted of the Mann Act (transporting an underage female across state lines for immoral purposes). Fortunately, his stint allowed a certain flexibility and space to continue his rock composing.

In his autobiography, Berry recalled: "I remember having extreme difficulty while writing 'Promised Land' in trying to secure a road atlas of the United States to verify the routing of the Po' Boy from Norfolk, Virginia, to Los Angeles. The penal institutions then were not so generous as to give a map of any kind, for fear of providing the route for an escape."

Introduced into their shows in 1971, "Promised Land" was a natural show opener or first-set closer with Weir reprising his role as the Berry vocal invocateur.

8/24/72, Berkeley Community Theater, Berkeley, California

3/25/91, Knickerbocker Arena, Albany, New York

- ## *Promontory Rider*/Robert Hunter
  Relix RRLP 2003, 1989.
  "Boys in the Bar Room," "That Train Don't Run Here Anymore," "Tiger Rose," "Hooker's Ball," "Standing at Your Door," "Promontory Rider," "Touch of Darkness," "It Must Have Been the Roses," "Rum Runners," "Drunkard's Carole," "Lady of Carlisle," "Prodigal Town"
  Robert Hunter–guitar, tin whistle, vocals. Jerry Garcia–guitar, piano, snythesizer. T. Will Claire, Maureen Aylett, Rodney Albin–backup vocals. Mickey Hart–drums. Barry Melton–guitar, harp. David Freiberg–bass. Keith Godchaux–keyboard. Donna Godchaux–vocals. Steven Schuster (and others)–reeds and horns. Marleen Molle and

Kathleen Klein–vocals. Kevin Morgenstern–guitar. Richard McNeese–keyboard. Larry Klein–bass. Pat Lorenzano–drums. David Torbert–bass. Buddy Cage–pedal steel guitar. Markee Shubb–mandolin. Rick Shubb–banjo. Peter Albin–bass.

Primarily a Robert Hunter anthology, *Promontory Rider* works as a retrospective of the poet's more obscure lyrics. Yet, with the beauty and style of a chameleon, Hunter alters his voice throughout this collection to match the color of the foliage of each song. Whether as the masterful storyweaver in "Rum Runners" or the deliriously overjoyed guest at the "Hooker's Ball," Hunter reveals the natural powers of an intuitive raconteur.

According to Hunter's notes in *A Box of Rain*, "Hooker's Ball" was "The official theme song for the final Hooker's Ball in 1978. The San Francisco city council decided such an annual event was unseemly and refused to rent its Brooks Hall facility to Margo St. James's Coyote prostitutes' support group anymore. A commercial venture called the Exotic Erotic Ball has taken its place and seems to be okay with them."

A couple of songs concern themselves with those souls who dwell in pubs. "Boys in the Barroom" poses the philosophical question, "Does God look down on the boys in the barroom?" while treating the listener to a gorgeous display of harmony. "Drunkard's Carole," a merry tune reminiscent of a British alehouse song, pays tribute to the occasional stumbles that befall a man on his way to salvation. Another criminally overlooked Bob Hunter collection.

- **"Proud Mary"** (JOHN FOGERTY)
  Creedence Clearwater Revival, *Bayou Country* (1969), *Chronicle* (1976), *The Concert*/'70 (1980)
  Elvis Presley, *On Stage—February* 1970 (1970), *Elvis Recorded Live at Madison Square Garden* (1972)
  Ike and Tina Turner, *Workin' Together* (1970), *Live at the Carnegie: What You Hear Is What You Get* (1971)
  Tina Turner, *Live in Europe* (1988), *What's Love Got to Do With It* (1993)

Written by John Fogerty and recorded by Creedence Clearwater Revival, "Proud Mary" sold over a million copies and reached No. 2 on the pop charts in 1969. A bar band special, John Fogerty's "Proud Mary" is representative of many CCR songs that celebrate nostalgia for a more innocent vision of America. Evoking the riverboat days of Mark Twain, "Proud Mary" is no doubt being sung by a Tina Turner wanna-be in a Bangkok dive or a karaoke parlor in Labrador as you read this. It's still that ubiquitous.

The Dead performed "Proud Mary" once and that was with Fogerty when he joined the band during their set at the BILL GRAHAM Memorial Concert.

11/3/91, Polo Field, Golden Gate Park, San Francisco

- ***Pulling Me Apart: Captain Credit***/Philo
  ABS Records 8824, 1973.

Kreutzmann played drums while DAN HEALY and Hart engineered this bit of early 1970s obscura.

- **Flora Purim**
  Born March 6, 1942, Rio de Janeiro

Brazilian vocalist Flora Purim has led a wondrous and sonically psychic life, journeying the world in search of musical harmony. Raised in a musical family, Purim studied with percussionist AIRTO MOREIRA, whom she married in 1972.

From her days singing in her native Brazil to her collaborations with the popular Return to Forever fusion group in the early 1970s and drum masters Mickey Hart, ZAKIR HUSSAIN and BABATUNDE OLATUNJI, Purim has created some of the spicier grooves this side of the mambo. Her music balances the joyous emotions of life in tribal dance-style jazz tunes with more subdued moments through traditional Brazilian ballads and lullabies.

Her romance with Moreira is one of the great bonds of the jazz world. They first met in 1965 in Brazil and again three years later when Purim was studying in California. Soon after their marriage, the two were recruited by Chick Corea into Return to Forever. Of her collaboration with that highly popular unit, Purim told Roger Len Smith of *RELIX* magazine in 1995, "It was very limiting because I had to sit down and I couldn't relax and lose my whole body. I sing with my body, unfortunately; some people can just sing. If I don't move, I don't have it. Chick's music and Airto's music are very intense, even though they do have great dynamics. On the original Return to Forever, Chick played a lot of acoustic piano. With the evolution of the band it became so loud and electric, I couldn't keep up. So now, I keep up with loudness, you know how? I have [an effects] rack! The minute they raise their volume, all I have to do is raise mine."

As of 1995, Purim and Airto had not only recorded twenty-eight albums, but both had also contributed to many recordings by a variety of prominent artists. Purim can be heard on albums by the likes of jazz pianist (and John Coltrane alumnus) McCoy Tyner, bassists Ron Carter and Stanley Clarke, George Duke (the pianist who made his name working with Frank Zappa), and tenor saxophonist Joe Farrell.

Purim's association with the Grateful Dead began in 1979 when she and Airto were enlisted by Mickey Hart to contribute to the soundtrack recordings for Francis Ford Coppola's film *Apocalypse Now*.

On December 13, 1980, the two made their first on-stage appearance with the Grateful Dead at the Long Beach Arena in Southern California. Thus began her five-concert contribution as well as a February 11, 1989, show at the Los Angeles Forum.

The work with Mickey Hart continued through and beyond their onstage powwows. Purim and Airto continued their recording relationship with the Dead's percussionist with their 1985 album *DÄFOS*, an intriguing percussion-based sound tapestry. The couple were also among the principal musicians of *Planet Drum*, Hart's 1991 expedition into world percussion and its many avenues.

- **"Queen Jane Approximately"** (BOB DYLAN)
  Bob Dylan, *Highway 61 Revisited* (1965), *Dylan and the Dead* (1987)
  The Four Seasons, *Big Hits by Bacharach, David & Dylan* (1965)

Wide open to interpretation, this puckish put-down song has been taken to connote everything from a JOAN BAEZ snub, a reworking of a classic early sixteenth-century English-Scottish ballad, a veiled reference to a marijuana score, or an invitation to a drag queen.

Weir handled the vocals after the Dead and Dylan worked up an arrangement for their 1987 concerts and the song stuck firmly in the band's first-set "Dylan slot," growing by leaps and bounds through the years.

  8/17/91, Shoreline Amphitheater, Mountain View, California

- **"Quinn the Eskimo (The Mighty Quinn)"** (BOB DYLAN)
  Bob Dylan, *Self Portrait* (1970), *The Basement Tapes/'67* (1975), *Biograph* (1985)
  Manfred Mann, single (1969, 1982), *The Mighty Quinn* (1969), *Watch* (1978), *Budapest* (1984), *20 Years of Manfred Mann Earth Band 1971–1991* (1991), *Chapter Two: The Best of the Fontana Years* (1994)

  The Hollies, *Hollies Sing Dylan* (1969)
  Leon Russell, *Leon Live* (1973)
  Little Angels, single (1993)

It was a bit of a *cause célèbre* when the English pop group Manfred Mann had a hit with this tune from Dylan's then hush-hush "Basement Tapes" bootleg in the summer of 1969. Its success was, apparently, a bit of a surprise to Dylan, who once commented on the song's odd qualities, "I don't know what it was about. I guess it was some kind of a nursery rhyme."

Actually, this betrays the important cultural history involved with the release and popularity of "Quinn." Some Dylan scholars point to the singer/songwriter's interest in film and the obscure flick *Attila the Hun*, in which the actor Anthony Quinn plays a character approximating the appearance of an Eskimo, as a partial inspiration for the song's composition. Additionally, there is some debate among Dylanists as to the song's significance, some insisting that it's trivial while others pointing to a messianic subtext.

With Garcia singing lead, the Dead performed "Quinn the Eskimo" dozens of times between 1985 and 1995 almost always as an upbeat encore.

  12/27/86, Henry J. Kaiser Convention Center, Oakland, California
  2/24/92, Coliseum Arena, Oakland, California

R

■ **"The Race Is On"** (Don Rollins)
Grateful Dead, *Reckoning* **(1981)**
George Jones, *I Get Lonely in a Hurry* **(1965),** *The Best*
of (1955–1967) **(1991)**
Jack Jones, single (1956)
Dave Edmunds, *Twangin'* **(1981)**

"The Race Is On" is a clever country novelty song that likens aspects of the human condition (pride, heartaches, falling tears, etc.) to a horse race. Buoyant, tearjerky, and tongue-in-cheek all at the same time, the song was an early hit for George Jones in 1964.

Universally known as "the Rolls-Royce" of country music, Jones is a singer's singer and is likely to appear on anybody's list of the top male crooners in his genre. Like Hank Williams and Lefty Frizzell, Jones is an interpreter of country archetypes—broken love, human feelings, sweet love gone sour—through personal experience.

Jones was born September 12, 1931, in Saratoga, Texas, and raised in that area of East Texas known as the "Big Thicket." His piano playing mother and a guitar playing father gave George his first six-string at age nine. Three years later, the boy was earning money playing on the streets of Beaumont, Texas, and appearing on an afternoon radio show in his middle teens. By the time he hit seventeen, Jones was headlining the Beaumont club scene, but a bad marriage led him to enlist in the U.S. Marines and a Korean War tour.

Upon his discharge in 1952, Jones resumed his career as a full-time performer, slowly emerging as one of country's stars with a string of popular and influential songs mixing honky-tonk, blues-drenched East Texas twang, and early country-rock. "White Lightning," his first No. 1 country hit in 1959, was an uptempo novelty written by J. P. Richardson, better known as "The Big Bopper."

After his star rose higher following the success of "The Race Is On" in 1964, Jones's productions became increasingly careless despite the high quality and influential power of the songs themselves. Though they were sometimes recorded with strings, songs such as "She Thinks I Still Care" and "A Good Year for the Roses" were later revived by artists as varied as Creedence Clearwater Revival and Elvis Costello.

For a time, Jones's hard-living and cavalier attitude about performing earned him the nickname "No Show Jones." But when he retained Billy Sherrill as his producer, married Tammy Wynette in 1969, and joined her label, his star power was reignited. For a time, George and Tammy were without question the king and queen of country. "We're Gonna Hold On" catapulted him back into No. 1 Land in 1973 and introduced a series of hits that took the Jones-Wynette union (and eventual breakup) as their subject, climaxing with "Golden Ring" and "Near You" in 1976, the year Wynette remarried.

Once again, Jones's drinking threatened his career but, under Sherrill's skillful handling, he again prospered and continued to score big country hits. As he pushed and eclipsed sixty, Jones kept his name fresh, by recording with some of his most accomplished peers including Linda Ronstadt, Emmylou Harris, Willie Nelson, Merle Haggard, James Taylor, Elvis Costello, and Garth Brooks.

The Dead performed "The Race Is On" several dozen times in the late 1960s and early 1970s before resurrecting it as a choice in the band's 1980 acoustic sets. Subsequently its performance was linked to Dead shows that fell on Kentucky Derby day.

> 6/16/74, State Fairgrounds, Des Moines, Iowa
> 10/4/80, Warfield Theater, San Francisco
> 5/4/91, Cal Expo Amphitheater, Sacramento, California

▪ "Railroading Across the Great Divide" (Traditional)

U. Utah Phillips, *Legends of Folk* (1968)
Critton Hollow String Band, *Great Dreams* (1976)

Another one-off from Bobby Ace and the Cards from the Bottom of the Deck, "Railroading Across the Great Divide" is a western folk song of vague origin celebrating the wide-open spaces, places, and possibilities of early-twentieth-century America.

> 6/11/69, California Hall, San Francisco

▪ "Rain" (Lennon/McCartney)

The Beatles, single (1966), *Hey Jude* (1969)
Todd Rundgren, *Faithful* (1976)
Bongwater, *Double Bummer* (1989)

"Rain" first appeared on an experimental Beatles' single with "Paperback Writer" in 1966. The music and the vocal were slowed down technically in the recording studio and one lyric ("Rain, when the rain comes they run and hide their heads") is heard in reverse at the end of the disc because John Lennon, as he was to later claim, inadvertently played the working tapes backwards when he was at home and liked the effect so much he wanted it re-created on the record. But George Martin, the Beatles' recording manager and musical guru, contradicted Lennon by laying claim to the idea, saying he decided to take the line of vocal by Lennon off the four-track and put it on another spool and experiment by playing it backwards.

"Rain" was one of several Beatles' tunes keyboardist Vince Welnick encouraged his band mates to perform and, after it was introduced in December 1992, was utilized primarily as an encore.

> 5/25/93, Cal Expo Amphitheater, Sacramento, California

▪ "Rainy Day Women #12 and 35" (BOB DYLAN)

Bob Dylan, *Blonde on Blonde* (1966), *MTV Unplugged* (1995)
Bob Dylan and THE BAND, *Before the Flood* (1974)
Tom Petty and the Heartbreakers, *Bob Dylan: The 30th Anniversary Celebration Concert* (1993)
A Subtle Plague, *Marijuana's Greatest Hits* (1992)
Little Mike and the Tornadoes, *Flynn's Place* (1995)

"Rainy Day Women #12 and 35" is not just one of Bob Dylan's crazier songs, it is also one of his most commercially successful, soaring to No. 2 in 1966 on the pop charts as did "Like a Rolling Stone" a year earlier. Considering this was written by the most accomplished lyricist of his generation, it is a delightful stroke of lunacy—refreshing and great fun for Dylan and his studio musicians during the *Blonde on Blonde* recording session.

Ironically, despite its popular refrain ("Everybody must get stoned"), the song would seem to satirize the sixties drug culture as much as it extols it. Even in his later performances of "Rainy Day Women," it is difficult to determine if Dylan wasn't having some fun at his audience's (sometimes oblivious) expense. Not to say that in the heat of the 1960s there wasn't a huge outcry accompanying the song's release. The controversy was so strong, in fact, that it prompted Dylan to announce: "I never have and never will write a 'drug song.'" Despite this questionable claim, "Rainy Day Women" was banned by American and British radio stations, prompting *Time* magazine to report: "In the shifting, multilevel jargon of teenagers, to 'get stoned' does not mean to get drunk, but to get high on drugs . . . a 'rainy-day woman,' as any junkie knows, is a marijuana cigarette."

Indeed, the *Blonde on Blonde* version conveys a woozy and boozy New Orleans street procession, complete with tambourines and oompah bass drum adding to the song's sensory abandon.

Given Deadheads' reputation as a "party" crowd, "Rainy Day Women" was a natural selection for the Dylan and Dead concerts in 1987, albeit one of their less successful ones. Not surprisingly, it saw no life at Dead shows until His Bobness paid a surprise Madison Square Garden visit in October 1994 to rouse the boys and the crowd with an encore performance of the song with the mantra that still seems dangerous.

7/19/87, Autzen Stadium, Eugene, Oregon

▪ "Ramble On Rose" (Garcia/Hunter)
Grateful Dead, *Europe '72* (1972), *What a Long Strange Trip It's Been* (1977)

Ripe with self-referential Grateful Dead symbolism, "Ramble On Rose" contains the primary iconographic image associated with the band in the title. "Ramble On Rose" also catalogues a number of cultural icons in its strange portrait of Americana. Charlie Chan, P. T. Barnum, Wolfman Jack, and Billy Sunday all make their cameos. Jack the Ripper even pops up to pay his transatlantic respects. But it also references the mystery of the blues in its mention of "mojo hand," which was a common term among rural blacks for a person with magical abilities.

Hunter admitted to David Gans in 1978 that "I think 'Ramble On Rose' is the closest to complete whimsy I've come up with. I just sat down and wrote numerous verses that tied around 'Did you say your name was Ramblin' Rose? Ramble on, baby, heh, settle down easy.'"

"Ramble On Rose" is an odd mix of folk ballad and country swing not unlike "Brown-Eyed Women" or "Sugaree" in its plucky plaintiveness. And, like those two songs also introduced in 1971, it was a solid first set regular with the odd second set demonstration. Its original arrangement was not toyed with much but the earlier renditions had a looser, quicker tempo and a spunky punch.

5/3/72, Olympia Theater, Paris
7/13/74, Dillon Stadium, Hartford, Connecticut
5/19/77, Fox Theater, Atlanta
4/24/78, Horton Field House, Normal, Illinois
7/8/78, Red Rocks Amphitheater, Morrison, Colorado
4/30/88, Frost Amphitheater, Palo Alto, California
9/17/93, Madison Square Garden, New York

▪ *Rare, Live & Classic*/JOAN BAEZ
Vanguard 125/127, 1993.

Garcia, Weir, Hart, and Mydland did a session with Joan Baez around the time the Dead shared some bills with her in 1981. Many years later, "JACK A ROE" and "Marriott USA" were released from that get-together as part of this mega Baez box set.

▪ "The Raven" (Edgar Allan Poe)

In honor of their 1982 visit to Edgar Allan Poe's neighborhood, Phil Lesh read "The Raven," the poet's creepy symbolic masterpiece, while his band mates churned out a broiling space jam behind his recitation. In the Grateful Dead universe, Poe's dark jewel holds something of the same place as their own "Dire Wolf." The bird is Poe's bête noire: a black beast and nemesis representing the extreme yang within himself and nature as a whole. For another postmodern take on "The Raven," check out "Po' Eddie and the Bugbird," Lord Buckley's hipster interpretation of the classic on his posthumous release *A Most Immaculately Hip Aristocrat.*

Poe (1809–49) was born in Boston, orphaned in 1811 and joined the army at eighteen but was court-martialed three years later for deliberate neglect of duty. He turned to writing and turned out an extraordinary body of work in the last half of his short life. His short stories are renowned for their horrific atmosphere, as in *The Fall of the House of Usher,* and for acute reasoning, as in *The Gold Bug* and *The Murders of the Rue Morgue,* in which the investigators Legrand and Dupin anticipate Sir Arthur Conan Doyle's Sherlock Holmes. His verse, of which "The Raven" is most celebrated and studied, is colored by haunting lyric beauty and influenced the French Symbolists at the turn of the century. But Poe failed to earn a living as a writer. He became an alcoholic, lost his wife, and was found in a stupor outside a Baltimore saloon on October 3, 1849. He died four days later.

4/19/82, Civic Center, Baltimore

▪ *Reckoning*
Arista A2L 8604, 1981.
"Dire Wolf," "The Race Is On," "Oh Babe, It Ain't No Lie," "It Must Have Been the Roses," "Dark Hollow," "China Doll," "Been All Around This World," "The Monkey and the Engineer," "Jack-a-Roe," "Deep Elem Blues," "Cassidy," "To Lay Me Down," "Rosalie McFall," "On the Road Again," "Bird Song," "Ripple"

The Dead played a series of critically acclaimed three-set shows in the fall of 1980 that featured their return to live acoustic performing in the opening sequence. Fortunately the band was savvy enough to record and release a document of this run with *two* double albums.

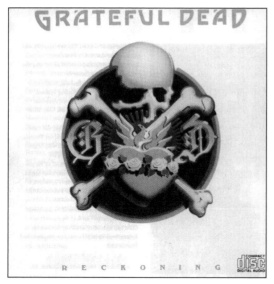

(Courtesy of Arista Records)

(© Grateful Dead Merchandising, Inc.)

The first and better of these efforts was *Reckoning*, a wonderful acoustic blend of soft Dead classics ("Bird Song," "Ripple," and "Dire Wolf") and choice country-blues chestnuts ("Rosalie McFall," "Dark Hollow," and "Oh Babe, It Ain't No Lie").

- ### Red Octopus/Jefferson Starship
  Grunt BFL 1-0999, 1975.

With Marty Balin and David Freiberg, Hunter cowrote the lyrics to "Tumblin'," one of many masterful songs on the Starship's best and most popular LP. Grace Slick's expressive singing and Marty Balin's reintegration to the group make this timeless recording a keeper. Around the same time, the threesome collaborated on "Nighthawks," a song that was to be the title track of an uncompleted Starship album but was performed by that group in the late 1970s.

- ### Reflections/Jerry Garcia
  Round RX-LA565-G/RX-107, 1976 (CD reissue Grateful Dead Merchandising GDCD 4009). Produced by Jerry Garcia.
  "Might as Well," "Mission in the Rain," "They Love Each Other," "I'll Take Melody," "It Must Have Been the Roses," "Tore Up over You," "Catfish John," "Comes a Time"

Nicky Hopkins–piano. JOHN KAHN–bass, synthesizer, vibes and clavinet. Ron Tutt–drums. Larry Knechtel–piano. Grateful Dead perform as a unit on "Might as Well," "They Love Each Other," "It Must Have Been the Roses," "Comes a Time."

Reflections is actually a hybrid Grateful Dead and JERRY GARCIA BAND album. The Dead perform on the tunes associated with their shows and Garcia's bar band tackle the numbers they performed in concert. Despite the thrown together quality of the album, *Reflections* is a too-often-overlooked studio disc as the groups are virtually indistinguishable from track to track and there isn't a dud in the mix. In fact, the Garcia Band numbers steal the show here and every one of the songs as a staple of both units.

Discussing the album's impetus with Blair Jackson in 1991, Garcia said, "Well, it was a continuation of what we were doing with *Blues for Allah*. We were having fun in the studio is what it boils down to, and that's pretty rare for us. The energy was there, and I thought, 'I've got a solo album coming up. Let's cut these tracks with the Grateful Dead. I've already taught them the tunes.'"

The album fared pretty well, hitting No. 42 in Billboard, charting for fourteen weeks.

Crosby, Stills, Nash and Young, Polo Field, Golden Gate Park, San Francisco, 11/3/91. (Photo: Chris Walklet)

▪ *Relix* (magazine)

The longest continually published Deadzine, and among the best ever, *Dead Relix* was founded in 1974 by Les Kippel, a trailblazer of the taping scene. Initially edited by Jerry Moore, *Dead Relix* drew together the disparate elements of the community during the Dead's touring hiatus. Starting out as little more than a crudely, but lovingly, designed chap book, *Relix* expanded to an impressive, four-color newsstand item by 1980 and shortened its name as a reflection of the wider focus it had adopted. While this sometimes included cover stories on the likes of Ozzy Osbourne, the magazine never strayed far from its original charter.

When Toni Brown took the helm in the 1980s, *Relix* sharpened its editorial focus and mandate, providing in-depth coverage not only of the Dead but all their related and various configurations as well. Naturally, the likes of Bob Dylan, the Allman Brothers Band, and Neil Young were well represented, but Brown made special efforts to make sure to spill some ink on up-and-coming sojourners such as Blues Traveler and Phish. Brown also took up the cause of those who had fallen victim to the harsh mandatory minimum-sentence drug laws enacted during the U.S. government's so-called "War on Drugs" by both speaking up against the legislation and publishing a list of incarcerated Deadheads yearning for correspondence. There is little doubt that Brown's loving perseverence with *Relix* in the years following Garcia's death helped keep the human Deadhead mandala intact.

▪ *Replay*/Crosby, Stills and Nash
Atlantic, 1980.

Garcia's pedal-steel contribution on the song "Change Partners" was released on a couple of Crosby, Stills and Nash albums including this compilation.

▪ "Reuben and Cherise" (Garcia/Hunter)
Jerry Garcia, *Cats Under the Stars* (1978)
Robert Hunter, *Jack O' Roses* (1979), *Box of Rain* (1991)

A popular Garcia Band song, "Reuben and Cherise" is one of Robert Hunter's great achievements as it recasts the Greek myth of Orpheus in New Orleans during Mardi Gras. Actually, the song owes just as much to the classic 1960 Marcel Camus film *Black Orpheus*, which tells the legend in modern day Rio during Carnival.

In the myth, Orpheus ventures into the Underworld to retrieve the body of his love Eurydice in a story that was reshaped by the great poets and writers through history starting with Homer, Virgil, and Dante.

"Reuben and Cherise" follows a similar path as Hunter places himself in the supreme literary tradition that modernizes a venerable archetypal tale and rejuvenates it for its transformative powers. James Joyce's *Ulysses*, which set Homer's *Odyssey* in 1906 Dublin, and Thomas Pynchon's *Gravity's Rainbow*, which also reinvented Orpheus in World War II Europe, are among the renowned twentieth-century examples of this literary method.

In Hunter's universe, Reuben takes on the mask of Orpheus and it is with his painted mandolin (his modernized lyre) that he unsuccessfully ventures into the Underworld of New Orleans to retrieve the doomed Cherise, the Eurydice of the songwriter's contemporary vision.

In their 1991 conversation with Blair Jackson, Garcia and Hunter gave an in-depth description of the song's genesis and meaning. Garcia said: "'Reuben and Cherise' started around the time of *Blues for Allah*, but it was completely different. I had a little riff I was fond of—a cute little thing where each time [the riff came around] it got a little shorter. It was a little trick, like a vanishing box; an optical illusion, or musical illusion. 'Hey look at this!' So I played it and Hunter studied it, and he came up with some lyrics. And the lyrics were so much better than my musical idea; the melody sounded diddley in comparison. He was already enunciating some of that *Black Orpheus* undercurrent. So I back-burnered it for a while. I came back and looked at it, and he'd changed it again, then I changed it, and we went back and forth. Then, when I started work on *Cats Under the Stars* it seemed right all of a sudden and it all clicked into place and I wrote that setting for it. It was one of those songs that had to be slammed and banged and adjusted before it was right. Usually if you work that long on something it ends up sounding forced, but in this case all that work became invisible and the result is a nice, sophisticated song that's invisibly complex. It slides right along and has a great narrative drive that exposes the lyrics in a nice way, and it also has some dramatic contour to it that makes it a better storytelling form than some things we've done."

Hunter was quick to point out that "I'd just like to add that 'Rube froze and turned to stone' does not mean that Ruby died. It just meant that she was in a state of shock at hearing her rival's voice through a mandolin. If you think she died there you're going to get the whole song wrong. I know there are people who are confused on that point."

"Reuben and Cherise" was a Jerry Garcia Band staple since 1978. The Dead, however, only broke the song out for four surprise concert showings in 1991.

12/1/89, Warfield Theater, San Francisco (Garcia Band with Clarence Clemons)

4/7/91, Orlando Arena, Orlando, Florida

■ "Revolution" (Lennon/McCartney)
The Beatles, *The Beatles* (The White Album) (1968), *Hey Jude* (1970)

John Lennon had been wanting to address his feelings about both the Vietnam War and his sense of uprising when he traveled to India in 1968. What followed was a complex composition not without its political fallout, precisely the effect he had probably desired.

As Lennon was to later say about "Revolution," "There were two versions of that song but the underground left only picked up the one that said, 'When you talk about destruction, don't you know that you can count me out.' The original version which ends up on the LP said 'Count me in' too; I put in both because I wasn't sure. There was a third version that was just abstract, *musique concrète*, kinds of loops and that, people screaming. I thought I was painting in sound a picture of revolution—but I made a mistake. You know. The mistake was that it was antirevolution."

As one might expect, the Dead chose the revolution of non-violence when they commenced performing the song as a shocking encore in 1983 and trotting it out eleven times over the next eleven years.

10/12/83, Madison Square Garden, New York

■ "Revolutionary Hamstrung Blues"
(Lesh/Mydland/PETERSEN)

Bobby Petersen's last lyrical contribution to Grateful Dead poetry, "Revolutionary Hamstrung Blues" was sung by Lesh and Mydland at one 1986 show. Petersen and Lesh had worked on the song in the early 1980s but, after hitting a creative logjam, they turned it over to Mydland. In 1986, Petersen told *The Golden Road* that the song was "sort of a period piece about people fighting amongst themselves, instead of fighting who they should be fighting."

3/27/86, Cumberland County Civic Center, Portland, Maine

■ The Rex Foundation
"Service in the Commonweal"

The Rex Foundation was created as a charitable foundation by members of the Grateful Dead and friends. It aims to help secure a healthy environment, promote individuality in the arts, provide support to critical and necessary social services, assist others less fortunate than ourselves, protect the rights of indigenous people and ensure their cultural survival, build a stronger community, and educate children and adults everywhere.

According to Mickey Hart, Rex draws its inspiration from two sources: a former roadie and an old television series. As he told the *New York Times* in 1994, "We named the foundation after Donald Rex Jackson, who was killed in a car crash in 1976. He embodied this great generous spirit. He was wild, a renegade who'd do anything, and I think Rex has some of that spirit. It's also like that old show *The Millionaire* where someone you don't know enters your life and gives you the chance to turn it around. I like to think we're doing that through Rex."

The Dead call it Lone Ranger philanthropy, Rex is unlike other charities because of what it doesn't do: it has no endowment, no fund-raising campaigns and no paid board or staff members. It solicits no grant proposals, rarely advertises its good works, and raises almost all of its money from Dead shows. Virtually all of their grant recipients are selected through the personal knowledge of the decision makers—as a result, unsolicited requests will not be considered. They have no application forms and no published guidelines. Grants are made once or twice a year, and their report and newsletter are published annually.

Most of the dozens of grants awarded each year go to recipients nominated by a body known as the Circle of Deciders, composed of the band members, their families, the Dead's office staff, and friends like former National Basketball Association great Bill Walton. All are guided by serendipity; inspiration to pursue a cause may stem from something as casual as a newspaper article.

The lion's share of the fund came from the Dead's annual Rex Foundation shows, usually held in June at the Shoreline Amphitheater in Mountain View, California. In 1995, the band's final year of touring, concert proceeds contributed $1,551,282 of the $1,753,140 accrued by Rex, and left the Foundation in a state of flux and uncertainty. But with a growing circle of donors Rex encourages donations to support their work and continues to welcome tax-deductible contributions, which amounted to $167,599 dollars in 1995. The nearly two hundred Rex recipients in 1995 included groups as diverse as the AIDS Information Network, Baseball Without Borders, Community House Mental Agency, the Duke Ellington School of the Arts, Forgotten Felines, Green Chimneys Children's Services, the Haight-Ashbury Food Program, the National Poetry Association, the Skokomish Indian tribe, the Wild Dolphin Project, and the Yerba Buena Jazz Band, with a couple of grants reaching as high as $20,000.

Commenting on the diversity of Rex's beneficiaries, Phil Lesh told the *New York Times* in 1994, "We look for things that have fallen through the cracks of the big charities, that need an angel to come down and give them a shot. There are no strings because if we trust them enough to give them the money, we trust them to know the best way to spend it."

Before the Dead had money to give away, the band played for free; in fact, its first show as the Grateful Dead was a benefit for the San Francisco Mime Troupe. In an era of limelight activism, when celluloid messiahs often draw less attention to their cause than their célèbre, the Dead had quietly donated time and money since they formed in 1965. And in an era when that decade is both overglamorized and rashly demonized, the Rex Foundation serves as a reminder that the decade's better impulses are always relevant.

In addition to their regular grants, the Rex Foundation also gives the Ralph J. Gleason Award to groups and individuals who have made an outstanding contribution to culture. Past recipients include Alan Lomax, Pharoah Sanders, the San Francisco Mime Troupe, the Hiero-glyphics Ensemble, David Grisman, the Sun Ra Arkestra, and Mike Seeger.

The Rex Foundation can be contacted at: P.O. Box 2204, San Anselmo, California 94979.

■ *The Rhythm Devils Play River Music: The Apocalypse Now Sessions*/Rhythm Devils

Passport PB 9844, 1980/Rykodisc 0109. Produced by Mickey Hart.

"Compound," "Trenches," "Street Gang," "The Beast," "Steps," "Tar," "Lance," "Cave," "Hell's Bells," "Kurtz," "Napalm for Breakfast"

Mickey Hart, Billy Kreutzmann, AIRTO MOREIRA, Michael Hinton, Jim Loveless, Greg Errico, Jordan Amarantha, FLORA PURIM, Phil Lesh

Rarely does ambient soundtrack music translate beyond the celluloid in which it is physically and artistically embedded. Yet this is such an album.

The Dead's involvement with this historic project began when film auteur Francis Ford Coppola attended a Grateful Dead show in the mid-1970s. He approached Mickey Hart and Bill Kreutzmann for a soundtrack to accompany what turned out to be the director's magnum opus on the Vietnam War, *Apocalypse Now*.

Hart described the project to Blair Jackson in 1990. "That was inspired by *Apocalypse Now*, of course, and that was a brutal, dark, foreboding image. It was the image of war, so it has all those nuances."

The film was partly responsible for engendering "The Beast," a huge array of percussion instruments assembled for the Rhythm Devils' contribution to the soundtrack. According to the album's liner notes, the music they made suggested "the single breath of war permeated every gesture, every movement, every thing. . . . Music not only relevant to Vietnam in the sixties, but also back in time to the first man." The music evoked the sense of the jungle, which Hart described as "a constant killing ground" whether or not human beings walked through it.

The group assembled a collection of instruments from across the globe and arranged them in the Dead's Club Front studio. The musicians viewed sequences from the film, spontaneously drawing on their instruments in response to the visuals and to each other's sounds.

For several years following the *Apocalypse Now* sessions, the Beast became a regular part of the Dead's stage setup. Although its size and configuration both shrank and altered over time, the Beast was still road-tested at every Dead show during the drummers' duet in the second set.

▪ "Riot in Cell Block #9" (LEIBER & STOLLER)
The Robins, single (1955)
Commander Cody, *Live from Deep in the Heart of Texas* (1974)
Johnny Winter, *Saints and Sinners* (1974), *The Johnny Winter Collection* (1988)
Dr. Feelgood, *As It Happens* (1979)

The Coasters were one of the most popular vocal groups of the 1950s. They started out professionally as the Robins, scoring hits under the writing and production care of Jerry Leiber and Mike Stoller. The duo's recordings with the Robins and the Coasters saw a marked development in their writing skills and production techniques. For songs like "Riot in Cell Block #9," "Smokey Joe's Cafe," and "SEARCHIN'," Leiber and Stoller wrote miniature dramas in which members of the group played different parts. In its original recording, the harrowing "Riot in Cell Block #9" was punctuated (like a modern rap track) by sirens and gunshots.

Both "Riot in Cell Block #9" and "Searchin'" were included in the Dead's famous set with THE BEACH BOYS during the last days of the Fillmore East.

4/27/71, Fillmore East, New York

▪ "Ripple" (Garcia/Hunter)
Grateful Dead, single, *American Beauty* (1971), *What a Long Strange Trip It's Been* (1977), *Reckoning* (1981)
Jerry Garcia Acoustic Band, *Almost Acoustic* (1989)
Chris Hillman, *Desert Rose* (1984)
Robert Hunter, *Box of Rain* (1991)
Jane's Addiction, *Deadicated* (1991)
NEW RIDERS OF THE PURPLE SAGE, *Live in Japan* (1991)

A medium-tempo Zen lullaby with a C&W bounce in the tradition of the Dead's best grooves, "Ripple" is a Deadhead favorite for its soft wisdom and folksy warmth. Like many Dead songs, "Ripple" doesn't pretend to provide the answers to life's great and small questions. Rather, it posits that each must follow their hearts to personal and spiritual fulfillment: "There is a road, no simple highway, that path is for your steps alone."

"Ripple" is filled with simple imagery as close to a musical representation of a Buddhist meditation garden as a song can get.

Yet there are levels of complexity and magic to the composition. As Garcia told Charles Reich in 1971, "'Ripple' is one of those things of having two halves of a thing and having them come together just perfectly. Bob Weir had a guitar custom-made for himself and I picked it up and that song came out, it just came out. Or at least the melody came out of the guitar and then when I saw Hunter—Hunter was in England at the time—next time I saw Hunter he says, 'Here, I have a couple of songs I'd like you to take a look at,' and he had 'Ripple' and it just . . . all of a sudden, just bam, there it was, it was just perfect. The interesting thing about that is the little bridge in there is a perfect haiku. The little 'Ripple in still water' part is a haiku, seventeen syllables. There's a lot of those kinds of things in our music that most people never get. Hunter is just a fantastic craftsman. He had lots of years of speed freaking, you know, to get really crazy about language."

It was Hunter, however, who recalled the elements that resulted in the song's completion. While discussing Garcia's habit of carrying around the lyrics with him for a while and working on them on the fly, Hunter told Blair Jackson that "The best example of that is 'Ripple,' which I wrote in England and brought back. They were on the trans-Canadian trip [summer 1970], Jerry woke up one morning, sat on the railroad tracks somewhere near Saskatoon and put it to music."

Of the lyrical composition, Hunter told Jackson that: "I wrote 'Ripple,' 'Brokedown Palace,' and 'To Lay Me Down' all in about a two-hour period of the first day I ever went to England. I sat there with a case of Retsina and I opened up a bottle of that stuff, and the sun was shining, I was in England, which I'd always wanted to visit, and for some reason this creative energy started racing through me and I could do no wrong . . ."

The Dead introduced "Ripple" as an acoustic offering in 1970. After a few attempts at electrifying it a year later, it was shelved until the band's 1980 acoustic revival when it found its place as a sweet set ender during that brief bicoastal run of shows. The Dead only played it at a couple of concerts after that but Garcia often included it as a selection in his acoustic gigs.

2/21/71, Capitol Theater, Port Chester, New York
4/29/71, Fillmore East, New York City
9/30/80, Warfield Theater, San Francisco

1/28/86, The Ritz, New York (Jerry Garcia solo with JOHN KAHN)

■ Road Runner

See "(I'm a) Road Runner"

■ "Roberta" (LEADBELLY)

Leadbelly, *The Legend of Leadbelly/*'39 (1976)
Midnight Special/'35 (1990)

Though Leadbelly is generally credited as the author of this dusky Louisiana blues, his biographers suggest that he learned the song on Fannin Street, Shreveport's rough and tumble thoroughfare, just after the turn of the century.

Leadbelly recorded "Roberta" numerous times and one of those old discs must have caught Bob Weir's attention as he performed it on two consecutive nights with his Grateful Dead spin-off band, Bobby Ace and the Cards from the Bottom of the Deck.

4/19/70, Family Dog, San Francisco

■ *Rock Columbia*/Robert Hunter

Relix RRLP 2019, 1984. Produced by Robert Hunter.
"Eva," "End of the Road," "I Never See You," "Aim at the Heart," "Kick It on Down," "What'll You Raise?," "Who, Baby, Who?," "Rock Columbia"
Robert Hunter–guitar, vocals. RICK MEYERS–keyboards, synthesizer. Johnny d'Fonseca–drums. Michael White–bass. DAVID NELSON–guitar, harmony. Jeanette Sartain, Joan Cashel, Annie Stocking–harmonies.

Instantly accessible, Hunter's fourth album in a two-year period contains some of his strongest melodies aided by a solid backup group. The vaguely Dylanesque "End of the Road," a couple of affecting ballads ("I Never See You" and "Aim at the Heart") and the metaphorical "What'll You Raise?" all contribute to another crafty and spit-shined offering from the Dead's wordsmith.

■ "Rockin' Pneumonia and Boogie Woogie Flu" (John Vincent/Huey Smith)

Huey "Piano" Smith, *Louisiana Piano Rhythms/*'57 (1994)
Jerry Lee Lewis, single (1965)
The Flamin' Groovies, *Supersnazz* (1969), *Flamingo* (1973)
The Crickets, *Bubblegum, Pop, Ballads & Boogies* (1973)
Professor Longhair, *Rock 'n' Roll* (1974)

The Meters, *Good Old Funky Music* (1979)
David Lindley, *El Rayo-X* (1981)
Art Neville, *His Specialty Recordings* (1992)
Sugar Beats, *Everybody Is a Star* (1995)

Born January 26, 1934, Huey "Piano" Smith was a rhythm & blues pianist whose rollicking live shows allowed him to make the crossover to rock & roll. A popular New Orleans session musician and bandleader in the 1950s, Smith's only two hits were "Rockin' Pneumonia and Boogie Woogie Flu" in 1957 and "Don't You Just Know It" a year later.

Reared on Crescent City gospel and blues, Smith began playing local clubs with Guitar Slim in 1950. But Slim bounced Smith from the piano bench in 1954, replacing him with the later-to-be-legendary Ray Charles. Smith floated around town as an in-demand gig and sessionman for a few notable groups, including Little Richard's.

However, his popularity rose rapidly when he formed the Clowns and hired Bobby Marchan to sing lead vocals. The commercial success of "Rockin' Pneumonia" and "Don't You Just Know It" garnered invitations to join R&B and rock & roll package tours in the late 1950s and early 1960s. Though some of his recordings during this period, with strange titles like "Little Chicken Wah-Wah" and "Tu-ber-cu-lucas and Sinus Blues," were marginally successful, Smith retired by decade's end to become a Jehovah's Witness. Several later comeback attempts failed.

With Garcia handling the lead vocals, the Dead only performed "Rockin' Pneumonia" about five times in 1972.

10/23/72, Performing Arts Center, Milwaukee

■ "Rollin' and Tumblin'" (Muddy Waters/Traditional)

Singles: Hambone Willie Newbern (1929), Charlie Patton (1929)
Muddy Waters, *The Real Folk Blues* (1966), *The Chess Box* (1989)
Elmore James, *The Complete Fire and Enjoy Sessions/*'63 (1989), *King of the Slide Guitar/*'63 (1992), *The Sky Is Crying/*'63 (1993)
Big Joe Williams, *Classic Delta Blues* (1964)
Cream, *Fresh Cream* (1966), *Live Cream, Vol. 1* (1970)
Johnny Winter, *The Progressive Blues Experiment* (1969)

Buddy Guy and Junior Wells, *Alone and Acoustic* (1981)
Canned Heat, *The Best of Canned Heat* (1987)
Eric Clapton, *Unplugged* (1992)
Howlin' Wolf, *Ain't Gonna Be Your Dog* (1994)

The last new cover song to get the call at a Dead show (two second-set appearances out of "Truckin'" in June 1995) was "Rollin' and Tumblin'"—a ragged, raucous, and updated Delta blues made famous by Muddy Waters and Elmore James but sometimes credited to Bobby Robinson, a Chicago producer who oversaw and engineered many of James's best sides in the late 1950s through Elmore's last session in 1963. Robinson was regarded as ahead of his time, easily the most technically advanced producer James worked with—recording almost everything in stereo as early as 1958, and in three- and four-track by 1963. Under Robinson's sympathetic guidance, James was finally able to give his penchant for playing "louder than God" free rein. The crashing fretboard slams, wrenched power chords, and screaming treble-string slides on the Robinson-produced gems have emerged as both anticipations and cornerstones of heavy metal. All headbangers, whether they know or not, are children of Elmore James.

But this great Delta-blues classic was first recorded by Hambone Willie Newbern in 1929 and was followed by Charley Patton's similar piece, "Down the Dirt Road Blues."

6/15/96, Franklin County Field, Highgate, Vermont

- ## *Rolling Thunder*/Mickey Hart
  Warner Bros. BS 2635, 1972. Relix RRLP 2026, 1986;
  Grateful Dead Records, GDC40114.
  "Rolling Thunder (Shoshone Invocation)," "The Main Ten (Playing in the Band)," "Fletcher Carnaby," "The Chase," "Blind John," "Young Man," "Deep, Wide and Frequent," "Pump Song (Greatest Story Ever Told)" "Grandma's Cookies," "Hangin' On"
  Mickey Hart–drums, field drums, timpani, percussion, water pump. Mike & Nancy Hinton–marimbas. Alla Rakha/ZAKIR HUSSAIN–rain. JOHN CIPOLLINA–guitar. Bob Weir–guitar, vocals. Tower of Power–horn section. Stephen Stills–bass. Carmel Garcia–timbales, congas. Robbie Stokes–guitar. David Freiberg–vocal, bass, piano, acoustic guitar, viola. Steve Shuster–flute. Grace Slick–piano, vocals. Greg Errricco–drums. Barry Melton–acoustic guitar,

vocals. Phil Lesh–vocals, bass. Jerry Garcia–guitar, insect fear. Terry Haggerty–guitar. Bill Champlin–organ.

An unconventional early stab at a conventional pop-rock album, Mickey Hart's *Rolling Thunder* features the Dead's extended musical family and early versions of "Greatest Story Ever Told" and "Playing in the Band." A well-recorded, if uneven, solo debut disc for the Dead's percussionist-at-large. Garcia's guitar parts also include "The Chase" and "Grandma's Cookies."

- ## "Rosalie McFall" (Traditional)
  Grateful Dead, *Reckoning* (1981)
  Dead Ringers, DEAD RINGERS (1981)
  Peter Rowan, *With the Red Hot Pickers* (1987)
  Country Gazette, *Keep on Pushing* (1991)

While Bill and Charlie Monroe are best known for leading their own bands, it was as the Monroe Brothers that they popularized bluegrass. Their recording of "Rosalie McFall" from the late 1930s exemplifies that "high lonesome" sound which was recaptured by the Grateful Dead when they performed the song, a shotgun shack lover's lament, in their 1970 and 1980 acoustic sets.

The song is sometimes credited to Charlie, but if any ink is going to be spilled on these pages for the Monroe family, it will have to be for Bill, who helped lay the foundation of modern country music and is the universally recognized grandpappy of bluegrass music.

Monroe, who played mandolin and sang in a signature tenor, created one of the most durable idioms in American music, as important to our cultural legacy as jazz. Bluegrass, named after his band, Blue Grass Boys, fused gospel, Celtic fiddling, blues, folk songs, Tin Pan Alley pop and jazz-tinged improvisations. In keening high harmony, the Blue Grass Boys sang about backwoods memories and stoic faith while they played brilliant filigreed tunes as if they were jamming on a back porch, swapping melodies between fiddle, banjo, and Monroe's steely mandolin. By drawing together rural nostalgia and rural and modern virtuosity, Monroe evoked an American Eden, pristine yet cosmopolitan.

Monroe stubbornly maintained the music he perfected in the 1940s and lived to see his revolutionary synthesis become the bedrock of a tradition that survives among enthusiasts and practitioners around the world. He was also an indefatigable traveling musician and a taskmaster who continually challenged his sidemen with difficult keys and tempos. Whether they knew it or not, anybody who has attempted playing bluegrass has drawn on Monroe's repertoire, his vocal style and notions of how a string band should be constructed. Naturally his influence echoes not just down through country music but from Elvis (who included Monroe's "Blue Moon of Kentucky" on his first single) to the Eagles and, of course, the Grateful Dead.

Born William Smith Monroe in Rosine, Kentucky, on September 13, 1911, the future progenitor of bluegrass grew up on a farm thirty miles north of Bowling Green. Bill was the youngest of eight children and, because one eye was crossed, a shy boy. Both his mother and an uncle, Pendleton Vandiver (later memorialized in Monroe's "Uncle Pen"), were fiddlers, and the young boy sometimes accompanied his uncle on guitar but was soon relegated to the mandolin as his older brother tended to monopolize the guitar. By the time he was sixteen, both his parents had died, leading Monroe to remember many years later: "It was a hard life, to come up with no money. You'd sing a lot of sad songs."

Following his brothers to the Chicago suburb of Whiting, Indiana, Monroe worked through the Depression in an oil refinery. He started performing with two of his brothers and in 1934 he began playing music full-time in a duo with brother Charlie on guitar, making their first recordings in 1936, but splitting up after two contentious years.

In 1939 Monroe put together the first version of the Blue Grass Boys and soon joined the Grand Ole Opry radio broadcasts, performing everything from hymns to fiddle tunes to comedy and touring thousands of miles between Saturday night broadcasts. A beloved performer, Monroe once described his audience as "people who get up in the morning and make biscuits."

By the early 1940s, the group took the lineup of the classic bluegrass quintet—mandolin, fiddle, guitar, bass, and banjo—even experimenting with the inclusion of harmonica and accordion for a spell. But it was when guitarist Lester Flatt and innovative banjoist Earl Scruggs joined the group in the mid-1940s that the Blue Grass Boys defined bluegrass music. With Chubby Wise on fiddle and Howard Watts on bass, that lineup of Monroe's group pushed each other to the limits of the genre and beyond. "Bluegrass is competition," Monroe once said, "with each man trying to play the best he can, be on his toes."

Tired of working for sixty dollars a week, Flatt and Scruggs left the band in 1948 but Monroe kept the unit fresh with his magic ability to recruit extraordinary players, among them banjoists Don Reno and Bill Keith, guitarists Mac Wiseman, Del McCoury, and Peter Rowan, and fiddle players Vassar Clements, Byron Berline, Richard Greene, Buddy Spicher, and Kenny Baker. Starting in the 1950s, Monroe sometimes expanded the group with two or three fiddles in harmony.

When the folk revival sprouted in the early 1960s, Monroe's traditionalism brought him a new audience among urban folkies and in 1967 he founded the annual bluegrass festival in Bean Blossom, Indiana. Bluegrass began spreading like wildfire across the globe among do-it-yourself musicians who would eventually support more than five hundred annual festivals even as the music became harder to find on the radio, pushed aside by modern country and rock 'n' roll.

Despite numerous awards late in his life, Monroe remained a fiercely private man and toured relentlessly despite poor health, his influence cemented when he recorded with performers such as Ricky Skaggs, who correctly acknowledged Monroe as a patriarch. Monroe's vintage 1923 Gibson F-5 mandolin was as symbolic an axe as Willie Nelson's weather-beaten guitar and, when the instrument was smashed after someone broke into his home in 1985, Gibson Guitars spent three months reassembling it with microscopes and tweezers. In 1994, bad investments led Monroe to sell the 288-acre homestead in Goodletsville, Tennessee, where he had lived for forty years; the company that owned the Grand Ole Opry bought it and agreed to let him stay there. And it was not far from the homestead that Monroe passed away on September 10, 1996.

As acolyte David Grisman remembered Monroe in the *New York Times*, "Like all great creators, Bill was a channeler, a direct connection to many deep roots. Centuries of fiddle tunes spun out of his mandolin, while his high, lonesome, bluesy singing echoed ancestral balladry, sacred and secular. Yet he was a heretic, creating a revolutionary sound. . . . Even more significant to a guy like me, who studied bluegrass but went on to do something different, is that Bill Monroe demonstrated the importance of being yourself. In doing so, he left his own indelible mark on American music and in the process helped send me on my own musical path."

Showing that a white mandolin player from Kentucky could wax just as mystical as a hoodoo-charmed bluesman from the Mississippi Delta, Bill Monroe once said, "I never wrote a tune in my life. All that music's in the air around you all the time. I was just the first one to reach up and pull it out."

9/20/70, Fillmore East, New York
11/8/70, Capitol Theater, Port Chester, New York
10/27/80, Radio City Music Hall, New York

- ### "Rosemary" (Garcia/Lesh/Hunter)
Grateful Dead, *Aoxomoxoa* (1969)

A beautiful, incredibly mysterious song with elliptical, elusive lyrics, "Rosemary" was recorded with experimental techniques that make it sound as though it was being played underwater. The Dead never performed "Rosemary" live.

- ### "Round & Round" (CHUCK BERRY)
Chuck Berry, *Chuck Berry Is on Top* (1958), *Chuck Berry's Golden Decade* (1967)
The Rolling Stones, *12 x 5* (1964), *Love You Live* (1977)
Grateful Dead, *Steal Your Face* /'74 (1976), *One from the Vault* /'75 (1991), *Dick's Picks Volume One* /'73 (1993), *Dick's Picks Volume Five*/'79 (1996), *Dozin' at the Knick*/'90 (1996)
Truth and Janey, *Live 4/8/76* (1976)
KINGFISH, *LIVE N' KICKIN'* (1977), *KINGFISH IN CONCERT*/'76 (1995)
Maureen Tucker, single (1981)

Injecting more dynamism into this minor Chuck Berry classic than the composer, Bob Weir utilized this barn-burning rocker as a show-ending raveup for twenty years.

Undoubtedly already familiar with the Berry cut, the Dead may have become interested in performing "Round and Round" after seeing the success (and fun) the Stones had with it. Additionally, the song provided an alternate Berry tune to complement their use of his best-known garage-band standard "Johnny B. Goode."

Like several of Berry's best, "Round and Round" had an informal genesis. Berry recalled that the song "sprouted from a jam session during a rehearsal before a concert. Sometimes I didn't jam before a concert, but these guys were on-the-ball musicians, and we almost had a concert before the concert started that evening. For nearly two hours we jammed, playing standard sweet songs to gut-bucket rock and boogie. One of the riffs we struck upon never left my memory, and I waxed in the tune with words about a dance hall that stayed open a lit-

tle overtime. 'Rocking 'til the early morning' had been used so ''til the moon went down' was the same time of day. Let it be known that at the actual experience, the police didn't knock."

11/19/72, Hofheinz Pavilion, Houston
5/26/73, Kezar Stadium, San Francisco
10/10/80, Warfield Theater, San Francisco
6/30/85, Merriweather Post Pavilion, Columbia, Maryland

- ### *Rowan Brothers*/Rowan Brothers
Columbia KC 31297, 1975 (reissued as *Livin' the Life*, Apaloosa 011, 1984.) Produced by David Grisman under the pseudonym "David Diadem."

Rejoining his younger brothers Chris and Lorin, Peter Rowan turned away from rock for the first of three albums of original songs and rich harmonies. This strong album features some of Peter's killer songs ("Midnight Moonlight," "Thunder on the Mountain," and "Beggar in Bluejeans") and includes Garcia and Kreutzmann. Garcia actually had a lot to do with the Rowans getting a monster deal from Clive Davis at Columbia when he said, "these guys could be the next Beatles." Davis shelled out a reported $350,000 (not exactly chump change in the mid-1970s) but the record was a flop and Davis soon took the fall.

- ### "Row Jimmy" (Garcia/Hunter)
Grateful Dead, *Wake of the Flood* (1973), *Dozin' at the Knick*/'90 (1996), *Dick's Picks Volume Seven*/'74 (1997)
Judy Mowatt, *Fire on the Mountain: Reggae Celebrates the Grateful Dead* (1996)

One of Robert Hunter's most enigmatic lyrics, "Row Jimmy" is a wistful ballad that recalls the gospel sentiments and themes of the old campfire song, "Michael Row Your Boat Ashore." The song had its lyrical birth as a line in "From Fair to Even Odds," an unrecorded Hunter poem written concurrently with "Friend of the Devil" in 1970.

Hunter's 1978 conversation with David Gans shed little light on the obtuse number. "I like the little setups in that, the characters. I like 'Julie catch a rabbit by his hair/come back step like to walk on air"—that's a whole song by itself. Then there's another song: 'Here's a half a dollar if you dare/double twist when you hit the air.'

"The main thrust of that is, do you dare jump in the air at all? And if you jump in the air, are you gonna have presence of mind enough to do a trick?"

Garcia was also proud of his musical contribution to the song. In his 1976 interview with Steve Weitzman for *Relix* he said, "There are songs that I really loved . . . like I really loved 'Row Jimmy Row.' That was one of my favorite songs of the ones that I've written. I *loved* it. Nobody else really liked it very much—we always did it—but no one liked it very much, at least in the same way I did."

Garcia began singing "Row Jimmy" in 1973 almost exclusively as a first-set downshift but, in the early days, as a sometimes second-set segue surprise. A minor masterpiece.

9/21/73, The Spectrum, Philadelphia
7/19/74, Selland Arena, Fresno, California
9/20/82, Madison Square Garden, New York
4/30/88, Frost Amphitheater, Palo Alto, California
12/16/92, Coliseum Arena, Oakland, California

"The Rub"

See "Ain't It Crazy"

Run for the Roses / Jerry Garcia

Arista AL 9603, 1982; (ARCD-8557). Produced by Jerry Garcia and JOHN KAHN.
"Run for the Roses," "I Saw Her Standing There," "Without Love," "Midnight Getaway," "Leave the Little Girl Alone," "Valerie," "Knockin' on Heaven's Door"
Jerry Garcia–guitar, slide guitar, vocals, arrangements. JOHN KAHN–bass, fretless bass, synthesizers, piano, arrangements. Ron Tutt–drums. Melvin Seals–organ. Jimmy Warren–piano, clavinet. Michael O'Martin–clavinets. MERL SAUNDERS–organ. Roger Neuman–trumpet, horn section leader. Liz Stires–vocals. Julie Stafford—vocals.

Regarded as possibly the weakest Garcia solo album, *Run for the Roses* has aged poorly. An incoherent gumbo of passable Garcia/Hunter originals ("Run for the Roses" and "Valerie") and cover tunes (a funky "I Saw Her Standing There" and a by-the-numbers "Knockin'

(Courtesy of Arista Records)

on Heaven's Door"), the album barely hangs together as a representation of the regenerating Garcia Band of the early 1980s.

The album suggested that Garcia had long since settled into the idea that his solo career was a side trip, enjoyable for him and Deadheads, but not in any serious competition with the Dead.

"Run Run Rudolph" (CHUCK BERRY)

Chuck Berry, single (1958), *The Collection*/'58 (1988)
Keith Richards, single (1978)

Holiday tunes, especially Christmas songs, are a common novelty marketing hook in the American popular music industry. The blues is especially rife with inclusions of this nature and Chuck Berry was following this path when he recorded "Run Run Rudolph" at the apex of his popularity. His Chess Records single was strategically released in December of 1958 and released with "Merry Christmas Baby," another rockin' Yuletide blues, on the disc's B side. As one would guess, the song describes in rollicking, honky-tonk style Santa's annual trip led by everyone's favorite red-nosed reindeer.

Pigpen handled the vocals when the Dead performed "Run Run Rudolph" four times in December of 1971.

12/15/71, Hill Auditorium, Ann Arbor, Michigan

"Sage and Spirit" (Bob Weir)
Grateful Dead, *Blues for Allah* (1975)

Many Deadheads complained that the band didn't perform enough instrumentals and point to "Sage and Spirit" as an example of the kind of direction the Dead would have done well to explore.

Owing more to Bach than bop, Weir developed the song's chord changes casually and formalized them for official release on the group's popular *Blues for Allah* LP in 1975. With its stylings recalling flamenco, this bright, complex exercise was all-too-briefly performed at the 1975 comeback show and at one of the Dead's 1980 acoustic sets.

In his 1981 *Guitar Player* interview with Jon Sievert, Weir revealed the developmental form and function of "Sage and Spirit." "I have a couple of warm-up things that I do, just running through a few major and minor scales and arpeggios," he said. "Once my fingers get a bit loose, I run through a little étude that I came up with a few years ago. It's actually been recorded on *Blues for Allah* as 'Sage and Spirit.' The guitar part was just a little study that we tried to do something relatively artsy-fartsy with. It puts me through all my paces—right and left. By the time I can do it without messing it up completely, I can play just about anything that I can play. I have to take it very slow at first and work into it. The whole thing is about three-and-a-half minutes, and I go through it a couple of times."

A final note concerns the song's title. "Sage" and "Spirit" were the names of children in the Dead family.

> 8/13/75, Great American Music Hall, San Francisco
> (*One from the Vault*)
> 10/21/80, Radio City Music Hall, New York

"Saint of Circumstance" (Weir/Barlow)
Grateful Dead, *Go to Heaven* (1980), *The Arista Years* (1996)

Devil-may-care, seat-of-the-pants optimism is the order of the day in "Saint of Circumstance." Often paired on the back end of a tandem jam with the phased-out "Lost Sailor" in the early readings of the song from 1979 until 1985, "Saint of Circumstance" came to stand on its own as a second set Weir rave.

"Saint of Circumstance" encapsulates the qualities of the seeker many Deadheads take to heart with its typically California hippie chorus: "Sure don't know what I'm going for but I'm gonna go for it for sure."

This sense of glad tidings awaiting just around the corner captures the essence of Grateful Dead spirit.

> 4/6/82, The Spectrum, Philadelphia
> 10/12/84, Civic Center, Augusta, Maine
> 7/6/86, RFK Stadium, Washington, D.C.

"Salt Lake City" (Weir/Barlow)
Bob Weir, *Heaven Help the Fool* (1978)

Rarely did any post-*Ace* Weir songs find their way into the Dead's repertoire, but "Salt Lake City," a scandalous commentary on the city's feminine populace, was dusted off for a one-time-only show-opening appearance at a Dead concert in that rather, ahem, strait-laced burgh.

2/21/95, Delta Center, Salt Lake City

■ "Samba in the Rain" (Welnick/Hunter)

"Samba in the Rain" isn't a samba as some musical purists may point out, yet the lush stomp from the pens of Vince Welnick and Robert Hunter has a get-up-off-your-ass-and-boogie flavor associated with the Latin genre in question.

Typical of the life-affirming songs Welnick brought to the Grateful Dead, "Samba in the Rain" immediately caught on with many Deadheads when the band began regularly performing it in 1994. A hall dancer's special.

7/20/94, Deer Creek Music Center, Noblesville, Indiana

■ "The Same Thing" (WILLIE DIXON)

Grateful Dead, *Historic Dead*/'66 (1971)
Bo Carter, *Greatest Hits, 1930–1940* (1970)
Muddy Waters, *Chess Masters* (1954), *The Real Folk Blues* (1966), *Fathers and Sons* (1969)
Koko Taylor, *I Got What It Takes* /'64(1975)
George Thorogood, *Move It on Over* (1973)
THE BAND, *Jericho* (1993)
Family, *He Was She Was You Was We Was* (1982)
THE ALLMAN BROTHERS BAND, *Second Set* (1995)

Usually attributed to Willie Dixon, "The Same Thing" is a slow blues of earlier Mississippi lineage which Dixon formalized (and copyrighted) with Muddy Waters in mind. But the earliest known recording of the ribald classic was cut by Bo Carter. Born Armenter Chathom, March 21, 1893, in Bolton, Mississippi, Carter was a member of a famous Delta musical family. Carter had an unequaled capacity for creating hilarious sexual metaphors in songs, specializing in suggestive imagery that resulted in such titles as "Banana in Your Fruit Basket," "Your Biscuits Are Big Enough for Me," "My Pencil Won't Write No More," "Pussy Cat Blues," and "Ram Rod Daddy." His skills are clear in the opening lyrics to "The Same Thing": "What makes a man go crazy when a woman wears her dress so tight? It's that same old thing that makes a bulldog fight all night."

Ironically, Carter was not known as a ladies' man. According to family members, writing racy blues was simply a way for Carter to earn a living after going blind in the late 1920s. Additionally, Carter was a talented multi-instrumentalist specializing on the banjo, bass, clarinet, and especially guitar with intricate and rhythmic riffs. He utilized a number of different keys and tunings on his recordings, which extended beyond the risqué to more traditional blues themes. He was, for instance, one of the first to record "Corrina Corinna" in 1928.

Carter continued performing with his family band, as a street musician and a sometime member of the esteemed Mississippi Sheiks, cutting more than a hundred titles for several labels through the 1930s. When his popularity waned during World War II, he retired from music, dying in Memphis, Tennessee on September 21, 1964.

Pigpen conservatively interpreted "The Same Thing" for the Dead in their early days and the song seemed to die in the band's repertoire with the vocalist's passing. So it was somewhat surprising when Weir pulled it out of the hat in 1991 and kept it in the band's song rotation.

11/19/66, Fillmore Auditorium, San Francisco
6/6/92, Rich Stadium, Orchard Park, New York

■ "Samson and Delilah" (Traditional/REV. GARY DAVIS)

Singles: Rev. T. E. Weems (1927), Rev. J. M. Gates (1927), Rev. T. T. Rose (1927), Mrs. L. C. Gatlin (1933), Norridge Mayhams (1936), Golden Gate Jubilee Quartet (1938), New Zion Baptist Church (1939), Dock Reed (1939), Deacon Sam Jackson (1941)
Reverend Gary Davis, *Pure Religion!* (1956), *Blues at Newport Folk Festival* (1959), *Live 1962–1964* (1964), *At Newport*/'65 (1967), *Gospel, Blues and Street Singers* (1987), *The Music Never Stopped: Roots of the Grateful Dead* (1995)
Grateful Dead, *Terrapin Station* (1977), *Dead Set* (1981), *Dick's Picks Volume Three*/'77 (1995), *The Arista Years* (1996)
Blind Willie Johnson, *Blues in the News*/'27 (1992), *The Complete Recordings of Blind Willie Johnson*/'27 (1993), *Dark Was the Night*/'27 (1995), *The Roots of Rap*/'27 (1996)
Peter, Paul and Mary, *Peter, Paul and Mary* (1962)
Dave Van Ronk, *Inside Dave Van Ronk* (1969)
The Blasters, *Hard Line* (1985)
The Washington Squares, *The Washington Squares* (1987)

The Staple Singers, *Freedom Highway* (1991), *They Sing Praises* (1995)

Clara Ward Singers, *Meetin' Tonight!* (1994)

The Mills Brothers, *The Anthology 1931–1968* (1995)

DAVID MURRAY, *DARK STAR (THE MUSIC OF THE GRATEFUL DEAD)* (1996)

The Reverend Gary Davis gathered the musical and literary shards of "Samson and Delilah" from the Negro spiritual and the blues of Blind Willie Johnson and fused it with his own take on Judges 13–16 to create one of the most powerful and influential songs in blues history.

After introducing their fast-paced, percussion-heavy arrangement of "Samson and Delilah" in 1976, the Dead went on to perform more than three hundred scorching versions, often as a second-set opener.

The song's lyric hook, "If I had my way I would tear this old building down," had particular immediacy in concert, localizing and humanizing the Grateful Dead event in a venue-specific manner.

Discussing the prospect of its imminent release with David Gans in 1977, Weir pointed out that "I'm not entirely sure that all those folks out there in those discos and stuff like that who are down into some heavy sinnin' want to hear a Bible story."

10/14/76, Shrine Auditorium, Los Angeles

4/11/78, Fox Theater, Atlanta

11/1/85, Coliseum, Richmond, Virginia

1/24/93, Oakland Coliseum, Oakland, California

7/3/94, Shoreline Amphitheater, Mountain View, California

▪ Carlos Santana
Born July 20, 1947, Autlan, Mexico

In that he is a musical and spiritual brother of the Grateful Dead, it is somewhat surprising that Carlos Santana only jammed with the band at a half dozen shows between 1980 and 1993.

A major figure in the San Francisco establishment of the late 1960s, Santana's major, ongoing achievement was the marriage of blues, rock, Latin, Afro-Cuban, and other indigenous musics into a vibrant, crystallized whole.

Like Garcia's, Santana's father was a musician, a Mexican mariachi violinist who moved his family to San Francisco when Carlos was fifteen. When the Fillmore West opened a few years later, young Carlos snuck in from the back window to catch his favorite bands, including the Dead. And like the Dead, the Santana Blues Band formed in 1967 as a group of equals with Carlos named as leader only because of the musicians' union requirement that such a designation be made. Gaining recognition in the same dance halls that hosted the era's and area's psychedelic groups, they never quite fit in with the stereotypical San Francisco sound because of their heavy Latin and African roots.

By the time they took Woodstock by storm (and with it a Columbia record deal) the band had grown to include six white-hot players: Gregg Rollie on vocals and keyboards, bassist Dave Brown, and drummer-percussionists Mike Shrieve, Armando Peraza, Mike Carabello, and Jose "Chepito" Areas. Bill Graham knew a good thing when he heard one and the band soon came under his direction, initiating a long-lasting bond between the impresario and the guitarist.

Concentrating on Afro-Cuban rhythms allied with Carlos' sweet, flowing guitar lines, *Santana*, their debut album, was a massive success piggybacked by the No. 4 hit single, "Evil Ways." Following up with the even better *Abraxas* in 1970 (featuring "Black Magic Woman" and Tito Puente's "Oye Como Va"), the band became one of the country's top acts for the next two years.

After *Santana III*, which completed the trilogy of the Woodstock-era Santana, and a couple of other transitional discs (including a live album with drummer Buddy Miles), the guitarist pursued a spiritual path, announcing his conversion to the Hinduism of Sri Chinmoy, adding Devadip to his name and recording *Love Devotion Surrender* with fellow adept John McLaughlin in 1973. Attempting jazz-fusion versions of John Coltrane and McLaughlin compositions, the album was the sixth straight Santana-related album to go gold.

In many respects Santana had the type of career Garcia would probably have enjoyed had not the Grateful Dead turned into the phenomenon, with its tour-heavy emphasis, that it did. Recording group and solo albums in parallel with mounting tours (including a couple with Bob Dylan) that spanned the globe, enhancing his already renowned international reputation, Santana put out a new album nearly every year. His luxurious position allowed him to put forth such efforts as *Borboleto* with AIRTO MOREIRA and FLORA PURIM in 1974; *The Swing of Delight*, which included Miles Davis's famed 1960s group, in 1980; and *Havana Moon*, a shockingly interesting turn to Tex-Mex and early rock with a guest artists as weirdly varied as Willie Nelson and Booker T. Jones in 1983.

Retaining both the deeply spiritual essence and political activism of his roots, Santana pursued projects that incorporated both sensibilities through the 1980s and mid-1990s. With a particular emphasis on the music of John Coltrane and the plight of Central America's struggles, Santana put out a series of related albums: *Freedom* and *Blues for Salvador* in 1987, *Spirits Dancing in the Flesh* (a Santana Blues Band reunion album) in 1990, *Milagro* in 1992, and *Santana Brothers,* a 1994 trio album recorded with his brother Jorge and his nephew Carlos Hernandez. In the midst of all this, Santana produced the music for *La Bamba*, the film based on the life of Ritchie Valens, which brought Latin-pop fusions to a new generation of listeners.

In the early days, Santana was a natural act to share bills with the Grateful Dead at the old Fillmores; yet, surprisingly, these instances were rare. It wasn't until the January 13, 1980, Oakland concert benefiting Cambodian refugees that Carlos and the Dead engaged in anything resembling a jam session, choosing "Not Fade Away," "Sugar Magnolia," and "U.S. Blues" as the catalysts towards musical nirvana. Seven years later, Santana opened a couple of August 1987 Northern California shows at which he offered *scorching* licks to "GOOD MORNING LITTLE SCHOOLGIRL," "MIDNIGHT HOUR," "IKO IKO," and "ALL ALONG THE WATCHTOWER" in what were arguably his most memorable appearances with the band. A 1991 Las Vegas "Birdsong" followed, as did a harrowing "Iko Iko">"Mona" extravaganza with the Dead and former Quicksilver guitarist Gary Duncan at the band's Oakland concert two days after their friend Bill Graham was killed in a helicopter crash. A spirited "Space"> "Jam">"The Other One">"Stella Blue"> "Love Light" roll followed by a smoking "GLORIA" encore at the 1993 Chinese New Year's show in Oakland rounded out Santana's formal concert relationship with the Grateful Dead.

In a warm gesture of solidarity following Garcia's passing, Santana offered to take Garcia's place in the Dead. Very few others could.

▪ *Sarangi: The Music of India*/Ustad Sultan Khan

360 Degrees Records 102, 1984 (Rykodisc RCD 10104, 1988). Produced by Mickey Hart and ZAKIR HUSSAIN.

"Raga: Bageshree," "Thumri"
Ustad Sultan Khan–sarangi. Shri Rij Ram–tabla.

Ustad Sultan Khan, along with his contemporary Ram Narayan, is one of a handful of Indian classical musicians keeping the sound of the sarangi alive. The son and grandson of India's two sarangi heroes, Khan is renowned for his extraordinary technical and melodic control over a difficult instrument. The sarangi is one of his country's most sonorous bowed string instruments, with a highly vocal sound and technique. But it has quickly been disappearing from the subcontinent's landscape. Fewer and fewer high-caliber sarangi practitioners appear on concert stages.

According to the album's liner notes: "In India, there is hardly a Saturday when Ustad Sultan Khan is not playing for vast audiences as a solo artist or as an accompanist to some great vocalist. Moreover, as a composer, he has scored music for many films and dance-dramas. He has been a staff member with All India Radio for many years. He has performed many times in Europe and the United States much to the delight of his classical music audiences, amazed at his dexterous bowing and his command over the tonal nuances of his instrument. During tours with Ravi Shankar, he gave sixty-eight concerts in the U.S. and Europe, as well as solo recitals throughout Western Europe, Hungary, Czechoslovakia, and East Germany."

The events that transpired to produce the album are almost as magical as the music itself. When Ravi Shankar and George Harrison collaborated with some of the greatest Indian musicians of our time on a fall 1974 American concert tour, Indian musicians were invited to perform at the Stone House in Marin County. This recording is a document of that unusual performance.

Sarangi: The Music of India shows many emotional sides of the living master of this ancient bowed instrument.

▪ *Saturday Night Live* (television program)

The heat the Grateful Dead were capable of generating never really translated all that well to the "cool medium." But the band was *on* for both of their *Saturday Night Live* appearances, which probably reached more people in the United States than anything they ever did.

The boys were fresh from their Egyptian adventure when they first appeared on November 11, 1978, and it shows in the loose enthusiasm they brought to their quick versions of "Casey Jones," "I Need a Miracle," and "Good Lovin'." This was before NBC banned drug references from its programming (though not necessarily drug use by its employees). The band's three-song display was the first and one of a very few times that any band was allowed to perform more than two songs on the popular program.

On April 5, 1980, a year and a half later, the Dead once again took the stage at Rockefeller Center for an equally loose crack at a couple of their newer songs, "Alabama Getaway" and "Saint of Circumstance." This was the *SNL* gig where Weir donned oversized rabbit ears for his own, if not the entire nation's, enjoyment.

▪ Merl Saunders

Born February 14, late 1930s, San Francisco

Getting caught in the Grateful Dead vortex was something that was meant to happen to Merl Saunders. He grew up and lived in the Haight-Ashbury section of San Francisco, only three blocks from the band, during the 1960s and though he was only dimly aware of them then, he did enjoy their music when they played in Golden Gate Park.

Merl's roots in jazz and rock are well documented and he acknowledges Wild Bill Davis and Count Basie as his early jazz inspirations and has recorded and performed with such diverse artists as HARRY BELAFONTE, the Statler Brothers, Lionel Hampton, Miles Davis, B.B. King, Sonny Stitt, Paul Butterfield, Mike Bloomfield, and Papa John Creach.

As a touring organist, Merl was on the road between 1965 and 1968, spanning the globe from Europe and the Far East to the United States blues house circuit laying down his Jimmy Smith–like licks on the Hammond B-3. Saunders actually studied with Smith in the late 1950s. As Saunders told Jeff Tamarkin of *RELIX* in 1988, "He showed me how to sit at the organ, how to relax, how to breathe, and how to use my hands and feet, how to listen to the bass pedal."

Soon after, Saunders was earning money, if not a living, as a jazz organist. Within short order he made a name for himself, working with the likes of jazz's preeminent vibraphonist, Lionel Hampton.

Looking for a change from the one-nighter grind, Saunders found it in New York as music director for *Big Time Buck White*, a play featuring Muhammad Ali. Miles Davis liked what he heard and invited Saunders to open for his band. Caught between his desire to play jazz or turn to rock music, Saunders was inspired by Davis's approach to music and his words: "Just take it where you want to take it." Davis had recently opened for the Dead

Merl Saunders *(Courtesy of Summertone Records)*

at the Fillmore West and, being impressed with their chops, suggested them as a group Saunders would do well to hook up with.

Returning to San Francisco in 1969, Merl began working with a jazz singer named Patty Urban who lived in Marin County near Michael Bloomfield, JOHN KAHN, and Nick Gravenites. Saunders began doing studio work with these musicians and a guitarist named "Jerry" whose personality and playing he liked very much. Laying down tracks on several albums and soundtracks, all Saunders knew about Jerry was that he gigged at the Matrix, a San Francisco club. It was only when Saunders began jamming with Jerry at the Matrix, that he began realizing that this was the "Captain Trips" he'd seen in the Haight several years earlier.

As Saunders told *Guitar Player* in 1993, "I was doing quite a few sessions around San Francisco back in the mid-sixties, and the player who stood out like a sore thumb on those sessions was Jerry. We hit it off, and he asked me to come by the Matrix to sit in with his band, the Dead, on organ. They were youngsters, and I was kind of abstract to them because I had just come from New York with all this high-powered energy. But they were eager to learn. And Jerry stayed right with me. He understood my music so quickly. I would do something, and he immediately knew what kind of complementing lines I wanted."

Pretty soon they had a tight little unit together and formed one of the early Saunders-Garcia bands, touring the East Coast and hitting all the Bay Area clubs that would take them in 1971. Commenting on the growth of the band's reputation, Saunders told Tamarkin, "I remember at first there were fifteen people at the gig. Then there'd be one hundred fifteen. Then two hundred fifteen. The next thing I knew some guy would be saying he came from Boston to see us, and I just went 'What!' People started coming from all over the country to hear us and we just decided to go out on tour."

Eventually coalescing into the quartet that included John Kahn on bass and drummer Billy Vitt and would record *LIVE AT KEYSTONE* in 1973, Saunders-Garcia music was an emotional roller-coaster with Saunders once commenting that "Sometimes I'd look over at Jerry and we would both have tears in our eyes."

Similarly, Garcia told Jon Sievert of *Guitar Player* magazine in 1978, "Playing with Merl gave me a real feeling of freshness that carried over to later work with other people."

(Courtesy of Summertone Records)

With members of the Dead frequently stopping by, Saunders bonded with Pigpen and the band at large, which invited him to lay down tracks on their *Grateful Dead* ("Skull and Roses") and *Europe '72* albums.

Surprisingly, though Saunders has been an inner-circle Grateful Dead family member for a quarter century, he only performed with the Dead on three occasions, but each one was memorable. With members of the ALLMAN BROTHERS, Saunders joined the Dead for the famous third set at Washington's RFK Stadium June 10, 1973, as the musicians blazed through "IT TAKES A LOT TO LAUGH," "THAT'S ALL RIGHT, MAMA," "PROMISED LAND," "JOHNNY B. GOODE," and a "NOT FADE AWAY">"GOIN' DOWN THE ROAD">"Not Fade Away" medley for the ages. A couple of years later, Saunders and Ned Lagin were added as the second and third keyboardist at the band's debut of some of the *Blues for Allah* material in a set that ranks with one of the band's jazziest. Finally, Saunders hit the Berkeley Community Theater bandstand with the boys in 1985 for a "Space">"The Other One" jam that featured a taste of their *Twilight Zone* collaboration.

- **"Saw Mill"** (Traditional/Horace Wheatley/Mel Tillis)
  Buck Owens, *On the Bandstand*
     (1963)
  Mel Tillis, *American Originals* (1989)

"Saw Mill," probably an early-twentieth-century Appalachian folk lament of the rigors of dangerous labor and tricky romance that was later updated by Mel Tillis and Horace Wheatley, appeared at only a couple of Dead shows in early 1970. Led by Weir on vocals, "Saw Mill" has those high harmony parts that suited it to the band's collaboration with members of the NEW RIDERS OF THE PURPLE SAGE who shared the stage with them on both occasions.

4/19/70, Family Dog, San Francisco

▪ "Scarlet Begonias" (Garcia/Hunter)

Grateful Dead, *From the Mars Hotel* **(1974),** *Dick's Picks Volume Six/'83* **(1996)**
Robert Hunter, *Box of Rain* **(1991)**
Sublime, *40 Oz. to Freedom* **(1992)**

A true Grateful Dead classic, "Scarlet Begonias" was a beloved concert constant since its introduction in 1974. Bubbling and rollicking, introspective and community concerned, the song deals with the consequences of lost romantic opportunity. Set in London's Grosvenor Square, the narrator passes a woman (part real, part apparition). Though the rings on her fingers and bells on her shoes beckon him to think twice before letting her pass by, the storyteller does just that. There are no regrets, however, the chance encounter being a fulfillment in itself.

Hunter lived in Great Britain for a period in the early 1970s and "Scarlet Begonias" is arguably the best of the songs from this adventure in the poet's flirtation with expatriation.

As further evidence of Hunter's interest and use of the nursery rhyme, the line in the song that reads "There were rings on fingers and bells on her shoes" appears almost verbatim in the British lullaby, "Ride a Cock Horse to Banbury Cross."

Discussing the song's melodic roots with Blair Jackson in 1991, Garcia said, "It definitely has a little Caribbean thing to it, though nothing specific. It's also its own thing. I wasn't thinking in terms of style when I wrote that setting, except that I wanted it to be rhythmic. I think I got a little of it from that Paul Simon 'Me and Julio Down by the Schoolyard' thing. A little from Cat Stevens—some of that rhythmic stuff he did on *Tea for the Tillerman* was kind of nice. It's an acoustic feel in a way, but we put it to an electric space, which is part of what made it interesting."

After its concert debut in 1974, "Scarlet Begonias"

was subsequently linked with "Fire on the Mountain," a musically and thematically related composition, in 1977. But it was utilized successfully on its own and in tandem with several other tunes. Its bright open-ended qualities provided band and audience alike with many glorious jams.

7/25/74, International Amphitheater, Chicago
8/6/74, Roosevelt Stadium, Jersey City, New Jersey
10/14/74, Shrine Auditorium, Los Angeles
5/8/77, Barton Hall, Ithaca, New York
4/11/78, Fox Theater, Atlanta
11/30/80, Fox Theater, Atlanta
4/3/82, The Scope, Norfolk, Virginia
6/18/83, Saratoga Performing Arts Center, Saratoga, New York
7/13/84, Greek Theatre, Berkeley, California
7/1/85, Merriweather Post Pavilion, Columbia, Maryland
6/28/88, Saratoga Performing Arts Center, Saratoga, New York
9/14/90, Madison Square Garden, New York
10/14/94, Madison Square Garden, New York

▪ "Searchin'" (LEIBER & STOLLER)

The Coasters, single (1957), *50 Coastin' Classics: Anthology* **(1992)**
The Crickets, *Something Old, Something New, Something Blue, Something Else!* **(1962)**
Spencer Davis Group, *First Album* **(1965),** *I'm A Man* **(1967)**
The Kingsmen, *15 Great Hits* **(1966)**
The Lovin' Spoonful, *What's Shakin'* **(1966)**
Lynyrd Skynyrd, *Gimme Back My Bullets* **(1976)**
Otis Blackwell, *All Shook Up* **(1977)**
The Hollies, *30th Anniversary Collection* **(1993)**
The Beatles, *Anthology 1* **(1995)**

Virtually the creation of songwriter-producers Jerry Leiber and Mike Stoller, the Coasters were one of the most popular vocal groups of the 1950s. Leiber and Stoller's comic playlets about ghetto, and then teenage, life were the mainstay of the group's period of greatest success.

"Searchin'" (along with such other gimmicky but great million-sellers as "Young Blood," "Yakety Yak," "Charlie Brown," and "Poison Ivy") saw members of the group creating (and reprising) vocal character parts resembling television situation comedies and animated cartoons familiar at the time.

The Dead are only known to have covered "Searchin'" twice but their last rendition of the novelty was a novelty in itself coming during the famous 1971 set with THE BEACH BOYS during the band's last run at the Fillmore East.

4/27/71, Fillmore East, New York (with the Beach Boys)

▪ "Seasons"

The Dead performed this song of vague origin at a couple of shows in 1969 and 1970.

12/31/69, Boston Tea Party, Boston

▪ *Seastones*/Phil Lesh/Ned Lagin

Round RX 106, 1975 (Reisssued Rykodisc RCD/RACS 40193 with six unreleased live sections recorded in December 1975). Produced by Ned Lagin.
"I," "II (Vocals)," "III A," "III B," "IV A (Vocals)," "IV B (Vocals)," "V," "V B," "VI (Vocals)," "VII"
Ned Lagin–piano, computers, synthesizers, keyboards. Phil Lesh–electric bass. Jerry Garcia–electric guitar, vocals. DAVID CROSBY–vocals, Alembic electric twelve-string guitar. GRACE SLICK–vocals. David Freiberg–vocals. Mickey Hart–gongs. Spencer Dryden–cymbals.

"Composed" by Ned Lagin, Phil Lesh's electronic avant-gardist crony from 1971–74, *Seastones* is perhaps *the* most challenging Grateful Dead–related release. Atonal and meandering, it is a good representation of the music Lesh and Lagin created during their special mini-sets at a slew of 1974 Dead shows when they performed a *Seastones* segment at halftime. Thereafter, Lagin joined the band for a memorable March 1975 "Blues for Allah" jam that also included MERL SAUNDERS and, later, he continued to experiment with Lesh through the mid-1980s.

Lagin has always been a bit of a mysterious footnote in the Dead's musical family tree with a background as diverse as any member in the band. He began playing piano when he was six, starting off with classical and then slowly graduating to Broadway show tunes. By the time he hit his teens, he was getting his feet wet in jazz and before long was a confirmed avant-gardist, a devotee of John Coltrane and Archie Shepp, and a student of Bill Evans, a *giant* of the jazz piano. After he came to Boston in 1966 to study science at M.I.T., jazz at the Berklee School of Music, and orchestration and compo-

sition at Harvard while keeping a foot in the performance arena by playing various jazz ensembles, Lagin's musical tastes and penchant for experimentation broadened exponentially.

Feeling no particular kinship with rock 'n' roll, this jazzster was more interested in making the art-jazz scene in New York and Boston than in making his mark with a maverick acid rock band hailing from Marin County. Yet when he was dragged kicking and screaming to a Dead show at the Boston Tea Party in 1969, he was tremendously impressed. So impressed, that he and some friends in the antiwar movement helped organize an M.I.T. show in May 1970 that was preceded by the famous free concert on the campus common.

Concurrently, Lagin composed a complex experimental piece of electronic music for eight speakers which was presented at the M.I.T. chapel, a performance attended by members of the band. Lagin had already impressed Garcia and Lesh with a letter conveying his musical ideas some months previously, so it was only natural that they should invite him to California for a little studio work.

In the summer of 1970, Lagin did just that, eventually spending a lot of time at both Lesh's and Garcia's houses learning Dead tunes and talking music theory. Remembering his first day in San Francisco, Lagin told Mick Skidmore of *RELIX*, "I got off of the Greyhound bus and walked a couple of blocks to a studio I had never heard of. Wally Heider's, and there were three studios. One had the Grateful Dead in it, and only Garcia was there. He was early, and I was early, and he said 'Good, you can play on our records,' which was *American Beauty*. In another studio was the Airplane, and part of the time in the third was Santana and part of the time was David Crosby. That was when everybody was one big happy family. If you weren't playing on one album, you ran around the corner to other studios and played on another album or just jammed."

It was during this period that Lagin contributed to *American Beauty* and began sitting in with the band at various gigs through the autumn of that magical year.

After a brief return to the East Coast to complete his education, Lagin moved back to the West Coast, where he began composing the pieces that would eventually become *Seastones*. Interestingly, the work was written and recorded over a four-year period.

Remembering the mixed response the album garnered on its release and the elongated, unorthodox process with which it was constructed, Lagin told Skidmore, "People either thought I was God or they absolutely hated me. . . . Recording each of the musicians for each of the sections we used a score, and there was verbal guidance, and in some cases I played with them. In only one or two sections did the whole group ever get together to play the sections. In other words the thing was layered together. It was impossible, due to other recording and travel commitments, to get all those people together, or for that matter to have enough time with those people to explain the music and what was trying to be achieved."

- ### "Seastones" (Lesh/Lagin)
  #### Phil Lesh and Ned Lagin, *Seastones*
  #### (1975)

A soothing title for the heavily "plugged-in" music Phil Lesh and Ned Lagin displayed between the first and second sets of many 1974 Grateful Dead concerts. But despite the brevity of this aspect of live presentation, the Dead have always included an atonal aural selection at their concerts. In the early days it was simply called "Feedback" when the guitarists would turn their instruments into their speakers and manipulate the seemingly random screeching emanating from their amps. Since the mid-1970s, high-tech gadgetry allowed them to traverse this challenging terrain with equal effectiveness in the "Space" segments of their concerts. But, in 1974 at least, it was left to Lesh and Lagin to take the music out there.

6/23/74, Jai-Alai Fronton, Miami
9/21/74, Palais des Sports, Paris

- ### *Second Sight*/Second Sight
  Shanachie 5716, 1996. Produced by BOB BRALOVE.
  "Night Fires," "Red Hills of Rwanda," "Dance to the Music," "A Knight Supreme," "Rosetta Rock," "Blood and Mercury," "Marble Moon Beams," "Tabla Rasa," "Dangerous Dream," "Sin City Circumstance," "If 6 Were 4"
  Bobby Strickland–sax. HENRY KAISER–guitar. Vince Welnick–keyboards, piano, synth harp. Bob Bralove–keyboards, electric piano, synths, processed vocals. Marc Van Wageningen–bass. Paul Van Wageningen–drums, electric tablas. Jerry Garcia–guitar on "Rosetta Rock" and "Dangerous Dream." Bob Weir–guitar on "Sin City Circumstance."

In the wake of the Grateful Dead's demise, a number of bands from the Dead camp stepped forward to extend the Dead's mission in various directions. Second Sight, a band formed before Garcia's death, is an innovative ensemble which developed a small but hardy West Coast following in the mid-1990s.

Led by Dead midi-master Bob Bralove (the guy who could make Garcia's guitar sound like a trumpet or Lesh's bass like a didjeridoo), Second Sight made its

(© Grateful Dead Merchandising, Inc.)

(Courtesy of Shanachie Records)

mark onstage and on this disc with wildly explortory performances of adventurous, groove-oriented music—just your average psychedelic space-jazz twenty-second-century music from Venus.

▪ "See That My Grave Is Kept Clean"

(Blind Lemon Jefferson)

Singles: Pete Harris (1934), Smith Casey (1939)

Blind Lemon Jefferson, *King of the Country Blues* (1985), *Complete Recorded Works, Vol. 1/'27* (1991)

Saunders/Garcia/Kahn/Vitt, KEYSTONE ENCORES/'73 (1989)

Joe Evans and Arthur McClain, *The Two Poor Boys* (1931)

LIGHTNIN' HOPKINS, *Lightnin' Hopkins* (1959)

BOB DYLAN, *Bob Dylan* (1962)

John Hammond, *John Hammond* (1964)

Peter, Paul and Mary, *In Concert* (1964)

Canned Heat, *Living the Blues* (1968)

Michael Bloomfield, *Michael Bloomfield* (1978)

Dream Syndicate, *Ghost Stories* (1988)

BLIND LEMON JEFFERSON

(Courtesy of R. Crumb/Shanachie Entertainment)

Chillingly portentous, "See That My Grave Is Kept Clean" may be Blind Lemon Jefferson's most famous recording. It's certainly his most harrowing.

Jefferson was among the first blues-guitar stars and the most famous bluesman of the Roaring Twenties—his popularity running from coast to coast after his 78s shattered racial barriers, influencing a generation of musicians. He was born July 11, 1897, in Couchman, Texas; little is known about his early life other than that he was born blind and was one of seven children. After teaching himself guitar as a means to scrape out a meager living playing at house parties, picnics, and dances around Worthman, Texas, Jefferson gravitated to Dallas's roustabout Deep Ellum section, where he busked for spare change on street corners. As the reputation of this singer/songwriter spread, he began attracting regular patrons, earning enough through the tin-cup offerings to support a wife and child.

By the time he was discovered by Sammy Price, a Dallas piano player and bazaar merchant, who facilitated a 1925 Chicago recording date, Jefferson's style was fully formed. His main vocal signature, an elastic, thinly veneered whine developed from the singing of cotton workers, transformed not only the blues but the religious hymns, spirituals, work songs, folk tunes, and other selections from the Southern songster tradition into something uniquely his. But as singular as Jefferson's vocalese was, it was his guitar style that impacted his peers and blues descendants most profoundly, becoming a second voice with its halting rhythms at the end of vocal lines, which would launch into elaborate solo flourishes. With its intricate construction that alternated pronounced bass notes with arpeggios inspired by the Mexican vaqueros, Jefferson was capable of jazz-like improvisation coloring his music and enhancing his charismatic rep.

Most significantly was Jefferson's top-rate songwriting, which helped establish the singer/songwriter as a permanent and accepted fixture on the American cultural landscape. While some of Jefferson's songs are merely clever takeoffs on standard folk-blues songs, his best portray vivid, imagistic lyrical accounts of early 1900s Southern black culture. Jefferson knew of what he spoke, as he is also remembered as a take-no-prisoners showman who anticipated the flash of Jimi Hendrix a half-century later and as a man well acquainted with liquor, gambling, loose women, and the establishments at which all three were available.

A spectral half-blues, half-spiritual piece played in arpeggio, "See That My Grave Is Kept Clean" is stuffed with the ominous symbolism that appealed to all succeeding generations of blues artists and interpreters. Interestingly, the song has its origins in the British folk tradition (as "Two White Horses in a Line"), but was adapted to the blues by blacks in the nineteenth century.

Some literary-minded blues scholars have traced the song's silver spade and golden chain imagery all the way back through a nineteenth-century sea-chantey to the old British song "Who Killed Cock Robin," and there are Old Testament and Negro Spiritual shades for many of the lyrics and motifs found in this very influential plea.

Blind Lemon Jefferson's death came, appropriately enough, at the end of the first great blues era. Despite legends imputing otherwise, Jefferson met his demise in December 1929, reputedly during a Chicago snowstorm, of what is generally regarded as a heart attack, although there are some who have suggested that he was hampered by the densely falling snow, became lost on the streets, and froze to death. Nearly forty years after his passing, the cult of Blind Lemon Jefferson formed a foundation that raised funds to discover where the bluesman's remains were interred and erect a memorial and ensure that his grave be kept clean.

Garcia sang "See That My Grave Is Kept Clean," a.k.a. "One Kind Favor," at a few early Dead shows and included it as a cover in his bar bands with Merl Saunders.

12/1/66, The Matrix, San Francisco

■ *Sentinel*/Robert Hunter
  Rykodisc RCD 20265, 1993.
  "Pride of Bone," "Gingerbread Man," "Idiot's Delight (excerpt)," "A Red Dog's Decoration Day," "Trapping a Muse," "Jaaz #3," "Toad in Love," "Rimbaud at Twenty," "Rain in a Courtyard," "Way of the Ride," "Sentinel," "Preserpie and Senti Yagoya," "Poets on Poets," "Like a Basket," "Yagritz," "Cocktails with Hindemith," "Blue Moon Alley," "The New Jungle," "Full Moon Cafe," "Tango Hit Palace," "Exploding Diamond Blues," "Rainwater Sea," "Holigomena"

Though some of these poems were excerpted from three of Hunter's books (*IDIOT'S DELIGHT*, *NIGHT CADRE*, and *Infinity Minus Eleven*), hearing the poet's commanding

(Courtesy of Rykodisc)

voice presenting this difficult material the way it was supposed to be heard—read aloud—is to experience it in a manner the printed word can never do justice to. Highly symbolic—even obscure—yet intangibly endearing and personal, Hunter's spoken-word disc is perfect for those introspective moments when the kids are in bed and a glass of cognac beckons.

■ *Sentinel* (book)/Robert Hunter
  154 pp. Penguin, 1993.
A recent addition to the Hunter canon, *Sentinel* contains thirty-five unprefaced works that predate Jerry Garcia's death. Some of the gems include "Black Sunflower," a reflection on lost time; "The Pool," a confessional puzzle; and the titular "Sentinel," which consists of several guard "watches." Hunter at his beatific, unpretentious best.

■ **"The Seven"** (Grateful Dead)
This rhythmic jam, similar in feel, concept, and intensity to "The Eleven," started life as a MICKEY AND THE HARTBEATS number in 1968 and found its way into a couple of Dead shows over the next two years.
  10/9/68, The Matrix, San Francisco

■ *Shady Grove*/Jerry Garcia/DAVID GRISMAN
  Acoustic Disc, ACD-21, 1996. Produced by Jerry Garcia and David Grisman.
  "Shady Grove," "Stealin'," "The Sweet Sunny South,"

(Courtesy of Acoustic Disc)

"Off to Sea Once More," "Louis Collins," "Fair Ellender," "Jackaroo," "Casey Jones," "Dreadful Wind and Rain," "I Truly Understand," "The Handsome Cabin Boy," "Whiskey in the Jar," "Down in the Valley," "Hesitation Blues"
Jerry Garcia–acoustic guitar, five-string banjo. David Grisman–mandolin, five-string banjo. Jim Kerwin–bass. Joe Craven–drums. Bryan Bowers–autoharp. Will Scarlett–mouth harp. Matt Eakle–flute.

During the last five years of his life, Jerry Garcia got together with David Grisman for over forty recording sessions at the mandolinist's Dawg Studios, playing blues, jazz, folk songs, pop tunes, country, bluegrass, weird fun stuff, and originals. As Grisman describes in the album's sleeve notes, "The sessions were scheduled sometimes and often not. Out of the blue, that voice would bark out of my answering machine, 'Hey Dawggie, this is Papa Doc Garcia, I know you're there, damn it!' He'd be cruising in his BMW and minutes later we'd be sitting face to face, playing old folk songs, jazz standards, country ballads, or whatever—music from our mutually entwined past, the music we both loved, the many roots of what long since transformed into our life's work and joy.

"This album is the first collection of tunes we recorded during this period to be released since Jerry's death . . . though some of the performances are more polished than others, I thought that all of them merited inclusion because they paint a fuller portrait of our

shared musical reminiscences, and especially show the breadth and depth of Jerry Garcia as one of the great interpretive American folk artists of this or any generation.

"Playing (and hanging) with Jerry during those last few years was an experience I feel privileged to have had. These sessions were a real high point for me; I'm pleased to be able to share some of those moments with you."

Additional and extensive liner notes by former New Lost City Rambler John Cohen packaged with lyrics and rare photos round out another incredible offering from Dawg Studios.

Drawn from Dawg's vaults, these are the tunes that inspired both musicians during their formative folkie years. This soulful set of thirteen classics includes memorable versions of the title track as well as a trio of tunes for the initiated: "Jackaroo," "Stealin'" and the haunting "Dreadful Wind and Rain." On a novelty note, "The Sweet Sunny South" features the two on five-string banjos. Finally, "Hesitation Blues" is an uncredited hidden track on the CD.

■ *Shakedown Street*
Arista AB 4198, 1978. Produced by Lowell George.
"Good Lovin'," "France," "Shakedown Street," "Serengeti," "Fire on the Mountain," "I Need a Miracle," "From the Heart of Me," "Stagger Lee,"

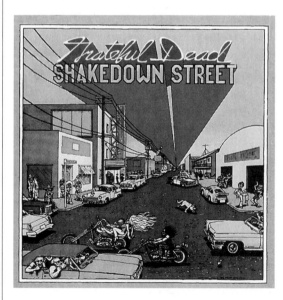

(Courtesy of Arista Records)

"All New Minglewood Blues," "If I Had the World to Give"

Even the Dead admitted that the production guidance of Little Feat legend Lowell George could not save this limp studio effort. Though some of the material (notably "Fire on the Mountain," "Stagger Lee," and "Shakedown Street") developed by leaps and bounds onstage, the record was correctly scored as poorly recorded and the performances cold and indifferent.

But at least one member of the band seemed to have enjoyed the process of making the album and working with George. In his 1989 interview with Blair Jackson, Bill Kreutzmann said, "I really liked Lowell a lot. Whereas Keith [Olsen] always wanted to be the director-producer type and wear the highest hat—to work in the upper office, so to speak—Lowell was really like a member of the band more. If we were working on a song and he didn't feel it was going right, he'd just grab a guitar and come in the studio and show us how he felt it. That was one of the ways he'd communicate, and it worked great. I had a tremendous amount of respect for him.

"Basically, though, I think the Grateful Dead produces itself best. It's not the fastest way for us to work, but that's not important."

Mickey Hart's assessment of Lowell was somewhat more circumspect. As he told David Gans in 1984, "Lowell George was mad. We wrote a great song one night, but we never recorded it. It was called 'My Drum Is a Woman.' We wrote this song about all my instruments and what I thought about them, how I address them. Lowell played good guitar, but he was no producer—certainly not for the Grateful Dead. He did too much coke. There's no way for him to have any kind of rational judgment."

■ **"Shakedown Street"** (Garcia/Hunter)
Grateful Dead, *Shakedown Street* (1978), *Dick's Picks Volume Five*/'79 (1996), *The Arista Years* (1996)
DAVID MURRAY, *DARK STAR (THE MUSIC OF THE GRATEFUL DEAD)* (1996)

The title tune of an otherwise forgettable album, "Shakedown Street" evolved in the Grateful Dead repertoire as a funky R&B boogie that featured Garcia trading fours with the band's keyboardist of the moment.

Used primarily as either a first or second set opening powerhouse, "Shakedown Street" had the ability to translate well to Anytown, U.S.A. Like "Terrapin Station" or "Franklin's Tower," "Shakedown Street" is more a state of mind than a specific locale. But, unlike the aforementioned compositions which portray a destination of visionary redemption, "Shakedown Street" is firmly rooted in the hard reality of gritty urban America. New York's Times Square, Boston's Combat Zone, and San Francisco's Tenderloin are all places where danger is omnipresent and life cheap. Yet the song searches for positive signs of life even on those desperate boulevards of broken dreams. "They tell me this town ain't got no heart" reads the chorus. "You just gotta poke around."

4/6/82, The Spectrum, Philadelphia

■ **"She Belongs to Me"** (BOB DYLAN)
Bob Dylan, *Bringing It All Back Home* (1965)
Grateful Dead, *Backstage Pass* (video) (1992)
West Coast Pop Art Experimental Band, *The Legendary Unreleased Album* (1966)
Duane Eddy, *Duane Goes Bob Dylan* (1966)
The Nice, *The Nice* (1969)
Rick Nelson, *In Concert* (1970)
Birdland, *Birdland* (1991)
Harry Connick Jr., *Blue Light, Red Light* (1991)
Pete Anderson, *Working Class* (1994)

This frequently quoted Dylan love ballad to a mysterious, aloof woman has an ironic title, as Dylan spends the entire song trying to convince the listener she doesn't belong to him. Adding to the irony is Dylan's delicate reading of the song both on its official release and in his many concert performances of it.

Weir is remembered as having sung "She Belongs to Me" with the WARLOCKS and the very early Grateful Dead. But it was Garcia who mournfully interpreted the song for nine 1985 shows. The band released an acoustic interpretation of the song on their video *Backstage Pass* with Garcia, Weir, and Lesh sharing lead vocals.

4/7/85, The Spectrum, Philadelphia

■ **"She's Mine"** (LIGHTNIN' HOPKINS)
Lightnin' Hopkins, *Lightnin' Hopkins* (1959)

Pigpen sang "She's Mine" during his solo dobro bit in the Dead's 1970 acoustic set. A put-up or shut-up love song from the muse of Lightnin' Hopkins, "She's Mine" has the sound and sensibility of an ancient blues.

5/15/70, Fillmore East, New York

■ "Shelter from the Storm" (BOB DYLAN)

Bob Dylan, *Blood on the Tracks* (1974), *Hard Rain* (1976), *Live At Budokan* (1978)
Mission, single (1987)

Like "Tangled Up in Blue," the disturbing masterpiece from *Blood on the Tracks*, his equally masterful 1974 album, Dylan's "Shelter from the Storm" is a painful look at a man's life and the shattering of a relationship. Describing his tempest-tossed state of being with elemental symbolism, the song is a tragic summing up of what once was but will never be again. The poet found shelter but now "it's doom alone that counts."

"Shelter from the Storm" was only played at one of the Dylan/Dead shows but was well handled by the short-lived combo.

7/24/87, Oakland Coliseum, Oakland, California (with Bob Dylan)

■ "Ship of Fools" (Garcia/Hunter)

Grateful Dead, *From the Mars Hotel* (1974), *Steal Your Face* (1976)
Elvis Costello, *Deadicated* (1971)

A thinly veiled political allegory, "Ship of Fools" is a bitter song celebrating staunch individuality. With a subtle allusion to Herman Melville's *Moby-Dick* in the first lines of the song ("Went to see the captain, strangest I could find"), "Ship of Fools" works as a powerful kiss-off song to ingrained socio-economic hierarchies with its cold warning: "Don't lend your hand to raise no flag atop no ship of fools."

The Dead debuted "Ship of Fools" in 1974 and performed it more than two hundred times in the next two decades—a second-set exclusive after 1977.

7/8/78, Red Rocks Amphitheater, Morrison, Colorado
12/30/86, Henry J. Kaiser Convention Center, Oakland, California

■ "Shit Happens" (Weir/Hunter)

A bumper sticker that became the title of an unreleased and unperformed Dead tune, "Shit Happens" featured a great Hunter lyric and a strange jazzy score.

■ *Siamese Twins*/Tom Constanten and HENRY KAISER

Cuneiform Records, Rune 72, 1995.

More space-alien music from these two masters of the universe. The press release for this interstellar album claimed the entire band met at a Vegas UFO convention, have the same luminous tattoos on the soles of their feet, and that, under hypnosis, wrote out the identical melody and chords for the first track of the album.

■ "Sick and Tired" (Fats Domino/Chris Kenner)

Fats Domino, *The Fabulous Mr. D* (1958)
Johnny Winter, *Hey, Where's Your Brother?* (1992)

Antoine "Fats" Domino (born February 26, 1928) may not be the best musician New Orleans produced, but his sound and name are the most recognizable. Years before the phrase "rock 'n' roll" came into the language, "The Fat Man" was writing and singing songs that became standards.

In 1949 the short, rotund pianist was discovered by Imperial Records president Lew Chudd during a three-dollars-a-week gig at the Hideaway Bar in the Crescent City. Through the coming decade, Domino became a one-man hit parade. In each of those years Domino achieved the unparalleled feat of hitting the top ten on the rhythm and blues or pop charts at least once with such memorable singles as "Ain't That a Shame," "Blueberry Hill," and "I'm Walking." Many of his songs were written with New Orleans band leader Dave Bartholomew with whom he united in the late 1940s and maintained a working relationship into the 1980s.

Domino was self-taught but he mastered many forms of popular piano techniques, including blues, boogie-woogie, and ragtime. He fused his own arrangements with these styles and began building the blocks for much of what followed, immeasurably influencing white and black rock artists.

Though he receded from the limelight by the mid-1960s, he continued to tour and record, finally racking up some three dozen Top 40 singles with sales totals in the one hundred million range.

"Sick and Tired" (which Domino wrote with New Orleans R&B vocalist Chris Kenner) was not one of the Dead's best-known covers but, with Pigpen's edgy vocals and zigzagging harp, was an effective if short-lived inclusion in their very early sets.

2/23/66, The Matrix, San Francisco

■ *Silver*

Arista 4076, 1975.

Some four years before he started performing and recording with the Grateful Dead, Brent Mydland was making a name for himself in this slick Los Angeles band which cut this sole commercial and overproduced release.

▪ "The Sidewalks of New York" (James W. Blake and Charles Lawlor)

Duke Ellington, *The Blanton-Webster Band* (1986), *Fargo, North Dakota, Nov. 7, 1940* (1940)
Cannonball Adderley, *Things Are Getting Better* (1958)

A one-time-only Dead encore of this ancient piece of business wrapped a glorious Big Apple run just before the band stormed Europe in '72.

Introduced by Lottie Gilson at the Old London Theater in New York's Bowery in the late nineteenth century, "The Sidewalks of New York" was the campaign song of Alfred E. Smith, the Democratic nominee for President in 1924. Though the song was not used in the Broadway musical of the same name, Betty Grable and June Haver sang it in the 1945 film *The Dolly Sisters*, and Jimmy Durante and Bob Hope performed it in *Beau James*, the Hollywood story of New York City Mayor Jimmy Walker, in 1957.

3/28/72, Academy of Music, New York

▪ "Silver Threads and Golden Needles" (Dick Reynolds/Jack Rhodes)

The Springfields, *Silver Threads and Golden Needles* (1962), *History of British Rock* (1962)
Horace Silver, *Songs for My Father* (1965)
Linda Ronstadt, *Hand Sown—Home Grown* (1969), *Don't Cry Now* (1973), *Greatest Hits* (1976)
Roy Clark, *Best of Roy Clark* (1971)
Sandy Denny, *Rendezvous* (1977)
Ferlin Huskey, *With Feelin'* (1991)
Dolly Parton and Tammy Wynette, *Honky Tonk Angels* (1993)
Skeeter Davis, *The Essential Skeeter Davis* (1995)

The Springfields, an early-'60s British folk trio, had the first hit with "Silver Threads and Golden Needles" and this saccharine piece of country poetry may have first attracted Bob Weir's attention as a teenager. The song concerns the narrator's sad realization that his humble roots put him at a fatal disadvantage in his attempts to woo a woman of considerably higher station. As a result, not even silver threads and golden needles could ever mend his permanently broken heart.

With Garcia often supplying some juicy *obbligato*

licks on his pedal steel guitar, Weir performed "Silver Threads and Golden Needles" in 1969 and 1970, often in the group's acoustic sets during that "Golden Age."

Next stop: Tear Jerk City.

5/15/70, Fillmore East, New York

▪ "Simple Twist of Fate" (BOB DYLAN)

Bob Dylan, *Blood on the Tracks* (1974), *At Budokan* (1978)
JOAN BAEZ, *Diamonds and Rust* (1975)

Bob Dylan's sad tale of lost love finds the poet at his most vulnerable. Dylan's delivery of the song on record is almost a whispered understatement, painfully recalling his loneliness through dreams and fractured imagination.

Though the Dead only performed "Simple Twist of Fate" in three of their six concerts with Dylan, Garcia had been regularly including it in his own band's concerts since the late 1970s, where it often showcased the solo chops of his "other bassist" JOHN KAHN.

7/26/87, Stadium, Anaheim, California (with Bob Dylan)
12/10/83, Capitol Theater, Passaic, New Jersey (Jerry Garcia Band)

▪ "Sing Me Back Home" (MERLE HAGGARD)

Merle Haggard, *Sing Me Back Home* (1967), *Okie from Muskogee* (1970)
The Everly Brothers, *Roots* (1968)
Cleo Laine, *Wordsongs* (1978), *Cleo at Carnegie* (1983)
Seldom Scene, *Best of the Seldom Scene* (1986)
Hubert Sumlin, *Heart and Soul* (1989)
Pat Travers, *Blues Tracks* (1992)
Dave Ray/Tony Glover, *Picture Has Faded* (1993)
JOAN BAEZ, *Rare, Live and Classic* (1993)

Merle Haggard didn't only sing from the heart, he sang about the true experiences of his gritty life. After an impoverished, hard-scrabble childhood, Haggard landed in San Quentin for burglary. In this tragedy, a death row prisoner's last night is darkly depicted.

In his autobiography (also entitled *Sing Me Back Home*), Haggard credits James Hendricks, a fellow prisoner nicknamed "Rabbit," with motivating him to develop his musical talents. Hendricks briefly escaped from the Big House shortly after and was quickly captured but not before killing a pursuing officer. For that he was sentenced to die in San Quentin's notorious gas chamber. Rabbit's final hours were the inspiration for Haggard's poignant ballad, "Sing Me Back Home."

"Years later," Haggard recalled in his autobiography, "when I wrote 'Sing Me Back Home,' it was because I believe I know exactly how he felt that night. Even now when I sing that song, it's for Rabbit and all those like him."

Indeed, his dry-as-dust delivery and unquestioned tough-guy credentials made it (and many more like it) instantly creditable to his audience.

Despite some off-key harmonizing with his band mates, Garcia dramatically rendered the song with the Dead in the early 1970s where it served as a late-second-set downshift, occupying a space in the concert that would later be filled with songs such as "Black Peter," "Wharf Rat," "Stella Blue," and "Standing on the Moon."

7/2/71, Fillmore West, San Francisco
5/18/72, Kongressaal, Munich
8/27/72, Old Renaissance Faire Grounds, Veneta, Oregon
3/24/73, The Spectrum, Philadelphia

■ "Sittin' on Top of the World"
(Traditional)
Grateful Dead, *Grateful Dead* (1967)
The Missisipi Sheiks, single (1930)
Howlin' Wolf, single (1957), *The Real Folk Blues* (1963), *The London Howlin' Wolf Sessions* (1971), *Live & Cookin at Alice's Revisited* (1972)
Doc Watson, *Old Timey Concert* (1967)
Bob Wills and the Texas Playboys, *Tiffany Transcriptions* (1988)

(Courtesy of R. Crumb/Shanachie Entertainment)

Cream, *Wheels of Fire* (1968), *Goodbye* (1969)
Jack Bruce, *Inazuma Super Session* (1988), *Cities of the Heart* (1994)
BOB DYLAN, *Good as I Been to You* (1992)
Taj Mahal, *Dancing the Blues* (1993)
Lonnie Smith and Band, *Sounds of the South/'40s* (1995)
Ray Charles, *Brother Ray "Rocks" Rhythm & Blues* (1995)
Memphis Slim, *Alone with My Friends* (1996)

There are almost as many versions of "Sittin' on Top of the World" as there are musicians who adapted this ancient country blues. In 1930, the highly influential Mississippi Sheiks had the first hit with the song, rendering it as a slow blues on the Okeh label. Their rendition was the inspiration for Howlin' Wolf's most famous take on the tune and his rendition, in turn, became the framework for Cream's 1969 adaptation. To bring the lineage full circle, Bob Dylan's 1992 arrangement is a clear tip of the hat to the Mississippi Sheiks.

Garcia acknowledged early in the Dead's career that their version owed much to Carl Perkins's high-spirited 1958 debut album. The Perkins rocker is cut out of the same mold as the one recorded by the incomparable Kings of Texas Swing, Bob Wills and his Texas Playboys.

The Dead performed "Sittin' on Top of the World" around forty times between 1966 and 1972. In many of the later versions, the Dead wedged the chestnut in the middle of their spaciest and most far-out compositions, "Dark Star" and "The Other One." This would create the uncanny and off-balance, gear-shifting sensation that Dead shows were famous for in the late 1960s and early 1970s.

4/21/69, The Ark, Boston
6/13/69, Convention Center, Fresno, California
12/5/71, Felt Forum, New York
12/10/71, Fox Theater, St. Louis
5/18/72, Kongressaal, Munich

■ *Skeleton Key: A Dictionary for Deadheads* (book)/David Shenk and Steve Silberman.
388 pp. Doubleday, 1994.

Part lexicon, part handbook, *Skeleton Key* is proof that the Dead's impact on society is so powerful that they virtually created a language and culture all its own. With thumbnail sketches of band members, albums, Dead-

(Courtesy of Warner Bros. Records)

head terminology, and in-jokes, the authors have ingeniously formalized the flexible linguistic shades of Deaddom for posterity.

▪ Skeletons from the Closet

Warner Bros. W 2764, 1974.
"TURN ON YOUR LOVE LIGHT" (edited), "Uncle John's Band,"
    "Friend of the Devil," "St. Stephen," "High Time,"
    "One More Saturday Night"

This justly criticized anthology was produced by Warner Bros. without the band's involvement as part of a contractual obligation. The edited version of "Turn on Your Love Light" is particularly painful. Ouch!

▪ McGannahan Skjellyfetti

The Grateful Dead used this pseudonym as a group credit for songs the unit composed together. Those with eagle eyes will notice that "The Golden Road (to Unlimited Devotion)" and "Cream Puff War" on their debut album and "Feedback" from *Live/Dead* receive the McGannahan Skjellyfetti authorship.

Kenneth Patchen's novel *Memoirs of a Shy Pornographer* is the source of the monicker.

▪ Skull and Roses

See **Grateful Dead** (a.k.a. "Skull and Roses" or "Skull Fuck")

▪ *Slewfoot*/David Rea

Columbia KC 32485, 1973. Produced by Bob Weir.

Weir, the Godchauxs, Charles Lloyd, and some of the New Riders show up on this pedestrian album from a former member of Fairport Convention.

▪ "Slipknot!" (Garcia)

**Grateful Dead, *Blues for Allah* (1975), *Without a Net*
    (1990), *One from the Vault* /'75 (1991), *Dick's Picks*
    Volume Three /'77 (1995)**

An intricate, propulsive, and percussive instrumental linking "Help on the Way" with "Franklin's Tower," "Slipknot!" is the jazzy musical equivalent of the titled knot. Actually, the 1974 concert appearance of "Slipknot!" slightly predates the development of the Dead's "Blues for Allah" material to which it was hinged just more than a hundred times through 1995.

The composition was, according to Weir, really honed in concert. As he told David Gans in 1981, "We'd take it and play it onstage, then think about it for a while, make some adjustments. The more time you have, obviously, the more you're going to be able to chisel away and sculpt it just the way you want."

Somewhat overlooked by casual Deadheads and the band's critics, "Slipknot!" is one of the band's most jazz-oriented compositions, recalling the best of Miles Davis's work from the late 1960s and early 1970s,

(Courtesy of Warner Bros. Records)

Weather Report, or even Frank Zappa's heavily orchestrated compositions.

Interestingly, this piece may have some roots in American folk. Woody Guthrie wrote a haunting, highly disturbing lament about a hanging called "Slip Knot," which, when recorded by Mark Spoelstra (an early colleague of Dylan's), had a deliberate and forbidding drone quality accounting for at least half of its remarkable effect. This drone and the similarity of the song titles could have informed the Dead's tight, Oriental-flavored instrumental.

9/27/76, Community War Memorial, Rochester, New York

5/9/77, War Memorial Auditorium, Buffalo, New York

3/29/83, Warfield Theater, San Francisco

10/8/89, Coliseum, Hampton, Virginia

6/14/91, RFK Stadium, Washington, D.C.

9/25/91, Boston Garden, Boston

■ "Slow Train" (BOB DYLAN)

Bob Dylan, *Slow Train Coming* (1979), *Dylan & the Dead* (1987)

Bob Dylan was a troubled man as the 1970s came to a close. Despite a successful return to recording and performing in the middle of the decade, his first feature film *Renaldo and Clara* was widely condemned as a confusing morass and, more saliently, his marriage had fallen apart.

At the instigation of either guitarist T-Bone Burnett or his then-girlfriend, actress Mary Alice Artes, Dylan became a born-again Christian late in 1978. In an interview two years later, Dylan said, "Jesus put his hand on me. It was a physical thing. I felt it. I felt it all over me. I felt my whole body tremble. The glory of the Lord knocked me down and picked me up."

Reiterating his experience in an interview with Robert Hilburn of the *Los Angeles Times* later in 1980, Dylan described an epiphany in a Phoenix, Arizona, hotel room: "There was a presence in the room that couldn't be anything but Jesus . . . I truly had a born-again experience if you want to call it that."

Dylan's public conversion was shocking. The ultimate cynic had found something to believe in. *Slow Train Coming*, recorded in ten days at Alabama's famed Muscle Shoals Studio, was his testament of faith.

With production assistance from Dire Straits guitarist Mark Knopfler and record biz legend Jerry Wexler, *Slow Train Coming* is regarded as Dylan's slickest studio recording. But it was not all smooth sailing in the studio. As Wexler once recalled, "I had no idea he was on this born-again Christian trip until he started to evangelize me. I said, 'Bob, you're dealing with a sixty-two-year-old confirmed Jewish atheist. Let's just make an album.'"

The album was made and became a surprise commercial smash but it was not without its fallout. Dylan drew a line in the sand that his fans never thought they would ever be challenged to cross. Either you were a believer or you weren't—there was no middle ground. It was a major shift in philosophy for an artist who had always encouraged his audience to think for themselves.

Ironically, "Slow Train," the album's title track, was a symbol Dylan first mentioned in the liner notes to his most iconoclastic album, *Highway 61 Revisited*. Dylan returned to the song off and on in the following years and his reinterpretation of "Slow Train" was one of the surprise treats of his 1987 concerts with the Grateful Dead.

7/4/87, Sullivan Stadium, Foxboro, Massachusetts (with Bob Dylan).

■ *Smoke* (film and soundtrack)

Directed by Wayne Wang and Paul Auster. Written by Paul Auster. Miramax Productions, 1995. Starring Harvey Keitel, William Hurt, Forrest Whitaker.

The Jerry Garcia Band recorded "Smoke Gets in Your Eyes" and "Coffee and Cigarettes" especially for this unusual film set in a Brooklyn, New York, cigar store that deals with serendipitous events intertwining the lives of an unlikely assortment of characters. The Garcia Band track ran over the film's closing credits and was included on the soundtrack album. Additionally, a Garcia Band video of the song was shown before some screenings of the film. "Smoke Gets in Your Eyes" was written by Jerome Kern and, in that Garcia was named after Kern, it was fitting that this was the last Garcia music released in his lifetime.

For the extra curious, Paul Auster's novels (especially *Moon Palace*) should appeal to Deadheads who experience high levels of meaningful coincidence. Synchronicity spoken here.

■ "Smokestack Lightnin'" (Howlin' Wolf)

Howlin' Wolf, *The Genuine Article—The Best of Howlin' Wolf* (1960), *The Real Folk Blues* (1963), *Moanin' In The Moonlight* (1964), *The Howlin' Wolf Album* (1969), *The Chess Box* (1991)

it: "Smokestack Lightinin'" is less a song than condensation of antique blues phrases and motifs, clipped and elliptical, like a half-distinct telegraph message from the past. But one imperishable image stands out: a train's smokestack glinting in the sun as the train threads through the landscape.

At six-foot-six and weighing in close to three hundred pounds, the Wolf possessed a voice that could shake a city down to its last transistor—a primal, ferocious sound that is without peer. His gripping histrionics and sheer, intimidating physical intensity redefined the genre with nearly every performance—acting out his most potent blues while whooping, hollering and wriggling on the floor as if succumbing or battling the worst demons.

Born Chester Arthur Burnett June 10, 1910, in West Point, Mississippi and named after the late nineteenth-century American president, Wolf learned of the blues early on but he was also a huge fan of the white country-blues singer Jimmie Rodgers, whose yodels and whoops were derived from the work chants and blues of black plantation workers.

Wolf's handle was derived from a series of nicknames that included "Bull Crow" and "Foot." But, as he once said, "I just stuck to the Wolf. I could do no yodelin' so I turned to Howlin'." On other occasions he boasted that he'd won his name after his father had killed a wolf and brought it home to show his son. Young Chester was terrified by the fearsome carcass and learned to imitate a wolf's howl, so that he could scare off any of its companions that might be out to get him.

A pupil of Charley Patton and Willie Brown, both of whom he saw perform at plantation picnics and the local juke joints he frequented, Wolf picked up the guitar and mouth harp and began playing the same places. Tilling the land on his father's farm during the week and singing the blues on the weekends, Wolf was itching for the chance to take his blues out of the Delta.

He moved to West Memphis, Arkansas, just across the river from Memphis, Tennessee and formed units that included harmonica-singers James Cotton and Junior Parker and guitarist Matt "Guitar" Murphy that began playing the blues and endorsing agricultural equipment on KWEM, a local radio station. Ike Turner (later of Ike and Tina fame), of all people, heard the band and steered Sam Phillips their way. It was Phillips, the legendary Memphis producer who went on to his greatest fame as Elvis Presley's guru, who once de-

Howlin' Wolf (Chester Burnett). *(Archive Photos/Frank Driggs Collection)*

Muddy Waters, single (1954), *Rare and Unissued* **(1989),** *Chess Box* **(1989)**

Grateful Dead, *History of the Grateful Dead, Vol. 1 (Bear's Choice)/'70* **(1973)**

The Yardbirds, *The Yardbirds Featuring Eric Clapton* **(1964),** *Five Live Yardbirds* **(1965),** *Having a Rave Up* **(1965)**

Manfred Mann, *The Five Faces of Manfred Mann* **(1964)**

John Hammond, *I Can Tell* **(1967)**

HENRY KAISER, *Devil in the Drain* **(1987)**

Soundgarden, *Ultramega OK* **(1988)**

George Thorogood, *Born to Be Bad* **(1988)**

The Burnin' Rain, *Visions* **(1989)**

Lynyrd Skynyrd, *Lynyrd Skynyrd 1991* **(1991)**

A simple, traditional blues riff of unknown origin, "Smokestack Lightinin'" is most closely associated with Howlin' Wolf, the bluesman who hot-wired rock 'n' roll and who had a hit with the song in the early 1960s. Not only is this one of Wolf's finest performances, it fleshes out the myth. Here he really does howl, in that throaty half-yodel, part feral, part borrowed voice from old Jimmie Rodgers records. Not that he doesn't have room for

scribed Wolf as "a force of nature," liked what he heard and brought Wolf and company into the studio in 1951 to record a couple of songs, "Moanin' at Midnight" and "How Many More Years," which were later leased to Chess Records.

Wolf churned out one classic after another and, in 1953, moved to Chicago, the city he would call home for the rest of his life. United with WILLIE DIXON, for whose songs he competed mightily with Muddy Waters, Wolf recorded many of the tunes that became virtual chapters in the blues Bible: "LITTLE RED ROOSTER," "SPOONFUL," "Back Door Man," "Evil," and "I AIN'T SUPERSTITIOUS." His Chess records, masterfully realized symphonies that combine molten-metal riffs with off-the-wall bebop rhythms, were used as blueprints by everyone from Led Zeppelin to the Rolling Stones, Captain Beefheart to Tom Waits. And ten years before Bob Dylan first opened up the imagery of rock lyrics, Wolf was using surreal, bizarre allusions and metaphors that came from both black folklore and the unfathomable recesses of his own psyche.

While some blues historians describe the relationship between Wolf and Waters as tense at best (both were proud men), others also suggest that, like Diz and Bird in the early fermentation of bebop, the competition existing between them may have forced the pair to achieve even greater heights.

Like Waters, Wolf slowly transformed himself from a scorching practitioner of the rural Southern blues into an avatar of the deep blues of Chicago's ghetto. But no matter what the style, he was always capable of simultaneously rocking the house and scaring the audience out of their wits. No shambling cotton-picker, Wolf was hip, as he had to be in the ruthlessly cut-throat arena of American black music in the 1940s and 1950s. Going electric with a vengeance and blowing their horn-oriented jump-blues rivals offstage, Wolf's band were the baddest motherfuckers around, and they made cutting-edge pop music as vital as Jimi Hendrix in the 1960s or Prince in the 1980s.

Just when his raw style, still deeply rooted in the Southern tradition, began to fall out of favor with his black audience who were turning to the more sophisticated R&B records, Wolf was discovered by young Europeans, namely the Rolling Stones who, in 1965, invited him to play on *Shindig*, the American rock television show, while they literally sat at his feet. These ties were strengthened through the end of the decade and

culminated with a couple of blues-rock albums in 1969 and 1970 recorded in London with all-star casts that included Eric Clapton, Steve Winwood, Ringo Starr, Bill Wyman, and Charlie Watts.

The last five years of Howlin' Wolf's life marked a slow decline in his output and health. A heart attack and a debilitating car accident seriously curtailed his touring schedule, yet he was able to record a few more albums which included the songs "Watergate Blues" and the autobiographical "Moving." Two months after his last November 1975 performance in Chicago with B. B. King, he died of kidney failure.

Twenty years after his death, Howlin' Wolf's 1950s recordings are still used by Madison Avenue as totems of authenticity for selling everything from beer to blue jeans. But no amount of homogeneity can tame the Wolf's howl, which comes from the very wellspring of American music, sourced directly from the plantation in the Mississippi Delta where the blues bubbled from the fertile earth.

Wolf was never considered a great blues composer but "Smokestack Lightnin'" is probably his most famous. The Grateful Dead versions of the song (first with Pigpen singing the lead and later with Weir) are considerably slower than the best-known versions, allowing Garcia, in particular, to search the folds of this wonderfully funky Mississippi Delta styling.

2/19/71, Capitol Theater, Port Chester, New York

8/17/91, Shoreline Amphitheater, Mountain View, California

- ## So Far (video)
  Produced by Len Dell'Amico, 1987.
  "Uncle John's Band">"Playing in the Band">"Lady with a Fan">"Space">"Rhythm Devils">"Throwing Stones">"Not Fade Away"

A panoramic sweep of Dead music and song-specific imagery, this tasty set combines footage from an audienceless shoot at the Marin County Civic Center and the 1985 New Year's show in a collage style format that captures the mid-1980s band in a video bottle.

- ## Solid Silver/Quicksilver Messenger Service
  Capitol SM 11820, 1975. Produced by John Palladino and Quicksilver.

Capitol reunited Quicksilver's best-known (though not best) unit when they released this passable LP, which included a song ("I Heard You Singing") cowritten by Robert Hunter and David Freiberg. The song can also be found on Hunter's *Tales of the Great Rum Runners*.

"So Many Roads" (Garcia/Hunter)

Part of the same musical tapestry as "Black Muddy River" and "Built to Last," "So Many Roads" is filled with lyrical allusions to the older musical styles that informed the Dead's aesthetic fomentation: the country blues and the jug band. Musically the song attempts the same Van Morrison–style build-up as "Standing on the Moon" and "Believe It or Not" and was successful in getting the desired emotional rise out of the crowd. The Dead introduced "So Many Roads" in 1992 and it was fluidly tapped in both sets.

With its road warrior sensibility, "So Many Roads" reads like a map to the band's soul and could almost be interpreted as a latter-day "Truckin'."

According to Robert Hunter's notes in *A Box of Rain*, the song had a long gestation period. "One afternoon, Jerry was playing some structured changes on piano. Figuring they might be forgotten otherwise, I clicked on my tape recorder. Ten years later I found the tape and listened to it, liked it, and set these words to it. Listening to the pitifully recorded and time-degraded tape, Jerry protested that, although he liked the words, his changes were not very good and unfinished besides. This didn't seem to be the case and I requested that he at least give it a run through. The result was one of the better received new GD songs and one that almost got away. Dozens of others did, but you can't go following people around with tape recorders—you get a reputation that way."

11/29/94, McNichols Sports Arena, Denver

Somebody to Love (with Mr. Twidge: Art & Antics) (song and computer screen saver)/Jerry Garcia Band
Rotten Rotty Entertainment, Inc., 1997.

A Jerry Garcia Band CD single disguised as some of the squirreliest computer screen-saving graphics ever (courtesy of Garcia's bizarre visual imagination) will ensure that the maestro's legacy will live on in yet another medium. The live track, a hot raveup of "Everybody Needs Somebody to Love," the Solomon Burke/Bert Berns/Jerry Wexler R&B soul chestnut, is almost reason enough to take the plunge.

Sonatas by Haydn, Schubert, Beethoven/Tom Constanten
Mauroy Records MR2001, 1991.

Traditional classicism with a twist has always been T.C.'s hallmark and he lets these talents shine on this small label outing.

Songs for Beginners/Graham Nash
Atlantic SD 7204, 1971.

Garcia and Lesh show up on a couple of tracks on Graham Nash's moving, personal solo debut, which is filled with lovely nuances and ideas and even lovelier melodies. On "I Used to Be a King," Lesh plays bass and Garcia plays pedal steel and piano. On "Man in the Mirror," Garcia contributes his patented pedal steel licks.

Sonic Roar Shock/BOB BRALOVE and Tom Constanten
Dose Hermanos Productions DH001. Recorded at The Knitting Factory, New York, January 12, 13, and 14, 1996; Wetlands Preserve, New York, January 16, 1996; Cabaloosa, New Paltz, New York, January 19, 1996. Produced by Bob Bralove and Tom Constanten.
"Velvet Jungle," "Meteor Blizzard," "Casbah Gardens," "Reorient Express," "Waltz of the Autumn Moon," "Swamp Thing," "Moonscape Earthrise," "Buddah Pest Rush-Hour," "Fire Dance," "Cartoon Spy," "Shadow of the Invisible Man," "Roar Shock"

Two keyboards plus four hands plus 196 keys equals One Mind. Such is the stuff of this fanciful yet deeply intuitive release from two of the more eccentric and unheralded members of the Dead's musical family.

"So Sad (to Watch Good Love Go Bad)" (Don Everly)
The Everly Brothers, *It's Everly Time* (1960), *Reunion Concert* (1983)

The Everly Brothers didn't miss a beat when they made the leap to an A-list recording company as they continued to keep churning out the Top 10 pop hits. "So Sad" was the first of their Warner Bros. chart-toppers.

Weir had a real affinity for this era of the Everly

Brothers but only is known to have sung "So Sad" during one 1970 acoustic set.

7/11/70, Fillmore East, New York

■ **"So What"** (Miles Davis)

Miles Davis, *Kind of Blue* (1959), *Saturday Night at the Blackhawk, Vol. 2* (1961), *Live at the Plugged Nickel/'65* (1995), *Live in Copenhagen/'59* (1991)

Eddie Jefferson, *Body and Soul* (1968), *There I Go Again* (1969)

Bill Evans, *Blue in Green* (1974)

John Stubblefield, *Morning Song* (1993)

Benny Golson, *I Remember Miles* (1993)

While the Dead only gamely but lamely attempted to tackle "So What," one of the most famously recognizable and infectiously mellow compositions in the jazz canon, it was a favored and inspired choice for Garcia's performances with DAVID GRISMAN in the 1990s.

Miles Davis composed and recorded "So What" in 1959 for his groundbreaking 1960 album *Kind of Blue*, which featured some of the most hallowed names in American music: John Coltrane on tenor saxophone, Julian "Cannonball" Adderley on alto, Bill Evans on pi-ano, Paul ("Mr. P.C.") Chambers on bass, and Jimmy Cobb on drums. This influential quintet had already be-gun experimenting with a new approach to jazz in which traditional chord changes as the foundation for the music were replaced by a modal orientation which allowed the musicians freer range for inspiration. This technique generated more thought and creativity along melodic lines and was an idea which the Dead took to heart for their more exploratory pieces such as "Dark Star."

As Davis wrote in his 1989 autobiography, "I didn't write out the music for *Kind of Blue*. [Instead I] brought in sketches for what everybody was supposed to play be-cause I wanted a lot of spontaneity in the playing, just like I thought was in the interplay between those drum-mers and the finger piano player [I'd seen] with the Bal-let Africaine. Everything was first take, which indicates the level everyone was playing on. It was beautiful.

"When I tell people that missed what I was trying to do on *Kind of Blue*, that I missed getting the exact sound of the African finger piano up in that sound, they just look at me like I'm crazy. Everyone said that record was a masterpiece—and I loved it too—and so they feel I'm just trying to put them on. But that's what I was trying to do on most of that album, particularly on 'All Blues' and 'So What.' I just missed."

Paul Chambers, bass; Julian "Cannonball" Adderley, alto sax; Miles Davis, trumpet; Jimmy Cobb, drums; John Coltrane, tenor sax; Newport Jazz Festival, 1958. *(Archive Photos/Frank Driggs Collection)*

This was an attitude that Miles Dewey Davis III seemed to carry with him from cradle to grave. Other than possibly BOB DYLAN (a fellow Gemini), with whom he shared the remarkable ability to continually transform and reinvent himself, nobody shed as many artistic or personal skins as the coolest of trumpeters and humans. More than any other player, Davis pushed jazz in new directions, defined and refined elements and sounds, explored and exploited new ideas and technologies. The defiant loner, Miles was the quintessential jazz icon—enigmatic, moody, brooding.

Born May 24, 1926, in Alton, Illinois, Davis was, like Duke Ellington, raised in an affluent African-American home. He took up the trumpet when he was thirteen, briefly played alongside Charlie "Bird" Parker in Billy Eckstine's big band in 1944 and won a scholarship to New York's Juilliard School of Music a year later. Studying music theory by day and combing the jazz clubs of Fifty-second Street by night, Miles eventually united with Parker and Dizzy Gillespie.

Bird and Diz were the storm troopers of the bebop revolution and among the greatest improvisers in the history of jazz—true musical geniuses of the twentieth century. Not surprisingly, Davis left Juilliard in the fall of 1945 to pursue a doctorate from the "University of Bebop under the tutelage of Professors Bird and Diz."

But while Bird was an inspiration to the young man with a horn, Diz was his teacher, showing him how to play piano and telling him that the reason Davis couldn't play in the highest registers as he did was because he couldn't "hear up there." It was evident even then that Davis's voice would be his own.

The years following World War II would prove to be pivotal in his musical development, as they saw him taking Diz's chair in Bird's quintet and jamming with the new music's other young turks (Thelonious Monk, Bud Powell, Fats Navarro, Charles Mingus, and Max Roach) as well as older, established cats like Coleman Hawkins.

It was during these studies in the informal laboratory of Fifty-second Street that Davis began to assemble an innovative unit that offered a stylistic alternative to bop. The idea for the nonet, culled from discussions with Gil Evans, resulted in *Birth of the Cool*, an album presaging the school of West Coast jazz in the 1950s.

But the early 1950s were tough times for Davis. He developed a heroin addiction and a bad rep while falling in and out of the scene. But he reemerged in 1954 and began to forge a remarkable sound and style that would stamp him forever as a giant, perfecting his sparse, staccato trumpet style. His crisp, concise and often unforgettable solos demonstrated just how strong an impact could be made through considered use of space and time as with speed and flash.

Davis simultaneously investigated two separate but related musical paths. With Gil Evans as an arranger, Davis's influence on big band orchestration was felt in a series of recordings culminating with *Sketches of Spain* that showed his ability to blend his captivating leads with a dynamic ensemble. In his great jazz combo of the late 1950s, Davis led Coltrane and company in a series of recordings (including *Kind of Blue*) seminally impacting inside and outside jazz.

During the 1960s and 1970s, Davis continued to break new ground while rejecting the "free jazz" innovations set forth by ORNETTE COLEMAN. With a younger stable of musicians that would dominate popular jazz in the coming decade (including pianist Herbie Hancock, tenor saxophonist Wayne Shorter, and drummer Tony Williams), the new Davis quintet flourished, working with a concept employing written themes but no prearranged harmonies. This allowed both the soloist and the answering rhythm section players to include whatever notes or chords they desired after the initial theme statement.

From the mid-1960s onward, Davis opted for longer pieces without composed structures. He used rock as a foundation, employed Indian and Asian instrumentation along with standard jazz pieces, and went electric, yet his trumpet solos remained as definitive and clear as in earlier, acoustic periods.

When the Dead had to follow Davis onstage during a string of three April 1970 Fillmore West gigs, Lesh recalled, "I don't want to hear anybody snivel about following anybody else, because we got the *one*. Made me feel so dumb. It was cold-blooded murder. Miles had his *Bitches Brew* band, a hot fucking band, and they played some stuff! Billy and Mickey and I were onstage for sure—I think everybody in our band was onstage, digging it, and trying to keep up with the music. It was some dense stuff. Then we had to *follow* these guys. It wasn't exactly stage fright I felt; it was like, 'How am I going to play this stuff after hearing that? I'd much rather listen to more!'"

Davis's own recollections of the concerts were not as devastating as relayed in his autobiography. "After I finished *Bitches Brew*, Clive Davis put me in touch with

Bill Graham, who owned the Fillmore in San Francisco and the Fillmore East in downtown New York. Bill wanted me to play San Francisco first, with the Grateful Dead, and so we did. That was an eye-opening experience for me, because there were about five thousand people there that night, mostly young, white hippies, and they hadn't hardly heard of me if they had heard of me at all. We opened for the Grateful Dead, but another group came on before us. The place was packed with these real spacey, high white people, and when we first started playing people were walking around and talking. But after a while they all got quiet and really got into the music. I played a little of something like *Sketches of Spain* and then we went into the *Bitches Brew* shit and that really blew them out. After that concert, every time I would play out there in San Francisco, a lot of young white people showed up at the gigs.

"So it was through Bill that I met the Grateful Dead. Jerry Garcia, their guitar player, and I hit it off great, talking about music—what they liked and what I liked—and I think we all learned something, grew some. Jerry loved jazz, and I found out that he loved my music and had been listening to it for a long time. Looking back, I think Bill Graham did some important things for music with those concerts, opened everything up so that a lot of different people heard a lot of different kinds of music that they wouldn't normally have heard."

Those who wondered what led the Garcia-Saunders unit to cover the old Rodgers and Hammerstein ballad "My Funny Valentine" in the early 1970s should realize that Davis was toying with the standard a good decade before.

Poor health dogged his career through the 1970s, forcing him to take a break from music for the last half of the decade. But while the results of his return to the studio were mixed, his reemergence on concert stages of the 1980s were triumphant. His playing seemed to get stronger and more interesting, especially in his use of the lower and middle register. Right up until the bitter end, each phrase of a Miles Davis solo seemed to encapsulate the spectrum of his music and his being: the sputtering foundling blowing with Bird, the suave composure of his work in 1950s, the strident quester of the 1960s, the gruff electric maverick of the 1970s, and the mellowed but never content yearning of his final years.

On September 28, 1991, Davis died of pneumonia, respiratory failure and a stroke while convalescing in Santa Monica, California.

3/27/88, Hamptom Coliseum, Hampton, Virginia
2/3/91, Warfield Theater, San Francisco (Garcia acoustic ensemble with David Grisman)

■ *Sonnets to Orpheus*
See Duino Elegies

■ "Space" (Grateful Dead)
Grateful Dead, *Dead Set* (1981), *Infrared Roses* (1991), *Dozin' at the Knick/'90* (1996)
Robert Hunter, *Box of Rain* (1991)
Saunders/Garcia, *Live at Keystone* (1974)

First there was "Feedback" and then there was "Space." The Dead always experimented with atonal, formless music that stretched the boundaries of sound, if sometimes their audience's patience. One thing for certain: it was during their nightly "Space" jams that the Dead were making all-new, first-of- and one-of-a-kind music never to be played again. As a roadmap, the band would sometimes, in their discussions of the events of the day or the latest entry in their reading lists, give themselves a topical theme with which to launch these serial quests.

Discussing the band's approach to this sometimes difficult-to-access portion of a Dead concert with Paul Krassner in 1984, Garcia said, "Our second half definitely has a shape which is, if not directly, at least partially, inspired by the psychedelic experience as a wave form. The second half for us is the thing of taking chances and going all to pieces and then coming back and reassembling . . . you might lose a few pieces but you don't despair about seeing yourself go completely to pieces—you don't despair about it—you just let go.

"We've been doing interesting things now . . . the last year or so—actually the last two years—our most free form, the stuff that's not really attached to any particular song but is just free form music—it's not rhythmic, it's not really attached to any musical norms—it's the completely weird shit. We've been doing stuff with that. We've been picking themes for that and thinking of that as a painting or a movie. I think our most recent theme was 'Reagan in China' . . . we just do it like that . . . One time we had the 'Qaddafi Death Squad' as our theme. Sometimes they're terribly detailed, but sometimes they're just a broad subject. We do this when we think about it, when we remember to. It's not a hard and fast rule. But it's made that part of the music at times tremendous on another level of organization that pulls it together. It makes it real interesting.

"It's current events. Whoever gets the idea will just say it: 'Hey, tonight it's blah.' We don't argue about it or anything—if someone just has an inspiration. You know so 'Tonight it's the Bongo Straits, 1940,' 'Pearl Harbor' or whatever . . . we usually just take it from just what's in the air like something in the news. Ya know, maybe it's somebody famous's birthday—any of those kind of things. There's always the thing of wanting to paint pictures, ya know and doing something that's more or less literal. A lot of times it doesn't come off that way. What it does is provide us an invisible infrastructure which everybody can interpret freely. It's a neat thing because anyone can interpret it however they want and it still provides a kind of centerpiece for us all to look at. It's a neat way to do it. It's provided for us more interesting shapes for that non-formed music, that shapeless music.

"Before we started using that idea, that music would tend to get dispersed so far that you couldn't relate to it at all. And sometimes it would make an effort to turn into something real fast—something familiar—real fast, so that it would hover between these two poles and turn into something not quite juicy, not quite as promising as it could be."

3/24/73, The Spectrum, Philadelphia

6/28/74, Boston Garden, Boston

1/22/78, McArthur Court, Eugene, Oregon

11/24/78, Capitol Theater, Passaic, New Jersey

8/4/79, Oakland Auditorium Arena, Oakland, California

3/20/81, Rainbow Theater, London

4/20/83, Providence Civic Center, Providence, Rhode Island

9/10/83, Sante Fe Downs, Sante Fe, New Mexico

9/11/85, Henry J. Kaiser Convention Center, Oakland, California

9/20/88, Madison Square Garden, New York

10/21/88, Reunion Arena, Dallas

5/6/89, Frost Amphitheater, Palo Alto, California

8/17/91, Shoreline Amphitheater, Mountain View, California

8/21/93, Frost Amphitheater, Palo Alto, California

12/18/93, Coliseum Arena, Oakland, California

7/2/94, Shoreline Amphitheater, Mountain View, California

3/18/95, The Spectrum, Philadelphia

▪ "Spanish Jam" (Weir)
Grateful Dead, *Dick's Picks Volume Six*/'83 (1996)

An appropriately titled, pensively mounting nine-chord instrumental jam which was an intermittent and always

Jerry Garcia, Bob Weir, and Bill Kreutzmann, Grand Prix Racecourse, Watkins Glen, New York, 7/28/73. *(Photo: Richard Berner)*

curious inclusion during the Dead's second set. From its first offerings in 1968, "Spanish Jam" never failed to surprise with its suspense power.

2/11/70, Fillmore East, New York

6/23/74, Jai-Alai Fronton, Miami

6/26/74, Providence Civic Center, Providence, Rhode Island

10/19/81, Sports Palace, Barcelona, Spain

■ The Spirit Cries—Musics from the Rainforests of South America and the Caribbean: The Library of Congress Endangered Music Project

Rykodisc RACS 0250, 1993. Produced by Mickey Hart and Alan Jabbour.

"Garfuna" (Belize, 1981), "Indians of the Choco" (Panama/Colombia, 1949), "Shipibo" (Peru, 1964), "Ashaninka" (Peru, 1964), "Aluku" (French Guiana), "Wayana" (Suriname, 1952), "Maroons" (Jamaica, 1978)

The Spirit Cries is part of a series of digitally remastered field recordings from the Library of Congress's vast Archive of Folk Culture. Many of the cultural traditions practiced by the people on these recordings are in danger of extinction. Others have vanished altogether, leaving only the songs behind. Compiled and edited by Mickey Hart, *The Spirit Cries* was recorded within the Rainforests of South America and the Caribbean over the course of a period of nearly forty years by Kenneth

The Library of Congress
Endangered Music Project
The Spirit Cries
*Music from the Rainforests
of South America & the Caribbean*

(Courtesy of Rykodisc)

Bilby, David Findlay, Per Host, Enrique Pinilla, and Carol and Travis Jenkins.

"Our archive as a people are locked up in a few places around the world," said Mickey in 1993. "One of them is the Library of Congress and now the bottle of champagne is opening. The cork is being pulled from the bottle. The Library of Congress has been gathering this for years, all these musics—it's the only place for it to settle."

Describing *The Spirit Cries* as "endangered music," Hart said the result was "a stunning representation of the musics of the rain forest. This is exciting because we are illuminating the plight of the people and their music. Their community is being ripped away and this is the last remnants we have of some of these disappearing cultures. Each one of them are masterpieces. They are fine arts—works of art being destroyed slowly just like the rain forest. The ecological disaster goes right along with the musical disaster. They're all endangered: the people are endangered, the culture is endangered, the music is endangered. So in this way we're trying to focus some light on this very, very important subject."

■ "Spoonful" (WILLIE DIXON)

Charley Patton, *Founder of the Delta Blues* (1969), *Roots of Rock* (1991), *The Music Never Stopped: Roots of the Grateful Dead* (1995)

ETTA JAMES, *Etta James* (1962)

Howlin' Wolf, *The Genuine Article: The Best of Howlin' Wolf* (1960), *The Howlin' Wolf Album* (1969), *The Chess Box* (1991)

Shadows of Knight, *Gloria* (1966), *Back Door Men* (1967)

Cream, *Fresh Cream* (1966), *Wheels of Fire* (1968), *Strange Brew: The Very Best of Cream* (1983)

John Hammond, *I Can Tell* (1967)

Ten Years After, *Ten Years After* (1967)

BO DIDDLEY/Muddy Waters/Howlin' Wolf, *The Super Super Blues Band* (1968)

Willie Dixon, *I Am the Blues* (1970), *Chess Box* (1991)

The Allman Joys, *Allman Joys*/'66 (1973)

The Blues Project, *Live at the Cafe Au Go-Go* (1966)

Paul Butterfield Blues Band, *Live* (1971), *Golden Butter* (1972)

The Index, *The Index* (1967)

Koko Taylor, *The Earthshaker* (1978)
Mountain, *Theme* (1988)
Jack Bruce, *Inazuma Super Session* (1988), *Cities of the Heart* (1994)
Alexis Korner, *The Collection* (1988)

Although Willie Dixon is rightly credited as the author of "Spoonful," the song has loose thematic precedents in ragtime and vaudeville. In whatever the oeuvre the song surfaces, it is always cryptic and mysteriously ambiguous, qualities which Dixon himself addressed in his 1989 autobiography, *I Am the Blues*. "The idea of 'Spoonful' was that it doesn't take a large quantity of anything to be good. If you have a little money when you need it, you're right there in the right spot, that'll buy you a whole lot. If a doctor give you less than a spoonful of some kind of medicine that can kill you, he can give you less than a spoonful of another one that will make you well.

"But after you write these songs, people who have bad minds, their minds will tell them what they want to believe. If it's blues and they've been trying to degrade the blues all the time, I don't care what title you come up with, they'll say it's a bad title. I remember a time years ago that if I said sex, my mama would beat the hell out of me. People who think 'Spoonful' was about heroin are mostly people with heroin ideas."

"Spoonful" would have been a natural for Pigpen, but it was Bob Weir who kept it in light rotation after introducing the song at Dead shows in 1981.

11/2/84, Berkeley Community Theater, Berkeley, California
9/22/91, Boston Garden, Boston

▪ "Stagger Lee" (Traditional/Garcia/Hunter)

Grateful Dead, single, *Shakedown Street* (1978)
Robert Hunter, *Jack O'Roses* (1980)
Singles: Ford and Ford (1924), Cliff Edwards (1924), Sol Hoopii's Novelty Trio (1926), Duke Ellington (1927), Papa Harvey Hull and Long "Cleve" Reed (1927), Ivory Joe Hunter (1933), Blind Pete and Partner (1934), Lucille Bogan (1934), John "Big Nig" Bray, (1934), Albert Jackson (1934), Lonnie Robertson (1936), Roscoe McLean (1936), Buena Flynn (1936), Vera Hall (1937), Tom Bell (1937), Blind Jesse Harris (1937), Johnny Dodds (1938), Lucious Curtis (1940), Willie Storks (1942), Pete Seeger (1958), Tommy Roe (1971), Dr. John (1972)

Ma Rainey, *Madame Gertrude "Ma" Rainey Master's Collection 1923–38* (1994)
Furry Lewis, *Furry Lewis 1927–1929* (1990)
Boyd Senter, *Solos and Senterpedes: 1927–1928* (1986)
Mississippi John Hurt, *1928 Sessions* (1990)
The Down Home Boys, *The Songster Tradition 1927–1935* (1991)
Cab Calloway, *Cab Calloway and his Orchestra 1931–1932* (1990)
Sidney Bechet, *The Best of Sidney Bechet/'30s* (1994)
Ray Noble, *Ray Noble and his American Dance Band/'30s* (1975)
Woody Guthrie, single (1944), *Hard Travelin'/'54* (1993), *Bound for Glory/'56* (1992)
JESSE FULLER, *Jazz, Folk Songs, Spirituals and Blues* (1958)
Lloyd Price, single (1959), *Greatest Hits* (1982, 1994)
Paul Clayton, *Bloody Ballads* (1960)
Dave Van Ronk, *Inside Dave Van Ronk* (1961)
Memphis Slim, *Broken Soul Blues* (1961)
Tex Johnson, *Gunfighter Ballads* (1961)
The New Lost City Ramblers, *New Lost City Ramblers* (1962)
The Isley Brothers, *The Famous Isley Brothers: Twisting and Shouting* (1964)
Alice Stuart, *All the Good Times* (1964)
Julius Lester, *Julius Lester* (1965)
Merle Travis, *Rough, Rowdy and Blue/'60s* (1986)
Tim Hardin, *This Is Tim Hardin/'62* (1966)
The McCoys, *(You Make Me Feel) So Good* (1966)
Wilson Pickett, single (1967), *I'm in Love* (1968)
JIM KWESKIN, *Jump for Joy* (1967)
James Brown, single, *Cold Sweat* (1967)
Taj Mahal, *Giant Step* (1969)
Roy Bookbinder, *Ragtime Millionaire* (1977)
Professor Longhair, *Live on the Queen Mary* (1975), *Big Chief* (1978)
Fats Domino, *Live at Montreux—Hello Josephine* (1974)
Neil Diamond, *September Morn* (1980)
Mary Wheeler, *Folk Songs of the River* (1982)
The Fabulous Thunderbirds, *Porky's Revenge* soundtrack (1985)
Doc Watson, *Ballads from Deep Gap* (1988)
Jerry Lee Lewis, *Killer: The Mercury Years Vol. 2* (1989)
Bob Brozeman, *A Truckload of Blues* (1992)
Willie and the Poor Boys, *Tear It Up—Live* (1992)
BOB DYLAN, *World Gone Wrong* (1993)

One of the most enduring songs and legends in the American folk lexicon, "Stagger Lee" is *the* Garcia/Hunter composition that masterfully nails their fascination with reinterpreting the classic chestnuts from earlier eras and traditions. The venerable "Stagger Lee" dates to the mid-nineteenth century when songs functioned not only as entertainment but as oral history and a brand of moral teaching.

There are so many different versions of "Stagger Lee" (or "Stacker Lee," "Stagolee," or other like variations) sung by so many different artists with almost as many different story lines that it could easily rank as *the* archetypal American folk song. Blacks and whites were singing it decades before recording equipment was even a gleam in anyone's eyes so, not surprisingly, its origins are murky. Stagger Lee's history is a window into a time when folk music was far more imbedded in the oral historical fabric of society and culture, when memory and creativity were relied upon to pass the song on.

Like many of the all-time great folk songs, the yarn seems to have a germ of historical truth. The Lee family of mid-nineteenth-century Memphis made its fortune as proprietors of a prosperous Southern steamboat line. Stacker Lee, one of the sons of the family patriarch, worked in the family business but evidently lacked his father's mettle, developing something of a reputation as a gambler who chased the skirts of white and black women. A son he sired by a black woman was also named Stacker Lee and it was he who became the archetypal antihero celebrated and damned in song. A one-eyed man of cruel disposition, he was remembered as "one of the niggers what fired up the engines on the Lee boats" by an acquaintance who was interviewed by folk-song historians John and Alan Lomax in the early 1930s.

Deprived of his birthright and trapped in a lowly station in life, Stacker Lee developed a white-hot temper that led first to incidents of violence and then several murderous rampages, including the event in Memphis around the turn of the century which left Billy Lyons shot to death after supposedly winning Stack's Stetson hat in a wager. Whether or not Billy Lyons was an actual person or a cipher from the folk mythos is a matter of debate, as are the reasons for how he came to be known in some renditions of the song as Billy de Lyon (or Lion), the most common theory being that "de" was a bastardization of "the" as the Lomaxes and other musicologists transcribed black speech.

One of the first serious attempts to ascertain the possible historical existence of Stacker Lee was made, in an article by Richard E. Buehler, "Stacker Lee: A Partial Investigation into the Historicity of a Negro Murder Ballad," published in the *Keystone Folklore Quarterly* in Fall 1967. Buehler identifies a Stacker Lee as a Confederate officer who became an upstanding member of the community, and who is unlikely to have been the model for the badman of legend. And while Buehler suggests several lines for further research, little if no pursuit seems to have been made in this area. Additionally, Buehler also suggests that the key to the history of the ballad may lie in the name "Billy Lyons," rather than in Stacker Lee.

The Lomaxes determined that the earliest known version of "Stagger Lee" dated back to the early twentieth century when it was "sung by Negroes on the Memphis levee while they were loading and unloading the river freighters, the words being composed by the singers," according to a letter they received from a Texas woman.

While the early versions of "Stagger Lee" find justice being duly meted, the tale was embellished over time to empower Stag with superhuman powers and/or portray him as the owner of a soul darker than even Beelzebub's. The Stetson hat (some versions imbue it with the most powerful mojo), the particular game being gambled (cards or craps) the number of children Billy's death left orphaned (two through five), and the police's willingness or unwillingness to pursue the accused are all variables in the song which transmogrify in the most outlandish ways. The only constant would seem to be the awe and dread with which Stagger Lee is held.

Gertrude "Ma" Rainey, Furry Lewis, and Mississippi John Hurt recorded very different but equally influential takes on the legend in the mid-1920s. Hurt's "Stagolee" had the biggest impact on the succeeding generation of Southern bluesmen and was a likely model for Robert Hunter, who adapted Hurt's original melody for the acoustic reading the songwriter released as "Billy de Lyons and Stagger Lee" on his *Jack O' Roses* album.

Hunter's "Stagger Lee" was written in the early to mid-1970s and is similar in spirit to his earlier

"Dupree's Diamond Blues," which is also drawn from early twentieth-century Negro story-songs. In both songs, Hunter invents his characters and employs vernacular dialogue to propel the story and protagonists to fitting, thoughtful finales.

Recalling the elements which informed his "Stagger Lee," Hunter told Blair Jackson in 1985, "I really didn't know very much more than what I'd heard on records and read in Lomax. Of course, I added the character of Delia [Billy's wife], who actually has some early songs about her, so I sort of interlaced myths. Basically, I just gave Billy de Lyon's wife a name and gave her some of the tough-mama characteristics of Delia."

Hunter's shaping of "Stagger Lee" is of particular note in that he literally and figuratively cuts the titled villain down to size in turning the tale into a dramatic revenge story that finds Billy de Lyon's widow settling the score by sidling up to Stag at the bar still wet with her dead husband's blood and shooting the savage tormentor in his most delicate gear.

Jackson's comments on "Stagger Lee" as printed in THE GOLDEN ROAD no. 8 (his excellent and sorely missed labor-of-love Grateful Dead fanzine) give further insight into Hunter's and the Dead's achievement. "What makes Hunter's 'Stagger Lee' a true masterpiece, and the reason it is in some ways a culmination of the entire tradition of the song, is the depth of the characters and its literate details. He has effectively taken it from the oral tradition and made it part of the *written* tradition, as befits a true poet influenced by the classics of literature. The slang he employs belies the cleverness of the song's construction. From the first lines he draws us into a story that is already moving at a furious pace, and then he builds his tale from there using almost cinematic images.

"But this discussion doesn't end with Hunter's lyrics, for in 1978, when the Dead were recording *Shakedown Street*, Garcia took Hunter's words, dispensed with the traditional blues melody, and placed the story in an utterly new setting. It still bears echoes of its blues heritage, yet the opening sounds like a combination of early American vaudeville music (the rolling piano lead-in) and a Storyville whorehouse romp. In fact, as the story takes place on Christmas Eve 1940 in Hunter's telling, it's easy to imagine the song being played by the Salvation Army–style band prominent in the song! Whatever Garcia's intention, 'Stagger Lee' stands as one of his best fusions of Americana and Grateful Dead rock & roll. It

all sounds familiar, but at the same time you know that something *very* strange is going on here. As usual."

The Christmas Eve setting has its precedent in some earlier versions of the song as well as in "Delia" and "Delia's Gone," two related compositions.

True to its title, in concert, "Stagger Lee" has a staggered history. Weir virtually learned how to play slide guitar on the tune when the Dead were first heavily airing it out it 1978 and 1979. As he told Jon Sievert of *Guitar Player* in 1981, his entree into that approach "came out of a desire to hear a sustain instrument in the band. When we were playing with Keith Godchaux, he played acoustic piano almost exclusively, and we didn't have a real sustain instrument except what Garcia was doing. I guess desperation is the mother of invention. I figured you could have quite a bit of sustain with a slide, especially if you throw in a little feedback and distortion. So I took up playing slide guitar pretty much for that reason, and I've had a lot of fun with it. It gives us a chance to get leads working with and against each other, sort of Dixieland style."

After a couple of feeble stabs in 1982, "Stagger Lee" returned to medium-light rotation in 1985 through 1995 as it developed into a surprisingly welcome standout with a great concluding jam.

> **11/24/78, Capitol Theater, Passaic, New Jersey**
> **5/7/79, Kirby Fieldhouse, Lafayette College, Easton, Pennsylvania**
> **3/27/88, Hampton Coliseum, Hampton, Virginia**
> **12/11/92, Oakland Coliseum Arena, Oakland, California**

■ "Standing on the Corner" (Frank Loesser)

> *The Most Happy Fella, Original Broadway Cast* (1956)
> Count Basie, *Kansas City Shout* (1980)
> The Four Lads, *The Most Requested Songs*/'56 (1991)
> Dean Martin, *Greatest Hits*/'56 (1992)

This piece of pop tripe was drawn from the Broadway musical *The Most Happy Fella* and was covered by Garcia during at least a couple of *very* early GD shows.

> **7/17/66, Fillmore Auditorium, San Francisco**

■ "Standing on the Moon" (Garcia/Hunter)

> Grateful Dead, *Built to Last* (1989), *The Arista Years* (1996)

Leave it to the Dead to write a political love song. Yet "Standing on the Moon" became one of the band's most compelling concert offerings since its debut in 1989. It is also one of the more overlooked gems from the latter phase of the Garcia/Hunter output. A lonely ballad, "Standing on the Moon" found its place as a late-show natural, a meditation similar in form and function to such songs as "Wharf Rat," "Black Peter," or "MORNING DEW."

The action begins on the Moon, with a sad narrator surveying the tragic and emotional landscape on Earth. As the song moves on, the action is slowly transported to a back porch in San Francisco with the narrator wishing he was with his love rather than on "this crescent in the sky," far from this confusing place humans call home.

8/21/93, Autzen Stadium, Eugene, Oregon

▪ "Stander on the Mountain" (BRUCE HORNSBY)
Bruce Hornsby and the Range, *A Night on the Town* (1990)

As a partial reward for helping them make the transition from the Brent Mydland era to the Vince Welnick reign, the Dead let the affable Bruce Hornsby perform a couple of songs in the fall 1990 tour. "Stander on the Mountain," a stark piece of visionary folk-rock, was one of these, sounding like it had been around forever. The Dead performed it just three times, placing it neatly at the end of the first set on all its outings. The band might have done well to keep this one around after Hornsby fulfilled his short tour of duty.

11/1/90, Wembley Arena, London

▪ "Stars and Stripes Forever" (John Philip Sousa)
John Philip Sousa, *Grand Sousa Marches* (1995)

The Dead would have made a great turn-of-the-century marching band so it is appropriate that they employed the most famous of Sousa's marches, and possibly of all American marches, as a rare tune-up exercise. Sousa's band had three successful recordings of the song with three different record companies in 1897, 1901, and 1917. Naturally, the song was featured in *Stars and Stripes Forever*, the 1952 Sousa biographical film with Clifton Webb portraying the noted bandleader/composer.

▪ "The Star-Spangled Banner" (Francis Scott Key)

The Dead performed America's national anthem as a warm-up time-killer now and then in the late 1960s and early 1970s. The song was originally published in the *Baltimore American* a week after the bombardment of Fort McHenry in 1814. The words were soon being sung to the tune of "The Anacreontic Song," by London composer John Stafford Smith.

▪ "Stealin' " (Traditional)
Grateful Dead, single (1966), *Historic Dead*/'66 (1970)
The Memphis Jug Band, *Double Album*/'28 (1990)
Jimmy Young, *Chicago Blues* (1965)
The Yardbirds, *Little Games* (1967)
Arlo Guthrie, *Running Down the Road* (1969), *Together in Concert (Live with Pete Seeger)* (1975)
Jeff Beck/Eric Clapton/Jimmy Page, *Guitar Boogie* (1971)
Taj Mahal, *Happy to Be Just Like I Am* (1971)
Uriah Heep, *Sweet Freedom* (1973), *Live at Shepperton '74* (1974)
Jerry Garcia/DAVID GRISMAN, *Shady Grove* (1996)

Another folk-blues relic of the nineteenth-century Southern tradition, "Stealin'" was first recorded by the Memphis Jug Band, one of the most popular and influential black jug bands spawned in the mid-South in the twenties.

"Stealin'" appeared on the Dead's first Scorpio Records single in 1965 and was a common choice for both the Warlocks and the early Grateful Dead. One of the song's lyrics "Put your arms around me like a circle 'round the sun" was rewritten by the band and nestled into one of their earliest compositions, "The Golden Road (to Unlimited Devotion)," as "Everybody's dancing in a ring around the sun . . ."

3/25/66, Trouper's Club, Los Angeles

▪ *Steal Your Face*
UA/Grateful Dead Records GD-LA629-J2 GD-104, 1976. Produced by Grateful Dead.
"THE PROMISED LAND," "Cold Rain and Snow," "AROUND AND AROUND," "Stella Blue," "Mississippi Half-Step Uptown Toodleoo," "Ship of Fools," "Beat It on Down the Line," "BIG RIVER," "Black-Throated Wind," "U.S. Blues," "EL PASO," "Sugaree," "It Must Have Been the Roses," "Casey Jones"

From the start, Deadheads disparagingly referred to this album as "Steal Your Money." Critics also joined the outcry, saying that the tepid live double-album drawn from the band's 1974 "Farewell" concerts at San Fran-

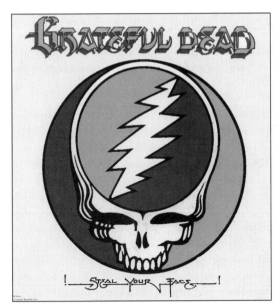

(© Grateful Dead Merchandising, Inc.)

cisco's long-gone Winterland deserved every bit of the flak it caught through the years. Though some of the album's negativity may be overrated (it comes off better on CD), a better representation of the band's music during this period can be gleaned from the excellent concert film, *THE GRATEFUL DEAD MOVIE* shot at these same shows. As Phil Lesh said, this was a "zits and all" affair.

■ "Stella Blue" (Garcia/Hunter)
Grateful Dead, *Wake of the Flood* (1973), *Steal Your Face* (1976), *Dick's Picks Volume One/'73* (1993), *Dick's Picks Volume Six/'83* (1996), *Dozin' at the Knick/'90* (1996)
Robert Hunter, *Box of Rain* (1991)

A somber, graceful ballad about time's passage and ravages, "Stella Blue" traditionally filled the role as a late show Garcia testimonial similar in function to "Wharf Rat" and "Black Peter." "Stella Blue" is an extremely enigmatic song which has been interpreted as everything from a meditation on lost love to an ode to a guitar. In regard to the latter, the Stella is a brand of guitar favored by many of the early country-blues greats and there are a couple of references to the instrument in the song: "A broken angel sings from a guitar" in the first verse, and in the break the singer beckons, "Dust off those rusty strings just one more time, gonna make 'em shine."

But even Garcia admitted to having trouble figuring out what the song was about during his 1988 interview with Blair Jackson. "I must've sung 'Stella Blue' for three or four years before I started to really come out of it," he said. "Because originally, I was taken with the construction of it, which is extremely clever, if I do say so myself. I was proud of it as a composer—'Hey, this is a slick song! This sucker has a very slippery harmonic thing that works nicely.' That's what I liked about it. It wasn't until later that I started to find other stuff in there. That's a good example of a song I sang before I understood it. I understood some of the sense of what the lyrics were about, but I didn't get into the pathos of it. It has a sort of brittle pathos in it that I didn't get until I'd been singing it for a while."

In 1988, Garcia told *Guitar Player* magazine, "'Stella Blue' is a mood piece. It's lovely, and it's unique—it's not like any other song. It doesn't owe anything to anything else. When Hunter gave me the lyrics, I sat on 'em and sat on 'em. Then when we were in Germany, I sat down with an acoustic early in the morning, and the song just fell together. It was so effortless writing it that I don't feel as though I wrote it. It's also one of those songs that I was born to sing. Every time I do it, I find something new in it, like a little thing in the phrasing or some little thing in the sense of it. And the way the Grateful Dead plays 'Stella Blue' is just gorgeous. Everybody plays so beautifully on it. At times it seems like a moment freezes on one of those chord changes, and I have to go a long way to find where I am and where the lyric is. Some moments are so beautiful. That song brings out a certain sensitivity and delicacy that only the Grateful Dead is capable of. Those guys will follow my lyric. If I change the tempo inside of a phrase, they'll be there. If I retard it slightly or pull it back, they'll be right there in the next bar. It's amazing. It's a special thing."

A final note on the song concerns the location of its lyrical composition. Like BOB DYLAN's "Sad-Eyed Lady of the Lowlands," "Stella Blue" was penned at the Chelsea Hotel in New York City.

6/18/74, Freedom Hall, Louisville, Kentucky
6/15/76, Beacon Theater, New York
3/18/88, Henry J. Kaiser Convention Center, Oakland, California
6/8/92, Coliseum, Richfield, Ohio

■ *Stephen Stills 2*/Stephen Stills
Atlantic SD 7206, 1971.

Though he is not credited on the album, Garcia is listed as the pedal-steel player on the song "Change Partners" when the song was rereleased on *Replay*, a Crosby, Stills and Nash compilation released in 1980.

■ "Stir It Up" (Bob Marley)
Bob Marley and the Wailers, *Catch a Fire* (1973), *Babylon by Bus* (1978), *Songs of Freedom* (1993)
Johnny Nash, *The Reggae Collection/'73* (1993)

Given a mutual love and support of ganja, it is no wonder that the Dead covered a Bob Marley song. It was only given, however, one rather ragged first-set outing in 1988 with Garcia handling the lead vocals. Three years later, the band was somewhat more successful in its incorporation of a "Stir It Up" instrumental jam as second-set segue fodder at a couple of shows.

Robert Nesta Marley was born February 6, 1945, in Nine Mile, St. Anns, Jamaica, and transcended the humility of his rural beginnings to become not merely a millionaire and the first pop star to emerge from the Third World, but also—more significantly—a spiritual figure whose pleas for brotherhood and justice achieved worldwide notice.

The son of an English army captain and a God-fearing Jamaican country girl, he was moved to Trenchtown, a poor area of Kingston, the country's capital, by his mother while still a young child. In the early 1960s, the young Marley was, like every other ghetto kid, excited by the nascent Jamaican music industry. "Judge Not," his first record made for producer Leslie Kong's Beverly label, was not a hit and neither were two follow ups: "One Cup of Coffee" and "Terror."

It was when he formed the Wailers, a vocal group under the tutelage of Trenchtown recording artist Joe Higgs, with his friend Neville O'Reilly (better known as Bunny Wailer), Junior Braithwaite (a younger singer with a voice like an unschooled Motown-era Michael Jackson), and Peter Tosh (another feisty youth), that Marley began finding local acclaim. Fashioning themselves after American vocal groups such as the Impressions and the Drifters, the Wailers recorded a series of records that were pure Jamaican. "Simmer Down" was their first hit in 1964 and was followed by "I Am Going Home," "Mr. Talkative," and many more regional successes.

After Braithwaite left the band in order to pursue a new life in the United States, the Wailers continued to

score with harmonies tight enough to compare with any of their Jamaican contemporaries, even if it didn't get them the studio time that their American peers were granted. Marley, Tosh, and Livingston swapped lead chores and all had plenty to offer, with Marley sounding like a sock-it-to-'em soulman, Tosh providing a raw, disdainful bark, and Bunny offering a tender, mellow tone guaranteed to melt the heart of their ever-growing female following. Hits like "Rude Boy" reinforced their grip on Jamaican youth, although, in reality, they were just one of many popular ska acts.

They formed their own label, Wail 'n Soul 'm, in 1966, and continued to impact the local charts with very little financial reward until they hooked up with the seminal oddball producer Lee Perry, who oversaw the release of an amazing series of singles that remain one of the group's finest hours. Using his studio band, the Upsetters, Perry gave the Wailers a new, tougher sound that suited the militancy of songs like "Duppy Conqueror," "Small Axe," and "400 Years." Perry brought out the best in the group, offering a sparing, funky backdrop for the Wailers' outlaw lyrics and searing harmonies.

Island Records president Chris Blackwell signed the Wailers in 1972, recorded the band, tinkered with the mix, and pulled *Catch a Fire* out of the can in 1973, the first reggae record conceived as an album and the premier Anglo-Jamaican record. With its democratic blend of rock, soul, blues, and funk with reggae, *Catch a Fire* was a critical smash and landed the Wailers on a major tour of Britain and the United States, which also proved to be their last. Bunny disliked life on the road and quit, as did a dissatisfied Peter Tosh, leaving Marley as the band's de facto leader. Adding the I-Threes, a supporting female vocal trio that included his wife Rita, Marley attained his first taste of international acclaim when Eric Clapton had a No. 1 hit with a world-weary cover of "I Shot the Sheriff," a take-no-shit Marley original.

By this point, Bob Marley had become a revolutionary standard-bearer and inheritor of the activist energy and hippie ganja enlightenment of the 1960s. A devout Rastafarian (a millenarian religion espousing Afrocentricism, marijuana consumption, and the growing of dreadlocks), Marley held strong to his Jamaican roots and retained the Caribbean island as a base of operations.

At once politically provocative and neutral, Marley was almost assassinated at his home by unknown raiders only weeks before the "Smile Jamaica" concert he had organized to reconcile the country's opposing political leaders in the tense year of 1976. He recovered sufficiently not only to appear but join the hands of Michael Manley and Edward Seaga onstage during the peak of his performance, and Marley's actions helped garner him the United Nations Peace Medal on behalf of 500 million Africans in 1978 for his humanitarian achievements. But, by his own account, Bob Marley's greatest honor came when he was invited to headline the Zimbabwe Independence Celebrations in 1980.

Though he outdrew the Pope in Milan, fathered eleven children by seven women, and sold tens of millions of records worldwide, Bob Marley could not beat the cancer that felled him on May 11, 1981.

Johnny Nash already had a Top 20 pop hit in 1973 with "Stir It Up," a soft, sexual appeal from Marley's rocksteady period, when the Wailers first released it on *Catch a Fire*, their 1973 breakthrough disc. This precise, neat version has an ease that Nash didn't come close to achieving. Considering its commercial potential, "Stir It Up" was not released as a single until 1976 and even then, not as an A side.

3/21/91, Capital Centre, Landover, Maryland

▪ "Stronger Than Dirt (Or Milkin' the Turkey)" (Lesh)
Grateful Dead, *Blues for Allah* (1975), *One from the Vault* /'75 (1991)

Grateful Dead jazz fusion at a pinnacle, the band's half-dozen dizzying jams in 1975 and 1976 on this dynamic and funky theme are the stuff of legend and cassette filler.

3/23/75, Kezar Stadium, San Francisco (with MERL SAUNDERS and Ned Lagin)

▪ "St. Stephen" (Hunter/Garcia/Lesh)
Grateful Dead, *Aoxomoxoa* (1969), *Live Dead* (1969), *What a Long Strange Trip It's Been* (1977), *Two from the Vault*/'68 (1992), *Dick's Picks Volume Two*/'71 (1995)
Solar Circus, *Juggling Suns* (1989)

Among the Dead's most talismanic songs, "St. Stephen" was temporarily dropped from the group's performances in 1971. The band resuscitated "St. Stephen" after that but with mixed results. The earliest versions in the late 1960s are regarded as the best. Refreshingly off-balance, "St. Stephen" served as the cornerstone of the Dead's most cosmic psychedelic jams during that period, often nestled between "Dark Star" and "The Eleven," a medley that was documented (but rarely equaled) on *Live Dead*. Many of these renditions included an untitled coda reminiscent of traditional folk bagpipe musics of the British isles. In fact, a Robert Hunter–performed bagpipe track can be found on the *Aoxomoxoa* outtakes.

But "St. Stephen" proved cumbersome to perform. As Garcia noted to Blair Jackson in 1988, "'St. Stephen' has some real goofy shit in it. . . . It's a piece of material that is unnecessarily difficult. It's been made tricky. It's got a bridge in the middle that doesn't really fit in. It's interesting and remains interesting historically because it has a couple of things that work *real* good. But finally, the stuff that doesn't work overpowers the stuff that does work, and the reason it does is just that thing of memory: 'Let's see, what verse is this?' They're not interchangeable; you have to do them in order. So in that sense, a song like St. Stephen is a cop. It's our musical policeman: If we don't do it the way it wants to go it doesn't work at all. That mean's it's inflexible. When you get good enough at these kind of pieces, people think, 'Wow, that's really far out and open.' But that's an illusion. It's just written complicated, which is something you can always do."

This didn't prevent the Dead from reviving "St. Stephen." The first and most successful of these rebirths was between 1976 and 1978 when the band eased the song's tempo and created a jazzy exploration which crackled with the old energy. The song was buried again for a period only to be briefly dusted off for a few shows in the fall of 1983. While still well-performed and nostalgically surprising, these last renditions paled by comparison to the early glory of "St. Stephen." Finally, the song was soundchecked in December 1994 but failed to make a concert reappearance.

An indication of the band's ambivalent attitude regarding the song was in evidence as early as 1973. At a 1973 Utica, New York, show, Weir explained to the crowd calling for "St. Stephen" that the band didn't play the song anymore because "You liked it too much." To this, one audience member responds by shouting back, "We'll *hate* it this time . . . we'll *despise* it this time, Bobby!"

Recalling the song's poetic genesis, Hunter told Jeff Tamarkin of *Relix* in 1986, "I had been working on this a long time before I gave it to the Grateful Dead, before

I took off to New Mexico, which is where I originally sent them the lyrics from. I don't know what to say about this song except that it was very important to me. It seemed to be saying oodles. It's still one of my favorites. I didn't know who the real St. Stephen was until I wrote it. He turned out to be the first Christian monk or something."

Sometimes thought to reference Stephen Gaskin, a leading hippie figure in the Haight during the late 1960s who founded an admired commune in Tennessee known as the Farm, Hunter's lyrics do, coincidentally, resonate with the St. Stephen of Christianity. For the historically minded, Stephen, a Christian martyr, was a Greek-speaking Jew chosen by the apostles to be one of seven men who would look after the needs of widows who tended to be neglected in the daily distribution of charity.

Stephen, "full of grace and power" as the Acts of the Apostles describes him, did many great wonders, so that his enemies amongst his former associates plotted to bring about his death. They accused him of planning to destroy the Jewish Temple.

When Stephen was called before the Jewish Council to defend himself, his speech was one of great provocation. He tried to show how always in the past the people had turned against those sent by God, just as finally they killed Jesus. "Which of the prophets did your fathers not prosecute?" asked Stephen. "They killed those who announced the coming of the Righteous One. Now you have betrayed and murdered him."

He accused his hearers of always resisting the Holy Spirit. They grew so angry with him that they threw him out of the city, especially when they heard him cry that he saw the heavens opened "and the Son of Man standing at the right hand of God."

Then they stoned Stephen to death. Holding the coats of those who threw stones was a man from Tarsus named Saul. This was the future St. Paul, still at this time one of the most dangerous enemies of the Christians.

As they were stoning Stephen he prayed, "Lord Jesus, receive my spirit." He knelt down and said, just as he died, "Lord, do not hold this sin against them."

Devout men buried Stephen and wept over him. Nearly four centuries later, in the year 415, his relics are said to have been found again at Paphargamala.

9/2/68, Betty Nelson's Organic Raspberry Farm, Sultan, Washington

3/1/69, Fillmore West, San Francisco

6/13/69, Convention Center, Fresno, California

5/6/70, Kresge Plaza, M.I.T., Cambridge, Massachusetts

9/19/70, Fillmore East, New York

8/26/71, Gaelic Park, Bronx, New York

6/9/76, Boston Music Hall, Boston

5/8/77, Barton Hall, Ithaca, New York

1/22/78, McArthur Court, Eugene, Oregon

10/15/83, Hartford Civic Center, Hartford

■ "(Stuck Inside of Mobile with the) Memphis Blues Again" (BOB DYLAN)

Bob Dylan, *Blonde on Blonde* (1966), *Hard Rain* (1976)

Moon Martin, *Lunar Samples* (1995)

One of Dylan's most perfectly realized songs was effectively covered by Bob Weir beginning almost immediately before the Dead's support for the composer during their 1987 concerts. This brilliantly funny portrait in black velvet of a world gone mad is delightfully upbeat, the perfect counterpoint to the chaos of the lyrics.

In his 1986 biography, *No Direction Home: The Life and Music of Bob Dylan*, the late Robert Shelton made these points about this unnerving composition: "In blues and country songs, there is recurring lamentation about places left behind. Whatever flights of imagery the song takes, the full title, and its mordant message of disruption, makes a jackhammer finish to each of the nine verses. The singing is blues shouting, moaning, drawling. Band support enhances the drive that makes a giant lyric speed. What a cast: the ragman, Shakespeare as a dandy, and a bunch of 'neon madmen.' If 'Desolation Row' has become Main Street, then 'Memphis Blues' has become the national condition of a mobile, lonely and lost society."

Dylan has never stopped returning to "Memphis Blues" for renewed and vigorous interpretation. But Weir's handling of the song was unique as well, perhaps the most interesting Dead cover of a Dylan song if only for Weir's hysterically histrionic approach, which captured the mounting insanity of the singer and the mad, mad, mad, mad world he is describing.

7/16/88, Greek Theatre, Berkeley, California

■ "Sugaree" (Garcia/Hunter)

Jerry Garcia, *Garcia* (1972)

Grateful Dead, *Steal Your Face* (1976), *One from the*

Vault /'75 (1991), *Dick's Picks Volume Three/'77*
(1995)
MERL SAUNDERS and the Rainforest Band, *Merl Saunders
Live: Still Having Fun* (1996)

With a nod to Elizabeth Cotten's "Shake Sugaree" and
the lullaby "Hush, Little Baby, Don't You Cry," "Sugaree" is a splendid ballad wistfully meditating on the
memory of a painful romance. Thought to loosely
reference Garcia's marriage to his first wife, Sarah, "Sugaree" was a potent ode with a musical openness that allowed the lead guitarist to explore solos that recalled the
stylings of gypsy jazz-guitar legend, Django Reinhardt.

It's been a first-set reliable since its 1971 debut (and
a mid-1970s and early '80s Garcia Band morsel), and
the Dead pulled some startlingly long versions of "Sugaree" out of the musical fargoneisphere, with several
clocking in at sixteen-plus minutes. While some of those
renditions may legitimately be accused of noodling, at
its best "Sugaree" was a soaring and passionate acceptance of lost love.

5/26/73, Kezar Stadium, San Francisco
3/18/77, Winterland Arena, San Francisco
5/19/77, Fox Theater, Atlanta
6/21/80, West High Auditorium, Anchorage, Alaska
**5/14/82, Keystone, Palo Alto, California (Jerry Garcia
Band)**
10/17/83, Olympic Center, Lake Placid, New York
**3/25/85, Springfield Civic Center, Springfield,
Massachusetts**
9/14/90, Madison Square Garden, New York

▪ "Sugar Magnolia" (Weir/Hunter)

Grateful Dead, *American Beauty* (1970), *Europe '72*
(1972), single (1973), *Dick's Picks Volume Two /'71*
(1995), *Hundred Year Hall/'72* (1995), *Dick's Picks
Volume Six/'83* (1996)
Pop-O-Pies, *Joe's Third Album* (1988)

An infectious skip, "Sugar Magnolia" is one of the
Dead's most recognizable songs and a long-serving Bob
Weir favorite show-ending stand-by favorite. Likening
the flower to a fiery but loyal female, the song is a jumpy
litany of balancing a relationship with life in a rock
band.

Remembering his initial dissatisfaction with the studio results, Weir told David Gans in 1977 that "I wasn't
altogether pleased with what it came out like. It wasn't
everything it should be. I didn't know how to tell anybody that, but as soon as we took it out on the road, it immediately evolved into a whole lot more than what we'd
just put down on vinyl, and became at that point exactly
what I had envisioned it as being."

"Sugar Magnolia" is one of a small handful of Grateful Dead compositions to include a coda usually performed with it. Entitled "Sunshine Daydream," this
sister composition is where the band pulled out all the
stops, opened up for some of their most dynamic playing,
and took their audiences into moments that rival the ecstasies usually associated with a Baptist revival meeting
or the mysteries of ancient Greek religion.

The Dead performed "Sugar Magnolia" close to six
hundred times beginning in 1970 but it took a few years
for the song to really stand up and grow some hair. The
versions with Donna Godchaux in the late 1970s are
particularly hot while the 1980s saw the tune formalize
into a complete Grateful Dead showcase.

"Sugar Magnolia" was concert promoter Bill Graham's favorite Dead tune and they commonly opened
their New Year's Eve concerts with the song on his behalf. They also opened their October 27, 1991, concert
with "Sugar Mag" in honor of Graham, who had died two
days before.

12/31/72, Winterland Arena, San Francisco
12/2/73, Boston Music Hall, Boston
6/28/74, Boston Garden, Boston
8/4/76, Roosevelt Stadium, Jersey City, New Jersey
4/11/78, Fox Theater, Atlanta
12/31/78, Winterland Arena, San Francisco
3/10/81, Madison Square Garden, New York
**6/24/84, Saratoga Performing Arts Center, Saratoga,
New York**
**6/30/85, Merriweather Post Pavilion, Columbia,
Maryland**
**8/11/87, Red Rocks Amphitheater, Morrison,
Colorado**
10/27/91, Coliseum Arena, Oakland, California
3/27/95, The Omni, Atlanta

▪ *Sunfighter*/Paul Kantner and Grace Slick

Grunt/RCA FTR 1002, 1971.

Decent, dated, and jumbled, Garcia's studio performances on *Sunfighter* are among his best ever, playing a
round, wiry lead-guitar style he never really used with
the Dead on "Million," "Holding Together," and "When
I Was a Boy I Watched the Wolves."

- ## "Sunrise" (Donna Godchaux)
  ### Grateful Dead, *Terrapin Station* (1977), *Dick's Picks Volume Three*/'77 (1995)

Donna Godchaux, despite her detractors, was a passionate singer and sensitive songwriter as this meditative introspection reveals. Godchaux sang "Sunrise," a song reportedly inspired by a Native American ceremony she attended, at about thirty Dead shows in 1977 and 1978.

  11/6/77, Broome County Coliseum, Binghamton, New York

- ## "Sunshine Daydream" (Weir/Hunter)

The instrumental and vocal coda to "Sugar Magnolia" was performed as a stand-alone about thirty times since 1974. On special occasions like New Year's Eve, it was not uncommon for the Dead to commence the second set with "Sugar Magnolia" and end it with "Sunshine Daydream."

  See also **"Sugar Magnolia"**

- ## *Sunshine Daydream* (film)
  ### Directed and produced by Phil De Guere, John Norris, Sam Field, and Far West Action Picture Service, 1973.

Easily the best moving-image document of the Grateful Dead at an early peak is *Sunshine Daydream*, a ninety-minute film of the Dead's fantastic August 27, 1972 concert staged by Ken Kesey and the Merry Pranksters as a benefit for Chuck Kesey's Springfield Creamery. The audio tape of this show is one of the Dead's best ever and it is a treat to see some of the actual doings from that glorious day during which the mercury rose to 103°. The music was even hotter and *Sunshine Daydream* is an onstage and behind-the-scenes glimpse of the show rendered in a style that owes much to the film *Woodstock*, with the band roaring through blazing renditions of "Playing in the Band," "Jack Straw," "Promised Land," "China Cat Sunflower">"I Know You Rider," and "Dark Star">"El Paso."

The project started out as the brainchild of two young Palo Alto filmmakers, Phil De Guere and John Norris, who were working, ironically enough, on a couple of Stanford University–backed drug education films. The two were Dead fans and, with Sam Field, a third film-minded (and well-heeled) friend, they decided to make a Grateful Dead movie. Though the Dead were much more accessible individually and as an organization back in those days, the trio had some difficulty in pinning anyone down for a straight answer. De Guere finally collared Garcia outside a club where the guitarist was set to play a gig with Merl Saunders. Though Garcia was bemused by the idea of anyone making a film about a group who just stood onstage and gazed into their guitars, he did give tacit approval to the filmmakers to pursue the project.

After accompanying the Dead on their Europe '72 tour, the filmmakers decided on the Creamery Benefit after De Guere met the Pranksters during an Oregon sojourn during the summer. They were impressed by the Pranksters' equipment and tech support, as well as what promised to be a happening for the ages, and the Kesey affair seemed to present itself as the optimum opportunity for capturing the tribal stomp.

With seven cameras rolling, the shoot was a breeze despite the stultifying weather. The only unexpected development was the acid which, as De Guere explained to Blair Jackson in 1986, "seemed to get into almost every drop of liquid, cool or warm, anywhere in the place. That accounts for some of the strangely unsteady camera work."

After they sank $15,000 into the project, a very rough cut of the work-in-progress was shown to the Dead and their large extended family and was met with an extremely negative response. De Guere and company persevered, returning to Oregon where they and the Pranksters attempted to shape the celluloid into something resembling a real film. The Pranksters gave de Guere access to thousands of hours of unedited footage from their mid-1960s heyday. Finding some choice footage of Neal Cassady driving Furthur and a Palo Alto Acid Test, De Guere inserted these into the final cut to evoke the historical/cultural continuum of the Creamery show.

But the damage had already been done with the Dead, who finally put the kibosh on *Sunshine Daydream* after only three Bay Area screenings. Though the filmmakers quietly folded their tents and went away with their tails between their legs, pirate copies of *Sunshine Daydream* have been circulating since the mid-1980s.

Adding further irony to the saga was that De Guere reunited with the Dead more than a decade later when, as producer of television's later incarnation of *The Twilight Zone*, he engaged the members of the band in contributing the theme and incidental music to the intelligent revival of the Rod Serling standard-setter.

Yes, the guitars are out of tune, everybody looks pretty stoned, and the final cut does have an amateurish homemade quality but, as a remembrance of hippies past, this is one for the time capsule.

■ *Superstitious Blues*/Country Joe McDonald
Ragbaby/Rykodisc RCD 10201, 1991.

Never forgetting his oldest musical friends, Garcia lent support on four songs to this Country Joe acoustic effort.

■ **"Supplication"** (Weir/Barlow)
KINGFISH, *KINGFISH* (1976), *KINGFISH IN CONCERT*/'76 (1995)
Grateful Dead, *Dick's Picks Volume Three*/'77 (1995)

The funky coda to "Lazy Lightnin'," the early Weir/Barlow paean to "misfit power," "Supplication" was sometimes employed as an instrumental segue from 1980 through 1991.

6/9/76, Boston Music Hall, Boston
5/8/77, Barton Hall, Ithaca, New York
12/28/82, Oakland Auditorium Arena, Oakland, California
5/22/93, Shoreline Amphitheater, Mountain View, California
See also: **"Lazy Lightning"**

■ *Surrealistic Pillow*/Jefferson Airplane
RCA LPM/LSP-3766. Produced by Rick Jarrard, 1967.

Garcia is listed as "Musical and Spiritual Adviser" on the back cover of this door-opening disc but that hardly begins to tell the story of his powerful influence on the Airplane's debut release. Not only does Garcia play high electric lead on "Today" and acoustic rhythm on "Plastic Fantastic Lover," "My Best Friend," and "Coming Back to Me," he rearranged "Somebody to Love" into hit material.

According to Jorma Kaukonen, the Airplane's lead guitarist, Garcia actually ran the recording session in place of the official producer, Rick Jarrard. "Jerry could be credited with really being the producer in the real sense of the word in that he was one of us and he knew what to do with the band. . . . He really was the producer who arranged those songs."

Additionally, Garcia gave the album its title describing it "as surrealistic as a pillow."

■ *Sweet Surprise*/Eric Andersen
Arista 4075, 1976. Produced by Eric Andersen.

Andersen cowrote "Weather Report Part I" with Bob Weir and made some interesting albums in his own right. Though *Sweet Surprise* doesn't rank as one of Andersen's most memorable, it is notable for the backing vocals on one song contributed by future Dead keyboardist Brent Mydland.

■ **"Swing Low Sweet Chariot"** (Traditional)
Jerry Garcia Acoustic Band, *Almost Acoustic* (1989)
Johnny Cash, *Hymns by Johnny Cash* (1960)
Elvis Presley, *His Hand in Mine* (1961)
Ruth Brown, *Gospel Time* (1963)
Duane Eddy, *Duane Eddy Does Bob Dylan* (1966)
Dizzy Gillespie, *Swing Low, Sweet Chariot* (1967)
Bill Monroe, *Bean Blossom* (1973)
Sonny Rollins, *The Cutting Edge* (1974)
Eric Clapton, *There's One in Every Crowd* (1975)
JOAN BAEZ, *From Every Stage* (1976), *Rare, Live and Classic* (1993)
Paul Robeson, *The Power and The Glory* (1991)
Gospel Hummingbirds, *Steppin' Out* (1991)
Harlem Spiritual Ensemble, *In Concert* (1991)
Solar Circus, *Twilight Dance* (1992)
Astro Zombies, *Viva La Vulva* (1993)
Albert Ayler, *Goin' Home* (1995)

A piece of gospel music turned campfire folk song, "Swing Low Sweet Chariot" received an acoustic bluegrass treatment complete with a banjo-pickin' Garcia at about ten shows in 1970. Jerry returned to the song almost two decades later with a similar high lonesome interpretation with his acoustic band.

"Swing Low Sweet Chariot" was arranged in 1917 by Henry Thacker Burleigh. Burleigh, in turn, based his arrangement on an old black spiritual that dates back to at least 1872.

7/11/70, Fillmore East, New York

T

▪ "Take a Step Back" (Traditional)

Just about every popular musical act has had to, at one time or another, plead with their overzealous constituency to refrain from crushing the human life forms standing between them and the stage but only the Grateful Dead could turn this exercise in safety to such lofty Pirandellian extremes.

▪ "Take It Off" (BO DIDDLEY)

This piece of classic raunch, reportedly from the pen and fuzz-toned strings of Bo Diddley, was only tackled by the Dead at one concert, their famous 1972 jam with Diddley himself.

> 3/25/72, Academy of Music, New York (with Bo Diddley)

▪ "Take Me Out to the Ballgame" (Jack Norworth/Albert Von Tilzer)
> Raffi, *One Light, One Sun* (1985)
> Doc and Merle Watson, *Baseball's Greatest Hits* (1989)
> Bruce Springstone, *Baseball's Greatest Hits* (1989)
> Ray Brown Trio, *Three Dimensional* (1992)
> *Baseball: A Film by Ken Burns, Original Soundtrack* (1994)

An occasional Grateful Dead tune-up goof, "Take Me Out to the Ballgame" was written in 1908 by Jack Norworth, who had never seen a major-league baseball game and wouldn't see one until thirty-three years later. He wrote the song in fifteen minutes after seeing a poster on a New York City subway which beckoned one and all to see a ballgame at the Polo Grounds. Norworth's friend, Al Von Tizler (né Albert Gumm), set the words to music, and thus an American classic was born.

There have been many versions of "Take Me Out to the Ballgame," and in 1949, MGM released a movie with the same name, starring Frank Sinatra and Gene Kelly. Now appearing at a seventh-inning stretch near you.

▪ "Take Me to the River" (Al Green/Mabon Hodges)
> Syl Johnson, single
> Al Green, *Al Green Explores Your Mind* (1974), *Greatest Hits, Volume Two* (1977)
> Foghat, *Night Shift* (1976)
> Talking Heads, *More Songs About Buildings and Food* (1978), *The Name of This Band Is Talking Heads* (1992)
> Bryan Ferry, *The Bride Stripped Bare* (1978)
> Levon Helm, *Levon Helm* (1978)
> Mitch Ryder, *Like Talkies* (1982)
> Exile, *Exile* (1983)

One of the crazier covers sported by the Dead in their last year of touring, Al Green's "Take Me to the River" was handled in true stump preacher mode by Weir in his early first-set blues slot at a few shows in the spring and summer of 1995. Walking that fine line between the sacred and the profane, "Take Me to the River" has the toughness of the inner city's back streets and the travails of modern romance with a twist of Baptist Revivalism.

Fittingly, Green's career has straddled the sacred and profane as both the supreme soul singer of the 1970s and a born again, gospel-singing preacher finding international success with a sound described by one critic as "the living embodiment of a dying tradition, a unique distillation of cold fire, raw emotion and technical refinement."

Green was born April 13, 1946, in Forest City, Arkansas, but grew up in Grand Rapids, Michigan. By age thirteen, he had started singing with a family gospel group, the Greene Brothers, but over the next seven years expanded his horizons, singing secular and solo while scoring a dual R&B and pop chart *marker* with "Back Up Train" as the leader of the Soul Mates. Green toured the chitlin circuit on the strength of the record, finding himself on the same Midland, Texas bill one night as Memphis trumpeter and producer Willie Mitchell, who signed Al to Hi Records.

Not only was the rest history, it made it. Green placed twenty-three records on the R&B and eighteen on the pop charts, including seven Top 10 hits. With a sound that was ultra-cool, if a little homogenous, the Green-Mitchell Hi rhythm section sound broke very little overt sweat, with Green's disjointed, slightly off-the-beat phrases as surprising as his falsetto was unearthly. Combine all this with some soft female back-up singing and a tom-tom-laden drum track and you have the stuff of legend and double platinum sales.

But from 1974 onward, with his personal life spinning out of control, Green's songs increasingly had a gospel edge, as in "Take Me to the River" in 1974. In 1976 he was ordained as a preacher and split with Mitchell a year later, refusing to record anything but gospel music (and good, best-selling gospel music at that) for most of the next fifteen years. His 1981 gospel album *Higher Plane*, for example, included a stellar version of the Impressions' "People Get Ready." In 1985 he reunited with Mitchell, the Hi rhythm section and the Memphis horns to deliver the goods once again on his last truly great recording, *He Is the Light*.

Talking Heads picked up on and covered "Take Me to the River" in 1978 and turned it into kind of a downtown, New Wave anthem with a slick, jittery rendition that gave the song renewed national play.

The connections between the popular Talking Heads and the Dead are not as far-flung as one might imagine.

David Byrne, the head Head, caught the Dead's June 22, 1986, Greek Theatre show, later reporting "Stella Blue" to be his personal favorite from the afternoon. Later, when engaged in a post-concert KPFA radio interview with Bob Weir, David Gans asked the two what they thought about the oft-spoken notion that the T-Heads were the GD of the 1980s. Weir quipped, "God help them!"

4/1/95, The Pyramid, Memphis, Tennessee

■ *Tales of the Great Rum Runners*/Robert Hunter

Round RX 101, 1974. Directed by Robert Hunter. Rykodisc RCD 10158, 1990.

"Lady Simplicity," "That Train," "Dry Dusty Road," "I Heard You Singing," "Rum Runners," "Children's Lament," "Maybe She's a Bluebird," "Boys in the Barroom," "It Must Have Been the Roses," "Arizona Lightning," "Standing at Your Door," "Mad," "Keys to the Rain"

Robert Hunter–vocals, guitar, pipes, songs. Mickey Hart–drums. Barry Melton–guitar. Jerry Garcia–guitar. David Freiberg–bass. Peter Albin–bass. Keith Godchaux–keyboard. Donna Godchaux–vocals. Steven Shuster–saxophone. Snooky Flowers–saxophone. Hadi El Sadoon–trumpet. Buddy Cage–pedal steel guitar. Rick and Markee Shubb–banjo and mandolin. Robbie Stokes–guitar. James Paris–harp.

(Courtesy of Rykodisc)

When Robert Hunter went into the studio to record his debut solo album, he had plenty of support from his best friends. Naturally, Garcia was involved, playing on "Standing at Your Door," the first version of "It Must Have Been the Roses" and the Dylanesque "Keys to the Rain," while also mixing the album.

Hunter is an acquired taste, and his earliest solo record is filled with songs that lean heavily on English ballads, sea chanteys, and Dylan, folkie vocals and rough melodies that can scare away the intrepid rock 'n' roller.

For "Lady Simplicity," according to Hunter's notes in *A Box of Rain*, "I laid down sixteen tracks of stacked vocals on the recording of this nursery rhyme, which opens my first solo album."

■ "Tangled Up in Blue" (BOB DYLAN)

Bob Dylan, *Blood on the Tracks* (1975), *Real Live* (1984), *Biograph* (1985), *The Bootleg Series: Volumes 1–3/1961–91* (1991), *Bob Dylan's Greatest Hits Volume 3* (1994)
Jerry Garcia Band, *Jerry Garcia Band* (1991)
Half Japanese, *1/2 Gentlemen Not Beasts* (1979)
The Phantoms, *The Phantoms* (1992)
Indigo Girls, *1200 Curfews* (1995)

An undisputed Bob Dylan masterpiece, "Tangled Up in Blue" exquisitely captured the sense of personal and political loss as the spirit of the 1960s ebbed into the void of America in the 1970s. Forlorn yet forward looking, "Tangled Up in Blue" is one of Dylan's most recognizable and best-loved songs. But nothing is sacred in the Dylan catalogue and "Tangled Up in Blue" has been open to continual reinterpretation and even rewriting. In fact, the *Blood on the Tracks* version, with which even the most casual Dylan-watcher is familiar, was reworked from an earlier draft.

Dylan recorded the songs for *Blood on the Tracks* in 1974 while living in New York City. Employing spare instrumentation, the result was ten songs pressed on a promo disc which was distributed in very limited quantities to select radio stations later that autumn. But, after reviewing the album over the Christmas holidays in Minnesota, he quickly grew dissatisfied with the results and rerecorded several of the tracks. "Tangled Up in Blue" was one of these.

On all three of his officially released versions of the song, as well as through two decades of performance display, Dylan has experimented with changing the pronouns in "Tangled Up," giving ever-shifting perspectives on the song's narrative. This unorthodox approach to both the song and the album as a whole, was reportedly inspired by Norman Raeben, a painting-cum-philosophy teacher with whom Dylan studied for a period in 1974.

Supporting this hypothesis while discussing the song's genesis, Dylan once said, "I guess I was just trying to make it like a painting where you can see the different parts, but then you also see the whole of it. With that particular song, that's what I was trying to do . . . with the concept of time, and the way the characters change from the first person to the third person, and you're never quite sure if the third person is talking or the first person is talking. But as you look at the whole thing, it really doesn't matter."

Though the Dead only performed "Tangled Up in Blue" a couple of times with Dylan during their 1987 tour, the Garcia Band played it (à la *Blood on the Tracks*) for years with a concluding jam that rivaled "Deal" for pure firepower.

5/87, Club Front, San Rafael, California (Dylan/Dead rehearsals)
7/19/87, Autzen Stadium, Eugene, Oregon (with Dylan)
10/23/87, Lunt-Fontanne Theater, New York (Jerry Garcia Band with Bob Weir)

■ *Tarkio*/Brewer and Shipley
Kama Sutra KSBS 2024. Produced by Nick Gravenites, 1971.

Regarded as a second-rate midwestern Simon and Garfunkel, (Mike) Brewer and (Tom) Shipley are still way more tolerable than Seals and Crofts. Garcia contributed the pedal steel licks to two tunes on this album, "Oh, Mommy" and "One Toke Over the Line."

■ *Tarot*
United Artists UA 5563, 1972.
"The Turtle," "The Old Fool's Reel," "Greed," "Harlequin (The Fool's Theme)," "The Philosopher and the Tree of Life," "The Maiden Waltz," "The Lovers Walk in the Magic Forest," "The Mystic Carpenter," "The Chariot/Space Voyage," "The Moon (Lunacy)," "Return of the Philosopher," "Death March," "Sun Prelude," "The Sun"

Tom Constanten composed and recorded for this semi-soundtrack album derived from a very off-Broadway production (a mime musical after the deck of cards and based on a book by Joe McCord) with which he was involved in 1970.

■ "Tastebud" (McKernan)

A common piece of tape filler, this outtake from the Dead's first album is air mail direct from Pigpen but never made it to the concert stage.

■ The Teddy Bears' Picnic (book and cassette)/Bruce Whatley
HarperCollins, 1996.

Featuring a furry parade of cuddly bears illustrated by children's book author Bruce Whatley, *The Teddy Bear's Picnic* is a picture book narrating the story from the old folk song covered by Garcia and David Grisman on their *Not for Kids Only* album. A cassette recording of their Dixieland-style recording was packaged with this book for Deadheads of all ages.

■ "Tell Mama" (Clarence Carter/Marcus Daniel/Wilbur Terrell)
ETTA JAMES, Tell Mama (1968), Sweet Peaches: The Chess Years (1972), Her Greatest Hits (1987)
Savoy Brown, Street Corner Talking (1971)

Though "Tell Mama" is famous as Etta James's signature tune, it isn't as highly touted by the artist. According to *Rage to Survive*, her 1995 autobiography written with David Ritz: "There are people who think 'Tell Mama' is the Golden Moment of the Golden Age of Soul; they rant and rage about the snappy horn chart and the deep-pocket guitar groove, about how I sang the shit out of the song. I wish I could agree. Sure, the song made me money. It warmed Leonard Chess's heart to see the thing cross over to the pop charts, where it lingered for a long time. You might even say it became a classic. But I have to confess that it never was a favorite of mine. Never liked it. Never liked singing it: not then, not now. I almost never perform it. It's not like I don't admire the chart and the songwriter. Clarence Carter, the blind guitarist who had hits of his own with 'Slip Away' and 'Patches,' is great. Maybe it's just that I don't like being cast in the role of the Great Earth Mother, the gal you came to for comfort and easy sex."

James's antipathy to the song did not prevent her from singing "Tell Mama" during a two-concert stint with the Dead during the 1982 New Year's run.
12/30, 31/82, Oakland Auditorium Arena, Oakland, California

■ Tell Me All That You Know: The Unauthorized Grateful Dead Trivia Book (book)/Brian A. Folker
124 pp. Pinnacle Books, 1996.

Quick, name two of Mickey Hart's solo bands . . . beep! You lose. These and hundreds of other questions (and answers) are collected in Folker's fun, pocket-sized, point-of-purchase item. When Deadheads become octogenarians and are lazing about Deadhead retirement homes, this may be their favorite book.

■ "Tennessee Jed" (Garcia/Hunter)
Grateful Dead, Europe '72 (1972), What a Long Strange Trip It's Been (1977), Dick's Picks Voume Seven/'74 (1997)

"Tennessee Jed," a light country rocker with some elements of ragtime, was a first set standard since 1971. Rendered in Hunter's vivid *Zap Comix* style, "Tennessee Jed" is a chronicle of woes suffered by the song's ragtag hero—the musical embodiment of the "Ice Cream Kid" depicted on the cover of the album on which the song first appeared, *Europe '72*. He falls down a flight of stairs, cracks his spine, and gets punched in the eye. Even his dog gets kicked. Yet he always seems ready for more of whatever life throws at him. A survivor in the best sense, "Tennessee Jed" is the plucky archetypal Grateful Dead character—always smiling through a personal apocalypse.

The song was one of many written by Robert Hunter when he was living and traveling in Europe in the very early 1970s. Recounting the unusual circumstances which resulted in the lyric's composition, Hunter recalled a night of carousing and drinking *vino tinto* with his girlfriend at the time, Christie Bourne. "We were staggering back to our hotel, through this little alleyway between two church buildings, and it's cavernous—any sound you make just resonates and resonates. And there was this guy walking ahead of us, playing a Jew's harp. It was so out of place in Barcelona at 2:00 A.M., I just made the verses up and jotted them down when we got to the hotel . . . It was a good place to write a country song. That Jew's-harp was so absurd in the context of Barcelona that it became realer than real."

As Hunter told Blair Jackson in 1991, "There's something about being in a foreign country that makes me more Western than I am here. 'Tennessee Jed' was written in Barcelona, for instance. Maybe it's a hunger for my own identity."

In *A Box of Rain,* Hunter remembered that "Tennessee Jed" "originated in Barcelona, Spain. Topped up on *vino tinto,* I composed it aloud to the sound of a jaw harp twanged between echoing building faces by someone strolling half a block ahead of me in the late summer twilight."

The song is very much American, however, with lines like "Baby won't you carry me back to Tennessee" having their antecedents in songs such as Sleepy John Estes's "Easin' Back to Tennessee."

Although the song is musically formulaic, the Dead traditionally worked their jam to rousing but predictable peaks in concert.

6/22/73, P.N.E. Coliseum, Vancouver, British Columbia

6/11/76, Boston Music Hall, Boston

5/7/77, Boston Garden, Boston

11/25/79, Pauley Pavilion, Los Angeles

8/20/83, Frost Amphitheater, Palo Alto, California

7/10/89, Giants Stadium, East Rutherford, New Jersey

3/24/93, Dean Smith Center, Chapel Hill, North Carolina

(Courtesy of Arista Records)

■ *Terrapin Station*

Arista AL 7001, 1977. Produced by Keith Olsen.

"Estimated Prophet," "Dancing in the Streets," "Passenger," "Samson and Delilah," "Sunrise," "Lady with a Fan," "Terrapin Station," "Terrapin," "Terrapin Transit," "At a Siding," "Terrapin Flyer," "Refrain"

Tom Scott–lyricon.

The Dead's first release for Clive Davis's Arista label, *Terrapin Station* was easily the Dead's best-sounding album when it hit the record stores in 1977. As with many of the Dead's albums, the material was new to the band and would only grow some hair in the coming years. And, like its predecessor, *Blues for Allah,* one side of *Terrapin* is single songs and the other an extended, experimental foray. "Estimated Prophet," "Dancin'," "Passenger," "Sunrise," and "Samson" were all being road-tested when the album was released, and the music roars out of the gate. But it is in the "Terrapin" suite that the music reaches its conceptual and musical heights, the first lengthy composition since "That's It for the Other One" to really give the group some stretching room. It still stands as one of Robert Hunter's most intriguing stories and this studio version remains the definitive version of the piece.

Terrapin was produced by mainstream producer Keith Olsen who tried his hardest to shape the band in his own image, which meant a final wash that would garner as much standard FM radio rock play as can be drawn from a Dead album. But the songs that had a looseness in concert were a bit stifled here with the dreaded "disco" mix of "Dancin'" as unlistenable today as it was at the pinnacle of Donna Summer fever. "Sunrise," Donna Godchaux's contribution to the album, doesn't exactly help matters either, sounding like an out-of-tune Mariah Carey throwaway.

The difficulty of Olsen's studio demands was not lost on everyone. According to Kreutzmann in his 1989 interview with Blair Jackson, "Everybody told us that he was a real motherfucker on drummers, and he made me do stuff I didn't want to do, like playing with big sticks. I think he wanted me to be some Top 40 drummer. He was kind of a megalomaniac, which isn't the kind of person who should be working with the Grateful Dead."

Hart was equally hard on Olsen in his 1982 discussion with David Gans. "Keith Olsen was a good producer, and a good engineer. He was the most qualified. But he had a problem; he didn't know the Grateful Dead, and he wanted to mold the Grateful Dead in his own image. He did something that was one of the most disrespectful things that has ever happened to me musically in my life. On the second side of *Terrapin*, 'At a Siding' and 'Terrapin Flyer' are mine. The 'Flyer' was supposed to be a timbal solo with me and Garcia doing duets, timbal and guitar. Olsen erased one of the beautiful timbal tracks in Europe and replaced it with all these strings. He played it for me, and my mouth *dropped* . . .

"He took a lot off, and then I put my timbal solo back on. But he didn't ask—he erased it off the master and replaced it all with strings."

■ "Terrapin Station" (Garcia/Hunter)

Grateful Dead, single, *Terrapin Station* (1977), *Dick's Picks Volume Three*/'77 (1995), *The Arista Years* (1996), *Dozin' at the Knick*/'90 (1996)
Robert Hunter, *Jack O'Roses* (1979)

"Terrapin Station" stands as one of Robert Hunter's crowning masterpieces and truly unusual compositions, intertwining the legends and traditions of both English and American folklore into an epic vision. For a heartrending and historically neat reading of the song form in an earlier incarnation, Basil May's late 1920s or early 1930s "Lady of Carlisle" (*The Music of Kentucky Vol. 2*) can't be missed or beat. Hunter, incidentally, performed and recorded his own version of the song.

The May interpretation of "Lady of Carlisle" lays out the simple story for the ages quite plainly: a fair lady is approached by two men, a brave soldier and a courageous seaman. The lady can't choose between them, so tests them by leading them to a lion's den into which she throws her fan, saying "Which of you to gain a lady will return her fan or die." In modern vernacular, the soldier basically replies, "Later for this!" But the sailor does venture into the beast's domain to prove his love. It is not only typical of Hunter's genius that he can take a spare tale and transform it into epic song, but that he leaves the outcome of the sailor's gambit in doubt. The storyteller's job, as Hunter relates in "Terrapin," is to "shed light, not to master."

Just as the song itself is an invocation of inspiration, Hunter recalled some of the magic involved in the channeling of the lyrics through his muse in his 1978 conversation with David Gans. "'Terrapin Station' came in

on a pure beam," he said. "I sat down at the typewriter with my electric guitar plugged in, put in a piece of paper, and typed 'Terrapin Station.' I started with an invocation to the muse, because if it wasn't going to come from there, it was going to come from nowhere. The invocation carried me all the way through. I must have written a thousand words on it, eight twelve-inch pages—song after song. That's the mark of a good song—the words just come. With 'Terrapin,' I was in a state of pure well-being for the three days while I wrote."

After finishing the song Hunter remembered that "I called Jerry, and he came right over. Chord changes that he'd been working on fit perfectly into it. He got the first page and a half and last page set. There are about seven pages in between that aren't set to music, and probably won't be."

Discussing their collaboration on the song with David Gans and Blair Jackson in 1981, Garcia said, "He actually writes more clearly than I let him. I mean he'll explain things if I let him. Like if you've ever heard his version of 'Terrapin,' he closes the door on the whole story; he brings it all the way back. I don't let him do that. He knows I like it [ambiguous] so he tends to juice that part of it up on the versions we do together. We're manipulating there, but only insofar as we're not being precise when precision is *not* what's called for."

Similarly, he told Mary Eisenhart in 1987, "I prefer the open—you don't know what happened, we don't know what happened. It's like—'the storyteller makes no choice'—and neither do you, and neither does anybody else. I prefer that. I prefer to be hanging. In folk music, I've always been fond of the fragment. The song that has one verse. And you don't know anything about the characters, you don't know what they're doing, but they're doing something important. I love that. I'm really a sucker for that kind of song."

The composition and its album recording produced one of the band's most unusual collaborations as the Mormon Tabernacle Choir was enlisted to help the final sequence of the title suite soar with elegiac ecstasy. In discussing the final mix with David Gans in 1977, Bob Weir commented, "Well, the first time I heard it, it was mixed way, way more prominently than it is now, and I was pissed off—or, not pissed off, but concerned that all the orchestration and choral stuff was going to be given too much prominence in comparison to the band. So we began the long negotiation, as it were, to put it in a more reasonable perspective. Keith [Olsen] was real stoked;

he'd gone over to England and gotten these parts. They're kinda nifty parts, anything but 101 Strings—it's off in a peculiar direction, but I think it serves the song well. I think what it sounds like is English court music, but it serves the song well, that particular grandiose conception of how the orchestration would be done. I didn't mind the parts—there were a couple of lines that I would have spent more time with, but it's real expensive to do a sixty-piece orchestra. That first violin line in 'Terrapin Flyer' was a bit rushed. If Mickey had been over there (Mickey and Phil pretty much came up with that part), if we'd all had a chance to work with [arranger Paul] Buckmaster, Mickey would have found a way to make known to the players that the feeling that he wanted there was a little more mechanical. If you know Mickey, you know that he has a mechanical feel that he likes to lay into that kind of stuff. It's neat, it makes everything sort of busy and clock-like. Anyway, I could find fault here and there, but in general, I like the lines. There was just too much of it, and I thought it had to be backpedaled considerably."

Even then, Bob Weir saw the instrumental possibilities of the composition, telling Gans, "That whole 'Terrapin' sequence can become endless. We can just string it out further and further and further. I guess the rules are set that you have a few thematic lines here and there. Maybe with each new approach to it we might introduce one new thematic line, and try to work that into variations of the older themes. That would be one approach. Like Mickey says, it's a jumping-off point. We can go from anywhere to anywhere—within or without it, for that matter. We can tie other songs into it. Eventually, we might get it long enough that we can start off the evening with it and end the evening with it, and work in most anything anybody would want to hear."

5/17/77, Memorial Coliseum, Tuscaloosa, Alabama
1/22/78, McArthur Court, Eugene, Oregon
4/6/82, The Spectrum, Philadelphia
8/31/85, Manor Downs, Austin, Texas
10/30/90, Wembley Arena, London
6/26/94, Sam Boyd Silver Bowl, Las Vegas

■ *Texican Badman*/Peter Rowan
Appaloosa 010, 1980.

Recorded in 1974 but not released until some years later (and in Italy of all places), Garcia and Kreutzmann

contributed studio parts to Rowan's ode to the Wild West.

■ *That High Lonesome Sound*/OLD & IN THE WAY
Acoustic Disc, ACD-19, 1996
Produced by David Grisman. Recorded at the Boarding House, San Francisco, October 1 and 8, 1973, by Owsley Stanley and Victoria Babcock.
Jerry Garcia–banjo, vocals. DAVID GRISMAN–mandolin, vocals. VASSAR CLEMENTS–fiddle. Peter Rowan–guitar, vocals. JOHN KAHN–acoustic bass.
"Hard Hearted," "The Great Pretender," "Lost," "Catfish John," "High Lonesome Sound," "Lonesome Fiddle Blues," "Love Please Come Home," "Wicked Path of Sin," "Uncle Pen," "I'm on My Way Back to the Old Home," "Lonesome L.A. Cowboy," "I Ain't Broke But I'm Badly Bent," "Orange Blossom Special," "Angel Band"

Twenty-one years after the release of one of the most popular bluegrass albums came *That High Lonesome Sound* on David Grisman's Acoustic Disk Archive Series. The new recording featured fourteen previously unreleased songs from the original live performances that produced the acoustic excitement captured on the first Old & in the Way album.

One of the great things about Old & in the Way was its eclectic and extensive repertoire. This recording includes hard-core bluegrass classics like Bill Monroe's "I'm on My Way Back to the Old Home" and "Uncle Pen," Jim and Jesee McReynolds's "Hard Hearted," Vassar Clements's amazing fiddling on his own "Lonesome Fiddle Blues" and "Orange Blossom Special," as well as Peter Rowan favorites like "High Lonesome Sound" and "Lonesome L.A. Cowboy." There's also an inventive bluegrass arrangement of the 1950 pop ballad, "The Great Pretender," and an evocative performance by Garcia of the gospel anthem "Angel Band." All this, plus a twenty-page booklet featuring rare photographs and detailed song-by-song liner notes by bluegrass scholar Neil Rosenberg, makes this release a must for bluegrassheads, Deadheads, Dawgheads, and lovers of American acoustic roots music.

■ **"That's All Right, Mama"** (ARTHUR CRUDUP)
Garcia and Saunders, *Live at Keystone* (1973)

Arthur "Big Boy" Crudup, *Mean Ole Frisco* (1962), *That's All Right Mama* (1991)

Elvis Presley, single (1954), *Elvis Recorded Live at Madison Square Garden* (1972), *Elvis—A Legendary Performer* (1974), *The Sun Sessions* (1976), *Elvis Aron Presley* (1980), *This Is Elvis* (1981), *A Golden Celebration* (1984), *The Complete Sun Sessions* (1987)

ERIC ANDERSEN, *Bout Changes and Things* (1966)

Shocking Blue, *Beat With Us* (1967)

Barry Goldberg, *Two Jews' Blues* (1969)

Canned Heat, *Canned Heat 1970 Concert* (1970)

Rod Stewart, *Every Picture Tells a Story* (1971)

Krokodil, *Sweat and Swim* (1973)

Carl Perkins, *Ol' Blue Suedes Is Back* (1978), *Carl Perkins* (1986)

This early rock 'n' roll hit established Elvis Presley in 1954 but it was Mississippi bluesman Arthur "Big Boy" Crudup, one of the King's most revered influences, who formalized the song in the 1930s and recorded it in 1946 as "I Don't Know It." After the King it became standard bar-band fare for years to come.

One of those bands to take a whack at "That's All Right, Mama" was the Garcia and Saunders quartet, who took the song on extended, frequent flyer journeys during their regular Monday night jam sessions at San Francisco's Keystone or at any one of their many shows in the early and mid-1970s. Garcia brought the number to the Dead only twice, once in 1973 and again in 1986, both at RFK Stadium in Washington, D.C. The '73 version is nothing short of miraculous, with Garcia and Dickey Betts trading juicy licks in a tour de force jam that rivals the hottest bebop sessions. Charlie Parker was smiling in jazz Heaven during that one.

6/10/73, RFK Stadium, Washington, D.C. (with the ALLMAN BROTHERS BAND and MERL SAUNDERS)

▪ "That Would Be Something" (Paul McCartney)

Paul McCartney, *McCartney* (1970), *MTV Unplugged* (1991)

Paul McCartney's beautiful little nothing of a song began popping up as a surprise second-set mid-jam afterthought at Dead concerts in 1991, similar to the way "NOBODY'S FAULT BUT MINE" was utilized.

9/17/93, Madison Square Garden, New York

▪ "There's Something on Your Mind"
(Big Jay McNeely)

Big Jay McNeely, single (1959)

Bobby Marchan, single (1960), *There's Something on Your Mind* (1964)

James Cotton, *3 Harp Boogie* (1987)

Freddy Fender, *Canciones de Mi Barrio* (1993)

Big Jay McNeely wrote this obscure entry in the Grateful Dead catalogue in 1959 (Weir sang it at a couple of 1966 shows) but it was the weirdly unique Bobby Marchan who brought it to national attention when he scored his sole No. 1 hit with the tune in 1960—a powerhouse of a recording at that! Marchan was a female impersonator and part of a troupe called the Powder Box Revue and played with Huey "Piano" Smith and the Clowns before going out on his own. After the success of "There's Something on Your Mind," Marchan continued to record for a series of tiny labels and returned to the Top 20 in 1966 with the R&B single "Shake Your Tambourine."

12/1/66, The Matrix, San Francisco

▪ "They Love Each Other" (Garcia/Hunter)

Jerry Garcia, *Reflections* (1976)

Grateful Dead, *Steal Your Face* (1976)

"They Love Each Other" is a low-key plaint by a jealous observer of young lovers in the rush of romance that was a first-set regular since 1973. The early spunky, uptempo versions of "They Love Each Other" are regarded as superior to the later, languid renditions.

12/29/77, Oakland Auditorium Arena, Oakland, California

9/18/83, Nevada County Fairgrounds, Grass Valley, California

▪ *Those Who Know History Are Doomed to Repeat It* / HENRY KAISER

SST 198, 1988.

"Mason's Children," "The Man Who Shot Liberty Valance," "The Andy Griffith Show Theme: Fishin' Hole," "Ode to Billie Joe," "Dark Star,"›"The Other One"

Eclecticism reigns supreme on Kaiser's breakthrough album. Kaiser's superb music boasts killer versions of favored and uncommon Dead, taking "Dark Star" and

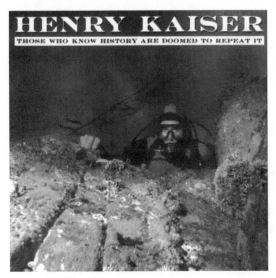

(Courtesy of SST Records)

"The Other One" to improvisational spaces even Garcia probably never imagined. Robert Hunter also guests on "Dark Star" reciting a verse of lyrics.

Mixing the ridiculous and oddball, Kaiser also includes "Ode to Billie Joe," "The Man Who Shot Liberty Valance," and "The Andy Griffith Show Theme" (a 1996 CD rererelease also contained five tunes from Captain Beefheart) on an album that demonstrates both Kaiser's chops and insanely cool tastes.

▪ "Throwing Stones" (Weir/Barlow)
Grateful Dead, *In the Dark* (1987), *The Arista Years* (1996)

Overt political messages are not standard fare in Grateful Dead songs. Although Weir deemed the composition "apolitical," "Throwing Stones" is the Dead's most pointedly eschatological tract. A finger-pointing, antifascist diatribe, "Throwing Stones" touches many bases: greed, gun-running, history, racism, cocaine trafficking, apathy, environmentalism, power-brokering, and, most saliently, nuclear annihilation. Yet the lyrics are deft and subtle with a chorus loosely based on "Ring Around the Rosey," the children's nursery rhyme which itself can be traced to the Great Plague.

Ultimately, "Throwing Stones" is a song not afraid to unflinchingly ask the biggest question: "What does it mean to be human?"

Musically the song is equally fascinating with odd time signatures and chord changes with a jam that allowed the band to soar with majestic drama.

Bob Weir shed some light on the song's genesis in his 1985 interview with Blair Jackson. "'Throwing Stones' is kind of weird because it starts out on the dominant," he said. "I don't know how I arrived at that. I think pretty obviously the diatribe part of the song came first because for a song to start out on the dominant is sort of a weird portent to begin with. Then I remember that it occurred to us that we were getting pretty thick pretty quick, and it was time to balance it a bit before the whole song became a full-blown diatribe and nothing but. The punks do that well enough. So it occurred to me that what I would do is temper all this by lifting a melody and a couple of words from an old Bahamian folk carol called 'Bye and Bye.' So the second half of the first verse uses those chord changes, and it's meant to counterbalance things. It had that softness I wanted. It has the punch from starting off on the dominant mode. When it finally resolved in the tonic mode, I wanted to cool it out for the second half of the verse.

"The world isn't all bad. But we wanted to paint a picture of the world as we both saw it that night. It took longer than a night, of course, but we had the form of it down in a night. It's just that sooner or later, whether they [the audience] knows it or not, that's what they're saying—sooner or later it's all going to collapse; the whole house of cards is going to collapse. I guess the thrust of the song is what we will or won't do in the face of that: 'We will leave this place an empty stone / Or that shiny ball of blue we call our home.' Sooner or later we'll emerge triumphant as a race or we'll make our own graves."

A final note concerns David Gans, whose uncredited contribution of the line "shipping powders back and forth/Black goes south and white come north" elucidates the concerns many people had regarding the guns and drugs coming into and out of Central America at the time.

10/10/82, Frost Amphitheater, Palo Alto, California
8/13/85, Manor Down, Austin, Texas
7/12/87, Giants Stadium, East Rutherford, New Jersey
6/20/91, Pine Knob Music Theater, Clarkston, Michigan

▪ *Tibetan Tantric Choir*/THE GYUTO MONKS
Windham Hill WH-2001, 1987. Produced by Mickey Hart.

THE GYUTO MONKS: TIBETAN TANTRIC CHOIR

WD-2001

(Courtesy of Windham Hill Records)

"Guhyasmaja Tantra, Chapter II," "Melody for Mahakala"

Mickey Hart's first formal release with the Gyuto Monks is astonishingly well recorded, sounding as if the monks are singing by your hearth. This entrancing and profound liturgical chanting is equally impressive with the monks coordinating both rhythm and seemingly impossible overtone signing. The very micropulses of the vocal waveforms are exactly in sync, precisely as if they were one voice guided by a universal computer. The first chant is from the "Guhyasamaja Tantra, Chapter II" and the second, "Melody for Mahakala," is interrupted with dramatic instrumental sections played by an ensemble of skull drum, small bell, several pairs of cymbals, a pair of conch shells, two long copper horns, a pair of short bone trumpets, and several large drums struck with sticks. Fasten seatbelts and when the oxygen sign flashes, you're on your own.

- **Ticket to New Year's** (video)
  Monterey Home Video 31988, 1996. Recorded December 31, 1987–January 1, 1988, Oakland Coliseum Arena, Oakland, California.
  "Bertha," "Cold Rain and Snow," "Little Red Rooster," "When Push Comes to Shove," "When I Paint My Masterpiece," "Bird Song">"The Music Never Stopped," "Hell in a Bucket">"Uncle John's Band">"Terrapin Station">"Drumz">"The Other

One">"Wharf Rat">"Throwing Stones">"Not Fade Away," "Knockin' on Heaven's Door."

Culling most of their 1987 year-end hullabaloo, the Dead rip through blazing versions of "Bertha," "Cold Rain and Snow," "When Push Comes to Shove," "Bird Song">"Music Never Stopped," "Uncle John's Band," "Terrapin," "The Other One," and "Wharf Rat" on this well-produced shoot that also includes some unrevealing interviews with the band and the de rigueur simulated psychedelic experience. Cultists will note that some of the rarity-filled third set that showcased the Neville Brothers sharing the stage on such nuggets as "Day-O" and "Do You Wanna Dance" is MIA on this release.

- **"Tico-Tico"** (Erwin Drake/Aloysio Oliveira/Zequinha Abreu)
  Ray Coniff, *'S Continental* (1962)
  Xavier Cugat, *16 Most Requested Songs* (1992)
  Charlie Parker, *South of the Border* (1995)

First heard in Disney's 1943 cartoon film *Saludos Amigos*, "Tico-Tico" was used by the Dead dozens of times as another upbeat tune-up exercise. The song appeared in several other films of the 1940s as well: *Thousands Cheer, Bathing Beauty, Kansas City Kitty*, and was sung by Carmen Miranda in *Copacabana*.

- **Tie-Died: Rock 'n' Roll's Most Dedicated Fans** (film)
  Directed by Andrew Behar, 1995.

An accurate eighty-minute portrait of "tourheads," the band's hardest-core followers, this serious documentary is an accurate road film shot in parking lots from Eugene to Vegas to Vermont in the summer of 1994. The classic stereotypes are here: the grizzled vets who have been checking in with the band since the 1960s, the dilated-pupil young'ns, drum circles, dancers, spinners, space cadets, Wharf Rats, communards, and tailgate chefs. But there is great humanity here too as even the most gnarly, unwashed characters are portrayed as seeking the same common goal: love and companionship.

While shooting the movie, the filmmakers relied heavily on original music donated by Deadheads themselves—usually recorded in concert-arena parking lots. When some film distributors expressed interest in making a deal with director Andrew Behar, provided that some commercially released Dead music be included in the soundtrack, the filmmaker remixed the film's soundtrack with five Dead songs—even making a pilgrimage to San Rafael to get the band's blessing. After a couple of screenings, Behar left under the impression that the Dead organization was more or less amenable to the project.

But then the filmmakers got a letter from the band's lawyer stating that they were not going to grant any music rights and wanted to put the kibosh on the entire project. At the time, the film's working title was *DeadHeads*—a term that the Dead had, in their infinite marketing wisdom, trademarked. Behar's lawyers pointed out that the term was trademarked only for merchandising and probably could be used as the movie's title. But because the band's lawyers might have been able to get an injunction against the film until a judge resolved the case, its debut at the Sundance Film Festival in 1995 was jeopardized. Even after the title was changed, Sundance received a letter from Dead attorneys threatening a suit if it screened the documentary.

According to Geoffrey Gilmore, the festival's director, "I have the sense that the Dead wish they had made the film themselves. I would certainly say it is rather ironic, given their stature in the counterculture over the years, that they view this as the only means with which to work."

Given that *Tie-Died*'s take on Deadheads is almost entirely positive, it's not clear why a band renowned for its free and easy ways would allegedly try to suppress the work of a few small independent filmmakers. Behar, who finally found nationwide art house distributorship only after Garcia's death, could only offer this: "I know it sounds strange, but they don't want to be associated with drugs and sex."

▪ *Tiger Rose*/Robert Hunter

Round RX-105, 1975 (Reissue-remix Rykodisc RCD 10115, 1989.) "Anti-produced" by Mickey Hart.
"Tiger Rose," "One Thing to Try," "Rose of Sharon," "Wild Bill," "Dance a Hole," "Cruel White Water," "Over the Hills," "Last Flash of Rock 'n' Roll," "Yellow Moon," "Ariel"
Robert Hunter–acoustic guitar, mandolin, vocal. (B. D.) Shot–drums. Mickey Hart–percussion. David Freiberg–bass, piano, synthesizer, vocals. Pete Sears–piano, organ, track piano & clavinet. Jerry Garcia–guitar, slide guitar, pedal steel guitar,

(Courtesy of Rykodisc)

synthesizer, vocals. Donna Godchaux–vocals. Dave Torbert–bass. DAVID GRISMAN–mandolin.

A smooth and engaging followup to his solo bow, Hunter's sophomore effort shows him still working out the kinks in his performance.

Garcia performs on each track from *Tiger Rose*, an artistic, if not sonic, success. Hunter never liked the vocal track and in 1989 rerecorded all of his vocals. As he told Blair Jackson in 1988, "There are vocals I detest on *Rum Runners* and *Tiger Rose* and I just can't live with them, but I won't change those, either. I just want to shine it all up a little. *Tiger Rose* still sounds good. Garcia and Bob Mathews did a good job on that, but my vocals are terrible. I can't listen to that record because of it."

A bit of trivia concerns the song "Ariel," which Hunter originally wrote in 1964. It was a Mickey Hart musical arrangement that brought it back to Hunter's mind and resulted in the song's inclusion on *Tiger Rose*.

The choice for Mickey Hart as the album's drummer was a strange one as Hart, himself, confessed in his 1982 interview with David Gans. "I was going through a catharsis here," he said. "Mickey Hart as Mickey Hart could never play straight drums on Bob Hunter's record. He couldn't play bass drum, snare drum, high-hat, and cymbals—Hart didn't play like that. Hart wasn't a straight drummer. Hart was a space drummer—up until that point.

"I was faced with an inner decision here. So what I did was split my personality. 'B. D. SHOT'—Bass Drum, Snare, High hat, Overhead, and Tom-tom—was the basic signature of the drums on the console. Shot's consciousness wasn't anything like Hart. Shot could play the straight stuff all day, because he wasn't Hart and it was no threat to Hart. Hart couldn't handle that then. Even the NEW RIDERS OF THE PURPLE SAGE was a lot more spacey than Hunter's stuff. I didn't want to play Hunter's stuff for the rest of my life, and Hart wouldn't do *anything* he didn't want to do. Ain't nothing like that in this body. I had to deal with it in my own space and time, so I thought schizophrenia was called for at this point. So I named myself B. D. Shot. And Hart played percussion.

"We finally made peace, and Hart and Shot became one again after that."

▪ "Till the Morning Comes" (Garcia/Hunter)
Grateful Dead, *American Beauty* (1970)

A buoyant but forgotten number from *American Beauty,* "Till the Morning Comes" was only performed five times in the latter part of 1970. The song is a harmonizer's special and one of the few Dead songs without a lead singer as Garcia, Weir, and Lesh simultaneously share the duties on this sweet rocker reminiscent of the Everly Brothers.

10/31/70, Gym, SUNY, Stony Brook, New York

▪ "The Times They Are a-Changin'"
(BOB DYLAN)
Bob Dylan, *The Times They Are a-Changin'* (1964), *At Budokan* (1978), *Biograph* (1985), *MTV Unplugged* (1995)
Peter, Paul and Mary, *In Concert* (1964)
The Byrds, *Turn! Turn! Turn!* (1966)
Simon and Garfunkel, *Wednesday Morning 3 A.M.* (1966)
THE BEACH BOYS, *Beach Boys Party!* (1966)
Sebastian Cabot, *Bob Dylan, poet* (1967)
The Hollies, *Hollies Sing Dylan* (1969)
Spirit, *Spirit of '76* (1975)
The Wanderers, *The Only Lovers Left Alive* (1981)
Richie Havens, *Sings Beatles and Dylan* (1987), *Cuts to the Chase* (1994)
Billy Joel, *In Concert: "Kohept"* (1987)
Billy Bragg, *Billy Bragg Goes to Moscow and Northern Virginia* (1991)

Because Dylan wrote and recorded "The Times They Are a-Changin'" on the eve of John F. Kennedy's assassination, the song would resonate with significance in the troubled months and years that followed. Indeed, along with "Blowin' in the Wind," "The Times They Are a-Changin'" became a virtual clarion call to political activism throughout the 1960s.

Acknowledging an intent, Dylan wrote in the *Biograph* liner notes: "This was definitely a song with a purpose. I knew exactly what I wanted to say and for whom I wanted to say it to. You know, it was influenced of course by the Irish and Scottish ballads . . . 'Come All Ye Bold Highway Men, Come All Ye Miners, Come All Ye Tender Hearted Maidens.' I wanted to write a big song, some kind of theme song, ya know, with short concise verses that piled up on each other in a hypnotic way . . . the civil rights movement and the folk movement were pretty close and allied together for a while at that time. Everybody knew almost everybody else. I had to play this song the same night that President Kennedy died. It sort of took over as the opening song and stayed that way for a long time."

As much as any of Dylan's other songs, "The Times They Are a-Changin'" (suffused with prophetic biblical imagery of imminent and irrevocable cataclysm and revolution) gave a generation its voice. But, probably because it is temporally clichéd and anthemic, the Dead never performed it outside of their 1987 concerts with Dylan.

7/4/87, Sullivan Stadium, Foxboro, Massachusetts (with Bob Dylan)

▪ "To Lay Me Down" (Garcia/Hunter)
Jerry Garcia, *Garcia* (1972)
Grateful Dead, *Reckoning* (1981)
Cowboy Junkies, *Deadicated* (1991)

A song that came to life in the studio, "To Lay Me Down" was recalled by Garcia in his 1981 interview with David Gans as part of a "group of songs I started writing using the keyboard. 'To Lay Me Down' is probably my first keyboard song."

"To Lay Me Down" had several lives with the Dead since its first acoustic performances in 1970. It returned as an electrified ballad in 1973 and 1974 before falling by the wayside until the Dead's 1980 acoustic sets. After that it made intermittent appearances, primarily as a mid-first-set surprise.

A melancholy wish by an estranged lover to rejoin a soulmate, "To Lay Me Down" is one of Hunter's most declarative romantic offerings.

9/18/74, Parc des Expositions, Dijon, France
10/25/80, Radio City Music Hall, New York
3/27/88, Hampton Coliseum, Hampton, Virginia

■ "Tomorrow Is a Long Time" (BOB DYLAN)
Bob Dylan, *Bob Dylan's Greatest Hits Volume II* (1971)
Sebastian Cabot, *Bob Dylan, poet* (1967)
Street, *Street* (1968)
Dion, *Dion* (1968)
Rod Stewart, *Every Picture Tells a Story* (1971)
Sandy Denny, *Sandy* (1972)

This song has a somewhat circuitous history in the Dylan recording canon. It was written and performed in the early 1960s but didn't make it to vinyl until 1971 when it appeared on *Bob Dylan's Greatest Hits Volume II* as a buyer's incentive.

This officially released version of "Tomorrow Is a Long Time" was originally to be included in *Bob Dylan in Concert*, an album which was planned but never released. The track listing was finalized, combining songs from two 1963 concerts at New York's Town Hall and Carnegie Hall. The reason for the album's non-release is a matter of some debate among Dylanists. The common theory is that when the album was to come out in late 1964 or 1965, the material, which was not exactly Dylan's strongest to start with, was definitely not representative of his then-current songs.

But, while "Tomorrow Is a Long Time" is a delicate song describing the poet's early vision of beauty in all things, it was more notable in its Dylan-Dead incarnation because it allowed Garcia to publicly demonstrate his pedal-steel chops for the first time in eons.

7/12/87, Giants Stadium, East Rutherford, New Jersey (with Bob Dylan)

■ "Tomorrow Is Forever" (Dolly Parton)
Porter Wagoner and Dolly Parton, *Sweet Harmony* (1970)

Dolly Parton and Porter Wagoner had a Top 10 hit with "Tomorrow Is Forever" just a couple of years before Donna Godchaux briefly performed it with the Grateful Dead.

9/24/72, Palace Theater, Waterbury, Connecticut

■ "Tomorrow Never Knows"
(Lennon/McCartney)
The Beatles, *Revolver* (1966)
Phil Manzanera and 801, *801 Live* (1976)
Phil Collins, *Face Value* (1980)

"Tomorrow Never Knows," the innovative closing track of the Beatles' groundbreaking *Revolver* LP, was composed by John Lennon while under the influence of Timothy Leary's version of *The Egyptian Book of the Dead*. Leary's book was a guide for people seeking to gain spiritual enlightenment, particularly through the use of LSD. It inspired Lennon and he incorporated a line from the book in his song.

Lennon brought many ideas to the April 1966 recording session that produced "Tomorrow Never Knows," which had to be technically translated to what could actually be achieved by the Beatles' chief sound gurus George Martin and Geoff Emerick. Lennon told them, "I want to sound as though I'm the Dalai Lama singing from the highest mountain top. And yet I still want to hear the words I'm singing."

Later, Lennon was to say that, "With 'Tomorrow Never Knows,' I'd imagine in my head that in the background you would hear thousands of monks chanting. That was impractical of course and we did something different. I should have tried to get my original idea, the monks' singing. I realize now that's what I wanted."

Still, the studio wizardry and ingenuity demonstrated by Martin and Emerick is nothing short of extraordinary. Their amazing results were achieved by the use of tape loops and playing several tape machines at various speeds. The birdlike sounds, for instance, were executed by the use of a tape loop of a laughing Paul McCartney.

The elliptical title came from Ringo Starr. "Tomorrow Never Knows" was Ringo-speak for "Tomorrow Never Comes."

"Tomorrow Never Knows" was brought to the Grateful Dead by Vince Welnick, who ingeniously linked it in concert with the Who's "Baba O'Riley." No doubt, the Dead's state-of-the-art MIDI technology allowed them to better re-create the unearthly aura of this very ethereal and classic Beatles tripfest.

5/25/92, Shoreline Amphitheater, Mountain View, California

■ *Tomorrow Show*
(television program)

Taking over Tom Snyder's usual snoozer of a program, the Dead's rambunctious May 7, 1981, appearance on the *Tomorrow Show* was highlighted by a four-song acoustic display: "On the Road Again," "Dire Wolf," "Deep Elem Blues," and "Cassidy." Ken Kesey was also on hand to further confuse and brighten matters.

■ "Tons of Steel" (Brent Mydland)
Grateful Dead, *In the Dark* (1987)

Trains inhabit many Grateful Dead songs, but "Tons of Steel" is the only one in which one is the actual subject. Somewhat heavy-handed in its metaphorical message connecting the train and a difficult romance, "Tons of Steel" was a rousing Brent Mydland concert selection while the Dead were performing it between 1984 and 1987.

> **4/19/87, Irvine Meadows Amphitheater, Irvine, California**

■ Too Loose to Truck
Showing every sign of stage itch during the Dead's year off, Phil Lesh formed this Bay Area bar band that performed in 1975 and early 1976. One of the songs featured in the band's repertoire was Dylan's "Just Like Tom Thumb's Blues," which Lesh dusted off and brought to the Dead a decade later.

■ "Touch of Grey" (Garcia/Hunter)
Grateful Dead, single, *In the Dark* (1987), *The Arista Years* (1996)
Mighty Diamonds, *Fire on the Mountain: Reggae Celebrates the Grateful Dead* (1996)

The Dead's most commercially successful song, this wistful but hopeful meditation on aging caught the fancy of hippies, yuppies, and Baby Boomers alike. Its triumph was the single reason for the band's rush to mass popularity in the late 1980s.

Discussing the collaborative give-and-take in composing the song, Garcia pointed out that "Hunter sang 'Touch of Grey' as a sort of dry, satirical piece with an intimate feel, but I heard something else coming through it. 'We will get by' said something to me, so I set it to play big. My version still has the ironic bite in the lyrics, but what comes across is a more celebratory quality."

After the song's phenomenal success, Hunter re-flected to David Gans in 1988, "I think 'Touch of Grey' was a hell of a hot little tune. I think it was very, very well recorded, and released well, followed up with a hell of a video. I think we genuinely got ourselves a hit, and a hit does what a hit's supposed to do: propels a band to the top. I think it's as simple as that: we got a hit record. . . . I wrote 'Touch of Grey' seven years ago. I've been performing it for years. Jerry saw the possibilities in it for being more than I was realizing, and reset it and made a monster out of it, I think."

Finally, according to Hunter, the line "Light a candle, curse the glare" was courtesy of Garcia.

> **7/13/84, Greek Theatre, Berkeley, California**
> **12/15/86, Coliseum Arena, Oakland Coliseum, Oakland, California**

■ *Transverse City*/Warren Zevon
Virgin Records America 91068, 1989.

An unusual supporting appearance by Garcia on Zevon's attempt to integrate the influence of Stravinsky on a complex, dense but absorbing blast of jagged rock, Garcia plays on one track, "They Moved the Moon."

■ *Tricker*/Ken Kesey
A Key-Z Production, 1988.

Aesop and Lord Buckley by way of Ken Kesey meet in this audio version of the author's story *Little Tricker the Squirrel Meets Double the Bear.* The B-side of this Kesey-produced tape includes three songs written by Kesey and performed by the Thunder Machine (a Prankster-specific contraption-instrument) with Jerry Garcia on lead guitar.

■ *Trios*/Rob Wasserman
MCA/GRP Records, MGD-4021, 1994. Produced by Rob Wasserman, John Cutler, Don Was, Clare Wasserman, Stephanie Clarke.
"Fantasy Is Reality"/"Bells of Madness," "Put Your Big Toe in the Milk of Human Kindness," "White-Wheeled Limousine," "Country (Bass Trilogy: Part 1)," "Zillionaire," "Dustin' Off the Bass," "Easy Answers," "Satisfaction (Bass Trilogy: Part 2)," "Home Is Where You Get Across," "Spike's Bulls (Bass Trilogy: Part 3)," "Gypsy One," "Gypsy Two," "American Popsicle"
Rob Wasserman with Carnie Wilson and Brian Wilson; Marc Ribot and Elvis Costello; BRUCE HORNSBY and

BRANFORD MARSALIS; Jerry Garcia and Edie Brickell; WILLIE DIXON and Al Duncan; Bob Weir and Neil Young; Les Claypool and Chris Whitely; Mat Haimovitz and Joan Jeanrenaud.

Following the road-tested formula that brought success to his *Duets* album, Rob Wasserman parlayed likely and unlikely settings for his collaborators in this tight enterprise.

On his collaborations with Garcia and Edie Brickell, Wasserman's liner notes are musically and personally insightful. "This was the first trio I recorded and I feel it set the tone for the entire record. I first met Edie when I picked her up at the San Francisco airport. My car door wouldn't open, so she proceeded to climb in through the window!—I liked her immediately. Later, when we jammed at Jerry's house, he and I were both astonished by her ability to spontaneously create a song at the very moment she was singing it. 'Zillionaire' was the first song that we came up with that night. Jerry played a grand piano as we were writing the song so he decided to record with it as well—a very rare occurrence. Several hours of music were recorded at that session. In fact, we all agreed that someday, just for fun, we would perform as an all improv band—no set lists, no material!

"This was a totally crazy, improvised jam session where 'American Popsicle' was one improv out of many we recorded that day, but perhaps the song that most represents the 'other side' of *Trios*—total spontaneity, no boundaries, improvisational musical madness."

- ### "Truckin'" (Garcia/Weir/Lesh/Hunter)
  Grateful Dead, single, *American Beauty* (1971), *Europe '72* (1972), *What a Long Strange Trip It's Been* (1977), *Dick's Picks Volume One/'73* (1993), *Hundred Year Hall/'72* (1995), *Dick's Picks Volume Seven/'74* (1997)
  Pop-O-Pies, *The White EP* (1983)
  Dwight Yoakam, *Deadicated* (1991)
  Tesla, *Five-Man Acoustical Jam* (1991)
  Dead Ringers, DEAD RINGERS (1993)

"Truckin'" is a Grateful Dead signature song and the band's popular testament to life on the road, chronicling many of their early adventures and misadventures. With its funky hook and humorous on-the-rag lyrics, "Truckin'" has served the Dead in many capacities. From a surprising show-opening jump start to a second-set explosion, the song has the distinction of contributing the line "What a long strange trip it's been" to the pop cultural lexicon.

The verses feature R&B inflected Berryisms that compare in scansion with the unmistakable monotone melody and the rhythmic phrasing of "No Particular Place to Go" or "School Days" and are juxtaposed with a light-hearted country feel in the lilting rhythmic groove and dulcet vocal harmonies of the choruses.

Discussing the collaborative elements that went into the song's composition, Garcia told Charles Reich and Jann Wenner in 1971, "When Hunter first started writing words for us originally, he was on his own trip and he was a poet. He was into the magical thing of words, definitely far out, definitely amazing. The early stuff he wrote that we tried to set to music was stiff because it wasn't really meant to be sung. After he got further and further into it, his craft improved and then he started going out on the road with us, coming out to see what life was like, to be able to have more of that viewpoint in the music, for the words to be more Grateful Dead words. 'Truckin'' is the result of that sort of thing. 'Truckin'' is a song that we assembled; it wasn't natural and it didn't flow and it wasn't easy and we really labored over the bastard, all of us together.

"You can see it happen if you hang around backstage. If you go to a concert you see there's the onstage part with the bright lights, the show, loud music, people screaming, all that stuff happening. And then you're backstage between sets and there's all kinds of milling crowds and people going, 'Hey man, hey man,' stuff coming at you and weird shit and you're having to duck and get out of the way and lie and talk fast—all these things to just be able to preserve a little composure, just so you don't have to be constantly putting out. That's just a way of saying that thing, I mean it's just a beautiful way of saying it."

Hunter's memory of writing the song was equally expansive. As he told Jeff Tamarkin of RELIX in 1986, "I wrote that in several different cities, starting off in San Francisco. I finished it up in Florida. I was on the road with the band and writing different verses in different cities, and when were in Florida I went outside and everybody was sitting around the swimming pool. I had finally finished the lyrics, so I brought them down and the boys picked up their guitars, sat down and wrote some rock & roll changes behind it. The bust in New Orleans happened about a year earlier.

"There was no lyrical change when the song got to the

band. It was fed to Bobby a line at a time when we got to the studio, with me telling him how to pronounce it. He'd go in and put a line down, then go back in and work out how to pronounce the next line. That's the one and only time such a thing has happened. The music was always like a Chuck Berry thing; they did it a little differently than I wrote it, put a different accent in. The 'Sometimes the lights all shinin' on me' part is definitely Grateful Dead."

But "Truckin'" is also a song with a pre-history. A popular, early-twentieth-century dance step, the word is also immortalized in several songs of the 1920s and 1930s, including the blues "Keep on Truckin'" and Blind Boy Fuller's "Truckin' My Blues Away."

4/28/71, Fillmore East, New York
7/18/72, Roosevelt Stadium, Jersey City, New Jersey
12/31/72, Winterland Arena, San Francisco
3/24/73, The Spectrum, Philadelphia
6/22/73, P.N.E. Coliseum, Vancouver, British Columbia
6/26/74, Providence Civic Center, Providence, Rhode Island
11/6/77, Broome County Arena, Binghamton, New York
5/9/79, Broome County Arena, Binghamton, New York
4/6/82, The Spectrum, Philadelphia
3/28/93, Knickerbocker Arena, Albany, New York

▪ *Truckin' with the Grateful Dead to Egypt* (book)/Robert Nichols
132 pp. 38 color and black and white photos. Bibliography, diagrams. Egyptian periods and dynasties and astrological overview. Moonbow Press, 1984.

Given the cosmic, political, and sheer devil-may-care spirit with which the Dead undertook their momentous Egyptian concert adventure, it's a shame that the only substantial reportage to emerge is this barely literate inconsequential hack job. Even the photographs are mediocre.

▪ **"Turn On Your Love Light"** (Scott/Malone)
Grateful Dead, *Live/Dead* (1969), *Skeletons from the Closet* (1974), *Two from the Vault*/'68 (1992), *Hundred Year Hall*/'72 (1995), *Dick's Picks Volume Four*/'70 (1996)
Bobby "Blue" Bland, *The Best of Bobby Bland* (1962), *The Music Never Stopped: Roots of the Grateful Dead*/'62 (1995)
Them, *Them Again* (1966)

Bobby "Blue" Bland. *(Archive Photos/Frank Driggs Collection)*

Jerry Lee Lewis, *Soul My Way* (1968)
Bob Seger, *Smokin' O.P.'s* (1972)
Gregg Allman, *The Gregg Allman Tour* (1974)
James Hunter, *. . . Believe What I Say* (1996)

The great Bobby "Blue" Bland first recorded and popularized "Turn On Your Love Light" in 1962, and it was covered many times thereafter. But nobody, even Bland, could touch what Pigpen and the Grateful Dead did with the saucy raveup.

Strutting his raunchiest stuff, Pigpen would turn "Love Light" into his invocation of the sexual muse with a rap to end all Pigpen raps with lines like "Take your hands out of your pockets and quit playin' pocket pool!"

But Bland's original was nothing to sneeze at, either. In fact, Bland was an original in his own right—one of the main creators of the modern soul-blues sound along with the likes of Sam Cooke, Ray Charles, and Junior Parker.

Born January 27, 1930, Bland was raised in Rosemark, Tennessee, a hamlet near Memphis. He moved to the city with his mother in 1947, where he began his career as a singer in the Miniatures, a gospel group. Not long after he moved to the Beale Streeters, a loose-knit blues unit which included such future marquee stars as Johnny Ace, B. B. King, and Junior Parker.

Bland made a few early recordings for the Modern and Chess labels between 1950 and 1952 before being drafted into the army. After his discharge, he came back with a vengeance. He began his long-time relationship with Duke Records that would lead to dozens of records and many hits. By 1957 he scored a No. 1 hit on the R&B charts with the seminal Texas shuffle "Further Up the Road."

Bland's high-water mark came in 1961 and 1963. In 1961 his "I Pity the Fool" also made it to No. 1 on the R&B charts while "Turn On Your Love Light" hit No. 2. In 1963 he had his third and final No. 1 R&B hit with "That's the Way Love Is."

By then Bland had fully developed his style: a sound that meshed gospel, blues, and R&B colored with a glittering soul sensibility, punctuated with big-band brassiness and slick guitar stylings reminiscent of B. B. King. Easily ranking as some of great soul-blues vocals of all time, Bland's impassioned singing ranged from a falsetto to the gospel howls of a stump preacher over the course of a single song.

Up until 1961 he had played the chitlin circuit with Junior Parker and with his own band, the Blue Flames. But it was when he split with Parker in '61 and set out on his own that he rose to his greatest popularity.

Bland didn't compose his own songs or even play an instrument so he had to rely on others for songs, impeccable instrumentation, and sharp musicianship for both his live shows and studio recordings. His bandleader, Joe Scott (who cowrote "Love Light"), and Duke label owner Don Robey's top talent scouts helped create Bland's brassy sound. The band's great R&B guitarist, Wayne Bennett, was equally as important to Bland with his clipped, jazz-influenced solos complementing the horns and his leader's vocals.

But Bland's alleged problems with alcohol resulted in the band falling apart in 1968. He revived his career without Bennett or Scott in 1972 with two commercially successful LPs on the ABC-Dunhill label, *California Album* and *Dreamer* in 1973 and 1974.

For many years after that Bland was constantly on the road, often sharing the bill with his old friend B. B. King. Despite rarely crossing over into the pop realm he was inducted into the Blues Foundation's Hall of Fame in 1981 and the Rock and Roll Hall of Fame in 1992, his influence on the idiom secure.

Weir revamped "Love Light" and the Dead resumed playing it in 1981 as a hoe-down show-closer, never having to remind the audience what to do with their love-light: "And leave it on!"

> **6/7/69, Fillmore Auditorium, San Francisco (with JANIS JOPLIN)**
>
> **2/13/70, Fillmore East, New York (*Dick's Picks Volume Four*)**
>
> **5/7/70, Dupont Gymnasium, M.I.T., Cambridge, Massachusetts**
>
> **4/27/71, Fillmore East, New York**
>
> **10/16/81, Melk Weg, Amsterdam**
>
> **3/29/90, Nassau Veterans Memorial Coliseum, Uniondale, New York (with BRANFORD MARSALIS)**

■ *The Twilight Zone*
(television program)

The Dead composed the title theme and most of the incidental or "spot" music to the provocative, well-crafted CBS program which aired in 1985 and 1986. Adding to the natural eeriness of the show, the Dead's musical contribution was most akin to their own "Space" jams. In true Dead high tech fashion, *The Twilight Zone* was the first television show to employ a then-new computer-processed sound treatment system known as "spatial reverberation," which gave viewers a sense of the localization of sound in a given scene. In other words, a plane flying overhead was made to sound like it's above the scene, rustling leaves below, etc.

Asked why he approved the choice of the Dead to do the music for the show, producer Phil DeGuere told *Mix* magazine in 1985, "The Grateful Dead has been responsible for my auditory awakening ever since the first time I heard them [in the late 1960s]. They are the state-of-the-art when it comes to the amplification of music. Nobody's in the same league with them."

For the trivia-minded, the heartbeat heard in the opening scene theme sequence belonged to Hart's son Taro, who was recorded by Dad while still in the womb. Additionally, Robert Hunter contributed some brief narrative segments to the *Zone* that could make even Rod Serling smile from the great beyond . . . or wherever.

■ *Two from the Vault*
Grateful Dead Merchandising, Inc. GDCD 40162, 1992. Produced by DAN HEALY. Recorded August 23–24, 1968, at the Shrine Exposition Hall, Los Angeles, California.

"Good Morning, Little Schoolgirl," "Dark Star">"St.

Stephen">"The Eleven">"Death Don't Have No Mercy," "The Other One">"New Potato Caboose">"Turn on Your Love Light," "(Walk Me Out in the) Morning Dew"

A superior follow-up to *One from the Vault*, *Two from the Vault* continues Healy's archival series with selections drawn from a pair of 1968 concerts—arguably the Dead's most musically inspired and exploratory period. *Two from the Vault* catches the Dead just as they are settling into this challenging, exuberant music. Anytime "Dark Star" could be considered the weakest tune on an offering must speak extra highly of the remaining selections and the band delivers in spades with a powerful "St. Stephen"> "The Eleven" and a momentous "The Other One">"New Potato Caboose" that is as joyously inspired as anything the Dead performed in this sublime era with climactic jam following climactic jam. Pigpen is also in rare form here with swaggering versions of "Good Morning, Little School Girl" and "Love Light."

A glimpse into the process of both the original recording and its subsequent digitizing for release a quarter century later is afforded in the liner notes written by Dan Healy and engineer Don Pearson. As an example of the type of detail attended to, they write, "This show was recorded on two consecutive nights. The band's equipment had been taken down at the end of one night and set up again the next. We were able to measure that the equipment was set up approximately one foot different than it was the night before. Because of the magic of today's technology, we are able to appreciate a tape that was unusable before. HOORAY!"

■ "Two Souls in Communion" (McKernan)

One of Pigpen's last original compositions, the gospel-inspired blues was featured during the Dead's 1972 European tour.

5/4/72, Olympia Theater, Paris

- **U./Incredible String Band**
  Elektra 7E 2002, 1970. Produced by Joe Boyd.

One of the most eclectic folk groups of the 1960s, the Incredible String Band began as a duo (Mike Heron and Robin Williamson) before expanding into an electrified folk-rock group. Tom Constanten performed with the group a few times after his departure from the Grateful Dead and is credited with the string arrangement on "Queen of Love" for this double album, which was written as music for a stage show.

- **"Unbroken Chain"** (Lesh/PETERSEN)
  Grateful Dead, *From the Mars Hotel* (1974)
  Joe Gallant and Illuminati, *Code of the West* (1994)

"Unbroken Chain" was one of those Grateful Dead songs most Deadheads never thought the band would perform. And, for virtually their entire run, it was perhaps the most significant unperformed selection from their vast catalogue. Then, an amazing thing happened. On their last spring tour in 1995, the band unexpectedly dusted it off and regularly displayed "Unbroken Chain" right up to and including their last show. The song wore well in concert with a jam reminiscent of Dave Brubeck's famous West Coast jazz piece "Take Five."

Like Lesh's "Box of Rain," "Unbroken Chain" addresses life's ephemeral qualities and is a subtle call to community.

Despite the high marks it has received from Dead-

Phil Lesh, Oakland Coliseum, 12/31/91. *(Robert Minkin)*

heads, Lesh remained displeased with the original release. "I gave up songwriting after *Mars Hotel,* because the results were disappointing. 'Unbroken Chain' could have been really something. Some people think it really is, but I wanted it be what I wanted it to be . . . It just didn't happen, so I decided to concentrate on playing the bass as best I can."

7/9/95, Soldier Field, Chicago

▪ *Unbroken Chain*
(magazine)

The most down-home of the Dead fanzines with a gentle charm all its own, this slim periodical offers set lists, concert reviews, gossip, and environmental columns. Like *Dupree's Diamond News*, *Unbroken Chain* is as much about Deadheads as it is about the Grateful Dead. One of its columns, "Deadheads Behind Bars," features regular exposition of the sizable community of incarcerated Heads, many of whom were targeted by law enforcement. An estimated 2,000 of them, many first-time offenders, are now serving long prison sentences with no hope of parole under mandatory-minimum sentencing laws.

▪ "Uncle John's Band" (Garcia/Hunter)
Grateful Dead, single, *Workingman's Dead* (1970),
   Dick's Picks Volume Five*/'79 (1996), *Dozin' at the
   ***Knick*/'90 (1996)**
Indigo Girls, *Deadicated* (1991)
Jimmy Buffett, *Fruitcakes* (1994)
Joe Higgs, *Fire on the Mountain: Reggae Celebrates the*
   ***Grateful Dead* (1996)**

Composed at the tail end of 1969 with the sense of community in the hippie counterculture quickly disappearing, "Uncle John's Band" is a clarion call to the tribes and a warning about those who seek to undermine them.

Despite the ease with which the song flows, Garcia told Charles Reich and Jann Wenner in 1971 that "'Uncle John's Band' was a *major* effort, as a musical piece. It's one we worked on for a really long time, to get it working right."

In 1991 he told Blair Jackson that the inspiration for the music came from an unlikely source. "I was listening to records of the Bulgarian Women's Choir and also this Greek-Macedonian music—these penny whistlers—and on one of those records there was a song that featured this little turn of melody that was so lovely that I thought, 'Gee, if I could get this into a song it would be so great.' So I stole it . . . Actually I only took a little piece of the melody, so I can't say I plagiarized the whole thing. Of course it became so transmogrified when Bob and Phil added their harmony parts it really was no

longer the part of the song that was special for me. That was the melodic kicker though."

The band made a rough cut of the tune and gave Hunter the tape that he played continuously as he tried writing to it. As he told Blair Jackson in 1991, "I kept hearing the words 'God damn, Uncle John's Band,' and it took a while for that to turn into 'Come hear Uncle John's Band,' and that's one of those little things where the sparkles start coming out of your eyes."

According to Hunter, "Uncle John was a Kansas City drifter who had a flea circus, little critters in band uniforms with instruments you could see under a magnifying glass. They didn't actually play them, but if they had, what a tiny music that tiny music would be. Technically, the song should go 'Come see Uncle John's band,' but I took poetic license with the verb. Also, the riverside is figurative, though he no doubt set up his flea circus wherever he felt he could draw a crowd, and I'm sure a riverside was as good a place to do so as any. He had some pretty hard times starting out, but learned to pick pockets while people tried to get their money's worth out of his gyp of a dead flea circus, which solved his financial worries."

"Uncle John's Band" served the Dead well in several different capacities: as a light acoustic number, a second-set extravaganza and even as encore fodder. In its very earliest incarnations during the fall of 1969, it was even used as a segue instrumental smack-dab in the middle of "Dark Star." Part of its musical charm is derived from the two very different instrumental constructions within the song, which allowed the band to stretch in many jazzy directions.

A message song with a committed but sentimental underbelly, "Uncle John's Band" conveys a pacifist ethos while taking heed of the very real dangers encountered in life. "Ain't no time to hate, barely time to wait," as one of the lyrics reads, sums up a worldview that the Dead and their extended family of Deadheads adopted to heart and practice.

10/4/70, Winterland Arena, San Francisco
11/17/73, Pauley Pavilion, Los Angeles
6/23/74, Jai-Alai Fronton, Miami
5/19/77, Fox Theater, Atlanta
6/8/80, Folsom Field, Boulder, Colorado
10/12/84, Civic Center, Augusta, Maine
9/28/93, Boston Garden, Boston

(© Grateful Dead Merchandising, Inc.)

■ **Upper Limbo**/KEN NORDINE
   Grateful Dead Records GDCD40172, 1993. Produced and
      mixed by Dan Healy.
   "Point of Time," "Kingdom of Noxt," "Emperor of Ice
      Cream," "Charlie Big Bang," "Ripple," "King of the
      Hill," "Speck of Dust," "Akond of Swat,"
      "Alphabet/Numbers," "I Sometimes Think,"
      "Operator," "Sing Me a Poem," "A Kind of Cry
      Blues," "Island"

A nifty follow-up to the Grammy-nominated *Devout Catalyst*, this spoken and musical offering finds word jazzster Ken Nordine still at the top of his game. Displaying his unusually usual charm and whimsy, the poet's sharp verbal constructs appear to rise from the primordial subconscious and fall back on themselves like a row of dominoes toppling over to infinity and back.

A selection of tracks recorded live at Chicago's Vic Theater, *Upper Limbo* is a colder and starker glimpse of Nordine's approach, especially when compared to the sun-porch warmth of *Devout Catalyst*.

Incidentally, Nordine's "Ripple" and "Operator" are not the songs that share identical titles in the Dead's catalogue.

■ **Uptown**/THE NEVILLE BROTHERS
   EMI-America/Rounder ST 17249, 1987.

The Neville Brothers and the Dead began forging an onstage musical relationship in 1986 so it was only a matter of time before the Crescent City brotherhood should invite Garcia to a record session which resulted in "You're the One," a song appearing on this album just before their mainstream ascension. Though a degree of eclecticism is displayed on this outing with the likes of BRANFORD MARSALIS, CARLOS SANTANA, and Keith Richards also contributing, *Uptown* failed to either get the Nevilles a big hit or faithfully recreate the fever pitch of their live shows.

■ **"U.S. Blues"** (Garcia/Hunter)
   Grateful Dead, single, *From the Mars Hotel* (1974), *Steal
      Your Face* (1976), *One from the Vault*/'75 (1991),
      Dick's Picks Volume Six/'83 (1996), *Dick's Picks
      Volume Seven*/'74 (1997)
   Harshed Mellows, *Deadicated* (1991)

This spunky rocker was a concert standard since 1974 and found its place as a riotous encore staple. In its earliest 1973 incarnation, the song was known as "Wave That Flag" and included a slightly different set of lyrics. Garcia and Hunter honed it over the next year, added a chorus and sharpened the words.

As Hunter told Jeff Tamarkin for *Relix* in 1986, "I originally wrote it for the song which became Weir's 'One More Saturday Night.' He took the lyrics and wrote some rock & roll changes, and then he decided to rewrite the lyrics. This was well and fine, but then he asked me if he could use the title 'United States Blues.' I said, 'No, man, that's mine.' So he called his song 'One More Saturday Night' and I took the title 'United States Blues' and rewrote it again. And I gave it to Jerry this time."

"U.S. Blues" is a humorous but ultimately dark litany of the trials and tribulations of late-twentieth-century American citizenship. Basically, expect but accept the worst. The boat is going to rock, your wife will be stolen and your life is not necessarily your own, so proceed with caution.

But, like the Dead's overtly political songs (few though they may be), "U.S. Blues" is tempered by its warmth and seat-of-the-pants optimism.

   6/23/74, Jai-Alai Fronton, Miami
   9/6/85, Red Rocks Amphitheater, Morrison, Colorado
   5/3/91, Cal Expo Amphitheater, Sacramento, California

▪ **"The Valley Road"** (R. B. Hornsby/John Hornsby)
BRUCE HORNSBY and the Range, *Scenes from the Southside* **(1988)**

As a Grateful Dead band member at large, Bruce Hornsby had every right to bring his own material to the concert stage. It was during his most intense relationship with the band, the months following Brent Mydland's death when Vince Welnick had just joined the Dead and they were in musical and emotional transition, that Hornsby trotted out "The Valley Road," a wonderful (and commercially successful) story song written with his brother, at six shows in the last months of 1990.

10/30/90, Wembley Arena, London

▪ *Venu* / Pandit Hariprasad Chaurasia / ZAKIR HUSSAIN
Rykodisc RCD 20113, 1989. Produced by Mickey Hart and Zakir Hussain.
"Rag Ahir Bhairav–alop and jor," "Rag Ahir Bhairav—fast gat in rupak tal, fast gat in tenntal"
Pandit Hariprasad Chaurasia–bansuri (bamboo flute).
Ustad Zakir Hussain–tabla.

Classical-flute master Chaurasia and Zakir Hussain, one of India's prodigal tabla players and a longtime friend of Mickey Hart's, recorded *Venu* at a 1974 concert. It stayed in the can for fifteen years before Hart and Hus-

(Courtesy of Rykodisc)

sain remixed and released it as part of Hart's Rykodisc series. The entire album is devoted to one early morning raga that mixes a well known piece of Indian classical music, "Bhairav," with a folk melody called "Ahir" drawn from the name of a pastoral tribe of India's mountainous areas. The composition's mixture of romantic and devotional moods with a touch of mystery evokes the expectant hush of the predawn hours when romantic thoughts of the night mix with a feeling of reverence for the return of life-giving forces.

Venu is the ancient name for the bamboo flute that is today called bansuri. Compared with a Western flute, with its complex technical design, the bansuri has the appearance of a relatively simple instrument: a piece of bamboo with finger holes and an extra hole near one end, across which the player takes his breath. Yet, in the hands of Chaurasia, this unassuming bamboo tube can express all the subtleties and intricacies for which Indian music is loved.

The bansuri was only recently developed as a classical instrument and its beauty on this recording is a testament to why its contemporary master now stands at the pinnacle of achievement in North Indian classical music.

■ "Victim or the Crime" (Weir/Gerrit Graham)
Grateful Dead, *Built to Last* (1989), *Without a Net* (1990)

Weir's maturity as a composer, lyricist, and musician was evident in many of his contributions to the Grateful Dead during the 1980s. One of these, "Victim or the Crime," is a complex, introspective piece that draws on avant-garde classical modernism while posing universal conundrums. Gerrit Graham, who cowrote the song with Weir, is an actor of some distinction having appeared in two dozen films including everything from *Phantom of Paradise* and *Walker* to *Police Academy 6* and *National Lampoon's Class Reunion.*

Weir gave some insight on the song's lengthy compositional history to Blair Jackson in 1989. "I had originally written it for the Grateful Dead in 1983 or 1984," he said. "I wrote a snatch of the chorus and then I showed it to my friend Gerrit Graham and we talked about it a little bit, and then he fleshed it out lyrically, and I fleshed out the music as well. When I originally brought it around to the band, the way I wrote it and the way it came together, it's a very complicated piece and it didn't get a whole lot of attention because there was a lot of other material we were working on at the time. So I did it a little bit with the Midnites, then did it solo, and then brought it around a few months ago to a warmer response. So at that point we started putting it together as a Grateful Dead song. It's introspective. It's just something that occurred to me. That chorus came to me—words and music—out of the blue, and then Gerrit and I

had at it. . . . There's that reference in the first line to the junkie, but that wasn't meant to be specific in any way. It's a line that had to be there. Hey listen, I tried to replace that like a billion different ways, but nothing would do it. It's a powerful, intact image that gets the point across with a great deal of ease, though not with kid gloves certainly.

"There's a lot of ground to be covered in the issue that we approached in this song. It takes the whole song to describe it. The chorus pretty much states it: 'What fixation feeds this fever / As the full moon pales and climbs / Am I living truth or rank deceiver / Am I the victim or the crime?' It's about self-doubt in the face of all that one amounts to. It points up moral terror and all that sort of stuff. I guess not everybody wants to hear about that, and I can surely understand that.

"Anyway, given the ground we were trying to cover in the tune, there isn't a whole lot of room to lightly suggest the subthemes that are going through it except by saying things plainly. If I were to try to pull that 'patience runs out on the junkie' line and replace it with something that gets to the same point with a little softer punch, it would take me the whole verse just to say that, and I just can't do that in that song.

"I gather some people were touchy about it because we had some problems with junk. But I wasn't pointing a finger at that. I wasn't shying away from it either. I was addressing a subject and that line came up. It was necessary to get to the place where we were going. I know some people stumble on that line and can't hear the rest of the song. In that case it's there as a challenge to either overcome or discount it if they don't want to look into it.

"I listen to a fair amount of twentieth-century music, and actually there's a thematic line that's sort of a suggestion of something I copped from Stravinsky's 'The Rite of Spring.' I'd actually been working on little permutations of it for a long time, and it's popped up in a couple of places. All that sort of stuff that I play on my bass strings . . . root and five, root and flat five, root and six or root and nine—and if I hammer those intervals on a quarter-pulse or sixteenth pulse, that's basically stuff I've lifted from 'The Rite of Spring,' which I consider to be early rock & roll.

"The ascending passage that happens after the second verse of 'Victim or the Crime,' and then again during the instrumental part at the end, is sort of a variation on a passage that Bartok did in 'Music for Strings, Percussion, and Celeste'—in a different key and with different intervals—of something he did in the first movement of that piece. I took a couple of lines and had them ascend in a sort of spiral so that whole feeling of the music there would point the listener up at the moon to set up that image in the chorus.

"The thing hangs together. I'm happy with it. But we'll see how it comes out on the recording and how it seasons as a performance piece for us. It's complicated."

Commenting on the song's difficult playability, Garcia told Jackson in 1988 that "it's a hideous song. It's very angular and unattractive sounding. It's not an accessible song. It doesn't make itself easy to like. It just doesn't sound good, or rather, it sounds strange. And it *is* strange. It has strange steps in it, but that's part of what makes it interesting to play.

"Bob's songs sometimes don't make musical sense in a direct, traditional way. Sometimes he writes songs that are completely out of the mark and you have to really stretch yourself to play in them."

12/6/89, Coliseum Arena, Oakland, California
8/16/91, Shoreline Amphitheater, Mountain View, California
3/21/94, Coliseum, Richfield, Ohio

▪ *Vietnam: A Television History*
(television program)

The PBS producers of this thirteen-part 1983 documentary about the Vietnam War were so impressed by what the Rhythm Devils did for Francis Ford Coppola's *Apocalypse Now* soundtrack that they engaged Mickey Hart, Bill Kreutzmann, bassist Bobby Vega, and others to do the same for them.

▪ *Vintage Dead*
Sunflower Records/MGM SUN-5001, 1971. Produced and engineered by Robert Cohen.

"I KNOW YOU RIDER," "IT HURTS ME TOO," "IT'S ALL OVER NOW, BABY BLUE," "DANCING IN THE STREETS," "IN THE MIDNIGHT HOUR"

Recorded live at the Avalon Ballroom in 1966, this quasi-legit release was the first taste many Deadheads had of the band's primordial stage. Though it might be a little painful for some to listen to in all its sonically flawed inglory, *Vintage Dead* is, nonetheless, a good glimpse of the band from a time that passed all too quickly. "Baby Blue," "Dancin'," and "Midnight Hour" still remain as passionate, if raw, performances.

"Those performances weren't meant to stand around forever," said an annoyed Garcia at the time of their release. "It's just a source of embarrassment."

*See also **Historic Dead** and **The History of the Grateful Dead.***

▪ *Vintage NRPS*/NEW RIDERS OF THE PURPLE SAGE
Relix Records RRLP 2025, 1986.

By February 1971, Garcia was the only original Grateful Dead member remaining with the New Riders, and this recording made at the Capitol Theater in Port Chester, New York, captures this incarnation of the group at a peak.

▪ "Viola Lee Blues" (Noah Lewis)
CANNON'S JUG STOMPERS, *The Complete Recordings*/'30 (1995)
GUS CANNON, *Complete Recorded Works, Vol. 1 (1927–29)* (1995)
Grateful Dead, *Grateful Dead* (1967)
JIM KWESKIN JUG BAND, *See Reverse Side for Title* (1966)
The Purple Gang, *Strikes* (1968)
Warm Dust, *Peace for Our Time* (1970)
Solar Circus, *Twilight Dance* (1992)
Ry Cooder, *Music by Ry Cooder* (1995)

The Dead probably copped this classic prison blues by Noah Lewis of Cannon's Jug Stompers from the Jim Kewskin Jug Band, who recorded it on their 1966 album *See Reverse Side for Title*. Cannon's Jug Stompers recorded "Viola Lee Blues" a couple of different times in styles similar to the Dead's. Geoff Muldaur of the Kweskin band found the tune on old 78s and it was he who introduced his leader to it. Garcia and Weir have often pointed to the Kweskin's jug band as being a formidable influence on their own jug band's endeavors. But the strains of the song stretch back before even Gus Cannon's group gained acclaim with "Some Got Six Months," a plaint from Louisiana's notorious Angola state-prison farm.

On this "lost classic" from the Dead's 1967 debut album, Garcia employed Freddie King guitar stylings while leading the band on a frenetic "surf" version of the song. Like their many concert versions between 1966 and 1970 of "Viola Lee Blues," the tempo of the jam increases with each measure, always on the verge of spiraling out of control. And, on more than one occasion, it did.

3/18/67, Winterland Arena, San Francisco

(Courtesy of CBS Records)

4/6/69, Avalon Ballroom, San Francisco

4/21/69, The Ark, Boston

5/2/70, Harpur College, Binghamton, New York

- *Virgin Beauty*/ORNETTE COLEMAN and Prime Time
  CBS-Portrait OR 44391, 1988.
  "Bourgeois Boogie," "Happy Hour," "Virgin Beauty,"
    "Healing the Feeling," "Honeymooners,"
    "Chanting," "Spelling the Alphabet," "Unknown
    Artist," "3 Wishes," "Singing in the Shower,"
    "Desert Players"

Adding some Django Reinhardt-on-Pluto-like phrases to "Desert Players," "Singing in the Shower," and "3 Wishes," Garcia is primarily a third guitar voice in Coleman's improvising ensemble on this, one of Prime Time's best releases.

With a more focused and conservative approach than their previous albums, the nature of Prime Time seemed to be changing here. Some of the complex rhythmic excitement of their earlier efforts was replaced by a no less infectious pop-music spirit, and Coleman's playing is for the most part especially lighthearted. "Bourgeois Boogie" hints at Charles Mingus's "Boogie Stop Shuffle"; the bubbly "Three Wishes" has a Middle Eastern theme over an exotic rhythm pattern—"Blues for Allah" as filtered through Coleman's sensibility; "Spelling the Alphabet" and "Happy Hour" offer clever Coleman—the

latter a fast country music piece. Two tracks, "Virgin Beauty" and "Chanting," are ballads played by Coleman over darker-colored variations of traditional-sounding folk harmonies. Loveliest of these performances is the ballad "Unknown Artist," which begins with Coleman's alto, alone, in a sorrowing theme.

Virgin Beauty is the most varied of Prime Time's albums, and perhaps for that reason (and Garcia's "special guest" appearance), it sold more copies in the first year of its release than any of Coleman's other recordings.

The experience was, according to Garcia, musically positive. As he told David Gans in 1988, "I learned so much and he was so graceful about letting me learn it. To work with him was a tremendous honor."

- **"Visions of Johanna"** (BOB DYLAN)
  Bob Dylan, *Blonde on Blonde* (1966), *Biograph/'66* (1985)
  Peter Laughner, *Take the Guitar Player for a Ride* (1994)

One of music's most otherworldly songs, "Visions of Johanna" is one of Bob Dylan's masterpieces. At the time of its composition, Dylan had begun writing longer songs, stringing together images and characters for verse after verse. The rarely performed gem has stunned audiences with an intricacy that remains intangible. But the writer never missed a beat on stage. Said Dylan, "I could remember a song without writing it down because it was so visual. I still sing that song every once in a while. It still stands up now as it did then, maybe even more in some kind of weird way."

With Garcia handling the vocals, the Dead had a short, two-concert go at "Visions of Johanna" in 1986 before returning to it with a flurry of excellent interpretations in 1995.

4/22/86, Berkeley Community Theater, Berkeley, California

4/7/95, Tampa Stadium, Tampa, Florida

- *Voices of the Rainforest*
  Rykodisc RCD 10173, 1991. Field recordings and
      research by Steven Feld. Produced by Mickey Hart.
  "From Morning Night to Real Morning," "Making
      Sago," "Cutting Trees," "Clearing the Brush,"
      "Bamboo Jew's Harp," "Relaxing by the Creek
      (Parts 1 & 2)," "From Afternoon to Afternoon

(Courtesy of Rykodisc)

**Darkening," "Evening Rainstorm," "Drumming,"
"Song Ceremony," "From Night to Inside Night"**

A soundscape of a day in the life of the Kaluli people of the Papua New Guinea rain forest. The voices here include the never-ending rhythms of birds, crickets, and frogs; the pulsing of rain, creeks, and streams; as well as the sounds of the Kaluli singing along and beating out their own rhythms with primal percussion.

Unlike most of the other releases in Hart's Rykodisc World series, *Voices of the Rainforest* was recorded by Steven Feld, director of the Center for Folklore and Ethnomusicology at the University of Texas in Austin. His research on Bosavi musical rituals and ecology is reported in *Sound and Sentiment: Birds, Weeping, Poetics and Song in Kaluli Expression* published by the University of Pennsylvania Press. His liner notes, rendered in the form of a long letter to Hart, are an invaluable overview of the music, culture and ecology of New Guinea.

■ ***Volunteers*** / **Jefferson Airplane**
RCA Victor LSP-4328, 1969.

Garcia contributed some straightforward pedal steel on "The Farm" to the Airplane's most stridently political album. A somewhat dated statement, the album is still a joyous and rewarding outing with "We Can Be Together" remaining a compelling anthem.

▪ "Wabash Cannonball" (A. P. Carter)

The Carter Family, *When the Roses Bloom in Dixieland,*
1929–1930 **(1995)**
Lonnie Donnegan, *Lonnie Donnegan Showcase*
(1956)
Johnny Cash, *Happiness Is You* **(1966)**
Nitty Gritty Dirt Band, *Will the Circle Be Unbroken*
(1972)
Doc Watson, *Memories* **(1975),** *The Vanguard Years*
(1995)
Arlo Guthrie, *Precious Friend* **(1982)**
U. Utah Phillips, *Good Though* **(1982)**
Roy Acuff, *Opry Legends* **(1991)**
Boots Randolph, *Live* **(1992)**
Townes Van Zandt, *Roadsongs* **(1992)**

The Carter Family *(Archive Photos/Frank Driggs Collection)*

Bobby Weir and company only covered this famous country music standard about a train at one 1969 Bobby Ace and the Cards from the Bottom of Deck show, but it was written by A.P. Carter, the patriarch of *the* most influential group in country music history: The Carter Family. With their unornamented, nasal harmonies born and bred in rural church music the Carter family are about as close as we are likely to get to a pure, white Appalachian sound.

Alvin Pleasant Carter was born in 1891 in Maces Spring, Virginia. As he grew up, married Sara Dougherty, and raised his daughters, A. P. naturally led them to his greatest love: music. From the 1920s through A.P.'s death in 1960, the Carter family (which also included sister-in-law Maybelle Carter) switched the emphasis of country music from hillbilly standards to vocals, made scores of their songs part of the genre's canon, and institutionalized a style of guitar-playing ("Carter-picking") that became the dominant approach to the instrument for decades. For the better part of a century, the Carters'

"Wildwood Flower" was the first song thousands of young country heads learned to play on the guitar.

The Carters' initial and greatest success came when they recorded for RCA Victor between 1927 and 1933. They were contemporaries of and collaborators with Jimmie Rodgers, with whom they were discovered. Although they did make a few comedy sketch records with Rodgers, the Carters were almost strait-laced in their approach to their music and, while Rodgers showed strong influences of jazz and blues, the Carters sang as if no African-Americans ever lived in the South. For some, this is excruciatingly bland; for many others, however, the group's beauty lies in the simplicity of their four-square approach. These down-home harmonies, which made them sound more like the folks next door than anything modern ears might associate with art and/or superstardom, were the models for hundreds of other family bands and helped change the shape of country music from a rural entertainment to a popular mainstream form.

A. P. Carter was also one of the region's first and most renowned musical historians, collecting hundreds of British-Appalachian folk songs and, in arranging these for recording, both enhanced the pure beauty of these "facts-of-life tunes" while at the same time saving them for future generations. The more than 300 sides they recorded became known as "Carter" songs, even though they were collected around their Virginia and Tennessee homes, and included "Worried Man Blues," "Will the Circle Be Unbroken," "Wildwood Flower," and "Wabash Cannonball."

The original Carter family disbanded in 1943, but their tradition was carried into a third generation by vocalist Carlene Carter, June's daughter by her first marriage to country singer Carl Smith, and, more notably, Rosanne Cash, the progeny of June's union with Johnny Cash.

6/11/69, California Hall, San Francisco

- ### *Wake of the Flood*
  Grateful Dead Records GD 01, 1973; (GDCD 4002, 1990). Produced by Grateful Dead.
  "Mississippi Half-Step Uptown Toodleoo," "Let Me Sing Your Blues Away," "Row Jimmy," "Stella Blue," "Here Comes Sunshine," "Eyes of the World," "Weather Report Suite: 'Prelude'›'Part 1'›'Let It Grow'"
  Bill Atwood–trumpet. Vassar Clements–violin. Joe

(© Grateful Dead Merchandising, Inc.)

Ellis–trumpet. Martin Fierro–alto, tenor, sax. Sarah Fulcher–vocals. Mathew Kelly–harmonica. Frank Morin–tenor sax. Pat O'Hara–trombone. Doug Sahm–twelve-string guitar. Benny Velarde–timbales.

Wake of the Flood is easily the Dead's most underrated album. Though recorded in the studio, the music has the spark and fluidity of a live show. Some of the beautiful songs here, "Here Comes Sunshine," "Eyes of the World," and "Weather Report Suite," became primal hippie anthems. The venture also marked the Dead's first major attempt at self-production.

- ### **"Wake Up Little Susie"** (Felice Bryant/Boudleaux Bryant)
  Grateful Dead, *Bear's Choice/'70* (1973)
  The Everly Brothers, single (1957), *The Very Best of the Everly Brothers* (1965), *The Everly Brothers Show* (1970)
  Simon and Garfunkel, *The Concert in Central Park* (1982)

The Everly Brothers had a number one hit with "Wake Up Little Susie" in 1957 but it was written by Felice and Boudleaux Bryant, the gifted husband and wife team who also gave the Everlys "BYE BYE LOVE," "ALL I HAVE TO DO IS DREAM," and "Poor Jenny."

A humorous 1950s period piece, "Wake Up Little

Susie" concerns a young couple who fall asleep at a drive-in movie and miss their curfew.

Weir sang the song with the Dead about a dozen times during their acoustic sets in 1970.

7/12/70, Fillmore East, New York

▪ "Walk Down the Street"

A song of undetermined origin, "Walk Down the Street" was performed semi-acoustically at one 1970 show.

4/18/70, Family Dog, San Francisco

▪ "Walkin' Blues" (Robert Johnson)

Robert Johnson, *The Complete Recordings/'36* (1990)

Grateful Dead, *Without a Net* (1990), *Dozin' at the Knick/'90* (1996)

Son House, *Library of Congress Recordings* (1942)

Muddy Waters, *Chess Masters* (1954), *The Real Folk Blues* (1966)

Paul Butterfield Blues Band, *East-West* (1966), *Live* (1971), *Golden Butter* (1972)

The Groundhogs, *Scratching the Surface* (1968), *Document Series Presents . . . the Groundhogs* (1992)

John Kay, *Forgotten Songs and Unsung Heroes* (1972)

Jorma Kaukonen, *Too Hot to Handle* (1985), *Magic* (1985)

Robert Johnson, the proverbial "King of the Delta Blues," recorded and is generally credited as the author of this cornerstone American composition. While "Walking Blues" may show its antecedents in its opening line ("Woke up this morning . . ."), *the* ultimate blues archetypal vocal hook, Johnson's extant rendition is as chilling as anything he left us.

All the mystique of the blues gurgling in the Mississippi Delta seems wrapped up in the smoky cipher and tantalizing myth that is Robert Johnson. It has been said that if Robert Johnson had never been born, the blues would have invented him. But though he is perhaps the most celebrated figure in blues history, very little is known about him. Yet his story is the archetype of blues life.

Despite some recent Johnson scholarship (Peter Guralnick's *Searching for Robert Johnson* and *Love in Vain: A Vision of Robert Johnson* are *must* reads), the date of the artist's birth is still debated, with May 8, 1911, being the consensus choice. Born out of wedlock in Hazlehurst, Mississippi, to Julia Dodds and Noah Johnson, young Robert was sent to live with his biological father, Charles Dodds, in Memphis, Tennessee, when he was three or four. But, because his father had taken a new name, Charles Spencer, the young boy was known alternately as Robert Dodds and Robert Spencer, eventually assuming the surname of his stepfather. No doubt this shifting of identity and rootless youth contributed to his later, itinerant proclivities.

First absorbing the rudiments of guitar by watching an older brother, Johnson went on to study the technique of some of the region's greats at Delta picnics and parties, including the likes of Charley Patton, Son House, and the almost equally mysterious Willie Brown.

The trail goes a little cold after that. It is known that by 1930 he had married and lost his wife (and baby) in childbirth in an event thought to presage his decision to become a bluesman, wandering around the Delta as the troubadours of yore traveled through medieval Europe. Upon re-encountering Son House and Willie Brown, Johnson shocked his friends with what he could play on guitar. In startlingly short order, Johnson had turned into a blues master, igniting the legend that he had made a deal with the Devil to acquire his impossible skills.

Even a casual listen to Johnson is still something of a shock to the uninitiated. His achingly eerie voice is difficult enough to confront, not unlike hearing the hardest of hard luck stories on a subway train at rush hour. But the guitar playing is the clincher, at times sounding like three pairs of hands working the demon box. Is it possible that one man could play those parts without help from some dark force?

These were Johnson's halcyon days. An inveterate skirt-chaser and drinker, he performed mostly at juke joints, levee camps, and street corners with a slide and finger-picking style that drew from but far surpassed his peers with an amazingly sophisticated finesse. Remembered as a human jukebox who could play almost anything after a single listen, Johnson could blend his guitar, voice, and lyrics into one inseparable being. But Johnson is also recalled as a tormented, unstable, and quarrelsome roustabout always seeking affection—often from the wives of others.

Though he occasionally moved about with a partner, Johnson was a loner who, as his reputation grew, visited St. Louis, Chicago, Detroit, and New York.

For someone whose imprint on the music was so lasting, that Johnson's reputation was etched for the ages at but two recording sessions makes his achievement all the more remarkable. The first of these took place in November 1936 in a San Antonio, Texas, hotel room where, over the course of three days, he cut sixteen sides for the American Record Company, including "I Believe I'll Dust My Broom," "Sweet Home Chicago," "Terraplane Blues," "Cross Road Blues," "Come on in My Kitchen," and "Walkin' Blues"—all celebrated classics. Half a year later he was at it again, this time in a Dallas warehouse in a session that preserved additional Johnson gold: "Traveling Riverside Blues," "Love in Vain," "Hell Hound on My Trail," and "Me and the Devil Blues."

Resuming his wandering ways soon after the last session, Johnson wound up in Greenwood, Mississippi, where he was poisoned with strychnine-laced whiskey after a short dalliance with the wife of a local juke-joint owner during a Saturday-night gig with Sonny Boy Williamson. By August 16, 1938, three painful days later, the King of the Delta Blues had faded into the gloam of the mystery whence he came and of which he sang.

A half century after his death, Johnson still possessed the power and magnetism to play a major role in the blues revival of the early 1990s. *The Complete Recordings of Robert Johnson,* combining all the previously haphazardly released material (forty-one tracks in all) from his two sessions, hit the market in 1990 with polish but modest commercial expectations. Half a million units and a Grammy later, Robert Johnson and his blues were back to stay.

The Dead started performing "Walkin' Blues" with a vengeance in 1987 but didn't even attempt to match Johnson's unduplicatable finger work on the fretboard (who but Beelzebub could?) opting for a fitting swamp-blues arrangement of the classic. What is extraordinary about the band's interpretation of "Walkin' Blues" is Bob Weir's spooky re-creation of Johnson's mercurial vocalese, almost as if the rhythm guitarist were conducting a rock séance in public, channeling the Delta cipher with some well-aimed hoodoo.

7/15/88, Greek Theatre, Berkeley, California
1/24/93, Oakland Coliseum, Oakland, California

■ "Walking the Dog" (Rufus Thomas)
Rufus Thomas, *Walking the Dog* (1963), *Doing the Push and Pull Live at P.J.'s* (1971), *Chronicle* (1986)
The Rolling Stones, *England's Newest Hit Makers* (1964)

The Everly Brothers, *Beat and Soul* (1965)
Mitch Ryder, *Breakout . . . !* (1966)
The Flamin' Groovies, *Flamingo* (1970), *Slow Death* (1972)
Aerosmith, *Aerosmith* (1973), *Pandora's Box* (1991)
Spirit, *Spirit of '76* (1975)
The Troggs, *Live at Max's Kansas City* (1981), *Au* (1990)
John Cale, *Sabotage Live* (1979)
Jimi Hendrix, *Last Night/'66* (1981)

When Rufus Thomas, the self-proclaimed "world's oldest teenager," had his first and only big hit with "Walking the Dog" in 1963, he was already pushing fifty!

From the minstrelsy to rap, Thomas's career is about as diverse and unusual as it can get on the American stage. Born March 28, 1917, in Collierville, Texas, Thomas began his career in 1935 as a comedian with the Rabbit Foot Minstrels and by the early 1940s was a DJ on WDIA, a black-owned station in Memphis known as "Mother Station to the Negroes," where B. B. King also had a show. Although the show was beamed at black audiences, Thomas made a considerable impact on white listeners as well. Steve Cropper, who later made his mark on the Stax sound, credited Thomas's show and the wide variety of black music he played on it as influencing his career choice. Remarkably, Thomas maintained the radio show through the many peaks and valleys of his career until the mid-1970s.

By 1952 he was singing at local R&B shows as well as on a few small label records, including the then-still-too-new-to-be-known Sun Records, which made its name issuing Elvis Presley's discs a year later. While these stabs at artistic opportunity may have been personally fulfilling, they did not result in professional success.

It wasn't until a new record firm was established in the old Capitol Theater in 1960 by Jim Stewart, a sometime accountant and country fiddler, and his sister, Mrs. Estelle Axton, that Thomas's fortunes were forever changed. The siblings had chosen the theater because it met their needs as a recording studio though, as Stewart later noted, neither had any familiarity with R&B: "We just happened to move into a colored neighborhood."

The city's soul musicians, some mistakenly thinking that because of the theater's name they were auditioning for Capitol Records, began dropping by looking for work. The die was cast when Rufus and his seventeen-year-old daughter Carla showed up and sang "'Cause I Love," a duet that caught Stewart's fancy and released it on Satellite, the name of the record label at the time. It was a hit, selling about twenty thousand records in the region and paving the way for their first taste of national glory, Carla Thomas's "Gee Whiz."

"Walking the Dog" was Rufus' first Top 10 hit on both the R&B and pop charts, establishing him as a star and landing him billings as a featured attraction on the soul and prestige nightclub circuit.

For the next decade, Thomas charted many soul and R&B singles. Nineteen seventy-one was a particularly big year, with such hits as "Do the Push and Pull," "The World Is Round," and "Breakdown, Part 1" bringing him to the peak of his renown.

"Walking the Dog" actually had its start with a previous Thomas release, "The Dog," which was a song tailored at capitalizing on the popular dance of the time that shared the same name. Rufus wrote "The Dog" on the bandstand while playing a dance. "There was a tall beautiful black girl, had a long waist line, and she was wearing a black leather skirt, very alluring, sleek and slick," he said. "She came right in front of the bandstand and started doing the dog. We were playing a rhythm at the time. There is nothing in my head about this song. When she started doing it I was just telling her to do the dog. I changed the rhythm pattern. I was putting it together as we went along. I couldn't think of but three dogs, bull dog, bird dog, hound dog. Then I got to the part where just do any kind of dog. We had three choruses and then just played the rhythm. I told everyone, 'You all just start barking like a dog' and, if you notice, on the records you hear the barking on one chorus and I was the lead dog with that bark up there."

"Walking the Dog" was followed by two more dog records in 1964, "Can Your Monkey Do the Dog" and "Somebody Stole My Dog." While the dog craze finally came to an end in 1966 with the Mar-keys' "Philly Dog," Thomas caught the funk wave in the early 1970s with such poultry-specific hits as "Do the Funky Chicken," which made the soul Top 10.

After the collapse of Stax/Volt, Thomas pretty much dropped off the map until the 1986 release of *Rappin' Rufus*, which showed him to be equally at home with a new generation's version of verbal showmanship.

With Weir handling the randy vocals, only seven Grateful Dead versions of "Walking the Dog" have been collected by the tapehead community, but they show the song used in a variety of settings: acoustic novelty in 1970, electric knockoff in 1970 and 1971, surprise show opener in 1984 and 1985, and as an encore in 1985.

11/9/70, Action House, Island Park, New York

11/25/85, Henry J. Kaiser Convention Center, Oakland, California

▪ "Walk in the Sunshine" (Weir/Barlow)
Bob Weir, *Ace* (1972)

"Walk in the Sunshine" was the one song from Weir's otherwise winning debut project that never saw the light of Grateful Dead performance.

Barlow had a few words on the album's lone dud: "There's a song on *Ace* called 'Walk in the Sunshine,' which neither Weir nor I is terribly fond of. He didn't like the lyric, and time was running out on the album. My father had just died and I had to go home, so Weir's old lady set me up with a bottle of whiskey and some other catalysts for one last twenty-four-hour plunge at trying to come up with something new. But nothing would come. All I wanted was for it to be so ugly that 'Walk in the Sunshine' would look good by comparison. It worked."

In 1986, Barlow told David Gans about writing "Walk in the Sunshine." "That's the worst song we ever wrote . . . at the time we were under duress, we were already in the studio, and Weir and I had been battling over this song, and my father died the night before that was written, and I had to write the song and get back, for obvious reasons. And I was feeling especially burnt out, and I wrote the first thing that came into my head, and it was *just terrible*. It was straight out of a greeting card. Sort of a hip cosmic greeting card. . . . It was like [a] fourteen-year-old's very earnest poetry. But it was all I could come up with. I was just shell-shocked. So I figured that the only way I could get Weir to do it so I could get out of the way, whatever the consequences, was to write something that was really twisted and perverse that would make the sunny sentiments of 'Walk in the Sunshine' seem much more palatable, and then he'd agree to do it, and then I could leave.

"So I wrote a song called 'The Dwarf' . . . based on the Pär Lagerkvist novel about a very twisted little man able to manipulate everybody in power around him. It's kind of a great song, now I see, but I figured if I gave Weir this twisted song it would work. "The pity was that I didn't throw away 'Walk in the Sunshine' and just give him 'The Dwarf' and let the devil take the hindmost."

▪ "Wang Dang Doodle" (WILLIE DIXON)

Willie Dixon, *Willie Dixon: 20 Greatest Blues Greats* (1987)
Howlin' Wolf, *The Genuine Article: The Best of Howlin' Wolf* (1960), *Poor Boy* (1965), *London Howlin' Wolf Sessions* (1971), *Collection: 20 Blues Greats* (1985)
Love Sculpture, *Blues Helping* (1969)
Koko Taylor, *South Side Lady* (1973), *What It Takes: The Chess Years* (1977)
Savoy Brown, *Greatest (Live) Hits* (1981)
PJ Harvey, single (1993)

Willie Dixon wrote "Wang Dang Doodle" for Howlin' Wolf when he first met the master bluesman in the early 1950s, although Wolf didn't record the tune until several years hence. But as Dixon recalled in his autobiography *I Am the Blues*, "I've been real lucky about writing people songs but a lot of times, if I picked the song, the guys didn't want the song for himself. Muddy didn't want the ones I was givin' him and Howlin' Wolf didn't want the ones I was givin' him. The one Wolf hated most of all was 'Wang Dang Doodle.' He hated that 'Tell Automatic Slim and Razor-Toting Jim.' He'd say, 'Man, that's too old-timey, sound like some old levee-camp number.'

"'Wang Dang Doodle' meant a good time, especially if a guy came in from the South. A wang dang doodle meant having a ball and a lot of dancing, they called it a rocking style so that's what it meant to wang dang doodle. There used to be a place up north of Vicksburg called the Rock House. It was built out of stone but it had a weak floor. On Saturday nights, people would crowd in there and when they would all get to dancin', the floor would rock up and down. Everybody was saying, 'Boy, the Rock House, I'm gonna pitch a wang dang up there.' After I left Vicksburg, I heard the kids were there dancing one day and the floor fell in."

Dixon elaborated on the catalogue of bizarre names recounted in the song when he told Blair Jackson, "I knew guys who had every name in that song. Automatic Slim was a guy who was supposedly great with a pistol. Razor Totin' Jim and a lot of people who carried razors. You see, years ago in the South, in Mississippi where I grew up, people had nicknames according to what they were involved in. People used nicknames and slang to talk around other people mainly. The blues was able to talk around, sing around the message they didn't want other folks understandin'. These languages were all to themselves. From the beginning, there were songs they didn't want the boss to know about what was really goin' on. The blues has always given a message to the people who understood the blues, and the people that don't have to make up what they think we meant."

Indeed, "Wang Dang Doodle" contains a covert quality as the narrator puts the word out to the likes of Washboard Sam, Abyssinia Ned, Pistol Totin' Pete, and Butcher Knife Totin' Annie that a wang dang doodle is about to be pitched all night long.

Weir started singing "Wang Dang Doodle" with the Dead in 1983 and the band performed it semi-regularly after that, primarily as Bobby's early-show blues cover.

9/11/83, Sante Fe Downs, Sante Fe, New Mexico
6/6/91, Deer Creek Music Center, Noblesville, Indiana

▪ *Wanted Dead or Alive* / DAVID BROMBERG
Columbia PC 32717, 1974.

A musician's musician, David Bromberg (born September 19, 1945, Philadelphia, Pennsylvania) has made as much of a career of being a sideman to the likes of Bob Dylan and Jerry Jeff Walker as he has fronting his own bands. Like the Dead, he brings equal passion to the blues, bluegrass, folk, country, and rock while drawing on a diverse range of influences as reflected in his recordings and performances, which can be a musical education.

As its title suggests, *Wanted Dead or Alive* features several members of the Dead (Garcia, Lesh, Kreutzmann, and Keith Godchaux) on the first side of the album, which contains some of Bromberg's strongest and most enduring material.

▪ The Warlocks

When Garcia and company exchanged their jug band instruments for electric axes in April 1965, it was as the Warlocks that they took part in the Acid Tests and made a name for themselves with local Bay Area gigs. It was at Pigpen's instigation that Garcia recruited Bob Weir, Bill Kreutzmann, and bassist Dana Morgan Jr., who was soon replaced by Phil Lesh even though Lesh had never played bass before.

Performing a few originals, the Warlocks began covering songs that would remain as part of the Dead's repertoire for the long haul: "King Bee," "LITTLE RED

ROOSTER," "PROMISED LAND," "IT'S ALL OVER NOW, BABY BLUE," and "JOHNNY B. GOODE."

After performing at Menlo College and Magoo's Pizza Parlor in Menlo Park, the Warlocks began dropping acid for a standard five-set-per-night engagement at Belmont, California's, In Room, where they began to see the possibilities of taking their music in a direction inspired by the chemically and artistically induced visions of the moment.

When Lesh claimed to have seen a record by another group with the name Warlocks, the band began searching for another name, settling on Grateful Dead after a chance flip of the pages through a dictionary at Lesh's house.

▪ "Warriors of the Sun" (JOAN BAEZ)
Joan Baez, *Speaking Of Dreams* (1989)

The Dead performed "Warriors of the Sun," a later Joan Baez rallying call, with its author during a 1981 acoustic set benefiting Nuclear Disarmament groups.

12/12/81, Fiesta Hall, San Mateo, California

▪ *Watchfire*/Pete Sears
Redwood RRCD 8806, 1988.

Garcia, Hart, and several other Grateful Dead family favorites appear on this ecologically correct album from the Jefferson Starship's former keyboardist Pete Sears. Garcia's three contributions ("Nothing Personal," "One More Innocent," and "Let the Dove Fly Free") do little to improve this earnest but saccharine release that proselytizes more than it pleases.

Regarding Garcia's involvement on the oh-so-PC album, Sears told Blair Jackson in 1988, "I think Garcia is reluctant to do political things a lot of the time . . . but we've been friends for a long time now. In fact, before I joined Starship we did a KSAN live jam together. And we worked on one of Bob Hunter's albums together. So he agreed to be on *Watchfire*, and it turns out he really got into it—he listened to the songs and he seemed to like the approach. These are more global issues."

Sears did practice what he preached, as a certain portion of the album's royalties ended up in the coffers of some very worthy causes, including the Environmental Defense Fund, Greenpeace, the World Wildlife Fund, and the Christic Institute.

▪ "Watching the River Flow" (BOB DYLAN)
Bob Dylan, *Bob Dylan's Greatest Hits, Vol. II* (1971)
Joe Cocker, *Luxury You Can Afford* (1978)

With a jaunty melody that perfectly suits this song about a man changing from a participant to an observer, "Watching the River Flow" popped up at two of the West Coast Dylan/Dead shows as a semi-successful surprise.

7/26/87, Stadium, Anaheim, California

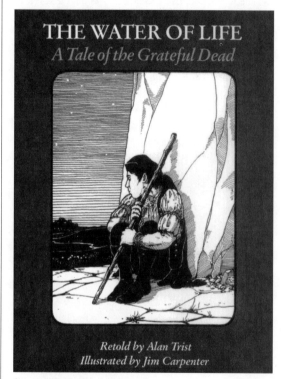

(Courtesy of Hulugos'i Communications)

▪ *The Water of Life: A Tale of the Grateful Dead* (book)/told by Alan Trist
Illustrations by Jim Carpenter.
Hulugos'i, 1989.

Merging the visible with the invisible is a profound and ancient folklore theme and Alan Trist's retelling of *The Water of Life*, an old hero tale in the Grateful Dead story cycle as well as the "Fisher King" and the "Holy Grail" motifs, is true to its publisher's claim of "A Children's Book for All Ages."

Trist worked at the upper levels of the Grateful Dead collective overseeing aspects of their in-house publishing concerns for many years after receiving his master's in social anthropology from Cambridge and it is apparent that the reconstruction of the fable came naturally to him. Carpenter's illustrations, which reinforce the mythic themes lacing the story, rate as high as Trist's reinterpretive skills with line drawings that simultaneously invoke Japanese prints, German woodcuts, and medieval illuminated manuscripts.

▪ "Wave That Flag" (Garcia/Hunter)
See "U.S. Blues"

▪ "Wave to the Wind" (Lesh/Hunter)

Every now and then the Dead broke out an original tune that refused to catch on with their audience. "Money, Money" was such a song in the 1970s, "Day Job" fit the bill in the 1980s, and "Wave to the Wind" was regarded as the clunker for the 1990s. Ironic, too, because the song's composer, Phil Lesh, had previously produced some of the group's most cherished nuggets.

Deadheads immediately disparaged "Wave to the Wind" as the "Love Boat Song" in reference to the theme song of the bizarrely schmaltzy television program of the early 1980s with which it shared a similar melody. Indeed, the song's chord changes are saccharine and the lyrics downright juvenile.

Some revisionist Deadheads, however, suggested that if the song was looked at as a children's song in the grand tradition of Woody Guthrie or Burl Ives then its goofy simplicity may be more palatable. Phil Lesh and Robert Hunter both had young children when the song was composed, and it is natural to assume that it could have been meant to please their youngsters. After all, the image of waving to the wind is exuberantly naive and environomorphically touching. Lesh himself once appeared on stage dressed as Barney the purple dinosaur of children's television fame, to entertain his youngsters, who were in attendance that evening, and blow an open mind or two. So considering this, it could be suggested that the song may have been better suited to their respective families' hearths than a larger venue.

After its initial performance in 1992, the Dead revamped and toughened the original arrangement with only slightly better results. As Hunter told Blair Jackson in 1993, "It's a tune that is very complex and will take a lot of dusting off and a lot of work. Regardless of what you might have heard on tapes or onstage, there's an excellent song there. It's one of those, though, that will take a lot of time for everybody to get in sync and bring it out, for it to be what it can be."

5/27/93, Cal Expo Amphitheater, Sacramento, California

▪ "Way to Go Home" (Welnick/Hunter/Bralove)

The first song keyboardist Vince Welnick composed for the Grateful Dead was a crowd pleaser from the get go. Hunter's bedraggled road lyrics captured the spirit of band and audience alike, especially those who toured extensively, with the sense of isolation and misunderstanding many counterculture refugees have experienced.

Welnick and Bralove wrote the music and melody on tour in a hotel room and then indicated with scat vocalization of "doo de doos" where they wanted Hunter's lyrics and phrasing to go. When the tape arrived in his mailbox, Hunter added his own oral audio spin.

8/21/93, Autzen Stadium, Eugene, Oregon

▪ "Weather Report Suite: Part One"
(Weir/Eric Andersen)
Grateful Dead, *Wake of the Flood* (1973), *Dick's Picks Volume One/'73* (1993), *Dick's Picks Volume Seven/'74* (1997)

A sorely missed ode with sweet harmonies and an earthy, naturalistic bent, this sweeping piece of Thoreauesque folk-rock was cowritten with ERIC ANDERSEN and performed as the centerpiece of the three-part suite it was composed with at about fifty shows in 1973 and 1974 before its premature shelving.

With the rerelease of *Ghosts Upon the Road*, the distinguished career of Eric Andersen once again brought his timeless quality to the public. Andersen is one of America's finest lyric-poet songwriters. With a career spanning almost thirty years, he stands with his contemporaries BOB DYLAN and Joni Mitchell as one of the few remaining pioneers of the 1960s singer/songwriter movement continuing to do important work. He was born February 14, 1943, in Pittsburgh, Pennsylvania, and grew up in Amherst, New York. After two years of college, he took his guitar and headed west in search of his Beat

Eric Andersen. *(Courtesy of Plump Records)*

and Jonal Fjeld, a Norwegian artist, resulted in the Rykodisc album *Danko Fjeld Andersen.* Their second trio album was released in Norway in 1995.

> **9/11/73, College of William and Mary, Williamsburg, Virginia**
> **11/10/73, Winterland Arena, San Francisco**
> **3/23/74, Cow Palace, Daly City, California**
> **7/19/74, Selland Arena, Fresno, California**

See also **"Let It Grow"**

- ## "Weather Report Suite: Prelude" (Weir)
  Grateful Dead, *Wake of the Flood* **(1973),** *Dick's Picks Volume One/'73* **(1993),** *Dick's Picks Volume Seven/'74* **(1997)**

Bob Weir's Bach-meets-flamenco–styled intro to "Weather Report Suite" never made it past the fifty-odd airings it was given in 1973 and 1974.

> **9/11/73, College of William and Mary, Williamsburg, Virginia**
> **10/25/73, Dane County Coliseum, Madison, Wisconsin**
> **11/25/73, Feyline Field, Tempe, Arizona**

See also **"Let It Grow"**

- ## "We Can Run, but We Can't Hide" (Mydland/Barlow)
  Grateful Dead, *Built to Last* **(1989)**

The Dead's emergence into the realm of environmental activism in the late 1980s was pointedly marked by "We Can Run, but We Can't Hide," a sober warning on the dangers of fouling the ecosystem's delicate balance. The song was displayed almost two dozen times in the eighteen months preceding Brent Mydland's death in 1990. Despite its good intentions, the song never caught on with many who, though in agreement with the message, found it an overbearing tract.

> **2/11/89, Great Western Forum, Los Angeles**
> **4/2/89, Pittsburgh Civic Arena, Pittsburgh**

- ## "The Weight" (J. R. Robertson)
  THE BAND, *Music from Big Pink* **(1968),** *Rock of Ages* **(1972),** *The Last Waltz/'76* **(1978),** *The Collection* **(1992)**
  The Staples Singers, *Soul Folk in Action* **(1968)**
  Michael Bloomfield and Al Kooper, *Live Adventures* **(1969)**
  King Curtis, *Instant Groove* **(1969)**

Generation literary heroes. In the early 1960s, Andersen was discovered in a San Francisco coffeehouse by Tom Paxton, who invited him to join the Phil Ochs–Bob Dylan writing circle. Soon his songs were being covered by such new folk luminaries as Judy Collins and Peter, Paul and Mary.

Throughout the 1960s and 1970s, Andersen recorded a variety of albums for Vanguard Records, Warner Bros., Columbia Records, and Arista. His collaborations included Patti Smith, Janis Joplin, Buddy Guy, the Band, and the Grateful Dead. Aside from the Dead, his songs were recorded by Linda Ronstadt, John Denver, and Rick Nelson. In 1966, Andersen appeared in the Andy Warhol film *Space,* starring Edie Sedgwick. In 1972, his recording career reached new heights with the release of *Blue River* on Columbia, which *Rolling Stone* called "the best example of the seventies singer/songwriter movement."

During the 1980s, Eric settled in Norway and recorded independently released solo albums, such as 1988's *Ghosts Upon the Road,* and his 1991 Columbia/Legacy album, *Stages: The Lost Album.* Also, in 1991, his collaboration with Rick Danko of the Band

Aretha Franklin, *This Girl's in Love with You* (1970);
Queen of Soul (1992)
BOB DYLAN and The Band, *Before the Flood* (1974)
Ringo Starr, *Ringo Starr and His All-Starr Band* (1990)
Joe Cocker, *The Long Voyage Home* (1995)

Arguably the Band's most beloved and recognizable song, "The Weight" was inspired not only by the group's association with Bob Dylan but by Robbie Robertson's fascination with cinema. As Robertson commented in the liner notes accompanying *To Kingdom Come*, the Band's 1989 CD anthology, "I was just as much influenced by Luis Buñuel or John Ford or [Akira] Kurosawa . . . [Buñuel, the Spanish neosurrealist] did so many films on the impossibility of sainthood—in *Viridiana* and *Nazarin* . . . there were these people trying to be good, and it's impossible to be good. In 'The Weight' it was a very simple thing. Someone says, 'Listen, would you do me this favor? When you get there will you say hello to somebody, or will you give somebody this, or will you pick up one of these for me? Oh, you're going to Nazareth; that's where the Martin guitar factory is. Do me a favor when you get there.' This is what it's all about. So the guy goes and one thing leads to another and it's like, 'Holy shit, what has this turned into? I've only come here to say hello for somebody and I've got myself in this incredible predicament.' It was very Buñuelish to me at the time."

The Dead began performing their interesting arrangement of "The Weight" in 1990 with each member of the Dead taking a different verse and the whole ensemble joining in for the final sing-along.

Recalling the song's Dead debut of the song, Lesh told Blair Jackson in 1990 that "When we did 'The Weight' for the first time I was terrified I was going to forget the words, so I was really nervous—and in fact I did. That was a lot of fun."

5/6/90, California State University at Dominguez Hills,
Carson, California
6/17/91, Giants Stadium, East Rutherford, New Jersey

▪ Bob Weir
Born October 16, 1947, Atherton, California

As the originator of "Misfit Power," a mantra that many Deadheads have long taken to heart, it would figure that Bob Weir's entire existence would have an aura of rootlessness about it. Some of these inclinations may have been exacerbated by an undiagnosed and severe case of

Bob Weir, Polo Field, Golden Gate Park, San Francisco, 6/21/67.
(Photo: Mike Polillo/Courtesy of Robert Minkin)

inherited dyslexia, which slowed his academic progress and kept him bouncing from school to school. A classic rich kid gone good, Weir was adopted as an infant and raised in Atherton, California, a wealthy suburb of San Francisco. But though his father was an engineer and his mother ran a successful export-import business, Weir had no urge to follow in either of his parents' footsteps.

To cover the root of his classroom failings, Weir adopted the persona of a yahoo, an uncontrollable adolescent who was only brought under control when he discovered the joys of the acoustic guitar. But it was during this period of itinerant schooling that Weir first crossed paths with two rebellious souls, John Barlow, a writer with whom Weir would cowrite most of his songs, and Mathew Kelly, a musician with whom he would form a couple of bands: KINGFISH and Ratdog.

In 1981, Weir recounted the events that resulted in encountering Jerry Garcia to Jon Sievert of *Guitar Player*. "I had a four-man group that wasn't much of a band—we performed, I think, once. We called ourselves the Uncalled Four. I was going to Pacific High School, and I actually met Garcia for the first time that night backstage at the Tangent in Palo Alto. It was a real brief thing. I didn't really meet him on concrete terms until two months later on New Year's Eve. I was walking around the back streets of Palo Alto with one of the guys in my group, and we walked past the back of Dana Morgan Music and heard banjo music coming from the inside. The light was on so we knocked on the door to see what was happening, and it was Garcia waiting for his students to show up, completely unmindful of the fact that it was New Year's Eve. Of course he was at a loss as to why none of the students were showing up, so he was just playing banjo. We talked for a while and then broke into the front of the store and got a bunch of instruments out and played for the rest of the evening. I think it had occurred to us by the end of the night that there was enough amateur talent around to start a jug band, which was a current popular trend in folk music."

Falling out of the path towards formal education, Weir fell in with the folkie scene blossoming in and around San Francisco in the early 1960s, jamming with the musicians in the Menlo Park area and performing in the loose knit jug bands spearheaded by Garcia. Weir eventually traded in his jug (at which he was unusually expert) for a guitar in MOTHER MCCREE'S UPTOWN JUG CHAMPIONS and then the electric guitar when that unit went electric as the WARLOCKS. With his high harmonies, straight-ahead rhythm guitar work, cowboy vocals, and pure teenage energy, Weir was the perfect combination of raw power and youthful frenzy to propel the Grateful Dead in its earliest gigs.

Weir described the fomation of the jug band in his 1981 interview with Sievert of *Guitar Player*. "We got a bunch of old jug band, country blues, and 'race' records that a friend's mother had collected, and I took them over to Garcia's house where we tried to figure out the words and chords. We actually got a fairly thorough understanding of what that kind of music was all about."

LSD was introduced into the scene around the same time they went electric. But when the music began to stretch, Weir's inexperience began to show. After several ultimatums, Weir buckled down and found the places in the sonic canopy where he could weave his off-kilter tapestries through the moving landscapes of the Dead's sound. With his enormous hands, Weir found he could voice atypical chords in unique ways as he began to lead driving jams and extend the possibilities of live Dead. "We never did buy the Hollywood stardom business," said Weir. "That's not how we want to live our lives—that's not how we want to be."

Never content merely to play the stage role of the Dead's androgynous space-child heartthrob cowboy, Bob Weir consistently alchemized his musical style and the

Bob Weir, Roosevelt Stadium, Jersey City, New Jersey, 8/1/73. *(Photo: Richard Berner)*

band's overall sound, evolving into one of the punchiest and most versatile rhythm guitarists on wheels.

Along with scads of cover songs drawn from folk, country music, and the blues, Weir brought to the band many of his own compositions, which became springboards for some of the Dead's most exploratory musical voyages. Written almost exclusively with John Barlow, Weir's legacy of original songs comprises a veritable song- cycle reflecting the ethos of "misfit power"—their own brand of iconoclastic individualism portraying a narrator attempting to connect with an indifferent world always spinning just out of his grasp.

Discussing his approach to and philosophy of songwriting in his 1981 *Guitar Player* interview with Jon Sievert, Weir said, "Sometimes the words will occur first, or maybe John Barlow has given me some words, and I'll try to find the music that serves the words. Most often the music comes first, when I'm sitting around playing guitar. Then I'll work on developing words that fit it. And I would say that my guitar style has pretty much developed from my writing. If I'm writing a song that I'm going to be singing and playing at the same time, then I go for a combination of the two that's more than the sum of its parts. That's what a song is, in my opinion. A SONG, in capital letters, is more than just the chords and the melody and the words. It's the way they all work together in a special, magical relationship that makes a great song. That's what I keep going for."

But Weir always had the heart of a rock 'n' roller and, after Pigpen's death, he assumed the mantle of the Dead's libido-vibrating frontman—invoking the gyrating muse of Elvis and the frothy passion of the stump preacher with the timely physical accentuation of the musical moment.

The only band member who never married, Weir is a major jock who, when not on the bandstand or in studio, can probably be found cruising the hills of Marin County on his mountain bike or running the flea-flicker in the backfield of his notorious touch-football team, the Tamalpais Chiefs.

But as with Garcia's, Weir's own musical callings kept him on tour for much of the time that the Dead did not. Through most of the 1970s and 1980s, Weir fronted his own diverse bands, from the rock-based KINGFISH and Bobby and the Midnites to the short-lived Bob Weir Band, releasing a quartet of solo albums. He also lent guest support to groups such as the jazzy Nightfood. In a continuing collaboration with bassist Rob Wasserman,

Bob Weir, Madison Square Garden, New York City, 9/19/87. *(Oliver Trager)*

Weir evolved a group from an acoustic duo into Ratdog—a full-fledged combo that eventually included Matt Kelly on harmonica and Chuck Berry alum Johnny Johnson on piano. Covering the gamut of Weir's original and cover-song catalogue, Ratdog's appearance at the Furthur Festival in 1996 was a highlight of the first Dead-related tour following Garcia's death.

Often referred to as the conscience of the Dead, Weir has been perhaps the most politically outspoken and environmentally active member of the group. He lobbied Congress hard in 1992 to turn back legislation that would have sacrificed more of America's old-growth forests to the timber industry. He is also intensely involved with the REX FOUNDATION and he has lent heavy personal support to a similar and related Marin County charity, the Seva Foundation, which funds eye clinics in India and Nepal and organizes empowerment projects for the helpless, homeless, and indigenous.

One manifestation of Weir's concerns for the vanishing rain forest was *Panther Dream*, an ecologically correct children's book combining his original story with his sister Wendy Weir's lush acrylic artwork, packaged with an audio cassette of Weir telling the story overdubbed with exotic sounds. All proceeds from the sales from

Panther Dream were earmarked to fund rain forest reforestation and educational projects in Africa. Weir was also equally involved in the preservation of forests in the United States with efforts ranging from authoring a *New York Times* op-ed piece to a fact-finding bicycle tour in which he was physically threatened by the strong-armed methods of local lumber interests. "The timber industry is wanton, reckless, and criminal in its activities. And it has subverted and corrupted the Forest Service to a frightening and pathetic degree. The Forest Service is an instrument, by and large, of the timber industry. It does not represent the interests of the American people."

In an unpublished 1993 discussion with William Myers, Weir described himself as being attracted to Buddhism but not a practicing Buddhist—and as being spiritual but not religious—and as an aspiring vegetarian but a practicing omnivore. He says he hates being preached at, and though in his wildly declamatory lyrics he may sometimes seem to be preaching, he says he's only playing a role. Mytho-historian Joseph Campbell once called him "the Conjurer" of the band. Weir's influence could be felt most strongly in its nonspecific moral force and poetic ambiguity. Weir once confirmed this notion, saying, "Music is a hallucinogenic realm. When I'm singing and playing, even if we're not doing it well, I'm hallucinating. I'm visiting another realm—a parallel world or something. And when it really gets good, it's like there's a bright, electric-blue white light that just radiates through everything and everybody and I can see through people, and I can see three hundred degrees around me. I can see everybody's face. I can feel everybody's smile. I can hear everybody's heart. That's a place where I go all the time. And I like it there.

"You have to sort of dodge or sidestep your own ego in order to get there. And you learn how to do that over the years if you're a musician. You have to leave all self-consciousness behind, because to get to that outer experience you just can't get that baggage through the door. You have to drop that stuff. And you go through that door naked—that's the only way you get there."

Weir showed no signs of letting up when the Dead called it quits after Garcia's death. Weir's longtime fascination with baseball pitching great Satchel Paige inspired the wide-ranging guitarist to join forces with jazz tenor-saxophonist DAVID MURRAY and bluesman Taj Mahal to compose music for a musical play based on the life of the legendary Negro Leagues Hall-of-Famer, which

was scheduled to open on Broadway in 1997. As Weir mused on the mercurial righty, "Satchel Paige is probably without any doubt the greatest pitcher who ever lived—and, well beyond that, one of the most colorful and amazing Americans who ever lived. He really belongs in the American pantheon, up there with Paul Bunyan and Marilyn Monroe. It's funny that the only black guy we got in the American pantheon is Uncle Remus, and that's bullshit. This guy was real. And he was truly great. Quite honestly, this might be the ghost of old Satch calling to me."

And his involvement with Ratdog and the environment promised to keep him on the road for years to come. "I want to live to be real, real old. I want to get good at living. I think it's going to take a long time to do that, and I want this place to be a livable place when I'm old. If nothing else, it's just impossibly poor form to trash this place when you leave it behind. For all those reasons, I won't even consider having kids until I'm satisfied that we've turned a corner environmentally, and that the curtain's not going to come down in the middle of the next century—which it could very easily do—with no more life on earth."

▪ *Welcome to Our World: 1990 Rykodisc Sampler of the World*
Rykodisc RCD PRO 9002.

Selections from Mickey Hart's Rykodisc releases were highlighted on this promotional compilation.

▪ Vince Welnick
Born February 21, 1951, Phoenix, Arizona

At first glance, Vince Welnick seemed an unlikely choice to replace Brent Mydland when the Dead's fourth keyboardist died in July 1990. As a veteran of the Tubes, one of the most flamboyantly theatrical and satirical rock acts to stomp this sweet, swingin' sphere, he didn't exactly seem to have the résumé to interest a band that had avoided flashy stage shows for over a quarter century. But upon closer inspection, he had the chops and touring experience to make him the prime candidate to hold down the Dead's piano chair in the last five years of their spectacular run.

A product of Phoenix, Arizona, Vince was introduced to music by a boogie-woogie piano-playing mother who

Vince Welnick, San Rafael, California, February 1991. *(Robert Minkin)*

schooled him in blues, jazz, and rock while urging him to play classical organ in his local church. His teenage band, the Equations, shared double bills with the Spiders, led by Vincent Furnier, who would later unleash his own brand of rock theater on an unsuspecting world as Alice Cooper.

Around the time he caught his first Dead show in 1970, Welnick was hooking up with a local band calling themselves the Beans. When they moved to San Francisco not long after, the Beans reinvented themselves as the Tubes, playing an over-the-top solution of hard rock and fusion jazz and gaining an immediate rep for their fluorescent stage show and hit debut single, "White Punks on Dope."

Though lead singer Fee Waybill's gonzo stage antics took their cue from Frank Zappa's Mothers of Invention and Parliament/Funkadelic (making them easy targets for the Moral Majorities of the world), the Tubes were among the first to bring performance art to arena rock. The band also lived communally in a musical marriage that kept its vows "for better or for worse" for over seventeen years.

And there were many tough times. The Tubes spent an entire summer playing bar gigs in order to pay back the road crew who got burned by the manager while they were out on a long tour. In the red $175,000, they worked all summer long to pay off the debt and when the tour was over, Waybill quit the band.

Still, the Tubes' long run was not without its many bizarre gigs, perhaps none so strange as performing "Sports Fan," one of their few hits, at half-time of the famed 1981 NFC title game when Dwight Clark's touchdown reception from Joe Montana sent the San Francisco 49ers to their first Super Bowl.

Heavily steeped in the music of John Coltrane and McCoy Tyner, Welnick became expert in most of the genres familiar to the Dead while with the Tubes. A stint with Todd Rundgren following the demise of the Tubes didn't exactly hurt matters either and resulted in two albums: *Nearly Human* and *Second Wind*. Still, when the opportunity arose to audition for a band with an active repertoire in excess of one hundred songs, Welnick knew he was up for a major challenge.

After passing the test with flying colors, Welnick was behind the keyboard when the Dead resumed touring on September 7, 1990, in Richfield, Ohio—a gig not without its eerie moments. According to Welnick "the bench that Brent used to sit on exploded before my first gig. After the soundcheck, one of our guys slid over to check out my microphone and as soon as he sat down, the bench splintered into a hundred pieces."

Welnick made his mark so quickly that he had to deal with few "new guy in the band" labels. Still, he once mused that "being the keyboardist in this band is like being the new guy in Nam."

With his intense but buoyantly hip persona, Welnick quickly won over every Deadhead who, to a number, seemed eager to like him. "There's so much love out there especially for the lowly keyboard player who normally sits in the back line and is seldom even heard over the rest of the band."

Welnick's discipline, acquired from his years in the rock 'n' roll trenches, made it easier for him to pick up on the Dead's 140-plus song list in less that two weeks of rehearsal. Discipline, on the other hand, can be fatal with the Dead unless coupled with a willingness to explore the sometimes ragged edges of collective improvisation. "I think when you're playing with this caliber of musicians and they're reaching out all the time too, that you tend to get beyond yourself, and it turns into more than the individual musicians."

The magic of the Dead's music soon hit Welnick on the deepest of personal levels when his terminally ill mother attended as many Grateful Dead concerts as her health would permit before her death. Welnick's sister credited the music with prolonging their mother's life for six months and Welnick was quoted in *Relix* as saying, "My mom swore that the music was healing."

Welnick's magic added greatly to the band's last five years. Along with his incisive, signature keyboard work, he collaborated with Robert Hunter on a couple of tunes ("Long Way to Go Home" and "Samba in the Rain") while spearheading the inclusion of some interesting Beatles tunes into the Dead's later repertoire: "RAIN," "TOMORROW NEVER KNOWS," "LUCY IN THE SKY WITH DIAMONDS," and "IT'S ALL TOO MUCH."

Between Dead tours, Welnick joined forces with several Bay Area units to keep his chops as loose as possible including the Affordables, the Valentines, Zero, and Second Sight, a freewheeling, experimental, electrified improv band that was the brainchild of keyboardist-producer-audio ace Bob Bralove, who was also a crucial behind-the-scenes presence with the Grateful Dead. After Jerry Garcia's passing, Welnick joined his old friend and collaborator from the Tubes, Prairie Prince, to form Missing Man Formation, a name referring to the flight pattern that pilots, flying in a group, assume in order to indicate that a pilot and plane have gone down. Playing many Dead tunes, originals, and covers, Missing Man Formation began performing and recording in 1996.

▪ "Werewolves of London" (Warren Zevon/Larry Marinell/Robert Wachtell)
Warren Zevon, *Excitable Boy* (1978), *Standing in the Fires* (1981), *Learning to Flinch* (1993)
Black Velvet Band, *The Rubaiyat* (1990)

Discussing the macabre element in his music, Warren Zevon once said, "I can't disagree that there's a violent quality in my work, and it may not be something that familiar in pop songs. But in any other art form, it's the artist's prerogative to inject the adrenaline. Restraint has never been one of my virtues."

Zevon's creative development and rise to fame is almost as bizarre as his songwriting. Born January 24, 1947, in Chicago he moved with his family to California at a young age and spent most of his formative years there. Zevon's father was a professional gambler, a career choice that kept the family on the move—often in picaresque fashion.

These experiences no doubt influenced Zevon's wickedly black sense of humor and love for tough rock 'n' roll. But he became a popular 1970s Los Angeles songwriting pro by tempering that dark streak with some evocative and personal ballads surveying the lifestyle trappings found in the City of Lost Angels.

"Werewolves of London," Zevon's gory Top 10 hit from his equally dark 1978 album *Excitable Boy*, is an anomaly in the Dead's cover-song repertoire both because of the song's bloody streak and because they started performing it at the peak of its popularity. Its appearances in the Dead's set lists is very sporadic, but "Werewolves of London" became something of a Halloween concert tradition, included, for example, in the October 31, 1990, show at London's Wembley Arena. The Jerry Garcia Band also took about a half dozen Halloween stabs at the spooky sendup.

7/7/78, Red Rock Amphitheater, Morrison, Colorado
10/31/90, Wembley Arena, London

▪ "West L.A. Fadeaway" (Garcia/Hunter)
Grateful Dead, *In the Dark* (1987), *The Arista Years* (1996)

Generally thought to loosely reference the death of John Belushi, "West L.A. Fadeaway" is a bluesy portrayal of the American underbelly. Life on the run, nefarious dealings with dangerous people, and no clear path of safe escape are the themes here. In his 1988 conversation with Blair Jackson, Hunter described the method of the song's composition. "I think the initial hit on that was the old song—not the one I wrote—that goes 'stop on the red and go on the green but get my candyman home, salty dog, candyman, salty dog, candyman.' I liked that; it was catchy. Little bits of old folk songs have a way of getting into my songs. But then I put that on an L.A. freeway. The character in there—his eyes are tombstones. Those are L.A. attitudes in there. Whew! And Jerry soft-pedaled those lyrics a little. There were verses he didn't do. I was out to create a real *bad* character, which is what I consider an L.A. way of looking at things. I'm not a great fan of L.A."

The song received much attention in concert during the mid-1980s but was only rarely performed by the early 1990s. Interestingly, "West L.A. Fadeaway" was a sometime selection for Bob Dylan during his "Never-Ending Tour" of the late 1980s and 1990s.

5/6/90, California State University at Dominguez Hills, Carson, California

■ "Wharf Rat" (Garcia/Hunter)

Grateful Dead, *Grateful Dead* (1971), *Dick's Picks Volume Three/'77* (1995), *Dick's Picks Volume Seven/'74* (1997)
Midnight Oil, *Deadicated* (1991)
Michael Rose, *Fire on the Mountain: Reggae Celebrates the Grateful Dead* (1996)

A Grateful Dead classic of 1971 vintage, "Wharf Rat" describes a common experience of the urban subterrain: an encounter with a down-on-his-luck street person with a story to tell. In this scenario, the subject is August West and it is by the docks of the city that he recounts his troubles with women, jail, and burgundy wine. But despite his pathetic situation, he is positive that, with a little luck and love, he can get back on his feet someday. The narrator of "Wharf Rat," who has patiently listened to the poignant tale, isn't as sure but is nonetheless uplifted by West's hopeful spirit.

Primarily a ballad, "Wharf Rat" has a languid gospel break which thematically carries the song to its bright conclusion.

One lyric of note concerns West's imprisonment because of "some other fucker's crime." As such it was the first song released by a major band on a major label to clearly enunciate the F word.

In regards to the use of expletives in art, Hunter told Blair Jackson in 1988 that "Well, I've thrown in a few forbidden words in my time. We got in 'some other fucker's crime' in 'Wharf Rat.' The Jefferson Airplane said they used that word [in 'We Can Be Together' from *Volunteers*], but did they really? I challenge you to listen to that closely. You can't hear it. I think we were the first ones to say 'fuck' on a record and get by with it. You know, it was fairly risqué to use the word 'cocaine' when we did, unless you were a folk song on public radio. And though it seems mild today, 'goddamn' was a heavy word to use when 'Uncle John's Band' came out. I don't like too many strictures on language. At the same time, I don't like using these kinds of words in a sloppy fashion. Sloppy language is usually indicative of sloppy thinking. You want language to be liberated, and I love what Lenny Bruce did, of course, but that doesn't mean you have to go act and talk like that. But you should *be able* to. It's a basic liberty."

Discussing the song's conversational elements, Garcia praised his songwriting partner, "Hunter is able to write that into just about everything—he's able to leave just enough *out*, so that you're not really sure whose side you're on, if it's a matter of taking sides. In 'Wharf Rat' you don't know if you're the guy who's hearing the story or the guy who's telling it. It really doesn't matter in the long run."

As with several Garcia/Hunter collaborations, "Wharf Rat" was one of those cases where the guitarist had an idea for something and Hunter had a literary version of the same idea and they got together and just worked it out over the course of an afternoon.

2/18/71, Capitol Theater, Port Chester, New York
5/3/72, Olympia Theater, Paris
9/28/72, Stanley Theater, Pittsburgh
6/8/74, Coliseum Stadium, Oakland, California
5/17/77, Memorial Coliseum, Tuscaloosa, Alabama
11/14/78, Boston Music Hall, Boston
6/24/84, Saratoga Performing Arts Center, Saratoga, New York
6/28/91, Mile High Stadium, Denver

■ *What a Long Strange Trip It's Been*

Warner Bros. 2W 3091, 1977.
"New, New Minglewood Blues," "Cosmic Charlie," "Truckin'," "Black Peter," "Born Cross-Eyed," "Ripple," "Doin' That Rag," "Dark Star," "High Time," "New Speedway Blues," "St. Stephen," "Jack Straw," "ME & MY UNCLE," "Tennessee Jed," "Cumberland Blues," "Playing in the Band," "Brown-Eyed Women," "Ramble on Rose"

Regarded as another useless corporate anthology redeemed only by the inclusion of two rare studio outtakes of "Dark Star" and "Born Cross-Eyed."

■ "What's Become of the Baby"
(Garcia/Lesh/Hunter)
Grateful Dead, *Aoxomoxoa* (1969)

Arguably the most unlistenable track on any Grateful Dead release, "What's Become of the Baby" is a six-minute atmospheric specter with echo-box lyrics that sound as if they are sung in a language more akin to Venusian than anything found on this particular planet.

Perhaps the most unfortunate aspect of the song's recorded murkiness is its obscuring of Hunter's minimalist reference to *The Thousand and One Nights*.

While Lesh once labeled this impenetrable song "a raunch classic," Garcia recalled: "I had a concept in my head but I had no idea of how to do it technically or how to communicate it. I wanted to contain the whole band just playing music inside the voice, where you'd hear some kind of Grateful Dead randomness replacing the voice, a guy opening his mouth and the Grateful Dead coming out. I know how to do it now, but it was impossible then."

In his 1991 conversation with Blair Jackson and Robert Hunter, Garcia said, "Well, 'What's Become of the Baby' was originally baroque. I had this melody worked out that had this counterpoint and a nice little rhythm. This original setting I'd worked out was really like one of those song forms from the New York Pro Musica."

"What's Become of the Baby" is known to have been performed live by the Grateful Dead at one 1969 concert.

4/26/69, Electric Theater, Chicago

▪ "What's Going On" (Marvin Gaye)
Marvin Gaye, single (1971), *What's Going On* (1971), *Marvin Gaye Live* (1974), *Live at the London Palladium* (1976), *Greatest Hits* (1983)

The quirks of fate have overshadowed the pop charts on numerous occasions. The deaths of Otis Redding, Jim Croce, and Kurt Cobain just at the time they were riding the wave of highest popularity certainly come to mind. But Marvin Gaye held the concept in near mystical perspective, believing that his triumphs were prophesied before his birth. As legend has it, Gaye's grandfather had told his mother that her child's fortune would lie "under the grapevine." By 1970, his recording of "I Heard It Through the Grapevine" had sold more than 4 million copies, he had performed the song on the *Tonight Show,* and a *Billboard* poll found him sharing the same rarefied air as Elvis in the eyes of the nation.

His soaring star helped him wrest artistic control of his product from Motown's executives and producers. The result, *What's Going On* yielded three singles that crossed over and hit the Top 10. Hitting the record stores at the height of the Vietnam War, the album was a brooding, sometimes bleak vision belying its pleasing melodic backdrops. Along with the war, *What's Going On* was steeped with such headline news anxiety as the environment, inner city strife and a concern for the world's children.

Though Gaye's popularity was never on the wane after that, it was never as politically hard-edged, with the possible exception of "He's the Man," a 1972 diatribe against President Richard Nixon. The pleasures and pains of sex were the obsessive focus of his recording career in the following years, and *Let's Get It On,* released in 1973, was the definitive late-night seduction album.

But Gaye was deeply mired in a web of drug addiction that led him to relocate to Belgium in the late 1970s and early 1980s. Returning to California in 1982, Gaye had his final great success with *Midnight Love,* which produced the megahit "Sexual Healing." By the end of a support tour for the album, Gaye was again severely strung-out and, in a bizarre twist, was shot to death by his father over an argument about his drug addiction on April 1, 1984. A year later, the elder Gaye, a diminutive, deeply religious man, was found guilty of involuntary manslaughter and released on probation.

During their 1988 Rainforest Benefit at Madison Square Garden, the Dead chose this perfect message song as the centerpiece for their set and performed it with surprise guests Hall and Oates.

9/24/88, Madison Square Garden, New York

▪ "The Wheel" (Garcia/Hunter)
Jerry Garcia, *Garcia* (1972)
Grateful Dead, *Dozin' at the Knick*/'90 (1996)
Toni Brown, *Blue Morning* (1996)

Drawing on one of civilization's most potent symbols, this enigmatic song was a concert staple beginning in 1976. The wheel has deep associations in the psyche of world history and culture. Obviously it was early man's greatest and most significant invention in its catalytic effect on survival and mobility. Probably because of this it became a natural iconographic emblem in ancient religions across the globe. From Buddhist mandalas and Hopi sand circles to Stonehenge and beyond, circular imagery evoking the mystic is an archetype fully integrated into the cycles and rituals of existence.

While not clearly referencing a specific tradition, the Dead's composition is a combination of the sublime and the silly—a perfect modern American blend of the wheel's vast resonance: Buddhism meets Harley-Davidson in an R. Crumb comic strip.

Remembering the song's genesis, Garcia told Blair Jackson in 1988, "Actually it was just one time through on the piano. I was playing the piano and I didn't even know what I was doing. Now the way I approached that side of the album [side two of *Garcia*] is that I sat down at the piano—which I *don't* play—and Billy sat down at the drums, which he *does* play. So at least one of us knew what he was doing. [*Laughs*] And I just played. When I'd get an idea, I'd elaborate on it and then go back and overdub stuff on it. But that side was really almost one continuous performance, pretty much. When a song would come up in there, or just a progression, we'd play with it and I'd work it through a few more times. And 'The Wheel' came out of that. It wasn't written, I didn't have anything in mind, I hadn't sketched it out or anything.

"So then, after that, Hunter came in and wrote the lyrics."

The Dead began performing "The Wheel" in 1976 and it quickly found its place as a second-set entry.

2/26/77, Swing Auditorium, San Bernardino, California
5/19/77, Fox Theater, Atlanta
12/5/81, Market Square Arena, Indianapolis
7/15/88, Greek Theatre, Berkeley, California
8/22/93, Autzen Stadium, Eugene, Oregon

▪ "When I Paint My Masterpiece" (BOB DYLAN)

Bob Dylan, *Greatest Hits Vol. Two* (1971)
Grateful Dead, *Dozin' at the Knick/'90* (1996)
THE BAND, *Cahoots* (1971), *Bob Dylan: The 30th Anniversary Celebration Concert* (1993)
Dead Ringers, *DEAD RINGERS* (1993)
Tim O'Brien and the O'Boys, *Oh Boy! O'Boy* (1993)

The Dead worked up an arrangement of Bob Dylan's literary-heavy composition prior to their concerts with him in 1987. Strangely, it was the only Dylan song they performed in their own sets without the maestro at a few of those shows and was never performed with the songster himself. The band evidently enjoyed performing "Masterpiece" because it stayed in heavy rotation after that. Weir sang the song with the Dead and included it on his playlist with Rob Wasserman.

Historically, the tune is a bit of an oddity in its own right. It was one of several tunes Dylan cut specifically for *Bob Dylan's Greatest Hits Vol. II* in a not-too-veiled marketing decision to move units. Dylan performed the song almost nightly during the Rolling Thunder Revue in 1975 and 1976 but has rarely revived it since then.

Lyrically, the song has a fractured, cubist sensibility with the angular imagery at once nonsensical and poig-

nant. In "Masterpiece," the narrator relates the monuments of an ancient culture to himself, a product of an emerging younger culture. Some Bobcats have made a cogent case for the song's narrator as an extension of Dick Diver in F. Scott Fitzgerald's *Tender Is the Night*. They point to what they describe as the novel's "fragmentary picture," most notably the Roman episode when Diver's affair with Rosemary collapses, and he watches Rome and its mystique disintegrate. The Dylan scholars link the song's "footprints" and "Spanish Stairs" directly to the novel arguing that while Diver is in Rome, he comes to admit to himself that he is never actually going to write the masterpiece that he's been aiming at. So Dylan's title assumes a fascinating double-edge: "when" may mean "never."

12/11/92, Coliseum Arena, Oakland, California

▪ "When Push Comes to Shove"
(Garcia/Hunter)
Grateful Dead, *In the Dark* (1987)

An eighties observation of alienation which recalls the musical spirit of the Dead's earlier composition "Ramble On Rose," "When Push Comes to Shove" is a wry but wary warning, a coaxing gestalt from one friend to another. The person to whom the song is addressed is not only afraid of love but inhabits a world where even roses in a garden pose an unreasonably paranoid threat. But the singer is a sensitive soul who gamely punctures the barricades of his acquaintance's foolish fears.

The Dead gave "When Push Comes to Shove" substantial concert treatment in the late 1980s but it had fallen out of the rotation by 1990.

12/15/86, Coliseum Arena, Oakland, California
3/18/88, Henry J. Kaiser Convention Center, Oakland, California

▪ "Where Have All the Flowers Gone?"
(Pete Seeger)
Pete Seeger, *Rainbow Quest* (1961)

A mournful antiwar song cut out of the same fabric as "Morning Dew," "Where Have All the Flowers Gone" was only covered by the Dead during one of their December 1981 acoustic sets with JOAN BAEZ.

According to a 1962 issue of the cherished folk-song magazine *Sing Out!*, Pete Seeger got the basic idea for this song from a line in *All Quiet Flows the Don* by the Russian novelist Mikhail Sholokhov.

Many might recall this as among the first songs questioning authority they ever heard. Sharing a mournful wistfulness similar to that found in Dylan's "Blowin' in the Wind," "Where Have All the Flowers Gone?" follows the path of some flowers which are picked by young girls who give them to their young men who enlist in the military to fight in a war from which they'll never return, left to push up their own bouquet of daisies in some distant, unnamed land.

12/12/81, Fiesta Hall, San Mateo, California (with Joan Baez)

- ### *Where the Beat Meets the Street*/ BOBBY
AND THE MIDNITES
Columbia BFC 39276, 1984.
"(I Want to Live) In America," "Where the Beat Meets the Street," "She's Gonna Win Your Heart," "Ain't That Peculiar," "Lifeguard," "Rock in the '80s," "Lifeline," "Falling," "Thunder and Lightning," "Gloria Monday"

This was a less-jazzy followup to the Midnites' debut disc, and a telling symbol of this album's flatness is that only "Ain't That Peculiar" ended up as a regular in Weir's solo tours with Rob Wasserman. The pickup band's final album was a weak stab for mid-'80s radio acceptance and, as he did with KINGFISH, Weir took a backseat in his own group, leaving most of the singing to Bobby Cochran while bringing in a host of outside song scribes. A set of by-the-numbers toe-tappers didn't catch on with the general public or Deadheads, sinking without a trace after a few weeks on the bottom of the charts, soon followed by the demise of the Midnites.

- ### "Who Do You Love" (Ellas McDaniel)
BO DIDDLEY, single (1956), *Roadrunner* (1964)
Ronnie Hawkins, single (1959), *The Best of Ronnie Hawkins and His Band* (1990)
Blues Project, *Live at the Cafe Au Go Go* (1966)
Howlin' Wolf, *Super Super Blues Band* (with Muddy Waters and Bo Diddley) (1968)
Quicksilver Messenger Service, *Happy Trails* (1969)
The Doors, *Absolutely Live* (1970)
George Thorogood, *Move It On Over* (1973), *Live: George Thorogood* (1986)
Ian Hunter, *Ian Hunter* (1975)

THE BAND with Ronnie Hawkins, *The Last Waltz*/'76 (1978)
Santana, *Havana Moon* (1983)
Iggy and the Stooges, *Live '71* (1988)
Jesus & Mary Chain, *Barbed Wire Compilation* (1988)

More closely associated with the Quicksilver Messenger Service, who transformed "Who Do You Love" into a snake dance special, this Bo Diddley stomp was paired by the Dead with their own "Caution" as a second-set jam segue at three Europe '72 concerts.

5/11/72, Civic Hall, Rotterdam, the Netherlands

- ### "Why Don't We Do It in the Road"
(Lennon/McCartney)
The Beatles, *The Beatles* (The White Album) (1968)
Lydia Lunch, single (1991)

Ostensibly a Paul McCartney solo effort, "Why Don't We Do It in the Road" was recorded on the fly at the Beatles' Abbey Road studios in October 1968. Aside from his vocals on which there was some double tracking, McCartney played guitar, piano, and bass. Ringo Starr later overdubbed his drums, handclaps, and some vocals.

A few years after the fact, John Lennon expressed the disappointment he felt when he discovered that McCartney proceeded on the track without inviting or even consulting either him or George Harrison.

Phil Lesh and Brent Mydland worked up a raunchy cover of "Why Don't We Do It in the Road" that was displayed at seven Dead shows between 1984 and 1986.

4/7/85, The Spectrum, Philadelphia

- ### "The Wicked Messenger" (BOB DYLAN)
Bob Dylan, *John Wesley Harding* (1968)
Small Faces, *First Step* (1970)
Mitch Ryder, *Live Talkies* (1982)

A scathing portrait of a heartless con man, "The Wicked Messenger" is rife with biblical allusion right down to its archaic diction. Dylan's lyrical conception is ancient and venerable. The Old Testament Eli was a high priest and judge of Israel, and teacher of the young Samuel. In Proverbs 13:17, "A wicked messenger falleth into mischief/But a faithful ambassador *is* health." In Shakespeare's *King Henry IV Part 2*, "The first bringer of unwelcome news/Hath but a losing office." It has been suggested that Dylan was drawing on these ideas in the song to speak of the poet's duty to tell the truth.

Musically, "The Wicked Messenger" is one of the most innovative tunes on Dylan's brilliantly somber *John Wesley Harding* album, with harsh descending contours that draw equally on the blues and the dirge.

The song's appearance in the Dylan/Dead shows was one of the tour's biggest surprises, though somewhat ill-chosen given the large venues the tour swung through. Garcia included it as an on-again off-again number in his own band's repertoire since the mid-1970s.

7/12/87, Giants Stadium, East Rutherford, New Jersey (with Bob Dylan)

4/19/75, Oriental Theater, Milwaukee (LEGION OF MARY)

▪ Wildwood Boys

See **Mother McCree's Uptown Jug Champions**

▪ "Willie and the Hand Jive" (Johnny Otis)

Johnny Otis, single (1958), *The Capitol Years* (1988)

Crickets, *Something Old, Something New, Something Blue, Something Else* (1962), *Rock n' Roll Masters: The Best of the Crickets* (1989)

NEW RIDERS OF THE PURPLE SAGE, *Powerglide* (1972)

Eric Clapton, *461 Ocean Boulevard* (1974)

George Thorogood, *Maverick* (1985)

The Master's Apprentices, *Jam It Up!* (1987)

The Dead only performed "Willie and the Hand Jive" a half-dozen times between 1986 and 1987 but the song has a remarkable history. Written and recorded by the one-of-a-kind Johnny Otis, "Hand Jive," with its familiar but always intoxicating "Bo Diddley beat," was a No. 1 hit in the summer of 1958.

The genesis of "Hand Jive" came in 1957 when Otis and his partner Hal Zeiger scored a surprise hit in England with a rock version of "Ma, He's Making Eyes at Me." The old standard, unbeknownst to Otis and Zeiger, had been a morale-boosting song for the British during World War II when people in the bomb shelters sang the song.

Zeiger traveled to England to arrange a supporting tour and was amazed to discover that kids weren't allowed to dance at the theaters where the early rock & roll extravaganzas were staged. He was even more astounded to see these teens using their hands in a manner that reminded him of the way a saxophonist would wave his hands while the trumpeter soloed in the old black jazz bands.

Returning home, Zeiger suggested Otis write a song

called "Hand Jive" with the belief that it would find further British success for the duo. Though Zeiger hated the song Otis came up with, the executives at Capitol Records (as well as Otis's four-year-old) loved it.

Recorded with a three-piece band along with Otis's wife and a couple of friends providing the hand-clapping and background vocals, the song rocketed to the top of the charts. "Hand Jive" was also reportedly one of the first rock songs to create a marketing craze, with Capitol putting out diagrams of how to do the hand jive and an avalanche of products, such as Hand Jive Shoes.

2/12/86, Henry J. Kaiser Convention Center, Oakland (with THE NEVILLE BROTHERS)

▪ *A Wing and a Prayer* /Matt Kelly

Relix RRLP 2010, 1985.

At some point in 1973, Garcia participated in recording sessions conducted by singer, harmonica player, and guitarist Matthew Kelly at the Record Plant in Sausalito that produced a lead guitar solo on one song from the album, "Dangerous Relations." The sessions would not be released for another dozen years. Kelly also enlisted, at various times, Weir and his buddies Keith Godchaux, Brent Mydland, and Bill Kreutzmann to help lay down some grooves on this solo project.

▪ *Without a Net*

Arista AL19-8634, 1990. Produced by John Cutler and Phil Lesh.

"Feel Like a Stranger," "Mississippi Half-Step Uptown Toodleoo," "Walkin' Blues," "Althea," "Cassidy," "Bird Song," "Let It Grow," "China Cat Sunflower">"I Know You Rider," "Looks Like Rain," "Eyes of the World," "Victim or the Crime," "Help on the Way">"Slipknot!">"Franklin's Tower," "One More Saturday Night," "Dear Mr. Fantasy"

BRANFORD MARSALIS–tenor saxophone on "Eyes of the World."

This album, drawn from concert recordings in 1989 and 1990, was widely hailed as the band's finest live release since *Europe '72* as it captured the Dead at a performance peak. Along with scorching renditions of "Mississippi Half-Step," "Bird Song," and "Let It Grow," the Dead stepped into a lush jam with saxophonist Branford Marsalis on "Eyes of the World" worthy of serving as background music to a sophisticated Park Avenue cocktail party.

(Courtesy of Arista Records)

(Courtesy of Warner Bros. Records)

Explaining to Blair Jackson in 1990 how he was enlisted as the album's coproducer, Lesh said, "It sort of fell to me by default. I wanted to do *something,* and I felt like we've been playing a lot better recently—especially on this last tour [1990 spring East Coast]—and Garcia's got other things he wants to do, like make a live Garcia Band album and actually take some time off. He practically lived in the studio when we were making the last record [*Built to Last*], plus he worked on our videos and all, so he deserves a break.

"John [Cutler] actually is the one who called and asked if I wanted to take a whack at it, and I said, 'Oh boy, yes!'"

The album is dedicated to Clifton Hanger, which was Brent Mydland's *nom de guerre* when checking into hotel rooms while on tour.

▪ *Woodstock*
(film) Directed by Michael Wadleigh, produced by Warner Bros., 1970.

The Dead's performance at the Woodstock cultural event was, as the tape still bears out, horrible to the nth de-

gree. It was for that reason that they refused to allow any representation of that performance disaster on vinyl or celluloid. There is, however, a brief shot of Garcia noodling on his guitar backstage and holding a suspicious looking cigarette while testifying, "Marijuana. Exhibit A."

▪ *Woodstock*
Cotillion SD 3-500, 1970.

Garcia's "Marijuana. Exhibit A" comment turns up on the popular three-disc document of the defining moment of the late 1960s.

▪ *Workingman's Dead*
Warner Bros. WB 1869, 1970. Produced by Bob Mathews, Betty Cantor, the Grateful Dead.
"Uncle John's Band," "High Time," "Dire Wolf," "New Speedway Boogie," "Cumberland Blues," "Black Peter," "Easy Wind," "Casey Jones."
DAVID NELSON—acoustic guitar on "Cumberland Blues."

The first of a tandem of acoustic-heavy, country-flavored outings, *Workingman's Dead* is considered to be representative of the band's best studio work. Filled with a thoughtful, neo-American folk sensibility and influenced by Crosby, Stills, Nash and Young, the disc unveiled some of the Dead's best and most often performed tunes.

Recalling the factors that resulted in *Workingman's Dead*, Garcia explained to Charles Reich and Jann Wenner in 1971, "After *Aoxomoxoa* we hadn't made a studio record for almost a year since *Live/Dead* came out in its place. We were anxious to go into the studio but we didn't want to incur an enormous debt making the record like we had been. When you make a record, you pay for the studio time out of your own royalties. That costs plenty. *Live/Dead* was not too expensive since it was recorded live. It ended up paying for the time on *Aoxomoxoa*, which was eight months or some really ridiculous amount of time. A hundred grand or even more than that—it was real expensive. And we ended up at our worst, in debt to Warner Bros. for around $180,000.

"So, when record time came around and we were getting new material together, we thought, 'Let's try to make it cheap this time.' So we rehearsed for a month or so before we went to make *Workingman's Dead*. We rehearsed and we were pretty far into the material and then we got busted in New Orleans. After we got busted, we went home to make our record. And while we were making our record, we had a big, bad scene with our manager. Actu-ally making the record was the only cool thing happening—everything else was just sheer weirdness. We were into a much more relaxed thing about that time. And we were also out of our pretentious thing. We weren't feeling so much like an experimental music group, but were feeling more like a good old band.

"I liked all those tunes. I loved them all, to give you the absolute and unashamed truth. I felt that they were *all* good songs. They were successful in the sense you could sing 'em, and get off and enjoy singing 'em."

Discussing the conceptual inspiration of the album, Robert Hunter told Blair Jackson in 1988 that "Robbie Robertson most certainly uncovered some germinally great ideas. The direction he went with the Band earlier was one of the things that made me think of conceiving *Workingman's Dead*. I was very much impressed with the area Robertson was working in. I took it and moved it to the West, which is the area I'm familiar with, and thought, 'Okay, how about modern ethnic?' Regional, but not the South, because *everyone* was going back to the South for inspiration at that time. I've done my share of back-to-the-South songs, too, of course."

Describing the collaborative elements that went into

Jerry Garcia, circa 1970. *(The New York Public Library for the Performing Arts)*

the album, Hunter told David Gans in 1978 that "One of the reasons *Workingman's Dead* had such a nice, close sound to it is that we all met every day and worked on the material with acoustic guitars and sang the songs. Phil would say, 'Why don't we use a G minor there rather than a C?' that sort of thing, and a song would pop a little more into perspective. That's a good band way of working a song out."

The Dead's new direction seems to have pleased everyone in the band. As Bill Kreutzmann told Blair Jackson in 1989, "It was a neat period, a lot of fun. We were adding so many new songs, and the whole feeling of the music was very different from what we'd been doing. For me, it was a lot more satisfying than playing the music of *Anthem*."

In their 1991 conversation with Blair Jackson, Garcia and Hunter recalled the creative process that produced the material for both *Workingman's Dead* and *American Beauty*. The band and extended family had moved into a large house in Larkspur, a small town in southern Marin County, in 1969 or early 1970 to escape the implosion of Haight-Ashbury. Hunter would sit upstairs banging on his typewriter, "picking up my guitar, singin' something, then going back to the typewriter. Jerry would be downstairs practicing guitar, working things out. You could hear fine through the floors there, and by the time I'd come down with a sheet and slap it down in front of him, Jerry already knew how they should go!"

Garcia was a bit more mystified. "You know, I have almost no recognition of the actual process of writing those songs. I listen to them now and I wonder, 'Where the hell did that come from?' Some of them seem to have appeared out of nowhere. Others I can remember the actual moment when they came together. And sometimes it was the thing of Hunter giving me the lyrics and I'd carry them around for a while, then sit down with them in a hotel room or some place and work it out."

■ *Yamantaka*/**Mickey Hart, Francis Wolff, and Nancy Hennings**
Celestial Harmonies 003, 1983.

Yamantaka is the Tibetan god of the dead and the lord of the underworld. Not surprisingly, this album joins Mickey Hart with Tibetan bells specialists Henry Wolff and Nancy Hennings in a tonally dark and other-worldly venture. Performed on rare and invented percussive instruments, *Yamantaka* is music that seems to build and appear from a vacuum.

Yamantaka is meditation music. Quiet, ethereal, and subtle, it reflects Hart's more introspective side. Hart was brought to the project by Wolff and Hennings, who are revered throughout the "new age" music community for their *Tibetan Bells* albums.

As Hart described the album—a work of supreme texture—to Blair Jackson in 1983, "I didn't use any membranes on it. It's a percussion record with no drums on it. It's bells, gong, Beam, but I never struck a membrane because it sometimes takes away that space of drifting, because it draws your attention to it. It's interesting music. We're used to more things 'happening' in music. With this, you have to really just sit back and listen. This music doesn't have anything to do with anything else. We're so inundated by western music and our own sounds that sometimes we can't hear the purity of other music."

■ **"You Ain't Woman Enough"** (Loretta Lynn)
Loretta Lynn, single (1966), *You Ain't Woman Enough* (1967), *Greatest Hits* (1968), *20 Greatest Hits* (1987)
Shirley Brown, single (1967)
Tina Turner, single (1977)

Loretta Lynn, the "Coal Miner's Daughter" herself, had a No. 2 hit with "You Ain't Woman Enough" in 1966. The song, a one-woman-to-another putdown, finds the narrator drawing the deepest line in the sand in defense of her man and was a perfect cover for Donna Godchaux, who sang the song with the Dead for a short while in 1973.
2/17/73, Auditorium, St. Paul, Minnesota

■ **"You Don't Have to Ask"** (WARLOCKS)
The Warlocks, *Emergency Crew* demo (1965)

A truly disastrous attempt at high harmonizing, this Warlocks bomb appears on a couple of early Dead tapes.
3/25/66, Trouper's Club, Los Angeles

■ **"You Don't Love Me"** (Katrina/Frederick)
Bloomfield/Stills/Kooper, *Super Session* (1968)
THE ALLMAN BROTHERS BAND, *Allman Brothers at Fillmore East* (1971), *Dreams* (1989), *2nd Set* (1995)

Garcia sang this popular piece of angry blues later made famous by the Allman Brothers Band during at least a couple of very early Dead shows. "You Don't Love Me" has the distinction of being part of the first known Grateful Dead segue, as the band took a "Good Morning, Little Schoolgirl" into the blues plaint and back again into "Schoolgirl."

12/1/66, The Matrix, San Francisco

▪ "(You Give Me) Fever"

(Davenport/Cooley/John)

Little Willie John, single (1956), *Fever: The Best of Little Willie John* (1993)

Elvis Presley, *Elvis Is Back!* (1960), *Aloha from Hawaii* (1973)

Peggy Lee, single (1958), *Capitol Collectors Series, Vol. 1* (1990), *Fever and Other Hits* (1992), *Spotlight on Peggy Lee* (1995)

Ben E. King, *Songs for Soulful Lovers* (1964)

The McCoys, *Hang On Sloopy* (1965)

The Kingsmen, *15 Great Hits* (1966)

James Brown, *Cold Sweat* (1967)

James Cotton, *100% Cotton* (1974)

Bobby "Blue" Bland, *The Soul of the Man* (1974)

Otis Blackwell, *All Shook Up* (1977)

Buddy Guy, *Hot and Cold* (1978), *My Time After Awhile* (1992)

Fever Tree, *Another Time, Another Place* (1979)

Brian Eno, *Music for Fans* (1979)

Toots and the Maytalls, *In the Dark* (1985)

Joe Cocker, *One Night of Sin* (1987)

THE NEVILLE BROTHERS, *Treacherous* (1988)

"Please, do not forget the man I was opening for in 1956, '57. Do not pass over one of the most important soulful voices. Little Willie John was a soul singer before anyone thought to call it that." So said James Brown about one of the true Gods of Soul, the man who cowrote and popularized one of pop music's most lustful hits.

William Edward John was born in 1937 in Camden, Arkansas, the last of seven children. After his father moved the family to Detroit to take a job at the Dodge auto plant, John began singing in a gospel quintet. When he was just fourteen years old, John was performing at a talent show at Motown's Paradise Theater when influential bandleader Johnny Otis caught his act and recommended him to Syd Nathan of King Records. It took a couple of years, but Nathan eventually signed the pint-sized solo act with the high, elastic tenor that stretched across a precious range of blues, love ballads, and goofy novelty songs.

After a couple of blustery hits in 1955, "Fever" re-vealed vulnerability and dependence in the soul man's performance delirium. Peggy Lee helped popularize "Fever," but Willie John's own single, his biggest seller, outsold Lee's by far, hanging tough in the 1956 R&B charts for six months.

Several minor hits followed, but by the end of the decade, Little Willie John had shot his hit-making wad. Though he is remembered as a quiet man, John's life ended tragically. After being convicted of manslaughter for stabbing a man to death in a Seattle cafe brawl, John died of pneumonia in Washington State Penitentiary May 28, 1968, six months short of his thirty-second birthday.

Bob Weir enjoyed singing "Fever" with his own bands, but he only trotted it out in the first set of one 1987 Dead show.

9/13/87, Capital Centre, Landover, Maryland

▪ "Your Mind Has Left Your Body"

(Kantner/Grateful Dead)

Grateful Dead, *Dozin' at the Knick/'90* (1996)

Kantner, Slick and Freiberg, *Baron von Tollbooth and the Chrome Nun* (1973)

Though Garcia, Hart, and Hunter all contributed to the album on which this song was released, it is still somewhat surprising that it should appear in the Dead musical universe very intermittently over a twenty-year period as an instrumental jam. For reasons that remain unclear (perhaps copyright), the Dead formally retitled this instrumental "Mud Love Buddy Jam" when they released it on *Dozin' at the Knick* in 1996.

11/11/73, Winterland Arena, San Francisco

12/2/73, Boston Music Hall, Boston

▪ "You See a Broken Heart"

Weir is known to have ripped through this number of unclear history at only one early Dead concert.

3/12/66, Danish Center, Los Angeles

▪ "You Win Again" (Hank Williams)

Hank Williams, single (1953), *40 Greatest Hits* (1978), *I Won't Be Home No More, Vol. 8* (1987)

Grateful Dead, *Europe '72* (1972)

Fats Domino, *Let the Four Winds Blow* (1961), *Whole Lotta Rock 'n' Roll* (1991)

Ray Charles, *Modern Sounds on Country & Western Music* (1962)

Jerry Lee Lewis, *The Greatest Live Show on Earth* (1964)

Gerry and the Pacemakers, *I'll Be There* (1965)

Hank Williams, Sr. (Archive Photos)

Del Shannon, *Del Shannon Sings Hank Williams*
(1965)
The Bee Gees, *ESP* (1987)
Mary-Chapin Carpenter, *Shooting Straight in the Dark*
(1990)
Hank Williams Jr., *Classic Songs* (1993)

The oddity of *Europe '72*, Garcia's cover of this Hank Williams special was only performed by the Dead at a score of shows between November 1971 and September 1972. Odd, too, that the Dead didn't include more Hank in their repertoire, as he was the alpha and omega of country music—a King-sized Main Day singer/songwriter whose death from the ravages of alcoholism at age twenty-nine on New Year's Day 1953 left an irreplaceable void in this America's musical culture.

If, as Dylan sang in "(STUCK INSIDE OF MOBILE WITH THE) MEMPHIS BLUES AGAIN," "Shakespeare's in the alley," he could also be found blazing through the southern United States of the mid-twentieth century. In a career that lasted less than a decade, Williams gave us a songbook bursting with American classics. Through tales of misery and joy, of love lost and won, Saturday-night dancing and Sunday-morning devotion, crafted

with grace and wisdom, the influence of Hank Williams still burns bright.

Truly, it is impossible to overstate the importance of Hank Williams to our nation's heritage, a statement that is as true today as it was at the height of his fame more than four decades down the lonesome highways he immortalized. As both a composer and recording artist, Williams left behind some of American popular music's most enduring standards and established Butler County, Alabama's, favorite son as the model of soulful, simple expression that artists across all musical genres, hopefully, will always continue to emulate.

Hiram King Williams was born September 17, 1923, in Mt. Olive, Alabama, a rural, dirt-poor community. Fatherless by the age of six when an old World War I injury forced his dad's commitment to long-term care at Biloxi, Mississippi's V.A. hospital, he was raised by his formidable mother, Lillie Williams. The hand-to-mouth experience of childhood in the Depression-era South forged William's character with a spirit of independence and compassion for society's forgotten. Moving to the more metropolitan town of Greenville, Alabama, Williams encountered Rufe Payne, a black street singer who gave him, as he was to later say, "all the musical training I ever had."

The family moved to Montgomery in 1937 where Williams made his first public appearance billed as "the Singing Kid," performing a topical blues about the Works Progress Administration (the New Deal agency) at a local amateur night. This led to a regular spot on local radio station WSFA and propelled him to try his hand at composing, the first known fruits of which were "Six More Miles (to the Graveyard)," a bluesy Roy Acuff knock-off which, nonetheless, showed Williams's unique sense of gallows humor. Performing a combination of Roy Acuff tunes and other popular songs of the day with his band, the Drifting Cowboys (a name that he would use for backup bands throughout his career), Williams became a familiar face at venues in southern Alabama.

World War II forced a temporary suspension of an active professional career but he was back in the saddle by 1943 with a return to music and a new band, featuring Audrey Sheppard Guy, a young female singer who was to become his first wife (and mother of Hank Williams Jr.). Taking over the very full-time job of managing her husband's career (a job that had, up to that time, been handled by his mother), Audrey learned how to play stand-up bass in the band, collected the admission at the door in the schoolhouses and roadside honky-tonks where the band played, and made sure Williams showed up for his gigs—sober or otherwise.

Williams's talent and Audrey's ambition led him, in 1946, to sign with Fred Rose, the Nashville power broker who masterminded Williams's highly successful career. A year later, after a couple of impressive sessions, Rose led Williams to an MGM contract and his first hit, the bluesy and ballsy "Move It On Over," which hit Number Five on the country charts in 1947. Rose would quickly become a major force in Williams's life, acting as an artistic and professional mentor as well as a father figure. To what extent Rose contributed to Williams's songs themselves remains a matter of debate amongst Williamsologists, though the common conclusion is, as one of Hank's biographers put it, that "Williams produced the gems and Rose polished them." Two of these were "Honky-Tonkin'," a low-life anthem, and "I Saw the Light," a recasting of a sacred song which became one of his best-known compositions.

A prestigious invitation to join Shreveport's *Louisiana Hayride* radio program in 1948 helped Hank spread his gospel among rural folk throughout the Southwest as did his cover of "Lovesick Blues," a 1920 novelty number, which hit No. 1 on the country charts a year later. Now he was a cinch for the *Grand Ole Opry* radio show, a spot that had previously been denied to him because of his reputation as a heavy drinker. The Opry propelled him to the heights of country stardom.

He began churning out hits at breakneck pace and made serious inroads in other avenues of the pop mainstream as Rose shrewdly peddled his songs to artists as varied as Tony Bennett, Frankie Laine, Tennessee Ernie Ford, Teresa Brewer, and Ray Charles, all of whom scored with Williams's material. Naturally, virtually every noteworthy country artist recorded an album of Williams songs, and standards like "Kaw-Liga," "Your Cheatin' Heart," "Jambalaya," "I'm So Lonesome I Could Cry," "Cold, Cold, Heart," "Hey Good Lookin'," and "You Win Again" still play on jukeboxes from Bangor to San Diego. Additionally, he recorded a series of spiritual and philosophic recitations in 1950, pseudonymously released under the name Luke the Drifter, though it was an open secret who the speaker was. In a recording career that lasted a mere six years, Hank Williams left about one hundred titles.

But if the final few years of Hank Williams's life were his most prolific, they were also easily his most tortured. Just when his opportunities for happiness were at their strongest, everything fell apart for him. His drinking took on a life of its own and painkillers (originally prescribed to alleviate the constant aggravation he experienced from spina bifida) were often dangerously mixed, leading to the dissolution of his already tempestuous marriage. Expelled from the Opry for showing up drunk once too often, Williams fell into the downward spiral from which he was never able to escape. There is much evidence suggesting that he probably never drew a sober breath during the last year of his life, which ended in the back of his new powder-blue Cadillac on his way to a New Year's Day gig in 1953. Ironically, Williams's last recording, "I'll Never Get Out of This World Alive," peaked at No. 1 just after his passing.

Put on a Hank Williams record late at night some time and experience the harrowing emotional intensity of this man and his music. Steeped in sincerity and imbued with all the joys and sorrows of everyday life, the vision of Hank Williams is as tangible as a page from the Book of Revelations. No joke!

7/26/72, Paramount Theater, Portland, Oregon

■ **"You Won't Find Me"** (JOAN BAEZ)

Another Joanie one-off for the Dead, performed while backing the composer at one of their 1981 concerts.

12/12/81, Fiesta Hall, San Mateo, California

■ **"Your Sons and Daughters"**
See **"Fire in the City"**

■ **"You Were Made for All of My Love"**
(Jackie Wilson)
Jackie Wilson, single (1960)

Pigpen is known to have belted this Jackie Wilson classic at one primordial Dead concert.

1/13/66, The Matrix, San Francisco

Zabriskie Point
(film soundtrack) MGM SE 4668ST, 1970. MCA 25032, 1986. Sony AK52417, 1992.

Hailed as one of the avant-garde curiosities of contemporary cinema, Michelangelo Antonioni's rambling study of the aggressive, materialistic, unflinching American lifestyle hasn't held up as well as its soundtrack, which includes an excerpt of "Dark Star" and "Love Song," a peaking one-take, seven-minute Jerry Garcia electric-guitar solo. The balance of the soundtrack is worth the plunge too, with selections from John Fahey ("Dance of Death"), Pink Floyd ("Come in Number 51, Your Time Is Up" and "Careful with That Axe, Eugene"), Kaleidoscope, and Patti Page.

"Zip-a-Dee-Doo-Dah" (Ray Gilbert/Allie Wrubel)
Harry Nilsson, *Stay Awake: Songs from Disney Films* (1991)
Phil Spector, *Back to Mono* (performed by Bobb. B. Soxx & the Blue Jeans) (1991)
Ric Ocasek, *Simply Mad About the Movie* (1991)
Michelle Shocked, *Arkansas Traveler* (1992)

A goofy tune-up exercise for the Dead from the creators of Goofy, "Zip-a-Dee-Doo-Dah" was introduced by James Baskett in Walt Disney's 1946 animation, *Song of the South.* A year later it won the Academy Award for best song in a motion picture.

Zero
See **Chance in a Million; Here Goes Nothin'**

Zodiacs
See **Mother McCree's Uptown Jug Champions**

Index